Color Image Processing: Models and Methods (CIP: MM)

Color Image Processing: Models and Methods (CIP: MM)

Topic Editors

Giuliana Ramella
Isabella Torcicollo

MDPI

Basel • Beijing • Wuhan • Barcelona • Belgrade • Novi Sad • Cluj • Manchester

Topic Editors

Giuliana Ramella
Institute for the Applications of Calculus "M. Picone"
National Research Council
Naples
Italy

Isabella Torcicollo
Institute for the Applications of Calculus "M. Picone"
National Research Council
Naples
Italy

Editorial Office
MDPI AG
Grosspeteranlage 5
4052 Basel, Switzerland

This is a reprint of the Topic, published open access by the journals *Applied Sciences* (ISSN 2076-3417), *Entropy* (ISSN 1099-4300), *Journal of Imaging* (ISSN 2313-433X) and *Optics* (ISSN 2673-3269), freely accessible at: https://www.mdpi.com/topics/6GC4CH653P.

For citation purposes, cite each article independently as indicated on the article page online and as indicated below:

Lastname, A.A.; Lastname, B.B. Article Title. *Journal Name* **Year**, *Volume Number*, Page Range.

ISBN 978-3-7258-7955-7 (Hbk)
ISBN 978-3-7258-7956-4 (PDF)
https://doi.org/10.3390/books978-3-7258-7956-4

Cover image courtesy of Giuliana Ramella

Contents

entropy

MDPI

Editorial

Topic: "Color Image Processing: Models and Methods (CIP: MM)"

Giuliana Ramella * and Isabella Torcicollo

Institute for the Applications of Calculus "M. Picone", National Research Council (CNR), Via P. Castellino 111, 80131 Naples, Italy; isabella.torcicollo@cnr.it

* Correspondence: giuliana.ramella@cnr.it

Color information plays a crucial role in digital image processing: it is a robust descriptor that can improve data compression and support scene understanding for both humans and automatic vision systems. Color Image Processing (CIP) has become a highly active research area with applications spanning biomedicine, cultural heritage, remote sensing, defense, and security, among others.

This Topic was conceived to provide an overview of the state of the art and stimulate present and future directions, explicitly bridging two aspects often treated separately: the mathematical modeling and computational design of methods. This Topic is hosted across four participating journals (*Applied Sciences*, *Entropy*, *Journal of Imaging*, *Optics*), reflecting the interdisciplinary nature of CIP research.

The Topic brings together 14 peer-reviewed open access papers published between 2022 and 2025, authored by researchers from a wide range of countries. Overall, the contributions highlight how advances in CIP emerge from continuous interplay between model-based formulations, optimization, and learning-based architectures, with strong ties to real-world constraints and application-driven evaluation. Taken together, the papers in this Topic confirm that CIP remains a fertile domain in which theory, computation, and data-driven methods mutually reinforce one another.

The published papers reflect the breadth of CIP models and methods and span several interconnected directions:

- Imaging systems, sensing, and multimodal perception, including hyperspectral imaging design/optimization and assistive perception systems.
- Segmentation, thresholding, and detection in complex scenes, covering optimization-driven color segmentation and cross-modal (RGB-thermal) object detection.
- Restoration and enhancement of challenging imagery, addressing dehazing, nighttime imaging/stitching, and quality-oriented fusion pipelines.
- Color transfer, representation, and multivariate operators, including example-based color transfer, order-statistics morphology for color data, and hue-driven pixel manipulations in graphics workflows.
- Learning-based reconstruction and detail recovery, including super-resolution and reference-guided multi-exposure fusion.
- Biomedical and medical imaging applications, from retinal fundus multi-label classification to pseudo-coloring of grayscale nuclear imaging for improved interpretability.
- Color analysis beyond pure vision tasks, such as quantitative chromaticity analysis in cultural and landscape contexts.

We would like to thank all authors for their valuable contributions and all reviewers for their careful evaluations and constructive feedback. We are also grateful to the Topic

Editors and the Editorial Offices of the participating MDPI journals for their support in managing and coordinating this cross-journal Topic initiative.

Conflicts of Interest: The authors declare no conflict of interest.

List of Contributions:

1. Li, Y.; Duan, J.; Zhao, X.; Peng, Y.; Luo, Y.; Zhang, D.; Chen, Y. Optimization of Convex Transmissive Volume Bragg Grating for Hyperspectral Imaging Applications. *Optics* **2025**, *6*, 49. https://doi.org/10.3390/opt6040049.
2. Seyyedabbasi, A. A Hybrid Multi-Strategy Optimization Metaheuristic Algorithm for Multi-Level Thresholding Color Image Segmentation. *Appl. Sci.* **2025**, *15*, 7255. https://doi.org/10.3390/app15137255.
3. Li, Y.; Zhan, W.; Jiang, Y.; Guo, J. RDCRNet: RGB-T Object Detection Network Based on Cross-Modal Representation Model. *Entropy* **2025**, *27*, 442. https://doi.org/10.3390/e27040442.
4. Wang, Z.; Zhou, J.; Wang, S.; Wang, N. A Comprehensive Method for Example-Based Color Transfer with Holistic-Local Balancing and Unit-Wise Riemannian Information Gradient Acceleration. *Entropy* **2024**, *26*, 918. https://doi.org/10.3390/e26110918.
5. Han, J.H.; Yoon, I.; Kim, H.S.; Jeong, Y.B.; Maeng, J.H.; Park, J.; Jeon, H.-J. Mobility Support with Intelligent Obstacle Detection for Enhanced Safety. *Optics* **2024**, *5*, 434–444. https://doi.org/10.3390/opt5040032.
6. Yan, Y.; Yang, L.; Huang, W. Fundus-DANet: Dilated Convolution and Fusion Attention Mechanism for Multilabel Retinal Fundus Image Classification. *Appl. Sci.* **2024**, *14*, 8446. https://doi.org/10.3390/app14188446.
7. Zeng, L.; Li, R.Y.M.; Li, R. Chromaticity Analysis on Ethnic Minority Color Landscape Culture in Tibetan Area: A Semantic Differential Approach. *Appl. Sci.* **2024**, *14*, 4672. https://doi.org/10.3390/app14114672.
8. Ma, Y.; Xu, Y.; Liu, Y.; Yan, F.; Zhang, Q.; Li, Q.; Liu, Q. Multi-Scale Cross-Attention Fusion Network Based on Image Super-Resolution. *Appl. Sci.* **2024**, *14*, 2634. https://doi.org/10.3390/app14062634.
9. Huang, Y.; Zhou, S.; Xu, Y.; Chen, Y.; Cao, K. Ref-MEF: Reference-Guided Flexible Gated Image Reconstruction Network for Multi-Exposure Image Fusion. *Entropy* **2024**, *26*, 139. https://doi.org/10.3390/e26020139.
10. Yan, M.; Qin, D.; Zhang, G.; Tang, H.; Ma, L. Nighttime Image Stitching Method Based on Image Decomposition Enhancement. *Entropy* **2023**, *25*, 1282. https://doi.org/10.3390/e25091282.
11. Sun, S.; Huang, Y.; Inoue, K.; Hara, K. Order Space-Based Morphology for Color Image Processing. *J. Imaging* **2023**, *9*, 139. https://doi.org/10.3390/jimaging9070139.
12. Xu, Y.; Zhang, H.; He, F.; Guo, J.; Wang, Z. Enhanced CycleGAN Network with Adaptive Dark Channel Prior for Unpaired Single-Image Dehazing. *Entropy* **2023**, *25*, 856. https://doi.org/10.3390/e25060856.
13. Koren Ivancevic, T.; Stanic Loknar, N.; Rudolf, M.; Bratic, D. Manipulating Pixels in Computer Graphics by Converting Raster Elements to Vector Shapes as a Function of Hue. *J. Imaging* **2023**, *9*, 106. https://doi.org/10.3390/jimaging9060106.
14. Rahimian, A.; Etehadtavakol, M.; Moslehi, M.; Ng, E.Y.K. Comparing Different Algorithms for the Pseudo-Coloring of Myocardial Perfusion Single-Photon Emission Computed Tomography Images. *J. Imaging* **2022**, *8*, 331. https://doi.org/10.3390/jimaging8120331.

optics

MDPI

Article

Optimization of Convex Transmissive Volume Bragg Grating for Hyperspectral Imaging Applications

Yueying Li †, Jiazhu Duan *,†, Xiangjie Zhao, Yingnan Peng, Yongquan Luo, Dayong Zhang and Yibo Chen

Institute of Fluid Physics, China Academy of Engineering Physics, Mianyang 621000, China; s109liyy@caep.cn (Y.L.)
* Correspondence: jzduan@caep.cn
† These authors contributed equally to this work.

Abstract

The Volume Bragg Grating (VBG) imaging technique provides a novel approach to gaze-type hyperspectral imaging. However, collimation constraints of the incident beam during narrow-band filtering and high-spatial-resolution imaging introduce system complexity, hindering miniaturization and modularization of the optical system. To address these limitations, this paper proposes a convex transmissive VBG structure with tunable design parameters to enhance the field of view (FOV), relax collimation requirements, improve imaging quality, narrow filter spectral bandwidth, and simplify the optical system design. For the precise analysis and optimization of convex VBG performance, we established a physical model for filtered imaging using a convex transmissive VBG with polychromatic extended sources. An evaluation metric termed the "Maximal Splitting Angle (MSA)" was introduced to quantify the dispersion extent of image spots. This approach was employed to investigate the intrinsic correlations between structural parameters (such as the radius of curvature, vector tilt angle, grating period, and thickness) and key system performance indicators (spatial resolution and spectral resolution). The necessity of optimizing these parameters was rigorously demonstrated. Theoretical analysis confirms that convex transmissive VBG achieves superior spatial and spectral resolution over planar VBG under reduced collimation constraints. The experimental results show a 58.5% enhancement in spatial resolution and a 63.6% improvement in spectral bandwidth for the convex transmissive VBG system. Crucially, while planar transmissive VBG suffers from stray fringe interference during wavelength tuning, its convex counterpart remains unaffected. This study proposes a novel device structure, offering new perspectives for optimizing VBG-filtered spectral imaging systems.

Keywords: convex transmissive VBG; spectral imaging systems; filter; vector tilt angle; radius of curvature

1. Introduction

Spectral imaging technology is an organic integration of optical imaging and spectroscopic analysis techniques. Unlike the finite-thickness negative-index slabs [1], it enables the simultaneous acquisition of two-dimensional spatial information and spectral-dimensional information of targets. It has a wide range of applications in remote sensing and telemetry [2–6], environmental surveying [7], agriculture [8,9], and medicine [10,11]. Among the various technical approaches to spectral imaging, surface array imaging can capture monochrome images across the entire image planar and construct two-dimensional spatial and spectral information about the target through wavelength scanning. This approach effectively increases the amount of information obtained through optical detection and avoids issues associated with image splicing and fusion, offering superior imaging capabilities.

As the core spectral separation component in focal planar array spectral imaging systems, the optical filter functions to separate incident polychromatic light by wavelength, thereby acquiring target image information across different spectral bands, directly impacting the performance of focal planar array spectral imaging. Among the various filters applicable to focal planar array imaging, aside from traditional filter wheels, mainstream technological approaches include diffraction gratings, acousto-optic tunable filters (AOTFs), liquid crystal tunable filters (LCTFs), and volume Bragg grating (VBG).

Diffraction gratings typically employ a push-broom imaging mechanism, where the sensor is moved along the spatial dimension to collect target spectral information line by line, followed by post-processing to reconstruct the complete spatial–spectral data cube through image stitching methods. Both AOTF and LCTF utilize electrically tunable filtering mechanisms, enabling wavelength selection without the need for mechanical movement. Thus, compared to filter wheel methods that rely on motor-driven rotation to switch filters, they significantly increase the number of available spectral channels and enhance system flexibility. However, they face challenges such as difficulty in narrowing the filter spectral bandwidth and a substantial decrease in transmittance as the filter spectral bandwidth narrows [12–15].

VBG-based surface-array spectral imaging leverages the superior wavelength-selective properties of Bragg gratings to achieve narrowband filtering for area-array detectors [16]. This approach attains filter bandwidths at nanometer or sub-nanometer scales, enabling high-spectral-resolution ($\lambda/100$) and even hyperspectral ($\lambda/1000$) imaging [17,18]. The technique delivers critical advantages, including high spectral resolution, exceptional spectral transmittance, and rapid data acquisition capability.

A prevalent approach for achieving high spatial and spectral resolution employs a grating-pair complementary method [19,20]. This technique partially mitigates image planar blurring and significantly enhances spatial resolution [21]. However, it introduces additional diffraction stages that cause substantial energy loss and reduced transmittance [22]. Critically, prior studies lack theoretical analysis correlating VBG structural parameters with dispersion characteristics. To address this gap, the MSA metric [23] was adopted to establish parametric relationships between VBG configurations and image-point dispersion magnitude. This framework quantifies the impacts of chromatic blurring, diffractive aberration, and central wavelength deviation on spatial resolution. Nevertheless, optimization demands ultra-narrow dispersion angles (milliradian-range), while practical applications such as remote sensing typically involve wide-angle incident illumination—fundamentally constraining the scheme's implementability.

However, attaining high spatial and spectral resolution in VBG systems imposes stringent specifications on front-end optical components. The conventional approach—enhancing collimation—constrains the FOV. Spatial–spectral dimensional scanning [24] offers an alternative that acquires 2D spatial–spectral data while relaxing front-end collimation requirements. Nevertheless, this method introduces three critical limitations: increased post-processing complexity, diminished spectral calibration accuracy, and inevitable transmittance degradation.

To advance system performance, this paper proposes a convex transmissive VBG structure with tunable parameters that reduces the incident beam divergence angle from 179.6 mrad to 4.5 mrad (97.5% decrease), simultaneously enhancing filtering imaging performance and reducing spectral imaging system complexity. Through constructing a physical model of planar VBG spectral imaging, we elucidate how grating structural parameters govern filtered imaging characteristics, with parameter optimization guided by the maximum separation angle evaluation function. The theoretical and experimental results demonstrate the convex VBG's dual capacity to enhance spatial resolution (58.5%↑) and spectral resolution (63.6%↑) while suppressing spurious interference fringes, all achieved with 40% reduced front-end collimation requirements—yielding significant advancements for performance-structure co-optimization in VBG spectral imaging systems.

2. Theoretical Analysis and Discussion

Broad-spectrum diffuse illumination represents a form of incoherent illumination. The diffractive imaging system formed by a complex-color extended light source passing through a convex transmissive VBG constitutes a linear space-invariant system. This extended light source can be decomposed into a series of point sources with varying spectral components and non-uniform intensities, where the resultant diffraction pattern emerges from the incoherent superposition of their individual images. This paper analyzes a high-pressure xenon lamp with a wavelength range covering the visible spectrum. By establishing a right-handed coordinate system under the assumption of grating fringes being uniformly distributed along the y-direction, the diffraction characteristics of the VBG can be investigated through analyzing the light-field diffraction process within the meridional planar (xz-planar). The fundamental physical model simplifies to the diffraction of a monochromatic point source (wavelength λ) located at spatial coordinates (x_0, z_0) by the convex transmissive VBG, as illustrated in Figure 1. (Note that the incident light is white light).

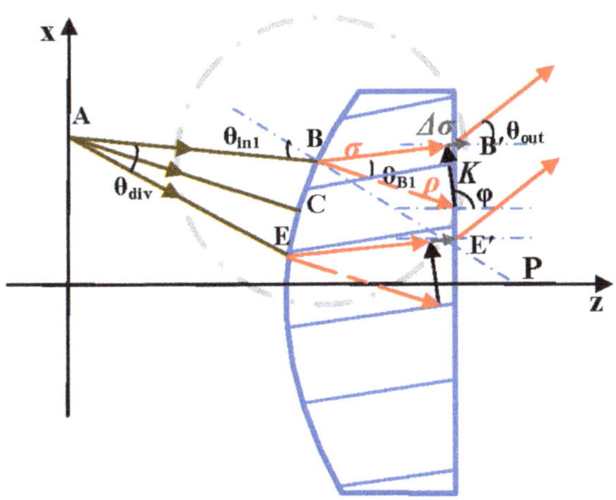

Figure 1. Schematic of convex transmissive VBG structure and k-vector relationship. θ_{div} is the divergence angle, θ_{B1} is the Bragg angle, ϕ is the vector tilt angle. Point A represents the point source; Point B is the incident point of the upper boundary ray of the light beam on the convex surface; Point B′ is the exit point of the upper boundary ray of the light beam on the planar surface; The center of the circular arc of the convex surface is located at point P.

First, the beam propagation process from polychromatic point sources at arbitrary spatial locations incident upon a VBG is investigated. Consider a point source A positioned at the focal point of a convex lens with focal length f and radius R, where an illumination spot of diameter D forms on the lens surface centered at point C. The distance L from A to C equals the lens focal length f and satisfies $f = R/(n_0 - 1)$. The divergence angle θ_{div} of the beam incident on the convex transmissive VBG adheres to $\tan(\theta_{div}/2) = (D/2)/L$, yielding

$$\theta_{div} = 2\tan^{-1}\left(\frac{D(n_0 - 1)}{2R}\right). \tag{1}$$

When the beam propagates to the front surface of the convex transmissive VBG, it is assumed that the incident direction of the central ray aligns with the local radius of curvature of the VBG surface, while the central wavelength λ satisfies the Bragg condition given by Equation (2):

$$\cos(\phi + \theta_{B0}) = -\frac{\lambda}{2n_0\Lambda}. \quad (2)$$

θ_{B0} is the Bragg angle, ϕ is the vector tilt angle of VBG, n_0 is the average refractive index of VBG, and Λ is the period of VBG.

For the upper marginal ray incident at point B on the convex surface (taking ray AB as representative case), θ_1 denotes the angle between the incident ray at B and the z-axis, while $\Delta\theta$ represents the angular deviation from the central ray. During beam scanning, $\Delta\theta$ varies dynamically and can be approximated as $\theta_{\text{div}}/2$. The incidence angle θ_{in1} at point B satisfies the geometric relationship given by Equation (3), where L (the distance from point source A to central ray incidence point C) adheres to $L = R/(n_0 - 1)$.

$$\theta_{in1} = \theta_{in} = \sin^{-1}\left(\frac{L+R}{R}\sin\Delta\theta\right). \quad (3)$$

Upon refraction through the convex surface, the refracted ray forms a Bragg angle θ_{B1} with the z-axis, exhibiting a wavevector $\boldsymbol{\rho}$ within the volume grating. According to Kogelnik's coupled-wave theory [15], the diffraction process modulated by grating vector $\mathbf{K}$ redirects the incident wavevector $\boldsymbol{\rho}$, yielding a diffracted wavevector $\boldsymbol{\sigma}$ that satisfies

$$\boldsymbol{\sigma} + \boldsymbol{\Delta\sigma} = \boldsymbol{\rho} + \mathbf{K}. \quad (4)$$

Herein, $\boldsymbol{\Delta\sigma}$ designates the phase mismatch, while $\boldsymbol{\rho}$ and $\boldsymbol{\sigma}$ exhibit identical magnitudes of $2\pi n_0/\lambda_{\text{in}}$. The grating vector $\mathbf{K}$ possesses a modulus $K = 2\pi/\Lambda$. Although Equation (2) determines the central wavelength at the Bragg angle, the inherent spectral selectivity bandwidth of the volume grating—quantified as $\Delta\lambda = \Lambda\lambda_0 \cot\theta_0/(2d)$, where d denotes grating thickness—must be incorporated. Consequently, the maximum incident wavelength at point B is derived as $\lambda_{\text{inl}} = -2n_0\Lambda\cos(\phi + \theta_{B1})$, and the resultant longest output wavelength post-VBG diffraction becomes $\lambda_l = \lambda_{\text{inl}} + \Lambda\lambda_0 \cot\theta_0/(2d)$, ultimately yielding Equation (5):

$$\lambda_l = -2n_0\Lambda\cos(\phi + \theta_{B1}) + \frac{\Lambda}{2d}\cot\theta_0 \cdot \lambda_0. \quad (5)$$

Substituting Equation (5) into the vector relation Equation (4) yields diffraction angles for polychromatic components. Applying Snell's law then determines the output angle θ_{out}. Similarly, for the marginal ray incident at point E, the minimum incident wavelength derivation must incorporate the volume grating's inherent spectral selectivity bandwidth—analogous to Equation (5). For convex transmissive VBG, the maximum angular separation maintains identical formulation to planar VBG, expressed as

$$\text{MSA} = \theta_{out}(\lambda_s,\theta_l) - \theta_{out}(\lambda_l,\theta_s), \quad (6)$$

where $\theta_{\text{out}}(\lambda_s, \theta_l)$ and $\theta_{\text{out}}(\lambda_l, \theta_s)$ denote the output angles after VBG diffraction for the shortest diffractable wavelength and longest diffractable wavelength at the beam margin, respectively (the exit angles of B′ and E′ in Figure 1). The derivation process above innovatively analyzes the diffraction relationships of light waves in the meridional planar of a convex VBG based on coupled-wave theory.

The degree of dispersion of image points is directly correlated with the MSA, meaning the MSA can be used to characterize the blurring extent of the image spot. As indicated by the expression for MSA, the convex surface radius of curvature, period, average refractive index of the grating medium, and thickness of the grating significantly influence the MSA. To analyze the impact of structural parameters of the convex volume grating on the MSA, a specific set of VBG parameters was selected, as detailed in Table 1 (where refractive index modulation Δn = 0.00028, and this is not reflected in the expression of MSA):

Table 1. Parameters of convex transmissive VBG.

Grating Structural Parameters	Λ (μm)	n_0	ϕ (°)	*d* (mm)	*R* (mm)
Before optimization	1	1.5	92	3	50

This study first investigates the influence of the radius of the convex VBG. Under incident conditions of a diffusely reflected light field with a large beam divergence angle, the divergence angle becomes the primary factor affecting the filtering spectral bandwidth due to central wavelength drift. Selecting an appropriate curvature radius can minimize the divergence angle after the beam is refracted into the VBG. As illustrated in Figure 2a, the MSA value decreases with the increase in the radius of curvature, and the results are in agreement with the anticipated model behavior. However, the rate of change slows down as the radius of curvature grows larger. Meanwhile, further analysis of the relationship between the FOV angle of the convex transmissive VBG and the radius of curvature, as shown in Figure 2b, reveals that the FOV angle decreases as the radius of curvature increases. When *R* is greater than 90 mm, the FOV angle is half that when R is 40 mm, which exacerbates the quasi-regime limitation of the spectral imaging system. Therefore, the curvature radius of curvature should be selected based on the MSA and FOV requirements.

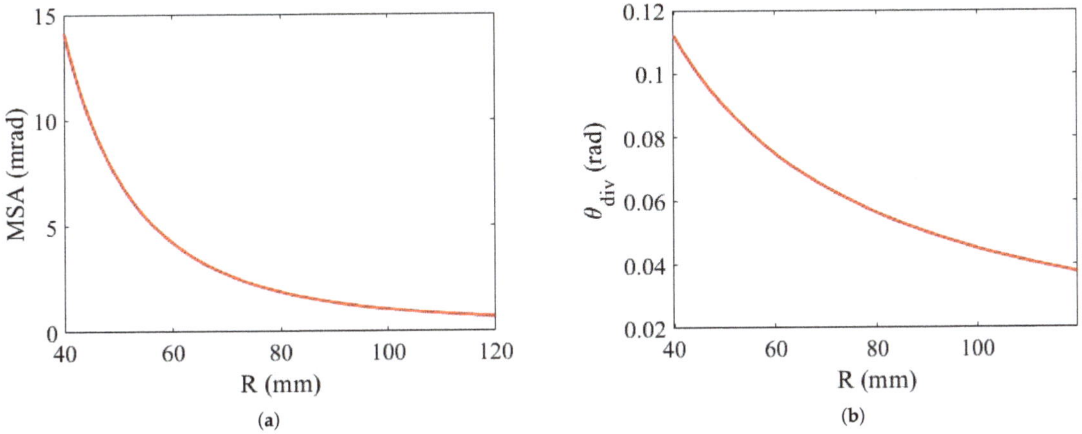

Figure 2. Impact of curvature radius on MSA and FOV. (**a**) The relationship between R and MSA. (**b**) The relationship between R and θ_{div}.

To ensure minimal central wavelength shift of diffracted light from various incident directions after grating diffraction, the vector tilt angle of the convex VBG requires optimized design. As derived from the Bragg condition, theoretically distinct optimal tilt angles should correspond to different central wavelengths for VBG with identical periods and refractive indices, where the MSA reaches its minimum value. As shown in Figure 3, the influence of the vector tilt angle on MSA was investigated across different radii. It is observed that the vector tilt angle significantly affects MSA. For a given radius of curvature of the convex surface, there exists an optimal tilt angle that minimizes the MSA, whereas for different radii of curvature, distinct optimal vector tilt angles are obtained; larger radii correspond to larger optimal tilt angles, which approach 90°.

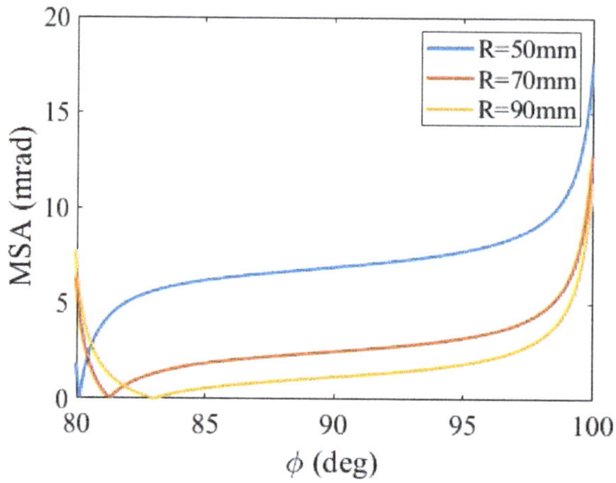

Figure 3. The relationships between ϕ and MSA for different R.

Combined with the Bragg condition, changes in the period affect the spectral bandwidth derived from the Bragg condition. Furthermore, when correlated with Equation (5), the influence of period variations ultimately manifests in the filtering spectral bandwidth obtained after wavelength shift, thereby affecting the degree of dispersion of the spot on the image planar. Figure 4 illustrates the influence of the grating period on both MSA and spectral bandwidth. It is evident that reducing MSA requires the selection of a smaller period, which aligns with the need to decrease the filter bandwidth—specifically, a smaller period narrows the wavelength selectivity. This relationship underscores the critical role of period optimization in controlling grating dispersion. Smaller periods enable tighter spectral confinement, proving particularly valuable for applications demanding high-resolution discrimination between closely spaced wavelengths.

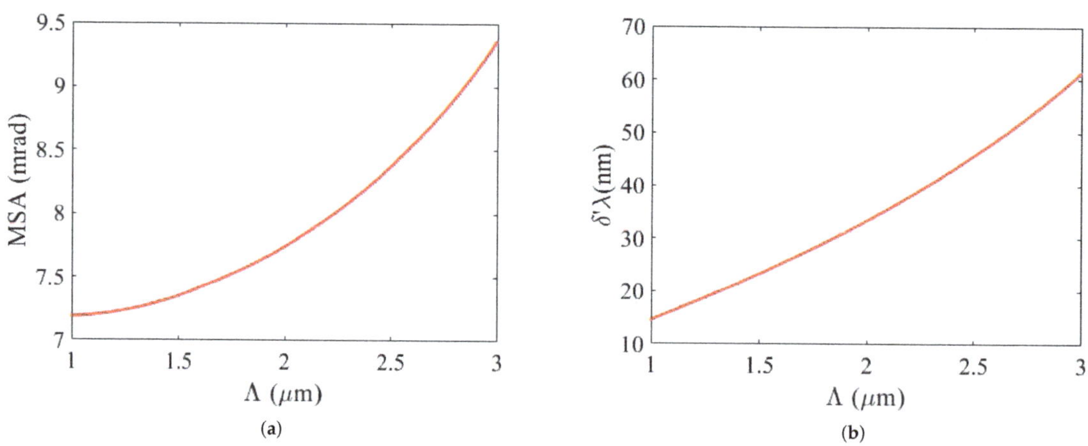

Figure 4. Impact of period on MSA and filtering spectral bandwidth at a central wavelength of 550 nm. (**a**) The relationships between Λ and MSA. (**b**) The relationships between Λ and wavelength selective width.

Similarly, according to Equation (5), the influence of thickness variations ultimately manifests in the filtering spectral bandwidth obtained after wavelength shift, thereby affecting the degree of dispersion of the spot on the image planar. The influence of VBG thickness on MSA is shown in Figure 5a; thicker VBG exhibits narrower spectral width, according to Equation (5). An increase in thickness reduces the intrinsic wavelength-selective width of the VBG, as illustrated in Figure 5b, ultimately leading to a reduction in MSA.

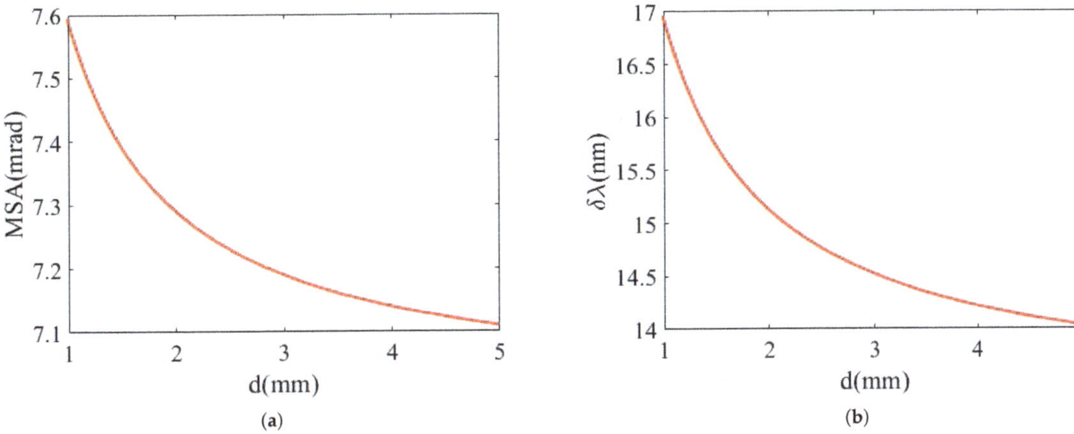

Figure 5. Impact of Thickness on MSA and Filtering Spectral Bandwidth at a Central Wavelength of 550 nm. (**a**) The relationships between thickness d and MSA. (**b**) The relationships between thickness d and wavelength selective width.

To reduce the divergence angle of the incident beam and achieve a wider field of view, it is necessary to select an appropriate radius of curvature. Based on the Bragg condition and the inherent wavelength selectivity of VBG, this requires an optimal tilt angle, smaller period, and greater thickness.

Due to its wavelength-selective properties, a VBG diffracts light of different wavelengths at distinct incident angles that satisfy the Bragg condition. This results in varying propagation directions for different wavelengths after diffraction, causing dispersion that degrades spatial resolution. Common dispersion reduction methods include minimizing the incident light divergence angle [25], with an ideal target compression to the milliradian (mrad) level [20]. To validate the effectiveness of convex transmissive VBG in enhancing spatial resolution, we conducted a comparative analysis of the minimum spot area (MSA) between convex and planar transmissive VBG with identical structural parameters. In the optical path of the planar VBG, a convex lens matching the curvature radius of the convex VBG was employed. While the planar VBG receives diverging light transmitted through this lens, the convex VBG directly intercepts the beam originating from a pinhole aperture. Using specified grating parameters, the beam divergence angle incident on the planar VBG surface after passing through a 50 mm radius-of-curvature lens was measured at 6.6 mrad. In contrast, the external divergence angle for the convex transmissive VBG reached 179.6 mrad. The internal divergence angle within the convex VBG—a function correlated with the external divergence angle—exhibits minor variations due to deflection within the grating, with theoretical calculations estimating it at approximately 4.5 mrad. Meanwhile, the computed internal divergence angle for the planar VBG remained consistently between 4.17 and 4.20 mrad. Results demonstrate that the convex transmissive VBG reduces the beam divergence angle from 179.6 mrad to 4.5 mrad, effectively mitigating chromatic blur. Although the convex VBG exhibits a marginally larger internal divergence angle than its planar counterpart, resolution can be further enhanced by optimizing the vector tilt angle.

During diffraction-limited imaging with a fixed focal length f of the imaging lens, the Point Spread Function (PSF) was established to evaluate the imaging spatial resolution of the convex transmissive VBG.

$$\mathrm{PSF} = f \times \mathrm{MSA}. \tag{7}$$

As indicated by the blue curve in Figure 6a, the planar transmissive VBG achieves an average resolvable line pair density of 3.18 lps/mm. The red curve in Figure 6a shows that the convex transmissive VBG without vector tilt angle optimization yields 2.78 lps/mm. After optimizing the vector tilt angle to $\phi = 83°$ (light blue curve, Figure 6a), the convex VBG demonstrates significantly enhanced resolution at 3.80 lps/mm. These results confirm that the optimized convex VBG exhibits superior PSF performance across the visible spectrum compared to the planar VBG.

Figure 6b demonstrates that after varying the radius of curvature, the optimal value of the vector tilt angle can be determined from the position of the minimum MSA value, indicating a compensation effect between the curvature radius and optimal vector tilt angle. The pre-compensation PSF inflection point (light blue curve in Figure 6a/Figure 6b) initially occurs before 400 nm. Increasing the curvature radius shifts this inflection point to 413 nm while improving PSF performance throughout the visible band—consistent with the conclusions in Figure 2a.

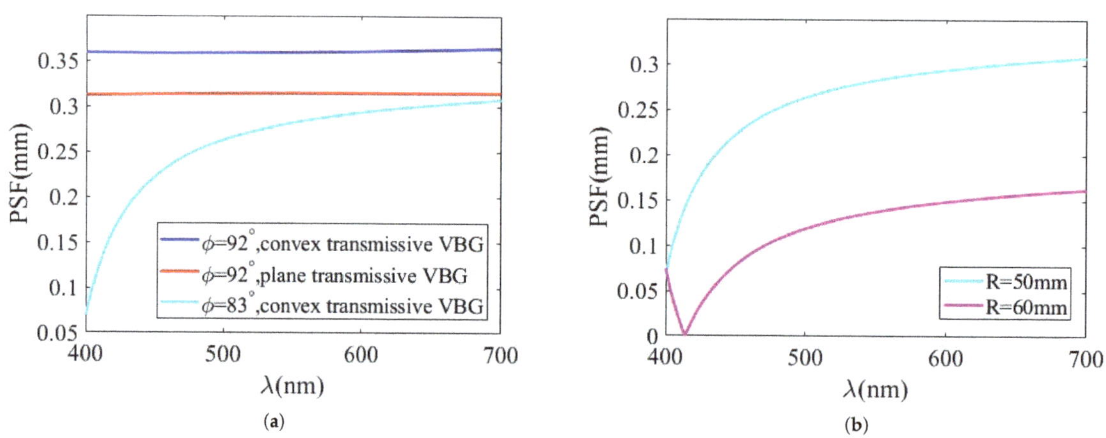

Figure 6. Variation in the VBG's PSF with incident wavelength. (**a**) Planar VBG vs. convex VBG with optimized vector tilt angle. (**b**) PSF before and after curvature radius compensation for vector tilt angle.

Table 2 compares the average imaging resolution of transmissive VBG with different structural parameters. The results demonstrate that after optimizing solely the vector tilt angle, the convex transmissive VBG achieves a 16.31% higher average resolution than its planar counterpart. Through co-optimization of the vector tilt angle and curvature radius, spatial resolution is further enhanced by 61.31% compared to planar VBG.

Table 2. Distinguishability of different transmissive VBG.

BG (ϕ, R)	planarVBG (ϕ = 92°)	ConvexVBG (ϕ = 92°, R = 50 mm)	ConvexVBG (ϕ = 83°, R = 50 mm)	ConvexVBG (ϕ = 83°, R = 60 mm)
Average lps/mm	3.18	2.78	3.80	8.22

3. Experimental Results and Analysis

To validate the theoretical analysis in Table 2, an experimental setup (Figures 7 and 8) was constructed using planar and convex transmissive VBG with identical pre-optimized structural parameters (Table 3) to compare theoretical and experimental spectral imaging performance. This verifies the convex VBG model's accuracy while establishing an experimental foundation for investigating the vector tilt angle and curvature radius effects. The convex VBGs were fabricated via standard amplitude-splitting interferometry: coherent-beam-interference inscription in photosensitive media followed by convex surface machining and anti-reflection coating to complete tunable filter prototypes. System configuration included a commercial camera lens (with a large field of view to enhance alignment tolerance, 108 mm focal length), convex lens L1/convex VBG (f_1 = 100 mm), and charge-coupled device (CCD)-front convex lens L2 (f_2 = 50 mm). Object light formed a sharp real image at the camera's rear focal planar; after divergence amplification, the focal-matched convex VBG collected and pre-collimated rays. Mounted on a 0.001°-precision rotation stage, the VBG enabled 0.1 nm spectral tuning through incident angle adjustment, diffracting Bragg-matched components to the CCD lens for imaging. Spectrometer substitution permitted direct filtering bandwidth measurement at the image planar.

The experiment employed a broad-spectrum halogen tungsten lamp to illuminate a USAF-1951 (which is come from Edmund Optics, Barrington, NJ, USA) resolution target, enabling calculation of the system's line-pair resolution (inverse of the PSF) through identification of the finest resolvable element at the imaging planar. Spectral analysis and imaging of this diffuse-reflective target yielded empirically measured PSF values and full-width at half-maximum (FWHM) data for quantitative assessment of spatial resolution performance.

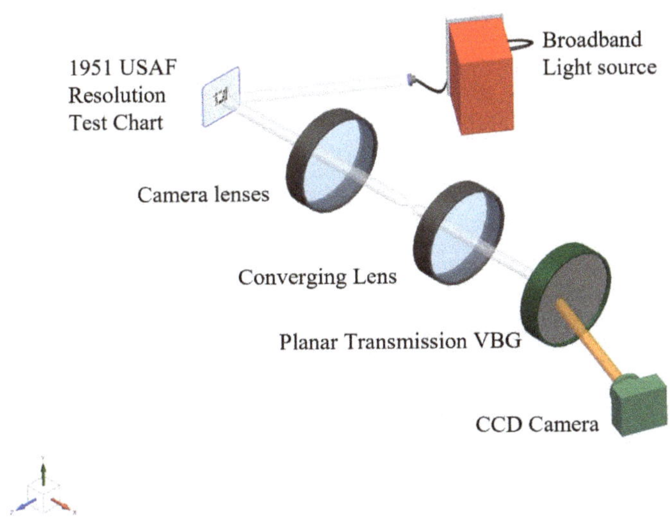

Figure 7. Planar transmissive VBG based spectral imaging system. Converging lens: L_1, f_1; CCD: f_2.

The USAF-1951 resolution target used in Figures 7 and 8 is widely employed to evaluate the resolution capability of optical imaging systems (such as microscopes and cameras). Figure 9 presents the imaging results for both planar and convex transmissive VBG. Due to aberrations in the imaging system, the image quality at the edges is inferior to that at the center. The image of the resolution target obtained with the planar transmissive VBG (the red dashed box in Figure 9a) allows identification up to group (0), element (5), corresponding to a measured line pair density of 1.59 lps/mm. However, the imaging quality is significantly degraded across the wavelength tuning range due to pronounced stray interference fringes. In contrast, the image acquired with the convex transmissive VBG (the red dashed box in Figure 9b) resolves features up to group (1), element (3), corresponding to a measured line pair density of 2.52 lps/mm. This represents a mere 9% deviation from the theoretical value of 2.77 lps/mm.

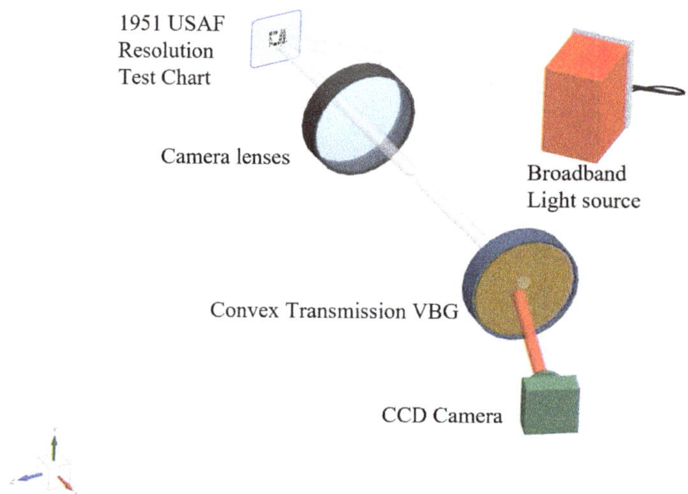

Figure 8. Convex transmissive VBG based spectral imaging system. Convex transmissive VBG: f_1; CCD: f_2.

Compared to similar spectral imaging systems, the compressive sensing hyperspectral imaging system based on LCTF significantly improves spatial and spectral resolution; however, the system is relatively complex, suffers from light energy attenuation, and is susceptible to stray light. The CubeSat hyperspectral imager based on freeform optics suppresses stray light while maintaining high spatial resolution and achieves miniaturization of the imaging system, but its design and manufacturing present certain challenges. The four common optical schemes based on AOTF require trade-offs among different key parameters: for instance, T-coll and D-coll offer high spectral resolution but suffer severe light loss, whereas S-coll provides high spectral resolution but exhibits significant chromatic shift, and S-conf cannot simultaneously achieve both high spatial resolution and high spectral resolution [26–28]. Compared to the planar VBG, the convex VBG achieves a 37% improvement in the measured resolution. Furthermore, imaging with the convex transmissive VBG is free from stray interference fringes, resulting in significantly superior image quality over the planar structure.

Table 3. Imaging resolution of planar vs. convex transmissive VBG on USAF-1951 reflective target at 624.8 nm.

BG	PSF	lps/mm
planar VBG	0.63	1.59
convex VBG	0.40	2.52

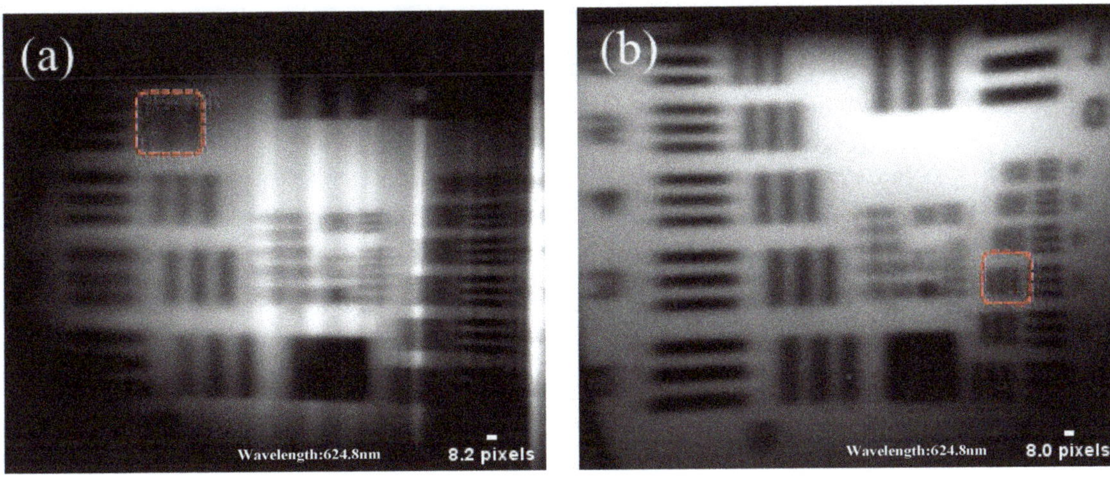

Figure 9. Monochromatic images of USAF-1951 resolution target. (**a**) Planar transmissive VBG. (**b**) Convex transmissive VBG.

To investigate the image quality issues associated with planar transmissive VBG, the focal length of lens L1 was adjusted to 50 mm in the experiment. The stray light patterns produced by planar transmissive VBGs with different structural parameters were then compared, as shown in Figure 10. The grating parameters in Figure 10a are identical to those in Figure 9a, while the parameters for Figure 10b are listed in Table 4. The experimental results demonstrate that stray interference fringes originating from the VBG itself are present in planar transmissive VBGs with both sets of structural parameters, indicating that the generation of such fringes is independent of the grating's structural parameters. In contrast, no stray light phenomena were observed in the imaging results obtained with the convex transmissive VBG. This occurs because light reflected from the rear surface of the planar VBG interferes with light reflected from the front surface, generating unintended stray fringes.

At the central wavelength indicated in Figure 9, spectral measurements were performed on the image planar of the spectral imaging system. In Figure 11, the red curve represents the measured data, while the black curve denotes the fitted result. Experimental data reveal that the spectral tuning range of the planar VBG is approximately 598–663 nm, while that of the convex VBG is approximately 600–630 nm. The planar transmissive VBG exhibits a filter FWHM of 28.42 nm (Figure 11a). In contrast, the convex transmissive VBG achieves a significantly narrower FWHM of 17.37 nm (Figure 11b), representing a 63.6% reduction in spectral bandwidth. Furthermore, the spectral distribution of the convex VBG more closely approximates a Gaussian profile. (The fitting was performed over the 550–700 nm range, resulting in an increase in R^2 from 0.90 to 0.93.) This observation further validates the performance advantage of the convex VBG structure in spectral selectivity.

Table 4. Parameters of planar VBG corresponding to Figure 10b.

Grating Structural Parameters	Λ (μm)	n_0	ϕ (°)	d (mm)
Before optimization	2	1.5	90	2.3

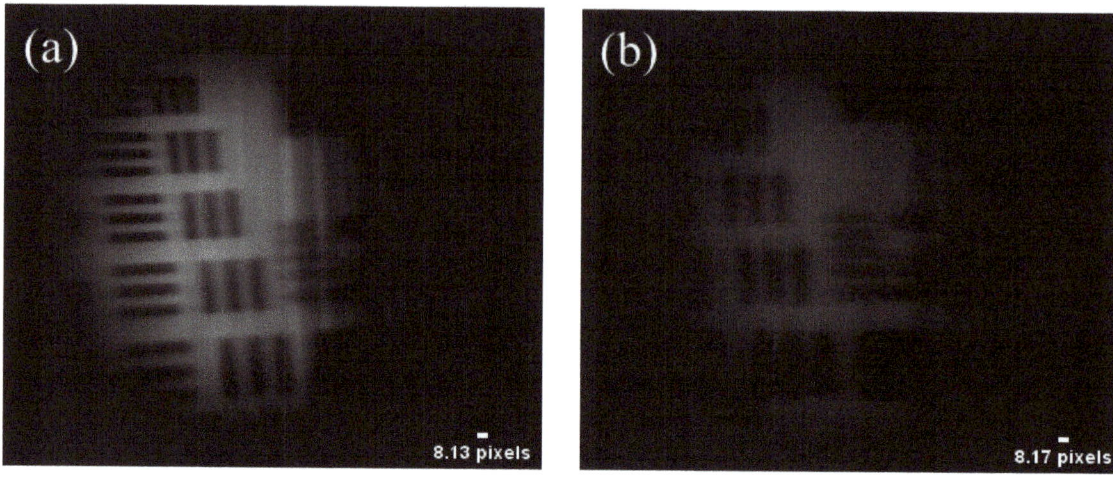

Figure 10. Spectral Imaging with planar transmissive VBG: variable lens focal lengths and grating parameters on USAF-1951 reflective target. (**a**) The planar transmissive VBG with structural parameters shown in Table 1. (**b**) The planar transmissive VBG with structural parameters shown in Table 4.

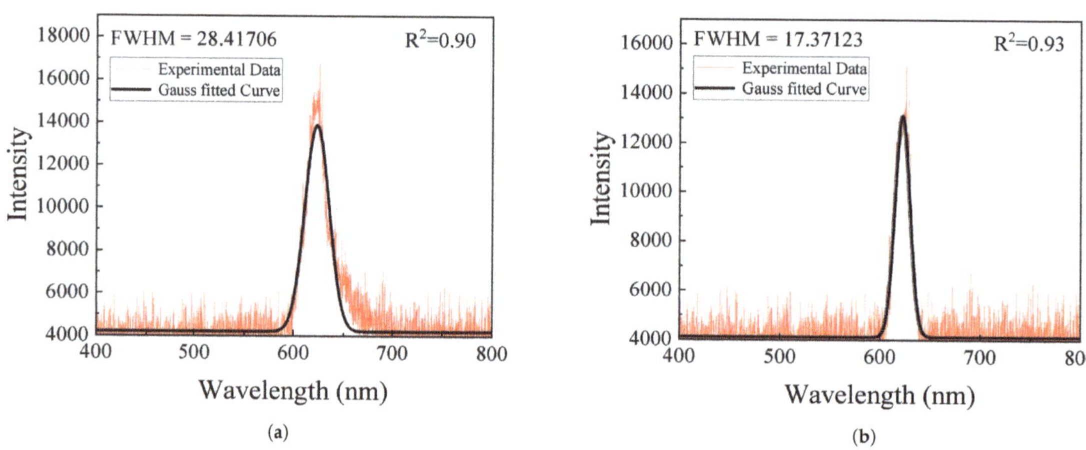

Figure 11. The planar and convex FWHM of VBG. (**a**) Planar transmissive VBG: 28.42 nm. (**b**) Convex transmissive VBG: 17.37 nm.

As can be seen from Table 5, from a theoretical perspective, the convex VBG obtained by optimizing the curvature radius and vector tilt angle (In Figure 1, ϕ represents the vector tilt angle. After optimization, ϕ was adjusted from 92° to 83°), which demonstrates improvements in both spatial and spectral resolution compared to a planar VBG. From an experimental standpoint, optimizing only the curvature radius can also enhance the spatial and spectral resolution of the VBG. (The convex surface was achieved through front-surface machining of the VBG, with the physical prototype shown in Figure 12).

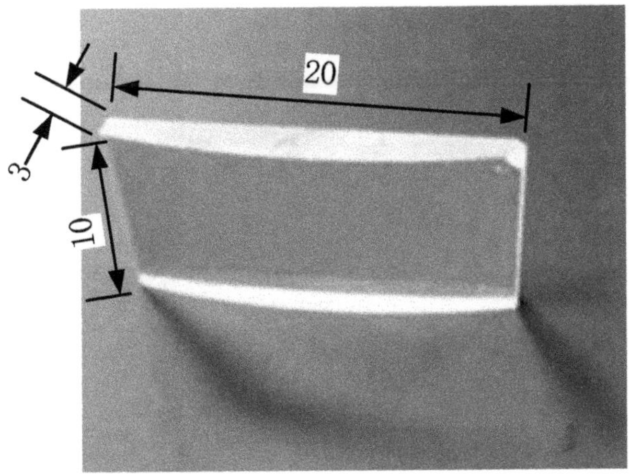

Figure 12. Physical prototype of the convex VBG.

Table 5. Summary table: spatial and spectral resolution comparison of planar vs. convex transmissive VBG (theoretical and experimental) with optimized curvature radius and vector tilt angle.

Spatial or Spectral Resolution	Convex Transmissive VBG	Planar VBG (ϕ = 92°)	Percentage Increase
Theoretical values lps/mm	3.80 (ϕ = 83°, R = 50 mm)	3.18	19.5%
Experimental values lps/mm	2.52 (ϕ = 92°, R = 50 mm)	1.59	58.5%
Spectral resolution nm	28.42 (ϕ = 92°, R = 50 mm)	17.37	63.6%

4. Conclusions

A new high-resolution spectral imaging component called convex transmissive VBG is designed in this paper. The filtered imaging model is established for describing the convex transmissive VBG. Two majority parameters, the curvature radius and vector tilt angle, are most important parameters affecting the resolution. Furthermore, a coupling relationship between curvature and the vector tilt angle is established, revealing that curvature affects the MSA by the divergence angle, while the vector tilt angle affects the MSA by the Bragg Condition.

The preferred method of the curvature radius and VTA was established and verified experimentally. The MSA was also introduced to characterize the degree of image planar dispersion, thereby optimizing and fabricating sample gratings with improved spatial and spectral resolution. The experimental results demonstrate that, with identical structural parameters, the imaging quality and spectral resolution of convex transmissive VBG surpass planar transmissive VBG by 58.5% and 63.6%, which closely matches theoretical predictions.

The method proposed in this paper can promote the development of miniaturized VBG spectral imaging systems, as increasing the radius of the curvature parameter can significantly reduce the complexity of the front-end optical system design. However, as this is a newly designed component, a phase difference exists in different optical axes. Due to factors such as manufacturing processes, the theoretical optimum value has not yet been achieved for the current sample. This must be accomplished in the next stage of the research.

Author Contributions: Conceptualization, Y.L. (Yueying Li) and J.D.; methodology, Y.L. (Yueying Li); software, Y.L. (Yueying Li); validation, X.Z. and Y.C.; formal analysis, Y.L. (Yueying Li); investigation, Y.L. (Yueying Li) and Y.P.; resources, Y.L. (Yueying Li), J.D. and D.Z.; data curation, Y.L. (Yueying Li); writing—original draft preparation, Y.L. (Yongquan Luo) and X.Z.; writing—review and editing, Y.L. (Yueying Li); visualization, Y.L. (Yueying Li); supervision, J.D.; project administration, Y.L. (Yongquan Luo) and D.Z.; funding acquisition, J.D. All authors have read and agreed to the published version of the manuscript.

Funding: This research was funded by National Natural Science Foundation grant number 61805224 and 61905229. This research was also funded by a certain innovative project with the number "C90202525".

Institutional Review Board Statement: Not applicable.

Informed Consent Statement: Not applicable.

Data Availability Statement: The data presented in this study are available on request from the corresponding author.

Conflicts of Interest: The authors declare no conflicts of interest.

Abbreviations

The following abbreviations are used in this manuscript:

VBG	Volume Bragg Grating
FOV	Field of View
AOTF	Acousto-Optic Tunable Filters
LCTF	Liquid Crystal Tunable Filters
MSA	Maximal Splitting Angle
PSF	Point Spread Function
CCD	Charge-Coupled Device
FWHM	Full-Width at Half-Maximum

References

1. Ahmadi, A.; Mosallaei, H. The image performance of a negative index slab and a layered slab using coupled surface modes. *J. Appl. Phys.* **2009**, *106*, 064502. [CrossRef]
2. Fang, L.; Jiang, Y.; Yan, Y.; Yue, J.; Deng, Y. Hyperspectral Image Instance Segmentation Using Spectral–Spatial Feature Pyramid Network. *IEEE Trans. Geosci. Remote Sens.* **2023**, *61*, 1–13. [CrossRef]
3. Wang, Z.; Zhou, J.; Liu, S.; Li, M.; Zhang, X.; Huang, Z.; Dong, W.; Ma, J.; Ai, L. A Land Surface Temperature Retrieval Method for UAV Broadband Thermal Imager Data. *IEEE Geosci. Remote Sens. Lett.* **2022**, *19*, 1–5. [CrossRef]
4. Zhou, T.-D.; Liang, X.-B.; Li, C.; Huang, Z.-H.; Feng, J.-S.; Zhao, L.; Wang, J.-J.; Jing, F. 2.5 kW average power, two-channel spectral-beam-combined output based on transmitting volume Bragg grating. *Acta Phys. Sincia* **2017**, *66*, 084204. [CrossRef]
5. Drachenberg, D.R.; Andrusyak, O.; Cohanoschi, I.; Divliansky, I.; Mokhun, O.; Podvyaznyy, A.; Smirnov, V.; Venus, G.B.; Glebov, L.B. Thermal tuning of volume Bragg gratings for high power spectral beam combining. In Proceedings of the Fiber Lasers VII: Technology, Systems, and Applications, San Francisco, CA, USA, 25–28 January 2010; Tankala, K., Ed.; International Society for Optics and Photonics, SPIE: Bellingham, WA, USA, 2010; Volume 7580, p. 75801U. [CrossRef]
6. Song, J.H.; Kwon, Y.H. Hyperspectral push-broom imager using a volume Bragg grating as an angular filter. *Opt. Express* **2024**, *32*, 8736–8750. [CrossRef]
7. Dumke, I.; Nornes, S.M.; Purser, A.; Marcon, Y.; Ludvigsen, M.; Ellefmo, S.L.; Johnsen, G.; Søreide, F. First hyperspectral imaging survey of the deep seafloor: High-resolution mapping of manganese nodules. *Remote Sens. Environ.* **2018**, *209*, 19–30. [CrossRef]
8. Guerri, M.F.; Distante, C.; Spagnolo, P.; Bougourzi, F.; Taleb-Ahmed, A. Deep learning techniques for hyperspectral image analysis in agriculture: A review. *ISPRS Open J. Photogramm. Remote Sens.* **2024**, *12*, 100062. [CrossRef]
9. Shitharth, S.; Manoharan, H.; Alshareef, A.M.; Yafoz, A.; Alkhiri, H.; Mirza, O.M. Hyper spectral image classifications for monitoring harvests in agriculture using fly optimization algorithm. *Comput. Electr. Eng.* **2022**, *103*, 108400. [CrossRef]
10. Sandasi, M.; Vermaak, I.; Chen, W.; Viljoen, A.M. Hyperspectral Imaging and Chemometric Modeling of Echinacea—A Novel Approach in the Quality Control of Herbal Medicines. *Molecules* **2014**, *19*, 13104–13121. [CrossRef]

11. Payne, G.; Langlois, N.; Lennard, C.; Roux, C. Applying visible hyperspectral (chemical) imaging to estimate the age of bruises. *Med. Sci. Law* **2007**, *47*, 225–232. [CrossRef]
12. Arablouei, R.; Goan, E.; Gensemer, S.; Kusy, B. Fast and robust pushbroom hyperspectral imaging via DMD-based scanning. *arXiv* **2016**, arXiv:1608.00361. [CrossRef]
13. Zhang, C.; Wang, H.; Zhang, Z.; Yuan, J.; Shi, L.; Sheng, Z.; Zhang, X. Narrowband double-filtering hyperspectral imaging based on a single AOTF. *Opt. Lett.* **2018**, *43*, 2126–2129. [CrossRef]
14. Yuan, J.; Fan, W.; Cheng, H.; Huang, D.; Du, T. Interference Spectral Imaging Based on Liquid Crystal Relaxation and Its Application in Optical Component Defect Detection. *Appl. Sci.* **2022**, *12*, 718. [CrossRef]
15. Wang, Y.; Tong, G.; Li, B.; Guo, X.; Song, X.; Zhao, Y.; Karim, S.; Deng, C.; Zhou, J.; Zhang, W.; et al. Miniaturized customized filtering-wheel-based multispectral imaging system for target detection. *Measurement* **2023**, *221*, 113506. [CrossRef]
16. Kogelnik, H. Coupled wave theory for thick hologram gratings. *Bell Syst. Tech. J.* **1969**, *48*, 2909–2947. [CrossRef]
17. Ludman, J.; Riccobono, J.R.; Reinhand, N.O.; Korzinin, Y.L.; Semenova, I.; Shahriar, S.M. Nonspatial filter for laser beams. *Quantum Electron.* **1996**, *26*, 1093–1096. [CrossRef]
18. Henrion, M.; Ludman, J.E.; Sobolev, G.A.; Shahriar, M.S.; Soboleva, S.B.; Hemmer, P.L. Two-dimensional holographic non-spatial filtering for laser beams. In Proceedings of the Photopolymer Device Physics, Chemistry, and Applications IV, Online, 15–16 July 1998. [CrossRef]
19. Ott, D.; SeGall, M.; Divliansky, I.; Venus, G.; Glebov, L. High-contrast filtering by multipass diffraction between paired volume Bragg gratings. *Appl. Opt.* **2015**, *54*, 9065. [CrossRef]
20. Blais-Ouellette, S.; Daigle, O.; Taylor, K. The imaging Bragg tunable filter: A new path to integral field spectroscopy and narrow band imaging. In Proceedings of the Ground-based and Airborne Instrumentation for Astronomy, Orlando, FL, USA, 25–29 May 2006. [CrossRef]
21. Duan, J.; Zhao, X.; Hu, Q.; Wu, F.; Luo, Y.; Zhang, D. Volume Bragg grating filters and its spectral imaging application. *High Power Laser Part. Beams* **2018**, *30*, 079001-1. [CrossRef]
22. Havermeyer, F.; Liu, W.; Moser, C.; Psaltis, D.; Steckman, G.J. Volume holographic grating-based continuously tunable optical filter. *Opt. Eng.* **2004**, *43*, 2017–2021. [CrossRef]
23. Duan, J.; Zhao, X.; Luo, Y.; Zhang, D. Improving the spatial resolution of volume Bragg grating two-dimensional monochromatic images. *Appl. Opt.* **2018**, *57*, 3159. [CrossRef] [PubMed]
24. Eckhard, J.; Eckhard, T.; Valero, E.M.; Nieves, J.L.; Contreras, E.G. Outdoor scene reflectance measurements using a Bragg-grating-based hyperspectral imager. *Appl. Opt.* **2015**, *54*, D15–D24. [CrossRef]
25. Chakraborty, D.; Georgiev, R.; Aspell, S.; Toal, V.; Naydenova, I.; Cody, D.; Martin, S. Modelling and Design of Holographic Optical Elements for Beam-Coupling Applications for a Range of Incident Beam Angles. *Photonics* **2022**, *9*, 936. [CrossRef]
26. Xi, W.; Zhang, Y.; Ma, X.; Xu, T.; Arce, G. Compressive spectral imaging system based on liquid crystal tunable filter. *Opt. Express* **2018**, *26*, 25226–25243. [CrossRef] [PubMed]
27. Liu, Y.; Bauer, A.; Viard, T.; Rolland, J. Freeform hyperspectral imager design in a CubeSat format. *Opt. Express* **2021**, *29*, 35915–35928. [CrossRef]
28. Batshev, V.; Machikhin, A.; Gorevoy, A.; Martynov, G.; Khokhlov, D.; Boritko, S.; Pozhar, V.; Lomonov, V. Spectral Imaging Experiments with Various Optical Schemes Based on the Same AOTF. *Materials* **2021**, *14*, 2984. [CrossRef]

applied sciences

MDPI

Article

A Hybrid Multi-Strategy Optimization Metaheuristic Algorithm for Multi-Level Thresholding Color Image Segmentation

Amir Seyyedabbasi

Computer Engineering Department, Faculty of Engineering and Natural Science, Istinye University, 34396 Istanbul, Turkey; amir.seyyedabbasi@istinye.edu.tr

Abstract

Hybrid metaheuristic algorithms have been widely used to solve global optimization problems, making the concept of hybridization increasingly important. This study proposes a new hybrid multi-strategy metaheuristic algorithm named COSGO, which combines the strengths of grey wolf optimization (GWO) and Sand Cat Swarm Optimization (SCSO) to effectively address global optimization tasks. Additionally, a chaotic opposition-based learning strategy is incorporated to enhance the efficiency and global search capability of the algorithm. One of the main challenges in metaheuristic algorithms is premature convergence or getting trapped in local optima. To overcome this, the proposed strategy is designed to improve exploration and help the algorithm escape local minima. As a real-world application, multi-level thresholding for color image segmentation—a well-known problem in image processing—is studied. The COSGO algorithm is applied using two objective functions, Otsu's method and Kapur's entropy, to determine optimal multi-level thresholds. Experiments are conducted on 10 images from the widely used BSD500 dataset. The results show that the COSGO algorithm achieves competitive performance compared to other State-of-the-Art algorithms. To further evaluate its effectiveness, the CEC2017 benchmark functions are employed, and a Friedman ranking test is used to statistically analyze the results.

Keywords: hybrid optimization algorithm; multi-strategy; multi-level thresholding; image segmentation

1. Introduction

Image segmentation aims to divide an image into several regions with similar features or semantic meanings for further processing and analysis [1]. This technique has attracted significant attention in various fields, including early disease detection [2], autonomous driving [3], and image processing applications [4]. To achieve accurate and robust segmentation, it is essential that the pixel characteristics within each region are consistent [1]. Threshold-based segmentation methods in image segmentation are typically divided into two categories [5]. Bi-level thresholding is a fundamental technique that segments an image into two separate classes by determining a single optimal threshold value. On the other hand, multi-level thresholding partitions the image into multiple segments by locating several threshold values.

Multi-threshold segmentation refers to the process of dividing an image into several object and background regions by determining multiple threshold values [6]. Existing image thresholding segmentation techniques primarily include two classical approaches: the Otsu method and the Kapur entropy method. The Kapur entropy approach selects thresholds based on the principles of information theory [1,6]. It operates by evaluating the entropy values of pixel distributions at various grey levels within the image. The threshold corresponding to the maximum entropy is chosen as the optimal point for image segmentation. The Otsu method is a popular technique for image segmentation that relies on analyzing greyscale distributions [1,6].

Its main strategy is to identify a threshold that separates the image into two groups, aiming to reduce the variance within each group as much as possible. By iteratively assessing intra-class variances, the method selects the threshold that yields the lowest total variance, leading to optimal binarization. The increase in the number of thresholds in multi-threshold image segmentation leads to an exponential rise in computational complexity, which in turn causes traditional multi-level thresholding techniques to suffer from reduced accuracy and slow convergence.

To address these limitations, metaheuristic algorithms have been employed in image segmentation tasks, demonstrating impressive performance. There have been many metaheuristic algorithms presented in the last few decades. Metaheuristic algorithms are used to solve real-world problems in different dimensions. It is possible to find the best or near-optimal solution using metaheuristic algorithms. Based on the No-Free-Lunch (NFL) theory [7], it has been concluded that there is no algorithm that can find all the possible solutions to optimization problems. There is a large difference between a heuristic algorithm and a metaheuristic algorithm in avoiding local optima trapping. Unlike heuristic algorithms, metaheuristic algorithms try to find a global optimum or optimal solution. Metaheuristic algorithms avoid being trapped in local optima through the use of exploration and exploitation phases. In each metaheuristic algorithm, these phases are the main operations. In addition, the trade-off between these two phases is important. The process of exploration involves looking for the most effective solution(s) for a given area(s), while the process of exploitation involves focusing on the most effective solution(s) for a given area(s) [8]. In most cases, the exploration ability of search agents must be increased in the initial iterations in order to locate potential areas and then exploit the optimum solution once discovered.

Metaheuristic algorithms can be divided into three categories: evolution-based, swarm-based, and physics-based. Evolutionary algorithms are largely based on natural laws and behaviors. Based on Darwin's theory of evolution, the genetic algorithm is a metaheuristic algorithm [9]. Another evolution-based metaheuristic algorithm is differential evolution (DE) [10], another algorithm based on Darwinian theory, although it differs from GA in its selection phase. Metaheuristic algorithms based on swarms and societies in nature are called swarm-based algorithms. In order to find a solution to these algorithms, members of groups interact with one another within a search space. One of the most well-known algorithms in this category is particle swarm optimization (PSO) [11]. PSO simulates flocking birds' social behavior. There are several possible solutions represented by each particle in the group. Among the other algorithms in this category are ant colony optimization (ACO) [12], grey wolf optimization [13], and Sand Cat Swarm Optimization [14]. Metaheuristic algorithms with physics-based inputs are derived from physical laws and theories, like gravity and particle movement. Among the well-known physics-based metaheuristic algorithms are the Gravitational Search Algorithm (GSA) [15], the Big-Bang Big-Crunch (BBBC) [16], and the Charged System Search (CSS) [17].

In [5], the proposed modified grey wolf optimizer (MGWO) is applied to multi-level thresholding color image segmentation to achieve the optimum threshold. The authors used some strategies in leader selection and position update; in addition, they used a mutation operator to lead search agents to the optimum solution. In [1], the authors proposed a hybrid algorithm based on crayfish optimization and a differential evolution algorithm named ACOADE to use in color multi-threshold image segmentation. This hybrid algorithm maximizes the foraging parameter of crayfish optimization and uses the base process of the differential evolution (DE) algorithm to achieve the optimum threshold value of the image segmentation technique using the Otsu and Kapur entropy methods as objective functions. The authors of [18] proposed an improved whale optimization algorithm to overcome the limitations of the classical WOA in color multi-threshold image segmentation. In this way, enhancement significantly improved the segmentation accuracy and robustness of the results.

In [19], the black widow optimization (BWO) algorithm is applied to a multi-level thresholding image segmentation problem. Similar to other studies in this field, the Otsu and Kapur entropy methods are used to evaluate as their objective function. Learning Enthusiasm-Based Teaching–Learning-Based Optimization (LebTLBO) is a recent meta-heuristic known for its simplicity and low computational cost [20]. Its effectiveness in image segmentation is evaluated using the Berkeley Segmentation Dataset 500 (BSDS500). This dataset provides diverse and high-quality images suitable for benchmarking. Objective functions such as Otsu's method and Kapur's entropy are employed to assess segmentation performance. Improved elephant herding optimization (IEHO) integrates opposition-based learning and chaotic sequences to enhance the exploration–exploitation balance [21]. Its efficiency is tested on multi-level thresholding (MTH) for image segmentation. Kapur's entropy, Otsu's method, and Masi entropy are used as objective functions to determine optimal thresholds.

Recently, a novel 3D memristive cubic map employing dual discrete memristors (3D-MCM) has been proposed, exhibiting rich dynamical behaviors, including coexisting attractors, making it suitable for secure image encryption tasks [22]. To address the growing demand for secure and efficient image transmission, a novel color image encryption algorithm based on the 2D Logistic–Rulkov Neuron Map (2D-LRNM) was proposed, offering enhanced complexity and unpredictability through a hybrid chaotic model [23]. PSEQADE is a quantum differential evolutionary algorithm that uses a quantum-adaptive mutation strategy and a population state evaluation framework to address excessive mutation in QDE. The experimental results show excellent convergence performance, high accuracy, and stability in solving high-dimensional complex problems [24].

MGAD is a novel adaptive evolutionary multitask optimization algorithm designed to address challenges in evolutionary multitask optimization, including dynamic control, inaccurate task selection, negative knowledge transfer, and decreased optimization performance due to increased uncertainty [25]. The TSLS-SCSO algorithm, an enhanced version of Sand Cat Swarm Optimization (SCSO), is proposed for autonomous path planning in dynamic environments. It incorporates a population initialization strategy, spiral search, Livy flight, tent chaotic mapping, and sparrow alert mechanism, achieving higher accuracy and competitiveness [26].

The method includes a PHFM-based domain transform strategy and the BHRN network structure. The input image is transformed into the PHFM domain for parsing and edge predictions. An encoder–decoder structure is used for mutual guidance learning across multiple stages. The shared encoder enhances feature propagation, while separate decoders predict parsing and edge results [27]. This study explores the use of chaotic systems in metaheuristic optimization techniques to improve search efficiency. The initial populations of the PSO and WSO algorithms are distributed according to Logistic, Chebyshev, Circle, sine, and Piecewise chaotic maps [28].

The paper proposes a Polynomial Chebyshev Symmetric Chaotic-based GJO (PC-SCGJO) algorithm to improve image segmentation in image processing. The PCSCGJO algorithm combines a chaotic generating function with the Golden Jackal Optimizer (GJO) algorithm, aiming to avoid local optima and improve segmentation results. The simulation results show the PCSCGJO method's effectiveness in dealing with medical color images outperforms other metaheuristic algorithms in terms of quality and accuracy [29]. This paper proposes an improved Transit Search algorithm based on a chaotic map and local escape operator (CLTS). The algorithm introduces chaos initialization, simplifies transit criteria, improves convergence speed in the neighborhood phase, and balances exploration and exploitation. The experimental results show the CLTS algorithm achieves faster convergence speed and higher accuracy compared to the TS algorithm and other advanced algorithms. It also outperforms advanced image segmentation algorithms in terms of convergence and segmentation effects [30].

To improve metaheuristic algorithm performance, hybrid metaheuristic algorithms are proposed. It is common for metaheuristic algorithms to integrate two or more metaheuristic algorithms to solve optimization problems. Hybrid metaheuristic algorithms have the primary objective of utilizing the advantages of both algorithms while minimizing their drawbacks. Hybrid metaheuristic algorithms generally fine-tune exploration and exploitation [31]. A hybrid metaheuristic algorithm is proposed in order to achieve a balance between exploration and exploitation of metaheuristic algorithms. The performance of the convergence curve and the optimal solution during algorithm execution are essential for achieving the best result. The metaheuristic algorithm finds the optimal solution by analyzing the initial search space, whereas the algorithm structure is used to determine the optimal solution. The diversity of solutions is also important in this way. On the other hand, there is a relationship between the diversity of solutions and the speed of convergence. Fast convergence is often caused by low diversity. Most hybrid metaheuristic algorithms perform solution diversity, and the algorithm structure further promotes solution diversity [31,32]. The most important issue to avoid is local trapping.

This study makes the following major contributions:

- A novel hybrid metaheuristic algorithm (COSGO) is proposed, which integrates grey wolf optimization (GWO) and Sand Cat Swarm Optimization (SCSO) to enhance global optimization performance.
- The COSGO algorithm is specifically designed to overcome the local optima problem by improving exploration capabilities. The adaptive characteristics of SCSO are used to increase the diversity of GWO, thereby achieving a better balance between exploration and exploitation.
- A chaotic opposition-based learning (COBL) strategy is incorporated into the hybrid metaheuristic algorithm to further improve convergence speed and solution quality by enhancing population diversity.
- The proposed algorithm is applied to the multi-level thresholding color image segmentation problem, aiming to reduce computational effort in finding optimal threshold values. Both Otsu's method and Kapur's entropy are employed as objective functions.
- Experimental validation is conducted using the BSD500 dataset (10 color images) to demonstrate the segmentation quality and effectiveness of the COSGO algorithm.
- Comprehensive performance evaluation is carried out using the CEC2017 benchmark suite, and statistical significance is assessed using the Friedman ranking test, confirming the competitive performance of the proposed approach.

2. Fundamentals

An overview of the GWO optimization algorithm is provided in the first part of this section. The second part of the presentation focuses on the SCSO optimization algorithm, which is explained in detail. At the end of this section, the multi-level thresholding image segmentation problem is defined.

2.1. Grey Wolf Optimization (GWO)

The grey wolf optimization (GWO) algorithm was described by Mirjalili et al. [13]. A simulation of GWO was conducted based on the leadership hierarchy and social behavior of grey wolves. Unlike other types of animals, grey wolves live and hunt in a unique habitat. There are usually 5–12 grey wolves in a group of grey wolves. In each group, there are four kinds of grey wolves, namely, alpha (α), beta (β), delta (δ), and omega (ω). In groups, each of these types of grey wolves has a different responsibility. Alpha (α) wolves have a powerful effect on their groups. The alpha (α) wolf is responsible for making decisions regarding hunting, sleep locations, and wake-up times. The group is responsible for making this decision. Beta (β) wolves are on the second level of the pack hierarchy. Co-leaders are wolves that are considered to be part of the group's leadership. Delta (δ) is categorized at the third level of the hierarchy. Delta wolves must follow the instructions of the upper-level wolves: alpha and beta. The delta is the last wolf capable of eating and hunting. It is important to say that if the delta wolf does not exist in a group, the group encounters internal chaos and problems. In the hierarchy of grey wolves, the omega grey wolf occupies the lowest position. A wolf is considered an omega if it does not include any of the above types.

The GWO algorithm consists of three phases: encircling, attacking, and hunting. Each phase has a different mathematical model. A number of parameters are included in the encircling model to allow the wolves to encircle their prey. As a result, the new location has been updated. The following equations represent encircling the prey mathematically:

$$\vec{D} = \left| \vec{C} \cdot \vec{X}_p(t) - \vec{X}(t) \right| \tag{1}$$

$$\vec{X}(t+1) = \vec{X}_p(t) - \vec{A} \cdot \vec{D} \tag{2}$$

$$\vec{A} = 2\vec{a} \cdot \vec{r_1} - \vec{a} \tag{3}$$

$$\vec{C} = 2 \cdot \vec{r_2} \tag{4}$$

$$\vec{a} = 2\left(1 - \frac{t}{T}\right) \tag{5}$$

In this regard, $\vec{A}$, $\vec{C}$ are coefficient vectors, and $\vec{X}$, $\vec{X}_p$ are the position vectors of the grey wolf and prey, respectively. Here, another important parameter is $\vec{a}$, which decreased from 2 to 0. This parameter is used to guide the search agents to the prey based on the iteration number. As in most metaheuristic algorithms, there are some random parameters between 0 and 1; in the GWO algorithm, $\vec{r_1}$ and $\vec{r_2}$ are random numbers:

$$\begin{aligned} \vec{D}_\alpha &= \left| \vec{C_1} \cdot \vec{X}_\alpha - \vec{X} \right|, \\ \vec{D}_\beta &= \left| \vec{C_2} \cdot \vec{X}_\beta - \vec{X} \right|, \\ \vec{D}_\delta &= \left| \vec{C_3} \cdot \vec{X}_\delta - \vec{X} \right| \end{aligned} \tag{6}$$

$$\begin{aligned} \vec{X_1} &= \vec{X}_a - \vec{A_1} \cdot \vec{D}_\alpha, \\ \vec{X_2} &= \vec{X}_\beta - \vec{A_2} \cdot \vec{D}_\beta, \\ \vec{X_3} &= \vec{X}_\delta - \vec{A_3} \cdot \vec{D}_\delta \end{aligned} \tag{7}$$

$$\vec{X}(t+1) = \frac{\vec{X_1}(t) + \vec{X_2}(t) + \vec{X_3}(t)}{3} \tag{8}$$

2.2. Sand Cat Swarm Optimization (SCSO)

Sand Cat Swarm Optimization (SCSO) is a metaheuristic algorithm inspired by the unique survival and hunting behaviors of sand cats, a species adapted to harsh desert environments [14]. Unlike domestic cats, sand cats can detect low-frequency sounds below 2 kHz, which plays a crucial role in locating prey in challenging conditions. SCSO simulates this remarkable sensory and hunting capability to navigate the search space and locate near-optimal solutions. Similar to other swarm-based optimization techniques, the algorithm begins with the random initialization of a population of search agents within defined lower and upper bounds. Each agent represents a potential solution in a matrix where rows correspond to individual agents and columns to the problem's dimensions. A fitness function is employed to evaluate how well each solution satisfies the optimization objective—whether minimization or maximization—and guides the search process across iterations. The algorithm iteratively updates the agents' positions based on fitness values until convergence, with the final solution representing the best outcome found. While the principal goal across metaheuristics is similar, the strategies employed, such as the foraging-inspired mechanism in SCSO, distinguish each algorithm in achieving optimal or near-optimal results.

Each search agent begins with a sensitivity range starting at 2 kHz, controlled by the $\vec{R_G}$ parameter, which linearly decreases over iterations to balance exploration and exploitation. Position updates are based on both the best candidate and the current position, modulated by the sensitivity range $\vec{r}$, ensuring adaptive movement across the search space. A circular movement strategy is employed using a random angle θ, enabling agents to effectively avoid local optima and converge toward the best solution:

$$\vec{r_G} = s_M - \left(\frac{S_M \times iter_c}{iter_{Max}}\right) \tag{9}$$

$$\vec{R} = 2 \times \vec{r_G} \times rand(0,1) - \vec{r_G} \tag{10}$$

$$\vec{r} = \vec{r_G} \times rand(0,\ 1) \tag{11}$$

$$\overrightarrow{Pos}(t+1) = \vec{r}.\left(\overrightarrow{Pos_{bc}}(t) - rand(0,1)\cdot \overrightarrow{Pos_c}(\mathrm{t})\right) \tag{12}$$

$$\begin{gathered} \overrightarrow{Pos_{rnd}} = \left| rand(0,1)\cdot \overrightarrow{Pos_b}(t) - \overrightarrow{Pos_c}(\mathrm{t}) \right| \\ \overrightarrow{Pos}(t+1) = \overrightarrow{Pos_b}(t) - \vec{r}.\overrightarrow{Pos_{rnd}}\cdot\cos(\theta) \end{gathered} \tag{13}$$

$$\vec{X}(t+1) = \begin{cases} \overrightarrow{Pos_b}(t) - \overrightarrow{Pos_{rnd}}\cdot\cos(\theta).\vec{r} & |R| \le 1; exploitation \\ \vec{r}.\left(\overrightarrow{Pos_{bc}}(t) - rand(0,1)\cdot \overrightarrow{Pos_c}(\mathrm{t})\right) & |R| > 1; exploration \end{cases} \tag{14}$$

2.3. Multi-Level Thresholding Image Segmentation

One of the most important and sensitive topics in image processing research is the multi-level thresholding problem, which can accurately capture complex details and structures in images. Additionally, it greatly enhances the impact of image segmentation. The segmentation approach is applied to images in the majority of medical sciences, such as pattern identification, medical image processing, and medical image analysis. The Otsu and Kapur methods are used in this study as objective functions in this problem.

2.3.1. Otsu Method

Otsu's multi-threshold image segmentation is a statistical, unsupervised, and non-parametric method used to determine the optimal threshold values in image processing [4]. The goal of this method is to maximize the between-class variance, ensuring that pixels within the same segment have similar intensity values while also achieving strong separation between different segments. Assume an image is to be divided into N classes. To achieve this segmentation, N − 1 thresholds $T_1, T_2, \ldots, T_{N-1}$ must be determined. Multi-thresholding separates pixels based on their greyscale intensity values using these thresholds. The normalized histogram of the image is defined below in Equation (15)

$$p_i = \frac{h_i}{NP}, \sum_{i=0}^{L-1} p(i) = 1 \tag{15}$$

Here, h_i is the histogram count for intensity level i, NP is the total number of pixels in the image, and L is the number of greyscale levels. For a single threshold T, the probability of occurrence (weights) for the two classes separated by T are given by:

$$w_0(T) = \sum_{i=0}^{T-1} p(i) \qquad w_1(T) = \sum_{i=T}^{L-1} p(i) \tag{16}$$

The class means are:

$$\mu_0(T) = \frac{1}{w_0(T)} \sum_{i=0}^{T-1} i.p(i) \quad \mu_1(T) = \frac{1}{w_1(T)} \sum_{i=T}^{L-1} i.p(i) \tag{17}$$

The total mean intensity of the image is:

$$\mu(T) = \sum_{i=0}^{L-1} i.p(i) \tag{18}$$

Otsu's method selects the threshold T* that maximizes the between-class variance:

$$\begin{gathered} \sigma_b^2(T) = w_0(T).w_1(T).\, [\mu_0(T) - \mu_1(T)]^2 \\ T^* = argmax\sigma_b^2(T) \end{gathered} \tag{19}$$

For multi-threshold segmentation (i.e., more than two classes), the principle is extended to maximize the sum of between-class variances for all N classes. This typically involves evaluating combinations of thresholds to find the set that yields the highest overall between-class variance.

2.3.2. Kapur Method

An additional popular technique for multi-level thresholding is Kapur's method, which is founded on the idea of Shannon entropy. Unlike Otsu's method, which relies on variance-based class separation, Kapur's method seeks to maximize the sum of entropies of the segmented regions, thus ensuring that each region contains the most information possible. The method utilizes the normalized histogram of the greyscale image to calculate the probability distribution of pixel intensities. Given a combination of thresholds $T_1, T_2, \ldots, T_{K-1}$, the total entropy H for K segmented regions is calculated as:

$$H = H_1 + H_2 + \cdots + H_K \tag{20}$$

The entropy of the final region is:

$$H_k = -\sum_{i=T_{k-1}+1}^{L-1} \frac{p_{(i)}}{W_K} log(\frac{p_{(i)}}{W_K}) \quad (21)$$

Based on the above equation, *pi* is the probability of the *i*th grey level, and L is the total number of grey levels. The probability sums (weights) for each segmented region are calculated as follows:

$$W_K = \sum_{i=T_{k-1}+1}^{L-1} p_{(i)} \quad (22)$$

The optimal set of thresholds is the one that maximizes the total entropy H, thereby achieving the most informative segmentation of the image. Kapur's method is particularly effective for images with complex intensity distributions and is often used in applications requiring the precise segmentation of textures or objects with varying brightness.

3. Hybrid Metaheuristic Algorithm

Here, the classic SCSO and GWO algorithms are used to propose a new hybrid algorithm that benefits from the advantages of these algorithms to create an efficient algorithm for solving global optimization. In addition, a chaotic opposition-based learning strategy is used in the proposed hybrid optimization algorithm.

3.1. Hybridization SCSO and GWO

The SCSO algorithm uses the R parameter to control the movement of search agents within the search space. This parameter also ensures a balance between exploration and exploitation. Inspired by the unique characteristics of sand cats in nature, the R parameter emphasizes the sensitivity range and decreases from 2 kHz to 0 over time. In contrast, the GWO algorithm uses the A parameter to control the movement of search agents. When the A parameter value is greater or less than 1, it influences the balance between exploration and exploitation. However, this mechanism can lead to drawbacks, such as trapping in local optima, especially in large search spaces. To address this issue, the hybrid algorithm incorporates the R parameter to enhance control over agent movement and improve the balance between exploration and exploitation.

In this context, the COSGO algorithm benefits from the R-value of the SCSO algorithm to switch dynamically between two well-known metaheuristic algorithm strategies. When the R-value is between -1 and 1, the search agents follow the behavior rules of the SCSO algorithm; otherwise, they update their positions based on the GWO algorithm. COSGO also includes a mechanism to validate the fitness of newly updated positions. Updated positions are first checked against the search space boundaries. If they fall outside the allowed limits, correction parameters are applied to move them back within boundaries. Subsequently, a sorting mechanism is employed to merge the new positions with the existing ones, resulting in a combined population of old and new individuals. Likewise, the fitness values of both the existing and new individuals are merged. All individuals are ranked in ascending order based on their fitness values, with the best individual placed at the top. The population is then updated by selecting the top individuals according to the original number of search agents, ensuring that the best solutions are retained.

Grey wolf optimization (GWO) was employed due to its effective global exploration capabilities, simple structure, and minimal parameter requirements, which make it highly adaptable across a variety of optimization problems. On the other hand, the Sand Cat Swarm Optimization (SCSO) algorithm has demonstrated efficient local search behavior and a balanced exploration–exploitation trade-off, making it a suitable candidate for hybridization. The integration of chaotic opposition-based learning further enhances diversity and helps avoid premature convergence. Comparative studies such as [13,14] have also highlighted the complementary strengths of these algorithms, supporting the rationale for their combination in the proposed framework.

3.2. Chaotic Opposition-Based Learning Strategy

One of the recently introduced techniques in optimization is opposition-based learning (OBL) [33]. OBL was first proposed by Tizhoosh to emphasize the evaluation of the opposite position of a search agent within the search space. In this approach, an optimization algorithm evaluates the fitness of both the current position and the opposite position of a search agent. This allows the algorithm to explore the search space more broadly, covering diverse regions and directions. Moreover, in complex optimization problems where multiple local optima exist, search agents can easily become trapped. OBL helps mitigate this issue by increasing the chances of escaping local optima, thus enhancing the global search capability of the algorithm. In Equation (23), which represents the initial population of the optimization algorithm, lb is lower bound, ub is upper bound, and r_i is a random number from a uniform distribution in the range [0, 1]. In equation 24, the opposite position of the current position is calculated:

$$pos_{t+1} = Lb + r_i \cdot (Ub - Lb) \tag{23}$$

$$Opos_{t+1} = Lb + Ub - pos_{t+1} \tag{24}$$

As mentioned earlier, OBL benefits from considering the opposite population based on fixed positions; however, this approach may face limitations. To address this issue, in [34], the authors proposed a modified version of OBL by introducing a random number, which adds a certain level of randomness to the solution and improves diversity. In the chaotic opposition-based learning strategy (COBLS), chaotic behavior is introduced to enhance population diversity and avoid premature convergence. A chaotic array is first generated by iteratively applying the sine map s times. This chaotic array is then used to replace the conventional random array, and opposite solutions are calculated accordingly. As a result, the search process is enriched by exploring different regions of the search space more effectively.

In this study, the sine map was selected as the chaotic map to enhance the diversity of the population during the optimization process. Compared to other chaotic maps such as the Logistic map, the sine map offers smoother and more uniformly distributed sequences, which can help to explore the search space more effectively. Previous studies have shown that the choice of chaotic map can significantly influence the convergence behavior and performance of metaheuristic algorithms [35,36]:

$$Opos_{t+1} = Lb + Ub - F_s \cdot pos_{t+1} \tag{25}$$

$$F_{i+1} = \sin(\pi F_i) \tag{26}$$

In Equation (25), the F_s is a chaotic array that has been mapped using a sine function s times. S is set at 20 in order to prevent the loss of diversity brought on by too few iterations or the increase in running time produced by too many iterations.

3.3. System Model

As aforementioned, this study proposes a new multi-strategy hybrid metaheuristic algorithm to address one of the np-hard problems, multi-level thresholding for color image segmentation. The aim of this problem is to partition a color image into meaningful regions based on pixel intensity values. Initially, it takes an RGB image as input and converts it to greyscale histograms. These histograms are then used to determine the optimal threshold values. This combinatorial optimization problem is modeled, and the goal is to select a set of threshold values that maximizes an image quality criterion. The proposed COSGO algorithm was employed to find these optimal thresholds. To evaluate the COSGO algorithm, a total of 10 real-world images were taken from the BSD500 dataset, which is one of the well-known datasets. The flowchart of the proposed COSGO algorithm is given in Figure 1.

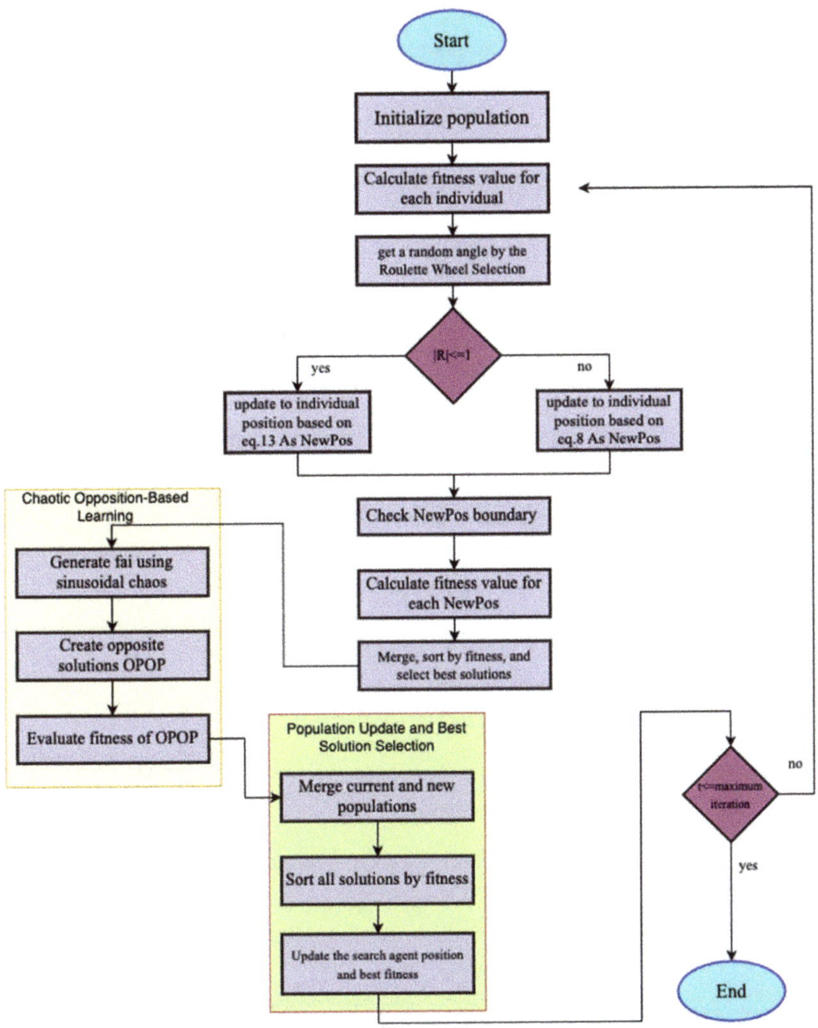

Figure 1. The flowchart of the COSGO algorithm.

In addition, in the simulation, the main parameters used in the system and COSGO algorithm are explained below:

- T: number of thresholds (3–5 in this study).
- MaxIter: maximum number of iterations (e.g., 100).
- PopulationSize: number of candidate solutions (e.g., 30).

- Objective Functions: Otsu method and Kapur entropy.
- Dataset: BSD500 (10 selected color images).
- Channels: R, G, and B (treated independently for thresholding).
- Evaluation Metric: PSNR, SSIM, and computation time.

It is possible to explain the problem formulation. Let h(i) be an image histogram for intensity level i ∈ [0, 255]. The objective is to determine a threshold vector for a multi-level thresholding problem with T thresholds:

$$T = \{t1, t2, \ldots, t_T\} \ with \qquad 0 < t1 < t2 < \cdots < t_T < 255$$

The goal is to maximize f(T), a fitness function that can be either Otsu's method or Kapur's entropy. Thus, the optimization problem is formulated as:

$$maxf(T) \ subject \ to \ \ t_1 < t_2 < \cdots < t_T$$

In order to determine the optimal threshold set T that produces the highest segmentation quality based on the chosen objective function, the COSGO algorithm searches the solution space.

4. Results and Analysis

This section evaluates the proposed algorithm using benchmark functions, which are commonly employed to assess metaheuristic algorithms due to their stochastic nature. To demonstrate the effectiveness of the proposed method, it is compared with several metaheuristic algorithms, including GWO [13], SCSO [14], and the WOA [37] and two hybrid metaheuristic algorithms, including AGWO_CS [38] and the PSOGSA [39]. The evaluation includes benchmark tests and statistical analyses. Each algorithm was run independently 30 times using identical control settings, and performance was measured based on the mean and standard deviation. All simulations were conducted on the same system using MATLAB R2020b. The simulation parameters for each metaheuristic algorithm are explained in Table 1.

Table 1. The simulation parameters.

Algorithm	Parameter	Value	Algorithm	Parameter	Value
GWO	a	[2, 0]	SCSO	Sensitivity range (r_G)	[2, 0]
	A	[2, 0]		Phase control range (R)	[$-2r_G$, $2r_G$]
AGWO_CS	a	$2 - \left(cos(rand) \cdot \frac{l}{Max_{iter}}\right)$	WOA	a	[2, 0]
PSOGSA	G_0	1		A	[2, 0]
	C1	0.5		C	2.rand (0, 1)
	C2	1.5		l	[−1, 1]
				b	1

4.1. Experimental Analysis Based on CEC2017

For numerical validation, a set of 29 benchmark functions from the CEC2017 test suite was employed, which are widely utilized for assessing the performance of metaheuristic algorithms. These functions are categorized into four groups: the unimodal functions range from F1 to F3, multimodal from F4 to F10, hybrid from F11 to F20, and composite from F21 to F30. The proposed COSGO algorithm was benchmarked using these functions and compared against several existing methods, including GWO, SCSO, the WOA, AGWO-CS, and the PSOGSA. Table 2 summarizes the experimental outcomes in terms of mean, worst, best, and standard deviation values. In this way, the Friedman ranking presented in Table 3 was used to compare the performance of COSGO to metaheuristic algorithms. For each benchmark function, the algorithms are ranked based on their performance, with the best-performing algorithm. These rankings were then averaged over all problems to compute the overall Friedman rank for each algorithm. A lower average rank indicates better overall performance. The Friedman test is a non-parametric statistical method that helps determine whether the observed differences in ranks among the algorithms are statistically significant. Based on Table 3, it is observed that the average ranking of the COSGO algorithm is lower than the other algorithms. It means the COSGO algorithm performance is better than the others.

Table 2. Results for F1-F30 algorithms (CEC17) D10.

Function		COSGO	GWO	SCSO	WOA	AGWO-CS	PSOGSA
F1	Mean	2840	35,700	1.9×10^9	37,800,000	14,600.00	108,000.00
	Worst	8420	54,800	1.92×10^9	1.14×10^9	210,000.00	240,000.00
	Best	126	17,300	1.89×10^9	134	16,600.00	19,500.00
	STD	2380	9430	9,280,000	207,000	38,500.00	45,000.00
F3	Mean	300	1410	2460	877	2520.00	877.00
	Worst	301	4300	27,500	3830	8500.00	3830.00
	Best	300	546	300	302	378.00	302.00
	STD	0.221	960	6000	937	2170.00	937.00
F4	Mean	424	418	421	402	424.00	409.00
	Worst	527	464	529	403	527.00	440.00
	Best	403	407	404	400	403.00	406.00
	STD	27.8	19.8	28.1	0.818	27.80	6.01
F5	Mean	521	520	535	515	521.00	516.00
	Worst	537	542	565	529	537.00	535.00
	Best	510	506	505	508	510.00	504.00
	STD	7.06	10.4	13.4	4.6	7.06	9.11
F6	Mean	600	601	613	613	604.00	601.00
	Worst	600	605	643	640	614.00	605.00
	Best	600	600	602	600	600.00	600.00
	STD	0.0234	1.11	11.4	11.6	3.13	1.08
F7	Mean	719	731	763	724	738.00	734.00
	Worst	729	746	803	749	765.00	756.00
	Best	713	717	730	712	715.00	716.00
	STD	3.52	10	20.5	9.88	12.00	11.10
F8	Mean	812	816	827	834	819.00	817.00
	Worst	824	837	838	857	829.00	835.00
	Best	805	805	814	818	811.00	805.00
	STD	5.41	8.11	7.33	8.04	4.94	7.66

Table 2. *Cont.*

Function		COSGO	GWO	SCSO	WOA	AGWO-CS	PSOGSA
F9	Mean	900	907	997	913	919.00	910.00
	Worst	900	969	1280	970	973.00	984.00
	Best	900	900	903	905	900.00	900.00
	STD	0.0124	14.3	88.8	11.4	24.10	21.70
F10	Mean	1500	1720	1890	1520	1900.00	1480.00
	Worst	2270	2840	2490	2000	2520.00	2500.00
	Best	1000	1180	1240	1250	1420.00	1130.00
	STD	450	412	296	156	308.00	317.00
F11	Mean	1150	1120	1100	1110	1150.00	1130.00
	Worst	1240	1150	1110	1130	1240.00	1310.00
	Best	1120	1100	1100	1100	1120.00	1110.00
	STD	31.3	11.3	2.01	5.82	31.30	44.20
F12	Mean	641,000	948,000	943,000	844,000	641,000.00	844,000.00
	Worst	2,820,000	7,210,000	3,890,000	2,740,000	2,820,000.00	2,740,000.00
	Best	13,200	27,700	46,100	8660	13,200.00	8660.00
	STD	740,000	1,410,000	999,000	901,000	740,000.00	901,000.00
F13	Mean	8300	13,000	11,600	8450	8450.00	12,600.00
	Worst	29,000	26,500	35,100	15,400	15,400.00	29,700.00
	Best	1360	2280	2500	3190	3190.00	3140.00
	STD	7650	7460	8740	2990	2990.00	6760.00
F14	Mean	1450	2900	2100	1470	3060.00	1540.00
	Worst	1480	7240	5230	1560	5560.00	1610.00
	Best	1440	1450	1440	1420	1450.00	1500.00
	STD	11.3	1860	1400	35.2	1740.00	24.00
F15	Mean	1540	4380	2710	1690	5230.00	4120.00
	Worst	1580	10,100	7690	2820	10,600.00	6020.00
	Best	1510	1650	1560	1520	1580.00	1640.00
	STD	16.1	2270	1420	255	2440.00	1150.00
F16	Mean	1770	1820	1800	1780	1770.00	1700.00
	Worst	1990	2240	2000	1960	1990.00	2050.00
	Best	1620	1600	1620	1600	1620.00	1610.00
	STD	118	178	108	111	118.00	115.00
F17	Mean	1760	1760	1760	1790	1760.00	1790.00
	Worst	1870	1890	1820	1880	1870.00	1880.00
	Best	1720	1720	1730	1740	1720.00	1740.00
	STD	34.2	37.1	19.1	34.4	34.20	34.40
F18	Mean	20,800	25,300	18,900	16,100	20,800.00	30,800.00
	Worst	41,200	55,300	50,500	40,900	41,200.00	55,600.00
	Best	3640	4060	2010	2480	3640.00	2930.00
	STD	13,600	13,900	12,500	12,100	13,600.00	16,200.00

Table 2. *Cont.*

Function		COSGO	GWO	SCSO	WOA	AGWO-CS	PSOGSA
F19	Mean	1930	8260	6690	2770	15,400.00	8380.00
	Worst	1970	18,600	14,700	10,100	258,000.00	18,900.00
	Best	1910	1930	1910	1900	1910.00	1920.00
	STD	13.2	6190	5640	1860	46,200.00	6530.00
F20	Mean	2020	2200	2100	2040	2090.00	2060.00
	Worst	2030	2280	2230	2150	2220.00	2150.00
	Best	2000	2180	2040	2000	2030.00	2020.00
	STD	7.51	19.8	55	46	58.40	43.10
F21	Mean	2270	2270	2260	2300	2310.00	2310.00
	Worst	2330	2330	2340	2340	2340.00	2340.00
	Best	2200	2100	2100	2200	2200.00	2200.00
	STD	53.7	63.2	69.6	48.5	30.40	21.70
F22	Mean	2300	2300	2300	2310	2310.00	2310.00
	Worst	2310	2320	2330	2340	2340.00	2330.00
	Best	2200	2220	2250	2300	2300.00	2300.00
	STD	18.7	16	14.1	8.76	8.76	6.33
F23	Mean	2620	2620	2640	2620	2620.00	2620.00
	Worst	2650	2640	2690	2630	2650.00	2650.00
	Best	2610	2600	2620	2610	2610.00	2610.00
	STD	8.73	9.8	14.4	7.75	8.73	11.20
F24	Mean	2750	2730	2750	2740	2750.00	2750.00
	Worst	2800	2780	2820	2780	2800.00	2770.00
	Best	2720	2510	2500	2500	2720.00	2730.00
	STD	14.3	61.8	67	53.5	14.30	13.00
F25	Mean	2930	2940	2940	2930	2930.00	2940.00
	Worst	2950	2950	3020	2950	2950.00	3020.00
	Best	2910	2900	2900	2900	2910.00	2900.00
	STD	13	14.2	22.7	22.8	13.00	22.80
F26	Mean	3040	2930	3010	2940	3040.00	2960.00
	Worst	4060	3190	3470	3830	4060.00	3840.00
	Best	2750	2900	2810	2600	2750.00	2900.00
	STD	289	59.6	128	186	289.00	171.00
F27	Mean	3100	3100	3100	3100	3100.00	3090.00
	Worst	3170	3120	3180	3160	3170.00	3100.00
	Best	3090	3090	3090	3090	3090.00	3090.00
	STD	17.5	5.8	18.6	16.4	17.50	3.02

Table 2. *Cont.*

Function		COSGO	GWO	SCSO	WOA	AGWO-CS	PSOGSA
F28	Mean	3370	3380	3280	3220	3370.00	3370.00
	Worst	3480	3450	3410	3410	3480.00	3410.00
	Best	3170	3180	3160	3100	3170.00	3170.00
	STD	99.7	62.6	109	144	99.70	83.90
F29	Mean	3200	3200	3250	3200	3200.00	3200.00
	Worst	3290	3320	3450	3310	3290.00	3300.00
	Best	3160	3150	3160	3150	3160.00	3140.00
	STD	38.5	50	70.2	44.1	38.50	42.50
F30	Mean	33,200	550,000	464,000	253,000	648,000.00	893,000.00
	Worst	831,000	1,920,000	2,270,000	821,000	6,730,000.00	2,450,000.00
	Best	3820	5430	7120	4520	8600.00	7470.00
	STD	151,000	715,000	658,000	378,000	1,460,000.00	621,000.00

Table 3. Friedman rankings of COSGO and the compared algorithms.

Function	COSGO	GWO	SCSO	WOA	AGWO_CS	PSOGSA
1	1	3	6	5	2	4
3	1	4	5	2.5	6	2.5
4	5	3	4	1	5	2
5	4	3	6	1	4	2
6	1	2.5	5.5	5.5	4	2.5
7	1	3	6	2	5	4
8	1	2	5	6	4	3
9	1	2	6	4	5	3
10	2	4	5	3	6	1
11	5	3	1	2	5	4
12	1.5	6	5	3.5	1.5	3.5
13	1	6	4	2.5	2.5	5
14	1	5	4	2	6	3
15	1	5	3	2	6	4
16	2	6	5	4	2	1
17	2.5	2.5	2.5	5.5	2.5	5.5
18	3	5	2	1	3	6
19	1	4	3	2	6	5
20	1	6	5	2	4	3
21	2.5	2.5	1	4	5.5	5.5
22	2	2	2	5	5	5
23	3	3	6	3	3	3
24	3	1	3	2	3	3
25	2.5	5	5	2.5	2.5	5
26	5.5	1	4	2	5.5	3
27	4	4	4	4	4	1
28	4	6	2	1	4	4
29	3	3	6	3	3	3
30	1	4	3	2	5	6
Total	66.5	106.5	119	85	120	102.5
Average Ranking	2.2931	3.6724	4.1034	2.9310	4.1379	3.5345

4.2. Experimental Analysis Based on Multi-Level Thresholding

To assess the performance of the proposed COSGO algorithm against other methods, multiple quantitative metrics were used, such as the Peak Signal-to-Noise Ratio (PSNR), the Feature Similarity Index (FSIM), the Structural Similarity Index Measure (SSIM), dice, and the Jaccard index and accuracy, along with the optimal objective function values and their associated variances. In this regard, ten images were selected from the BSD500 dataset [40]. For ease of interpretation and comparative analysis, the best results averaged over 10 independent runs are highlighted in bold in the subsequent tables. Table 4 presents the average and standard deviation fitness function values for all compared methods across thresholding levels 2, 3, 4, and 5 evaluated on all images using two objective functions: Otsu's method and Kapur's entropy. Moreover, the proposed COSGO algorithm demonstrates lower computational time at threshold level 2 and level 3. Based on the obtained results of the running time of each algorithm, which are presented in Table 5, the COSGO algorithm achieves superior performance in terms of execution time.

The segmentation results based on Otsu and Kapur entropy are shown in Table 6, along with the PSNR, SSIM, and FSIM values. A traditional statistic for assessing image quality is the PSNR. It determines how segmented and original photos differ from one another. The segmented image is more like the original when the PSNR value is higher. In this way, the higher value of the PSNR proves the algorithm efficiently. In addition, the mean square error (MSE) was calculated for each algorithm with two objective functions. The obtained results were also in the same running condition, with 100 iteration numbers and 30 search agent numbers. It was observed that the proposed COSGO algorithm showed better performance in terms of higher PSNR and lower MSE values in comparison to the other algorithms.

The Structural Similarity Index Measure (SSIM) evaluates the perceived quality of an image by incorporating luminance, contrast, and structural information. A higher SSIM value closer to 1 indicates a greater structural similarity between the segmented image and the original image. The Feature Similarity Index Measure (FSIM), which is widely used for image quality assessment, particularly in terms of texture and detail preservation, quantifies the similarity based on low-level image features, such as phase congruency and gradient magnitude. Table 7 presents the obtained value for each algorithm with two different objective functions as Otsu and Kapur entropy functions.

In Table 8, the dice coefficient and Jaccard index are shown. The dice coefficient and Jaccard index (intersection over union) are widely used metrics for evaluating image segmentation performance by measuring the similarity between the predicted segmentation and the ground truth. In contrast, the Jaccard index measures the ratio of the intersection to the union of the same sets. Both metrics range from 0 to 1, with higher values indicating greater similarity, and they are especially important in assessing the spatial accuracy of segmentation methods.

Table 9 presents the quantitative evaluation of the segmentation accuracy achieved by each algorithm across the test image dataset. The evaluation is based on two widely recognized overlap-based similarity metrics: the dice coefficient and the Jaccard index. These metrics assess how closely the segmented regions produced by the algorithms align with the ground truth masks. Higher values in both metrics indicate superior segmentation performance, reflecting better boundary adherence and region consistency. The table highlights the comparative strengths of each method and provides a comprehensive understanding of their effectiveness in accurately delineating the target regions.

Table 4. The fitness values of the algorithms.

Level	Image		COSGO		GWO		SCSO		WOA		AGWO_CS		PSOGSA	
			Otsu	Kapur	Otsu	Kapur	Otsu	Kapur	Otsu	Kapur	Otsu	Kapur	Otsu	Kapur
2	118031	Value	−18,504.54	−5.15	−18,504.54	−5.15	−18,504.54	−5.15	−18,504.51	−5.15	−18,504.32	−5.15	−18,504.54	−5.15
		STD	0.00	0.00	0.00	0.00	0.00	0.00	0.05	0.00	0.15	0.00	0.00	0.00
	118072	Value	−9517.97	−5.04	−9517.97	−5.04	−9517.97	−5.04	−9517.96	−5.04	−9517.91	−5.04	−9517.97	−5.04
		STD	0.00	0.00	0.00	0.00	0.00	0.00	0.02	0.00	0.06	0.00	0.00	0.00
	326025	Value	−6334.31	−4.88	−6334.31	−4.88	−6334.31	−4.88	−6334.31	−4.88	−6334.25	−4.88	−6334.31	−4.88
		STD	0.00	0.00	0.00	0.00	0.00	0.00	0.00	0.00	0.08	0.00	0.00	0.00
	120003	Value	−26,805.11	−5.22	−26,805.11	−5.22	−26,805.11	−5.22	−26,805.08	−5.22	−26,804.92	−5.22	−26,805.11	−5.22
		STD	0.00	0.00	0.00	0.00	0.00	0.00	0.06	0.00	0.05	0.00	0.00	0.00
	253092	Value	−15,027.04	−4.99	−15,027.01	−4.99	−15,027.04	−4.99	−15,027.04	−4.99	−15,026.96	−4.99	−15,027.04	−4.99
		STD	0.00	0.00	0.08	0.00	0.00	0.00	0.01	0.00	0.09	0.00	0.00	0.00
	8068	Value	−12,529.92	−4.65	−12,529.92	−4.65	−12,529.92	−4.65	−12,529.92	−4.65	−12,529.85	−4.65	−12,529.92	−4.65
		STD	0.00	0.00	0.00	0.00	0.00	0.00	0.01	0.00	0.10	0.00	0.00	0.00
	81095	Value	−15,094.56	−5.16	−15,094.56	−5.16	−15,094.56	−5.16	−15,094.56	−5.16	−15,094.53	−5.16	−15,094.56	−5.16
		STD	0.00	0.00	0.00	0.00	0.00	0.00	0.00	0.00	0.06	0.00	0.00	0.00
	92014	Value	−14,961.03	−4.55	−14,961.03	−4.55	−14,961.03	−4.55	−14,961.03	−4.55	−14,960.91	−4.55	−14,961.03	−4.55
		STD	0.00	0.00	0.00	0.00	0.00	0.00	0.01	0.00	0.13	0.00	0.00	0.00
	365072	Value	−17,439.29	−5.48	−17,439.29	−5.48	−17,439.29	−5.48	−17,439.29	−5.48	−17,439.23	−5.48	−17,439.29	−5.48
		STD	0.00	0.00	0.00	0.00	0.00	0.00	0.00	0.00	0.09	0.00	0.00	0.00
	384022	Value	−15,896.95	−5.16	−15,896.95	−5.16	−15,896.95	−5.16	−15,896.93	−5.16	−15,896.90	−5.16	−15,896.95	−5.16
		STD	0.00	0.00	0.00	0.00	0.00	0.00	0.05	0.00	0.03	0.00	0.00	0.00

Table 4. *Cont.*

Level	Image		COSGO		GWO		SCSO		WOA		AGWO_CS		PSOGSA	
			Otsu	Kapur	Otsu	Kapur	Otsu	Kapur	Otsu	Kapur	Otsu	Kapur	Otsu	Kapur
3	118031	Value	−18,730.87	−5.15	−18,730.74	−5.15	−18,730.87	−5.15	−18,730.84	−5.15	−18,730.08	−5.15	−18,730.87	−5.15
		STD	0.00	0.00	0.29	0.00	0.00	0.00	0.05	0.00	0.33	0.00	0.00	0.00
	118072	Value	−9640.56	−5.04	−9640.56	−5.04	−9640.54	−5.04	−9640.52	−5.04	−9639.99	−5.04	−9640.56	−5.04
		STD	0.00	0.00	0.00	0.00	0.04	0.00	0.05	0.00	0.31	0.00	0.00	0.00
	326025	Value	−6504.93	−4.88	−6504.93	−4.88	−6504.92	−4.88	−6504.85	−4.88	−6504.16	−4.88	−6504.93	−4.88
		STD	0.00	0.00	0.00	0.00	0.01	0.00	0.09	0.00	0.87	0.00	0.00	0.00
	120003	Value	−27,071.72	−5.22	−27,071.70	−5.22	−27,071.71	−5.22	−27,071.54	−5.22	−27,070.76	−5.22	−27,071.72	−5.22
		STD	0.00	0.00	0.04	0.00	0.03	0.00	0.40	0.00	0.94	0.00	0.00	0.00
	253092	Value	−15,184.31	−4.99	−15,183.55	−4.99	−15,184.31	−4.99	−15,184.30	−4.99	−15,183.08	−4.99	−15,184.31	−4.99
		STD	0.00	0.00	1.67	0.00	0.00	0.00	0.01	0.00	0.85	0.00	0.00	0.00
	8068	Value	−12,611.96	−4.65	−12,611.96	−4.65	−12,611.96	−4.65	−12,611.91	−4.65	−12,611.23	−4.65	−12,611.96	−4.65
		STD	0.00	0.00	0.00	0.00	0.00	0.00	0.09	0.00	0.55	0.00	0.00	0.00
	81095	Value	−15,261.54	−5.16	−15,261.38	−5.16	−15,261.53	−5.16	−15,261.44	−5.16	−15,260.17	−5.16	−15,261.54	−5.16
		STD	0.00	0.00	0.35	0.00	0.02	0.00	0.11	0.00	0.66	0.00	0.00	0.00
	92014	Value	−15,071.07	−4.55	−15,070.85	−4.55	−15,071.09	−4.55	−15,071.08	−4.55	−15,070.23	−4.55	−15,071.09	−4.55
		STD	0.04	0.00	0.55	0.00	0.00	0.00	0.02	0.00	0.76	0.00	0.01	0.00
	365072	Value	−17,685.43	−5.48	−17,685.43	−5.48	−17,685.42	−5.48	−17,685.34	−5.48	−17,684.14	−5.48	−17,685.43	−5.48
		STD	0.00	0.00	0.00	0.00	0.03	0.00	0.13	0.00	1.18	0.00	0.00	0.00
	384022	Value	−16,124.65	−5.16	−16,124.65	−5.16	−16,124.65	−5.16	−16,124.62	−5.16	−16,123.64	−5.16	−16,124.65	−5.16
		STD	0.00	0.00	0.00	0.00	0.01	0.00	0.04	0.00	0.77	0.00	0.00	0.00

Table 4. *Cont.*

Level	Image		COSGO		GWO		SCSO		WOA		AGWO_CS		PSOGSA	
			Otsu	Kapur	Otsu	Kapur	Otsu	Kapur	Otsu	Kapur	Otsu	Kapur	Otsu	Kapur
4	118031	Value	−18,805.074	−5.152	−18,804.707	−5.152	−18,805.081	−5.152	−18,804.720	−5.152	−18,801.351	−5.152	−18,805.082	−5.152
		STD	0.009	0.000	0.845	0.000	0.020	0.000	0.394	0.000	2.147	0.000	0.011	0.000
	118072	Value	−9695.921	−5.036	−9695.365	−5.036	−9695.908	−5.036	−9695.822	−5.036	−9693.808	−5.036	−9695.941	−5.036
		STD	0.019	0.000	1.271	0.000	0.040	0.000	0.164	0.000	1.821	0.000	0.000	0.000
	326025	Value	−6593.882	−4.885	−6593.882	−4.885	−6593.886	−4.885	−6593.854	−4.885	−6592.268	−4.885	−6593.886	−4.885
		STD	0.014	0.000	0.014	0.000	0.005	0.000	0.044	0.000	1.137	0.000	0.005	0.000
	120003	Value	−27,163.825	−5.220	−27,163.808	−5.220	−27,163.801	−5.220	−27,163.555	−5.220	−27,161.155	−5.220	−27,163.828	−5.220
		STD	0.003	0.000	0.038	0.000	0.054	0.000	0.244	0.000	1.277	0.000	0.000	0.000
	253092	Value	−15,254.533	−4.990	−15,254.046	−4.990	−15,254.540	−4.990	−15,254.434	−4.990	−15,252.271	−4.990	−15,254.543	−4.990
		STD	0.015	0.000	1.078	0.000	0.008	0.000	0.105	0.000	1.013	0.000	0.000	0.000
	8068	Value	−12,666.569	−4.645	−12,666.569	−4.645	−12,666.571	−4.645	−12,666.394	−4.645	−12,664.976	−4.645	−12,662.381	−4.645
		STD	0.004	0.000	0.004	0.000	0.000	0.000	0.215	0.000	1.148	0.000	9.369	0.000
	81095	Value	−15,321.807	−5.156	−15,321.806	−5.156	−15,321.817	−5.156	−15,321.695	−5.156	−15,320.714	−5.156	−15,321.807	−5.156
		STD	0.028	0.000	0.031	0.000	0.023	0.000	0.161	0.000	0.590	0.000	0.028	0.000
	92014	Value	−15,132.280	−4.552	−15,132.276	−4.552	−15,132.281	−4.552	−15,132.270	−4.552	−15,129.595	−4.552	−15,132.276	−4.552
		STD	0.005	0.000	0.006	0.000	0.005	0.000	0.031	0.000	1.515	0.000	0.007	0.000
	365072	Value	−17,791.010	−5.483	−17,790.996	−5.483	−17,791.033	−5.483	−17,790.846	−5.483	−17,787.168	−5.483	−17,791.008	−5.483
		STD	0.032	0.000	0.051	0.000	0.000	0.000	0.275	0.000	1.619	0.000	0.041	0.000
	384022	Value	−16,180.251	−5.160	−16,180.238	−5.160	−16,169.119	−5.160	−16,179.835	−5.160	−16,177.785	−5.160	−16,179.035	−5.160
		STD	0.009	0.000	0.009	0.000	24.859	0.000	0.661	0.000	1.126	0.000	2.727	0.000

Table 4. *Cont.*

Level	Image		COSGO		GWO		SCSO		WOA		AGWO_CS		PSOGSA	
			Otsu	Kapur	Otsu	Kapur	Otsu	Kapur	Otsu	Kapur	Otsu	Kapur	Otsu	Kapur
5	118031	Value	−18,843.8	−5.15164	-1.88×10^4	-5.15×10^0	−18,836	−5.15164	−18,843.5	−5.15164	−18,843.8	−5.15164	-1.88×10^4	-5.15×10^0
		STD	0.024575	0	2.185805	6.28×10^{-16}	17.26396	0	0.432428	0	0.024575	0	2.185805	6.28×10^{-16}
	118072	Value	-9.73×10^3	-5.04×10^0	-9.72×10^3	-5.04×10^0	-9.72×10^3	-5.04×10^0	-9.73×10^3	-5.04×10^0	-9.73×10^3	-5.04×10^0	-9.72×10^3	-5.04×10^0
		STD	0.015209	8.88×10^{-16}	1.713792	4.44×10^{-16}	13.31547	4.44×10^{-16}	0.437801	8.88×10^{-16}	0.015209	8.88×10^{-16}	1.713792	4.44×10^{-16}
	326025	Value	−6640.82	−4.88486	-6.64×10^3	-4.88×10^0	-6.64×10^3	-4.88×10^0	-6.64×10^3	-4.88×10^0	−6640.82	−4.88486	-6.64×10^3	-4.88×10^0
		STD	0.02325	0	0.000355	6.28×10^{-16}	0.007064	7.69×10^{-16}	0.321744	7.69×10^{-16}	0.02325	0	0.000355	6.28×10^{-16}
	120003	Value	-2.72×10^4	-5.22×10^0	-2.72×10^4	-5.22×10^0	-2.72×10^4	-5.22×10^0	−27,219.5	−5.21957	-2.72×10^4	-5.22×10^0	-2.72×10^4	-5.22×10^0
		STD	0.062141	7.69×10^{-16}	0.138989	8.88×10^{-16}	0.239523	8.88×10^{-16}	1.980433	0	0.062141	7.69×10^{-16}	0.138989	8.88×10^{-16}
	253092	Value	-1.53×10^4	-4.99×10^0	−15,292.5	−4.99043	−15,293.9	−4.99043	−15,285.9	−4.99043	-1.53×10^4	-4.99×10^0	−15,292.5	−4.99043
		STD	0.088749	4.44×10^{-16}	3.140839	0	0.001474	0	17.53074	0	0.088749	4.44×10^{-16}	3.140839	0
	8068	Value	-1.27×10^4	-4.65×10^0	-1.27×10^4	-4.65×10^0	-1.27×10^4	-4.65×10^0	-1.27×10^4	-4.65×10^0	-1.27×10^4	-4.65×10^0	-1.27×10^4	-4.65×10^0
		STD	0.005499	4.44×10^{-16}	2.946929	4.44×10^{-16}	0.022274	1.09×10^{-15}	0.901476	8.88×10^{-16}	0.005499	4.44×10^{-16}	2.946929	4.44×10^{-16}
	81095	Value	-1.54×10^4	-5.16×10^0	-1.54×10^4	-5.16×10^0	-1.54×10^4	-5.16×10^0	-1.54×10^4	-5.16×10^0	-1.54×10^4	-5.16×10^0	-1.54×10^4	-5.16×10^0
		STD	0.006642	7.69×10^{-16}	0.421632	4.44×10^{-16}	16.24358	6.28×10^{-16}	0.66682	4.44×10^{-16}	0.006642	7.69×10^{-16}	0.421632	4.44×10^{-16}
	92014	Value	-1.52×10^4	-4.55×10^0	−15,159.7	−4.55222	-1.52×10^4	-4.55×10^0	−15,160.5	−4.55222	-1.52×10^4	-4.55×10^0	−15,159.7	−4.55222
		STD	0.057762	6.28×10^{-16}	1.830489	0	0.017674	4.44×10^{-16}	0.052781	0	0.057762	6.28×10^{-16}	1.830489	0
	365072	Value	-1.78×10^4	-5.48×10^0	−17,848.9	−5.48253	-1.78×10^4	-5.48×10^0	-1.78×10^4	-5.48×10^0	-1.78×10^4	-5.48×10^0	−17,848.9	−5.48253
		STD	0.036263	4.44×10^{-16}	0.030867	0	0.116513	1.09×10^{-15}	0.150933	8.88×10^{-16}	0.036263	4.44×10^{-16}	0.030867	0
	384022	Value	-1.62×10^4	-5.16×10^0	−16,225.7	−5.16025	-1.62×10^4	-5.16×10^0	−16,226	−5.16025	-1.62×10^4	-5.16×10^0	−16,225.7	−5.16025
		STD	0.020737	6.28×10^{-16}	2.203184	0	0.211542	4.44×10^{-16}	0.704882	0	0.020737	6.28×10^{-16}	2.203184	0

Table 5. The running time of each algorithm.

Level	Image	COSGO		GWO		SCSO		WOA		AGWO_CS		PSOGSA	
		Otsu	Kapur	Otsu	Kapur	Otsu	Kapur	Otsu	Kapur	Otsu	Kapur	Otsu	Kapur
2	118031	0.8769	0.9559	0.2855	0.3186	0.2969	0.3218	0.2884	0.3146	0.3003	0.3298	0.2900	0.3198
	118072	0.8331	0.9563	0.2861	0.3181	0.2898	0.3223	0.2802	0.3136	0.2966	0.3290	0.2842	0.3195
	326025	0.8368	0.9590	0.2862	0.3197	0.2938	0.3225	0.2825	0.3143	0.2943	0.3316	0.2940	0.3191
	120003	0.8435	0.9637	0.2842	0.3189	0.2879	0.3268	0.2821	0.3152	0.2973	0.3295	0.2824	0.3220
	253092	0.8432	0.9507	0.2859	0.3173	0.2913	0.3215	0.2791	0.3101	0.2938	0.3275	0.2840	0.3171
	8068	0.8437	0.9573	0.2831	0.3190	0.2913	0.3236	0.2809	0.3133	0.2930	0.3292	0.2878	0.3189
	81095	0.8351	0.9547	0.2794	0.3187	0.2902	0.3253	0.2815	0.3117	0.2932	0.3295	0.2949	0.3202
	92014	0.8507	0.9520	0.2860	0.3181	0.2919	0.3254	0.2846	0.3135	0.2951	0.3307	0.2859	0.3193
	365072	0.8325	0.9484	0.2786	0.3162	0.2830	0.3203	0.2828	0.3104	0.2919	0.3273	0.2839	0.3181
	384022	0.8334	0.9470	0.2813	0.3272	0.2872	0.3237	0.2815	0.3144	0.2912	0.3306	0.2899	0.3201
3	118031	0.8883	0.9767	0.2931	0.3254	0.2945	0.3329	0.2934	0.3228	0.3139	0.3457	0.2949	0.3223
	118072	0.8539	0.9695	0.2835	0.3258	0.2935	0.3288	0.2843	0.3256	0.3030	0.3432	0.2874	0.3237
	326025	0.8739	0.9839	0.2876	0.3290	0.2912	0.3324	0.2929	0.3260	0.3068	0.3430	0.2976	0.3245
	120003	0.8653	0.9769	0.2879	0.3265	0.2934	0.3373	0.2887	0.3277	0.3056	0.3451	0.2912	0.3251
	253092	0.8573	0.9601	0.2892	0.3198	0.2933	0.3295	0.2886	0.3206	0.3025	0.3352	0.2895	0.3199
	8068	0.8559	0.9788	0.2886	0.3257	0.2950	0.3330	0.2853	0.3247	0.3066	0.3376	0.2958	0.3290
	81095	0.8618	0.9609	0.2858	0.3259	0.2942	0.3347	0.2907	0.3215	0.3045	0.3396	0.2978	0.3251
	92014	0.8698	0.9725	0.2877	0.3270	0.2952	0.3323	0.2850	0.3238	0.3080	0.3436	0.2950	0.3256
	365072	0.8560	0.9618	0.2847	0.3252	0.2915	0.3322	0.2835	0.3212	0.3022	0.3418	0.2869	0.3213
	384022	0.8608	0.9753	0.2856	0.3246	0.2891	0.3333	0.2842	0.3265	0.3028	0.3391	0.2866	0.3258
4	118031	0.9017	1.0080	0.2921	0.3369	0.2969	0.3355	0.2897	0.3271	0.3137	0.3503	0.3019	0.3348
	118072	0.8971	0.9984	0.2908	0.3428	0.2975	0.3410	0.2858	0.3339	0.3101	0.3500	0.2942	0.3341
	326025	0.8771	1.0022	0.2892	0.3335	0.2933	0.3361	0.2896	0.3365	0.3105	0.3519	0.2980	0.3373
	120003	0.8722	0.9890	0.2991	0.3349	0.3004	0.3394	0.2889	0.3338	0.3160	0.3533	0.2955	0.3375
	253092	0.8793	0.9681	0.2998	0.3309	0.2947	0.3412	0.2890	0.3299	0.3079	0.3503	0.2948	0.3290
	8068	0.8901	0.9726	0.2894	0.3327	0.2974	0.3363	0.2852	0.3265	0.3094	0.3488	0.3010	0.3295
	81095	0.8797	0.9799	0.2907	0.3320	0.2980	0.3343	0.2864	0.3278	0.3073	0.3491	0.3021	0.3356
	92014	0.8896	1.0001	0.2932	0.3307	0.2961	0.3505	0.2912	0.3269	0.3113	0.3579	0.3006	0.3328
	365072	0.8610	0.9931	0.2892	0.3348	0.2938	0.3334	0.2892	0.3334	0.3063	0.3501	0.2931	0.3297
	384022	0.8790	0.9992	0.3008	0.3340	0.2968	0.3365	0.2919	0.3298	0.3055	0.3489	0.2950	0.3353

Table 5. *Cont.*

Level	Image	COSGO		GWO		SCSO		WOA		AGWO_CS		PSOGSA	
		Otsu	Kapur	Otsu	Kapur	Otsu	Kapur	Otsu	Kapur	Otsu	Kapur	Otsu	Kapur
5	118031	0.8970	0.9917	0.3113	0.3451	0.3047	0.3399	0.2965	0.3275	0.3205	0.3559	0.3045	0.3325
	118072	0.8763	0.9898	0.3134	0.3415	0.2968	0.3365	0.2899	0.3288	0.3092	0.3631	0.2958	0.3310
	326025	0.8902	0.9990	0.3129	0.3465	0.3018	0.3399	0.2882	0.3254	0.3146	0.3597	0.3013	0.3326
	120003	0.8857	0.9936	0.3203	0.3486	0.3007	0.3337	0.2918	0.3315	0.3131	0.3546	0.3006	0.3329
	253092	0.9002	0.9818	0.3062	0.3390	0.2965	0.3347	0.2892	0.3282	0.3155	0.3731	0.2979	0.3289
	8068	0.8874	0.9833	0.3024	0.3401	0.2985	0.3323	0.2890	0.3261	0.3134	0.3605	0.3014	0.3330
	81095	0.8722	0.9910	0.3097	0.3348	0.2964	0.3393	0.2885	0.3291	0.3174	0.3679	0.3039	0.3286
	92014	0.8786	0.9942	0.3070	0.3421	0.2971	0.3399	0.2921	0.3394	0.3151	0.3699	0.2996	0.3276
	365072	0.8606	0.9963	0.2984	0.3395	0.2974	0.3364	0.2875	0.3285	0.3072	0.3522	0.2987	0.3273
	384022	0.8866	1.0177	0.2969	0.3346	0.2936	0.3376	0.2860	0.3283	0.3098	0.3548	0.2972	0.3271

Table 6. The PSNR and MSE values of the algorithms.

Level	Image		COSGO		GWO		SCSO		WOA		AGWO_CS		PSOGSA	
			Otsu	Kapur	Otsu	Kapur	Otsu	Kapur	Otsu	Kapur	Otsu	Kapur	Otsu	Kapur
2	118031	PSNR	19.51	16.14	19.51	16.76	19.51	16.23	19.50	16.47	19.42	15.46	19.51	16.18
		MSE	727.94	1603.79	727.94	1416.16	727.94	1561.26	729.86	1484.20	743.18	1919.64	727.94	1588.24
	118072	PSNR	19.54	16.80	19.54	17.66	19.54	17.91	19.54	16.87	19.54	15.06	19.54	17.08
		MSE	723.02	1498.45	723.02	1225.43	723.02	1223.50	723.09	1420.47	723.36	2130.41	723.02	1317.66
	326025	PSNR	21.54	19.70	21.54	16.26	21.54	15.33	21.55	16.04	21.54	16.87	21.54	15.22
		MSE	455.85	761.11	455.85	2075.13	455.85	2277.03	455.55	1862.70	456.18	1659.86	455.85	3026.49
	120003	PSNR	20.21	14.85	20.21	14.55	20.21	13.83	20.20	15.55	20.16	12.44	20.21	16.58
		MSE	619.69	2412.10	619.69	2619.17	619.69	2693.16	620.89	2017.50	627.36	4020.18	619.69	1658.73
	253092	PSNR	15.16	14.42	15.16	14.35	15.16	14.35	15.17	14.17	15.17	13.81	15.16	14.81
		MSE	1981.66	2378.72	1979.69	2411.36	1981.66	2393.70	1979.08	2519.82	1975.38	2721.10	1981.66	2152.47
	8068	PSNR	16.14	10.55	16.14	10.55	16.14	11.46	16.14	10.95	16.14	10.55	16.14	12.04
		MSE	1582.45	5747.19	1582.45	5737.83	1582.45	4724.23	1582.64	5410.56	1583.09	5919.62	1582.45	4177.89
	81095	PSNR	20.00	15.64	20.00	16.07	20.00	16.52	20.00	16.84	19.99	14.97	20.00	15.98
		MSE	649.97	1775.69	649.97	1667.19	649.97	1506.76	649.97	1375.75	651.71	2083.89	649.97	1668.81
	92014	PSNR	9.74	9.59	9.74	9.45	9.74	9.52	9.75	9.43	9.75	9.51	9.74	9.43
		MSE	6898.32	7156.04	6898.32	7382.34	6898.32	7269.33	6895.70	7433.11	6894.52	7287.66	6898.32	7432.31
	365072	PSNR	20.67	12.86	20.67	12.53	20.67	13.04	20.67	14.42	20.66	13.50	20.67	16.95
		MSE	557.46	3465.46	557.46	3683.50	557.46	3291.42	557.46	2572.63	558.16	3347.27	557.46	1614.96
	384022	PSNR	19.93	16.89	19.93	16.40	19.93	17.29	19.92	17.97	19.94	15.85	19.93	16.72
		MSE	661.26	1426.22	661.26	1589.15	661.26	1283.28	661.92	1091.16	659.15	1795.36	661.26	1527.68

Table 6. *Cont.*

Level	Image		COSGO		GWO		SCSO		WOA		AGWO_CS		PSOGSA	
			Otsu	Kapur	Otsu	Kapur	Otsu	Kapur	Otsu	Kapur	Otsu	Kapur	Otsu	Kapur
3	118031	PSNR	22.9351	16.1268	22.9395	16.8132	22.9351	17.8432	22.9771	16.4218	23.0017	17.0766	22.9351	16.7904
		MSE	330.8066	1587.5032	330.4663	1388.9745	330.8066	1081.3988	327.6347	1500.8736	325.8938	1308.5358	330.8066	1450.2195
	118072	PSNR	21.8671	19.0321	21.8671	20.4082	21.8688	20.8823	21.8721	18.7467	21.8783	18.3972	21.8671	18.8232
		MSE	423.0325	857.9918	423.0325	609.7335	422.8679	573.7079	422.5413	921.7215	422.3121	1254.7416	423.0325	954.7287
	326025	PSNR	24.0745	19.5266	24.0745	19.2204	24.0684	19.6495	24.0650	18.1740	24.0191	18.6720	24.0745	18.4796
		MSE	254.4667	768.5329	254.4667	947.5201	254.8246	754.1504	255.0223	1163.7450	257.7481	978.2080	254.4667	970.3092
	120003	PSNR	23.5687	17.2643	23.5664	17.9989	23.5678	18.3603	23.5650	16.6042	23.5177	13.9925	23.5687	19.9053
		MSE	285.8943	1519.4354	286.0463	1195.9356	285.9580	1040.8176	286.1398	1836.8011	289.2805	2599.2134	285.8943	697.5528
	253092	PSNR	15.6191	14.2779	15.6303	15.1022	15.6191	15.1786	15.6193	14.7340	15.5954	14.6339	15.6191	14.9065
		MSE	1783.0651	2450.0577	1778.4972	2014.7354	1783.0651	1985.2576	1783.0104	2188.1618	1792.8673	2267.9789	1783.0651	2107.3803
	8068	PSNR	16.4546	11.0887	16.4546	12.5159	16.4546	11.8508	16.4526	11.2104	16.4597	10.1321	16.4546	12.1029
		MSE	1471.0292	5093.5785	1471.0292	3961.2185	1471.0292	4329.9797	1471.6988	4978.9180	1469.3146	6633.4375	1471.0292	4327.0509
	81095	PSNR	23.5034	15.8988	23.4930	15.9230	23.5235	16.9943	23.5246	18.2818	23.5496	16.2688	23.5034	18.4466
		MSE	290.2267	1679.0968	290.9304	1693.7111	288.9014	1403.3690	288.8323	1116.9040	287.1832	1618.6846	290.2267	1002.2381
	92014	PSNR	9.9854	9.8244	9.9835	9.8756	9.9855	9.6024	9.9837	9.6813	9.9798	9.8877	9.9854	9.6678
		MSE	6524.4049	6773.2089	6527.2132	6691.6330	6524.1913	7135.6674	6527.0265	7000.3487	6532.7637	6674.3300	6524.3526	7024.2659
	365072	PSNR	23.2644	13.1461	23.2644	15.3812	23.2635	14.4680	23.2638	12.3608	23.2482	15.9268	23.2644	19.0736
		MSE	306.6449	3344.1274	306.6449	2150.0121	306.7088	2687.2560	306.6893	3777.8059	307.7983	2194.2999	306.6449	1173.5723
	384022	PSNR	24.6464	16.2940	24.6464	17.2054	24.6443	18.0827	24.6481	16.4700	24.6232	17.7313	24.6464	18.0721
		MSE	223.0680	1558.4437	223.0680	1277.8032	223.1773	1046.8039	222.9844	1499.4587	224.2729	1210.3236	223.0680	1060.0297
4	118031	PSNR	24.53	17.50	24.56	18.93	24.52	17.82	24.54	17.66	24.48	15.88	24.53	18.40
		MSE	229.08	1177.38	227.77	922.91	229.69	1135.00	228.78	1131.68	232.16	1716.31	228.92	1005.15
	118072	PSNR	24.03	19.06	24.02	21.97	23.99	20.34	24.08	21.37	23.93	19.97	24.02	19.57
		MSE	256.87	935.98	257.66	438.79	259.48	658.31	254.19	638.95	263.56	807.32	257.63	876.66
	326025	PSNR	25.98	22.17	25.98	19.93	25.97	19.83	25.98	21.05	25.94	17.46	25.97	19.21
		MSE	164.02	422.00	164.02	880.27	164.37	742.25	164.04	542.57	165.60	2176.26	164.37	926.52
	120003	PSNR	25.26	16.71	25.26	20.61	25.27	17.52	25.25	19.97	25.20	13.14	25.27	18.46
		MSE	193.71	1893.83	193.61	621.12	193.38	1472.89	193.96	670.40	196.22	3350.84	193.18	1321.95
	253092	PSNR	15.98	15.10	15.96	15.38	15.98	15.46	15.97	14.58	15.89	14.46	15.98	15.04
		MSE	1642.72	2017.10	1649.54	1898.59	1642.61	1854.57	1643.00	2306.10	1673.70	2356.26	1642.55	2066.07
	8068	PSNR	16.46	10.98	16.46	12.07	16.46	13.60	16.47	11.64	16.45	9.96	16.49	12.68
		MSE	1469.12	5234.30	1469.12	4248.12	1468.47	3167.39	1466.01	4648.60	1472.55	6886.64	1459.92	3715.07
	81095	PSNR	24.88	16.57	24.86	19.58	24.88	17.47	24.87	19.15	24.86	16.86	24.88	17.32
		MSE	211.34	1514.17	212.51	780.56	211.52	1278.55	211.78	868.95	212.49	1527.53	211.34	1352.85
	92014	PSNR	10.10	9.83	10.10	9.97	10.10	10.05	10.10	9.65	10.10	9.88	10.10	9.85
		MSE	6356.41	6772.50	6356.94	6554.16	6356.25	6424.65	6356.11	7058.70	6355.09	6686.68	6357.70	6727.22
	365072	PSNR	25.18	12.72	25.18	17.39	25.19	14.90	25.18	16.82	25.09	13.95	25.18	17.74
		MSE	197.06	3535.42	197.19	1317.40	196.95	2608.09	197.43	1726.96	201.56	2873.21	197.15	1578.84
	384022	PSNR	25.61	16.98	25.64	19.43	25.37	20.50	25.52	17.88	25.52	17.29	25.66	20.30
		MSE	178.72	1321.67	177.47	884.30	189.47	672.84	182.51	1193.42	182.59	1274.93	176.83	699.73

Table 6. *Cont.*

Level	Image		COSGO		GWO		SCSO		WOA		AGWO_CS		PSOGSA	
			Otsu	Kapur	Otsu	Kapur	Otsu	Kapur	Otsu	Kapur	Otsu	Kapur	Otsu	Kapur
5	118031	PSNR	26.05	18.60	26.05	20.34	26.14	18.51	26.16	21.66	25.96	18.63	26.02	19.27
		MSE	161.68	1008.74	161.58	648.90	158.23	1011.57	157.78	469.07	165.38	1037.91	162.54	865.14
	118072	PSNR	25.69	20.56	25.62	21.42	25.63	20.81	25.61	21.68	24.97	21.34	25.57	23.31
		MSE	175.60	681.95	178.19	495.47	178.10	694.31	178.67	449.19	208.81	504.80	180.20	315.30
	326025	PSNR	27.63	19.80	27.63	22.53	27.63	18.87	27.61	22.49	27.39	20.11	27.64	22.14
		MSE	112.25	1023.23	112.18	395.52	112.23	1243.14	112.68	403.09	118.59	651.54	111.92	460.49
	120003	PSNR	26.94	18.99	26.94	19.30	26.93	14.72	26.92	17.39	26.67	14.10	26.91	21.18
		MSE	131.66	846.31	131.44	998.71	131.75	2343.70	132.24	1702.88	139.94	2545.59	132.34	541.65
	253092	PSNR	16.24	15.11	16.23	15.70	16.23	15.07	16.21	15.46	16.26	14.95	16.20	15.51
		MSE	1544.16	2021.33	1550.36	1770.17	1547.55	2028.60	1554.61	1856.85	1537.96	2106.70	1561.64	1850.45
	8068	PSNR	16.62	11.69	16.62	14.12	16.62	13.98	16.61	12.71	16.63	10.85	16.63	13.34
		MSE	1414.48	4476.09	1414.45	2726.31	1414.55	2954.99	1418.46	3795.22	1413.46	5740.31	1413.74	3287.62
	81095	PSNR	26.48	16.31	26.49	22.07	26.41	19.98	26.43	21.23	25.98	15.40	26.09	18.99
		MSE	146.24	1534.75	145.93	428.28	148.49	779.80	148.11	630.37	164.10	1958.40	161.68	952.29
	92014	PSNR	10.15	9.72	10.14	9.87	10.15	9.81	10.14	9.94	10.15	9.94	10.15	9.82
		MSE	6285.96	6942.66	6289.18	6701.73	6287.07	6793.33	6298.67	6598.72	6288.24	6592.38	6288.95	6772.64
	365072	PSNR	26.74	14.63	26.72	18.40	26.74	16.99	26.71	16.60	26.51	16.14	26.74	19.83
		MSE	137.74	2659.72	138.39	1148.47	137.89	1879.41	138.57	1962.17	145.11	2454.43	137.72	747.78
	384022	PSNR	27.16	18.26	27.16	20.40	27.12	21.67	26.82	16.89	26.85	19.13	27.12	21.90
		MSE	125.14	1058.45	125.01	655.66	126.19	502.82	136.74	1398.76	134.34	1062.81	126.24	605.26

Table 7. The SSIM and FSIM values of the algorithms.

Level	Image		COSGO		GWO		SCSO		WOA		AGWO_CS		PSOGSA	
			Otsu	Kapur	Otsu	Kapur	Otsu	Kapur	Otsu	Kapur	Otsu	Kapur	Otsu	Kapur
2	118031	SSIM	0.6929	0.5421	0.6929	0.5533	0.6929	0.5196	0.6928	0.5139	0.6914	0.5079	0.6929	0.5061
		FSIM	0.2940	0.1850	0.2940	0.1880	0.2940	0.1657	0.2939	0.1546	0.2934	0.1595	0.2940	0.1507
	118072	SSIM	0.6188	0.4424	0.6188	0.4880	0.6188	0.5280	0.6188	0.4528	0.6188	0.4095	0.6188	0.4891
		FSIM	0.2884	0.1795	0.2884	0.2099	0.2884	0.2310	0.2886	0.1866	0.2889	0.1587	0.2884	0.1906
	326025	SSIM	0.6185	0.5693	0.6185	0.4385	0.6185	0.4504	0.6185	0.4638	0.6179	0.4957	0.6185	0.4215
		FSIM	0.2750	0.2596	0.2750	0.2068	0.2750	0.2267	0.2749	0.2212	0.2744	0.2418	0.2750	0.2058
	120003	SSIM	0.7224	0.5991	0.7224	0.6345	0.7224	0.7003	0.7222	0.6900	0.7223	0.6302	0.7224	0.6400
		FSIM	0.2486	0.2017	0.2486	0.2066	0.2486	0.2126	0.2487	0.2256	0.2487	0.1988	0.2486	0.2258
	253092	SSIM	0.6207	0.5251	0.6204	0.5164	0.6207	0.5360	0.6206	0.5077	0.6200	0.4693	0.6207	0.5718
		FSIM	0.2382	0.2104	0.2381	0.2039	0.2382	0.1926	0.2382	0.2076	0.2381	0.1985	0.2382	0.2117
	8068	SSIM	0.6597	0.4088	0.6597	0.3951	0.6597	0.4357	0.6597	0.4190	0.6597	0.4091	0.6597	0.4586
		FSIM	0.1519	0.1122	0.1519	0.1222	0.1519	0.1340	0.1520	0.1278	0.1520	0.1331	0.1519	0.1357
	81095	SSIM	0.6595	0.5813	0.6595	0.5884	0.6595	0.5971	0.6595	0.6088	0.6594	0.5811	0.6595	0.5911
		FSIM	0.2454	0.1447	0.2454	0.1595	0.2454	0.1739	0.2454	0.1746	0.2455	0.1591	0.2454	0.1629
	92014	SSIM	0.4599	0.4518	0.4599	0.4252	0.4599	0.4311	0.4602	0.4120	0.4605	0.4376	0.4599	0.4295
		FSIM	0.2915	0.2856	0.2915	0.2794	0.2915	0.2787	0.2915	0.2479	0.2912	0.2772	0.2915	0.2794
	365072	SSIM	0.5763	0.2447	0.5763	0.2289	0.5763	0.2529	0.5763	0.3175	0.5762	0.2845	0.5763	0.4335
		FSIM	0.2507	0.0686	0.2507	0.0555	0.2507	0.0742	0.2507	0.1098	0.2504	0.0893	0.2507	0.1712
	384022	SSIM	0.6890	0.6061	0.6890	0.5992	0.6890	0.6185	0.6888	0.6375	0.6887	0.5652	0.6890	0.6073
		FSIM	0.2167	0.1901	0.2167	0.1801	0.2167	0.2012	0.2167	0.2086	0.2159	0.1779	0.2167	0.1790

Table 7. *Cont.*

Level	Image		COSGO		GWO		SCSO		WOA		AGWO_CS		PSOGSA	
			Otsu	Kapur	Otsu	Kapur	Otsu	Kapur	Otsu	Kapur	Otsu	Kapur	Otsu	Kapur
3	118031	SSIM	0.7799	0.4921	0.7800	0.5559	0.7799	0.6644	0.7807	0.5536	0.7799	0.5898	0.7799	0.5601
		FSIM	0.3657	0.1477	0.3654	0.1896	0.3657	0.2854	0.3661	0.1932	0.3661	0.2298	0.3657	0.2006
	118072	SSIM	0.7114	0.5245	0.7114	0.5536	0.7115	0.5900	0.7116	0.5410	0.7114	0.5227	0.7114	0.5292
		FSIM	0.3764	0.2133	0.3764	0.2387	0.3764	0.2664	0.3765	0.2422	0.3762	0.2282	0.3764	0.2315
	326025	SSIM	0.6949	0.5779	0.6949	0.5488	0.6948	0.5800	0.6943	0.5480	0.6934	0.5941	0.6949	0.5332
		FSIM	0.3420	0.2748	0.3420	0.2564	0.3419	0.2776	0.3417	0.2682	0.3419	0.2947	0.3420	0.2520
	120003	SSIM	0.7804	0.6609	0.7807	0.6761	0.7805	0.6989	0.7805	0.7075	0.7794	0.7071	0.7804	0.6996
		FSIM	0.2816	0.2267	0.2817	0.2318	0.2817	0.2438	0.2817	0.2376	0.2816	0.2257	0.2816	0.2514
	253092	SSIM	0.6424	0.5250	0.6422	0.5604	0.6424	0.5597	0.6425	0.5621	0.6419	0.5574	0.6424	0.5635
		FSIM	0.2914	0.1965	0.2920	0.2379	0.2914	0.2372	0.2915	0.2068	0.2906	0.2369	0.2914	0.2186
	8068	SSIM	0.6826	0.4258	0.6826	0.4713	0.6826	0.4549	0.6829	0.4415	0.6830	0.4060	0.6826	0.4437
		FSIM	0.1769	0.1364	0.1769	0.1620	0.1769	0.1364	0.1771	0.1224	0.1777	0.1157	0.1769	0.1582
	81095	SSIM	0.7343	0.5850	0.7346	0.5823	0.7344	0.6016	0.7340	0.6334	0.7347	0.5932	0.7343	0.6395
		FSIM	0.2989	0.1477	0.2991	0.1550	0.2989	0.1742	0.2988	0.2092	0.2977	0.1732	0.2989	0.2195
	92014	SSIM	0.5434	0.4970	0.5434	0.5062	0.5433	0.4645	0.5431	0.4666	0.5422	0.5351	0.5433	0.4583
		FSIM	0.3791	0.3279	0.3785	0.3139	0.3785	0.3075	0.3782	0.3088	0.3801	0.3602	0.3786	0.2978
	365072	SSIM	0.6767	0.2648	0.6767	0.3720	0.6767	0.3314	0.6765	0.2267	0.6771	0.3965	0.6767	0.5367
		FSIM	0.3437	0.0821	0.3437	0.1403	0.3436	0.1263	0.3437	0.0575	0.3430	0.1620	0.3437	0.2575
	384022	SSIM	0.7331	0.5930	0.7331	0.6193	0.7331	0.6481	0.7331	0.6122	0.7337	0.6202	0.7331	0.6317
		FSIM	0.2655	0.1636	0.2655	0.2153	0.2655	0.2219	0.2656	0.1827	0.2661	0.2270	0.2655	0.2186
4	118031	SSIM	0.8091	0.5763	0.8091	0.6388	0.8087	0.6033	0.8088	0.5841	0.8091	0.5256	0.8090	0.6160
		FSIM	0.4271	0.1933	0.4274	0.2584	0.4275	0.2255	0.4270	0.1985	0.4265	0.1845	0.4274	0.2529
	118072	SSIM	0.7726	0.5478	0.7712	0.6395	0.7719	0.5693	0.7724	0.6018	0.7701	0.6233	0.7720	0.5608
		FSIM	0.4487	0.2572	0.4480	0.3116	0.4483	0.2569	0.4486	0.2829	0.4465	0.3167	0.4485	0.2620
	326025	SSIM	0.7630	0.6302	0.7630	0.5599	0.7631	0.6022	0.7625	0.6105	0.7622	0.5289	0.7631	0.5469
		FSIM	0.4012	0.3053	0.4012	0.2695	0.4014	0.3037	0.4010	0.3044	0.4008	0.2752	0.4014	0.2654
	120003	SSIM	0.7857	0.6343	0.7848	0.7208	0.7846	0.7198	0.7844	0.7311	0.7860	0.6679	0.7849	0.6765
		FSIM	0.3042	0.2303	0.3047	0.2695	0.3046	0.2480	0.3049	0.2621	0.3111	0.2175	0.3046	0.2526
	253092	SSIM	0.6774	0.5709	0.6775	0.6138	0.6774	0.6208	0.6776	0.5475	0.6772	0.5458	0.6772	0.5887
		FSIM	0.3402	0.2303	0.3399	0.2630	0.3401	0.2554	0.3403	0.2174	0.3394	0.2141	0.3400	0.2291
	8068	SSIM	0.6587	0.4305	0.6587	0.4561	0.6586	0.5285	0.6619	0.4454	0.6567	0.3812	0.6648	0.4835
		FSIM	0.3118	0.1277	0.3118	0.1609	0.3118	0.1635	0.3128	0.1282	0.3106	0.1406	0.2889	0.1552
	81095	SSIM	0.7626	0.6011	0.7623	0.6673	0.7625	0.6171	0.7621	0.6556	0.7612	0.6030	0.7626	0.6287
		FSIM	0.3406	0.1691	0.3404	0.2625	0.3407	0.1921	0.3402	0.2357	0.3385	0.1876	0.3406	0.2028
	92014	SSIM	0.6157	0.4900	0.6155	0.5324	0.6159	0.5521	0.6158	0.4787	0.6136	0.5404	0.6149	0.5047
		FSIM	0.4472	0.3242	0.4469	0.3464	0.4475	0.3552	0.4473	0.3164	0.4443	0.3784	0.4466	0.3290
	365072	SSIM	0.7510	0.2413	0.7508	0.4616	0.7509	0.3474	0.7510	0.4534	0.7506	0.3174	0.7509	0.4956
		FSIM	0.4279	0.0688	0.4278	0.1946	0.4277	0.1383	0.4278	0.2064	0.4277	0.1211	0.4278	0.2445
	384022	SSIM	0.7924	0.6092	0.7920	0.6482	0.7797	0.6696	0.7894	0.6338	0.7903	0.6168	0.7856	0.6756
		FSIM	0.3903	0.2026	0.3900	0.2371	0.3649	0.2754	0.3887	0.2434	0.3875	0.2491	0.3713	0.2970
5	118031	SSIM	0.8395	0.6154	0.8387	0.7160	0.8334	0.7094	0.8398	0.6402	0.8395	0.6154	0.8387	0.7160
		FSIM	0.4763	0.2464	0.4753	0.3365	0.4664	0.3278	0.4764	0.2594	0.4763	0.2464	0.4753	0.3365
	118072	SSIM	0.8122	0.6165	0.8120	0.6296	0.8042	0.6322	0.8127	0.6016	0.8122	0.6165	0.8120	0.6296
		FSIM	0.5033	0.3023	0.5029	0.3116	0.4925	0.3316	0.5025	0.3046	0.5033	0.3023	0.5029	0.3116
	326025	SSIM	0.8134	0.5348	0.8128	0.6301	0.8132	0.6167	0.8124	0.5774	0.8134	0.5348	0.8128	0.6301
		FSIM	0.4531	0.2606	0.4523	0.3083	0.4528	0.3086	0.4521	0.2867	0.4531	0.2606	0.4523	0.3083
	120003	SSIM	0.8120	0.6719	0.8133	0.6995	0.8130	0.7228	0.8132	0.7207	0.8120	0.6719	0.8133	0.6995
		FSIM	0.3363	0.2490	0.3372	0.2632	0.3369	0.2588	0.3361	0.2514	0.3363	0.2490	0.3372	0.2632
	253092	SSIM	0.7084	0.6279	0.7070	0.6101	0.7087	0.6317	0.7079	0.6452	0.7084	0.6279	0.7070	0.6101
		FSIM	0.3793	0.2801	0.3786	0.2604	0.3790	0.2708	0.3727	0.2590	0.3793	0.2801	0.3786	0.2604
	8068	SSIM	0.6687	0.4700	0.6738	0.6228	0.6685	0.5219	0.6660	0.4685	0.6687	0.4700	0.6738	0.6228
		FSIM	0.3303	0.1374	0.3288	0.1845	0.3298	0.2212	0.3296	0.1457	0.3303	0.1374	0.3288	0.1845
	81095	SSIM	0.7926	0.5921	0.7923	0.6331	0.7873	0.6778	0.7927	0.6838	0.7926	0.5921	0.7923	0.6331
		FSIM	0.3796	0.1602	0.3802	0.2173	0.3721	0.2640	0.3786	0.2652	0.3796	0.1602	0.3802	0.2173
	92014	SSIM	0.6517	0.5027	0.6460	0.4980	0.6550	0.5219	0.6511	0.5497	0.6517	0.5027	0.6460	0.4980
		FSIM	0.5040	0.3392	0.4993	0.3236	0.5069	0.3398	0.5033	0.3755	0.5040	0.3392	0.4993	0.3236
	365072	SSIM	0.8041	0.3094	0.8040	0.5740	0.8044	0.3850	0.8037	0.3905	0.8041	0.3094	0.8040	0.5740
		FSIM	0.4900	0.1134	0.4903	0.2870	0.4907	0.1630	0.4894	0.1639	0.4900	0.1134	0.4903	0.2870
	384022	SSIM	0.8167	0.6448	0.8178	0.6815	0.8167	0.6675	0.8148	0.6324	0.8167	0.6448	0.8178	0.6815
		FSIM	0.4212	0.2337	0.4247	0.2641	0.4211	0.2740	0.4229	0.2411	0.4212	0.2337	0.4247	0.2641

Table 8. The dice and Jaccard index values of the algorithms.

Level	Image		COSGO		GWO		SCSO		WOA		AGWO_CS		PSOGSA	
			Otsu	Kapur	Otsu	Kapur	Otsu	Kapur	Otsu	Kapur	Otsu	Kapur	Otsu	Kapur
2	118031	Dice	0.0000	0.0000	0.0000	0.0000	0.0000	0.0000	0.0000	0.0000	0.0000	0.0000	0.0000	0.0000
		Jaccard	0.0000	0.0000	0.0000	0.0000	0.0000	0.0000	0.0000	0.0000	0.0000	0.0000	0.0000	0.0000
	118072	Dice	0.4398	0.0685	0.4398	0.1109	0.4398	0.3996	0.4398	0.1181	0.4413	0.6776	0.4398	0.4003
		Jaccard	0.2819	0.0394	0.2819	0.0610	0.2819	0.2867	0.2819	0.0708	0.2831	0.5871	0.2819	0.3060
	326025	Dice	0.1742	0.1537	0.1742	0.1175	0.1742	0.4232	0.1737	0.2987	0.1707	0.4385	0.1742	0.0676
		Jaccard	0.0954	0.0857	0.0954	0.0626	0.0954	0.3002	0.0951	0.1918	0.0933	0.3096	0.0954	0.0357
	120003	Dice	0.5013	0.1165	0.5013	0.5108	0.5013	0.8966	0.5013	0.7504	0.5036	0.9373	0.5013	0.4133
		Jaccard	0.3344	0.0679	0.3344	0.4155	0.3344	0.8126	0.3344	0.6331	0.3365	0.8863	0.3344	0.2755
	253092	Dice	0.0000	0.0000	0.0000	0.0000	0.0000	0.0000	0.0000	0.0000	0.0000	0.0000	0.0000	0.0000
		Jaccard	0.0000	0.0000	0.0000	0.0000	0.0000	0.0000	0.0000	0.0000	0.0000	0.0000	0.0000	0.0000
	8068	Dice	0.2835	0.1693	0.2835	0.1878	0.2835	0.2080	0.2835	0.3133	0.2835	0.4783	0.2835	0.2166
		Jaccard	0.1652	0.0928	0.1652	0.1037	0.1652	0.1165	0.1652	0.2326	0.1652	0.3980	0.1652	0.1219
	81095	Dice	0.0000	0.0000	0.0000	0.0000	0.0000	0.0000	0.0000	0.0000	0.0000	0.0000	0.0000	0.0000
		Jaccard	0.0000	0.0000	0.0000	0.0000	0.0000	0.0000	0.0000	0.0000	0.0000	0.0000	0.0000	0.0000
	92014	Dice	0.0000	0.0000	0.0000	0.0000	0.0000	0.0000	0.0000	0.0000	0.0000	0.0000	0.0000	0.0000
		Jaccard	0.0000	0.0000	0.0000	0.0000	0.0000	0.0000	0.0000	0.0000	0.0000	0.0000	0.0000	0.0000
	365072	Dice	0.4339	0.0785	0.4339	0.0783	0.4339	0.0992	0.4339	0.2734	0.4338	0.6731	0.4339	0.2790
		Jaccard	0.2771	0.0429	0.2771	0.0426	0.2771	0.0542	0.2771	0.1755	0.2770	0.6398	0.2771	0.1670
	384022	Dice	0.5636	0.1131	0.5636	0.2598	0.5636	0.2914	0.5641	0.1617	0.5636	0.7277	0.5636	0.2853
		Jaccard	0.3923	0.0617	0.3923	0.2079	0.3923	0.2170	0.3929	0.0892	0.3923	0.6345	0.3923	0.2280
3	118031	Dice	0.0000	0.0000	0.0000	0.0000	0.0000	0.0000	0.0000	0.0000	0.0000	0.0000	0.0000	0.0000
		Jaccard	0.0000	0.0000	0.0000	0.0000	0.0000	0.0000	0.0000	0.0000	0.0000	0.0000	0.0000	0.0000
	118072	Dice	0.3193	0.0049	0.3193	0.0372	0.3193	0.0803	0.3193	0.0568	0.3159	0.4178	0.3193	0.1969
		Jaccard	0.1900	0.0025	0.1900	0.0193	0.1900	0.0448	0.1900	0.0329	0.1877	0.3343	0.1900	0.1485
	326025	Dice	0.1215	0.2055	0.1215	0.1100	0.1212	0.1149	0.1212	0.1964	0.1192	0.3547	0.1215	0.0971
		Jaccard	0.0647	0.1224	0.0647	0.0586	0.0645	0.0631	0.0645	0.1281	0.0634	0.2262	0.0647	0.0516
	120003	Dice	0.4536	0.0578	0.4536	0.1417	0.4536	0.2036	0.4536	0.7026	0.4516	0.8944	0.4536	0.3224
		Jaccard	0.2933	0.0298	0.2933	0.0859	0.2933	0.1182	0.2933	0.5937	0.2917	0.8091	0.2933	0.2086
	253092	Dice	0.0000	0.0000	0.0000	0.0000	0.0000	0.0000	0.0000	0.0000	0.0000	0.0000	0.0000	0.0000
		Jaccard	0.0000	0.0000	0.0000	0.0000	0.0000	0.0000	0.0000	0.0000	0.0000	0.0000	0.0000	0.0000
	8068	Dice	0.2664	0.1334	0.2664	0.2150	0.2664	0.2223	0.2664	0.1884	0.2666	0.4935	0.2664	0.1945
		Jaccard	0.1537	0.0715	0.1537	0.1219	0.1537	0.1260	0.1537	0.1042	0.1538	0.4425	0.1537	0.1085
	81095	Dice	0.0000	0.0000	0.0000	0.0000	0.0000	0.0000	0.0000	0.0000	0.0000	0.0000	0.0000	0.0000
		Jaccard	0.0000	0.0000	0.0000	0.0000	0.0000	0.0000	0.0000	0.0000	0.0000	0.0000	0.0000	0.0000
	92014	Dice	0.0000	0.0000	0.0000	0.0000	0.0000	0.0000	0.0000	0.0000	0.0000	0.0000	0.0000	0.0000
		Jaccard	0.0000	0.0000	0.0000	0.0000	0.0000	0.0000	0.0000	0.0000	0.0000	0.0000	0.0000	0.0000
	365072	Dice	0.3283	0.0372	0.3283	0.1340	0.3283	0.1491	0.3291	0.0313	0.3234	0.1742	0.3283	0.3767
		Jaccard	0.1964	0.0196	0.1964	0.0847	0.1964	0.1014	0.1970	0.0161	0.1929	0.1043	0.1964	0.2438
	384022	Dice	0.2029	0.0299	0.2029	0.0989	0.2029	0.1251	0.2020	0.0458	0.2078	0.6233	0.2029	0.0624
		Jaccard	0.1129	0.0153	0.1129	0.0529	0.1129	0.0675	0.1123	0.0236	0.1160	0.5076	0.1129	0.0325

Table 8. *Cont.*

Level	Image		COSGO		GWO		SCSO		WOA		AGWO_CS		PSOGSA	
			Otsu	**Kapur**	**Otsu**	**Kapur**	**Otsu**	**Kapur**	**Otsu**	**Kapur**	**Otsu**	**Kapur**	**Otsu**	**Kapur**
4	118031	Dice	0.0000	0.0000	0.0000	0.0000	0.0000	0.0000	0.0000	0.0000	0.0000	0.0000	0.0000	0.0000
		Jaccard	0.0000	0.0000	0.0000	0.0000	0.0000	0.0000	0.0000	0.0000	0.0000	0.0000	0.0000	0.0000
	118072	Dice	0.2203	0.0565	0.2188	0.0818	0.2218	0.0179	0.2172	0.0117	0.2232	0.3537	0.2203	0.1650
		Jaccard	0.1238	0.0327	0.1228	0.0458	0.1247	0.0091	0.1219	0.0059	0.1256	0.2466	0.1238	0.1196
	326025	Dice	0.1058	0.0491	0.1058	0.0841	0.1055	0.1440	0.1055	0.0816	0.1061	0.4591	0.1055	0.0835
		Jaccard	0.0558	0.0253	0.0558	0.0444	0.0557	0.0834	0.0557	0.0429	0.0561	0.3564	0.0557	0.0444
	120003	Dice	0.3272	0.1262	0.3315	0.2263	0.3300	0.6132	0.3302	0.2667	0.3638	0.9171	0.3300	0.2370
		Jaccard	0.1956	0.0691	0.1987	0.1389	0.1976	0.5011	0.1978	0.1635	0.2228	0.8496	0.1976	0.1397
	253092	Dice	0.0000	0.0000	0.0000	0.0000	0.0000	0.0000	0.0000	0.0000	0.0000	0.0000	0.0000	0.0000
		Jaccard	0.0000	0.0000	0.0000	0.0000	0.0000	0.0000	0.0000	0.0000	0.0000	0.0000	0.0000	0.0000
	8068	Dice	0.2645	0.1306	0.2645	0.1901	0.2643	0.2053	0.2650	0.1762	0.2632	0.6294	0.2549	0.1967
		Jaccard	0.1524	0.0699	0.1524	0.1053	0.1523	0.1159	0.1527	0.0975	0.1516	0.5654	0.1462	0.1097
	81095	Dice	0.0000	0.0000	0.0000	0.0000	0.0000	0.0000	0.0000	0.0000	0.0000	0.0000	0.0000	0.0000
		Jaccard	0.0000	0.0000	0.0000	0.0000	0.0000	0.0000	0.0000	0.0000	0.0000	0.0000	0.0000	0.0000
	92014	Dice	0.0000	0.0000	0.0000	0.0000	0.0000	0.0000	0.0000	0.0000	0.0000	0.0000	0.0000	0.0000
		Jaccard	0.0000	0.0000	0.0000	0.0000	0.0000	0.0000	0.0000	0.0000	0.0000	0.0000	0.0000	0.0000
	365072	Dice	0.2651	0.0250	0.2669	0.2223	0.2669	0.0529	0.2642	0.1118	0.2574	0.4217	0.2660	0.1919
		Jaccard	0.1528	0.0129	0.1540	0.1331	0.1540	0.0281	0.1522	0.0628	0.1478	0.4042	0.1534	0.1292
	384022	Dice	0.1930	0.0125	0.1902	0.1161	0.1957	0.1256	0.1921	0.1970	0.1927	0.6454	0.1738	0.1601
		Jaccard	0.1068	0.0063	0.1051	0.0637	0.1085	0.0722	0.1062	0.1615	0.1067	0.5135	0.0957	0.0940
5	118031	Dice	0.0000	0.0000	0.0000	0.0000	0.0000	0.0000	0.0000	0.0000	0.0000	0.0000	0.0000	0.0000
		Jaccard	0.0000	0.0000	0.0000	0.0000	0.0000	0.0000	0.0000	0.0000	0.0000	0.0000	0.0000	0.0000
	118072	Dice	0.1618	0.0338	0.1633	0.0311	0.1633	0.0377	0.1663	0.0108	0.1901	0.1550	0.1649	0.0082
		Jaccard	0.0880	0.0184	0.0889	0.0165	0.0889	0.0198	0.0907	0.0055	0.1053	0.0865	0.0898	0.0042
	326025	Dice	0.0875	0.0366	0.0874	0.0720	0.0877	0.1240	0.0869	0.0304	0.0909	0.1805	0.0879	0.0787
		Jaccard	0.0457	0.0187	0.0457	0.0388	0.0458	0.0728	0.0454	0.0156	0.0476	0.1042	0.0460	0.0410
	120003	Dice	0.2915	0.0998	0.2931	0.3265	0.2929	0.7665	0.2875	0.2988	0.2943	0.8929	0.2971	0.2040
		Jaccard	0.1706	0.0537	0.1717	0.2437	0.1716	0.6782	0.1679	0.2279	0.1730	0.8066	0.1745	0.1236
	253092	Dice	0.0000	0.0000	0.0000	0.0000	0.0000	0.0000	0.0000	0.0000	0.0000	0.0000	0.0000	0.0000
		Jaccard	0.0000	0.0000	0.0000	0.0000	0.0000	0.0000	0.0000	0.0000	0.0000	0.0000	0.0000	0.0000
	8068	Dice	0.2119	0.1307	0.2106	0.2127	0.2113	0.2149	0.2143	0.2150	0.2045	0.4184	0.2119	0.2064
		Jaccard	0.1185	0.0706	0.1177	0.1207	0.1181	0.1215	0.1200	0.1211	0.1140	0.3532	0.1185	0.1159
	81095	Dice	0.0000	0.0000	0.0000	0.0000	0.0000	0.0000	0.0000	0.0000	0.0000	0.0000	0.0000	0.0000
		Jaccard	0.0000	0.0000	0.0000	0.0000	0.0000	0.0000	0.0000	0.0000	0.0000	0.0000	0.0000	0.0000
	92014	Dice	0.0000	0.0000	0.0000	0.0000	0.0000	0.0000	0.0000	0.0000	0.0000	0.0000	0.0000	0.0000
		Jaccard	0.0000	0.0000	0.0000	0.0000	0.0000	0.0000	0.0000	0.0000	0.0000	0.0000	0.0000	0.0000
	365072	Dice	0.2315	0.0418	0.2287	0.1382	0.2324	0.0502	0.2342	0.0373	0.2501	0.3051	0.2315	0.2013
		Jaccard	0.1309	0.0217	0.1292	0.0843	0.1315	0.0262	0.1327	0.0196	0.1431	0.2488	0.1309	0.1191
	384022	Dice	0.0923	0.0440	0.0913	0.1413	0.0910	0.1359	0.1112	0.0142	0.0963	0.4080	0.0916	0.1170
		Jaccard	0.0484	0.0228	0.0478	0.0772	0.0477	0.0748	0.0593	0.0071	0.0506	0.3274	0.0480	0.0637

Table 9. The accuracy values of the algorithms.

Level	Image	COSGO		GWO		SCSO		WOA		AGWO_CS		PSOGSA	
		Otsu	Kapur	Otsu	Kapur	Otsu	Kapur	Otsu	Kapur	Otsu	Kapur	Otsu	Kapur
	118031	0.9079	0.8720	0.9079	0.9299	0.9079	0.9558	0.9078	0.9468	0.9075	0.5480	0.9079	0.9297
	118072	0.2819	0.0394	0.2819	0.0610	0.2819	0.2867	0.2819	0.0708	0.2831	0.5871	0.2819	0.3060
	326025	0.0954	0.0857	0.0954	0.0626	0.0954	0.3002	0.0951	0.1918	0.0933	0.3096	0.0954	0.0357
	120003	0.3344	0.0679	0.3344	0.4155	0.3344	0.8126	0.3344	0.6331	0.3365	0.8863	0.3344	0.2755
2	253092	0.8717	0.8214	0.8722	0.7572	0.8717	0.8516	0.8717	0.6697	0.8727	0.5685	0.8717	0.9111
	8068	0.1652	0.0928	0.1652	0.1037	0.1652	0.1165	0.1652	0.2326	0.1652	0.3980	0.1652	0.1219
	81095	0.7998	0.9898	0.7998	0.9911	0.7998	0.9342	0.7998	0.9858	0.7988	0.4300	0.7998	0.9897
	92014	0.8781	0.8340	0.8781	0.7775	0.8781	0.8981	0.8781	0.7017	0.8781	0.7675	0.8781	0.7659
	365072	0.2771	0.0429	0.2771	0.0426	0.2771	0.0542	0.2771	0.1755	0.2770	0.6398	0.2771	0.1670
	384022	0.3923	0.0617	0.3923	0.2079	0.3923	0.2170	0.3929	0.0892	0.3923	0.6345	0.3923	0.2280
	118031	0.9173	0.9430	0.9176	0.9146	0.9173	0.8150	0.9168	0.9244	0.9168	0.9202	0.9173	0.9382
	118072	0.1900	0.0025	0.1900	0.0193	0.1900	0.0448	0.1900	0.0329	0.1877	0.3343	0.1900	0.1485
	326025	0.0647	0.1224	0.0647	0.0586	0.0645	0.0631	0.0645	0.1281	0.0634	0.2262	0.0647	0.0516
	120003	0.2933	0.0298	0.2933	0.0859	0.2933	0.1182	0.2933	0.5937	0.2917	0.8091	0.2933	0.2086
3	253092	0.9062	0.9282	0.9033	0.9118	0.9062	0.9134	0.9062	0.9293	0.9057	0.7059	0.9062	0.9261
	8068	0.1537	0.0715	0.1537	0.1219	0.1537	0.1260	0.1537	0.1042	0.1538	0.4425	0.1537	0.1085
	81095	0.8412	0.9959	0.8412	0.7968	0.8420	0.7980	0.8428	0.9389	0.8481	0.7754	0.8412	0.9752
	92014	0.8860	0.8846	0.8857	0.8871	0.8863	0.7606	0.8863	0.8934	0.8863	0.8558	0.8861	0.8921
	365072	0.1964	0.0196	0.1964	0.0847	0.1964	0.1014	0.1970	0.0161	0.1929	0.1043	0.1964	0.2438
	384022	0.1129	0.0153	0.1129	0.0529	0.1129	0.0675	0.1123	0.0236	0.1160	0.5076	0.1129	0.0325
	118031	0.9212	0.9545	0.9211	0.9068	0.9214	0.9288	0.9214	0.9372	0.9207	0.7522	0.9212	0.9349
	118072	0.1238	0.0327	0.1228	0.0458	0.1247	0.0091	0.1219	0.0059	0.1256	0.2466	0.1238	0.1196
	326025	0.0558	0.0253	0.0558	0.0444	0.0557	0.0834	0.0557	0.0429	0.0561	0.3564	0.0557	0.0444
	120003	0.1956	0.0691	0.1987	0.1389	0.1976	0.5011	0.1978	0.1635	0.2228	0.8496	0.1976	0.1397
4	253092	0.9199	0.9246	0.9194	0.9340	0.9199	0.9254	0.9194	0.8374	0.9204	0.7524	0.9202	0.9118
	8068	0.1524	0.0699	0.1524	0.1053	0.1523	0.1159	0.1527	0.0975	0.1516	0.5654	0.1462	0.1097
	81095	0.8619	0.9968	0.8631	0.9542	0.8625	0.9973	0.8632	0.9716	0.8618	0.5212	0.8619	0.8155
	92014	0.8945	0.9152	0.8943	0.8838	0.8945	0.8903	0.8945	0.8433	0.8955	0.8454	0.8948	0.8886
	365072	0.1528	0.0129	0.1540	0.1331	0.1540	0.0281	0.1522	0.0628	0.1478	0.4042	0.1534	0.1292
	384022	0.1068	0.0063	0.1051	0.0637	0.1085	0.0722	0.1062	0.1615	0.1067	0.5135	0.0957	0.0940
	118031	0.9237	0.9744	0.9262	0.9121	0.9239	0.9438	0.9234	0.9098	0.9247	0.9265	0.9240	0.9150
	118072	0.0880	0.0184	0.0889	0.0165	0.0889	0.0198	0.0907	0.0055	0.1053	0.0865	0.0898	0.0042
	326025	0.0457	0.0187	0.0457	0.0388	0.0458	0.0728	0.0454	0.0156	0.0476	0.1042	0.0460	0.0410
	120003	0.1706	0.0537	0.1717	0.2437	0.1716	0.6782	0.1679	0.2279	0.1730	0.8066	0.1745	0.1236
5	253092	0.9298	0.9589	0.9298	0.9390	0.9294	0.7943	0.9279	0.9153	0.9348	0.7211	0.9397	0.9135
	8068	0.1185	0.0706	0.1177	0.1207	0.1181	0.1215	0.1200	0.1211	0.1140	0.3532	0.1185	0.1159
	81095	0.9047	0.9978	0.9053	0.9824	0.9034	0.9726	0.9021	0.9366	0.8826	0.2147	0.8948	0.9511
	92014	0.9000	0.9309	0.9007	0.9138	0.9003	0.9137	0.8996	0.9123	0.9029	0.8596	0.9014	0.9049
	365072	0.1309	0.0217	0.1292	0.0843	0.1315	0.0262	0.1327	0.0196	0.1431	0.2488	0.1309	0.1191
	384022	0.0484	0.0228	0.0478	0.0772	0.0477	0.0748	0.0593	0.0071	0.0506	0.3274	0.0480	0.0637

As shown in Figures 2–5, the comparisons of SSIM and FSIM values across 10 test images demonstrate significant variations among different algorithms at threshold levels 2–5.

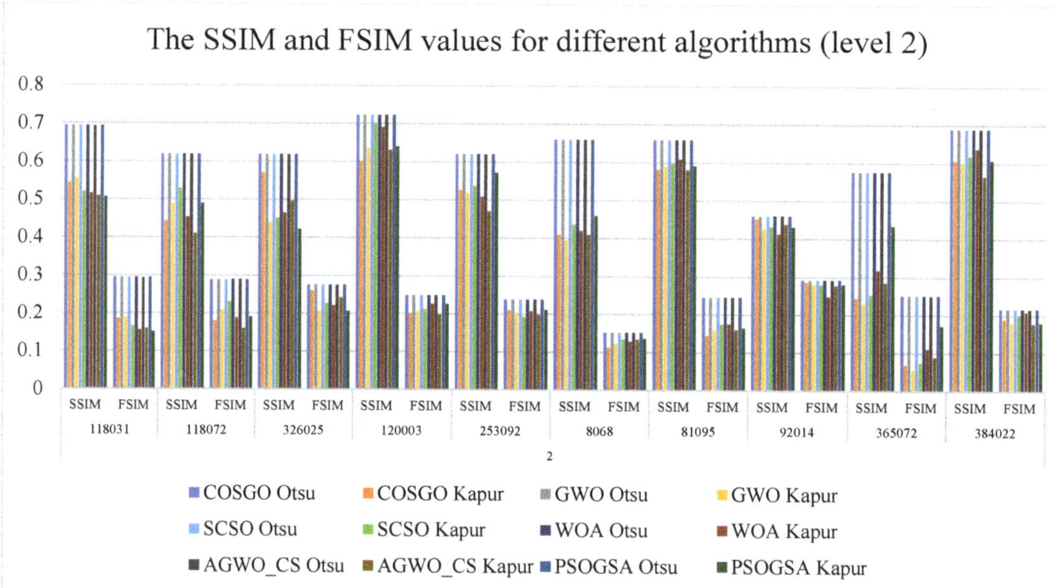

Figure 2. Comparison of SSIM and FSIM values obtained from 10 test images using different algorithms at threshold level 2.

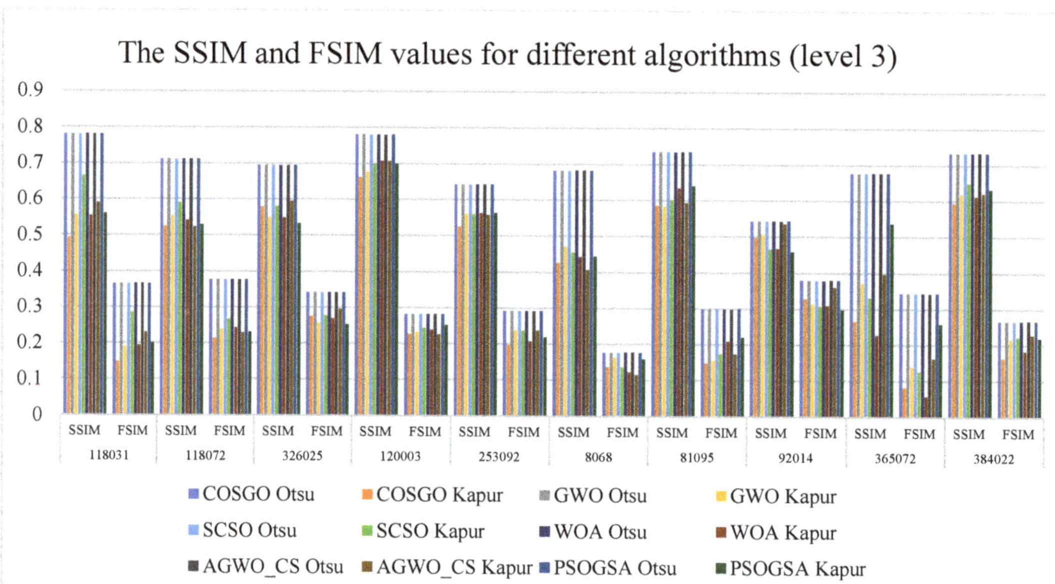

Figure 3. Comparison of SSIM and FSIM values obtained from 10 test images using different algorithms at threshold level 3.

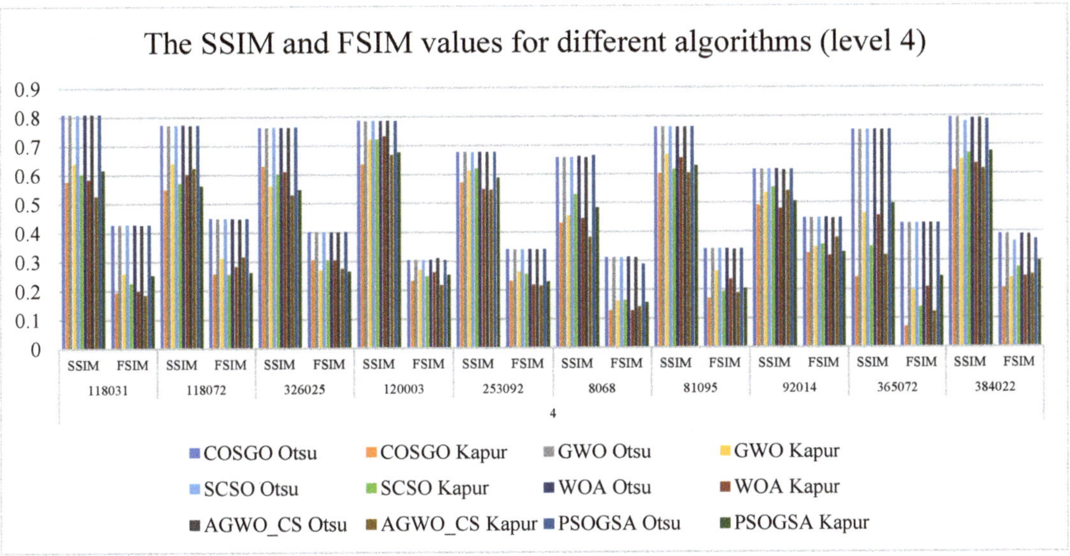

Figure 4. Comparison of SSIM and FSIM values obtained from 10 test images using different algorithms at threshold level 4.

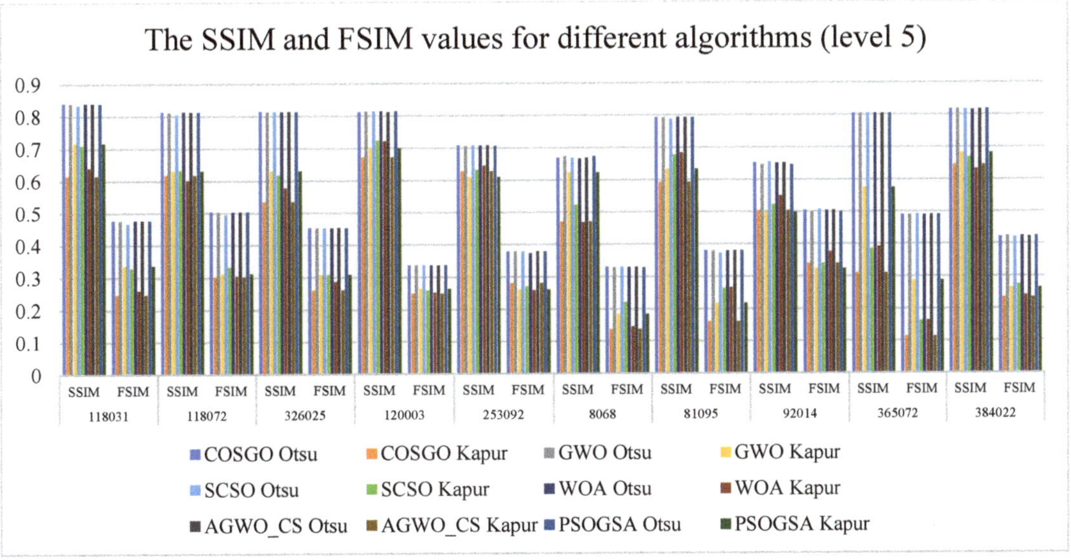

Figure 5. Comparison of SSIM and FSIM values obtained from 10 test images using different algorithms at threshold level 5.

4.3. Performance Analysis

Based on the results, it should be noted that the COSGO algorithm performed significantly in finding the threshold value in images. In this problem, the image levels were studied on levels 2, 3, 4, and 5, respectively. The findings obtained for the algorithm in concern were near to one, which shows good improvement of the algorithm and a considerable performance of the algorithm, according to Tables 6 and 7, which have been analyzed on the PSNR, SSIM, and FSIM criteria. An increase in the number of threshold levels generally results in more vivid and detailed segmented images. While images segmented using the COSGO algorithm are often visually distinguishable, the method exhibits certain weaknesses in specific regions. In addition, Figure 6 shows the segmented images with different metaheuristic algorithms.

Figure 6. The segmented images with different algorithms.

4.4. Objective Function Analysis

In this section, the results obtained for the Otsu and Kapur entropy objective functions are analyzed. Based on Figures 7–9, it can be noted that the COSGO algorithm performed better. In Figure 7, which is based on the PSNR results, the Otsu function obtained superior results over the COSGO algorithm and WOA. In the case of the Kapur function, the GWO and SCSO algorithms obtained better results, respectively. Based on the level of the images, the COSGO algorithm with the Otsu function at level 2, the SCSO algorithm with the Otsu function at level 3, the COSGO algorithm with the Otsu function at level 4, and the COSGO algorithm with the Otsu function at level 5 obtained promising results in the PSNR.

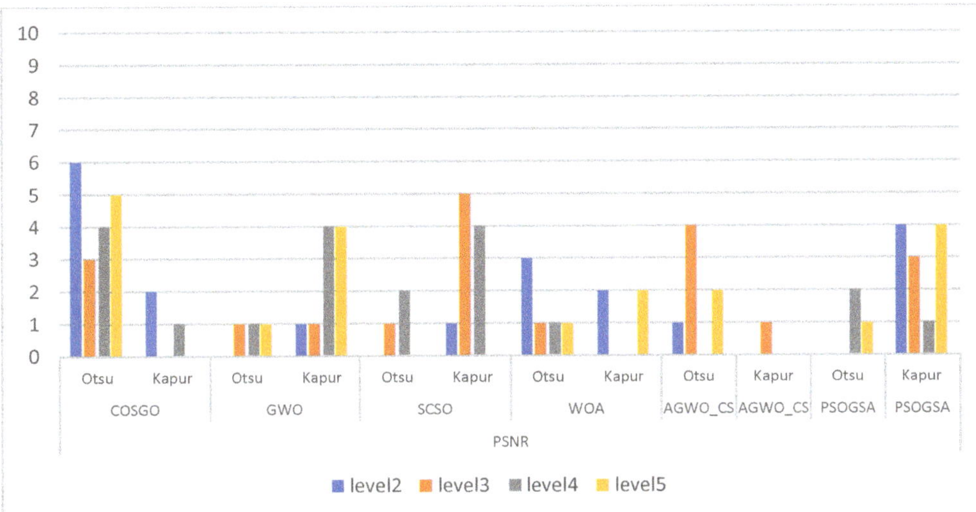

Figure 7. Comparative PSNR analysis across different threshold levels (levels 2–5) using Otsu and Kapur methods with four algorithms. COSGO consistently outperforms other methods, especially under the Otsu-based segmentation, indicating its robustness in preserving image quality.

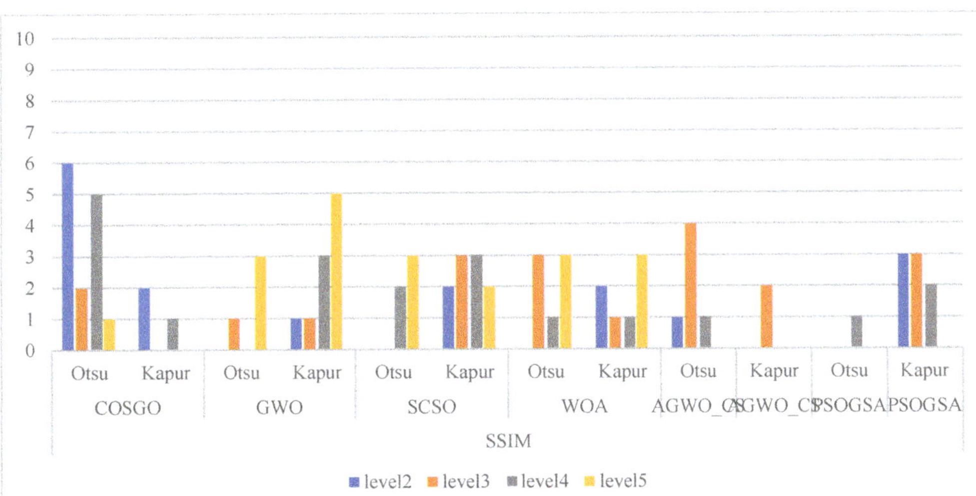

Figure 8. SSIM analysis for multiple threshold levels (levels 2–5) using Otsu and Kapur methods with various metaheuristic algorithms. COSGO again shows superior structural similarity performance, particularly under the Otsu thresholding strategy, indicating its effectiveness in preserving structural details.

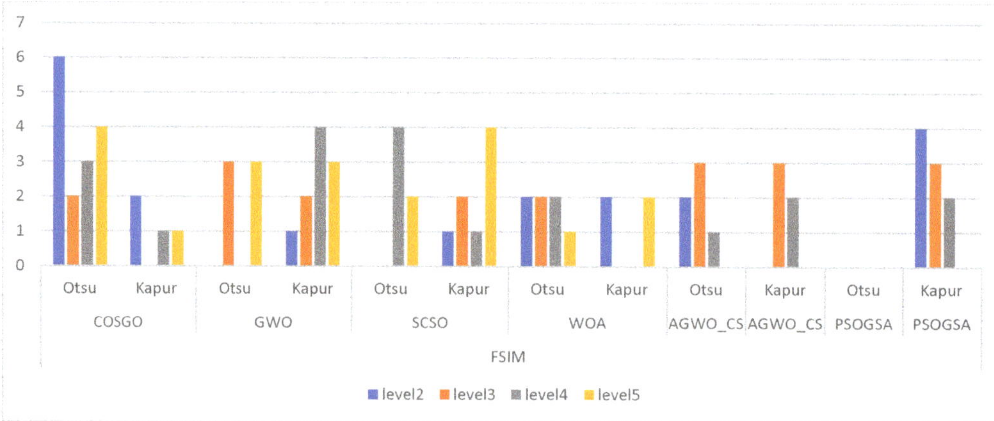

Figure 9. FSIM analysis across different threshold levels (levels 2–5) using Otsu and Kapur methods with various algorithms. COSGO consistently outperforms others in feature similarity, especially when combined with Otsu, highlighting its robustness in preserving perceptual image quality.

In Figure 8, the Structural Similarity Index Measure (SSIM) values were analyzed for different metaheuristic algorithms in combination with two distinct objective functions: Otsu and Kapur entropy. The results reveal that the proposed COSGO algorithm, when used with the Otsu objective function, generally exhibits strong performance in terms of structural similarity. Notably, at the multi-level thresholding level of 5, COSGO demonstrates superior performance with both Otsu and Kapur entropy compared to the other algorithms. This indicates that the COSGO algorithm is more capable of preserving structural information, such as luminance, contrast, and texture consistency, particularly at higher threshold levels. The effectiveness of COSGO under these conditions highlights its potential for more accurate and visually coherent image segmentation.

In Figure 9, the Feature Similarity Index Measure (FSIM) values obtained from various algorithms are presented and analyzed. The results indicate that the proposed COSGO algorithm demonstrates superior performance compared to other competing methods. Particularly, when integrated with the Otsu objective function, COSGO achieves the highest FSIM values across multiple test images. This suggests that COSGO is more effective in preserving low-level visual features, such as texture and edge information, during the segmentation process. The enhanced FSIM scores further confirm that the proposed approach maintains a high degree of similarity between the segmented and original images, thus contributing to improved perceptual quality and segmentation accuracy.

4.5. Theoretical Insights into the COSGO Algorithm

The COBL method improves the suggested hybrid GWO-SCSO algorithm, which provides unique theoretical contributions beyond the simple combination of two metaheuristics. The hybrid structure achieves a more balanced search process by combining the local exploitation strength of SCSO with the global exploration capabilities of GWO. The algorithm can converge more quickly while being resilient against local optima due to this combination. Additionally, the population diversity is enhanced by the chaotic opposition-based learning (COBL) method, which results in improved initialization and more consistent convergence behavior across runs. Our approach combines a complementary dynamics hierarchical leadership-based search in GWO with adaptive motion in SCSO, which improves the optimization performance in hybrid metaheuristic algorithms that frequently mix similar search behaviors. The COSGO hybridization process collectively offers advantages in both convergence speed and stability, which is established by our experimental findings.

5. Conclusions

In this study, the COSGO metaheuristic algorithm is proposed as a hybrid multi-strategy metaheuristic algorithm. This algorithm benefits from the advantages of the grey wolf optimization and sand cat swarm optimization algorithms to create an efficient meta-heuristic algorithm to solve global optimization problems. Also, chaotic opposition-based learning was used to enhance the search agents' search ability and obtain balanced exploration and exploitation phases. The COSGO algorithm displays better performance in comparison with the GWO and SCSO algorithm, the WOA, and two hybrid metaheuristic algorithms, AGWO-CS and the PSOGSA, in the CEC 2017 benchmark functions. Based on the obtained results in the Freidman ranking test, the COSGO algorithm's 1.862068966 average ranking shows its competitive efficiency in the benchmark functions. In addition, one of the well-known np-hard problems—multi-level thresholding color image segmentation—was studied with the proposed COSGO algorithm. Two objective functions named Otsu and Kapur were used to find the optimum values. This technique was evaluated with four performance criteria—the PSNR, MSE, SSIM, FSIM, dice coefficient, Jaccard index, and segmentation accuracy—to investigate the COSGO algorithm's performance in comparison with other metaheuristic algorithms. It was observed that the COSGO algorithm shows good performance with the Otsu method in multi-level thresholding color image segmentation.

Funding: This research received no external funding.

Institutional Review Board Statement: Not applicable.

Informed Consent Statement: Not applicable.

Data Availability Statement: The data presented in this study are available on request from the corresponding author.

Conflicts of Interest: The author declares no conflict of interest.

References

1. Dong, Y.; Li, M.; Zhou, M. Multi-Threshold Image Segmentation Based on the Improved Dragonfly Algorithm. *Mathematics* **2024**, *12*, 854. [CrossRef]
2. Akay, R.; Saleh, R.A.; Farea, S.M.; Kanaan, M. Multilevel thresholding segmentation of color plant disease images using metaheuristic optimization algorithms. *Neural Comput. Appl.* **2022**, *34*, 1161–1179. [CrossRef]
3. Oliva, D.; Abd Elaziz, M.; Hinojosa, S. *Metaheuristic Algorithms for Image Segmentation: Theory and Applications*; Springer International Publishing: Berlin/Heidelberg, Germany, 2019; pp. 59–69.
4. Abualigah, L.; Almotairi, K.H.; Elaziz, M.A. Multilevel thresholding image segmentation using meta-heuristic optimization algorithms: Comparative analysis, open challenges and new trends. *Appl. Intell.* **2023**, *53*, 11654–11704. [CrossRef]
5. Hu, P.; Han, Y.; Zhang, Z. Multi-Level Thresholding Color Image Segmentation Using Modified Gray Wolf Optimizer. *Biomimetics* **2024**, *9*, 700. [CrossRef] [PubMed]
6. Zhang, C.; Pei, Y.H.; Wang, X.X.; Hou, H.Y.; Fu, L.H. Symmetric cross-entropy multi-threshold color image segmentation based on improved pelican optimization algorithm. *PLoS ONE* **2023**, *18*, e0287573. [CrossRef]
7. Wolpert, D.H.; Macready, W.G. No free lunch theorems for optimization. *IEEE Trans. Evol. Comput.* **1997**, *1*, 67–82. [CrossRef]
8. Yang, X.S. *Nature-Inspired Metaheuristic Algorithms*; Luniver Press: Bristol, UK, 2010.
9. Holland, J.H. Genetic algorithms. *Sci. Am.* **1992**, *267*, 66–73. [CrossRef]
10. Storn, R.; Price, K. Differential evolution–a simple and efficient heuristic for global optimization over continuous spaces. *J. Glob. Optim.* **1997**, *11*, 341–359. [CrossRef]
11. Kennedy, J.; Eberhart, R. Particle swarm optimization. In Proceedings of the ICNN'95-International Conference on Neural Networks, Perth, WA, Australia, 27 November–1 December 1995; Volume 4, pp. 1942–1948.
12. Dorigo, M.; Birattari, M.; Stutzle, T. Ant colony optimization. *IEEE Comput. Intell. Mag.* **2007**, *1*, 28–39. [CrossRef]

13. Mirjalili, S.; Mirjalili, S.M.; Lewis, A. Grey wolf optimizer. *Adv. Eng. Softw.* **2014**, *69*, 46–61. [CrossRef]
14. Seyyedabbasi, A.; Kiani, F. Sand Cat swarm optimization: A nature-inspired algorithm to solve global optimization problems. *Eng. Comput.* **2023**, *39*, 2627–2651. [CrossRef]
15. Rashedi E, Nezamabadi-Pour H, Saryazdi S GSA: A gravitational search algorithm. *Inf. Sci.* **2009**, *179*, 2232–2248. [CrossRef]
16. Erol, O.K.; Eksin, I. A new optimization method: Big bang–big crunch. *Adv. Eng. Softw.* **2006**, *37*, 106–111. [CrossRef]
17. Kaveh A, Talatahari S A novel heuristic optimization method: Charged system search. *Acta Mech.* **2010**, *213*, 267–289. [CrossRef]
18. Ma, G.; Yue, X. An improved whale optimization algorithm based on multilevel threshold image segmentation using the Otsu method. *Eng. Appl. Artif. Intell.* **2022**, *113*, 104960. [CrossRef]
19. Houssein, E.H.; Helmy, B.E.D.; Oliva, D.; Elngar, A.A.; Shaban, H. A novel black widow optimization algorithm for multilevel thresholding image segmentation. *Expert Syst. Appl.* **2021**, *167*, 114159. [CrossRef]
20. Singh, S.; Mittal, N.; Singh, H. A multilevel thresholding algorithm using LebTLBO for image segmentation. *Neural Comput. Appl.* **2020**, *32*, 16681–16706. [CrossRef]
21. Chakraborty, F.; Roy, P.K. An efficient multilevel thresholding image segmentation through improved elephant herding optimization. *Evol. Intell.* **2025**, *18*, 17. [CrossRef]
22. Gao, S.; Iu, H.H.C.; Erkan, U.; Simsek, C.; Toktas, A.; Cao, Y.; Wu, R.; Mou, J.; Li, Q.; Wang, C. A 3D memristive cubic map with dual discrete memristors: Design, implementation, and application in image encryption. *IEEE Trans. Circuits Syst. Video Technol.* **2025**. *Early Access*. [CrossRef]
23. Gao, S.; Zhang, Z.; Iu, H.H.C.; Ding, S.; Mou, J.; Erkan, U.; Toktas, A.; Li, Q.; Wang, C.; Cao, Y. A Parallel Color Image Encryption Algorithm Based on a 2D Logistic-Rulkov Neuron Map. *IEEE Internet Things J.* **2025**, *12*, 18115–18124. [CrossRef]
24. Deng, W.; Wang, J.; Guo, A.; Zhao, H. Quantum differential evolutionary algorithm with quantum-adaptive mutation strategy and population state evaluation framework for high-dimensional problems. *Inf. Sci.* **2024**, *676*, 120787. [CrossRef]
25. Song, Y.; Song, C. Adaptive evolutionary multitask optimization based on anomaly detection transfer of multiple similar sources. *Expert Syst. Appl.* **2025**, *283*, 127599. [CrossRef]
26. Deng, W.; Feng, J.; Zhao, H. Autonomous path planning via sand cat swarm optimization with multi-strategy mechanism for unmanned aerial vehicles in dynamic environment. *IEEE Internet Things J.* **2025**. *Early Access*. [CrossRef]
27. Liu, Y.; Wang, C.; Lu, M.; Yang, J.; Gui, J.; Zhang, S. From simple to complex scenes: Learning robust feature representations for accurate human parsing. *IEEE Trans. Pattern Anal. Mach. Intell.* **2024**, *46*, 5449–5462. [CrossRef]
28. Serbet, F.; Kaya, T. New comparative approach to multi-level thresholding: Chaotically initialized adaptive meta-heuristic optimization methods. *Neural Comput. Appl.* **2025**, *37*, 8371–8396. [CrossRef]
29. Hamza, A.; Grimes, M.; Boukabou, A.; Lekouaghet, B.; Oliva, D.; Dib, S.; Himeur, Y. A chaotic variant of the Golden Jackal Optimizer and its application for medical image segmentation. *Appl. Intell.* **2025**, *55*, 295. [CrossRef]
30. Li, C.; Liu, H. A transit search algorithm with chaotic map and local escape operator for multi-level threshold segmentation of spleen CT images. *Appl. Math. Model.* **2025**, *141*, 115930. [CrossRef]
31. Ting, T.O.; Yang, X.S.; Cheng, S.; Huang, K. Hybrid Metaheuristic Algorithms: Past, Present, and Future. In *Recent Advances in Swarm Intelligence and Evolutionary Computation*; Springer: Berlin/Heidelberg, Germany, 2015; pp. 71–83.
32. Amirsadri, S.; Mousavirad, S.J.; Ebrahimpour-Komleh, H. A Levy flight-based grey wolf optimizer combined with back-propagation algorithm for neural network training. *Neural Comput. Appl.* **2018**, *30*, 3707–3720. [CrossRef]
33. Tizhoosh, H.R. Opposition-based learning: A new scheme for machine intelligence. In Proceedings of the International Conference on Computational Intelligence for Modelling, Control and Automation and International Conference on Intelligent Agents, Web Technologies and Internet Commerce (CIMCA-IAWTIC'06), Vienna, Austria, 28–30 November 2005; Volume 1, pp. 695–701.
34. Long, W.; Jiao, J.; Liang, X.; Cai, S.; Xu, M. A random opposition-based learning grey wolf optimizer. *IEEE Access* **2019**, *7*, 113810–113825. [CrossRef]
35. Rani, G.S.; Jayan, S.; Alatas, B. Analysis of chaotic maps for global optimization and a hybrid chaotic pattern search algorithm for optimizing the reliability of a bank. *IEEE Access* **2023**, *11*, 24497–24510. [CrossRef]
36. Lu, H.; Wang, X.; Fei, Z.; Qiu, M. The effects of using chaotic map on improving the performance of multiobjective evolutionary algorithms. *Math. Probl. Eng.* **2014**, *2014*, 924652. [CrossRef]
37. Mirjalili, S.; Lewis, A. The whale optimization algorithm. *Adv. Eng. Softw.* **2016**, *95*, 51–67. [CrossRef]
38. Sharma, S.; Kapoor, R.; Dhiman, S. A novel hybrid metaheuristic based on augmented grey wolf optimizer and cuckoo search for global optimization. In Proceedings of the 2021 2nd International Conference on Secure Cyber Computing and Communications (ICSCCC), Jalandhar, India, 21–23 May 2021; pp. 376–381.

39. Mirjalili, S.; Hashim, S.Z.M. A new hybrid PSOGSA algorithm for function optimization. In Proceedings of the 2010 International Conference on Computer and Information Application, Tianjin, China, 3–5 December 2010; pp. 374–377.
40. Martin, D.; Fowlkes, C.; Tal, D.; Malik, J. A database of human segmented natural images and its application to evaluating segmentation algorithms and measuring ecological statistics. In Proceedings of the Proceedings Eighth IEEE International Conference on Computer Vision. ICCV 2001, Vancouver, BC, Canada, 7–14 July 2001; Volume 2, pp. 416–423.

entropy

MDPI

Article

RDCRNet: RGB-T Object Detection Network Based on Cross-Modal Representation Model

Yubin Li †, Weida Zhan *,†, Yichun Jiang † and Jinxin Guo †

The College of Electronic and Information Engineering, Changchun University of Science and Technology, Changchun 130022, China; lyb_cust@163.com (Y.L.); jiangyichun@cust.edu.cn (Y.J.); guojinxin@cust.edu.cn (J.G.)

* Correspondence: zhanweida@cust.edu.cn; Tel.: +86-135-9612-5007

† These authors contributed equally to this work.

Abstract: RGB-thermal object detection harnesses complementary information from visible and thermal modalities to enhance detection robustness in challenging environments, particularly under low-light conditions. However, existing approaches suffer from limitations due to their heavy dependence on precisely registered data and insufficient handling of cross-modal distribution disparities. This paper presents RDCRNet, a novel framework incorporating a Cross-Modal Representation Model to effectively address these challenges. The proposed network features a Cross-Modal Feature Remapping Module that aligns modality distributions through statistical normalization and learnable correction parameters, significantly reducing feature discrepancies between modalities. A Cross-Modal Refinement and Interaction Module enables sophisticated bidirectional information exchange via trinity refinement for intra-modal context modeling and cross-attention mechanisms for unaligned feature fusion. Multiscale detection capability is enhanced through a Cross-Scale Feature Integration Module, improving detection performance across various object sizes. To overcome the inherent data scarcity in RGB-T detection, we introduce a self-supervised pretraining strategy that combines masked reconstruction with adversarial learning and semantic consistency loss, effectively leveraging both aligned and unaligned RGB-T samples. Extensive experiments demonstrate that RDCRNet achieves state-of-the-art performance on multiple benchmark datasets while maintaining high computational and storage efficiency, validating its superiority and practical effectiveness in real-world applications.

Keywords: object detection; multimodal; cross-modal representation; pretraining

1. Introduction

Object detection, a critical branch of computer vision, has been extensively studied and is widely applied in fields such as autonomous driving [1,2], remote sensing [3,4], and military defense [5,6]. Typically, high-quality images captured by devices provide abundant target information. However, under low-light or adverse weather conditions, traditional RGB cameras often fail to capture sufficient effective information [7]. In contrast, thermal infrared imaging technology can function effectively in environments with insufficient lighting and is unaffected by common visual disturbances such as smoke and dust [8]. Consequently, researchers have increasingly explored multimodal perception technologies, combining visible light and thermal infrared sensors to develop RGB-T (RGB-thermal) sensing systems that overcome the limitations of single-modality systems.

Nevertheless, significant differences exist between the imaging mechanisms of RGB-T infrared images [9]. These differences manifest not only in the visual appearance of the images but also in how they fundamentally influence subsequent analysis and processing

https://doi.org/10.3390/e27040442

tasks [10,11]. Therefore, in object detection applications, effectively integrating RGB-T data and addressing the inherent structural and semantic disparities between the two modalities remains a major challenge in the research community. Since Ha et al. [12] pioneered the first end-to-end model MF-Net for RGB-T image object detection, substantial advancements have emerged in this domain [13–15]. Numerous state-of-the-art models have been innovated in network architecture design, introducing various efficient modal interaction mechanisms that significantly enhance the processing capabilities for RGB-T images [16–18]. However, these methods predominantly rely on precisely registered RGB-T infrared image datasets, restricting their applicability to more commonly available unaligned RGB-T devices.

In recent years, several researchers have addressed this challenge by proposing network architectures that adapt to slight misalignments between modalities, enabling effective interaction across different spatial and modal domains [19–21]. However, the scarcity of labeled RGB-T datasets often leads to overfitting during model training, resulting in suboptimal detection performance and limited generalization capabilities. Furthermore, current approaches frequently fail to fully account for the inherent distributional disparities between RGB and thermal infrared images during architectural design, leading to inadequate or inappropriate information fusion strategies that ultimately compromise the accuracy and robustness of detection systems.

To address the aforementioned challenges, we propose the RGB-T Object Detection Network Based on Cross-Modal Representation Model (RCDRNet), featuring a novel pipeline architecture and an innovative pretraining methodology. Specifically, we designed a Cross-Modal Representation Network (CRN) as the backbone, which initially encodes multimodal features independently through multilevel dense residual modules with shared parameters. These features then flow through a meticulously crafted Cross-Modal Aggregation Module (CAM) to enhance inter-modal information interaction. Within the CAM, we introduce Cross-modal Feature Remapping (CFR) and a Cross-Modal Refinement and Interaction Module (CRIM), which effectively address significant distribution disparities between cross-modal features and enable more efficient and robust information fusion.

Furthermore, we developed a cross-scale feature integration module that maximizes feature utilization efficiency by leveraging cross-modal features at multiple scales, thereby ensuring reliable multiscale prediction outputs. To strengthen the CRN's feature extraction and cross-modal information fusion capabilities, we propose a cross-modal pretraining strategy that integrates masked reconstruction with semantic consistency loss functions. This approach adaptively learns semantic priors from unlabeled, unaligned RGB-T images. Beyond conventional reconstruction loss for pixel prediction, our method employs generative adversarial networks to capture implicit distributions from limited sample data.

2. Related Work

2.1. Traditional Object Detection Methods

In recent years, object detection has evolved from traditional machine learning methods to deep learning approaches. Early techniques relied on handcrafted features and classifiers like SVM [22] or AdaBoost [23], which, despite their effectiveness in specific scenarios, were computationally expensive and lacked generalization capabilities, rendering them inadequate for complex real-world environments.

The emergence of deep learning, particularly Convolutional Neural Networks (CNNs) [24], has revolutionized object detection, primarily categorized into two-stage and single-stage methods. A prominent two-stage method is R-CNN [25], which employs selective search to generate candidate regions and CNNs for feature extraction, substantially enhancing accuracy and efficiency. Fast R-CNN [26] and Faster R-CNN [27] further optimized the process by sharing feature extraction computations and introducing the Region Proposal Network (RPN), improving both speed and accuracy. More recent advances, such as the rotation-based framework by Xie et al. [28] and the sparse object detection by Sun et al. [29], have introduced sophisticated optimizations, including generating high-quality rotated boxes and eliminating the need for non-maximum suppression (NMS).

In the realm of single-stage methods, object detection is formulated as a regression problem that simultaneously handles bounding box prediction and classification. The YOLO family [30–33] directly predicts bounding boxes and class probabilities, achieving end-to-end detection with remarkable speed improvements. SSD [34] combines YOLO's regression approach with Faster R-CNN's anchor mechanism, enhancing small object detection by making predictions across multiple feature map scales. Subsequent innovations, such as FCOS [35], eliminated predefined anchor boxes in favor of direct bounding box regression from pixel points, while EfficientDet [36] introduced BiFPN (Bidirectional Feature Pyramid Network) for efficient multiscale feature fusion, striking an optimal balance between accuracy and computational efficiency. Cascade-DETR [37] enhanced Transformer-based detectors through cascade attention layers and an IoU prediction mechanism, significantly improving generalization capabilities and localization accuracy.

Despite these significant advancements, enhancing feature extraction alone cannot fully address the challenges posed by degraded image quality. Therefore, in the following sections, we will explore RGB-T object detection algorithms that leverage complementary thermal information.

2.2. RGB-T Object Detection Methods

In recent years, object detection has undergone a paradigm shift from conventional machine learning approaches to deep-learning-based methods. Early techniques predominantly relied on handcrafted features coupled with classifiers such as SVM [22] or AdaBoost [23]. While demonstrating efficacy in constrained scenarios, these methods suffered from computational inefficiency and limited generalization capacity, significantly restricting their applicability in complex real-world environments.

The advent of deep learning, particularly Convolutional Neural Networks (CNNs) [24], has fundamentally transformed the landscape of object detection, giving rise to two principal categories: two-stage and single-stage detection frameworks. Among two-stage methods, R-CNN [25] represents a seminal work that pioneered the integration of selective search for region proposal generation with CNN-based feature extraction, achieving substantial improvements in both accuracy and computational efficiency. Subsequent refinements including Fast R-CNN [26] and Faster R-CNN [27] introduced critical innovations such as shared convolutional features and the Region Proposal Network (RPN), further optimizing the speed–accuracy trade-off. Contemporary advancements exemplified by Xie et al.'s rotation-based framework [28] and Sun et al.'s sparse detection approach [29] have introduced sophisticated mechanisms for generating precise rotated bounding boxes and eliminating the computational overhead of non-maximum suppression (NMS).

Single-stage detectors formulate object detection as a unified regression problem encompassing simultaneous bounding box prediction and classification. The YOLO series [30–33] established a new paradigm through direct prediction of bounding coordinates and class probabilities, enabling real-time end-to-end detection. SSD [34] enhanced this framework by incorporating multiscale feature maps and anchor-based detection, significantly improving performance on small objects. Recent innovations such as FCOS [35] have further simplified the detection pipeline by eliminating anchor boxes entirely, while EfficientDet [36] introduced the BiFPN architecture for optimized multiscale feature fusion, achieving state-of-the-art efficiency. The Cascade-DETR framework [37] represents a significant advancement in Transformer-based detection, employing cascaded attention mechanisms and IoU-aware prediction to enhance both generalization capability and localization precision.

Despite these remarkable advancements, conventional approaches relying solely on improved feature extraction remain inadequate for addressing challenges posed by severe image quality degradation. This limitation motivates our subsequent investigation into RGB-T object detection methods that exploit complementary multimodal information.

3. Method

Current state-of-the-art RGB-T object detection models predominantly adopt end-to-end architectures to streamline both training and inference procedures. While this design paradigm offers operational convenience, it exhibits strong dependence on large-scale training datasets with precise manual annotations. Such heavy reliance on annotated data imposes significant constraints on further advancements in this field. Particularly in RGB-T multimodal fusion scenarios, the inherent data scarcity exacerbates these challenges. Theoretically, transfer learning could alleviate this data insufficiency by introducing relevant prior knowledge through pretraining on datasets from related tasks. However, the application of transfer learning in RGB-T object detection remains relatively unexplored, primarily due to the absence of large-scale annotated thermal infrared datasets. Moreover, establishing effective cross-modal prior knowledge constitutes a critical research challenge that demands immediate attention.

To effectively exploit complementary information in RGB-T data and adaptively construct semantic representations from unlabeled samples, we propose RDCRNet—a novel network architecture that enhances model performance through representation–interpretation decoupling and differentiated training strategies. Figure 1 illustrates RDCRNet's design and inference pipeline. The architecture comprises three key components: (1) a Cross-Modal Representation Network serving as the backbone, (2) a multiscale aggregation module for inference, and (3) a Representation Feature Reconstruction mechanism for training. Through coordinated operation enabled by joint training strategies, these components collectively capture implicit prior knowledge from RGB-T data, substantially improving the detection system's overall performance and robustness. Subsequent sections detail these components' mechanisms, functionalities, and specific training methods.

3.1. Cross-Modal Representation Network

As depicted in Figure 1a, the Cross-Modal Representation Network (CRN) consists of two principal elements: a feature extractor and the Cross-Modal Attention Module (CAM). The feature extractor is designed to derive high-level features from individual modalities, while CAM facilitates inter-modal information transfer and fusion. Although Transformer architectures demonstrate superior performance, they typically require extensive training data to effectively capture local image characteristics—a requirement impractical for RGB-T applications given dataset limitations. To address this, we implement a hybrid architecture combining CNNs and Transformers in the feature extractor and CAM, respectively, ensuring adequate contextual relationship modeling while preserving local inductive biases.

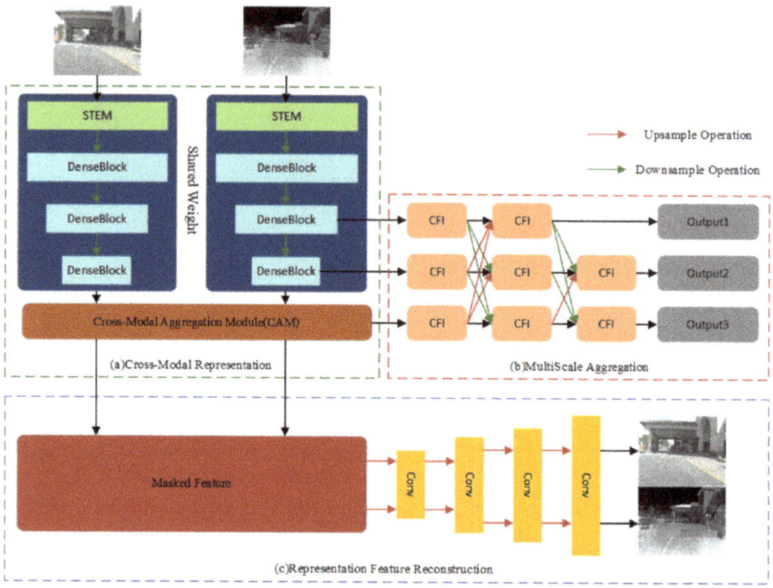

Figure 1. The overall network architecture of RDCRNet.

The CRN processes RGB images $I_{RGB} \in R^{H\times W\times 3}$ and thermal infrared images $I_T \in R^{H\times W\times 1}$, where the single-channel thermal input is replicated across three channels to maintain architectural consistency. Feature extraction initiates with an STEM module that projects input images into a high-dimensional latent space, generating shallow features $f_{RGB,0} \in R^{H/2\times W/2\times C_0}$ and $f_{T,0} \in R^{H/2\times W/2\times C_0}$ through the transformation:

$$f_{T,0} = STEM(I_T) \tag{1}$$

$$f_{RGB,0} = STEM(I_{RGB}) \tag{2}$$

where the parameter-shared $STEM(\cdot)$ operator performs simultaneous preliminary feature extraction and spatial downsampling for both modalities.

Following the design of most backbone networks, the entire network is divided into three stages, each processing RGB-T image features at different scales. To improve feature utilization and enhance representational capacity, we incorporate dense residual modules at each stage. Given the high dimensionality of infrared and visible light image data, which can lead to substantial computational and memory overhead, we integrate downsampling layers at multiple stages. These layers reduce the data dimensionality while enlarging the receptive field, enabling the model to output features at varying scales and depths. The features produced at each stage of the two branches are denoted as $f_{RGB,i} \in R^{H_i\times W_i\times C_i}$ and $f_{T,i} \in R^{H_i\times W_i\times C_i}$ (where $i = 1,2,3$), with feature resolutions progressively reduced to 1/4, 1/8, and 1/16 of the original image size. Concurrently, the channel dimensions increase to 128, 256, 512, and 1024, ensuring sufficient information density in the extracted features. This operation can be represented as follows:

$$f_{RGB,i} = F_i(f_{RGB,i-1}) \tag{3}$$

$$f_{T,i} = F_i(f_{T,i-1}) \tag{4}$$

where parameter-shared $F_i(\cdot)$ represents the function of the dense residual block at the i-th stage. At the final stage of the network, the RGB and thermal infrared features $f_{RGB,3} \in$

$R^{H_3 \times W_3 \times C_3}$ and $f_{T,3} \in R^{H_3 \times W_3 \times C_3}$ are embedded and transformed into feature vector sets $v_{RGB,i} \in R^{n \times C_3}$ and $v_{T,i} \in R^{n \times C_3}$. These feature vectors are subsequently processed through the CAM for feature refinement. By normalizing and integrating the cross-modal information, the transformed feature vector sets $\widehat{v}_{RGB,i} \in R^{n \times C}$ and $\widehat{v}_{T,i} \in R^{n \times C}$ are derived. For downstream processing, we restructure these feature vector collections back into feature maps, yielding $f_{RGB,out} \in R^{H_3 \times W_3 \times C}$ and $f_{T,out} \in R^{H_3 \times W_3 \times C}$. The inference and training phases employ distinct processing pipelines, with detailed procedures discussed in subsequent sections.

3.2. Cross-Modal Aggregation Module

In existing RGB-T object detection models, information interaction between different modality features is typically achieved through feature addition or concatenation, followed by refinement using learnable layers. While this approach is simple and effective, it struggles when processing non-registered RGB-T images, and lacks a standardized methodology. To address these limitations, we propose the Cross-Modal Aggregation Module within the CRN, which aims to overcome these shortcomings. As illustrated in Figure 2, the CAM comprises a series of stacked components, with the primary function of mitigating modality discrepancies and enhancing RGB-T feature fusion. The main functional components of the CAM include two parts: cross-modal feature remapping and information aggregation.

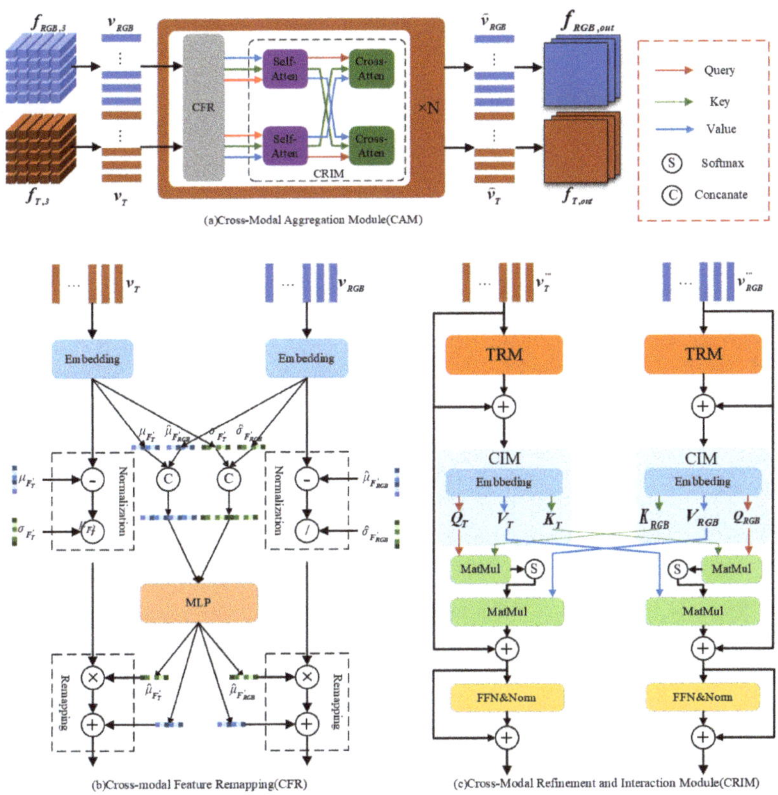

Figure 2. The structure of the Cross-Modal Aggregation Module.

Cross-Modal Feature Remapping (CFR). In the CRN, we employ feature extractors with shared parameters to process RGB-T images, effectively reducing the network's spatial complexity. However, due to the inherent differences in the imaging mechanisms of RGB and thermal infrared modalities, models without adaptive capabilities are susceptible to distributional discrepancies between these modalities during feature extraction, potentially degrading model performance significantly. To address this issue, we propose a Cross-Modal Feature Remapping Module, which adaptively recalibrates RGB-T features based on their statistical distributions. This remapping process helps mitigate modality discrepancies, ensuring more consistent feature representations for subsequent cross-modal information fusion.

The detailed architecture of the CFR module is depicted in Figure 4. Initially, after passing through an embedding layer, the extracted RGB and thermal infrared features are obtained, which can be mathematically represented as follows:

$$v'_{RGB} = W_1 v_{RGB} + b_1, \tag{5}$$

$$v'_T = W_2 v_T + b_2, \tag{6}$$

where W represents the weight parameters of the embedding layer, and b is the bias term. Inspired by prior research, modality differences are predominantly manifested in the statistical distribution properties of feature vectors, with mean and variance being the most characteristic parameters. To mitigate such modality discrepancies, we apply an initial normalization process to the extracted features, ensuring that feature vectors from both modalities conform to a standard normal distribution with zero mean and unit variance. This operation can be represented as follows:

$$v''_{RGB} = \frac{v'_{RGB} - \mu_{v'_{RGB}}}{\sigma_{v'_{RGB}}} \tag{7}$$

$$v''_T = \frac{v'_T - \mu_{v'_T}}{\sigma_{v'_T}} \tag{8}$$

where $[\mu_{v'_{RGB}}, \mu_{v'_T}]$ and $[\sigma_{v'_{RGB}}, \sigma_{v'_T}]$ represent the mean and variance of the feature vectors v''_{RGB} and v''_T, respectively. The aforementioned normalization method processes each feature vector independently. However, in practical applications, target objects are typically represented by multiple feature vectors. Therefore, we preserve the mean and variance information of the RGB and thermal infrared feature vectors across different channels and concatenate these statistics into a composite feature vector. Subsequently, through a two-layer multilayer perceptron (MLP), we correlate these key statistics and adaptively generate correction parameters $[\mu_{RGB}, \mu_T]$ and $[\sigma_{RGB}, \sigma_T]$ based on the global cross-modal information. This operation can be represented as follows:

$$[\mu_{RGB}, \mu_T] = f^1_{MLP}([\mu_{v'_{RGB}}, \mu_{v'_T}]) \tag{9}$$

$$[\sigma_{RGB}, \sigma_T] = f^2_{MLP}([\sigma_{v'_{RGB}}, \sigma_{v'_T}]) \tag{10}$$

where $f_{MLP}(\cdot)$ represents the equivalent function of the MLP. Finally, we perform the remapping operation on the normalized features using the correction parameters to obtain the output dual-band features v'''_{RGB} and v'''_T. This operation can be expressed as follows:

$$v'''_{RGB} = v'_{RGB} \cdot \sigma_{RGB} + \mu_{RGB} \tag{11}$$

$$v'''_T = v'_T \cdot \sigma_T + \mu_T \tag{12}$$

Cross-Modal Refinement and Interaction Module(CRIM). After completing the RGB-T feature remapping, a critical challenge emerges: determining how to effectively process and fuse these cross-modal features. To address this, we propose the Cross-Modal

Refinement and Interaction Module (CRIM), whose detailed architecture is illustrated in Figure 2c. CRIM comprises three core components: the Trinity Refinement Module (TRM), the Cross-Attention Interaction Module (CIM), and the Feed-Forward Network (FFN).

For both modalities, we first employ a shared-parameter encoder for preliminary feature processing. To further enhance intra-modal and inter-modal information extraction, we designed the Trinity Refinement Module, which refines feature granularity while strengthening both contextual information and inter-channel relationships. The architecture of TRM is detailed in Figure 3.

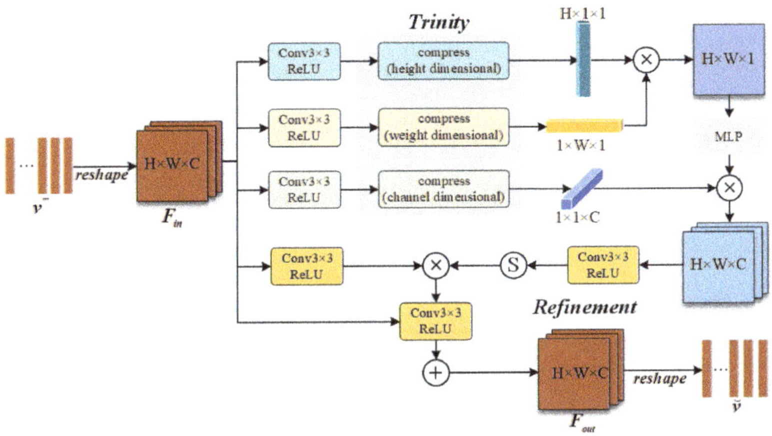

Figure 3. The structure of the Trinity Refinement Module.

The vector v''' is reshaped into an input feature map F_{in}, which undergoes dimensional compression to capture global contextual information. Through two matrix multiplication operations, the information extracted from three dimensions is aggregated to obtain a robust global feature representation. This process effectively captures long-range dependencies, significantly enhancing the modal features' expressive power. The integrated global information serves as pixel-level attention weights, applied to input features via element-wise multiplication for key information extraction.

To mitigate information loss and gradient vanishing, we incorporate local skip connections. The final output feature map F_{out} is converted back to vector form $\breve{v}$ for subsequent processing. These operations are formulated as follows:

$$F_d = f_{conpress,d}(f_{conv}(F_{in})), \forall d \in (H, W, C) \tag{13}$$

$$F_G = f_{conv}(f_{MLP}(F_H F_W) F_C) \tag{14}$$

$$F_{out} = f_{conv}(F_G \cdot f_{conv}(F_{in})) + F_{in} \tag{15}$$

where $f_{\text{compress},d}(\cdot)$ denotes the dimension-wise compression operation employing adaptive average pooling across height, width, and channel dimensions. While maintaining robust detection performance for unaligned RGB-T images remains our objective, the aforementioned operations alone prove insufficient for facilitating effective cross-modal interaction between RGB and thermal modalities.

Existing approaches predominantly focus on aligned RGB-T image pairs, lacking the capability for feature matching under spatial misalignment. To address this limitation, we propose a Cross-Modal Self-Attention Mechanism that enables comprehensive feature matching and fusion between misaligned RGB-T modalities. The mechanism operates as follows:

$$Q_{RGB} = W_Q \breve{v}_{RGB} \quad K_{RGB} = W_K \breve{v}_{RGB} \quad V_{RGB} = W_V \breve{v}_{RGB} \tag{16}$$

$$Q_T = W_Q \breve{v}_T \quad K_T = W_K \breve{v}_T \quad V_T = W_V \breve{v}_T \tag{17}$$

$$\tilde{v}_T = \text{Softmax}(\frac{Q_T \cdot {K_{RGB}}^T}{\sqrt{d_k}})\text{V}_{\text{RGB}} + v'''_T \tag{18}$$

$$\tilde{v}_{RGB} = \text{Softmax}(\frac{Q_{RGB} \cdot {K_T}^T}{\sqrt{d_k}})\text{V}_{\text{T}} + v'''_{RGB} \tag{19}$$

where $\breve{v}_{RGB}$ and $\breve{v}_T$ represent the input feature vectors from the RGB and T modalities, respectively; Q_{RGB}, K_{RGB}, and V_{RGB} represent the query, key, and value vectors derived from $\breve{v}_{RGB}$; W_Q, W_K, and W_V are learnable linear transformation matrices. Similarly, Q_T, K_T, and V_T denote the query, key, and value vectors obtained from $\breve{v}_T$. d_k represents the feature dimension for each attention head, and $\sqrt{d_k}$ serves as a scaling factor to prevent excessively large values in the dot product. The cross-modal attention computes similarity scores between the RGB key K_{RGB} and the TIR query Q_T via dot product, followed by normalization with factor $\sqrt{d_k}$ to obtain attention weights. These weights are then applied to perform a weighted summation of the RGB value V_{RGB} to update the TIR features, denoted as $\tilde{v}_T$. Similarly, RGB features are updated via the TIR key and value to obtain $\tilde{v}_{RGB}$. v'''_T and v'''_{RGB} represent residual connections that preserve original feature information.

In the RGB-T cross-attention mechanism, the query vector Q_T from the TIR modality interacts with the key vector K_{RGB} from the RGB modality to compute similarity scores through dot product operations. These scores are subsequently normalized using a softmax function to generate attention weights. The weighted summation of RGB value vectors V_{RGB} is then computed to update the TIR features. Conversely, the query vector Q_{RGB} interacts with the TIR key K_T, and the weighted summation of V_T updates the RGB features. This bidirectional cross-modal attention facilitates effective feature matching and fusion between RGB and TIR modalities, ensuring robust feature alignment even under conditions of spatial misalignment.

To further enhance the representational capacity of the model, we incorporate an FFN at the end of the CRIM module. By introducing additional non-linear transformations, the FFN significantly improves the model's performance. This operation can be mathematically expressed as follows:

$$\widehat{v} = \text{LayerNorm}(f_{FFN}(\tilde{v})) + \tilde{v} \tag{20}$$

where $\text{LayerNorm}(\cdot)$ denotes the layer normalization function, and $f_{FFN}(\cdot)$ represents the function implemented by the Feed-Forward Neural Network (FFN).

3.3. Cross-Modal Representation PreTraining

Although the CRN we designed exhibits strong potential for information complementarity, its performance heavily depends on the implementation of appropriate training methodologies. In existing RGB-T datasets, the quantity of registered and annotated samples is substantially smaller than that of unaligned and unannotated ones. To address this imbalance, we aim to develop an effective approach that can extract useful prior knowledge from a broader spectrum of datasets. Our proposed pretraining method, as illustrated in Figure 4, comprises two primary steps, in addition to training the CRN on the conventional ImageNet and COCO datasets to provide it with foundational capabilities.

Inspired by Masked Autoencoders (MAEs) [38,39], we propose a cross-modal masked reconstruction method. This approach facilitates collaborative learning of cross-modal features by strategically applying partial masking to the encoded features of both modalities.

Regarding mask generation, unlike traditional MAEs, we introduce additional constraints during the generation process to ensure that critical information required for reconstruction must simultaneously originate from both the source modality and the reference modality. This significantly enhances the model's feature extraction capabilities and the complementary information between modalities. To achieve this, we impose constraints on the minimum and maximum overlap rates during mask generation. This unique design ensures a balanced information sharing between source and reference modalities: on one hand, it effectively prevents the model from over-relying on information from a single modality, encouraging full exploration and leveraging of each modality's unique advantages; on the other hand, it significantly enhances the model's sensitivity and adaptability to cross-modal information, thereby establishing a more robust foundation for subsequent downstream tasks.

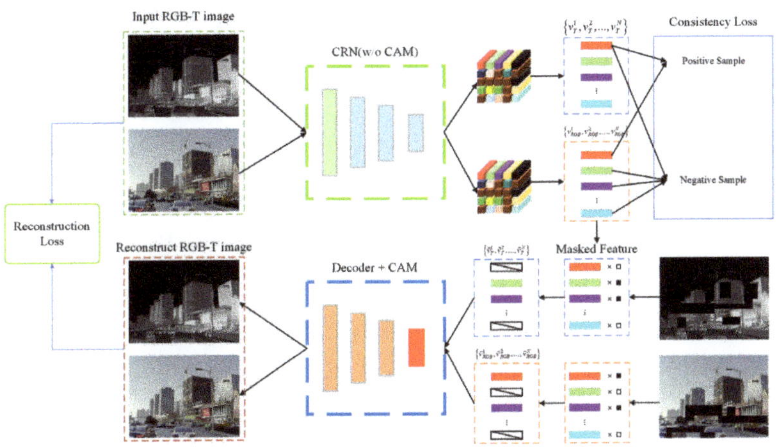

Figure 4. A schematic diagram of cross-modal representation pretraining.

During the pretraining stage, we refined and optimized the CRN structure to more efficiently extract and integrate multimodal information. Specifically, in the encoding component of the CRN, we removed certain elements of the CAM that focus exclusively on image feature encoding, and applied masking to the features. After feature encoding is completed, the masked encoded features are transmitted to the decoder, which incorporates the CAM, for reconstruction. The CAM serves a pivotal function in this process: it dynamically captures semantic correlations between source and reference modalities, excavates and leverages the complementary characteristics of both modalities, and achieves efficient cross-modal information fusion. This architecture requires the decoder not only to restore masked image information but also to fully utilize cross-modal synergy for precise comprehensive modeling of the overall content. This integration of modality interaction with preservation of image self-information enables the model to demonstrate enhanced cross-modal understanding capabilities in the reconstruction task while improving self-supervised learning effectiveness.

We employ the root mean square error (RMSE) as the primary reconstruction loss:

$$l_{rec} = \lambda_1 \cdot \frac{1}{p_{RGB}} \left\| I_{RGB} - I'_{RGB} \right\| + \lambda_2 \cdot \frac{1}{p_T} \left\| I_T - I'_T \right\| \tag{21}$$

where I'_{RGB} and I'_T represent the reconstructed RGB and thermal infrared images, and p_{RGB} and p_T denote the total number of pixels in the RGB and infrared images. However, due to the limited scale of collected RGB-T samples, which represent only a restricted subset of real-world scenarios, relying solely on MSE may neglect semantic information and complex patterns in the data. Therefore, we incorporate Generative Adversarial Learning (GAN) [40,41] to learn the implicit data distribution and capture richer patterns, which is validated in subsequent experiments. Beyond adversarial loss, we also introduce perceptual loss to ensure semantic consistency between reconstructed and real images. The expression for perceptual loss is as follows:

$$l_{adv} = \left\|1 - D(G(I'_{RGB}, I'_T))\right\|^2 \tag{22}$$

$$l_{per} = \sum_{j \in \Omega} \left\|\phi_j(G(I'_{RGB}, I'_T)) - \phi_j(I'_{RGB}, I'_T)\right\|^2 \tag{23}$$

where $G(\cdot)$ denotes the CRN functioning as the generator, $D(\cdot)$ represents the discriminator model, and $\varphi_j(\cdot)$ indicates the features extracted from the j-th layer of the VGG network. Although unaligned samples significantly outnumber registered samples, the registered samples spatially align the semantic and texture information of RGB-T modalities, thereby providing more robust supervisory signals.

To ensure semantic consistency during the reconstruction process of registered RGB-T images, we incorporate a contrastive loss [42,43] to aggregate semantic information from corresponding regions across the two modalities. Specifically, we select N sets of feature vectors from different spatial locations, designating feature vectors from identical locations as positive samples and optimizing them to be maximally proximate in the feature space during training. Conversely, feature vectors from different locations are designated as negative samples and are optimized to be maximally distant in the feature space. The expression for this contrastive loss function is as follows:

$$l_{ct} = -\log \frac{\exp(sim(v_{RGB,i}, v_{T,i})/\tau)}{\sum_1^N 1_{[i \neq j]} \exp(sim(v_{RGB,i}, v_{T,j})/\tau)} \tag{24}$$

where $sim(\cdot,\cdot)$ denotes the similarity measurement function, and the cosine similarity $sim(x,y) = x^T y/(\|x\| \cdot \|y\|)$ is employed in this work. Ultimately, we formulate a hybrid loss function that integrates the aforementioned losses to govern the CRN training process. The expression for this comprehensive loss is as follows:

$$l = l_{rec} + l_{adv} + l_{per} + s(I_{RGB}, I_T) \cdot l_{ct} \tag{25}$$

where $s(\cdot,\cdot)$ represents the indicator function that outputs 0 for unaligned samples and 1 for aligned samples. Through this methodology, we can effectively extract latent information from a substantial volume of unaligned RGB-T images while simultaneously leveraging the semantic and texture information embedded in registered samples for effective supervision.

3.4. Object Detection

After extracting the requisite features through the CRN, the subsequent task involves decoding these abstract representations into precise target localization and dimensional information. This decoding process is implemented via a meticulously designed decoder architecture, which is elaborated in the following sections.

Cross-Scale Feature Integration. Numerous research efforts have demonstrated that enhancing the processing and aggregation of multiscale features constitutes a pivotal strategy for addressing the challenge of target scale variation. Building upon this established approach, we introduce the Cross-Scale Feature Integration Module (CFI), which performs dense fusion of features across various scales and generates three feature maps at different resolutions. The architectural framework of the CFI is illustrated in Figure 5.

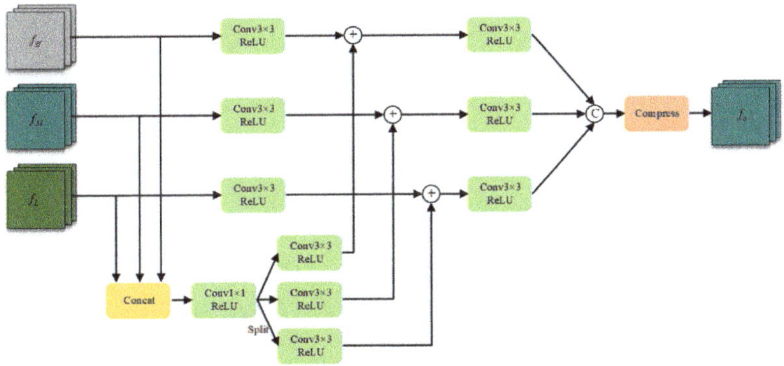

Figure 5. The structure of the Cross-Scale Feature Integration Module.

The feature maps processed by the output head ultimately encode the positional coordinates, dimensional parameters, and categorical attributes of targets at multiple scales. Through this architectural design, we ensure comprehensive information exchange across different scales, substantially enhancing the model's capacity to detect targets of varying dimensions and improving overall detection accuracy and robustness across diverse operational scenarios.

Loss Function. In object detection tasks, precise localization loss is indispensable. Therefore, we adopt the loss function from the YOLOv8 model [33], which has demonstrated excellent performance. The total loss function is defined as follows:

$$l = l_{VFL} + l_{CIoU} + l_{DFL} \tag{26}$$

where l_{VFL} represents the classification loss and $l_{CIoU} + l_{DFL}$ constitute the regression loss. The expressions for these components are

$$l_{VFL} = \frac{1}{N}\sum_{i=1}^{N}(q_i \cdot \log(p_i) + (1 - q_i) \cdot \log(1 - p_i)) \tag{27}$$

$$l_{CIoU} = 1 - IoU + \frac{\rho^2(b, b^{gt})}{c^2} + \alpha v \tag{28}$$

where N denotes the total number of samples, q_i represents the ground truth label of sample i (1 for positive samples and 0 for negative samples), and p_i indicates the predicted probability of sample i. In the CIoU loss, IoU measures the intersection over union between the predicted bounding box and the ground truth box, $\frac{\rho^2(b,b^{gt})}{c^2}$ quantifies the normalized Euclidean distance between the centers of the predicted box b and ground truth box b^{gt}, c represents the diagonal length of the smallest enclosing box covering both boxes, v measures the consistency of aspect ratios between the two boxes, and α serves as a weighting coefficient.

4. Experiment

4.1. Experimental Setup

Datasets and Metrics. During the pretraining phase of CRN, we utilized aligned datasets MFNet [12] and KAIST [44], which contain 1569 and 15,000 infrared-visible image pairs, respectively. Additionally, the unaligned FLIR ADAS dataset, comprising a total of 31,569 image samples, was incorporated. To further enhance CRN's training performance, we also collected a large number of unaligned and unlabeled RGB-T image samples, totaling 4200 images, some examples of which are shown in Figure 6. For the object detection task, we used the KAIST and FLIR ADAS datasets during both the training and testing phases, providing precise annotations for vehicles, pedestrians, and various road targets. The datasets were split into training, validation, and test sets in a 6:2:2 ratio. Notably, in the experiments involving the FLIR ADAS dataset, infrared images were used as the primary input data for object detection.

Figure 6. Examples of collected unaligned and unlabeled RGB-T image samples.

To comprehensively evaluate model performance, we employed standard detection metrics including accuracy, recall, precision, F1 score, mean intersection over union (mIoU), and mean average precision (mAP) to quantitatively assess the effectiveness of both multi-modal fusion and object detection capabilities.

Implementation Details. All experiments were conducted on a high-performance computing platform featuring an Intel(R) Core™ i9-13900KF processor, 64 GB RAM, and an NVIDIA GeForce RTX 4090 GPU. The software environment consisted of the Windows 11 operating system with PyCharm 2021.3.2 as the integrated development environment and PyTorch 2.1.0 as the deep learning framework.

For the Cross-Modal Representation Network pretraining phase, we employed the ADAM optimizer with parameters $\beta_1 = 0.9$, $\beta_2 = 0.999$, and $\epsilon = 8 \times 10^{-8}$ to ensure stable convergence. We configured the training with a minibatch size of 16 and an initial learning rate of 5×10^{-4}. The network was trained for 400 epochs, with learning rate decay to 10% of its current value implemented at the 200th and 300th epochs. Regarding the masking strategy, we set the masking rate at 0.6, with maximum and minimum overlaps for RGB-T masks configured at 0.5 and 0.2, respectively.

During the object detection training phase, we maintained the ADAM optimizer with identical parameter settings ($\beta_1 = 0.9$, $\beta_2 = 0.999$, and $\epsilon = 8 \times 10^{-8}$). We increased the minibatch size to 64 and utilized an initial learning rate of 1×10^{-2}. The training process spanned 200 epochs, with learning rate reductions to 10% of the current value scheduled at the 100th and 150th epochs.

4.2. Comparison with SOTA Methods

As our approach optimizes the network structure and pretraining methods for unaligned data, it is applicable to both aligned and unaligned object detection. We conducted comparative experiments on both scenarios.

Aligned Datasets. For aligned RGB-T datasets, we compared our method with state-of-the-art RGB-T object detection approaches, including IAF R-CNN [45], Midway Fusion [46], CIAN [47], AR-CNN [48], LRAF-Net [49], CAGTDet [50], and CMX [14]. Additionally, we evaluated single-modal object detection methods such as Faster R-CNN and RetinaNet. All methods were trained on the same dataset using the experimental setups provided by their respective authors. The quantitative results are presented in Table 1.

These results demonstrate that RGB-T object detection methods consistently outperform single-modal approaches, with the integration of cross-modal information significantly enhancing detection accuracy. Despite the varying architectures and fusion strategies employed by the RGB-T object detection networks used for comparison, the performance improvements across existing methods remain relatively modest. Among all the RGB-T detection methods, our approach achieved the best performance, with improvements in mIoU, F1 score, and mAP of 5.3%, 1.7%, and 3.5%, respectively, over the second-best method. This success can be attributed to our proposed cross-modal information interaction structure and effective pretraining strategy.

Table 1. Quantitative analysis results of various algorithms under the registered dataset (KAIST). The best and second-best values are highlighted in bold red and blue, respectively.

Method	Modality	mIoU	Recall	Precision	F1 score	mAP	FLOPS (G)	Param (M)
Faster R-CNN	RGB	0.7239	0.7962	0.7675	0.7816	0.6947	16.0	41.0
RetinaNet	RGB	0.7453	0.8325	0.7948	0.8132	0.7337	24.0	35.0
Faster R-CNN	Thermal	0.7520	0.8392	0.8046	0.8216	0.7422	16.0	41.0
RetinaNet	Thermal	0.7515	0.8396	0.8050	0.8219	0.7464	24.0	35.0
IAF R-CNN	RGB-T	0.8013	0.8753	0.8332	0.8537	0.8405	30.0	50.0
Halfway Fusion	RGB-T	0.8040	0.8775	0.8503	0.8637	0.8441	28.0	48.0
CIAN	RGB-T	0.8065	0.8837	0.8597	0.8715	0.8472	70.36	55.0
AR-CNN	RGB-T	0.8109	0.8892	0.8696	0.8793	0.8573	66.0	53.0
LRAF-Net	RGB-T	0.8085	0.8889	0.8693	0.8790	0.8529	40.5	18.8
CMX	RGB-T	0.8122	0.8895	0.8753	0.8834	0.8611	**104.3**	28.7
CAGTDet	RGB-T	0.8248	0.8998	0.8800	0.8898	0.8655	58.60	35.0
RDCRNet(Ours)	RGB-T	**0.8688**	**0.9302**	**0.8992**	**0.9046**	**0.8962**	101.7	**16.4**

To provide a visual demonstration, several detection examples are presented in Figure 7. Detection using only infrared or visible modalities often resulted in missed or false detections due to insufficient brightness or contrast, respectively. Consistent with the quantitative evaluation metrics, RGB-T detection methods produced superior results. Among all the methods, ours accurately identified targets, achieved precise object boundaries, and demonstrated high-confidence responses. The qualitative and quantitative analyses are in strong agreement.

Unaligned Datasets. Unaligned RGB-T data are more prevalent in real-world applications, but they present significant challenges for algorithms. We conducted comparative experiments on unaligned datasets to evaluate our algorithm's capability in addressing the issue of spatial misalignment in RGB-T data. Most existing methods struggle to handle unaligned data effectively due to the absence of structural design and training strategies tailored to matching disparate spatial features. As a result, we selected AR-CNN, LRAF-Net, and CAGTDet as comparative methods, as they can tolerate a certain degree of misalignment. To ensure that these methods performed optimally, we applied a rough alignment to the images from the FLIR dataset, mitigating excessive scale and spatial discrepancies. Additionally, we included several single-modal object detection methods, such as Faster R-CNN, RetinaNet, EfficientDet, and Cascade-DETR, which were trained and tested on infrared images, serving as baselines.

The results of the quantitative analysis, presented in Table 2, demonstrate that our method achieved the highest performance in all metrics, with improvements of 3.3% in mIoU, 6.2% in the F1 score, and 6.6% in mAP compared to the best results. Furthermore, visualizations of selected examples in Figure 8 illustrate that our method's advantages are even more pronounced on unaligned datasets such as FLIR ADAS, producing fewer errors than other methods. These visual results corroborate the quantitative findings, further validating the superiority and effectiveness of our approach.

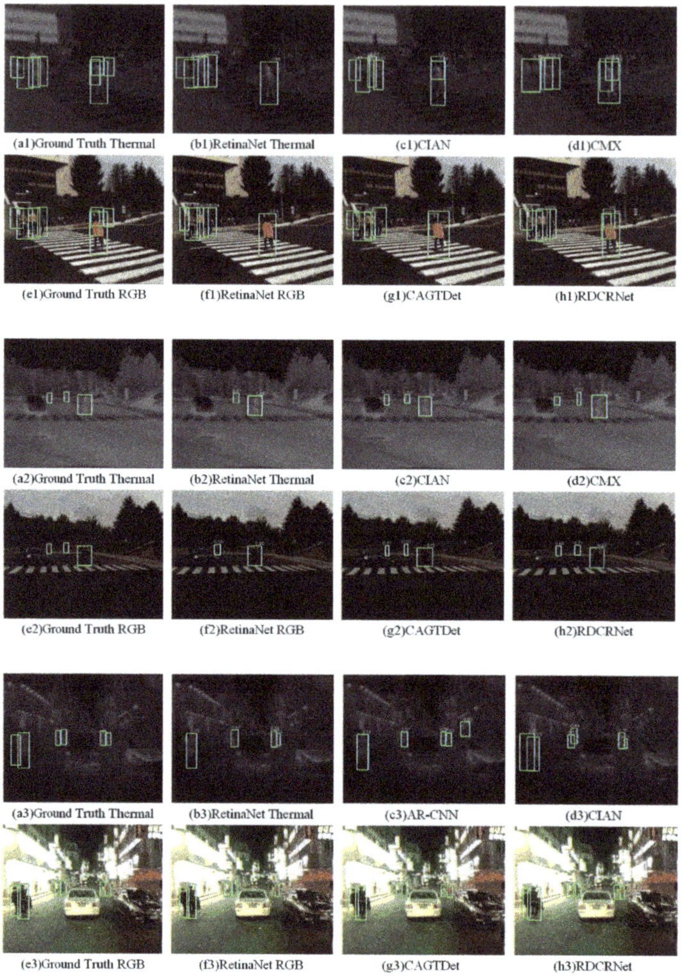

Figure 7. Qualitative comparison of various algorithms under the registration dataset (KAIST).

Table 2. Quantitative analysis results of various algorithms under the unaligned dataset (FLIR ADAS). The best and second-best values are highlighted in bold red and blue, respectively.

Method	Modality	mIoU	Recall	Precision	F1 score	mAP
Faster R-CNN	Thermal	0.6931	0.7409	0.7644	0.7524	0.5664
RetinaNet	Thermal	0.6960	0.7312	0.7603	0.7455	0.5732
FCOS	Thermal	0.7105	0.7478	0.7824	0.7647	0.5952
EfficientDet	Thermal	0.7099	0.7439	0.7927	0.7675	0.6098
Cascade-DETR	Thermal	0.7150	0.7723	0.8134	0.7923	0.6491
AR-CNN	RGB-T	0.7397	0.8039	0.8403	0.8217	0.6655
LRAF-Net	RGB-T	0.7406	0.8487	0.8645	0.8262	0.6823
CAGTDet	RGB-T	0.7840	0.8824	0.8937	0.8378	0.7195
RDCRNet	RGB-T	**0.8096**	**0.9119**	**0.9241**	**0.8897**	**0.7671**

Detail of the Result. To further analyze the detection performance, additional data analysis was performed. A total of 2000 test images were randomly selected from the KAIST and FLIR datasets, with 1000 images each from daytime and nighttime scenes. The miss rate (MR) of various methods under these conditions is presented in Figure 9. In daytime scenes, nearly all cross-modal detection methods exhibited low MR values on both datasets, as the high quality of RGB images in daylight provides abundant target information. In contrast, night-time MR values were higher due to the diminished information from RGB images, although cross-modal methods still outperformed single-modal approaches. RDCRNet achieved the lowest MR values in both scenarios, with less performance degradation at night, indicating its ability to efficiently extract and utilize the limited RGB features available in low-light conditions.

Figure 8. Qualitative comparison of various algorithms under the unregistration dataset (FLIR ADAS).

Furthermore, the detection performance for primary categories in the FLIR dataset was analyzed, as shown in Table 3. Pedestrian and vehicle classes, which appear frequently and benefit from strong complementary RGB-T features, were detected more accurately by RDCRNet. This can be attributed to the robust information interaction and aggregation capabilities of our network architecture. For other categories with fewer training samples, all methods demonstrated reduced effectiveness. However, RDCRNet, with its cross-modal pretraining, adapted better to small-sample data, demonstrating superior robustness across diverse object categories.

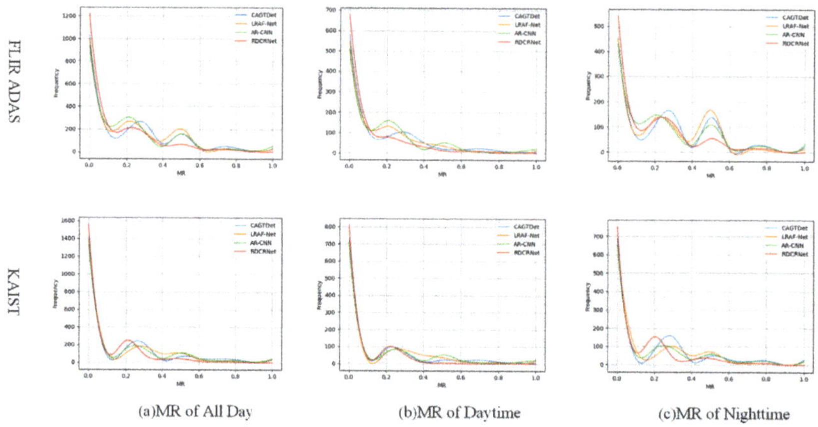

Figure 9. MR values of daytime and nighttime samples for different methods across two datasets.

Table 3. Detection accuracy of various algorithms for different categories of targets under the registration dataset (KAIST). The specific number of each category is indicated after the category name. The best and second-best values are highlighted in red and blue bold, respectively.

Method	People (5779)	Bicycles (471)	Cars (5432)	Dogs (14)	Total
AR-CNN	0.6813	0.3227	0.6794	0.2857	0.6655
LRAF-Net	0.6791	0.2929	0.6771	0.4285	0.6623
CAGTDet	0.6810	0.4140	0.6802	0.3571	0.6695
RDCRNet	**0.6860**	**0.7430**	**0.6830**	**0.8571**	**0.6871**

Cross-Domain Dataset. Experiments conducted on the surveillance scene dataset (LLVIP) further validate the cross-domain generalization capability of RCDRNet. Compared to the ADAS dataset, the LLVIP dataset presents more complex scenes, diverse environmental features, and significant variations in lighting conditions, such as low light, strong light, and shadows, thereby mitigating potential data biases present in road scene datasets. The experimental results demonstrate that RCDRNet exhibits remarkable performance advantages in object detection tasks within surveillance contexts, maintaining high accuracy and robustness under both complex backgrounds and varying lighting conditions. Quantitative analysis, as shown in Table 4, indicates that RCDRNet outperforms the second-best method, achieving an improvement of 3.5% in mIoU, 4.6% in F1 score, and 4.0% in mAP. Qualitative analysis illustrated in Figure 10 showcases selected detection results across different scenarios, revealing that RCDRNet achieves higher detection rates and precision. These experiments indicate that RCDRNet demonstrates strong adaptability to diverse scenes, with performance gains not limited to the specific characteristics of the ADAS domain, but, rather, stemming from the model's superior architectural design and generalization capabilities. This finding further substantiates the broad applicability of RCDRNet in cross-domain tasks and its potential for deployment in various real-world applications.

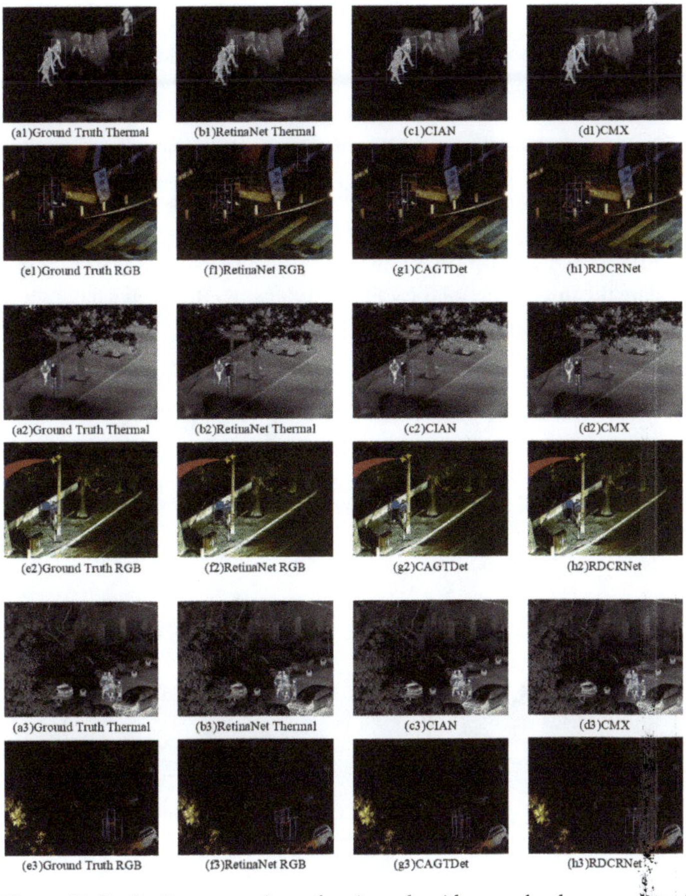

Figure 10. Qualitative comparison of various algorithms under the cross-domain dataset (LLVIP).

Table 4. Quantitative analysis results of various algorithms under the cross-domain dataset (LLVIP). The best and second-best values are highlighted in bold red and blue, respectively.

Method	Modality	mIoU	Recall	Precision	F1 score	mAP
Faster R-CNN	Thermal	0.6712	0.7234	0.7456	0.7343	0.5893
RetinaNet	Thermal	0.6853	0.7351	0.7582	0.7465	0.5967
FCOS	Thermal	0.6968	0.7513	0.7771	0.7633	0.6056
EfficientDet	Thermal	0.6897	0.7442	0.7834	0.7661	0.6102
Cascade-DETR	Thermal	0.7056	0.7601	0.8024	0.7816	0.6234
AR-CNN	RGB-T	0.7256	0.7943	0.8311	0.8122	0.6411
LRAF-Net	RGB-T	0.7348	0.8297	0.8591	0.8341	0.6583
CMX	RGB-T	0.7542	0.8563	0.8722	0.8286	0.6741
CAGTDet	RGB-T	0.7732	0.8745	0.8926	0.8361	0.7257
RDCRNet	RGB-T	**0.8012**	**0.8971**	**0.9152**	**0.8763**	**0.7556**

4.3. Ablation Study

To validate the effectiveness and robustness of key modules in the proposed RDCRNet, several ablation experiments were conducted. For consistency, all ablation experiments followed identical training and testing procedures.

Effectiveness of CFR. To determine if the CFR module effectively facilitates cross-modal feature remapping and enhances network performance, three experimental setups were designed: without remapping, with layer normalization only, and with complete CFR integration. As shown in Table 5, the addition of layer normalization resulted in limited performance improvement, indicating that normalization alone cannot fully address the modality discrepancies. However, when the complete CFR module was introduced, significant performance gains were observed. Visualization of features before and after remapping, illustrated in Figure 11, demonstrates that CFR effectively reduces the distinct differences between infrared and visible features, mapping them to a similar feature space. These results underscore the importance of the CFR module, as it effectively enables the model to harness the complementary capabilities of RGB-T information.

Table 5. Ablation study results of CFR.

Method	KAIST		FLIR ADAS	
	mIoU	mAP	mIoU	mAP
Without remapping	0.8012	0.8503	0.7418	0.6617
Layer normalization	0.8025	0.8581	0.7426	0.6682
CFR	0.8688	0.8962	0.8096	0.7671

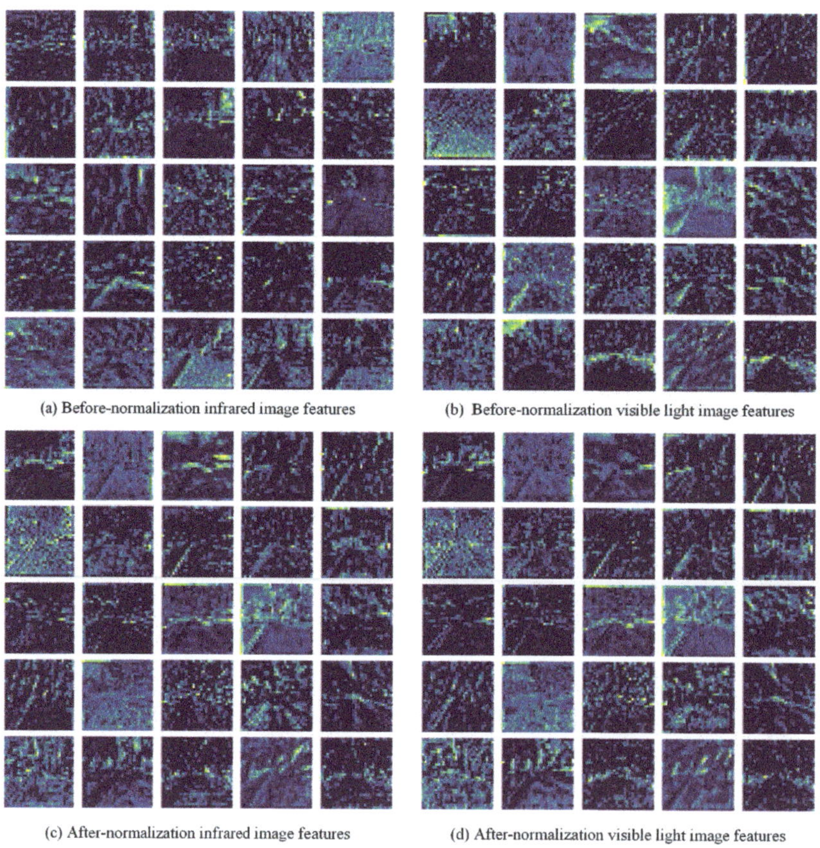

Figure 11. Comparison of infrared and visible light image features before and after normalization.

Effectiveness of CRIM. To test the design and necessity of the CRIM module, an ablation study was conducted on various combinations of TRM, CIM, and Feed-Forward Networks (FFNs) within the CRIM module. The results, as shown in Table 6, demonstrate that TRM, by establishing extensive contextual relationships within a single modality, yields moderate performance improvement. However, CIM serves as the core component for cross-modal information interaction, with its absence causing notable performance degradation. To visually demonstrate the effect of information interaction, an RGB-T image pair was selected to observe the cross-modal attention responses within the CRIM module in RDCRNet. As shown in Figure 12, by averaging response values across all CRIM layers and displaying them as red and blue heatmaps, it becomes evident that RDCRNet effectively captures complementary semantic information from the RGB images.

Table 6. Ablation study results of CRIM.

Method			KAIST		FLIR ADAS	
FFN	TRM	CIM	mIoU	mAP	mIoU	mAP
×	×	×	0.7631	0.7567	0.7025	0.5944
✓	×	×	0.7652	0.7588	0.7198	0.6458
✓	✓	×	0.8098	0.8119	0.7839	0.7118
✓	✓	✓	0.8688	0.8962	0.8096	0.7671

Result for the number of CRIM. The influence of CRIM layers on network performance was examined to determine optimal hyperparameter settings. As shown in Figure 13, network performance improved gradually with an increase in CRIM layers, but eventually reached a point of diminishing returns. Therefore, to maintain computational efficiency in RDCRNet, N = 6 layers was chosen as the optimal configuration, effectively balancing network complexity and detection accuracy.

Effectiveness of Cross-Modal Representation Pretraining. The effectiveness of cross-modal representation pretraining was explored by analyzing four main configurations: no pretraining, no cross-modal reconstruction loss, no semantic consistency loss, and full cross-modal pretraining. The results in Table 7 indicate that the cross-modal pretraining method effectively leverages extensive RGB-T data to acquire prior knowledge, significantly improving detection accuracy. Furthermore, encoder pretraining on the ImageNet dataset was performed for the CRN, which further enhanced the model's overall performance.

Table 7. Ablation study results of Cross-Modal Representation Pretraining.

Pretraining Step			KAIST		FLIR ADAS	
Classification	CCL	CMAE	Precision	mAP	Precision	mAP
×	×	×	0.7787	0.7982	0.7528	0.6675
✓	×	×	0.8003	0.8013	0.7543	0.6708
✓	✓	×	0.8251	0.8301	0.7889	0.6725
✓	✓	✓	0.8688	0.8692	0.8096	0.7671

Study of the Dependence of Pretraining Strategies on Unlabeled Data. To investigate the impact of unlabeled data quantity on model performance during the pretraining process, we designed and conducted a series of ablation experiments. First, we incrementally increased the number of samples within a single dataset; the experimental results are shown in Figure 14. The experiments revealed that model performance improved significantly in the initial stages, particularly after adding approximately 2000 samples, where a substantial enhancement in network performance was observed. However, due to the relatively homogeneous scenes in publicly available datasets (e.g., KAIST and FLIR ADAS), the amount of novel prior knowledge that could be provided diminished gradually. Consequently, when the number of pretraining samples exceeded half the total size of the each dataset, the performance gains began to plateau.

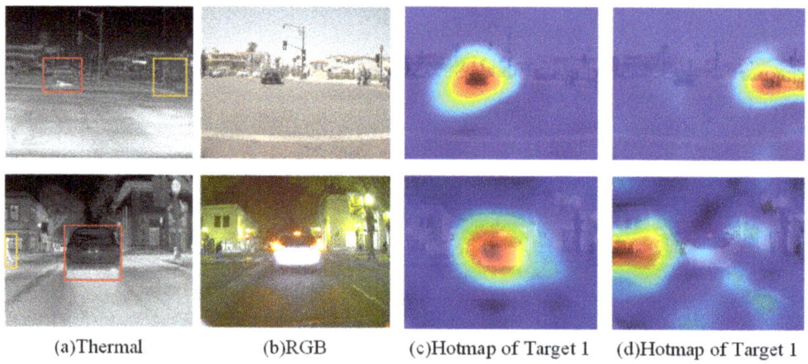

Figure 12. The visualization of semantic feature matching results in CAM.

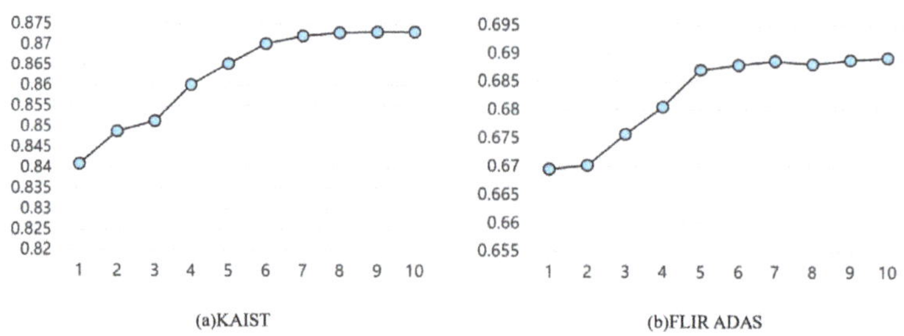

Figure 13. The performance variation curve of detection with respect to the quantity of CRIM and CFI.

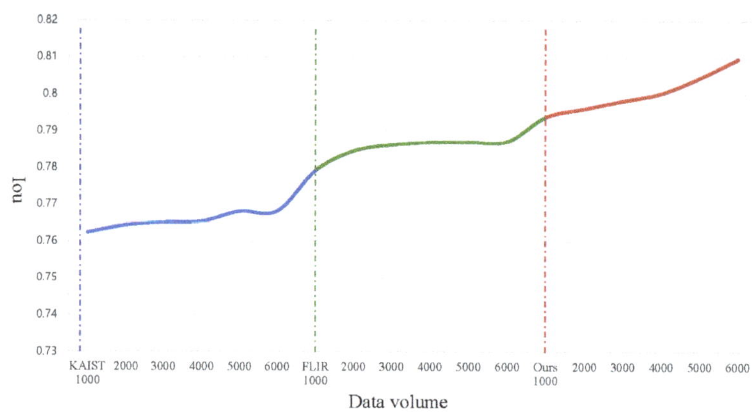

Figure 14. The curve of the effect of the number of unlabeled data on the model performance during pretraining.

Finally, we conducted a detailed analysis of aligned and non-aligned pretraining samples by categorizing them into three scenarios: (1) only non-aligned samples, (2) only aligned samples, and (3) a combination of aligned and non-aligned samples. To eliminate the influence of sample quantity on the experimental results, we strictly controlled the sample size across the three scenarios, ensuring that they remained at the same order of magnitude. The results, summarized in Table 8, indicate that RDCR-Net achieved the best performance under Scenario 3. This suggests that mixed samples provide richer prior knowledge and effectively enhance the network's ability to extract and fuse cross-modal information.

Table 8. Ablation experiment results on aligned and unaligned pretraining samples.

Method	KAIST		FLIR	
	mIoU	**mAP**	**mIoU**	**mAP**
scenarios 1	0.8234	0.8755	0.7789	0.6920
scenarios 2	0.8215	0.8740	0.7766	0.6943
scenarios 3	0.8688	0.8962	0.8096	0.7671

Effectiveness of the CFI Module. We evaluated the effectiveness of the CFI module by replacing it with two alternative fusion methods: element-wise addition and channel-wise concatenation, while preserving the multiscale feature fusion. Furthermore, we examined the effect of completely removing the multiscale fusion, opting instead for a basic upsampling and fusion strategy similar to the one employed in YOLO. The results, as presented in Table 9, demonstrate that both the CFI module and multiscale feature fusion substantially improve detection performance, confirming that these architectural enhancements are both effective and essential for optimal RGB-T object detection.

Table 9. Ablation study results of CFI.

Method	KAIST		FLIR	
	mIoU	**mAP**	**mIoU**	**mAP**
w/o Multiscale	0.8023	0.8526	0.7601	0.6754
Add	0.8113	0.8667	0.7678	0.6818
Concat	0.8103	0.8652	0.7655	0.6831
CFI	0.8688	0.8962	0.8096	0.7671

5. Conclusions

In this paper, we proposed RDCRNet, a novel framework for RGB-T object detection that addresses critical challenges in cross-modal feature alignment, distribution discrepancy mitigation, and efficient fusion under both aligned and unaligned conditions. The core innovation lies in the Cross-Modal Representation Model, which integrates several key components: the Cross-Modal Feature Remapping Module, for statistical normalization and adaptive correction of modality-specific distributions; the Cross-Modal Refinement and Interaction Module, enabling bidirectional feature fusion through trinity refinement and cross-attention mechanisms; and the Cross-Scale Feature Integration Module, for multiscale detection capability enhancement. To overcome data scarcity in RGB-T tasks, we introduced a self-supervised pretraining strategy combining masked reconstruction with adversarial learning and semantic consistency constraints, effectively leveraging both aligned and unaligned multimodal data. Extensive experiments on KAIST, FLIR ADAS, and LLVIP datasets demonstrated state-of-the-art performance, with RDCRNet achieving significant improvements in mIoU, F1 score, and mAP over existing methods while maintaining computational efficiency. The framework's robustness was particularly evident in challenging low-light scenarios and cross-domain applications, validating its ability to exploit complementary RGB-T information through effective cross-modal representation learning. These advancements establish RDCRNet as a practical solution for real-world applications requiring reliable object detection under diverse environmental conditions.

Author Contributions: Conceptualization, Y.L., W.Z., and Y.J.; methodology, Y.L., W.Z., and J.G.; data curation, Y.L., Y.J., and J.G.; writing—original draft preparation, Y.L. and W.Z.; writing—review and editing, Y.J. and W.Z.; supervision, W.Z.; project administration, W.Z.; funding acquisition, W.Z. All authors have read and agreed to the published version of the manuscript.

Funding: This research was supported by the Jilin Provincial Science and Technology Department Development Program, China. Project name: Research and development of vehicle multiband intelligent fusion enhanced imaging and processing system. Project number: 20240302029GX.

Institutional Review Board Statement: Not applicable.

Data Availability Statement: The original contributions presented in this study are included in the article. Further inquiries can be directed to the corresponding author.

Conflicts of Interest: The authors declare no conflicts of interest.

References

1. Chen, K.; Liu, J.; Zhang, H. IGT: Illumination-guided RGB-T object detection with transformers. *Knowl.-Based Syst.* **2023**, *268*, 110423. [CrossRef]
2. Zhang, J.; Zhang, R.; Yuan, W.; Liu, Y. Rgb-t semantic segmentation based on cross-operational fusion attention in autonomous driving scenario. *Evol. Syst.* **2024**, *15*, 1429–1440. [CrossRef]
3. Wu, Y.; Guan, X.; Zhao, B.; Ni, L.; Huang, M. Vehicle detection based on adaptive multi-modal feature fusion and cross-modal vehicle index using RGB-T images. *IEEE J. Sel. Top. Appl. Earth Obs. Remote. Sens.* **2023**, *16*, 8166–8177. [CrossRef]
4. Li, G.; Wang, Y.; Liu, Z.; Zhang, X.; Zeng, D. RGB-T semantic segmentation with location, activation, and sharpening. *IEEE Trans. Circuits Syst. Video Technol.* **2022**, *33*, 1223–1235. [CrossRef]
5. Jiang, N.; Wang, K.; Peng, X.; Yu, X.; Wang, Q.; Xing, J.; Li, G.; Guo, G.; Ye, Q.; Jiao, J.; et al. Anti-uav: A large-scale benchmark for vision-based UAV tracking. *IEEE Trans. Multimed.* **2021**, *25*, 486–500. [CrossRef]
6. Wang, G.; Jiang, Q.; Jin, X.; Wozniak, M.; Yao, P.; Wang, S. RTM-UAVDet: A Real-Time Multimodal UAV Detector. *IEEE Trans. Aerosp. Electron. Syst.* **2025**, *61*, 473–489. [CrossRef]
7. Zhu, D.; Zhan, W.; Jiang, Y.; Xu, X.; Guo, R. IPLF: A novel image pair learning fusion network for infrared and visible image. *IEEE Sens. J.* **2022**, *22*, 8808–8817. [CrossRef]
8. Zhang, X.; Demiris, Y. Visible and infrared image fusion using deep learning. *IEEE Trans. Pattern Anal. Mach. Intell.* **2023**, *45*, 10535–10554. [CrossRef]
9. Zhang, Z.; Wang, J.; Han, Y. Saliency prototype for rgb-d and rgb-t salient object detection. In Proceedings of the 31st ACM International Conference on Multimedia, Ottawa, ON, Canada, 29 October–3 November 2023; pp. 3696–3705.
10. Jiang, Y.; Liu, Y.; Zhan, W.; Tang, Y.; Li, J.; Liu, Y. Cross-modal texture transformer for thermal infrared reference-based super-resolution reconstruction. *Opt. Laser Technol.* **2024**, *176*, 110914. [CrossRef]
11. Zhou, W.; Gong, T.; Lei, J.; Yu, L. DBCNet: Dynamic bilateral cross-fusion network for RGB-T urban scene understanding in intelligent vehicles. *IEEE Trans. Syst. Man Cybern. Syst.* **2023**, *53*, 7631–7641. [CrossRef]
12. Ha, Q.; Watanabe, K.; Karasawa, T.; Ushiku, Y.; Harada, T. MFNet: Towards real-time semantic segmentation for autonomous vehicles with multi-spectral scenes. In Proceedings of the 2017 IEEE/RSJ International Conference on Intelligent Robots and Systems (IROS), Vancouver, BC, Canada, 24–28 September 2017; pp. 5108–5115.
13. Zhou, W.; Liu, J.; Lei, J.; Yu, L.; Hwang, J.-N. GMNet: Graded-feature multilabel-learning network for RGB-thermal urban scene semantic segmentation. *IEEE Trans. Image Process.* **2021**, *30*, 7790–7802. [CrossRef] [PubMed]
14. Zhang, J.; Liu, H.; Yang, K.; Hu, X.; Liu, R.; Stiefelhagen, R. CMX: Cross-modal fusion for RGB-X semantic segmentation with transformers. *IEEE Trans. Intell. Transp. Syst.* **2023**, *24*, 14679–14694. [CrossRef]
15. Feng, D.; Haase-Schütz, C.; Rosenbaum, L.; Hertlein, H.; Glaeser, C.; Timm, F.; Wiesbeck, W.; Dietmayer, K. Deep multi-modal object detection and semantic segmentation for autonomous driving: Datasets, methods, and challenges. *IEEE Trans. Intell. Transp. Syst.* **2020**, *22*, 1341–1360. [CrossRef]
16. Zhang, Q.; Huang, N.; Yao, L.; Zhang, D.; Shan, C.; Han, J. RGB-T salient object detection via fusing multi-level CNN features. *IEEE Trans. Image Process.* **2019**, *29*, 3321–3335. [CrossRef]
17. Wang, J.; Song, K.; Bao, Y.; Huang, L.; Yan, Y. CGFNet: Cross-guided fusion network for RGB-T salient object detection. *IEEE Trans. Circuits Syst. Video Technol.* **2021**, *32*, 2949–2961. [CrossRef]
18. Wang, H.; Song, K.; Huang, L.; Wen, H.; Yan, Y. Thermal images-aware guided early fusion network for cross-illumination RGB-T salient object detection. *Eng. Appl. Artif. Intell.* **2023**, *118*, 105640. [CrossRef]
19. Wang, K.; Lin, D.; Li, C.; Tu, Z.; Luo, B. Alignment-Free RGBT Salient Object Detection: Semantics-guided Asymmetric Correlation Network and A Unified Benchmark. *IEEE Trans. Multimed.* **2024**, *26*, 10692–10707. [CrossRef]

20. Tian, C.; Zhou, Z.; Huang, Y.; Li, G.; He, Z. Cross-Modality Proposal-guided Feature Mining for unaligned RGB-Thermal Pedestrian Detection. *IEEE Trans. Multimed.* **2024**, *16*, 6449–6461. [CrossRef]
21. Chen, G.; Shao, F.; Chai, X.; Chen, H.; Jiang, Q.; Meng, X.; Ho, Y.-S. Modality-induced transfer-fusion network for RGB-D and RGB-T salient object detection. *IEEE Trans. Circuits Syst. Video Technol.* **2022**, *33*, 1787–1801. [CrossRef]
22. Kyrkou, C.; Theocharides, T. A parallel hardware architecture for real-time object detection with support vector machines. *IEEE Trans. Comput.* **2011**, *61*, 831–842. [CrossRef]
23. Kyrkou, C.; Theocharides, T. A flexible parallel hardware architecture for AdaBoost-based real-time object detection. *IEEE Trans. Very Large Scale Integr. (VLSI) Syst.* **2010**, *19*, 1034–1047. [CrossRef]
24. Li, Z.; Liu, F.; Yang, W.; Peng, S.; Zhou, J. A survey of convolutional neural networks: Analysis, applications, and prospects. *IEEE Trans. Neural Networks Learn. Syst.* **2021**, *33*, 6999–7019. [CrossRef] [PubMed]
25. Girshick, R.; Donahue, J.; Darrell, T.; Malik, J. Rich feature hierarchies for accurate object detection and semantic segmentation. In Proceedings of the IEEE Conference on Computer Vision and Pattern Recognition, Columbus, OH, USA, 23–28 June 2014; pp. 580–587.
26. Girshick, R. Fast R-CNN. In Proceedings of the IEEE International Conference on Computer Vision, Santiago, Chile, 7–13 December 2015; pp. 1440–1448.
27. Ren, S.; He, K.; Girshick, R.; Sun, J. Faster R-CNN: Towards real-time object detection with region proposal networks. *IEEE Trans. Pattern Anal. Mach. Intell.* **2016**, *39*, 1137–1149. [CrossRef] [PubMed]
28. Xie, X.; Cheng, G.; Wang, J.; Yao, X.; Han, J. Oriented R-CNN for object detection. In Proceedings of the IEEE/CVF International Conference on Computer Vision, Montreal, QC, Canada, 11–17 October 2021; pp. 3520–3529.
29. Sun, P.; Zhang, R.; Jiang, Y.; Kong, T.; Xu, C.; Zhan, W.; Tomizuka, M.; Yuan, Z.; Luo, P. Sparse r-cnn: An end-to-end framework for object detection. *IEEE Trans. Pattern Anal. Mach. Intell.* **2023**, *45*, 15650–15664. [CrossRef]
30. Redmon, J. You only look once: Unified, real-time object detection. In Proceedings of the IEEE Conference on Computer Vision and Pattern Recognition, Las Vegas, NV, USA, 27–30 June 2016; pp. 779–788.
31. Redmon, J.; Farhadi, A. YOLO9000: Better, faster, stronger. In Proceedings of the IEEE Conference on Computer Vision and Pattern Recognition, Honolulu, HI, USA, 21–27 July 2017; pp. 7263–7271.
32. Farhadi, A.; Redmon, J. Yolov3: An incremental improvement. *Comput. Vis. Pattern Recognit.* **2018**, *1804*, 1–6.
33. Varghese, R.; Sambath, M. YOLOv8: A novel object detection algorithm with enhanced performance and robustness. In Proceedings of the 2024 International Conference on Advances in Data Engineering and Intelligent Computing Systems (ADICS), Chennai, India, 18–19 April 2024; pp. 1–6.
34. Liu, W.; Anguelov, D.; Erhan, D.; Szegedy, C.; Reed, S.; Fu, C.-Y.; Berg, A.C. SSD: Single shot multibox detector. In Proceedings of the Computer Vision–ECCV 2016: 14th European Conference, Amsterdam, The Netherlands, 11–14 October 2016; pp. 21–37; Proceedings, Part I 14.
35. Tian, Z.; Shen, C.; Chen, H.; He, T. FCOS: A simple and strong anchor-free object detector. *IEEE Trans. Pattern Anal. Mach. Intell.* **2020**, *44*, 1922–1933. [CrossRef]
36. Tan, M.; Pang, R.; Le, Q.V. EfficientDet: Scalable and efficient object detection. In Proceedings of the IEEE/CVF Conference on Computer Vision and Pattern Recognition, Seattle, WA, USA, 13–19 June 2020; pp. 10781–10790.
37. Ye, M.; Ke, L.; Li, S.; Tai, Y.-W.; Tang, C.-K.; Danelljan, M.; Yu, F. Cascade-DETR: Delving into high-quality universal object detection. In Proceedings of the IEEE/CVF International Conference on Computer Vision, Paris, France, 2–3 October 2023; pp. 6704–6714.
38. He, K.; Chen, X.; Xie, S.; Li, Y.; Dollár, P.; Girshick, R. Masked autoencoders are scalable vision learners. In Proceedings of the IEEE/CVF Conference on Computer Vision and Pattern Recognition, New Orleans, LA, USA, 18–24 June 2022; pp. 16000–16009.
39. Bachmann, R.; Mizrahi, D.; Atanov, A.; Zamir, A. Multimae: Multi-modal multi-task masked autoencoders. *Eur. Conf. Comput. Vis.* **2022**, *13697*, 348–367.
40. Tao, M.; Bao, B.-K.; Tang, H.; Xu, C. Galip: Generative adversarial clips for text-to-image synthesis. In Proceedings of the IEEE/CVF Conference on Computer Vision and Pattern Recognition, Vancouver, BC, Canada, 17–24 June 2023; pp. 14214–14223.
41. Sun, X.; Wang, Z.; Lu, Z.; Lu, Z. Self-supervised graph representations with generative adversarial learning. *Neurocomputing* **2024**, *592*, 127786. [CrossRef]
42. Radford, A.; Kim, J. W.; Hallacy, C.; Ramesh, A.; Goh, G.; Agarwal, S.; Sastry, G.; Askell, A.; Mishkin, P.; Clark, J.; et al. Learning transferable visual models from natural language supervision. In Proceedings of the International Conference on Machine Learning, Virtual, 18–24 July 2021; pp. 8748–8763.
43. Li, J.; Li, D.; Xiong, C.; Hoi, S. Blip: Bootstrapping language-image pretraining for unified vision-language understanding and generation. In Proceedings of the International Conference on Machine Learning, Baltimore, MD, USA, 17–23 July 2022; pp. 12888–12900.

44. Hwang, S.; Park, J.; Kim, N.; Choi, Y.; So Kweon, I. Multispectral pedestrian detection: Benchmark dataset and baseline. In Proceedings of the IEEE Conference on Computer Vision and Pattern Recognition, Boston, MA, USA, 7–12 June 2015; pp. 1037–1045.
45. Li, C.; Song, D.; Tong, R.; Tang, M. Illumination-aware Faster R-CNN for robust multispectral pedestrian detection. *Pattern Recognit.* **2019**, *85*, 161–171. [CrossRef]
46. Liu, J.; Zhang, S.; Wang, S.; Metaxas, D.N. Multispectral deep neural networks for pedestrian detection. In Proceedings of the IEEE Conference on Computer Vision and Pattern Recognition, Las Vegas, NV, USA, 27–30 June 2016; Volume 1611, p. 02644.
47. Zhang, L.; Liu, Z.; Zhang, S.; Yang, X.; Qiao, H.; Huang, K.; Hussain, A. Cross-modality interactive attention network for multispectral pedestrian detection. *Inf. Fusion* **2019**, *50*, 20–29. [CrossRef]
48. Zhang, L.; Zhu, X.; Chen, X.; Yang, X.; Lei, Z.; Liu, Z. Weakly aligned cross-modal learning for multispectral pedestrian detection. In Proceedings of the IEEE/CVF International Conference on Computer Vision, Seoul, Republic of Korea, 27 October–2 November 2019; pp. 5127–5137.
49. Fu, H.; Wang, S.; Duan, P.; Xiao, C.; Dian, R.; Li, S.; Li, Z. LRAF-Net: Long-range attention fusion network for visible–infrared object detection. *IEEE Trans. Neural Networks Learn. Syst.* **2023**, *35*, 13232–13245. [CrossRef]
50. Yuan, M.; Shi, X.; Wang, N.; Wang, Y.; Wei, X. Improving RGB-infrared object detection with cascade alignment-guided transformer. *Inf. Fusion* **2024**, *105*, 102246. [CrossRef]

entropy

MDPI

Article

A Comprehensive Method for Example-Based Color Transfer with Holistic–Local Balancing and Unit-Wise Riemannian Information Gradient Acceleration

Zeyu Wang [1], Jialun Zhou [1,*], Song Wang [1,2] and Ning Wang [1]

[1] School of Electrical and Information Engineering, Zhengzhou University, Zhengzhou 450001, China; wzy_00000@gs.zzu.edu.cn (Z.W.); ieswang@zzu.edu.cn (S.W.); ienwang@zzu.edu.cn (N.W.)
[2] Department of Computer Science, Toronto Metropolitan University, Toronto, ON M5B 2K3, Canada
* Correspondence: seiezjl@zzu.edu.cn

Abstract: Color transfer, an essential technique in image editing, has recently received significant attention. However, achieving a balance between holistic color style transfer and local detail refinement remains a challenging task. This paper proposes an innovative color transfer method, named BHL, which stands for Balanced consideration of both Holistic transformation and Local refinement. The BHL method employs a statistical framework to address the challenge of achieving a balance between holistic color transfer and the preservation of fine details during the color transfer process. Holistic color transformation is achieved using optimal transport theory within the generalized Gaussian modeling framework. The local refinement module adjusts color and texture details on a per-pixel basis using a Gaussian Mixture Model (GMM). To address the high computational complexity inherent in complex statistical modeling, a parameter estimation method called the unit-wise Riemannian information gradient (uRIG) method is introduced. The uRIG method significantly reduces the computational burden through the second-order acceleration effect of the Fisher information metric. Comprehensive experiments demonstrate that the BHL method outperforms state-of-the-art techniques in both visual quality and objective evaluation criteria, even under stringent time constraints. Remarkably, the BHL method processes high-resolution images in an average of 4.874 s, achieving the fastest processing time compared to the baselines. The BHL method represents a significant advancement in the field of color transfer, offering a balanced approach that combines holistic transformation and local refinement while maintaining efficiency and high visual quality.

Keywords: color transfer; statistical modeling; GMM; optimization on Riemannian manifold

1. Introduction

Example-based image color style transfer methods have emerged as powerful tools in computer graphics and image processing. Their significance lies in their ability to transfer the color characteristics from the example image to the source image. This allows for various key applications, such as artistic effects transformation [1], photorealistic image stylization [2], image illuminance adjustment [3,4], and underwater image enhancement [5,6].

Pioneering work in example-based image color style transfer was presented in [7]. The authors achieved the decorrelation of color channels by transforming RGB images into the Lab color space, leveraging simple statistics, such as mean and standard deviation, to linearly map the color characteristics from one image to another. Building on this foundation, the method introduced in [8] retained operations within the RGB space and utilized mean and covariance to account for the inherent correlations between the three color channels. Furthermore, the method detailed in [9] accomplished one-to-one color mapping by transferring the color palette of the example image to the source image through an iterative algorithm that transforms one probability density function into another. In [10], a linear color transformation derived from the Monge–Kantorovich theory was proposed. Following this, Ref. [11] introduced a regularized discrete optimal transport formulation for color transformation, effectively addressing challenges such as mass conservation relaxation and regularization. The method in [12] employed illuminant matching and optimal color palette mapping to achieve color transfer. Moreover, Ref. [13] tackled the limitations of relaxed optimal transport in color transfer by implementing a non-convex regularized optimal transportation method that enforced one-to-one feature matching while minimizing transport dispersion. The authors of [14] introduced a transformation between Multivariate Generalized Gaussian Distributions (MGGDs), consisting of optimal transportation of the second-order statistics and a stochastic-based shape parameter transformation.

While optimal transportation algorithms offer advantages in computational efficiency and ease of use, they have limitations. Notably, the application of a uniform processing method across all pixels hinders the ability to ensure the reasonableness of transformation results in all image regions. This may lead to artifacts, unnatural colorization, irrational luminosity relationships, biased color positioning, and color vignetting in the output image.

To overcome this limitation, an Expectation-Maximization (EM)-based segmentation method for regional color transfer was introduced in [15]. In [16], a soft color segmentation method was presented for color transfer, using a Gaussian Mixture Model (GMM) to capture broad color patterns with soft labels. The method proposed in [17] utilized an improved EM algorithm and a GMM for the automatic selection of appropriate reference colors within target regions. Focusing on local style variations, the method introduced in [18] leveraged Gaussian clustering to capture fine-grained light and color details within images. This method employed novel source-example cluster mapping policies and achieved style transfer through a combination of parametric color transfer and local chromatic adaptation, allowing for seamless image synthesis while preserving spatial and color coherence. A content-based color transfer method introduced in [19] performed high-level scene analysis for semantic region correspondence and utilized a novel optimization framework to achieve color transfer while preserving spatial layout and visual coherence. For applications in cartoon and fabric color transfer, the method presented in [20] improved color transfer vividness and enhanced detail preservation through image segmentation and the incorporation of a total generalized variation regularizer. A representative superpixel-based method for color transfer was presented in [21], utilizing a fast method that employed approximate nearest neighbor matching with enforced diversity and a fusion framework. Lastly, an L2 divergence-based method for color transfer was described in [22], offering flexibility by accommodating color correspondences and ensuring performance despite potential outlier pairs.

Building upon differential geometry concepts, Ref. [23] introduced a method for per-frame color transform interpolation that minimized curvature. In contrast, the method presented in [24] employed iterative probabilistic color mapping with self-learning filtering and multiscale detail manipulation, minimizing the Kullback–Leibler divergence to enhance color fidelity and detail preservation. To improve robustness, the method in [25] leveraged scattered point interpolation with moving least squares and probabilistic modeling in 3D RGB space, enabling robust color transfer across varying conditions. For more compelling results, the method in [26] considered scene illumination and target gamut constraints, utilizing white balancing, illuminant-aware tone mapping, and gamut-based color mapping techniques. Based on the color homography theorem, the method in [27] decomposed color transfer into chromaticity shift and shading adjustment, represented by a global shading curve. Additionally, a 3D color homography model was introduced in [28], approximating the transformation as a combination of a 3D perspective transform and mean intensity mapping. Addressing color transfer in a two-stage process, the method in [29] first prioritized similarities between source image pixel colors and dominant colors during color mapping, followed by an L0 gradient-preserving detail preservation step to refine large gradients at color region boundaries while maintaining small gradients within regions. The method in [30] tackled color transfer estimation with pixel-to-pixel correspondences using a robust feature-based method. This method utilized an optimal inlier maximization algorithm for outlier handling, combined with a novel structure tensor-based feature detector and descriptor, ensuring reliable color distribution matching across images.

Convolutional Neural Networks (CNNs) have proven remarkably adept at capturing the underlying features of images. This proficiency makes them particularly well suited for image style transfer tasks. Their advantage stems from their ability to learn complex image representations, often referred to as deep features. The most common method leverages these deep features to establish correspondences between the source and example images, subsequently implementing the style transfer [31–36].

Under this framework, a method for visual attribute transfer between images with different appearances was introduced in [37], focusing on images with similar semantic structures. This method leveraged deep image analogy and extended PatchMatch to guide semantically meaningful transfers. Similarly, the method proposed in [38] was designed for accurate and coherent color transfer in images with similar semantic structures, employing dense correspondences and local linear models. A local colorization method that allowed for customizable results by incorporating different example images was presented in [39]. Beyond CNN-based methods, a self-supervised Generative Adversarial Network (GAN) for High Dynamic Range (HDR) image color transfer was introduced in [40]. A style representation learning method for arbitrary image style transfer using contrastive learning was proposed in [41]. Meanwhile, a multichannel correlation network (MCCNet) for arbitrary video and image style transfer, which ensures temporal consistency and addresses flickering effects, was proposed in [42]. Detailed reviews of different color transfer techniques can be found in [43,44].

While deep learning methods generally achieve superior performance, they have certain limitations. Extensive training datasets and substantial computational resources are required to train these models. Additionally, their performance is hindered when the source image type is not present in the training data. Once trained, these networks may struggle to adapt to different source image sizes.

Existing methods for color transfer each have their own advantages. However, it is difficult to achieve good performance in all aspects, such as texture preservation, color brightness, and time efficiency. To overcome these challenges, this paper makes the following contributions:

1. This paper proposes a method that balances holistic and local costs, named BHL. The BHL method captures the color information of example images more comprehensively at a holistic level while better preserving the texture details of the source images.
2. A customized optimization method is introduced, based on the Riemannian information gradient and called the uRIG method, to address the high computational time associated with parameter estimation for the MGGD and GMM probability models. By leveraging the second-order acceleration effect of the Riemannian information metric (matrix), the uRIG method significantly enhances the time efficiency of the BHL algorithm.
3. In the preprocessing stage, SLIC (Simple Linear Iterative Clustering) is used to sample mini-batches for subsequent iterations. This ensures that the colors of the image will not be too monotonous when refining local areas.
4. Extensive numerical experiments demonstrate that the BHL method achieves a significant advantage in time complexity over existing color transfer techniques while matching or even surpassing the visual quality of existing methods.

2. Methodology

This paper aims to achieve fast and high-quality image color transfer by leveraging the complementary strengths of holistic and local methods. To this end, we formulate the engineering problem as a numerical optimization problem, as shown in the following equation:

$$\min(C_h + C_\ell), \tag{1}$$

where C_h and C_ℓ represent the costs associated with holistic and local color transformations, respectively. Minimizing both terms in Equation (1) theoretically leads to the optimal color transfer solution.

2.1. Holistic Cost

In this work, image pixels are represented as 3-dimensional vectors (i.e., corresponding to the 3 channels in the CIE Lab color space). By statistically modeling all pixel values in the example image, its holistic color features are described by a probability distribution, denoted as P_e. Similarly, the color features of the source image are represented by a distribution P_s. The holistic color transfer is accomplished through an optimal transport map between P_s and P_e, as optimal transport guarantees that mapping samples from P_s to P_e minimizes the color difference (i.e., the transport cost). As a result, the color distribution of the transformed image closely aligns with that of the example image. Mathematically, this problem is expressed as:

$$\min_T \mathbb{E}_{x\sim P_s}[c(x, T(x))], \tag{2}$$

where x represents a random vector following P_s, $T(x)$ is the optimal transport mapping to be found, and $c(x, T(x))$ denotes the transport cost. In this work, the Multivariate Generalized Gaussian Distribution (MGGD) is selected as an appropriate probability distribution to model the source image and example image. The MGGD is a generalization of the multivariate Gaussian distribution; since it inherits the advantages of the Gaussian distribution, it offers a more accurate fit to the real probability density of the dataset due to its adjustable shape parameter. The probability density function of the MGGD is defined as follows [45]:

$$p(\boldsymbol{x}|\boldsymbol{\theta}) = c|\boldsymbol{\Sigma}|^{-\frac{1}{2}} g_\beta(\delta) \quad \text{with} \quad \boldsymbol{\theta} = (\boldsymbol{\mu}, \boldsymbol{\Sigma}, \beta), \tag{3}$$

where the d-dimensional vector $\boldsymbol{\mu} \in \mathbb{R}^d$ is the location (mean) parameter. The $d \times d$-dimensional scatter matrix $\boldsymbol{\Sigma}$ is symmetric positive definite, and $|\boldsymbol{\Sigma}|$ denotes the determinant of $\boldsymbol{\Sigma}$. The real positive value β is the shape parameter. The coefficient c is the normalizing constant

$$c = \beta\pi^{-\frac{d}{2}} 2^{-\frac{d}{2\beta}} \Gamma(d/2)/\Gamma(d/2\beta), \tag{4}$$

where Γ is the Gamma function. The symbol δ denotes the Mahalanobis distance for simplicity

$$\delta = (\boldsymbol{x} - \boldsymbol{\mu})^\dagger \boldsymbol{\Sigma}^{-1} (\boldsymbol{x} - \boldsymbol{\mu}), \tag{5}$$

where $\dagger$ denotes the vector or matrix transpose. Then, the real-valued function $g_\beta(\delta)$ is

$$g_\beta(\delta) = \exp\left(-\delta^\beta/2\right). \tag{6}$$

To conceptually distinguish between the source image and the example image, denote the random vector corresponding to the source image as $\boldsymbol{x}$ and the random vector corresponding to the example image as $\boldsymbol{e}$. We define $\mathcal{X} = \{\boldsymbol{x}_1, \cdots, \boldsymbol{x}_M\}$ as a sample set of $\boldsymbol{x}$, representing the source image (whose color is to be transferred), and $\mathcal{E} = \{\boldsymbol{e}_1, \cdots, \boldsymbol{e}_N\}$ as a sample set of $\boldsymbol{e}$, representing the example image. It is assumed that $\mathcal{X}$ is distributed according to an MGGD, and the same assumption holds for $\mathcal{E}$. The transformation equation of two MGGDs, i.e., the minimum of Equation (2), is given in [14]. This transformation of MGGDs incorporates the following two key elements:

1. The MK (Monge–Kantorovich) linear transportation associated with the scatter matrices of $\boldsymbol{x}$ and $\boldsymbol{e}$;
2. A stochastic transformation of the shape parameters of $\boldsymbol{x}$ and $\boldsymbol{e}$.

Denote $\mathcal{U} = \{u_1, \cdots, u_M\}$ as the image that was transformed by MK mapping, $\forall m \in \{1, \cdots, M\}$. The expression of MK transportation is

$$T_{MK} : \boldsymbol{x}_m \mapsto \boldsymbol{u}_m = \boldsymbol{\Lambda}(\boldsymbol{x}_m - \boldsymbol{\mu}_x) + \boldsymbol{\mu}_e \tag{7a}$$

where

$$\boldsymbol{\Lambda} = \boldsymbol{\Sigma}_x^{-\frac{1}{2}} \left(\boldsymbol{\Sigma}_x^{\frac{1}{2}} \boldsymbol{\Sigma}_e \boldsymbol{\Sigma}_x^{\frac{1}{2}} \right)^{\frac{1}{2}} \boldsymbol{\Sigma}_x^{-\frac{1}{2}}. \tag{7b}$$

Since MK transportation is independent of the shape parameter β_e of the example image, we need to perform a second transfer operation related to β_x and β_e. Here, we denote T_s as this second transfer operation and $\boldsymbol{v}_m = T_s(\boldsymbol{u}_m), \forall m \in \{1, \cdots, m\}$, as the output of this transformation. To incorporate the shape parameter β_e of the example image into the transportation result $\boldsymbol{v}$, we first need to eliminate the influence of β_x on the current result $\boldsymbol{u}$. Then, we apply the influence of β_e to $\boldsymbol{u}$ to obtain the output result $\boldsymbol{v}$ with the full parameter influence of $\boldsymbol{e}$. Therefore, we need to introduce the stochastic representation of $\boldsymbol{u}$ [45]

$$\boldsymbol{u} \stackrel{\mathrm{d}}{=} \boldsymbol{\mu}_e + \tau_x \boldsymbol{\Sigma}_e^{\frac{1}{2}} \boldsymbol{r}. \tag{8}$$

where $\stackrel{\mathrm{d}}{=}$ denotes stochastic equality. The d-dimensional random vector $\boldsymbol{r}$ follows a uniform distribution on the unit sphere, and τ_x is a positive random variable (independent of $\boldsymbol{r}$) satisfying the following condition:

$$\tau_x^{2\beta_x} \sim \Gamma\left(\frac{d}{2\beta_x}, 2\right). \tag{9}$$

According to (8), the expression of T_s is obtained as follows:

$$\forall m \in \{1, \cdots, M\}, \qquad T_s : \boldsymbol{u}_m \mapsto \boldsymbol{v}_m = \frac{\tau_e(\boldsymbol{u}_m - \boldsymbol{\mu}_e)}{\|\boldsymbol{\Sigma}_e^{-\frac{1}{2}}(\boldsymbol{u}_m - \boldsymbol{\mu}_e)\|} + \boldsymbol{\mu}_e, \tag{10}$$

where τ_e is randomly sampled according to (9). By combining and T_s, we can obtain T_h:

$$\forall m \in \{1, \cdots, M\}, \qquad T_h : \boldsymbol{x}_m \mapsto \boldsymbol{v}_m = T_s(T_{MK}(\boldsymbol{x}_m)). \tag{11}$$

Ultimately, this optimal transportation problem is equivalent to an optimization problem: the estimation problem of $\boldsymbol{\theta}_x = (\boldsymbol{\mu}_x, \boldsymbol{\Sigma}_x, \beta_x)$ and $\boldsymbol{\theta}_e = (\boldsymbol{\mu}_e, \boldsymbol{\Sigma}_e, \beta_e)$

$$\min C_{h,x}(\boldsymbol{\theta}_x) \quad \text{with} \quad C_{h,x}(\boldsymbol{\theta}_x) = -\frac{1}{M} \sum_{m=1}^{M} \ln p(\boldsymbol{x}_m | \boldsymbol{\theta}_x), \tag{12a}$$

$$\min C_{h,e}(\boldsymbol{\theta}_e) \quad \text{with} \quad C_{h,e}(\boldsymbol{\theta}_e) = -\frac{1}{N} \sum_{n=1}^{N} \ln p(\boldsymbol{e}_n | \boldsymbol{\theta}_e). \tag{12b}$$

2.2. Local Costs

After the holistic transformation, a local transformation method is expected to adjust the details. In this work, we employ the framework introduced in [46], which achieves state-of-the-art performance. The interest of this framework not only resides in its performance but also in its operational simplicity.

Here, the output of T_h is used as the input for the local transformation. The local transformation leverages the assumption that the example image dataset $\mathcal{E} = \{\boldsymbol{e}_1, \cdots, \boldsymbol{e}_N\}$ follows a specific Gaussian Mixture Model (GMM). The means of this GMM are hypothesized to correspond to the source image. In this way, the matching of pixels and the color transformation between the source image and the example image can be performed simultaneously and adaptively during the parameter estimation process of the GMM, without the need for additional segmentation operations.

Denote $\mathcal{Z} = \{z_1, \cdots, z_M\}$ as the means of this GMM. The probability density function of the GMM followed by the random vector e_n is defined as follows:

$$\begin{aligned} p(e_n|\omega) &= \sum_{m=1}^{M} \frac{1}{M} p(e_n|\omega_m), \\ \text{with } \omega &= \{\omega_1, \cdots, \omega_M\}, \omega_m = (z_m, \sigma_m I), \end{aligned} \tag{13}$$

where $p(e_n|\omega_m)$ denotes the m-th Gaussian component of the GMM and M represents the total number of components in the mixture. Following [46], a vector $z_m \in \mathbb{R}^d$ is used as the mean (location parameter) of the m-th component, and a diagonal covariance matrix $\sigma_m I$ serves as its scatter matrix. Since the covariance involves only one parameter σ_m to be estimated, we denote ω_m as (z_m, σ_m) in the following sections for simplicity and ignore the identity matrix I. Additionally, all components are assigned equal weights of $1/M$ in [46]. The local cost is defined as the negative log-likelihood of the GMM:

$$\begin{aligned} &\min C_\ell(\omega), \\ &\text{with} \quad C_\ell(\omega) = -\sum_{n=1}^{N} \ln\left[\frac{1}{M}\sum_{m=1}^{M} p(e_n|\omega_m)\right], \end{aligned} \tag{14}$$

and for each component of the GMM,

$$p(e|\omega_m) = \frac{1}{(2\pi)^{\frac{d}{2}}} \sigma_m^{-\frac{d}{2}} \exp\left(-\frac{1}{2}\sigma_m^{-1}\|e - z_m\|^2\right). \tag{15}$$

Then, the color transformation is achieved through a GMM estimation process, utilizing $\mathcal{E} = \{e_1, \cdots, e_N\}$ as the sample data and $\mathcal{V} = \{v_1, \cdots, v_M\}$ (output of T_h) as the initial value for the means $\mathcal{Z} = \{z_1, \cdots, z_M\}$. In the minimization algorithm, we set

$$\{z_1^{(0)}, \cdots, z_M^{(0)}\} = \{v_1, \cdots, v_M\}. \tag{16}$$

While the Expectation-Maximization (EM) algorithm was applied to address this problem in [46], it is no longer suitable in this context. In Section 3, the uRIG method is introduced, specifically tailored to this problem.

3. Optimization Algorithm

3.1. Main Algorithm

To minimize the cost function in Equations (12) and (14), a two-stage optimization process is introduced. Figure 1 illustrates the overall workflow.

During the first stage, we employ Multivariate Generalized Gaussian Distributions (MGGDs) to independently model the source image $\mathcal{X} = \{x_m; m = 1, \cdots, M\}$ and the example image $\mathcal{E} = \{e_n; n = 1, \cdots, N\}$. We then estimate the parameters for these respective models. Utilizing these estimated parameters, we construct the holistic transformation equation T_h and subsequently apply it to achieve holistic color transfer.

The output of the first stage, denoted as $\mathcal{V} = \{v_m; m = 1, \cdots, M\}$, serves as the input for the second stage. Here, a GMM with means denoted by $\mathcal{Z} = \{z_m; m = 1, \cdots, M\}$ is leveraged. We posit that the example image $\mathcal{E}$ constitutes a sample set for this GMM. Through an iterative maximum likelihood estimation process initialized with $\mathcal{Z}^{(0)} = \mathcal{V}$, the estimated $\hat{\mathcal{Z}}$ represents the refined result, which is also the final transformed image. The BHL method is summarized in the Algorithm 1 as below.

Algorithm 1 The BHL method

Require: Source image $\mathcal{X} = \{x_1, \cdots, x_M\}$, example image $\mathcal{E} = \{e_1, \cdots, e_N\}$;
1: $\hat{\boldsymbol{\theta}}_x \leftarrow$ MGGDESTIMATION($\mathcal{X}$);
2: $\hat{\boldsymbol{\theta}}_e \leftarrow$ MGGDESTIMATION($\mathcal{E}$);
3: $\{v_1, \cdots, v_M\} \leftarrow$ TRANSMGGD($\mathcal{X}, \hat{\boldsymbol{\theta}}_x, \hat{\boldsymbol{\theta}}_e$);
4: $\{\hat{z}_1, \cdots, \hat{z}_M\} \leftarrow$ GMMESTIMATION($\mathcal{E}, \mathcal{V}$);
Ensure: Edited image $\hat{\mathcal{Z}} = \{\hat{z}_1, \cdots, \hat{z}_M\}$;
5: **procedure** TRANSMGGD($\mathcal{X}, \hat{\boldsymbol{\theta}}_x, \hat{\boldsymbol{\theta}}_e$)
6:     Holistic transformation via (11);
7:     **return** $\mathcal{V} = \{v_1, \cdots, v_M\}$;
8: **end procedure**

This color transfer method necessitates solving three optimization problems: (12a), (12b), and (14) (refer to Steps 1 and 2 in Algorithm 1). Traditionally, these problems are addressed using the fixed-point iteration method for (12a) and (12b), and the Expectation-Maximization (EM) algorithm for (14). However, these methods become computationally expensive, particularly for high-resolution images, due to increased time and memory demands. To overcome this computational bottleneck, the unit-wise Riemannian information gradient (uRIG) method is introduced. The core idea of uRIG leverages two key mathematical concepts: the Riemannian manifold and the Fisher information metric [47,48]. Updates on the Riemannian manifold effectively bypass numerical instabilities often encountered with nonlinear constraints, such as positive definite matrices, leading to a more robust algorithm. Additionally, the use of the Fisher information metric (matrix) as a replacement for the Hessian matrix eliminates the need for computationally expensive numerical approximations, thereby accelerating the convergence of the estimation process [49].

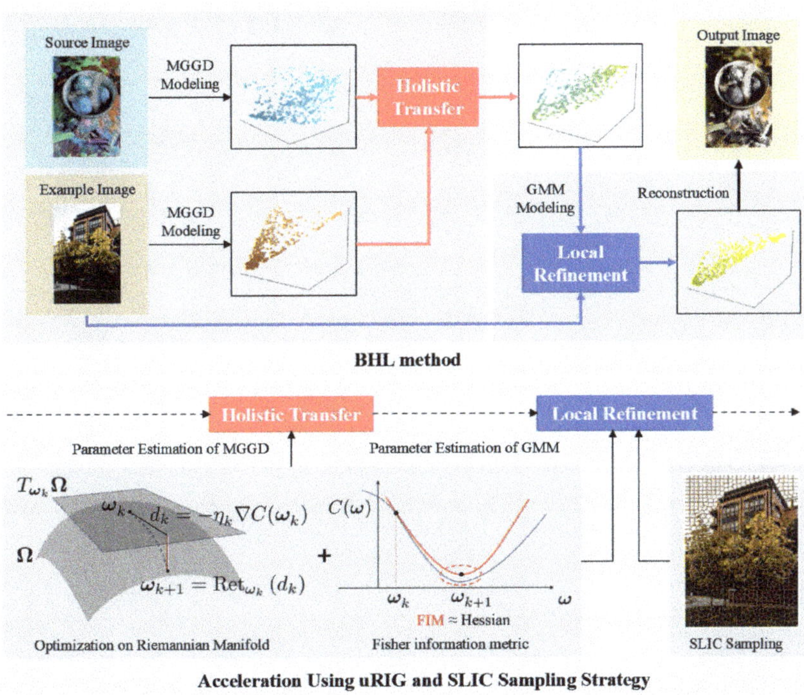

Figure 1. Overview of the BHL method.

3.2. Minimization of the Holistic Cost

While the shape parameter of an MGGD is known, such as in the Gaussian ($\beta = 1$) and Laplace ($\beta = 0.5$) distributions, its closed-form Fisher information metric exists, as detailed in [50,51]. However, when the shape parameter is unknown, its FIM requires solving a system of partial differential equations, which currently lacks a closed-form solution [52]. Inspired by [53], this paper proposes utilizing a unit-wise Riemannian information metric to address both Problem (12) and the subsequent Problem (14). In Problem (12), the MGGD parameters reside in a product space encompassing $\mathbb{R}^d$ for the location parameter $\boldsymbol{\mu}$, the set $\mathcal{P}_d$ of $d \times d$-dimensional symmetric positive definite (SPD) matrices for scatter matrix $\boldsymbol{\Sigma}$, and $\mathbb{R}_+$ for the shape parameter β. The spaces $\mathbb{R}^d$ and $\mathbb{R}_+$ are special Riemannian manifolds with zero curvature. The space $\mathcal{P}_d$ is a matrix (Riemannian) manifold with negative curvature. The product of these three spaces is then a Riemannian manifold [47]. We call a subspace in the product space $\mathbb{R}^d \times \mathcal{P}_d \times \mathbb{R}_+$ a unit since it has a closed-form FIM.

Definition 1. *For the MGGD model, the following spaces are defined: (i) The space $\mathbb{R}^d$ for the location parameter $\boldsymbol{\mu}$ is called a unit; (ii) The space $\mathcal{P}_d$ for the scatter matrix $\boldsymbol{\Sigma}$ is called a unit; (iii) The space $\mathbb{R}_+$ for the shape parameter β is called a unit.*

While the interesting manifold (parameter space) is well defined, the proposition below gives the unit-wise FIM.

Proposition 1. *Denote $\Theta = \mathbb{R}^d \times \mathcal{P}_d \times \mathbb{R}_+$ as the parameter space of an MGGD and $T_\theta\Theta = T_\mu\mathbb{R}^d \times T_\Sigma\mathcal{P}_d \times T_\beta\mathbb{R}_+$ as the tangent space of $\boldsymbol{\theta} \in \Theta$. The unit-wise FIM of this MGGD is*

$$\left\langle \boldsymbol{u}_\theta, \boldsymbol{v}_\theta \right\rangle = \left\langle \boldsymbol{u}_\mu, \boldsymbol{v}_\mu \right\rangle_\mu + \left\langle \boldsymbol{u}_\Sigma, \boldsymbol{v}_\Sigma \right\rangle_\Sigma + \left\langle u_\beta, v_\beta \right\rangle_\beta, \tag{17}$$

with

$$\left\langle \boldsymbol{u}_\mu, \boldsymbol{v}_\mu \right\rangle_\mu = I_\mu \boldsymbol{u}_\mu^\dagger \boldsymbol{\Sigma}^{-1} \boldsymbol{v}_\mu, \tag{18a}$$

$$\left\langle \boldsymbol{u}_\Sigma, \boldsymbol{v}_\Sigma \right\rangle_\Sigma = I_{\Sigma,1} \mathrm{tr}\left(\boldsymbol{\Sigma}^{-1}\boldsymbol{u}_\Sigma\boldsymbol{\Sigma}^{-1}\boldsymbol{v}_\Sigma\right) + I_{\Sigma,2} \mathrm{tr}\left(\boldsymbol{\Sigma}^{-1}\boldsymbol{u}_\Sigma\right)\mathrm{tr}\left(\boldsymbol{\Sigma}^{-1}\boldsymbol{v}_\Sigma\right), \tag{18b}$$

$$\left\langle u_\beta, v_\beta \right\rangle_\beta = I_\beta u_\beta v_\beta, \tag{18c}$$

where tr *is the matrix trace. The vectors $\boldsymbol{u}_\theta = (\boldsymbol{u}_\mu, \boldsymbol{u}_\Sigma, u_\beta)$ and $\boldsymbol{v}_\theta = (\boldsymbol{v}_\mu, \boldsymbol{v}_\Sigma, v_\beta)$ are elements in $T_\theta\Theta$.*

To simplify the notations, we use the symbols I_μ, $I_{\Sigma,1}$, $I_{\Sigma,1}$, and I_β to represent the coefficients in the three inner products above. The following remark gives the values of the three information coefficients.

Remark: The three inner products involved in Proposition 1 all have closed-form expressions for the constant coefficients, which can be directly used without any numerical approximation. The information constant with respect to $\boldsymbol{\mu}$ is

$$I_\mu = \frac{[2(\beta-1)+d]\Gamma\left(\frac{d-2}{2\beta}\right)}{2^{\frac{1}{\beta}} d(d-2)^{-1}\Gamma\left(\frac{d}{2\beta}\right)}, \tag{19a}$$

where d is the dimension of the image color vector and $\Gamma(\cdot)$ is the Gamma function. The information constants with respect to $\boldsymbol{\Sigma}$ are

$$I_{\Sigma,1} = \frac{d+2\beta}{2(d+2)} \quad \text{and} \quad I_{\Sigma,2} = \frac{\beta-1}{2(d+2)}, \tag{19b}$$

The information constant with respect to β is

$$I_\beta = \frac{1}{\beta^2}\left\{1 + \left(\frac{d}{2\beta}\right)^2 \Psi_1\left(\frac{d}{2\beta}\right) + \frac{d}{\beta}\left[\ln 2 + \Psi_0\left(\frac{d}{2\beta}\right)\right] + \frac{d}{2\beta}\left[(\ln 2)^2 + \Psi_0\left(1+\frac{d}{2\beta}\right)\left[\ln 4 + \Psi_0\left(1+\frac{d}{2\beta}\right)\right] + \Psi_1\left(1+\frac{d}{2\beta}\right)\right]\right\}, \tag{19c}$$

where Ψ_0 and Ψ_1 are the digamma and trigamma functions. The proof of Proposition 1 and its remark can be found in Appendix A. After defining the uFIM on the parameter space Θ, we are able to derive the associated Riemannian gradient based on this metric, i.e., the unit-wise Riemannian information gradient.

Proposition 2. *The uRIG of the holistic cost in Equation (12) is under the following form:*

$$\nabla C_h(\boldsymbol{\theta}) = \begin{pmatrix} \nabla_{\boldsymbol{\mu}} C_h(\boldsymbol{\theta}) \\ \nabla_{\boldsymbol{\Sigma}} C_h(\boldsymbol{\theta}) \\ \nabla_\beta C_h(\boldsymbol{\theta}) \end{pmatrix}, \tag{20}$$

where the components of the three parameters are as follows:

$$\nabla_{\boldsymbol{\mu}} C_h(\boldsymbol{\theta}) = -\frac{1}{L}\sum_{i=1}^{L} \beta I_{\boldsymbol{\mu}}^{-1} \delta_i^{\beta-1} (\boldsymbol{x}_i - \boldsymbol{\mu}), \tag{21a}$$

$$\nabla_{\boldsymbol{\Sigma}} C_h(\boldsymbol{\theta}) = -\frac{1}{L}\sum_{i=1}^{L}\left[\frac{\beta\delta_i^{\beta-1}}{2I_{\boldsymbol{\Sigma},1}}(\boldsymbol{x}_i - \boldsymbol{\mu})(\boldsymbol{x}_i - \boldsymbol{\mu})^\dagger - \frac{I_{\boldsymbol{\Sigma},1} + I_{\boldsymbol{\Sigma},2}\beta\delta_i^{\beta+1}}{2I_{\boldsymbol{\Sigma},1}(I_{\boldsymbol{\Sigma},1} + dI_{\boldsymbol{\Sigma},2})}\boldsymbol{\Sigma}\right], \tag{21b}$$

$$\nabla_\beta C_h(\boldsymbol{\theta}) = \frac{1}{L}\sum_{i=1}^{L}\frac{1}{I_\beta}\left\{\frac{1}{\beta}\left[1 + \frac{d}{2\beta}\left(\Psi_0\left(\frac{d}{2\beta}\right) + \ln 2\right)\right] - \frac{1}{2}\beta\delta_i^{\beta-1}\right\}. \tag{21c}$$

The values of the coefficients $I_{\boldsymbol{\mu}}$, $I_{\boldsymbol{\Sigma}}$, and I_β are presented in (19). We recall that the symbol δ_i denotes the Mahalanobis distance, defined as $\delta_i = (\boldsymbol{x}_i - \boldsymbol{\mu})^\dagger \boldsymbol{\Sigma}^{-1} (\boldsymbol{x}_i - \boldsymbol{\mu})$. The symbol Ψ_0 denotes the digamma function. The proof of Proposition 2 can be found in Appendix B.

Having established the relevant metric and gradient on the manifold, we now turn to the retraction map, which plays an important role in optimization algorithms. The retraction map serves as a bridge between the tangent space and the manifold itself, enabling us to efficiently perform gradient descent.

In Euclidean space, no special treatment is usually required for gradient descent. However, on a manifold, after moving in the direction of descent (i.e., typically the gradient) in the tangent space, a 'retraction' operation is needed to ensure that the parameters always remain within the constrained space. Therefore, the ideal retraction map is the geodesic map that performs the 'retraction' operation along geodesics. In particular, the geodesic map for Euclidean space is simply vector addition. Then, for the geodesic map on $\mathcal{P}_d$, we employ the form introduced in [54] in this work. Since each of the three units possesses its own intrinsic geodesic map, the most natural retraction map on Θ is the product of the three geodesic maps.

Proposition 3. *The following map is a retraction on $\Theta = \mathbb{R}^d \times \mathcal{P}_d \times \mathbb{R}_+$:*

$$\begin{array}{rccc} \mathrm{Ret}_{\boldsymbol{\theta}}: & T_{\boldsymbol{\theta}}\Theta & \to & \Theta \\ & \begin{pmatrix} \boldsymbol{u}_\mu \\ \boldsymbol{u}_\Sigma \\ u_\beta \end{pmatrix} & \mapsto & \begin{pmatrix} \boldsymbol{\mu} + \boldsymbol{u}_\mu \\ \boldsymbol{\Sigma}\mathrm{Exp}(\boldsymbol{\Sigma}^{-1}\boldsymbol{u}_\Sigma) \\ \beta\exp(u_\beta/\beta) \end{pmatrix}, \end{array} \tag{22}$$

where $T_{\boldsymbol{\theta}}\Theta = T_{\boldsymbol{\mu}}\mathbb{R}^d \times T_{\boldsymbol{\Sigma}}\mathcal{P}_d \times T_\beta\mathbb{R}_+$ is the tangent space at the point $\boldsymbol{\theta} = (\boldsymbol{\mu}, \boldsymbol{\Sigma}, \beta)$, and the vector $(\boldsymbol{u}_\mu, \boldsymbol{u}_\Sigma, u_\beta)$ is an element of $T_{\boldsymbol{\theta}}\Theta$.

In Proposition 3, exp denotes the natural exponential function on the real number field, while Exp refers to the matrix exponential map. The proof of Proposition 3 is presented in Appendix C.

With the foundation of necessary components in place, we now turn our attention to the specific iterative method employed for the estimation of the MGGD.

In the Algorithm 2, $\mathrm{Ret}_{\boldsymbol{\theta}}$ is given in (22). Indeed, in practical applications, in pursuit of time efficiency, the iteration is carried out in the form of mini-batch stochastic gradient descent, i.e., the constant L in (21) is the mini-batch size. Its convergence analysis and the selection of the coefficient a are discussed in Section 3.4, along with the optimization of C_ℓ.

Algorithm 2 MGGD estimation using the uRIG method

Require: Dataset $\mathcal{X} = \{x_1, \cdots, x_M\}$;
Ensure: estimate $\hat{\boldsymbol{\theta}}_x$;
1: **for** $k = 1, 2, 3, \cdots$ **do**
2: Compute uRIG via (20);
3: Define learning rate $\eta_k = a/k$;
4: Update $\boldsymbol{\theta}^{(k+1)} \leftarrow \mathrm{Ret}_{\boldsymbol{\theta}^{(k)}}\left(-\eta_k \nabla C_h(\boldsymbol{\theta}^{(k)})\right)$
5: **end for**

3.3. Minimization of the Local Cost

We assumed in Section 2.2 that all the component weights of the GMM are equal to 1/M, where M is the number of components. So, the EM algorithm is no longer the most suitable choice when the component weights are pre-set.

Instead, we adopt the uRIG method in the stochastic gradient descent framework. Specifically, for any component, the GMM, $p(e|\omega_m)$ is a Gaussian distribution, which is a special case of the MGGD with the shape parameter $\beta = 1$. Therefore, we can directly apply the uRIG of the MGGD to the estimation of the GMM.

Due to the complex parameters of the GMM, we declare the following symbols for the sake of convenience in expression and understanding:

- Parameter: $\omega = \prod_{m=1}^M \omega_m$, with $\omega_m = (z_m, \sigma_m)$;
- Parameter space: $\Omega = \prod_{m=1}^M \Omega_m$, with $\Omega_m = \mathbb{R}^d \times \mathbb{R}_+$;
- Tangent space at point ω: $T_\omega\Omega = \prod_{m=1}^M T_{\omega_m}\Omega_m$, with $T_{\omega_m}\Omega_m = \mathbb{R}^d \times \mathbb{R}$.

Similar to the case of the MGGD, we start with the definition of a unit.

Definition 2. *For any component $p(e|z_m, \sigma_m)$ of the GMM defined in Equation (13), we define the following spaces:*

- *The space $\mathbb{R}^d$ for the location parameter z_m is a unit;*
- *The space $\mathbb{R}_+$ for the covariance σ_m is a unit.*

In fact, each unit of the GMM parameter space is simply a Euclidean space; therefore, its uFIM is easier to derive. The uFIM is able to be obtained in the following form by taking the second differential of the log-likelihood with respect to each unit.

Proposition 4. *The unit-wise Fisher information metric of the GMM is*

$$\langle \boldsymbol{u}_\omega, \boldsymbol{v}_\omega \rangle_\omega = \sum_{m=1}^{M} \left(\frac{1}{\sigma_m} \boldsymbol{u}_{z_m}^\top \boldsymbol{v}_{z_m} + \frac{d}{2\sigma_m^2} u_{\sigma_m} v_{\sigma_m} \right). \tag{23}$$

The vectors $\boldsymbol{u}_\omega$ and $\boldsymbol{v}_\omega$ are elements in $T_\omega\Omega$, and $\boldsymbol{u}_{z_m}$ and $\boldsymbol{v}_{z_m}$ are elements in $T_{\omega_m}\Omega_m$.

The proof can be found in Appendix A. Then, the unit-wise information gradient can be easily derived based on the inner product in Equation (23).

Proposition 5. *The unit-wise information gradient of the GMM is*

$$\begin{aligned} \nabla C_\ell(\omega) = &(\nabla_{z_1} C_\ell(\omega_1), \nabla_{\sigma_1} C_\ell(\omega_1), \cdots, \\ &\nabla_{z_m} C_\ell(\omega_m), \nabla_{\sigma_m} C_\ell(\omega_m), \cdots, \\ &\nabla_{z_M} C_\ell(\omega_M), \nabla_{\sigma_M} C_\ell(\omega_M))^\dagger, \end{aligned} \tag{24}$$

where

$$\nabla_{z_m} C_\ell(\omega_m) = -\frac{1}{N} \sum_{n=1}^{N} o_{m,n} (\boldsymbol{e}_n - z_m), \tag{25a}$$

$$\nabla_{\sigma_m} C_\ell(\omega_m) = \frac{1}{N} \sum_{n=1}^{N} o_{m,n} \left(\sigma_m - \frac{\|\boldsymbol{e}_n - z_m\|^2}{d} \right), \tag{25b}$$

where $o_{m,n}$ represents the posterior probabilities

$$o_{m,n} = \frac{p(\boldsymbol{e}_n | \omega_m)}{\sum_{i=1}^{M} p(\boldsymbol{e}_i | \omega_i)}.$$

The proof of Proposition 5 is presented in Appendix B. For the means z_m, the retraction map is vector addition in the Euclidean space $\mathbb{R}^d$. For the coefficient σ_m of the covariance, we follow the same treatment as for the shape parameter β in (22). Using their product, the retraction shown below can be obtained.

Proposition 6. *The following map is a retraction on the parameter space of the GMM:*

$$\begin{array}{cccc} \mathrm{Ret}_\omega : & T_\omega\Omega & \to & \Omega \\ & \begin{pmatrix} \boldsymbol{u}_{z_1} \\ u_{\sigma_1} \\ \vdots \\ \boldsymbol{u}_{z_m} \\ u_{\sigma_m} \\ \vdots \\ \boldsymbol{u}_{z_M} \\ u_{\sigma_M} \end{pmatrix} & \mapsto & \begin{pmatrix} z_1 + \boldsymbol{u}_{z_1} \\ \sigma_1 \exp(\sigma_1^{-1} u_{\sigma_1}) \\ \vdots \\ z_m + \boldsymbol{u}_{z_m} \\ \sigma_m \exp(\sigma_m^{-1} u_{\sigma_m}) \\ \vdots \\ z_M + \boldsymbol{u}_{z_M} \\ \sigma_M \exp(\sigma_M^{-1} u_{\sigma_M}) \end{pmatrix}. \end{array} \tag{26}$$

The Algorithm 3 below gives the update rule for parameter estimation of the GMM.

Algorithm 3 GMM estimation using the uRIG method

Require: Dataset $\mathcal{E} = \{e_1, \cdots, e_N\}$;
Ensure: estimate $\hat{\omega}$;
1: **for** $k = 1, 2, 3, \cdots$ **do**
2: Compute uRIG via (24);
3: Define learning rate $\eta_k = a/k$;
4: Update $\omega^{(k+1)} \leftarrow \mathrm{Ret}_{\omega^{(k)}}\left(-\eta_k \nabla C_\ell(\omega^{(k)})\right)$
5: **end for**

In the above algorithm, $\nabla C_\ell(\omega^{(k)})$ and Ret_ω are given in (24) and (26), respectively. For the GMM, the uRIG method also performs under the form of mini-batch stochastic gradient descent. The convergence analysis and selection of the coefficient a of Algorithms 2 and 3 are discussed in the following subsection.

3.4. Convergence Analysis

To simplify the presentation and enhance the clarity of the convergence analysis of Algorithms 2 and 3, we unify the notations in this subsection. In the following part of this subsection, we use ω to represent the parameters and Ω to denote the parameter space (regardless of whether it is MGGD or GMM). Consider a statistical model with M units, and let N be the number of observed samples.

Since the conditions (1–3) shown below hold, the high time efficiency and robustness of Algorithm 1 can be established, as shown in Proposition 7.

The conditions are as follows:

1. The cost $C(\omega)$ has an isolated stationary point at $\omega = \omega^*$, where ω^* is the true parameter;
2. There exists a compact and convex neighborhood $\mathcal{U} \subset \Omega$ of ω^* such that the sequence generated by Algorithm 1 remains within $\mathcal{U}$.
3. The learning rate $\eta_k = a/k$, $a > 0$, verifies the usual condition for stochastic approximation:
$$\sum_{k=1}^{+\infty} \eta_k = +\infty, \qquad \sum_{k=1}^{\infty} \eta_k^2 < +\infty.$$

Proposition 7. *With these three conditions, we have*

$$\lim_{k \to \infty} \omega^{(k)} = \omega^*. \tag{27}$$

The proof of Proposition 7 is shown in Appendix D.

4. Experiment

In this section, the BHL method is evaluated from two perspectives: visual assessment and objective quantitative analysis. The BHL method is benchmarked against five state-of-the-art methods known for their high performance. In terms of holistic transformation methods, we chose the representative MGGD transformation method in [14]. In the domain of local transformation methods, we chose two top-performing methods: the GMM-based transformation technique [46] and the method derived from L2 divergence [22]. Two state-of-the-art deep neural network-based methods, specifically the CAST method [41] and MCCNet [42], were also included in the comparative experiments for evaluation.

We randomly selected five groups of images for experimental comparison, i.e., 10 different images, with 5 as the source images and 5 as the example images. All experiments were conducted on a regular laptop with an AMD Ryzen 7 6800H processor and a main frequency of 3.2 GHz.

4.1. Parameter Setting

For the uRIG algorithm, the initialization $\boldsymbol{\theta}^{(0)}$ of Algorithm 2 was determined using the method of moments [55], while the initialization of Algorithm 3 was obtained from the output of holistic transformation $\mathcal{V}$, i.e., $\mathcal{Z}^{(0)} = \mathcal{V}$. The coefficient a of the learning rate was estimated according to Proposition 2 in [56].

To facilitate gradient descent, a preprocessing step was introduced in [46] to select the mini-batch. Prior to commencing the iterations, for each pixel in $\mathcal{Z}^{(0)}$, b nearest neighbors are chosen from $\mathcal{E}$. Notably, b corresponds to the size of the mini-batch, and these selected b pixels from $\mathcal{E}$ then comprise the mini-batch employed for gradient descent. While this method effectively captures color information, it results in a significant computational burden in the preprocessing stage due to the need to sort $M \times N$ pixels.

To address this limitation, we proposed a distinct mini-batch sampling strategy that leverages the Simple Linear Iterative Clustering (SLIC) algorithm. Initially, we applied the SLIC algorithm for superpixel segmentation on the example image $\mathcal{E}$, partitioning it into 1000 superpixels. For each pixel in $\mathcal{Z}^{(0)}$, we computed the distance to the mean of each superpixel in $\mathcal{E}$. Based on these distances, the b' nearest superpixels were selected to replace the first b pixels during the iteration (typically, $b' \leqslant b$). This method offers two main advantages. First, it significantly reduces the sorting time, particularly for high-resolution images. Second, by utilizing all pixels within the superpixels, the hyperparameter b' becomes less sensitive to the final output. Specifically, extreme values of b' mainly affect the algorithm's runtime rather than the color richness of the output. Therefore, it is possible to choose a relatively smaller b' to reduce time costs. In the experiments, we set $b = 100$ and $b' = 50$.

This method substantially reduced the preprocessing time complexity, as detailed in Section 4.4. In addition, to incorporate spatial information, the Laplacian regularization term introduced in [46,57] was also applied to Equation (14).

4.2. Quantitative Comparison

In existing research [12,18,25,46,58], the Structural Similarity Index Measure (SSIM) and Peak Signal-to-Noise Ratio (PSNR) are commonly employed to assess the textural similarity between the output image $\mathcal{V}$ and the source image $\mathcal{X}$. Specifically, the SSIM quantifies the level of artifacts introduced by the color transfer method, while the PSNR measures the mean squared error between the two images. The color style similarity between the output image and the example image is typically evaluated using the Frechet Inception Distance (FID) and Perceptual Hash Value (PHV) [59,60].

The five methods involved in the comparative experiment have their own advantages due to their different processing techniques and optimization goals. However, no method performed well across all four quantitative evaluation criteria at the same time. For example, MCCNet achieved superior structural fidelity visually because it enhanced the edges of objects in the image (such as the edges of petals). However, excessive enhancement led to large artifacts. The L2 method provided bright-colored visual results, but because it requires local matching of the color palette, its output sometimes contained local color deviations. The results of the MGGD method and the BHL method show that their PSNR values were not relatively high. This is because the processing of these two methods requires a resampling operation combined with the parameters of the example image. Noise that differs from the source image will result in a low PSNR value [58].

To evaluate the performance of these methods, we introduced a comprehensive evaluation technique: the Technique for Order Preference by Similarity to Ideal Solution (TOPSIS) [61]. TOPSIS is a multi-criteria decision analysis technique that assesses the performance of candidate methods by calculating their distances to the ideal and negative-ideal solutions, thereby providing a comprehensive assessment.

Quantitative comparisons between the BHL method and five other methods are presented in Tables 1–5. When calculating the TOPSIS score, we performed the necessary order adjustments and normalization steps. The final TOPSIS scores range from 0 to 1, with higher values indicating better overall performance. As shown in Tables 1–5, the BHL method, which balances holistic and local information, achieved the highest TOPSIS scores. Due to its modeling and optimization techniques, the GMM algorithm achieved the best results in terms of the SSIM and PSNR. However, the performance of this algorithm varied with different hyperparameter settings, resulting in differing color effects. Consequently, the GMM method did not perform very well in the FID and PHV criteria. In contrast, the two deep learning methods, CAST and MCCNet, benefited from the robust color feature-capture capabilities of deep neural networks, achieving higher FID and PHV scores. However, these methods fell short in obtaining high textural similarity scores. The L2 divergence-based method showed severe distortions and artifacts in some images, leading to a low PHV score and, consequently, a lower comprehensive evaluation score. The MGGD method, which is based on optimal transport, performed well across all criteria. However, its lack of attention to detail resulted in numerous local artifacts, adversely affecting its evaluation score. Detailed visual comparisons are provided in the next subsection.

Table 1. $\mathcal{X} \rightarrow \mathcal{E} : purpleflower \rightarrow tomato.$

Method	GMM [46]	L2 [22]	MGGD [14]	CAST [41]	MCCNet [42]	BHL
SSIM↑	0.972	0.918	0.904	0.610	0.808	0.881
PSNR↑	29.4	22.9	22.1	19.0	22.9	20.3
FID↓	0.037	0.018	0.006	0.014	0.027	0.004
PHV↓	0.730	0.756	0.717	0.691	0.746	0.732
TOPSIS↑	0.260	0.231	0.596	0.211	0.149	**0.809**

The method with the highest TOPSIS score is highlighted in bold. An upward arrow following a criterion indicates that a higher score on this criterion represents better performance. Conversely, a downward arrow indicates that a lower score on this criterion represents better performance.

Table 2. $\mathcal{X} \rightarrow \mathcal{E} : blueflower \rightarrow mountain.$

Method	GMM [46]	L2 [22]	MGGD [14]	CAST [41]	MCCNet [42]	BHL
SSIM↑	0.902	0.782	0.809	0.488	0.574	0.706
PSNR↑	27.6	15.7	24.6	19.5	18.7	22.5
FID↓	0.066	0.119	0.012	0.020	0.020	0.007
PHV↓	0.715	0.758	0.736	0.701	0.682	0.720
TOPSIS↑	0.337	0.187	0.608	0.304	0.308	**0.816**

The bold and arrows are the same as Table 1.

Table 3. $\mathcal{X} \rightarrow \mathcal{E} : clusters \rightarrow parrot.$

Method	GMM [46]	L2 [22]	MGGD [14]	CAST [41]	MCCNet [42]	BHL
SSIM↑	0.957	0.688	0.832	0.477	0.566	0.844
PSNR↑	30.9	16.3	19.5	17.5	16.9	19.9
FID↓	0.056	0.045	0.015	0.016	0.135	0.013
PHV↓	0.792	0.769	0.807	0.733	0.723	0.803
TOPSIS↑	0.475	0.240	0.673	0.525	0.097	**0.707**

The bold and arrows are the same as Table 1.

Table 4. $\mathcal{X} \rightarrow \mathcal{E} : pinkflower \rightarrow sunflower.$

Method	GMM [46]	L2 [22]	MGGD [14]	CAST [41]	MCCNet [42]	BHL
SSIM↑	0.616	0.542	0.404	0.292	0.277	0.434
PSNR↑	22.6	16.3	10.4	11.4	12.6	11.2
FID↓	0.175	0.053	0.007	0.007	0.032	0.003
PHV↓	0.735	0.743	0.684	0.669	0.635	0.662
TOPSIS↑	0.350	0.257	0.317	0.305	0.103	**0.706**

The bold and arrows are the same as Table 1.

Table 5. $\mathcal{X} \to \mathcal{E}$: *bouquet* $\to$ *seaside.*

Method	GMM [46]	L2 [22]	MGGD [14]	CAST [41]	MCCNet [42]	BHL
SSIM↑	0.775	0.600	0.524	0.318	0.298	0.532
PSNR↑	32.1	17.6	12.9	13.6	14.1	12.5
FID↓	0.186	0.046	0.003	0.012	0.029	0.003
PHV↓	0.712	0.699	0.715	0.675	0.612	0.709
TOPSIS↑	0.457	0.256	0.499	0.156	0.098	**0.589**

The bold and arrows are the same as Table 1.

4.3. Visual Comparison

Figures 2–6 present the visual results of the five experiments. Due to its modeling approach, the GMM method excelled at preserving the texture of the source images. This advantage was also reflected in the quantitative evaluation. However, its output was highly sensitive to hyperparameter selection, such as the number of iterations (set to 50 for all five experiments, consistent with [46]). As shown in Figures 4(3) and 6(3), the colors of the example images were not accurately transferred, and the results retained the color style of the source images. Furthermore, in Figures 5(3) and 7(2), significant white artifacts can be observed in the GMM results.

Compared to other methods, the L2 method produced a brighter color style in its results. For example, in Figure 3(4), the L2 result has a significantly brighter color style, but it also deviates from the color style of the example image. This is because the L2 method relies on local matching of the color palettes, and the accuracy of color transfer depends on the precision of this local matching. In Figure 7(3), green shadows are visible on the yellow petals in the L2 result. A similar issue occurs in Figure 7(10), where the petals exhibit a cyan tint.

The MGGD method shares some visual similarities with the BHL method, which also employs a similar modeling technique in its first stage. The key distinction between the MGGD and BHL methods lies in the local refinement in the subsequent steps of the BHL method. Specifically, as shown in Figure 7(4), the MGGD method produces unnatural purple hues on the water droplets, and the black area to the right of the droplets appears opaque and blurry due to the lack of local color adjustments.

(1) Source image (2) Example image (3) GMM (4) L2

(5) MGGD (6) CAST (7) MCCNet (8) BHL

Figure 2. Source image: purple flower; Example image: tomato.

Leveraging the powerful ability of convolutional neural networks to extract structural features from images, CAST and MCCNet demonstrated excellent structural fidelity. However, due to the inherent limitations of deep neural networks, such as rigidity in input and output sizes and challenges with generalization, some flaws were present in their results. For instance, in Figure 3(6,7), sharp black blocks appear in the background, which should have been blurred. Similarly, in Figure 7(5,6), the edges of the water droplets in the results of both methods appear as rigid straight lines rather than as curves.

The BHL method achieves a good balance between holistic color style and local structural details. By utilizing a more efficient training method (uRIG) and an innovative sampling strategy, it delivers a more robust color transfer effect. The advantages in terms of time efficiency are demonstrated in the subsequent section.

(1) Source image (2) Example image (3) GMM (4) L2

(5) MGGD (6) CAST (7) MCCNet (8) BHL

Figure 3. Source image: blue flower; Example image: mountain.

(1) Source image (2) Example image (3) GMM (4) L2

(5) MGGD (6) CAST (7) MCCNet (8) BHL

Figure 4. Source image: clusters; Example image: parrot.

(1) Source image (2) Example image (3) GMM (4) L2

(5) MGGD (6) CAST (7) MCCNet (8) BHL

Figure 5. Source image: pink flower; Example image: sunflower.

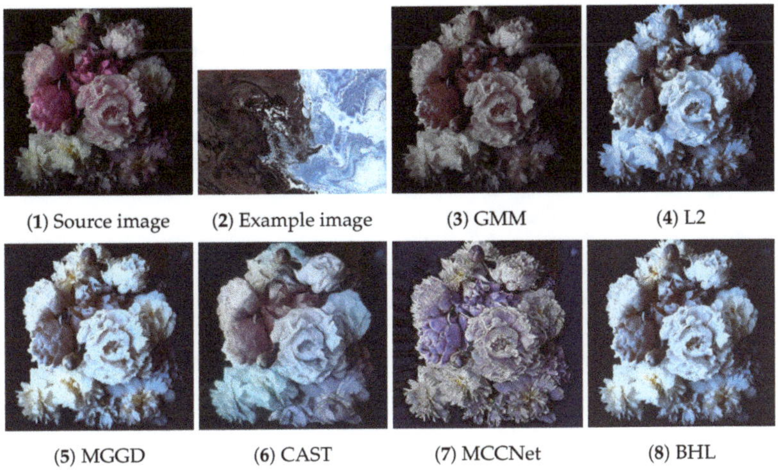

Figure 6. Source image: bouquet; Example image: seaside.

Figure 7. Comparison of details with zoomed-in images.

4.4. Time Efficiency

We also assessed the runtime efficiency of the six methods, with the results presented in Table 6. For deep learning methods, the runtime is generally divided into two phases: training and inference. In contrast, probabilistic methods estimate parameters dynamically for each individual dataset or image rather than relying on a pre-trained model. Consequently, their runtime cannot be compared to that of deep learning methods in the same manner, and the results are, therefore, presented differently.

For the four probabilistic methods, the first two rows of Table 6 display the average runtimes across five experiments. This analysis accounts for all processing steps involved in the four comparative methods, including data preprocessing, parameter estimation, and color transformation. The total number of pixels across the five image sets (i.e., the sample size for a single experiment) ranged from 5×10^5 to 1.6×10^6. The results indicate that due to the BHL method's use of the uRIG method and a novel sampling strategy based on SLIC, its average runtime across the five experiments was only 4.874 s, demonstrating a significant advantage over the other three probabilistic methods.

Table 6. Running times of different methods. For the MGGD method, parameter estimation is performed using a fixed-point iteration method.

Probabilistic methods	BHL	L2	GMM	MGGD
Running time	4.874 s	7.523 s	348.754 s	54.897 s
Deep learning methods	CAST		MCCNet	
Training time	18 h		59 h	
Inference time	0.011 s		0.013 s	

In contrast, for the two deep learning methods, CAST and MCCNet, the training times were 18 h and 59 h, respectively, with inference times of 0.011 s and 0.013 s. Compared to the probabilistic methods, CAST and MCCNet exhibited a substantial advantage in inference speed. However, the extended training times and the limited scope of the training datasets clearly constrained their ability to address all scenarios. For instance, in Figure 3(6), large black smudges obscure the petal contours, and in Figure 7(5,6), the water droplet contours are transformed into rigid lines. These issues did not arise with any of the four probabilistic methods.

To further validate the time efficiency benefits of the uRIG method, we conducted a simulation comparison experiment with other commonly used stochastic gradient-based optimization methods. The comparison included classic Stochastic Gradient Descent (SGD), Adam [62], and Affine-Invariant Gradient Descent (AIG) [63], which is equivalent to the classic Riemannian gradient descent method. The simulation involved 150 Monte Carlo simulations. Each experiment's data followed a randomly generated MGGD, with the initial values provided by the method of moments. The averaged results are presented in Figure 8. The horizontal axis represents the number of iterations, while the vertical axis depicts the error calculated using the empirical Kullback–Leibler divergence.

As evident from Figure 8, the uRIG method demonstrates a clear advantage for the parameter estimation task in statistical models. This advantage becomes increasingly pronounced as the number of iterations grows, highlighting the accelerating effect of the Fisher information metric.

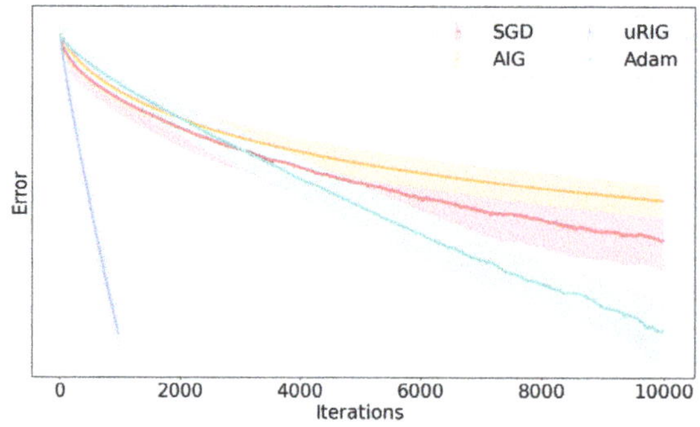

Figure 8. Comparison of uRIG with SGD, AIG, and Adam.

5. Conclusions

In conclusion, this paper presents a novel color transfer method that effectively balances holistic color style and local detail preservation within a statistical framework. By integrating optimal transport theory in the first stage for holistic color style transfer and utilizing a GMM in the second stage for local detail refinement, the BHL method addresses the inherent challenges of color transfer. The implementation of the unit-wise Riemannian information gradient (uRIG) method successfully tackles the complex optimization problems associated with these stages.

Extensive experimental results demonstrate that the BHL method significantly outperforms existing state-of-the-art techniques in both visual quality and objective evaluation criteria. The proposed method is not only effective but also efficient, with the capability to process high-resolution images in an average time of 4.874 s, making it suitable for practical applications where time constraints are critical.

Overall, the BHL method provides a robust and efficient solution for color transfer in image editing, paving the way for future advancements in the field. Future work may explore further optimization techniques and extend the method to other related image processing tasks.

Author Contributions: Conceptualization, J.Z. and N.W.; methodology, J.Z., Z.W. and S.W.; software, Z.W.; data curation, Z.W.; writing—original draft preparation, J.Z.; writing—review and editing, Z.W. and S.W.; supervision, N.W. All authors have read and agreed to the published version of the manuscript.

Funding: This work is supported by the National Natural Science Foundation of China (grant no. 42301401, 62301497), and the China Postdoctoral Science Foundation (grant no. GZC20232385, 2024T170823).

Institutional Review Board Statement: Not applicable.

Data Availability Statement: The original contributions presented in the study are included in the article, further inquiries can be directed to the corresponding author.

Conflicts of Interest: The authors declare no conflicts of interest.

Appendix A. Proof of Proposition 1 and Proposition 4

For the Multivariate Generalized Gaussian Distribution (MGGD), the Fisher information metric (FIM) of the scatter matrix $\mathbf{\Sigma}$ for elliptical distributions was first introduced in its general form in [50]. By substituting the parameters specific to the MGGD, the expression in Equation (18b) can be directly obtained. The FIM for the location parameter μ was previously introduced in [51] for the Gaussian distribution. Here, we derive the FIM of μ using the first two derivatives of the log-likelihood function of the MGGD. Recall the log-likelihood function of the MGGD:

$$\ell(x|\boldsymbol{\theta}) = \ln c - \frac{1}{2}\ln|\mathbf{\Sigma}| + \ln g_\beta(\delta) \tag{A1}$$

where the symbol δ and function g_β are defined in Equations (5) and (6), respectively. The first and second derivatives of Equation (A1) with respect to μ are

$$\mathrm{d}\ell = -2\frac{\partial \ln g_\beta}{\partial \delta}\mathrm{d}\mu^\dagger\Sigma^{-1}(x-\mu) \tag{A2a}$$

$$\begin{aligned}\mathrm{d}^2\ell =& 4\frac{\partial^2 \ln g_\beta}{\partial \delta^2}\mathrm{d}\mu^\dagger\Sigma^{-1}(x-\mu)(x-\mu)^\dagger\Sigma^{-1}\mathrm{d}\mu \\ &+ \frac{\partial \ln g_\beta}{\partial \delta}\mathrm{d}\mu^\dagger\Sigma^{-1}\mathrm{d}\mu\end{aligned} \tag{A2b}$$

Then, the negative expectation of the second derivative, $-\mathbb{E}_{\theta}[\mathrm{d}^2\ell]$, provides the FIM with respect to μ. By employing the stochastic expression in Equation (8), a closed-form solution for this integral (expectation) can be obtained:

$$\begin{aligned} -\mathbb{E}_{\theta}[\mathrm{d}^2\ell] &= -\mathbb{E}_{\theta}\left[\frac{4\delta}{d}\frac{\partial^2 \ln g_{\beta}}{\partial \delta^2} + 2\frac{\partial \ln g_{\beta}}{\partial \delta}\right]\mathrm{d}\mu^{\dagger}\Sigma^{-1}\mathrm{d}\mu \\ &= \frac{[2(\beta-1)+d]\Gamma\left(\frac{d-2}{2\beta}\right)}{2^{\frac{1}{\beta}}d(d-2)^{-1}\Gamma\left(\frac{d}{2\beta}\right)}\mathrm{d}\mu^{\dagger}\Sigma^{-1}\mathrm{d}\mu \end{aligned} \tag{A3}$$

Finally, for the shape parameter β, which is a positive real number, its Fisher information is also a real-valued scalar. The value of the Fisher information for β is provided in [55] and can be directly used in Equation (18c).

Moving on to Gaussian Mixture Models (GMMs), the FIM for any m-th component ($m \in \{1, \cdots, M\}$) is a special case of Equation (17). By setting $\mu = z_m$, $\Sigma = \sigma_m^2 I$, and $\beta = 1$, the information coefficient and the FIM with respect to z_m is

$$I_{z_m} u_{z_m}^{\top} (\sigma_m I)^{-1} v_{z_m} = \frac{u_{z_m}^{\top} v_{z_m}}{\sigma_m^2}, \quad I_{z_m} = 1 \tag{A4}$$

For the variance σ_m^2, its information coefficients are

$$I_{\sigma_m,1} = \frac{1}{2}, \quad I_{\sigma_m,2} = 0 \tag{A5}$$

Then, its FIM is

$$I_{\sigma_m,1}\mathrm{tr}\left(\frac{u_{\sigma_m} v_{\sigma_m}}{\sigma_m^4} I\right) = \frac{d\, u_{\sigma_m} v_{\sigma_m}}{2\sigma_m^4} \tag{A6}$$

Since the parameter space is a product of these individual units, the uFIM is simply the sum of the FIMs for each unit.

Appendix B. Proof of Proposition 2 and Proposition 5

The Riemannian information gradient (RIG) of C_g with respect to the scatter matrix Σ was established in [56]. The RIG with respect to the location parameter μ associated with uFIM is given by the derivative

$$\begin{aligned} \langle \nabla_{\mu} C_h, u_{\mu} \rangle_{\mu} &= \left.\frac{\mathrm{d}}{\mathrm{d}\varepsilon}\right|_{\varepsilon=0} C_h(\mu + \varepsilon u_{\mu}) \\ &= -u_{\mu}^{\dagger}\frac{1}{L}\sum_{i=1}^{L}\beta\delta_i^{\beta-1}\Sigma^{-1}(x_i - \mu) \\ &= \left\langle -\frac{1}{L}\sum_{i=1}^{L}\beta I_{\mu}^{-1}\delta_i^{\beta-1}(x_i - \mu), u_{\mu} \right\rangle_{\mu} \end{aligned} \tag{A7}$$

Solving this equation yields the RIG in Equation (21a). An analogous computation can be applied in the univariate case to obtain the RIG for parameter β.

Each individual component of a GMM is, in fact, a special case of the MGGD, i.e., a Gaussian distribution. Given that $I_{z_m} = 1$, the RIG with respect to z_m is

$$\begin{aligned} \nabla_{z_m} C_{\ell} &= -\frac{1}{N}\sum_{n=1}^{N} o_{m,n} I_{z_m}^{-1}\delta_{m,n}^{0}(e_n - z_m) \\ &= -\frac{1}{N}\sum_{n=1}^{N} o_{m,n}(e_n - z_m) \end{aligned} \tag{A8}$$

Then, for σ_m, by solving the following equation:

$$\frac{d\,\nabla_{\sigma_m} C_\ell\, v_{\sigma_m}}{2\sigma_m^2} = -\frac{1}{N}\sum_{n=1}^{N}\frac{o_{m,n}}{2\sigma_m}\left(d - \frac{\|e_n - z_m\|^2}{\sigma_m}\right) \tag{A9}$$

the expression in Equation (25b) can be obtained.

Appendix C. Proof of Proposition 3 and Proposition 6

In the context of the MGGD, a retraction on the manifold Θ is defined as a smooth mapping Ret_{θ} from the tangent space $T_{\theta}\Theta$ onto Θ, satisfying the following two specific properties (Definition 4.1.1 of [47]):

1. Ret_{θ} maps the zero element $\mathbf{0}_{\theta}$ of $T_{\theta}\Theta$ back to $\boldsymbol{\theta}$:

$$\forall \boldsymbol{\theta} \in \Theta, \quad \mathrm{Ret}_{\theta}(\mathbf{0}) = \boldsymbol{\theta}. \tag{A10}$$

2. For any element $\boldsymbol{u}_{\theta}$ in $T_{\theta}\Theta$, the curve $\gamma(t) : t \mapsto \mathrm{Ret}_{\theta}(t\boldsymbol{u})$ satisfies $\dot{\gamma}(0) = \boldsymbol{u}_{\theta}$, where

$$\dot{\gamma}(0) = \left.\frac{\mathrm{d}}{\mathrm{d}t}\right|_{t=0} \gamma(t).$$

Setting $\boldsymbol{u}_{\theta} = (u_{\mu}, u_{\Sigma}, u_{\beta})^{\top} = \mathbf{0}_{\theta}$, for any point $\boldsymbol{\theta}$, we have

$$\mathrm{Ret}_{\theta}(\mathbf{0}_{\theta}) = \begin{pmatrix} \boldsymbol{\mu} + \mathbf{0} \\ \boldsymbol{\Sigma}\,\mathrm{Exp}\left(\boldsymbol{\Sigma}^{-1}\mathbf{0}\right) \\ \beta \exp(0/\beta) \end{pmatrix} = \begin{pmatrix} \boldsymbol{\mu} \\ \boldsymbol{\Sigma} \\ \beta \end{pmatrix} = \boldsymbol{\theta}$$

which verifies property 1. Additionally, for the curve $\gamma(t) = \mathrm{Ret}_{\theta}(t\boldsymbol{u}_{\theta})$,

$$\begin{aligned} \dot{\gamma}(\mathbf{0}_{\theta}) &= \begin{pmatrix} u_{\mu} \\ \boldsymbol{\Sigma}\mathrm{Exp}(\boldsymbol{\Sigma}^{-1}\mathbf{0}_{\Sigma})\boldsymbol{\Sigma}^{-1}\boldsymbol{u}_{\Sigma} \\ \beta \exp(0/\beta)\beta^{-1}u_{\beta} \end{pmatrix} \\ &= (\boldsymbol{u}_{\mu}, \boldsymbol{u}_{\Sigma}, u_{\beta})^{\top} \\ &= \boldsymbol{u}_{\theta} \end{aligned}$$

which aligns with our choice of $t = 0$. This confirms property 2 for the retraction in Equation (22) of the MGGD.

Similar arguments can be extended to the case of a GMM with multiple components ($m = 1, \ldots, M$). Both properties 1 and 2 can be verified:

$$\mathrm{Ret}_{\omega}(\mathbf{0}_{\omega}) = \begin{pmatrix} \vdots \\ z_m + \mathbf{0}_{z_m} \\ \sigma_m \exp(0/\sigma_m) \\ \vdots \end{pmatrix} = \begin{pmatrix} \vdots \\ z_m \\ \sigma_m \\ \vdots \end{pmatrix} = \omega \tag{A11a}$$

$$\begin{aligned} \dot{\gamma}(\mathbf{0}_{\omega}) &= \begin{pmatrix} \vdots \\ \boldsymbol{u}_{z_m} \\ \sigma_m \exp(0/\sigma_m)\sigma_m^{-1}u_{\sigma_m} \\ \vdots \end{pmatrix} \\ &= \left(\cdots, \boldsymbol{u}_{z_m}, u_{\sigma_m}, \cdots\right)^{\top} = \boldsymbol{u}_{\omega} \end{aligned} \tag{A11b}$$

Since properties 1 and 2 are verified, Equation (26) is a retraction on Ω. Equation (26) is established as a valid retraction in the context of a GMM as well.

Appendix D. Proof of Proposition 7

In this proof, we utilize the notations introduced in Section 3.4: ω denotes the parameter, and Ω denotes the parameter space. The proof is based on Remark 2 in [56]. Let $u(w^{(k)})$ be the current descent direction. According to Remark 2 in [56], if the following condition holds:

$$\mathbb{E}\left[\left\langle u(w^{(k)}), \nabla C(\omega^{(k)})\right\rangle\right] < 0, \quad \forall k > 0 \tag{A12}$$

then, almost surely, we have

$$\lim_{k\to\infty} \omega^{(k)} = \omega^* \tag{A13}$$

As we declared in Section 3.4, the cost $C(\omega)$ has an isolated stationary point at $\omega = \omega^*$, and there exists a compact and convex neighborhood $\mathcal{U} \subset \Omega$ of ω^* such that the sequence generated by Algorithm 2 (or Algorithm 3) remains within $\mathcal{U}$. For any k, we have $u(\omega^{(k)}) = -\nabla C(\omega^{(k)})$:

$$\mathbb{E}\left[\left\langle u(w^{(k)}), \nabla C(\omega^{(k)})\right\rangle\right] = -\mathbb{E}\left[\|\nabla C(\omega^{(k)})\|^2\right] < 0 \tag{A14}$$

This verifies the condition of Remark 2 in [56], and therefore,

$$\mathbb{P}\left(\lim_{k\to\infty} \omega^{(k)} = \omega^*\right) \tag{A15}$$

References

1. Kotovenko, D.; Sanakoyeu, A.; Lang, S.; Ommer, B. Content and style disentanglement for artistic style transfer. In Proceedings of the IEEE/CVF International Conference on Computer Vision, Seoul, Republic of Korea, 27 October–2 November 2019; pp. 4422–4431.
2. Li, Y.; Liu, M.Y.; Li, X.; Yang, M.H.; Kautz, J. A closed-form solution to photorealistic image stylization. In Proceedings of the European Conference on Computer Vision (ECCV), Munich, Germany, 8–14 September 2018; pp. 453–468.
3. Nam, S.; Ma, C.; Chai, M.; Brendel, W.; Xu, N.; Kim, S.J. End-to-end time-lapse video synthesis from a single outdoor image. In Proceedings of the IEEE/CVF Conference on Computer Vision and Pattern Recognition, Long Beach, CA, USA, 15–20 June 2019; pp. 1409–1418.
4. Shih, Y.; Paris, S.; Durand, F.; Freeman, W.T. Data-driven hallucination of different times of day from a single outdoor photo. *ACM Trans. Graph. (TOG)* **2013**, *32*, 1–11. [CrossRef]
5. Li, C.; Guo, C.; Ren, W.; Cong, R.; Hou, J.; Kwong, S.; Tao, D. An underwater image enhancement benchmark dataset and beyond. *IEEE Trans. Image Process.* **2019**, *29*, 4376–4389. [CrossRef] [PubMed]
6. Li, K.; Wu, L.; Qi, Q.; Liu, W.; Gao, X.; Zhou, L.; Song, D. Beyond single reference for training: Underwater image enhancement via comparative learning. *IEEE Trans. Circuits Syst. Video Technol.* **2022**, *33*, 2561–2576. [CrossRef]
7. Reinhard, E.; Adhikhmin, M.; Gooch, B.; Shirley, P. Color transfer between images. *IEEE Comput. Graph. Appl.* **2001**, *21*, 34–41. [CrossRef]
8. Xiao, X.; Ma, L. Color transfer in correlated color space. In Proceedings of the 2006 ACM International Conference on Virtual Reality Continuum and Its Applications, Hong Kong, China, 14–17 June 2006; pp. 305–309.
9. Pitié, F.; Kokaram, A.C.; Dahyot, R. Automated colour grading using colour distribution transfer. *Comput. Vis. Image Underst.* **2007**, *107*, 123–137. [CrossRef]
10. Pitie, F.; Kokaram, A. The linear Monge-Kantorovitch linear colour mapping for example-based colour transfer. In Proceedings of the 4th European Conference on Visual Media Production, London, UK, 27–28 November 2007; pp. 1–9.
11. Ferradans, S.; Papadakis, N.; Peyré, G.; Aujol, J.F. Regularized discrete optimal transport. *SIAM J. Imaging Sci.* **2014**, *7*, 1853–1882. [CrossRef]
12. Frigo, O.; Sabater, N.; Demoulin, V.; Hellier, P. Optimal transportation for example-guided color transfer. In Proceedings of the Asian Conference on Computer Vision, Singapore, 1–5 November 2014; Springer: Berlin/Heidelberg, Germany, 2014; pp. 655–670.
13. Rabin, J.; Papadakis, N. Non-convex relaxation of optimal transport for color transfer between images. In *Proceedings of the Geometric Science of Information: Second International Conference (GSI 2015), Palaiseau, France, 28–30 October 2015*; Proceedings 2; Springer: Berlin/Heidelberg, Germany, 2015; pp. 87–95.

14. Hristova, H.; Le Meur, O.; Cozot, R.; Bouatouch, K. Transformation of the multivariate generalized Gaussian distribution for image editing. *IEEE Trans. Vis. Comput. Graph.* **2017**, *24*, 2813–2826. [CrossRef]
15. Tai, Y.W.; Jia, J.; Tang, C.K. Local color transfer via probabilistic segmentation by expectation-maximization. In Proceedings of the 2005 IEEE Computer Society Conference on Computer Vision and Pattern Recognition (CVPR'05), San Diego, CA, USA, 20–25 June 2005; Volume 1, pp. 747–754.
16. Tai, Y.W.; Jia, J.; Tang, C.K. Soft color segmentation and its applications. *IEEE Trans. Pattern Anal. Mach. Intell.* **2007**, *29*, 1520–1537. [CrossRef]
17. Xiang, Y.; Zou, B.; Li, H. Selective color transfer with multi-source images. *Pattern Recognit. Lett.* **2009**, *30*, 682–689. [CrossRef]
18. Hristova, H.; Le Meur, O.; Cozot, R.; Bouatouch, K. Style-aware robust color transfer. In Proceedings of the CAe@ Expressive, Istanbul, Turkey, 20–22 June 2015; pp. 67–77.
19. Wu, F.; Dong, W.; Kong, Y.; Mei, X.; Paul, J.C.; Zhang, X. Content-based colour transfer. In *Proceedings of the Computer Graphics Forum*; Wiley Online Library: New York, NY, USA, 2013; Volume 32, pp. 190–203.
20. Han, Y.; Xu, C.; Baciu, G.; Li, M.; Islam, M.R. Cartoon and texture decomposition-based color transfer for fabric images. *IEEE Trans. Multimed.* **2016**, *19*, 80–92. [CrossRef]
21. Giraud, R.; Ta, V.T.; Papadakis, N. Superpixel-based color transfer. In Proceedings of the 2017 IEEE International Conference on Image Processing (ICIP), Beijing, China, 17–20 September 2017; pp. 700–704.
22. Grogan, M.; Dahyot, R. L2 divergence for robust colour transfer. *Comput. Vis. Image Underst.* **2019**, *181*, 39–49. [CrossRef]
23. Bonneel, N.; Sunkavalli, K.; Paris, S.; Pfister, H. Example-based video color grading. *ACM Trans. Graph.* **2013**, *32*, 1–12. [CrossRef]
24. Su, Z.; Zeng, K.; Liu, L.; Li, B.; Luo, X. Corruptive artifacts suppression for example-based color transfer. *IEEE Trans. Multimed.* **2014**, *16*, 988–999. [CrossRef]
25. Hwang, Y.; Lee, J.Y.; So Kweon, I.; Joo Kim, S. Color transfer using probabilistic moving least squares. In Proceedings of the IEEE Conference on Computer Vision and Pattern Recognition, Columbus, OH, USA, 23–28 June 2014; pp. 3342–3349.
26. Nguyen, R.M.; Kim, S.J.; Brown, M.S. Illuminant aware gamut-based color transfer. In *Proceedings of the Computer Graphics Forum*; Wiley Online Library: New York, NY, USA, 2014; Volume 33, pp. 319–328.
27. Gong, H.; Finlayson, G.D.; Fisher, R.B. Recoding color transfer as a color homography. *arXiv* **2016**, arXiv:1608.01505.
28. Gong, H.; Finlayson, G.D.; Fisher, R.B.; Fang, F. 3D color homography model for photo-realistic color transfer re-coding. *Vis. Comput.* **2019**, *35*, 323–333. [CrossRef]
29. Wang, D.; Zou, C.; Li, G.; Gao, C.; Su, Z.; Tan, P. $\mathcal{L}0$ gradient-preserving color transfer. In *Proceedings of the Computer Graphics Forum*; Wiley Online Library: New York, NY, USA, 2017; Volume 36, pp. 93–103.
30. Oskarsson, M. Robust image-to-image color transfer using optimal inlier maximization. In Proceedings of the IEEE/CVF Conference on Computer Vision and Pattern Recognition, Nashville, TN, USA, 20–25 June 2021; pp. 786–795.
31. Luan, F.; Paris, S.; Shechtman, E.; Bala, K. Deep photo style transfer. In Proceedings of the IEEE Conference on Computer Vision and Pattern Recognition, Honolulu, HI, USA, 21–26 July 2017; pp. 4990–4998.
32. Liu, D.; Jiang, Y.; Pei, M.; Liu, S. Emotional image color transfer via deep learning. *Pattern Recognit. Lett.* **2018**, *110*, 16–22. [CrossRef]
33. Lee, J.; Son, H.; Lee, G.; Lee, J.; Cho, S.; Lee, S. Deep color transfer using histogram analogy. *Vis. Comput.* **2020**, *36*, 2129–2143. [CrossRef]
34. Zhou, Y.; Barnes, C.; Shechtman, E.; Amirghodsi, S. Transfill: Reference-guided image inpainting by merging multiple color and spatial transformations. In Proceedings of the IEEE/CVF Conference on Computer Vision and Pattern Recognition, Nashville, TN, USA, 20–25 June 2021; pp. 2266–2276.
35. Xia, X.; Zhang, M.; Xue, T.; Sun, Z.; Fang, H.; Kulis, B.; Chen, J. Joint bilateral learning for real-time universal photorealistic style transfer. In *Proceedings of the Computer Vision–ECCV 2020: 16th European Conference, Glasgow, UK, 23–28 August 2020*; Proceedings, Part VIII 16; Springer: Berlin/Heidelberg, Germany, 2020; pp. 327–342.
36. Wan, D.; Shen, F.; Liu, L.; Zhu, F.; Huang, L.; Yu, M.; Shen, H.T.; Shao, L. Deep quantization generative networks. *Pattern Recognit.* **2020**, *105*, 107338. [CrossRef]
37. Liao, J.; Yao, Y.; Yuan, L.; Hua, G.; Kang, S.B. Visual attribute transfer through deep image analogy. *arXiv* **2017**, arXiv:1705.01088. [CrossRef]
38. He, M.; Liao, J.; Chen, D.; Yuan, L.; Sander, P.V. Progressive color transfer with dense semantic correspondences. *ACM Trans. Graph. (TOG)* **2019**, *38*, 1–18. [CrossRef]
39. He, M.; Chen, D.; Liao, J.; Sander, P.V.; Yuan, L. Deep exemplar-based colorization. *ACM Trans. Graph. (TOG)* **2018**, *37*, 1–16. [CrossRef]
40. Huang, Y.; Qiu, S.; Wang, C.; Li, C. Learning representations for high-dynamic-range image color transfer in a self-supervised way. *IEEE Trans. Multimed.* **2020**, *23*, 176–188. [CrossRef]
41. Zhang, Y.; Tang, F.; Dong, W.; Huang, H.; Ma, C.; Lee, T.Y.; Xu, C. Domain enhanced arbitrary image style transfer via contrastive learning. In Proceedings of the ACM SIGGRAPH 2022 Conference Proceedings, Vancouver, BC, Canada, 7–11 August 2022; pp. 1–8.
42. Kong, X.; Deng, Y.; Tang, F.; Dong, W.; Ma, C.; Chen, Y.; He, Z.; Xu, C. Exploring the temporal consistency of arbitrary style transfer: A channelwise perspective. *IEEE Trans. Neural Netw. Learn. Syst.* **2023**, *35*, 8482–8496. [CrossRef]

43. Faridul, H.S.; Pouli, T.; Chamaret, C.; Stauder, J.; Trémeau, A.; Reinhard, E. A Survey of Color Mapping and its Applications. *Eurographics (State Art Rep.)* **2014**, *3*, 1.
44. Liu, S. An overview of color transfer and style transfer for images and videos. *arXiv* **2022**, arXiv:2204.13339.
45. Fang, K. *Symmetric Multivariate and Related Distributions*; CRC Press: Boca Raton, FL, USA, 2018.
46. Gu, C.; Lu, X.; Zhang, C. Example-based color transfer with Gaussian mixture modeling. *Pattern Recognit.* **2022**, *129*, 108716. [CrossRef]
47. Absil, P.A.; Mahony, R.; Sepulchre, R. Optimization on Matrix Manifolds. In *Optimization Algorithms on Matrix Manifolds*; Princeton University Press: Princeton, NJ, USA, 2008.
48. Amari, S.I. *Information Geometry and Its Applications*; Springer: Berlin/Heidelberg, Germany, 2016; Volume 194.
49. Amari, S.I. Natural gradient works efficiently in learning. *Neural Comput.* **1998**, *10*, 251–276. [CrossRef]
50. Berkane, M.; Oden, K.; Bentler, P.M. Geodesic estimation in elliptical distributions. *J. Multivar. Anal.* **1997**, *63*, 35–46. [CrossRef]
51. Besson, O.; Abramovich, Y.I. On the Fisher information matrix for multivariate elliptically contoured distributions. *IEEE Signal Process. Lett.* **2013**, *20*, 1130–1133. [CrossRef]
52. Verdoolaege, G.; De Backer, S.; Scheunders, P. Multiscale colour texture retrieval using the geodesic distance between multivariate generalized Gaussian models. In Proceedings of the 2008 15th IEEE International Conference on Image Processing, San Diego, CA, USA, 12–15 October 2008; pp. 169–172.
53. Ollivier, Y. Riemannian metrics for neural networks. *Inf. Inference J. IMA* **2013**, *2*.
54. Pennec, X.; Fillard, P.; Ayache, N. A Riemannian framework for tensor computing. *Int. J. Comput. Vis.* **2006**, *66*, 41–66. [CrossRef]
55. Verdoolaege, G.; Scheunders, P. Geodesics on the Manifold of Multivariate Generalized Gaussian Distributions with an Application to Multicomponent Texture Discrimination. *Int. J. Comput. Vis.* **2011**, *95*, 265–286. [CrossRef]
56. Zhou, J.; Said, S. Fast, Asymptotically Efficient, Recursive Estimation in a Riemannian Manifold. *Entropy* **2019**, *21*, 1021. [CrossRef]
57. Burt, P.J.; Adelson, E.H. The Laplacian pyramid as a compact image code. In *Readings in Computer Vision*; Elsevier: Amsterdam, The Netherlands, 1987; pp. 671–679.
58. Wang, Z.; Bovik, A.C.; Sheikh, H.R.; Simoncelli, E.P. Image quality assessment: From error visibility to structural similarity. *IEEE Trans. Image Process.* **2004**, *13*, 600–612. [CrossRef]
59. Heusel, M.; Ramsauer, H.; Unterthiner, T.; Nessler, B.; Hochreiter, S. Gans trained by a two time-scale update rule converge to a local nash equilibrium. *Adv. Neural Inf. Process. Syst.* **2017**, *30*.
60. Liu, S.; Zhang, B.; Liu, Y.; Han, A.; Shi, H.; Guan, T.; He, Y. Unpaired stain transfer using pathology-consistent constrained generative adversarial networks. *IEEE Trans. Med Imaging* **2021**, *40*, 1977–1989. [CrossRef]
61. Alaoui, M. *Fuzzy TOPSIS: Logic, Approaches, and Case Studies*; CRC Press: Boca Raton, FL, USA, 2021.
62. Kingma, D.P.; Ba, J. Adam: A method for stochastic optimization. *arXiv* **2014**, arXiv:1412.6980.
63. Bonnabel, S. Stochastic gradient descent on Riemannian manifolds. *IEEE Trans. Autom. Control* **2013**, *58*, 2217–2229. [CrossRef]

optics

MDPI

Article

Mobility Support with Intelligent Obstacle Detection for Enhanced Safety

Jong Hyeok Han [1,†], Inkwon Yoon [1,†], Hyun Soo Kim [2], Ye Bin Jeong [2], Ji Hwan Maeng [2], Jinseok Park [1,†] and Hee-Jae Jeon [1,2,*]

1 Department of Smart Health Science and Technology, Kangwon National University, Chuncheon 24341, Republic of Korea
2 Department of Mechanical and Biomedical Engineering, Kangwon National University, Chuncheon 24341, Republic of Korea
* Correspondence: jeon22@kangwon.ac.kr; Tel.: +82-33-250-6313
† These authors contributed equally to this work.

Abstract: In recent years, assistive technology usage among the visually impaired has risen significantly worldwide. While traditional aids like guide dogs and white canes have limitations, recent innovations like RFID-based indoor navigation systems and alternative sensory solutions show promise. Nevertheless, there is a need for a user-friendly, comprehensive system to address spatial orientation challenges for the visually impaired. This research addresses the significance of developing a deep learning-based walking assistance device for visually impaired individuals to enhance their safety during mobility. The proposed system utilizes real-time ultrasonic sensors attached to a cane to detect obstacles, thus reducing collision risks. It further offers real-time recognition and analysis of diverse obstacles, providing immediate feedback to the user. A camera distinguishes obstacle types and conveys relevant information through voice assistance. The system's efficacy was confirmed with a 90–98% object recognition rate in tests involving various obstacles. This research holds importance in providing safe mobility, promoting independence, leveraging modern technology, and fostering social inclusion for visually impaired individuals.

Keywords: image processing; convolution neural network; visually impaired; cane

1. Introduction

Despite the considerable challenges the visually impaired encounter in their daily lives, tactile paving blocks, an essential road infrastructure for the blind, are increasingly vanishing from urban areas [1–4]. This change significantly risks the walking safety of the visually impaired, presenting a major obstacle to their independent mobility in daily life. Over the past few years, various assistive tools have been developed to aid the visually impaired in environmental exploration [4–8]. Traditional aids such as guide dogs and white canes are helpful but offer limited information about the broader environment [9]. Additionally, while cane-based navigation systems have been introduced, canes can only detect obstacles at lower heights and fail to provide information about specific types of obstacles, such as a tree bent in shape or signs [10]. They also have limitations in detecting obstacles at upper body height, leaving a risk of collision for the user. The current cane technology does not offer sufficient environmental awareness, making it difficult for visually impaired individuals to reach their destinations safely and efficiently [10]. For instance, when crossing a heavy road, they face challenges in accurately gauging the speed and distance of oncoming vehicles, putting them at risk of accidents. These issues greatly restrict their mobility and hinder their full participation in social activities.

In recent times, there has been a notable surge in interest towards wearable blindness-assistive devices, some of which have already been commercialized [11]. Technological advancements have paved the way for innovative systems designed to aid the visually impaired, such as RFID-based indoor navigation and haptic feedback devices [12–15]. These innovative solutions, encompassing smart glasses [16], voice recognition apps [16], and cane-based navigation [17,18], strive to offset sensory impairments through alternative sensory modalities. A significant advancement in this area is the deployment of ultrasound sensors in wearable devices that detect obstacles and provide tactile feedback, thereby enhancing obstacle detection accuracy and minimizing collision incidents.

To support the claims made in this study, it is essential to reference statistical data, previous research, and case studies that highlight the need for improved walking safety for the visually impaired [19,20]. Numerous technologies have been developed to enhance mobility and safety, including systems where ultrasonic sensors are attached to canes to detect obstacles and deliver alerts to the user [21,22]. These alerts are typically transmitted through wireless communication with other electronic devices or conveyed directly through sound or vibration [23–25]. However, existing solutions do not yet provide a means of recognizing specific types of obstacles, leaving a gap in enabling visually impaired individuals to navigate safely with more detailed environmental awareness. Unlike conventional technologies, our proposed system goes a step further by identifying obstacle types, allowing users to respond with tailored actions. This advancement is expected to substantially improve user safety by facilitating more informed navigation.

While recent advancements in assistive technology have incorporated image processing and sound conversion systems—often combined with ultrasonic distance sensors to translate distance into vibration feedback—these solutions have shown promising initial results but also come with limitations [7]. Many of these systems require users to carry multiple devices, which can be impractical and uncomfortable. Moreover, feedback mechanisms in these systems, while innovative, can sometimes overwhelm or distract users. Coupled with high costs and maintenance demands, these factors raise concerns about the practicality and accessibility of such technology for widespread adoption.

To address these multifaceted challenges, we have developed an innovative deep learning-based walking assistance device and AI algorithm specifically designed for the visually impaired. The primary advantage of our approach lies in integrating multiple sensor components into a single, chest-mounted device, greatly enhancing user convenience. Moreover, we incorporated a deep learning-based object detection method into the camera, enabling real-time object recognition and obstacle differentiation. Unlike traditional aids, this feature allows the device to recognize and distinguish various objects and obstacles, including those at different heights and shapes that a cane cannot detect, providing immediate feedback to the user. Additionally, the system's real-time video analysis, coupled with voice assistance, supports visually impaired individuals in navigating complex scenarios—such as crossing busy streets—fostering a more inclusive, comprehensive, and safe experience in daily life. In this paper, we address the key challenges faced by visually impaired individuals, followed by a detailed explanation of the system's design and the integration of modern sensing technologies and artificial intelligence. The performance of the device is validated, highlighting its effectiveness in improving user safety, independence, and social participation.

2. Materials and Methods

2.1. A Configuration of the Walking Assistance Device

The walking assistance device developed in this study is designed to attach an ultrasonic sensor to a cane (Zhenjiang kimtex industrial, Zhenjiang, China) and is intended for attachment to the front chest area of the visually impaired individual in Figure 1a. To identify obstacles appearing around the user's upper body and provide immediate information, the device integrates an ultrasonic sensor (Shenzhen Wufang Electronic Technology Co., Shenzhen, China), a camera (DFRobot, Wuhan, China), and a portable battery (Xiaomi,

Beijing, China). The frame of the walking assistance device was fabricated using a 3D printing material suitable for attachment to the human body. Such a design approach maximizes user convenience and minimizes discomfort during prolonged wear. The device is manufactured in a type of band, making it easy to put on and take off. With overall dimensions of 110 × 110 × 121 mm in Figure 1b, its lightweight design ensures that even the elderly and children can use it easily. The primary material of the device is EN-PLA, and its total weight is 750 g.

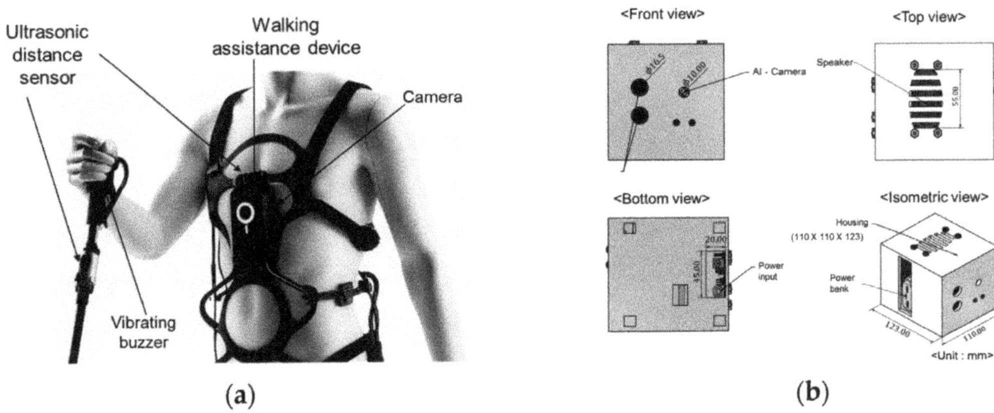

Figure 1. A configuration picture and schematic overview of the assistive device for visually impaired individuals. (**a**) The configuration picture of the walking assistance device for the visually impaired. This image shows the actual setup of an assistive device designed for visually impaired individuals that is worn or positioned on the user. (**b**) This schematic diagram illustrates the basic components and layout of the assistive device for visually impaired individuals. It provides an overview of the internal structure and integration of various sensors, technologies, and components aimed at assisting visually impaired individuals in their daily activities.

2.2. Deep Learning Network Structure

In this study, the YOLO algorithm was employed for object detection. Figure 2 illustrates the machine learning network structure and operating principle of the camera used in this research [26,27]. Traditional object detection systems operate through multiple stages of a pipeline [28]. In contrast, YOLO scans the image only once to simultaneously predict the location and type of objects. This is achieved by dividing the image into a grid and predicting multiple bounding boxes and class probabilities within each grid cell. One of YOLO's main advantages is its rapid processing speed, making it especially suited for applications that require real-time processing [29,30]. Additionally, because YOLO considers the overall context of the image, it is effective in accurately recognizing small or overlapping objects. YOLO comprises a single convolutional neural network (CNN) that predicts bounding box coordinates, object class, and the probability of the object's presence, providing faster and more accurate results compared to other algorithms [31–33].

For this study, we employed the YOLOv2 model, which integrates a Darknet-19 backbone architecture consisting of 19 convolutional layers, 5 max pooling layers, and anchor boxes optimized via k-means clustering for bounding box detection. A passthrough layer further enhances detection accuracy by allowing low-level feature reuse, while the model initially trains on 224 × 224 inputs then finetunes on 448 × 448 for improved feature extraction. This multi-scale training regime was applied to ensure robust detection performance across varying image sizes. In our experiment, we selected a set of four objects—cars, trees, KRW 10,000 bills, and motorcycles—from 200 images, all in color, to test the model's detection accuracy in a controlled, static environment.

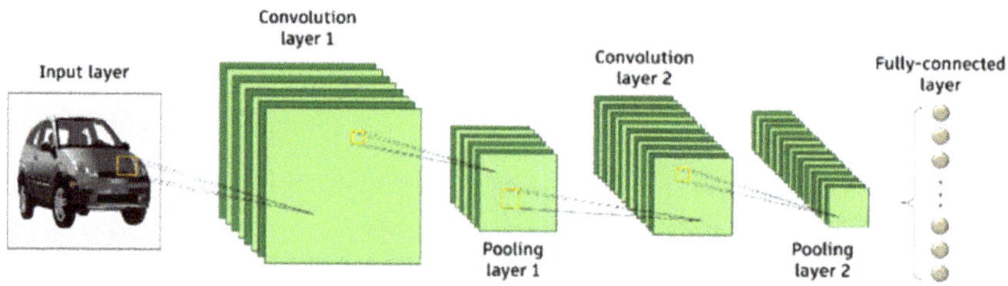

Figure 2. Convolutional neural network frameworks for obstacle classification and detection.

Recent studies have validated YOLOv2's versatility in real-time applications across various fields [34–36]. Research such as "Performance Evaluation of YOLOv2 and Modified YOLOv2 Using Face Mask Detection" has demonstrated YOLOv2's effectiveness in accurately identifying objects in cluttered or overlapping environments [37–39]. Additionally, studies like "Edge Detective Weights Initialization on Darknet-19 Model for YOLOv2-based Face Mask Detection" [32] and "Helmet Detection System Using YOLOv2" [33] further confirm YOLOv2's utility in fast-paced applications requiring accurate object recognition. While YOLOv2 has been used widely in these contexts, its application in assistive devices, specifically walking aids for the visually impaired, remains relatively unexplored. Therefore, this study focuses on YOLOv2's potential for enhancing user safety in a mobility support system, where real-time object detection is vital. However, future studies could explore testing newer versions of YOLO or other algorithms to further enhance accuracy and adaptability in dynamic environments.

2.3. Device Obstacle Detection and Voice Information Transmission Using Various Sensors

The operating principle of this system is detailed in Figure 3. When an obstacle appears in front of a visually impaired person, the ultrasonic sensor detects the distance to the obstacle in real-time. The ultrasonic sensor used in this study measures 45 mm $\times$ 20 mm $\times$ 15 mm and has a ranging distance of 2 cm to 400 cm, with a resolution of 0.3 cm, and operates at an ultrasonic frequency of 40 kHz. This capability allows for precise distance measurement, which is critical for effective obstacle detection [40–42]. As the system detects the distance to an object, it emits varying warning sounds that change in frequency and duration based on how close the obstacle is. Specifically, the warning sounds are designed to sound at a faster rate as the object approaches, providing the user with immediate auditory cues to facilitate timely responses. In addition to auditory alerts, a vibrating motor attached to the cane's handle activates, offering tactile feedback to the user. This dual feedback mechanism ensures that users receive alerts through both sound and touch, significantly enhancing their awareness of nearby obstacles, especially in environments where auditory cues may be less effective due to noise. This system is also equipped with a camera utilizing the Husky Lens (DFRobot, Wuhan, China), enabling it to detect and identify obstacles. Through image processing and machine learning algorithms, it precisely identifies the type of obstacle and converts this information into voice feedback for the visually impaired user. The identified information is relayed to the user through a speaker. In this study, a total of 4 types of objects, including nearby cars and trees, were trained with 400 sets of images and tested with 200 sets of images to validate the effectiveness of the system.

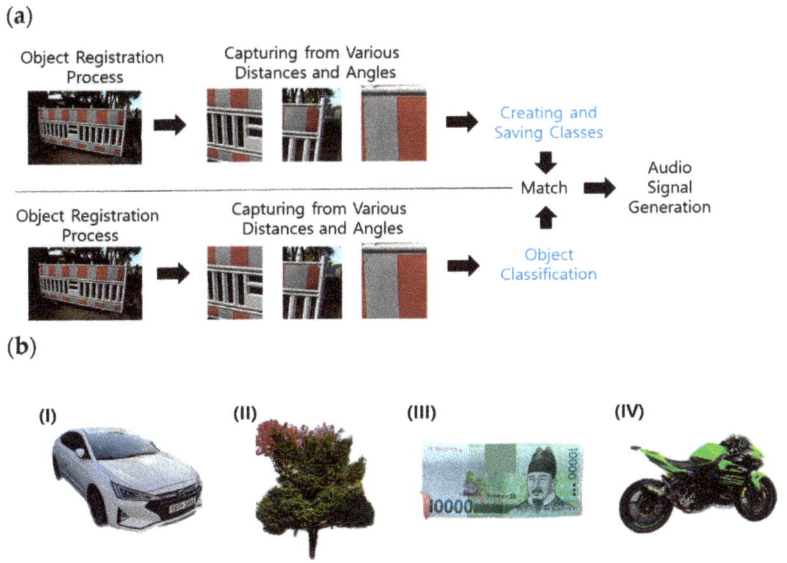

Figure 3. Deep learning-based recognition conceptual framework and sample of obstacle images. (**a**) Conceptual framework of system. (**b**) Obstacle image samples: (**I**) car, (**II**) tree, (**III**) korean 10,000 won bill, (**IV**) motorcycle.

2.4. Obstacle Detection and Voice Feedback via a Sensor, Camera, and Speaker in a Cane

The video recognition system of the walking assistance device for the visually impaired combines obstacle detection and recognition to deliver real-time feedback. When an obstacle is detected via an ultrasonic sensor mounted on the chest, the distance between the user and the object is measured, and warning sounds are emitted through a buzzer. These sounds vary by proximity, with longer warning sounds indicating closer obstacles. To address potential challenges in noisy environments, a vibration sensor attached to the cane handle provides additional tactile feedback in sync with the warning sounds, ensuring the user is alerted through both sound and touch.

The system's obstacle recognition is activated when an object appears within the camera's field of view, classifying it in real time using the YOLO algorithm. The classification result is then transmitted to the user through a speaker, enabling the user to understand both the type and distance of the obstacle. The video recognition system can categorize outcomes as either positive or negative. A positive outcome indicates a match with the acquired video's database, while a negative outcome denotes a non-match.

To evaluate these results, a performance evaluation technique called a confusion matrix is utilized [23,24]. The confusion matrix consists of four outcomes: True Positive (*TP*), False Positive (*FP*), True Negative (*TN*), and False Negative (*FN*). True Positives refer to instances when the system correctly identifies a photo within the database. True Negatives indicate when the system correctly determines that a photo is not in the database. False Positives occur when the system incorrectly associates an unregistered photo with a face in the database, while False Negatives refer to the system failing to recognize a photo that actually exists within the database. We assessed these outcomes through various performance metrics using Equations (1)–(4), which include Accuracy, True Positive Rate (*TPR*), False Positive Rate (*FPR*), True Negative Rate (*TNR*), and False Negative Rate (*FNR*).

$$TPR = \frac{TP}{TP + FN} \tag{1}$$

$$FPR = \frac{FP}{FP + FN} \quad (2)$$

$$TNR = 1 - FPR \quad (3)$$

$$FNR = 1 - TPR \quad (4)$$

3. Results

3.1. The Performance of the Walking Assistance Device

In this experiment, ultrasonic sensors were introduced for the integrated purposes of obstacle detection, the recognition of stairs and slopes, the provision of environmental information, and walking assistance. The cane for the visually impaired, equipped with this ultrasonic sensor, contributes to enhancing the user's independence and safety. When an obstacle appears in front of the user, the device generates a warning sound through the object detection function. This sound varies in frequency depending on the distance, allowing users to gauge proximity. Additionally, the object recognition function informs the user of the type of obstacle, enabling them to take appropriate measures. By providing both distance and object type, the device helps users respond effectively to their surroundings, enhancing walking safety. To facilitate smoother movement in daily life, the sensor mounted on the stick detects changes in the distance of the surrounding environment in real-time. As depicted in Figure 4a, the actual predicted distance recognition rate was converted to sound based on changes in obstacle distance and was measured. Such changes in distance are immediately reflected as changes in sound. In Figure 4b, the accuracy of the predicted distance was analyzed. As a result of the experiments, in measurements up to a maximum distance of 300 cm, the R^2 value was 0.99986, confirming the excellent performance of the sensor.

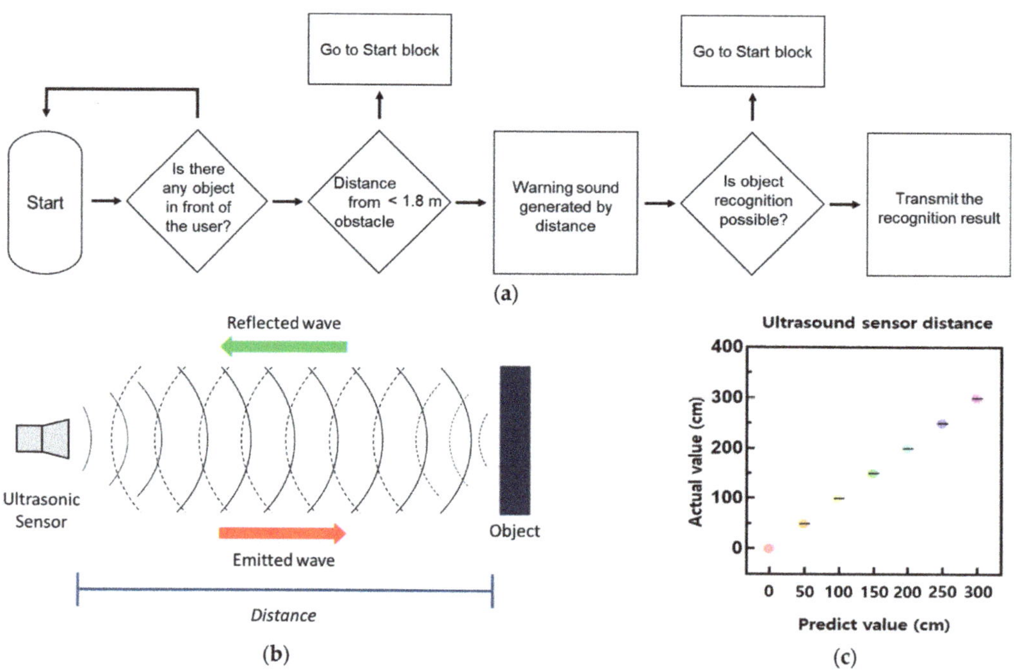

Figure 4. A flow chart of the proposed algorithm, distance measurement-utilizing ultrasonic sensor, and working principle, with measurement results based on distance (**a**). When there is an object in front of the user, object detection is performed by measuring the distance. And object recognition is performed on the type of object. (**b**) The ultrasonic sensor distance measurement method. (**c**) The detection rate based on actual distance.

3.2. Confusion Matrix of Object Recognition Results

To evaluate the performance and object recognition capability of the camera model, we utilized a confusion matrix. The training data included four objects: 'Car', 'Tree', 'Automobile', and '10,000 Won'. To confirm the efficacy of the model, we tested it using both real object images and photographic images. The image sensor used for object recognition uses a two-megapixel CMOS camera. The object recognition executed in Figure 5 was tested by setting the distance between camera objects to 1 m. Figure 5a,b depict the confusion matrices of the test set results predicted based on real object images and photographic images, respectively. Diagonal values in the confusion matrix represent the number of instances correctly classified. The results from Figure 5 show a high accuracy of 100% from 200 tests, indicating that the model is very effective in tests based on photographic images. In contrast, the results in Figure 5a show an average accuracy of 91.5% when using real object images, meaning that it has a slightly lower accuracy compared to tests using photographic images. These results suggest that expanding the diversity of data and further improving the model could yield higher accuracy.

	Car	Tree	Auto mobile	₩ 10,000	Un known	Sum
Car	45	0	0	0	5	50 90% 10%
Tree	0	43	0	0	7	50 86% 14%
Auto mobile	0	0	46	0	4	50 92% 8%
₩ 10,000	0	0	0	49	1	50 98% 2%
Sum	45 100% 0%	43 100% 0%	46 100% 0%	49 100% 0%	17	183/200 91.5% 8.5%

(**a**)

	Car	Tree	Auto mobile	₩ 10,000	Sum
Car	50	0	0	0	50 100% 0%
Tree	0	50	0	0	50 100% 0%
Auto mobile	0	0	50	0	50 100% 0%
₩ 10,000	0	0	0	50	50 100% 0%
Sum	50 100% 0%	50 100% 0%	50 100% 0%	50 100% 0%	200/200 100% 0%

(**b**)

Figure 5. The object recognition confusion matrix results, using real and photo images. (**a**) Physical images, (**b**) photographic images. The number at the top of Sum is the number of tests performed (black), the number in the middle is the true positive rate (green), and the number at the bottom is the true negative rate (red). * Green means *TP*, *FN* and Red means *TN*, *FP*.

3.3. Analysis of Object Recognition Performance

Figure 6 illustrates the results concerning the system's performance in evaluating the capability and performance of the camera model in object recognition. In this study, we distinguish between object detection and object recognition. Object detection refers to measuring the distance to an object, achieved with an ultrasonic sensor that provides feedback to the user based on the detected distance. In contrast, object recognition involves classifying the type of object in front of the user, utilizing an artificial intelligence algorithm to deliver this classification result. For the actual KRW 10,000 note, the TPR, FPR, TNR, and FNR are 98%, 2%, 0%, and 0%, respectively. For trees, the TPR, FPR, TNR, and FNR are 86%, 14%, 0%, and 0%, respectively. For cars, the TPR, FPR, TNR, and FNR stand at 90%, 10%, 0% and 0%, respectively. For motorcycles, the TPR, FPR, TNR, and FNR are 92%, 8%, 0%, and 0%, respectively. Comparing each, we observe variations of 91.5% in the TPR and 8.5% in the TNR. This suggests that the system's ability to accurately recognize actual obstacles is notably high. Thus, this system can be useful and effective in detecting and recognizing obstacles. Additionally, Figure 6e represents the recognition accuracy for each object in percentages. The banknote displayed the highest recognition rate at 98%, followed by trees at 86%, cars at 90%, and motorcycles, with an accuracy of 92%. The higher TPR observed in recognizing the KRW ten-thousand bill can be attributed to the bill's uniform shape and consistent color, which facilitate feature extraction. To improve the TPR for other objects, we propose two key strategies: enhancing data preprocessing and increasing data quality and quantity. Data preprocessing will address missing values, eliminate outliers, and ensure data balance to optimize feature recognition. Additionally, expanding the dataset and refining the quality of existing samples are expected to further improve recognition rates across diverse object types.

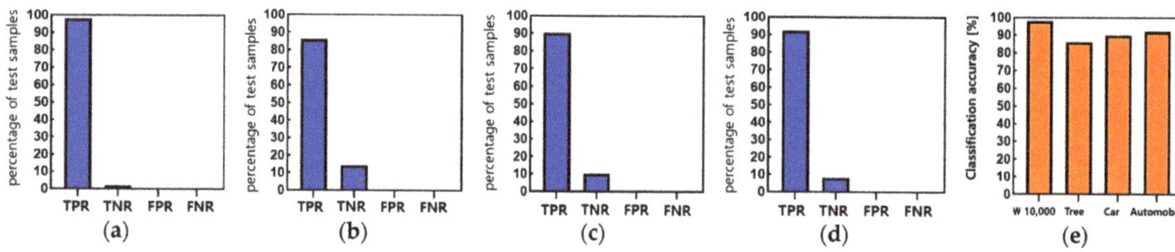

Figure 6. The object recognition accuracy: (**a**) KRW ten-thousand note, (**b**) tree, (**c**) car, (**d**) motorcycle, (**e**) classification results of all objects.

4. Discussion

This research evaluated the effectiveness of object detection and recognition capabilities through the integration of ultrasonic sensors and a camera model in a walking assistance device specifically designed for visually impaired individuals. The incorporation of ultrasonic sensors has demonstrated significant potential in enhancing user safety and independence. By detecting real-time changes in the distances of nearby obstacles, these sensors provide immediate auditory alerts, significantly minimizing the risk of collisions. The system's design allows for varying warning sounds that increase in frequency as obstacles approach, effectively guiding users in dynamic environments. In addition to auditory cues, a vibrating motor attached to the cane's handle delivers tactile feedback, ensuring that alerts are perceptible even in noisy conditions. This dual-feedback approach enhances situational awareness, empowering users to navigate their surroundings with greater confidence and security.

Moreover, our performance evaluation of the camera model revealed high accuracy rates in object recognition, which is crucial for ensuring user safety. Utilizing a confusion matrix to analyze recognition accuracy, we confirmed the system's apability to identify various obstacles effectively. A notable feature of this system is its ability to recognize currency notes, allowing visually impaired users to engage in financial transactions independently. This functionality not only promotes greater autonomy in managing daily activities but also supports social inclusion by reducing the stigma often associated with visual impairments. The integration of advanced technologies, such as ultrasonic sensors and machine learning algorithms [43], highlights a significant shift in the design of assistive devices for the visually impaired. The positive outcomes of our object detection and recognition system underscore its potential to enhance user autonomy and safety across a variety of environments. As the device successfully distinguishes between different obstacles, it plays a vital role in improving navigation skills and fostering user confidence in diverse social settings.

Furthermore, the findings align with previous research emphasizing the importance of real-time feedback systems in assistive technologies. Studies have shown that devices utilizing multi-modal feedback mechanisms—combining auditory, visual, and tactile elements—significantly enhance user performance and confidence in navigation tasks [2,4]. The incorporation of machine learning algorithms, particularly the YOLO algorithm for object recognition, has also been validated in various applications, showcasing its effectiveness in real-time object detection [26,27]. Looking ahead, future research should explore further enhancements to the device's capabilities by integrating additional sensors or advanced algorithms that can adapt to a wider range of scenarios. For instance, incorporating GPS technology could improve spatial awareness and navigation in unfamiliar environments, providing users with real-time guidance and support. Furthermore, studies focusing on user feedback can optimize the design and functionality of the device, ensuring that it meets the diverse needs of visually impaired individuals. Such advancements not only promise to improve technology but also aim to create a more inclusive society where all individuals can navigate their environments with confidence and ease.

5. Conclusions

In conclusion, the technological fusion of ultrasonic sensors and the camera model is anticipated to make a significant contribution to enhancing the mobility and daily life of the visually impaired. In particular, through additional features like currency recognition, their independence and convenience can be further elevated. Building on this research, if a program capable of perceiving in real-time through camera-based image processing technology is developed, there are high expectations for the development of integrated walking aids with diverse functionalities for the visually impaired in the future, offering more effective safety and convenience.

Author Contributions: Conceptualization, H.-J.J., J.H.H., H.S.K., Y.B.J., J.H.M. and I.Y.; methodology, H.-J.J., J.H.H., I.Y. and J.P.; software J.H.H., I.Y. and J.P.; validation, J.H.H., I.Y. and J.P.; formal analysis, J.H.H., I.Y. and J.P.; investigation, H.-J.J., J.H.H., I.Y. and J.P.; resources, H.-J.J., J.H.H., I.Y. and J.P.; data curation, J.H.H., I.Y. and J.P.; writing, H.-J.J., J.H.H., I.Y. and J.P.—original draft preparation, J.H.H., I.Y. and J.P.; writing—review and editing, H.-J.J., J.H.H., I.Y. and J.P.; visualization, J.H.H., I.Y. and J.P.; supervision, H.-J.J.; project administration, H.-J.J.; funding acquisition, H.-J.J. All authors have read and agreed to the published version of the manuscript.

Funding: This research was jointly supported by the 2023 Research Grant from Kangwon National University, the "Innovative Human Resource Development for Local Intellectualization" support program (IITP-2023-RS-2023-00260267), the IITP and funded by the Ministry of Science and ICT (MSIT), Korea, the National Research Foundation of Korea (NRF) grant under the auspices of the Korea government (MEST) (RS-2023-00213379) and Korea and Regional Innovation Strategy (RIS) through the National Research Foundation of Korea (NRF), funded by the Ministry of Education (MOE) (2022RIS-005).

Data Availability Statement: The data supporting the findings of this study are available from the corresponding author upon reasonable request.

Conflicts of Interest: The authors declare no conflicts of interest.

References

1. Johnston, A.D. *Sensory Augmentation for Navigation in Difficult Urban Environments by People With Visual Impairment*; Open University (United Kingdom): Milton Keynes, UK, 2013.
2. Zimring, C.; Templer, J. Wayfinding and orientation by the visually impaired. *J. Environ. Syst.* **1983**, *13*, 333–352. [CrossRef]
3. Zimmermann-Janschitz, S.; Mandl, B.; Dückelmann, A. Clustering the mobility needs of persons with visual impairment or legal blindness. *Transp. Res. Rec.* **2017**, *2650*, 66–73. [CrossRef]
4. Jiang, B.; Yang, J.; Lv, Z.; Song, H. Wearable vision assistance system based on binocular sensors for visually impaired users. *IEEE Internet Things J.* **2018**, *6*, 1375–1383. [CrossRef]
5. Tapu, R.; Mocanu, B.; Zaharia, T. Wearable assistive devices for visually impaired: A state of the art survey. *Pattern Recognit. Lett.* **2020**, *137*, 37–52. [CrossRef]
6. Hakobyan, L.; Lumsden, J.; O'Sullivan, D.; Bartlett, H. Mobile assistive technologies for the visually impaired. *Surv. Ophthalmol.* **2013**, *58*, 513–528. [CrossRef]
7. Kleinberg, D.; Abekasis, I.; Israel, Y.; Yozevitch, R.; Holdengreber, E. A Haptic Feedback System for Spatial Orientation in the Visually Impaired: A Comprehensive Approach. *IEEE Sens. Lett.* **2023**, *7*, 1–4. [CrossRef]
8. Modzelewski, M.; Kaiser, E.B. Hand gesture recognition interface for visually impaired and blind people. In Proceedings of the 2012 IEEE/ACIS 11th International Conference on Computer and Information Science, Shanghai, China, 30 May–1 June 2012; pp. 201–206.
9. Deshen, S.; Deshen, H. On social aspects of the usage of guide-dogs and long-canes1. *Sociol. Rev.* **1989**, *37*, 89–103. [CrossRef]
10. Kandil, M.; AlAttar, F.; Al-Baghdadi, R.; Damaj, I. AmIE: An ambient intelligent environment for blind and visually impaired people. In *Technological Trends in Improved Mobility of the Visually Impaired*; Springer: Berlin/Heidelberg, Germany, 2020; pp. 207–236.
11. Kumar, N.; Jain, A. A Deep Learning Based Model to Assist Blind People in Their Navigation. *J. Inf. Technol. Educ. Innov. Pract.* **2022**, *21*, 095–114. [CrossRef]

12. Simões, W.C.; Machado, G.S.; Sales, A.M.; de Lucena, M.M.; Jazdi, N.; de Lucena, V.F., Jr. A review of technologies and techniques for indoor navigation systems for the visually impaired. *Sensors* **2020**, *20*, 3935. [CrossRef]
13. Plikynas, D.; Žvironas, A.; Gudauskis, M.; Budrionis, A.; Daniušis, P.; Sliesoraitytė, I. Research advances of indoor navigation for blind people: A brief review of technological instrumentation. *IEEE Instrum. Meas. Mag.* **2020**, *23*, 22–32. [CrossRef]
14. See, A.R.; Costillas, L.V.M.; Advincula, W.D.C.; Bugtai, N.T. Haptic Feedback to Detect Obstacles in Multiple Regions for Visually Impaired and Blind People. *Sens. Mater.* **2021**, *33*, 1799–1808. [CrossRef]
15. Rodríguez, A.; Yebes, J.J.; Alcantarilla, P.F.; Bergasa, L.M.; Almazán, J.; Cela, A. Assisting the visually impaired: Obstacle detection and warning system by acoustic feedback. *Sensors* **2012**, *12*, 17476–17496. [CrossRef]
16. Joshi, R.C.; Yadav, S.; Dutta, M.K.; Travieso-Gonzalez, C.M. Efficient multi-object detection and smart navigation using artificial intelligence for visually impaired people. *Entropy* **2020**, *22*, 941. [CrossRef] [PubMed]
17. Valencia, G.; Diego, J. A Computer-Vision Based Sensory Substitution Device for the Visually Impaired (See ColOr). Ph.D. Thesis, University of Geneva, Geneva, Switzerland, 2014. Available online: https://nbn-resolving.org/urn:nbn:ch:unige-345689 (accessed on 4 July 2021).
18. Hu, M.; Chen, Y.; Zhai, G.; Gao, Z.; Fan, L. An overview of assistive devices for blind and visually impaired people. *Int. J. Robot. Autom.* **2019**, *34*, 580–598. [CrossRef]
19. Mocanu, A.; Sita, V.; Avram, C.; Aştilean, A. Enhanced Cane for Blind People Mobility Assistance. In Proceedings of the 2024 IEEE International Conference on Automation, Quality and Testing, Robotics (AQTR), Cluj-Napoca, Romania, 16–18 May 2024; pp. 1–6.
20. Muktha, D.; Niveditha, G.; Pinto, N.A.; Sinha, S. Enhancing Mobility: A Smart Cane with Integrated Navigation System and Voice-Assisted Guidance for the Visually Impaired. In Proceedings of the 2024 IEEE 13th International Conference on Communication Systems and Network Technologies (CSNT), Jabalpur, India, 6–7 April 2024; pp. 1124–1129.
21. Baldonado, J. An Enchanced Audio-Based Smart Cane For Visually Impaired People. *Educ. Adm. Theory Pract.* **2024**, *30*, 8087–8102.
22. Panazan, C.-E.; Dulf, E.-H. Intelligent Cane for Assisting the Visually Impaired. *Technologies* **2024**, *12*, 75. [CrossRef]
23. Kazi, W.; Limu, T.J.; Rakibuzzaman, M. Smart Cane: A Low Cost Assistive Device for the Visually Impaired. *EAI Endorsed Trans. Internet Things* **2023**, *8*, e5. [CrossRef]
24. Mai, C.; Xie, D.; Zeng, L.; Li, Z.; Li, Z.; Qiao, Z.; Qu, Y.; Liu, G.; Li, L. Laser Sensing and Vision Sensing Smart Blind Cane: A Review. *Sensors* **2023**, *23*, 869. [CrossRef]
25. Devi, A.; Hassan, M.A.; Ahmad, I.; Sohail, M.; Mahoob, M.A.; Junaid, H. Assistive Smart Cane for Visually Impaired People Based on Convolutional Neural Network (CNN). In *IoT-Enabled Convolutional Neural Networks: Techniques and Applications*; River Publishers: Aalborg, Denmark, 2023; pp. 125–147.
26. Jiang, P.; Ergu, D.; Liu, F.; Cai, Y.; Ma, B. A Review of Yolo algorithm developments. *Procedia Comput. Sci.* **2022**, *199*, 1066–1073. [CrossRef]
27. Huang, R.; Pedoeem, J.; Chen, C. YOLO-LITE: A real-time object detection algorithm optimized for non-GPU computers. In Proceedings of the 2018 IEEE International Conference on Big Data (Big Data), Seattle, WA, USA, 10–13 December 2018; pp. 2503–2510.
28. Zhao, Z.-Q.; Zheng, P.; Xu, S.-t.; Wu, X. Object detection with deep learning: A review. *IEEE Trans. Neural Netw. Learn. Syst.* **2019**, *30*, 3212–3232. [CrossRef]
29. Fang, W.; Wang, L.; Ren, P. Tinier-YOLO: A real-time object detection method for constrained environments. *IEEE Access* **2019**, *8*, 1935–1944. [CrossRef]
30. Gupta, S.; Devi, D.T.U. YOLOv2 based real time object detection. *Int. J. Comput. Sci. Trends Technol.* **2020**, *8*, 26–30.
31. Parupalli, S.; Akhsitha, S.; Naval, D.; Kasam, P.; Yavagiri, S. Performance evaluation of YOLOv2 and modified YOLOv2 using face mask detection. *Multimed. Tools Appl.* **2024**, *83*, 30167–30180. [CrossRef]
32. Ningthoujam, R.; Pritamdas, K.; Singh, L.S. Edge detective weights initialization on Darknet-19 model for YOLOv2-based facemask detection. In *Neural Computing and Applications*; Springer: Berlin/Heidelberg, Germany, 2024; pp. 1–14.
33. Arun, M.; Jaitly, V. Helmet Detection System Using Yolo V2. In Proceedings of the 2024 IEEE International Conference on Information Technology, Electronics and Intelligent Communication Systems (ICITEICS), Bangalore, India, 28–29 June 2024; pp. 1–6.
34. Kang, C.H.; Kim, S.Y. Real-time object detection and segmentation technology: An analysis of the YOLO algorithm. *JMST Adv.* **2023**, *5*, 69–76. [CrossRef]
35. Boudjit, K.; Ramzan, N. Human detection based on deep learning YOLO-v2 for real-time UAV applications. *J. Exp. Theor. Artif. Intell.* **2022**, *34*, 527–544. [CrossRef]
36. Tun, N.K.; Myat, A.M.; Oo, H.N.; Thu, A.M.; Win, K.T. Deep Learning-Based Real-Time Face Mask Detection for Human Using Novel YOLOv2 with Higher Accuracy. In Proceedings of the International Conference on Computer & Communication Technologies, Warangal, India, 6–7 October 2023; pp. 213–222.
37. Aamir, S.M.; Ma, H.; Khan, M.A.A.; Aaqib, M. Real-Time Object Detection in Occluded Environment with Background Cluttering Effects Using Deep Learning. *arXiv* **2024**, arXiv:2401.00986.
38. Banerjee, A.; Bhattacharjee, D.; Das, N.; Behra, S.; Srinivasan, N.T. CARP-YOLO: A Detection Framework for Recognising and Counting Fish Species in a Cluttered Environment. In Proceedings of the 2023 4th International Conference for Emerging Technology (INCET), Belgaum, India, 26–28 May 2023; pp. 1–7.

39. Chatrasi, A.L.V.S.S.; Batchu, A.G.; Kommareddy, L.S.; Garikipati, J. Pedestrian and object detection using image processing by yolov3 and yolov2. In Proceedings of the 2023 7th International Conference on Trends in Electronics and Informatics (ICOEI), Tirunelveli, India, 11–13 April 2023; pp. 1667–1672.
40. Nesti, T.; Boddana, S.; Yaman, B. Ultra-sonic sensor based object detection for autonomous vehicles. In Proceedings of the IEEE/CVF Conference on Computer Vision and Pattern Recognition, Vancouver, BC, Canada, 17–24 June 2023; pp. 210–218.
41. Essien, J.; Chimezie, C. Ultrasonic Sensor-Based Embedded System for Vehicular Collusion Detection and Alert. *J. Comput. Commun.* **2023**, *11*, 44–57. [CrossRef]
42. Chandrasegar, V.; Koh, J. Estimation of Azimuth Angle Using an Ultrasonic Sensor for Automobile. *Remote Sens.* **2023**, *15*, 1837. [CrossRef]
43. Busaeed, S.; Katib, I.; Albeshri, A.; Corchado, J.M.; Yigitcanlar, T.; Mehmood, R. LidSonic V2.0: A LiDAR and deep-learning-based green assistive edge device to enhance mobility for the visually impaired. *Sensors* **2022**, *22*, 7435. [CrossRef]

applied sciences

MDPI

Article

Fundus-DANet: Dilated Convolution and Fusion Attention Mechanism for Multilabel Retinal Fundus Image Classification

Yang Yan *, Liu Yang and Wenbo Huang

Institution of Computer Science and Technology, Changchun Normal University, Changchun 130000, China; qx202200158@stu.ccsfu.edu.cn (L.Y.); huangwenbo@sina.com (W.H.)
* Correspondence: yanyang2016@hotmail.com

Abstract: The difficulty of classifying retinal fundus images with one or more illnesses present or missing is known as fundus multi-lesion classification. The challenges faced by current approaches include the inability to extract comparable morphological features from images of different lesions and the inability to resolve the issue of the same lesion, which presents significant feature variances due to grading disparities. This paper proposes a multi-disease recognition network model, Fundus-DANet, based on the dilated convolution. It has two sub-modules to address the aforementioned issues: the interclass learning module (ILM) and the dilated-convolution convolutional block attention module (DA-CBAM). The DA-CBAM uses a convolutional block attention module (CBAM) and dilated convolution to extract and merge multiscale information from images. The ILM uses the channel attention mechanism to map the features to lower dimensions, facilitating exploring latent relationships between various categories. The results demonstrate that this model outperforms previous models in classifying fundus multilocular lesions in the OIA-ODIR dataset with 93% accuracy.

Keywords: attention mechanism; dilated convolution; classification of multiple fundus lesions

1. Introduction

Nearly half the cases of 2.2 billion people worldwide who experience visual impairment can be averted with early detection and treatment, according to the 2021 World Health Organization (WHO) report [1]. Thus, it is crucial to inspect for fundus lesions early and diagnose and treat them quickly. Optical Coherence Tomography (OCT), which creates high-resolution tomography pictures by scanning the reflected signals from the retinal fundus tissue, is the most widely utilized technique for fundus inspection. However, the limited number of ophthalmologists restricts widespread fundus lesion screening and prevention. Hence, there is an urgent need to develop techniques for automated diagnosis of fundus lesions.

Relevant research has proven that deep learning methods, including convolutional neural networks, perform well for classifying fundus lesions. As an illustration, Bogacsovics et al. [2] created a model that combined the characteristics from convolutional networks and hand-extracted data to improve the prediction of conditions like diabetic macular edema and diabetic retinopathy. Key elements of the BFPC-Net designed by Li et al. [3] combined channel and spatial attention mechanics with an emphasis on fundus lesions. To improve the classification accuracy of each target, Huo et al. [4] proposed a three-branch hierarchical multiscale feature fusion network architecture (HiFuse) for medical image classification. This architecture fused the advantages of the Transformer and convolutional neural network (CNN) at a multiscale level without destroying the corresponding modeling. A Discriminative Kernel Convolution Network (DKCNet) was created by Bhati et al. [5] to train the multiscale discriminative features using attention blocks. Yet, there is still a significant potential for improvement in classification accuracy and model generalization as the current approaches cannot extract the same morphological features exhibited by various lesions in the fundus pictures.

Therefore, this paper proposes Fundus-DANet with the following contributions:

1. A dilated-convolution convolutional block attention module (DA-CBAM) is designed to feature the representation in the convolutional neural network that is enhanced using the convolutional block attention module (CBAM) [6] after extracting and fusing the multiscale image features using dilated convolution to effectively extract the multiscale features within the image.
2. An interclass learning module (ILM) is designed to adapt the channel attention method to solve problems, such as the difficulty of effectively capturing the important features between classes by the traditional feature extraction method of convolutional neural networks.
3. Asymmetric polynomial loss (APL) [7] is used to apply different weights to the positive and negative samples to improve the model's ability to recognize rare categories. Specifically, this paper enhances the model's focus on positive samples by giving greater penalty to positive samples, which improves the model's performance.

The rest of the paper is organized as follows: Section 2 presents the related work on CNNs and graph neural networks in multi-disease fundus classification. Section 3 details the methodology and evaluation metrics. Section 4 presents the dataset, experimental information, and results. Finally, Section 5 summarizes the paper and emphasizes the importance of the method.

2. Related Work

Fundus lesions have gained increasing interest due to recent advancements in deep learning-based algorithms for fundus picture classification. CNN is a type of deep learning neural network architecture commonly utilized in classification tasks due to its ability to accurately capture the spatial properties of fundus images through convolutional computation. Furthermore, the attention mechanism is widely used in image processing because it reduces redundant information, prioritizes important regions, and enhances classification accuracy.

2.1. Dilated-Convolution-Based Methods

A new multiscale dilated-convolution-based ensemble learning (MDCEL) method was proposed by You et al. [8]. It involved introducing dilated convolution and different expansion rates in a traditional CNN with transfer learning, training multiple learners simultaneously through an aggregation strategy, and obtaining the final result using a weighted-voting method. Unfortunately, this approach could not retain information with higher precision and had a limited capacity for feature collection. To solve this issue, Sun et al. [9] applied a multiple parallel dilated-convolution multiscale fusion of contextual information in the bottleneck layer of the network and utilized a U-shaped network to fully collect the image multiscale features. However, this approach was unable to fuse the features properly. To gather more data, enhance the fundamental features, and broaden the sensory field, Panchal et al. [10] created the residual multi-kernel dilation convolution U-Net model (ResMU-Net), which combined the U-shaped network structure with hopping connections and cavity convolution at each layer. Furthermore, Tu et al. [11] proposed a method based on residual dense and dilated convolution (RDDC-3DCNN) for classifying hyperspectral images. The authors created a method that effectively extracts the spatial–spectral features of hyperspectral images by fusing different levels of spatial–spectral features through a dilated convolution of the residual dilated dense block. These two approaches, however, were very sophisticated, prone to overfitting issues for datasets with few samples, and had limited capacity for generalization. Consequently, by highlighting discriminative characteristics, Madarapu et al. [12] suggested the multiresolution convolutional attention network (MuR-CAN) to enhance the overall performance. This network demonstrated superior performance on two datasets with fewer samples by initially extracting features from the backbone network and subsequently extracting features using dilated convolution.

2.2. Attention Mechanism-Based Methods

By concentrating on the bright and dark structures in the retinal images independently, Romero-Ora et al. [13] developed a novel attentional method to produce independent attentional maps. However, this method could only handle photos with significant variations in the feature color, like fundus images, and it might be challenging to apply to other kinds of image classifications. To improve the feature differences between lesions and background while focusing on lesion feature information, Li et al. [14] created a Binocular Fundus Photographs Classifying Network (BFPC-Net) model with improved generalization. They specifically added a residual network and an attention mechanism fusion module. However, that approach, which employed dual channel and spatial attention mechanisms, may lead to information loss or an overemphasis on specific local elements. This could cause the model to overlook other significant features and reduce its overall comprehension of the input data. Hence, Madarapu et al. [15] no longer confined themselves to focusing on local features but instead proposed a parallel connection of channel and spatial attention mechanisms. They then used the self-attention mechanism to model the interactions between all the locations of the feature mapping to capture the remote dependencies in the input feature mapping. This approach was also based on the fusion of residual networks and attention mechanisms. Nevertheless, the channel attention mechanism with considerable modeling overhead was implemented using two tightly coupled modules. As a result, rich discriminative and stage-specific features were selectively implemented from the lesion region by Das et al. [16] in their design of a novel adapter and enhanced self-attention-based CNN framework (AES-Net) model, which was based on parallel connectivity by pooling and three 1 × 1 convolutional kernels. This significantly reduced the model overhead issue. As shown in Table 1, previous studies and key contributions can be found, providing a comprehensive overview of the research landscape in this field.

Table 1. Overview of previous studies and key contributions of this research.

Study	Objective	Method	Findings	Limitations	Contribution of This Study
You et al. (2020) [8]	To propose a new multiscale dilated-convolution-based ensemble learning method (MDCEL)	Introduced dilated convolution and different expansion rates in a traditional CNN with transfer learning, training multiple learners simultaneously through an aggregation strategy, and obtaining the final result using a weighted voting method	Improved classification performance	Limited information retention and feature collection capacity	Enhanced feature extraction capabilities
Sun et al. (2021) [9]	To apply multiple parallel dilated-convolution multiscale fusion of contextual information	Utilized a U-shaped network to fully collect the image multiscale features	Enhanced multiscale feature extraction	Inadequate feature fusion	Used a convolutional block attention module (CBAM) and dilated convolution to extract and merge multiscale information from images.
Panchal et al. (2022) [10]	To create the residual multi-kernel dilation convolution U-Net model (ResMU-Net)	Combined U-shaped network structure with hopping connections and cavity convolution at each layer	Broadened sensory field and enhanced feature extraction	High complexity, prone to overfitting	Reduced model complexity

Table 1. *Cont.*

Study	Objective	Method	Findings	Limitations	Contribution of This Study
Tu et al. (2022) [11]	To propose a method based on residual dense and dilated convolution (RDDC-3DCNN) for hyperspectral image classification	Fused different levels of spatial–spectral features through a dilated convolution of the residual dilated dense block	Effectively extracted spatial–spectral features	High complexity, prone to overfitting	Reduced model complexity
Madarapu et al. (2022) [12]	To propose the multiresolution convolutional attention network (MuR-CAN)	Extracted features from the backbone network and then used dilated convolution	Superior performance on two datasets with fewer samples	Small sample size	Validated on larger datasets
Romero-Ora et al. (2023) [13]	To develop a novel attentional method for retinal images	Generated independent attentional maps focusing on bright and dark structures	Improved classification accuracy	Applicable only to images with significant feature color variations	Addressed the issue of small interclass differences
Li et al. (2023) [14]	To create the BFPC-Net model with improved generalization	Added a residual network and an attention mechanism fusion module	Enhanced feature information extraction	Risk of information loss, overemphasis on local features	Fused multiscale features
Madarapu et al. (2023) [15]	To propose a parallel connection of channel and spatial attention mechanisms	Modeled interactions between all locations of the feature mapping using self-attention	Improved feature extraction and classification performance	High modeling overhead	Reduced model complexity
Das et al. (2023) [16]	To design the AES-Net model based on parallel connectivity by pooling and three 1×1 convolutional kernels	Selectively implemented rich discriminative and stage-specific features from the lesion region	Reduced model overhead	High complexity	Reduced model complexity

3. Methods

This section describes Fundus-DANet in detail. The general framework diagram of the network is depicted in Figure 1. It comprises four components: the image preprocessing module, DA-CBAM, ILM, and loss function. This study aimed to solve the problem of accurately classifying the multilocular lesions in the fundus. First, InceptionResnet-v2 was used as the main network to extract feature F from the previously processed images. Feature F was simultaneously inserted into the DA-CBAM and ILM. In the DA-CBAM, local and global image features were extracted and fused, while in the ILM, interclass features were extracted using the SE attention mechanism [17]. Each module generated prediction results, denoted as prediction1 and prediction2, respectively. Finally, an APL function was used to derive the final loss by independently summing and averaging the two outcomes.

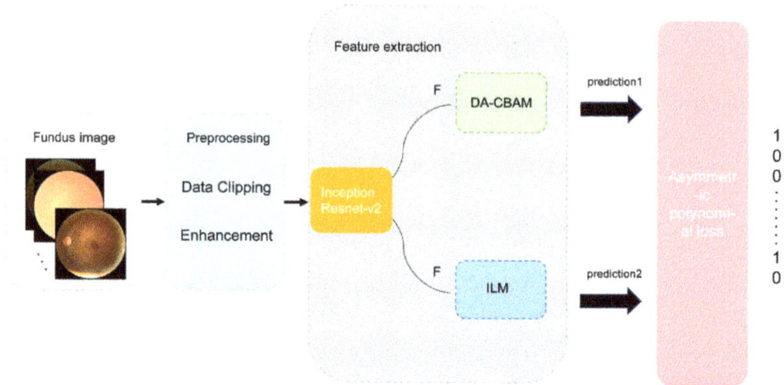

Figure 1. The overall structure of Fundus-DANet, DA-CBAM is the spatial feature learning module (green), ILM is the interclass learning module (dark blue), and the asymmetric polynomial loss is represented in pink.

3.1. Fundus-DANet

3.1.1. DA-CBAM

We designed the DA-CBAM for spatial feature learning in images. Without reducing the resolution of the feature maps, this module leveraged three dilated convolution layers and channel and spatial attention mechanisms of the CBAM [6] to focus on significant aspects and acquire multiscale features for learning and fusion. Specifically, Figure 2 depicts the general architecture of the DA-CBAM. First, the channels of feature F were divided into two groups, and the channels within these groups were rearranged to facilitate the exchange and combination of information between the different channels. Then, a dilated convolution layer with a convolution kernel of 3 and expansion rates of 1, 2, and 3 was applied to the channel-shuffled feature F'.

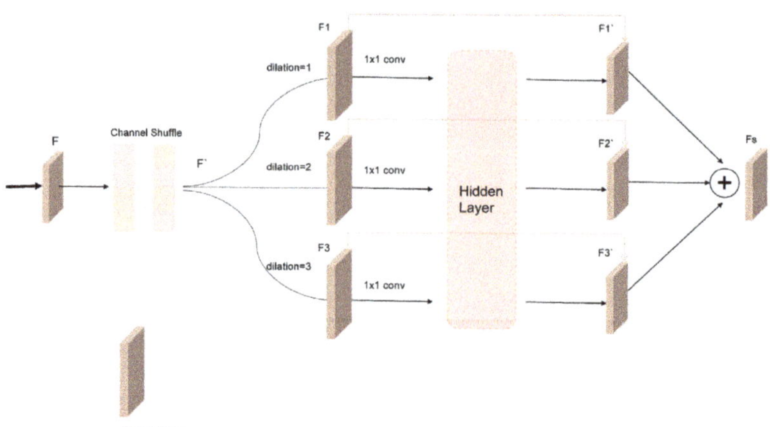

Figure 2. The overall architecture of the DA-CBAM. The channels are shuffled between the two groups. Dilated convolutions are then used to extract the features at different scales from each group. These features are processed through hidden layers, and the final results are summed up.

The dilated convolution kernel, depicted in Figure 3, incorporates spacing between the filters to expand the sensory field of the network without increasing the number of parameters and computational requirements. Dilated convolutions with different dilation rates can simultaneously capture the local details and global information, enhancing the perception of features at various scales. This capability is crucial for handling the fine and diverse characteristics present in images. Given that the image was transformed into a tensor with 1536 channels and a spatial size of 8 × 8 after processing through the backbone network, the selection of dilation rates required careful consideration. Excessive dilation rates could exceed the original spatial dimensions and adversely affect the experimental results. Therefore, we constrained the dilation rates to 1, 2, and 3. This ensured an appropriate receptive field while avoiding spatial inconsistencies. On this basis, we obtained three feature vectors, F1, F2, and F3, and the feature maps of these three scales were batch-normalized and then activated by the RELU function as shown in Equations (1) and (2):

$$Y_d[i,j] = \sum_{0}^{k-1}\sum_{0}^{k-1} X[i + m \times d, j + n \times d] \times W[m,n](k = 3, d = 1,2,3), \tag{1}$$

where i, j denotes the row and column indices of the output feature map Y_d, k is the size of the dilated convolution kernel, and d is the dilated convolution rate.

$$F_1, F_2, F_3 = \sigma\left(BN\left(Conv(F')\right)\right), \tag{2}$$

where σ is the activation function, and Conv is the dilated convolution.

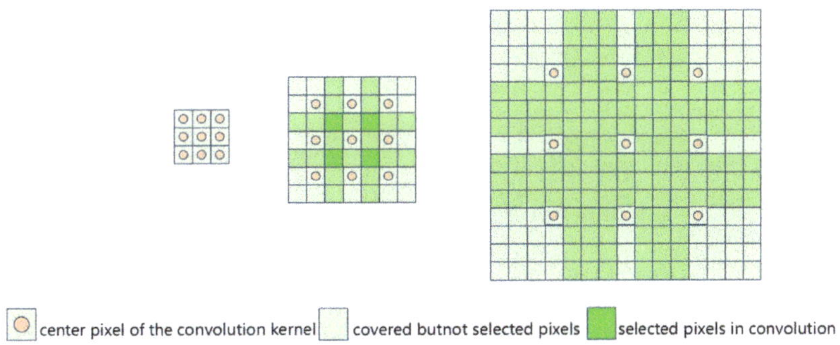

Figure 3. The receptive field with different dilation rates for a 3 × 3 kernel size.

As seen in Figure 4, each of the three feature maps obtained was subjected to a layer of 1 × 1 convolution to reduce the number of channels. The feature maps were then joined at the channel level using the maximum and average pooling, as indicated by Equation (3). This fused the feature maps in the channel and preserved the data from the various feature map categories, enhancing the model's representation and generalization capabilities. This research included the attention mechanism of the CBAM, which determined the significance of each spatial location in the image and improved the focus on the relevant spatial places, helping the network focus on the important aspects of the image. Ultimately, these three features were residual connections and summed up to produce F_1', F_2', and F_3'. This process was carried out to improve the network's representation capability and training efficiency by directly passing features from the lower layer to the higher layer and fusing global semantic information with local detail information. Eventually, full connectivity was used to produce the prediction results after the features Fs were reduced in feature size by average pooling while maintaining the overall features of the image.

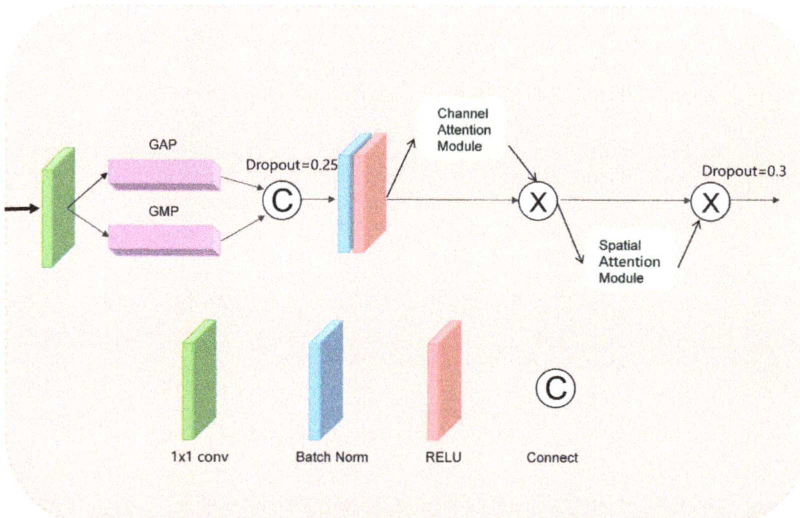

Figure 4. The architecture of the DA-CBAM hidden layer. The parallel processing consists of two pooling layers, two dropout layers, and an attention mechanism.

In addition, to prevent the model from an overfitting problem, a dropout function was added to randomly discard 0.25 and 0.3 neurons after pooling and before feature summation, respectively:

$$F_{pool} = \sigma(BN(AvgPool(x) + MaxPool(x))), \tag{3}$$

where x denotes the input feature map.

3.1.2. ILM

We developed an ILM that attempted to identify the critical characteristics between various classes for precise classification, focusing on the label dependency of the training set and the issue of interclass similarity in medical images. A 1×1 convolution operation was performed on the features collected using the InceptionResnet-v2 to further understand the variability in features between various classes and prepare for additional classification tasks, as illustrated in Figure 5. After mapping the original 1536-dimensional features to a lower-dimensional 8-dimensional feature space with a convolution kernel of size 1×1, the interclass features $\mathrm{F_a}$ were obtained through an average pooling operation, which transformed the data in the original feature space into higher-level abstract features and improved the feature representation of different classes. This enhanced the model's ability to capture subtle interclass differences.

The full connectivity relationship between the input and output features was established multiple times through the channel attention mechanism, which also used the maximum and parallel global pooling to improve the model's ability to characterize the input features. This enhanced the model's focus on critical differences between classes, improving its ability to capture interclass dependencies. Finally, the inter-channel correlation was dynamically acquired using the global and maximum pooling, and the input features were weighted to obtain the feature vector $F'_{\mathrm{a}.}$ resultant from integrating the F_{a} and F'_{a} residuals:

$$F'_{\mathrm{a}} = ILM(F_{\mathrm{a}}) = ILM(W \times F') \tag{4}$$

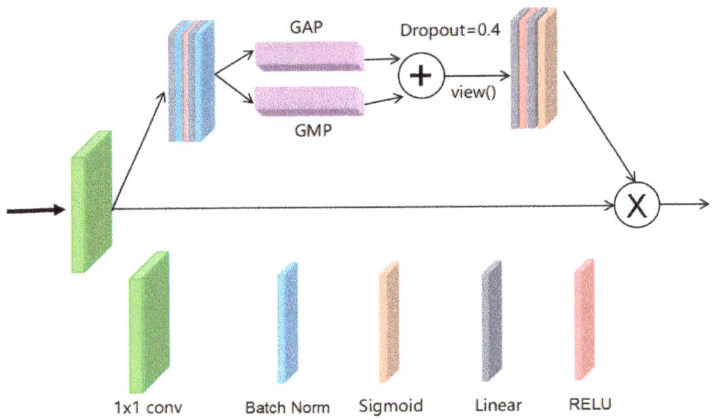

Figure 5. Structure of interclass learning module.

3.2. APL

An unbalanced data distribution results from a significant difference in the number of samples from each category in the existing public fundus datasets. This imbalance can negatively impact the performance and training of deep learning models, as the models are biased towards learning features from categories with a higher number of samples, ignoring categories with a lower number of samples, or even misclassifying such samples into categories with a higher number of samples.

We used APL [7,18] to address the issue of the dataset's uneven distribution. It achieved this by discarding the negative samples with low prediction probabilities and separating the gradient contributions of the positive and negative samples by varying the focusing parameters for the Taylor expansion of the BCE loss. Two hyperparameters with different scaling factors $\gamma^{+/-}$ were first used to adjust the loss $L^{+/-}$ for positive and negative categories and discard the categories with less impact on the experiment, as shown in Equation (5):

$$L- = \sum_{n=1}^{\infty} \beta_{i,n} \max(p_i - p_{th}, 0)^{n+\gamma^-}, \tag{5}$$

where p_i is the predicted probability, p_{th} is the hard threshold, and β is the coefficient for negative samples. When p_i is less than the threshold, it does not participate in the loss calculation, and based on that, the loss function was obtained as:

$$L_{APL} = \sum_{i=0}^{C} \{y_i(1-p_i)^{\gamma^+}[-logp_i + (\alpha_1 - 1)(1-p_i) + (\alpha_2 - \tfrac{1}{2})(1-p_i)^2] + (1-y_i)p_{res}^{\gamma^-}[-log(1-p_i) + (\beta_1 - 1)p_{res}]\}/C, \tag{6}$$

where α_1 and α_2 are adjustable parameters for positive samples, β_1 is a parameter for negative samples, C is the number of categories, and p_{res} denotes $\max(p_i - p_{th}, 0)$.

The loss function in this paper's method consists of two parts, the image learning module loss and interclass learning module loss. The total network loss formula in this paper is given by:

$$L_{total} = \frac{1}{N} \sum_{n=1}^{N} (L_s + L_a) \tag{7}$$

where L_s is the loss of the image learning module, L_a is the loss of the interclass learning module, and N is the number of samples under an epoch.

3.3. Evaluation Metrics

The six evaluation criteria that we employed in this work were the area under the curve (AUC), κ, final_ and F1_scores, hamming loss (HL), and classification accuracy (ACC).

ACC measures the proportion of samples the model correctly classifies in its predictions. The formula to calculate ACC is as follows:

$$Accuracy = \frac{TP + TN}{TP + FP + TN + FN}, \tag{8}$$

where TP, TN, FP, and FN represent the true positive, true negative, false positive, and false negative samples, respectively.

$F1\_score$ was calculated by the formula:

$$F1\_score = \frac{2TP}{2TP + FP + FN} \tag{9}$$

$Final\_score$ was calculated by the formula:

$$Final\_score = \frac{F1\_score + Kappa + AUC}{3} \tag{10}$$

κ is the degree to which the model's predictions and actual categorization outcomes agree. This statistic can be useful to evaluate how successfully the model classifies minor categories in unbalanced datasets. The confusion matrix, which has a value between −1 and 1 and is often greater than 0, is used to compute κ. The formula is as follows:

$$\kappa = \frac{p_0 - p_e}{1 - p_e}, \tag{11}$$

where p_0 is the accuracy of the prediction, and p_e is the sum of the product of the actual and predicted numbers divided by the square of the total number of samples.

By dividing the total number of labels by the number of elements that are not equal between the two, the Hamming loss metric was used to evaluate the discrepancy between true and predicted labels. The smaller the ratio, the more accurate the model's prediction. The formula is as follows:

$$HL_{(y,\hat{y})} = \frac{1}{n * m} \sum_{i=0}^{n-1} \sum_{j=0}^{m-1} 1\left(\hat{y}_{i,j} \neq y_{i,j}\right) \tag{12}$$

4. Experiments and Results

This section provides the details of the experiment and results. Section 4.1 explains the dataset in depth. Section 4.2 provides the experimental setups and hyperparameter selection information. Section 4.3 describes the data's preprocessing in depth. Section 4.4 thoroughly examines the experimental results, including the choice of several backbone models, attention mechanisms, ablation studies, and comparisons with current systems. A thorough analysis of the data shows that the model used in this work produces the best outcomes in these areas.

4.1. Datasets

This experimental dataset, OIA-ODIR (https://github.com/nkicsl/OIA-ODIR) (accessed on 3 August 2024) [19], contains OCT of both eyes of 5000 patients, totaling 10,000 images. As shown in Figure 6, the dataset comprises normal images (N) and six diseases, such as diabetic retinopathy (D), glaucoma (G), cataract (C), AMD (A), myopia (M), and hypertension (H), as well as other diseases (O). Labels for a single eye were initially created based on the diagnostic results because the dataset only contained labels for binocular images and diagnostic results for a single eye. This led to the retention of 9476 images as the dataset after removing images with shifted images, poor image quality, dusty lenses, abnormal camera exposures, optic discs that were not visible in photos, and controversial images regarding the pathology. The dataset, comprising 7574 images in the training set, 951 images in the validation set, and 941 images in the test set, was randomized into training, validation, and test sets at a ratio of 8:1:1.

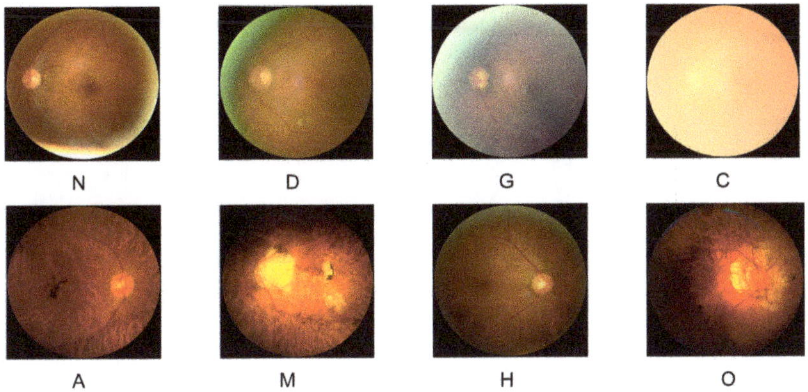

Figure 6. Fundus images of different categories randomly selected from the OIA-ODIR [19] dataset containing normal images (N) and six diseases, such as diabetic retinopathy (D), glaucoma (G), cataract (C), AMD (A), myopia (M), and hypertension (H), as well as other diseases (O).

4.2. Implementation Details

The hardware used for the study was an AMD EPYC 7402 24-core CPU, an A30 GPU graphics card, 24 GB video memory, and 86 GB RAM. The model was constructed using the Pytorch 2.0 framework based on Python 3.9 and CUDA 11.7. To make the raw data compatible with the experimental hardware and acceptable to the model, it was first scaled to 299 pixels × 299 pixels.

Table 2 illustrates how the hyperparameters were set up during the model training phase. The learning rate was first set at 0.0007 and was dynamically adjusted via StepLR. It was then refined based on the validation set results. The APL loss function was used to independently calculate and average the loss values for each module, with a complete connection utilized as the output layer.

Table 2. Hyperparameter settings in training.

Hyperparameter	Value
Epochs	30
Batch size	16
Optimizer	SGD
Learning rate	0.0007
Momentum parameter	0.9
Weight decay parameter	1×10^{-6}
Learning rate scheduler	StepLR
Scheduler step size	5
Learning rate decay factor	0.9

4.3. Image Preprocessing

Significant variations in resolution and contrast across the photos in the OIA-ODIR dataset occurred as different pieces of equipment were not used to capture them simultaneously. Other issues included uneven illumination and lens blurring. Since the model was prone to overfitting and the fundus images had little data, this paper aimed to improve the images before submitting them to the network for training.

Since most of the photos in the dataset were rectangular and the input model was square, as shown in Figure 7a, directly scaling the cropped extra black region would result in the distortion issue depicted in Figure 7c. Thus, as illustrated in Figure 7b, we first searched for non-black pixels in the four directions before cropping the image to create a square that only included the bottom of the eye. This was used to scale and crop the image to the dimensions needed by the network. Next, random flipping of the image's horizontal and vertical axes increased its diversity. The overfitting problem was resolved by adjusting the image's brightness, contrast, saturation, and hue. Finally, the image was normalized using the mean and standard deviation to quicken the model's convergence.

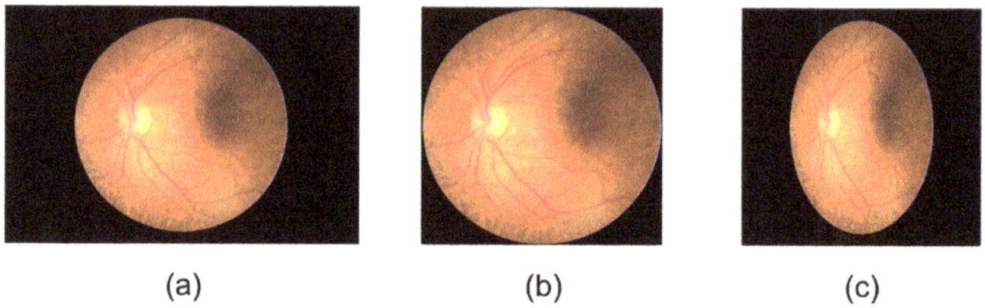

Figure 7. Fundus image preprocessing. The images in (**a**–**c**) are the original, cropped, and uncropped directly trained images, respectively.

4.4. Results

4.4.1. Performance Evaluation of Different Backbone Networks

This paper compared multiple backbone models to attain the best classification performance. Due to the extensive and difficult lesions' distribution in the fundus images, we prioritized Inception-ResNet-v2 [20]. With its residual connections, this hybrid architecture solves the gradient vanishing problem in deep networks and performs very well at capturing the features at various sizes. This preserves training stability for deeper networks. This paper also compared VGG16 [20], Inception-v3 [21], ResNet101 [22], and EfficientNet-B4 [23], four additional high-performing models, to strengthen the persuasiveness of our findings. The best results were obtained when using InceptionResnetV2 as the backbone network, as shown in Table 3, with a 93% ACC, 82.13% Final_score, 83.74% F1_score, 67.52% κ, 7% HL, and 95.12% AUC. Among the models compared, Inception-v3 and ResNet101 had their strengths, with ACCs of 92.28% and 90.70%, respectively. However, they slightly underperformed compared to the composite InceptionResNetV2. EfficientNet-B4 focuses on computational efficiency and resource utilization, which tends to sacrifice some feature extraction capabilities in complex tasks, resulting in poorer performance. VGG16 lacks an explicit multiscale feature extraction mechanism and residual connections, leading to relatively inferior results.

Table 3. Results of comparative experiments of the backbone model.

Backbone	No Preprocessing						Preprocessing					
	ACC	AUC	F1_Score	Final_Score	κ	HL	ACC	AUC	F1_Score	Final_Score	κ	HL
Vgg16 [20]	88.15	85.66	73.38	68.60	46.77	11.85	89.97	91.42	74.86	72.08	49.96	10.03
Inception-v3 [21]	90.42	90.68	77.44	74.35	54.94	9.58	92.28	94.62	82.49	80.70	65.00	7.72
Resnet101 [22]	89.35	90.45	71.99	68.95	44.42	10.65	90.70	93.52	78.02	75.88	56.11	9.30
EfficientNet-B4 [23]	88.58	89.39	65.47	62.43	32.43	11.42	89.50	91.46	70.32	67.75	41.48	10.50
InceptionResnetV2 [24]	90.95	92.69	77.52	85.15	55.23	9.05	93.00	95.12	83.74	82.13	67.52	7.00

Table 3 also illustrates the impact of the preprocessing module on experimental outcomes. The results demonstrated that incorporating the preprocessing module improved all the metrics by 1–3%. This indicated that addressing the input image distortion could significantly enhance the model's feature recognition capability. Furthermore, by significantly augmenting the diversity of image data and improving the quality of input images, the preprocessing module effectively reduced the risk of model overfitting.

4.4.2. Ablation Experiment

We conducted ablation experiments using the DA-CBAM, ILM, and APL functions to better demonstrate how each module affected the classification model outcomes. This paper's experiments used the cross-entropy loss function instead of the APL function, as illustrated in Table 4. The first row shows the outcome of using only the backbone model InceptionResnetV2, and the evaluation indexes like ACC and F1-score were slightly improved after adding the DA-CBAM. However, the results were not significantly improved because the problem of dataset imbalance had not been resolved yet, and it also failed to capture the interclass feature connection. A substantial 1–6% improvement was seen for all the measures when APL was added to the DA-CBAM. All the measures did not significantly improve when the ILM was added to the DA-CBAM, indicating that proper data balancing improved the experimental findings. The results of the experiment with the ILM but without the DA-CBAM were lower because the ILM and DA-CBAM had to collaborate to enhance the system's performance. The system's overall performance suffered when the ILM was utilized alone. The confusion matrix in Figure 8 for the experiment, including an APL, clearly showed that the classification results for the category with fewer samples greatly improved. Additionally, the results greatly improved when the DA-CBAM and ILM were put together. However, when the backbone model was introduced with the ILM alone, the results marginally declined. This was because by complementing each other's shortcomings and offering extra information, the two modules increased overall system performance and substantiated the need for concurrently extracting intra- and interclass features.

Table 4. Results of ODIR ablation experiments.

	ACC	AUC	F1_Score	Final_Score	κ	HL
InceptionResnet-V2	91.29	93.62	77.62	77.59	55.52	8.70
InceptionResnet-V2 + DA-CBAM	91.40	93.16	77.89	75.70	56.06	8.60
InceptionResnet-V2 + ILM	90.42	92.70	74.28	72.00	49.05	9.58
InceptionResnet-V2 + APL	92.90	94.61	84.10	82.31	68.22	7.10
InceptionResnet-V2 + DA-CBAM + APL	92.81	94.54	83.25	81.44	66.54	7.19
InceptionResnet-V2 + ILM + APL	90.53	92.70	74.59	72.30	49.66	9.5
InceptionResnet-V2 + DA-CBAM + ILM	91.77	93.68	79.18	77.14	58.56	8.23

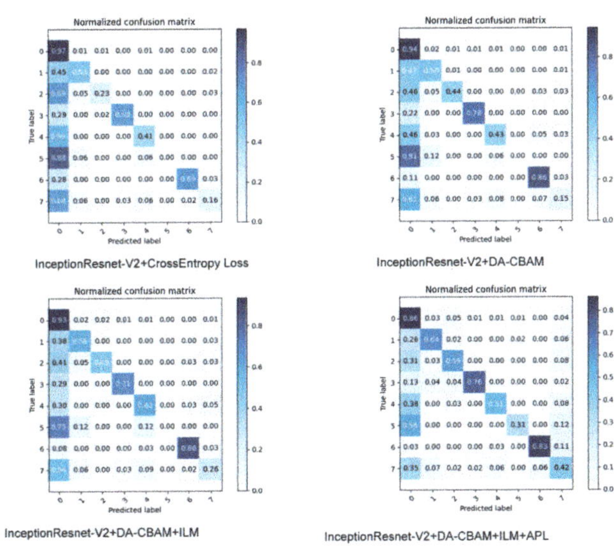

Figure 8. Ablation experiment confusion matrix of OIA-ODIR.

4.4.3. Comparative Experiments between Different Attentional Mechanisms

By giving distinct weights to different aspects, the attention mechanism can effectively increase the accuracy of medical picture categorization. This allows the model to focus more on those features. By analyzing the current state-of-the-art attention mechanisms, this research sought to determine the best scheme for the model to apply to the interclass and picture learning modules. This paper compared methods for the image learning module, such as CBAM, self-attention mechanism [25], spatial attention with channel attention removed [26], and SGE. For the interclass learning module, this paper compared ECA-Net [27] and existing improved methods by Zhang et al. [28] based on SE-Net. Table 5 displays the results of the experiment. Various attention mechanisms were found to increase the accuracy of the model. The most successful method was the combination of the CBAM and the SE-Net-improved method, which maximized the consideration of the features on the graph space and more effectively captured the important information in the image, thereby improving the model's performance.

Table 5. Comparative results of attentional mechanisms.

	ACC	AUC	F1_Score	Final_Score	κ	HL
Self-attention mechanism [25]	92.39	94.58	82.59	80.79	65.20	7.61
Spatial attention mechanism [26]	92.40	94.81	82.14	80.42	64.33	7.60
ECA-Net [27]	92.68	94.92	83.62	81.93	67.25	7.32
SGE [28]	92.55	94.39	82.62	80.76	65.28	7.45

4.4.4. Comparative Testing of Different Models

In this paper, Fundus-DANet was compared with the EfficientNetB3 model of Wang et al. [29], the MCGL-Net model of Sun et al. [30], the MCGS-Net model of Lin et al. [31], and the DCNet of Li et al. [32]. The results of the experiments are shown in Table 6. The experiment yielded an ACC score of 94.46% for the MCGL-Net, which was 1.46% higher than the model in this paper. However, the model performed worse regarding AUC and κ metrics, coming in at 1.62% and 3.22% lower, respectively, than the experimental model. These results indicate that the model in this paper performed better regarding dataset balance. Both DCNet and MCGL-Net performed better in terms of the F1_score, striking a better balance between comprehensiveness and accuracy while demonstrating significant generalization capabilities.

Table 6. Comparative experiments.

	ACC	AUC	F1_Score	Final_Score	κ	HL
EfficientNetB3 [29]	92.00	74.00	89.00	72.00	52.00	–
MCGL-Net [30]	94.46	93.50	91.60	–	64.30	–
MCGS-Net [31]	–	78.16	89.66	–	57.65	–
DCNet [32]	–	93.00	91.30	82.70	63.70	–
CNN-Trans [33]	80.68	95.9	–	–	–	–
Our	93.00	95.12	83.74	82.13	67.52	7.00

5. Discussion and Limitations

In this study, we proposed a Fundus-DANet model. Although our model showed promising outcomes in capturing subtle interclass differences and enhancing overall classification accuracy, implementing it in real-world scenarios still has several limitations and challenges. First, the quality of fundus images was inconsistent, and the number of samples across different classes was severely imbalanced, making model training challenging. The limited data reduced the model's robustness, making it difficult to maintain consistent performance across various application scenarios. Second, deploying Fundus-DANet requires substantial computational resources due to the complexity of the model and its extensive use of convolutional and attention mechanisms, which may result in longer inference times and higher hardware requirements. This limits its applicability in clinical settings requiring rapid diagnosis or real-time analysis. Lastly, the continuous updating and maintenance of the model are crucial for adapting to new data and evolving medical standards. This necessitates ongoing efforts in both technology and human resources.

To address these issues, we aim to collaborate with hospitals to acquire more data for model training, enhancing the model's generalization capability and robustness. In addition, we will strive to reduce the model's computational cost and inference time without compromising its accuracy to better suit the needs of real-time clinical applications.

6. Conclusions

This paper investigated a dilated-convolution fundus multi-disease classification model incorporating an attention mechanism, aiming at solving the problem of accurate recognition for multiple diseases of the retinal fundus. The model extracted the input image's spatial and categorical properties, which then applied the appropriate spatial and channel attention mechanisms. The final prediction result was calculated by averaging the two prediction outcomes. Furthermore, the APL function resolved the issue of category imbalance and enhanced the classification outcomes for some categories. The experimental results demonstrated that the model achieved an accuracy of 93% in classifying multiple lesions in fundus images, and all the metrics were enhanced compared to the existing fundus multi-disease classification model, validating the capability of the model proposed in this paper to accurately classify fundus multi-disease. The model efficiently balances the different data categories and can be a reliable clinical tool.

Author Contributions: Conceptualization, Y.Y., L.Y. and W.H.; methodology, L.Y.; software, Y.Y., L.Y. and W.H.; validation, Y.Y., L.Y. and W.H.; writing—original draft preparation, Y.Y. and L.Y.; writing—review and editing, Y.Y.; supervision, W.H.; project administration, Y.Y.; funding acquisition, Y.Y. All authors have read and agreed to the published version of the manuscript.

Funding: This research was funded by the Natural Science Foundation of Jilin Province, grant number YDZJ202401350ZYTS.

Institutional Review Board Statement: Not applicable.

Informed Consent Statement: Not applicable.

Data Availability Statement: The dataset used in this study, OIA-ODIR, is publicly available and can be accessed at [https://github.com/nkicsl/OIA-ODIR] (accessed on 3 August 2024). The data and code used to support the findings of this study are available from the corresponding author upon request (yanyang2016@hotmail.com).

Acknowledgments: We thank the OIA-ODIR project for providing the dataset used in this study, which is available at [https://github.com/nkicsl/OIA-ODIR] (accessed on 3 August 2024).

Conflicts of Interest: The authors declare no conflicts of interest.

References

1. Burton, M.J.; Ramke, J.; Marques, A.P.; Bourne, R.R.; Congdon, N.; Jones, I.; Tong, B.A.A.; Arunga, S.; Bachani, D.; Bascaran, C. The lancet global health commission on global eye health: Vision beyond 2020. *Lancet Glob. Health* **2021**, *9*, e489–e551. [CrossRef] [PubMed]
2. Bogacsovics, G.; Toth, J.; Hajdu, A.; Harangi, B. Enhancing CNNs through the use of hand-crafted features in automated fundus image classification. *Biomed. Signal Process. Control.* **2022**, *76*, 103685. [CrossRef]
3. Meng, Q.; Zhang, W. Multi-label image classification with attention mechanism and graph convolutional networks. In Proceedings of the 1st ACM International Conference on Multimedia in Asia, Beijing China, 15–18 December 2019; pp. 1–6.
4. Huo, X.; Sun, G.; Tian, S.; Wang, Y.; Yu, L.; Long, J.; Zhang, W. HiFuse: Hierarchical multi-scale feature fusion network for medical image classification. *Biomed. Signal Process. Control* **2024**, *87*, 105534. [CrossRef]
5. Bhati, A.; Gour, N.; Khanna, P.; Ojha, A. Discriminative kernel convolution network for multi-label ophthalmic disease detection on imbalanced fundus image dataset. *Comput. Biol.* **2023**, *153*, 106519. [CrossRef]

6. Woo, S.; Park, J.; Lee, J.-Y.; Kweon, I.S. Cbam: Convolutional block attention module. In Proceedings of the European Conference on Computer Vision (ECCV), Munich, Germany, 8–14 September 2018; pp. 3–19.
7. Huang, Y.; Qi, J.; Wang, X.; Lin, Z. Asymmetric polynomial loss for multi-label classification. In Proceedings of the ICASSP 2023–2023 IEEE International Conference on Acoustics, Speech and Signal Processing (ICASSP), Rhodes Island, Greece, 4–10 June 2023; pp. 1–5.
8. You, G.-R.; Shiue, Y.-R.; Su, C.-T.; Huang, Q.-L. Enhancing ensemble diversity based on multiscale dilated convolution in image classification. *Inf. Sci.* **2022**, *606*, 292–312. [CrossRef]
9. Sun, M.; Li, K.; Qi, X.; Dang, H.; Zhang, G. Contextual information enhanced convolutional neural networks for retinal vessel segmentation in color fundus images. *J. Vis. Commun. Image Represent.* **2021**, *77*, 103134. [CrossRef]
10. Panchal, S.; Kokare, M. ResMU-Net: Residual Multi-kernel U-Net for blood vessel segmentation in retinal fundus images. *Biomed. Signal Process. Control* **2024**, *90*, 105859. [CrossRef]
11. Tu, C.; Liu, W.; Jiang, W.; Zhao, L. Hyperspectral image classification based on residual dense and dilated convolution. *Infrared Phys. Technol.* **2023**, *131*, 104706. [CrossRef]
12. Madarapu, S.; Ari, S.; Mahapatra, K. A multi-resolution convolutional attention network for efficient diabetic retinopathy classification. *Comput. Electr. Eng.* **2024**, *117*, 109243. [CrossRef]
13. Romero-Oraá, R.; Herrero-Tudela, M.; López, M.I.; Hornero, R.; García, M. Attention-based deep learning framework for automatic fundus image processing to aid in diabetic retinopathy grading. *Comput. Methods Programs Biomed.* **2024**, *249*, 108160. [CrossRef]
14. Li, Z.; Xu, M.; Yang, X.; Han, Y. Multi-label fundus image classification using attention mechanisms and feature fusion. *Micromachines* **2022**, *13*, 947. [CrossRef] [PubMed]
15. Madarapu, S.; Ari, S.; Mahapatra, K. A deep integrative approach for diabetic retinopathy classification with synergistic channel-spatial and self-attention mechanism. *Expert Syst. Appl.* **2024**, *249*, 123523. [CrossRef]
16. Das, D.; Nayak, D.R.; Pachori, R.B. AES-Net: An adapter and enhanced self-attention guided network for multi-stage glaucoma classification using fundus images. *Image Vis. Comput.* **2024**, *146*, 105042. [CrossRef]
17. Hu, J.; Shen, L.; Sun, G. Squeeze-and-excitation networks. In Proceedings of the IEEE Conference on Computer Vision and Pattern Recognition, Salt Lake City, UT, USA, 18–22 June 2018; pp. 7132–7141.
18. Ridnik, T.; Ben-Baruch, E.; Zamir, N.; Noy, A.; Friedman, I.; Protter, M.; Zelnik-Manor, L. Asymmetric loss for multi-label classification. In Proceedings of the IEEE/CVF International Conference on Computer Vision, Montreal, BC, Canada, 11–17 October 2021; pp. 82–91.
19. Li, N.; Li, T.; Hu, C.; Wang, K.; Kang, H. A benchmark of ocular disease intelligent recognition: One shot for multi-disease detection. In Proceedings of the Benchmarking, Measuring, and Optimizing: Third BenchCouncil International Symposium, Bench 2020, Virtual Event, 15–16 November 2020; pp. 177–193.
20. Szegedy, C.; Ioffe, S.; Vanhoucke, V.; Alemi, A. Inception-v4, inception-resnet and the impact of residual connections on learning. In Proceedings of the AAAI Conference on Artificial Intelligence, San Francisco, CA, USA, 4–9 February 2017.
21. Simonyan, K.; Zisserman, A. Very deep convolutional networks for large-scale image recognition. *arXiv* **2014**, arXiv:1409.1556.
22. Szegedy, C.; Vanhoucke, V.; Ioffe, S.; Shlens, J.; Wojna, Z. Rethinking the inception architecture for computer vision. In Proceedings of the IEEE Conference on Computer Vision and Pattern Recognition, Las Vegas, NV, USA, 27–30 June 2016; pp. 2818–2826.
23. He, K.; Zhang, X.; Ren, S.; Sun, J. Deep residual learning for image recognition. In Proceedings of the IEEE Conference on Computer Vision and Pattern Recognition, Las Vegas, NV, USA, 27–30 June 2016; pp. 770–778.
24. Tan, M.; Le, Q. Efficientnet: Rethinking model scaling for convolutional neural networks. In Proceedings of the International Conference on Machine Learning, Long Beach, CA, USA, 9–15 June 2019; pp. 6105–6114.
25. Vaswani, A.; Shazeer, N.; Parmar, N.; Uszkoreit, J.; Jones, L.; Gomez, A.N.; Kaiser, Ł.; Polosukhin, I. Attention is all you need. *Adv. Neural Inf. Process. Syst.* **2017**, *30*. [CrossRef]
26. Chen, B.; Zhang, Z.; Liu, N.; Tan, Y.; Liu, X.; Chen, T. Spatiotemporal convolutional neural network with convolutional block attention module for micro-expression recognition. *Information* **2020**, *11*, 380. [CrossRef]
27. Wang, Q.; Wu, B.; Zhu, P.; Li, P.; Zuo, W.; Hu, Q. ECA-Net: Efficient channel attention for deep convolutional neural networks. In Proceedings of the IEEE/CVF Conference on Computer Vision and Pattern Recognition, Seattle, WA, USA, 14–19 June 2020; pp. 11534–11542.
28. Zhang, Y.; Luo, L.; Dou, Q.; Heng, P.-A. Triplet attention and dual-pool contrastive learning for clinic-driven multi-label medical image classification. *Med. Image Anal.* **2023**, *86*, 102772. [CrossRef]
29. Wang, J.; Yang, L.; Huo, Z.; He, W.; Luo, J. Multi-label classification of fundus images with efficientnet. *IEEE Access* **2020**, *8*, 212499–212508. [CrossRef]
30. Sun, K.; He, M.; Xu, Y.; Wu, Q.; He, Z.; Li, W.; Liu, H.; Pi, X. Multi-label classification of fundus images with graph convolutional network and LightGBM. *Comput. Biol. Med.* **2022**, *149*, 105909. [CrossRef]
31. Lin, J.; Cai, Q.; Lin, M. Multi-label classification of fundus images with graph convolutional network and self-supervised learning. *IEEE Signal Process. Lett.* **2021**, *28*, 454–458. [CrossRef]

32. Li, C.; Ye, J.; He, J.; Wang, S.; Qiao, Y.; Gu, L. Dense correlation network for automated multi-label ocular disease detection with paired color fundus photographs. In Proceedings of the 2020 IEEE 17th International Symposium on Biomedical Imaging (ISBI), Iowa City, IA, USA, 3–7 April 2020; pp. 1–4.
33. Liu, S.; Wang, W.; Deng, L.; Xu, H. Cnn-trans model: A parallel dual-branch network for fundus image classification. *Biomed. Signal Process. Control.* **2024**, *96*, 106621. [CrossRef]

applied sciences

MDPI

Article

Chromaticity Analysis on Ethnic Minority Color Landscape Culture in Tibetan Area: A Semantic Differential Approach

Liyun Zeng [1,*], Rita Yi Man Li [2] and Rongjia Li [1]

1 Civil and Architectural Engineering Institute, Panzhihua University, Panzhihua 617000, China
2 Sustainable Real Estate Research Center, Hong Kong Shue Yan University, Hong Kong 999077, China; ymli@hksyu.edu
* Correspondence: nonsar@foxmail.com; Tel.: +86-15600912550

Abstract: The color–area ratio in ethnic minority areas is one way to perceive cultural elements visually. The openness of spaces, sense of rhythm, and richness of color affect people's emotions and induce different psychological perceptions. Despite many ethnic minority areas being more colorful than the main traits of Han, there is no systematic quantitative study for the color elements in ethnic minority areas' landscapes, not to mention the research on the color–area ratio, main and auxiliary colors and embellishments, and layouts. Therefore, this paper studies the color–area ratio of Xiangcheng County in the Tibetan area of Ganzi Prefecture in Sichuan Province. Colors are extracted and quantitatively analyzed from six different aspects using the semantic differential (SD) method and color quantitative analysis method. In this way, low-scored (B group) and high-scored (A group) color landscape samples were extracted from the landscape image library and quantitatively analyzed by ColorImpact V4.1.2. The results show that the ethnic minority group's color layout is characterized by richer colors and stronger contrasts than the Han group. This paper contributes to academic scholarship regarding color culture in ethnic minority areas. It also provides theoretical support for preserving ethnic minority groups' cultural heritage and practical insights into color planning for urban and landscape designs.

Keywords: semantic differential; color quantification; colorimetry; chromaticity; color–area ratio; public aesthetics; Tibetan areas

1. Introduction

1.1. The Cultural and Environmental Context of Colorscape

Color is a significant component of urban landscapes. It contains vital information of their history, culture, and perception of aesthetics [1]. It plays an essential role in visual landscapes and affects the emotional perceptions of the nation's landscapes [2]. National culture and social background influence people's psychology, aesthetics, and colour characteristics [3,4]. Satio (1996) suggested that cultural, regional, and environmental aspects might influence color preference and formation [5]. Thus, various color landscapes are observed in different ethnic regions with different political systems, cultures, and customs [6]. The characteristics of a color landscape are also affected by the living or/and the natural environment, which influences people's aesthetic concepts in many ways, such as in local folk customs, and living habits [4].

1.2. The Dilemma of the Color Landscape Development

Today, urban color landscape design has become essential to differentiate or symbolize a city's characteristics or atmosphere [7]. With the rapid development of urbanization and large-scale urban construction activities, urban color landscapes face a series of problems [8]. First, the traditional color landscape in some cities has been strongly impacted by natural geographic situation, climate, local building materials, ethnic culture and religious consciousness, social and economic development, and other humanistic environmental factors [9]. Second, the problem of color pollution is prominent in cityscapes, adversely affecting people physically and psychologically, through the use of, for example, bright, solid-color buildings, billboards and lighting clusters [10]. Karim, Paymane, and Alireza (2020) suggested a unifying cityscape in Tehran. Third, colors are similar between cities and the cultural identity of many places is lost [10]. Many modern buildings have similar colors [11], diluting a local culture's characteristics.

1.3. Color Landscape of Ethnic Minority Area in China

Since the 20th century, China's landscape design grounded in its local traditions, culture, and geographic conditions [12]. Traditional ethnic minority landscapes are the carriers of the ancient civilization's artistic style, technological level, and historical information in China in different ethnic minority regions, due to three natural elements (i.e., geography, environment and climate) and three artificial elements (i.e., economy, social culture and customs) ethnic minority's landscapes have distinguished color aesthetic concepts [13]. For China's ethnic minority areas, the color types are richer than other Han regions and have rich cultural and regional connotations. The special color–area ratio in Tibetan areas is reflected in costumes, architecture, and environments, expressing certain local conventions and cultural characteristics. Therefore, the Tibetan color–area ratio is a vital factor in the external space [14] and an important part of the characteristic landscape.

1.4. Research Purpose, Questions, Value, Innovation and Structure

1.4.1. Research Purpose

To preserve the culture and regional characteristics, these color landscapes need to be analyzed in ethnic minority areas in China. The study researches the landscape of Xiangcheng County in Tibetan areas and discusses the technical strategies of color planning in ethnic minority areas. The sample selection, aesthetic evaluation, color quantification processing, and landscape factor inspection are explored from different landscape views using the Semantic Differential (SD) method and color quantitative analysis method. SD allows non-specialists to evaluate the aesthetics of landscape [15]. Then it conducts the quantitative analysis of the colors of the selected excellent and poor samples to obtain the main and auxiliary colors, embellish color layout, and offer suggestions for the color landscape design.

1.4.2. Research Questions

RQ1. *What are the colour layout about ethnic minority color-area ratio features groups of the built environment in the Tibetan area?*

RQ2. *What is the relative importance of color richness, brightness, attraction, sense of rhythm, and spatial openness in the perception of color landscape aesthetics?*

1.4.3. Theoretical and Practical Value

This study integrates theories from landscape design, psychology, cultural studies, and more, offering a new perspective for interdisciplinary research. Employing a methodological approach to studying the color landscapes of minority areas, it provides theoretical support for preserving and transmitting cultural heritage. A systematic color–area ratio quantification model was constructed in this research. Through the model, objective color perception can offer useful information for urban design. The color environment shares historical and cultural information and showcases the city's cultural and artistic characteristics [16]. The research outcomes can be directly applied to urban culture and art research.

The practical significance of the article is that it provides a theoretical to quantify color in a way that translates the laymen's perceptual color understanding into an actionable, data-driven color landscape plan. It provides landscape designers and architects with the idea of new color–area ratio designs in the Tibetan region. As conservation of these uniquely colored landscapes has the potential to attract more tourists, the results of this research may be used to boost the region's tourism and subsequent economic development. Furthermore, it can increase public awareness of environmental stewardship by protecting and highlighting the importance of ethnic minority groups' special landscape colors.

By integrating theoretical with practical concerns, this research demonstrates rigor and cutting-edge qualities in the academic field, as well as importance in practical applications. Its outcomes not only offer useful insights to designers and planners but also provide a significant theoretical and practical foundation for the protection of minority landscape cultural heritage. Moreover, by involving public participation and quantifying emotional cognition, this study pioneers a new direction in landscape design, creating new possibilities for the display of urban culture and art, as well as for creating a healthy color environment conducive to mental and physical well-being.

1.4.4. Innovation

The study focuses on the color landscapes of China's minority regions, a relatively rare focus in the field of landscape research. The innovative research method that combines traditional color quantitative analysis methods with the semantic differential technique provides a novel methodological approach to color landscape research. Moreover, this research not only focuses on the quantitative analysis of color but also values qualitative human perceptions and emotional responses, making the study more comprehensive.

1.4.5. Research Structure

The rest of this paper is structured as follows: Section 2 presents the conceptual background of color landscape; Section 3 describes the research areas and methods; Section 4 presents data collection and analysis, as well as color–area ratio factor analysis; Section 5 shows the quantitative process of color–area ratio; Section 6 is the discussion; Section 7 is the conclusion; Section 8 presents future research directions.

2. Literature Review

2.1. Color Landscape

2.1.1. Definition of Color Landscape

Color landscape synthesizes artificial decoration, such as buildings, roads, squares, and pavements, and natural colors like mountains, forests, plants, sky, and rivers [17–19]. The composition of a color landscape mainly includes distant and near views [6]. The color landscape affects people's emotions. Coupled with unique locality and nationality, the color landscape is an important part of the local landscape [20]. Color design is the focus of modern landscape design, and color can impact people's vision and psychology [16,21]. Some researchers pointed out that the regional and personalized urban landscape can be expressed through controlled color planning and design in the surroundings [22]. The color number, ratio, and layout differences can form varied color–area ratios and convey different emotional tones [14,15]. Human beings obtain 80% of their information through vision, while color is the most sensitive and direct visual information symbol, affecting people's psychological perceptions [23]. Existing studies rarely quantify landscape colors through image analysis [24]. Wang and Hu (2014) analyzed the components of community landscape colors, the specialty of design, factors influencing community landscape color, and the application of color in residential community landscape design [25]. Lengen (2015) studied the effect of colors, shapes, and boundaries of landscapes on perceptions, emotions based on space and place, and connected light aspects such as color hue, saturation, and brightness, all of which play an essential role in the perception of therapeutic landscape [6]. Cuixia (2018) analyzed the main contents and principles of color design in the landscape, providing a reference for landscape architecture designers [16].

2.1.2. Elements of Color Landscape

(1) Hue (H), Saturation (S) and Brightness (B)

Using color quantitative index HSB data analysis of hue, saturation, and brightness for analyzing landscape color environment has special research significance [4]. It is believed that hue, brightness, saturation of color, and color–area ratio of constituent color can influence color harmony and users' perception of color design [14]. (1) Hue (H) is used to distinguish different types of colors and determine the characteristics of a color landscape, and is the most easily captured by people's vision; (2) Saturation (S) is the freshness of the color perception, reflecting the vividness of the city's colors in the external space, and the purity of a city's color can fully demonstrate ambiguity and express emotion; (3) Brightness (B) refers to the perceived degree of lightness and darkness of colors, and is key objective in urban color visual design [4,26]. This article uses the HBS as an essential factor to extract color information from photographs for the next step, analysis.

(2) Color–area ratio and layout

This study adopts the color–area ratio, a color design element in product color design [14], to study landscape color. The color ratio refers to the proportional relationship between each part's length and area in the color combination design [14]. It is produced with the changes in form, position, and space, and plays a decisive role in the overall style and beauty of the color design scheme [27]. Due to the different color ratios, it is possible to create diverse landscape appearances despite using the same color. The proportion of the area occupied by the color greatly influences the effect of color layout in the landscape. Man and Wei (2019) pointed out that a color layout form should match the users' emotions for product design [15]. All in all, color layout is the spatial arrangement and distribution of colors within a composition, focusing on how colors are positioned relative to each other to achieve visual balance and harmony. In contrast, color ratio pertains to the quantitative relationship between different colors in a composition, emphasizing the proportion of one color to another to create desired visual effects or to convey specific emotions and meanings.

(3) Main color, auxiliary color, and decorative color

The three constituent colors are main color, auxiliary color, and decorative color, occupying about 70%, 25%, and 5% of the surface area of the product, respectively, which is widely adopted in the color design of color–area ratios [14]. The dominant color features determine landscapes' presentation and visual experience [24]. Urban tones are the overall effect constructed by the three colors and their combined relationships [28], as follows: (1) the primary color is a color that best reflects its cultural and landscape characteristics, which accounts for more than 70% of the ratio, and it has a certain degree of stability and sense of inheritance; (2) the colors that account for more than 20% and less than 70% can be summarized as the city's auxiliary colors, which play a role in color transition and coordination, and are determined by the color co-frequency rule in color design; and (3) the colors that account for less than 5% can be summarized as urban decorative tones, playing a role in highlighting themes.

2.1.3. Psychological Perception Elements of Color Landscape

Jonauskaite, Tremea and et al. (2020) made full use of the emotional characteristics of color for color therapy and human psychology, and rationally arranging the surrounding environment, which can effectively improve the impact of drug treatments [29]. In today's era of economic globalization, Man and Wei (2019) believed that when similar products' functions, structure, and production technology have no significant gap, their design and aesthetics must rely on the differentiation of form and color to differentiate them in the market [15]. If a research product wants to gain a foothold in the international market, it is necessary to understand the national culture of the country that the product is sold in and master its color psychology [30]. Color can express emotions intuitively, conveniently, and can directly affect people's psychology and emotions.

In addition to the importance of color to the urban landscape, color recognition is also critical. Frank Mahnke, Chairman of the International Association of Color Consultants, pointed out that seeing colors is not a simple visual process but a complex experience process [31]. It can be expressed as a physiological reaction, subconsciousness, association, cultural influence, fashion influence, and self-experience (Figure 1). From the bottom to the top of Figure 1, is the order in which color directly affects emotions and physical states (a physiological reaction); subtly affects psychology (subconsciousness); triggers specific things or emotional associations (association). Different cultures have different interpretations of colors (cultural influence). These are affected by fashion trends (fashion influence), and reflect personal preferences, personality and identity (self-experience). From the elementary to advance pyramid series, we can grasp the context that affects people's color and psychology, from physiology to psychology via the process of cultural influence. Regarding the colors: (1) white often symbolizes purity and sanctity and is commonly seen in religious buildings and ceremonies. Studying the use of white can offer deeper insights into Tibetan religious beliefs and cultural values; (2) Red brown, a color frequently found in Tibetan architecture and artifacts, is typically associated with the earth and stability, aids in understanding Tibetan lifestyles and artistic expression. (3) Yellow in Tibetan culture is associated with authority and nobility, especially in Buddhism. Studying the distribution of yellow can reveal aspects of religious and social structures. (4) Black and grey are often linked with winter, resilience, and survival challenges. Researching these colors can help others to understand how Tibetans express their relationship with the natural environment through color, etc. [15,30].

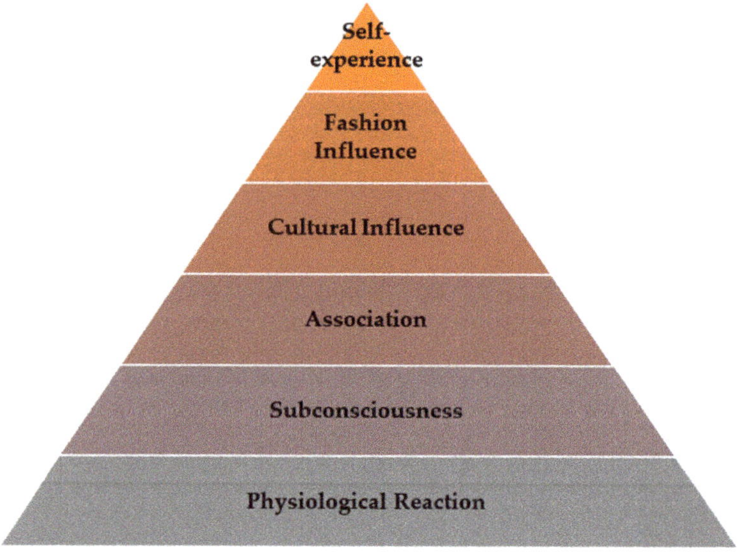

Figure 1. The process of color experience.

2.1.4. Color Quantitative Analysis Method

The color landscape can be categorized in cities and blocks, down to the building materials' details, and there is rich color information. The recording and research of this color information generally fall into qualitative and quantitative categories. Lengen (2015) studied the effect of colors, shapes and boundaries of landscapes on emotion perception by in-depth qualitative interviews [6]. The progressive development of contemporary digital technology in software and hardware has assisted landscape research in transforming from qualitative descriptions of color to quantitative instrumental data [4]. Tan (2021) proposed an automatic extraction method for color features from landscape images based on image processing through experiments [24]. Shen, Yao and Li (2021) quantitatively evaluated the color harmony and suitability degree of the plant community and external environment according to the Moon–Spencer (M-S) color harmony theory [2]. Cheng and Tan (2018) used the quantitative analysis of the color of the Ming Dynasty City Wall in Nanjing as a case study [4]. The study of Zhu, Zhang, Lan and et al. (2020) used Xunpu Village in southern Fujian as an example with which to conduct a quantitative analysis of color features and a qualitative evaluation of public perception [20]. Zhang, Chen et al. (2020) assessed the aesthetic quality of autumn landscape forest using scenic beauty estimation and analyzed the effects of color characteristics on ornamental value of autumn landscape forests based on color composition and color spatial pattern according to human visual characteristics [32]. There are many methods to describe color quantitatively and qualitatively, such as the hue, value, and chroma (HVC) model of the Munsell color system; the red, green and blue (RGB) model of the ratio of the 3-element color light; the hue, saturation, brightness (HSB) model using human eyes as the detector; the cyan, magenta, yellow, key (CMYK) model based on the mixture ratio of inks; and the Commission Internationale de l'Éclairage (CIE) color system described by pure mathematical models, etc., [4].

How to reasonably quantify and create rich color landscapes to achieve the best visual perception of the color landscape at different visual scales to meet the aesthetic needs of the public better based on culture and regional context has become a challenging issue of the landscape color design and application in ethnic minority areas. There are no studies on color landscape/color–area ratios in an ethnic minority in China. Therefore, the aim of this paper was analyze HSB, color area ratio, primary and secondary colors, and embellishment color landscape modes in ethnic minority areas. The study focuses on the color landscapes of minority regions in China, particularly the landscapes of Xiangcheng County in the Tibetan region.

2.2. SD Method

Semantic differential (SD) analysis was used to evaluate the characteristics of landscape aesthetics [33]. The SD, also known as the feeling record method, was proposed to measure psychological feelings in psychophysics [34]. The SD method uses the subject's psychological perception of language scale as the basis for evaluation and constructs quantitative data through the subject's psychological and physical perception factors [35]. In the SD method, it is necessary to design an evaluation that can objectively describe things and expand pairs of adjectives and antonyms. Some researchers studied color design by obtaining the user's color image perception based on semantic difference (SD) analysis [15]. The evaluation of landscape aesthetic quality is a crucial step in managing color landscapes [32]. In China, color is essential to distinguished ethnic minority landscapes, such as the Tibetan area of Ganzi Prefecture in Sichuan Province. Utilizing the semantic differential (SD) method, this study incorporates public aesthetic judgment into academic research, offering a new democratic path in landscape studies. Based on the color composition, color space pattern, and the SD method, it assessed the aesthetic quality. It analyzed the impact of color on the landscape values of ethnic minority areas.

The article uses the SD method to analyze the characteristics of landscape aesthetics in public spaces. It then extracts the high-quality and low-quality samples to be quantified by HSB, color ratio, and color layouts. The results of the high-quality groups can be used as typical samples for color landscape.

3. Research Area and Methods

3.1. Research Location

Xiangcheng County is in the Ganzi Tibetan Autonomous Prefecture in the West of Sichuan Province. It is located on the southwestern edge of the Qinghai–Tibet Plateau, in the north-central section of the Hengduan Mountains, spanning the 99°22′~100°04′ east longitude and 28°34′~29°39′ north latitude. It borders Daocheng to the east, Litang to the north, Batang and Derong counties to the west, and Shangri-La City, Yunnan to the south. The name is derived from the local terrain. The Chinese translation of the Tibetan word "Kashen" means the 'Buddhist beads in hand'. Xiangcheng County has a history of more than 2100 years. It is a national historical and cultural city and a famous tourist city. It is rich in historical and cultural relics. The magnificent mountain scenery and the Liujiang River form the most colorful urban landscape in Xiangcheng County [36].

3.2. Color Culture of the Study Areas

According to the people's government of Xiangcheng (http://www.xcx.gov.cn, accessed on 5 May 2023), the local cultural context is related to the colors in Xiangcheng. The "Three Wonders in Xiangcheng County" are the Fengzhuang, Baizangfang and Sangpiling Temples. First, Fengzhuang is a traditional dress worn by Xiangcheng Tibetan women. The rich color is its main feature, showing the unique ethnic culture of Xiangcheng, with colors such as red, yellow, green, black, and gold on the left and right breasts, representing the good life, land, prophets, livestock, and wealth. Second, as one of the significant architectural landscapes, the Baizangfang is the most popular type of architecture in Xiangcheng. It is characterized by white exterior walls, flat roofs, and wooden window frames, a design that accommodates the unique climatic conditions of the high-altitude region. In terms of color application, the primary use of white for the external walls contrasts with the blue and red of window frames and decorations. This color scheme reflects the aesthetic preferences inherent in Tibetan culture. The Baizangfang's white color is prominent in the natural environment. This vibrant hue has now become an integral part of the landscape, serving as a vital decoration. Its sacred and pure colors harmoniously blend to create a unique Tibetan scenery that is enriched with ethnic culture, adding depth and beauty to the surroundings. Third, Sangpiling Temple is one of the largest Gelug temples in Eastern Tibet and has a lofty status in Xiangcheng. The religious beliefs of the Tibetans affect the architectural colors. Ascending in a majestic sequence, the colors adorning the main building facade are arranged from top to bottom: golden, red, white, and black. Each hue symbolizes a profound meaning, representing loftiness, holiness, and unwavering faith. These sacred colors are held in utmost reverence by both monks and fervent believers, embodying their deep respect and profound devotion. Diverging from the conventional composition of residential buildings, the facade of this structure distinguishes itself with a trio of colors: red, white, and black. These colors artfully combine to form a three-part facade, imbuing the building with a unique visual appeal. Notably, the expansive white walls command attention, drawing the eye with their prominence. The infusion of a warm brown-red hue serves to invigorate the spirits of worshippers, fostering an atmosphere conducive to reverence. The colors of the "Three Wonders in Xiangcheng County" mirror the distinctive Tibetan landscape, convey profound national beliefs, and offer spiritual nourishment.

3.3. Sample Collection and Research Method

The research methods employed in this study center around the chromaticity measurement of images [37]. These methods enable precise and calibrated assessment of the visual attributes of samples. This research uses meticulous data analysis to extract the color spectrum that aligns with the traditional hues found in landscapes associated with ethnic minority groups. Researchers make field observations, photographs, and video recordings of landscape elements such as buildings, mountains, water bodies, vegetation, etc., extract image and image color information (removal of color deviations caused by weather, light, cameras, and other related factors), establish a color database for observation points, and analyze and summarize database information. Then, the current color database can be summarized to objectively reflect Xiangcheng County.

The landscapes in the research were classified into landscape aerial view, residential buildings, religious buildings, streets, farmland, and local materials [38–40]. Moreover, the landscape was segmented into three categories according to the distance of sight: distant view, middle view, and nearby view [41,42] The distant view type is mainly an aerial view;

the middle view type includes residential and temple buildings, streets, and farmlands; and the nearby view type mainly includes the local material details of landscape architecture (Table 1).

Table 1. Sample classification and selection basis.

Landscape View	Color Landscape Elements	Basis and Key Points for Sample Selection in Xiangcheng	Sources
Distant view	Aerial View	**Large-area color landscape data are selected from commanding heights in the core area of Xiangcheng by a bird's-eye view to collect: S1 and S2.** • The aerial view shows the terrain and natural colors, such as the farmland's green contrasting with the Baizangfang's white. • It can reflect the connection between Tibetan culture and the natural environment. From a high altitude, one can see how buildings and farmland blend harmoniously with the natural landscape.	A bird' s-eye view can provide a color layout of the main study area [43–45]. It can also observe the overall harmony and contrast of colors in natural and man-made environments—for example, the color boundaries between urban and natural areas [46].
Middle view	Architecture	**The local representative residential buildings and temples are selected, almost designed and constructed by local people: S3, S4, S5.** • Baizangfang is a unique residential architectural form of the Garze Tibetan people. Its white exterior walls and wooden frame reflect Tibetan living habits and aesthetics. • Religious buildings such as the Sangpiling Temple use traditional red and golden colors. Temples' architectural style and decorative details are important for studying Tibetan cultural identity and religious beliefs.	Architecture is an integral part of the urban/rural landscape, and architectural color becomes the protagonist of urban/rural color [47,48]. It sometimes even determines the color construction of the entire city/countryside [49].
	Street	**This study selected streets with core landscape nodes: S6, S7, and S8.** • Bright colored shops and religious symbols, such as prayer flags and colorful flags, are common on streets in Xiangcheng, reflecting Tibetan religious and daily life. • The use of color on the street is an expression of visual aesthetics and a reflection of community cohesion and cultural heritage.	Streets are landscape corridors and important activity spaces in cities, and their color analysis helps to understand the vitality and functionality of cities and rural areas [50,51]. This analysis includes pavement materials, street trees, street buildings, and other elements [52].
	Farmland	**This study selected angles that can reflect the overall farmland layout and detailed characteristics of the crop landscape: S9, S10, and S11.** • Farmland color shows a harmonious integration with the natural environment. For example, the color of crops forms a visual coordination with the surrounding sky, mountains and other natural landscapes. • Farmland layouts often follow traditional terrain utilization, demonstrating the relationship between topography and water sources.	The changing colors of farmlands reflect the changing seasons and the type of agricultural activity [53].

Table 1. *Cont.*

Landscape View	Color Landscape Elements	Basis and Key Points for Sample Selection in Xiangcheng	Sources
Nearby view	Local Materials	**Materials such as landscape retaining walls, building walls, painted wooden beams, and carved door lintels are selected: S12, S13, and S14.** • The natural materials used in Tibetan architecture and landscapes, such as stone, wood, etc., their natural colors and processed colors demonstrate Tibetan environmental adaptability and aesthetics. • These materials maintain their natural color and texture.	The natural and processed colors of materials (such as stone, wood, metal, etc.) used in architecture and landscape design directly affect the color effect of the overall landscape [54,55].

Note: The above sample collection basis and key points come from the People's Government of Xiangcheng (http://www.xcx.gov.cn, accessed on 15 April 2024).

From 6 different landscape perspectives, a total of 14 color–area ratio samples were selected from landscape research area and numbered S1, S2, S3, S4, S5, S6, S7, S8, S9, S10, S11, S12, S13, and S14, respectively (Table 2). The selection process was conducted by interviewing three landscape design specialists who research color landscape design and cultural heritage protection. The sample comprised 58 pictures, among which 14 samples were selected.

Table 2. Selected samples.

Type	No.	Sample Photographs	Type	No.	Sample Photographs
Aerial View	S1		Street	S8	
	S2		Farmland	S9	
Residential architecture	S3			S10	

Table 2. *Cont.*

Type	No.	Sample Photographs	Type	No.	Sample Photographs
Residential architecture	S4			S11	
Religious architecture	S5		Local Materials	S12	
Street	S6			S13	
	S7			S14	

Note: The research samples were collected via key landscape nodes in the main local tourist routes, and the landscape samples were collected based on the basis listed in Table 1.

4. Color–Area Ratio Factor Analysis

4.1. SD Factor Analysis

4.1.1. Selection of SD Evaluation Factors

Fourteen landscape samples (S1 to S14) were used for the analysis. Respondents scored each of these from −2 to 2. The results were then tabulated and calculated to obtain their average values. Those average values were plotted into an SD graphic and analyzed by factor analysis. This factor analysis was used to reduce landscape characteristic variables. This analysis found six factor (X_1 to X_6) variables, presented in Table 3, including the set of color landscape aesthetic characteristics [56]. This research project collected adjective pairs when designing the evaluation scale and constructing the questionnaire, understanding the SD method's specific meaning, and referring to the SD method in landscape color, artistic color, architecture, and gardens. The word pairs used above, combined with SPSS for principal component analysis, finally adopted six groups of adjective pairs; that is, six common factors from X_1 to X_6 were screened out (Table 3). The six common factors formed two groups: (1) the physical perception of human vision—spatial openness, sense of rhythm, color richness; and (2) psychological perception—attractiveness, shading and aesthetic degree.

Table 3. SD factor adjective pairs.

No.	SD Evaluation Factor	SD Evaluation Adjective Pair
X_1	Spatial openness	Open--------Closed
X_2	Sense of rhythm	Strong--------Weak
X_3	Color richness	Colorful--------Monotonous
X_4	Attraction	Attractive--------Unattractive
X_5	Color brightness	Bright--------Dark
X_6	Aesthetic degree	Aesthetic--------Not aesthetic

Xiangcheng's landscape and urban color–area ratio samples in the original state decide the SD evaluation factors. These factors comprise spatial openness (X_1), sense of rhythm (X_2), and color richness (X_3); psychological perception includes attraction (X_4), color brightness (X_5), and aesthetic degree (X_6). A total of six pairs of adjectives were constructed according to the Tibetan characteristics of Xiangcheng's landscapes, (1) "Open" and "Closed" were used to describe spatial openness (X_1); (2) "Strong" and "Weak" were used to describe the sense of rhythm (X_2); (3) "Colorful" and "Monotonous" were used to describe color richness (X_3); (4) "Attractive" and "Unattractive" were used to describe psychological perceptions, including attraction (X_4); (5) "Bright" and "Dark" were used to describe color brightness (X_5); (6) and "Aesthetic" and "Not aesthetic" were used to describe aesthetic degree (X_6). (Table 3).

4.1.2. Evaluation Scale and Questionnaire Design

The evaluation scale was based on the "bi-polar" principle to facilitate quantitative statistical analysis. Generally, the evaluation scale of adjective pairs is divided into 5–7 levels to conduct quantitative statistics [57,58]. To increase the accuracy and convenience of the evaluation, this paper set the evaluation scale at five levels to carry out the questionnaire design and quantitative statistics [14]. The 5-level evaluation scale was set to symmetrical: 2, 1, 0, −1, −2, as shown in Table 4. Among all 18 questions, 14 used the five-level scale to score 14 figure samples from S1 to S14, as shown in Tables 2 and 4.

Table 4. Evaluation scale and questionnaire design.

		Very Poor	Poor	Average	Good	Very Good	
No.	**Right Adjective Pair**	**−2**	**−1**	**0**	**1**	**2**	**Left Adjective Pair**
1	Open						Closed
2	Strong						Weak
3	Colorful						Monotonous
4	Attractive						Unattractive
5	Bright						Dark
6	Aesthetic						Not aesthetic

4.1.3. Subject Selection and Questionnaire Survey

To improve the accuracy of the research results, this research conducted questionnaire surveys on gender, occupation, age, scope, and number of subjects. Using purposeful sampling methods, this survey study included 274 professionals in the landscape design industry and non-professionals in the non-landscape sector, accounting for 30% and 70% of the total subjects, respectively. Table 5 reveals that there were more women than men and most were between 18 and 29 years old (73.36%). The survey sample mainly were from students major in landscape and related subjects (23.72%) and students of other majors (35.04%) with Bachelor's degrees (72.63%).

Table 5. Data analysis of Samples.

Item	Classification	Number of People	Percentage
Gender	Male	97	35.40%
	Female	177	64.60%
Age	12–17 Years Old	4	1.46%
	18–29 Years Old	201	73.36%
	30–45 Years Old	40	14.60%
	45–59 Years Old	25	9.12%
	Over 60 Years Old	4	1.46%
Degree	Primary School	1	0.36%
	Junior Middle School	7	2.55%
	Junior High School	16	5.84%
	Bachelor	199	72.63%
	Master	45	16.42%
	Ph.D.	6	2.19%
Work	Landscape And Related Fields Work	29	10.58%
	Other Areas Of Work	44	16.06%
	Students Majoring In Landscape And Related Majors	65	23.72%
	Students Of Other Majors	96	35.04%
	Unemployment	4	1.46%
	Retiree	6	2.19%
	Others	30	10.95%

4.1.4. Average Analysis

The questionnaire was analyzed, and the scale evaluation data of each sample from S1 to S4 were extracted using the SPSS 22.0 software. The data of the six evaluation factors of spatial openness (X_1), sense of rhythm (X_2), color richness (X_3), attraction (X_4), color brightness (X_5), and aesthetic degree (X_6) were averaged and weighted via SPSS 22.0 to obtain a sample statistics table (Table 6). The sample of S5 (weighted value 1.098) represents the characteristic religious buildings in rural areas, and the sample of S13 (weighted value 0.425) represents the details of landscape materials. Among the various evaluation indicators, spatial openness (X1) is the highest (S10, 1.29); the lowest is (S14, 0.09); the sense of rhythm (X2) is the highest (S4, 1.13), the lowest is (S1, 0.20); the highest color richness value is S5 (1.21), the lowest is (S1, 0.02); the most attractive is (S14, 1.1.0), the lowest is (S1, 0.22); the color brightness (X5) is the highest is (S14, 1.17), the lowest is (S10, 0.54); the highest aesthetic is (S13, 1.17), and the lowest is (S8, 0.33). It can be concluded that: among all the samples, S10 makes the public feel the most open and spatial; S4 gives the most comfortable rhythm of landscape; S5 consists of the most kinds of colors; S14 is the most attractive among them; S14 makes the public experience brightest landscape; and S13 is the most aesthetic landscape. The final comparison of the weighted scores from high to low is: S5 > S3 > S14 > S6 > S9 > S12 > S4 > S7 > S11 > S10 > S2 > S8 > S1 > S13. Therefore, the results show that the evaluator's sense of identity with the landscape samples gradually weakens from S5 to S13.

Table 6. SD method analysis results of Xiangcheng's color–area ratio.

		X_1	X_2	X_3	X_4	X_5	X_6	Weighted Value
		Spatial Openness	Sense of Rhythm	Color Richness	Attraction	Color Brightness	Aesthetic Degree	
Sample Statistics	S_1	1.13	0.20	0.02	0.22	0.68	0.39	0.449
	S_2	1.09	0.30	0.12	0.27	0.70	0.39	0.490
	S_3	0.85	0.95	1.20	1.08	1.21	1.17	1.092
	S_4	0.87	1.13	0.66	0.44	0.85	0.67	0.766
	S_5	1.04	1.06	1.21	1.05	1.07	1.02	1.098

Table 6. Cont.

		X_1 Spatial Openness	X_2 Sense of Rhythm	X_3 Color Richness	X_4 Attraction	X_5 Color Brightness	X_6 Aesthetic Degree	Weighted Value
Sample Statistics	S_6	0.66	0.75	1.32	0.92	0.98	0.94	0.985
	S_7	0.83	0.49	0.74	0.72	0.87	0.78	0.761
	S_8	0.70	0.45	0.23	0.35	0.76	0.33	0.474
	S_9	1.27	0.76	0.66	0.73	1.02	0.76	0.881
	S_{10}	1.29	0.42	0.32	0.57	0.54	0.65	0.626
	S_{11}	0.94	0.64	0.57	0.52	0.78	0.58	0.689
	S_{12}	0.78	0.62	0.72	0.67	1.00	0.75	0.776
	S_{13}	0.55	0.37	0.25	0.29	0.65	0.44	0.425
	S_{14}	0.09	1.01	1.43	1.10	1.17	1.13	1.005
Average		0.86	0.65	0.68	0.64	0.88	0.71	0.715

4.2. Data and Analysis

4.2.1. Kaiser–Meyer–Olkin (KMO) and Bartlett's Test

Kaiser–Meyer–Olkin (KMO), Bartlett's sphericity test, and factor analysis for dimensionality reduction ensures that the evaluation factors have high correlation and low overlap [15]. The questionnaire data were imported into the SPSS22.0 to perform KMO and Bartlett sphere detection using factor analysis (Table 7). The KMO value was 0.781 > 0.5, and the significance of Bartlett's sphericity test (Sig) was 0.000 < 0.05, indicating good validity of the questionnaire setting and strong SD factor correlation. Therefore, factor analysis for dimensionality reduction could be performed to analyze data.

Table 7. KMO and Bartlett's test.

KMO Sampling Suitability Quantity		0.781
Bartlett Sphericity Test	Approximate chi-square	228.289
	Degree of freedom (DF)	15
	Significance (sig)	0.000

4.2.2. SD Factor Analysis

The total variance explanation was obtained by the factor analysis for dimensionality reduction using SPSS 22.0 software, showing that just one factor can be chosen as the common factor, and the common factor can evaluate 76.9% of the internal relationship of color–area ratio quantification (Table 8). Therefore, when the number of landscape factors is small, and the independence of a few factors is high, these factors can also reflect the validity of quantification of the original data of color–area ratio factors in ethnic minority areas.

Table 8. Total variance explanation.

	Initial Eigenvalue			Extract the Sum of Squares of the Load		
	Total	Variance%	Total %	Total	Variance%	Total %
1	4.616	76.934	76.934	4.616	76.934	76.934
2	0.847	14.122	91.056			
3	0.318	5.304	96.359			
4	0.170	2.830	99.189			
5	0.031	0.521	99.710			
6	0.017	0.290	100.000			

The correlation matrix of color–area ratio evaluation factors (Table 9) can intuitively reflect the correlation between various color–area ratio factors and show that human vision and landscape interaction will change psychological perception. Therefore, colors are related to a person's psychological feelings. While color gives people a sense of beauty, it also affects people's psychological activities in many ways. Color psychological feelings can be generated from direct visual stimuli or obtained through simple associations and symbols. In short, it unconsciously influences people's emotions, thoughts, and behaviors [6]. The X1 in the SD factor is low, with a low load. Therefore, X_1 has a relatively weak relationship with X_2, X_3, X_4, X_5, and X_6, showing that the effect of spatial openness on the evaluation of color visual perception and psychological perception is weak.

Table 9. Factor correlation matrix.

	Spatial Openness	Sense of Rhythm	Color Richness	Attraction	Color Brightness	Aesthetic Degree
X_1	1.000	−0.289	−0.472	−0.312	−0.390	−0.316
X_2	−0.289	1.000	0.815	0.736	0.772	0.779
X_3	−0.472	0.815	1.000	0.953	0.873	0.951
X_4	−0.312	0.736	0.953	1.000	0.863	0.976
X_5	−0.390	0.772	0.873	0.863	1.000	0.863
X_6	−0.316	0.779	0.951	0.976	0.863	1.000

4.2.3. Establishment of Evaluation Model

According to the above analysis, a common factor was extracted from the cumulative contribution rate of the variance of each color–area ratio evaluation factor, and the proportion of the total variance contribution rate of the common factor was used as the weight for a weighted summary:

(1) Standardized value of landscape evaluation factor: $F1 = \sqrt{|Xi * 76.934|}$
(2) Comprehensive landscape evaluation factor $F = 76.934 \times F1/76.934$

Table 10 shows that the SD evaluation factors, including space openness, sense of rhythm, color richness, attraction, color brightness, and aesthetic degree, can significantly impact the color–area ratio evaluation in Xiangcheng. Among the six SD factors, color richness has the highest score and has the most significant impact on color evaluation. Secondly, spatial openness has the lowest impact factor on color evaluation. These factors reflect a unique Tibetan cultural style and the unique colour artistic value of the colour–area ratio in Xiangcheng. Compared with the sense of rhythm, color richness, attractiveness, brightness, and aesthetics, the evaluation score of spatial openness is low, and the gap is large. The results show that spatial openness did not receive much attention when evaluating the landscape. In addition, the evaluators are more concerned about color richness than spatial openness. Thus, color plays a vital role in landscape design; color richness is the most important influencing factor to impact color landscape based on public aesthetics evaluation. According to the results, it is necessary to analyze the color characteristics quantitatively.

Table 10. Factor score coefficient and ranking.

X_i	X (Factor Score)	F (Overall Score)	Ranking
(X_1)	0.100	0.2300	6
(X_2)	0.186	0.596	5
(X_3)	0.213	0.713	1
(X_4)	0.207	0.607	3
(X_5)	0.209	0.609	2
(X_6)	0.201	0.601	4

5. Color Quantitative Analysis

The color–area ratio quantification method uses Photoshop, ColorImpact, etc., to objectively analyze HSB color and RGB values in the landscape, which differs from subjective judgment through the perception of human vision [59]. Data obtained from the color quantification samples were screened and classified to obtain typical samples. Color–area ratio quantitative data, such as hue (H), saturation (S), brightness (B), etc., were analyzed to obtain the quantitative standard of the color–area ratio in Xiangcheng.

5.1. Color–Area Ratio

Three samples were imported into Photoshop to pixelize them. The sample pixel file, as the value according to the pixel square 100 unit, was rasterized, and the digitized image was extracted. Finally, the digitized image was imported into ColorImpact V4.1.2. The distribution range of each color was highlighted, and the proportions of its color areas were quantified (Table 11).

Table 11. The distribution range of each color HSB.

Type	No.	Samples	Type	No.	Samples
Aerial View	S1	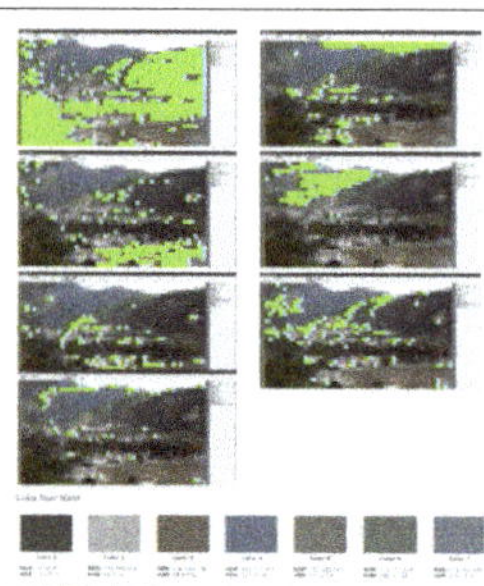	Street	S8	
	S2	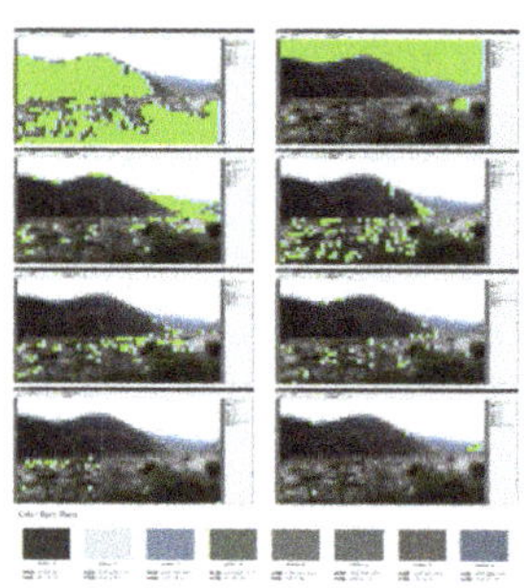	Farmland	S9	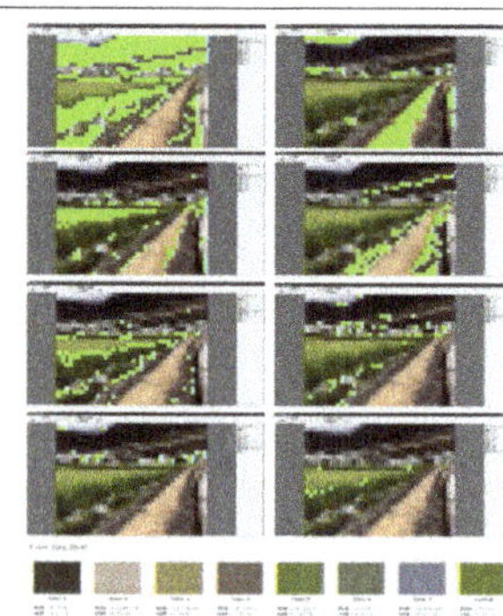

Table 11. *Cont.*

Type	No.	Samples	Type	No.	Samples
Residential architectures	S3	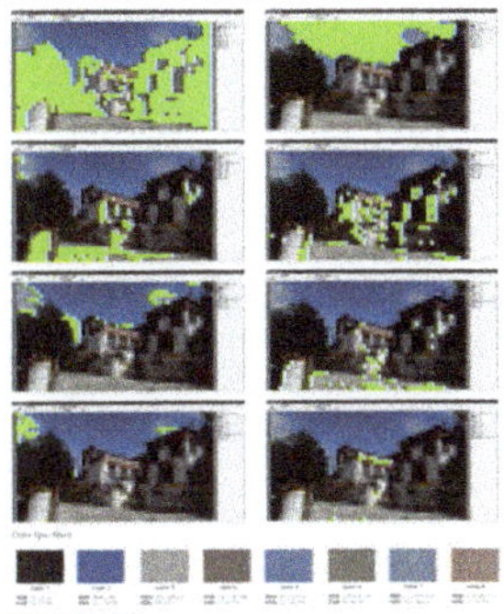	Farmland	S10	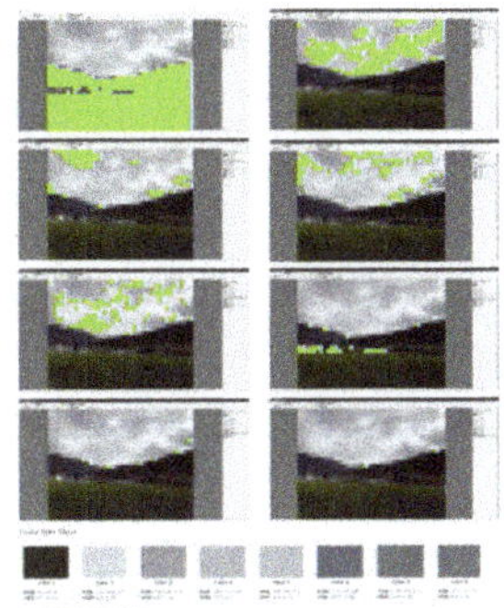
Religious Architectures	S4	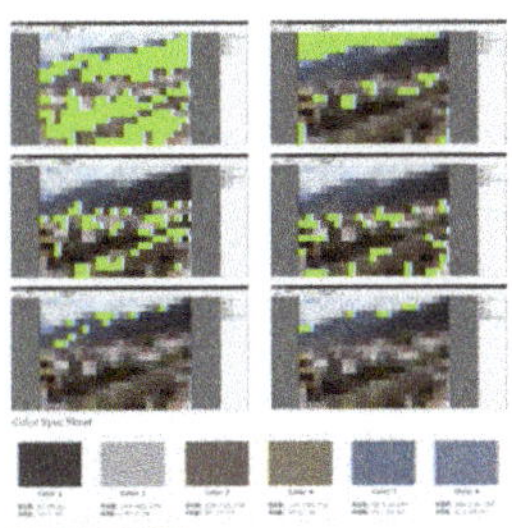		S11	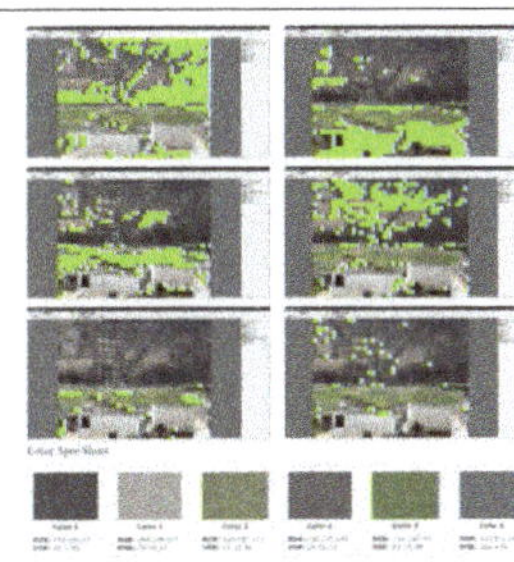
	S5	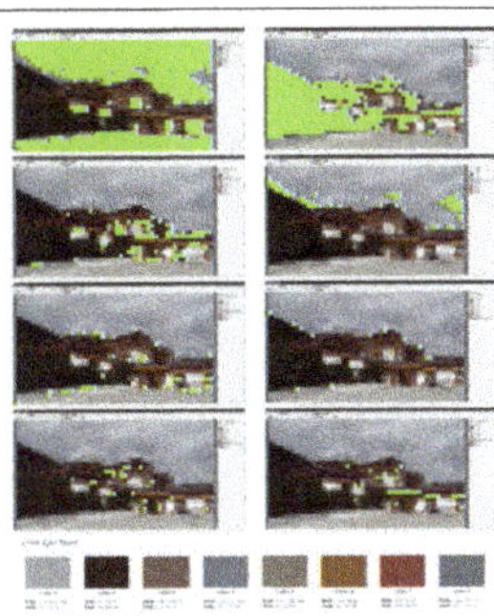	Materials	S12	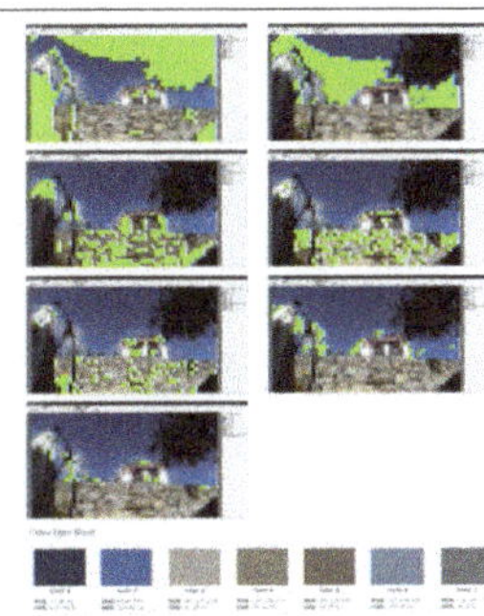
Street	S6	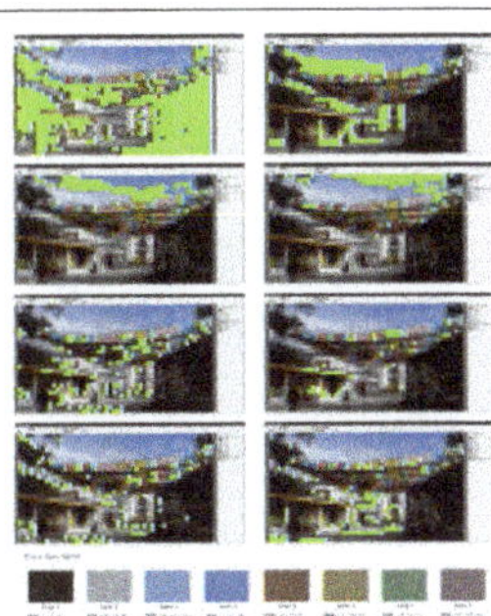		S13	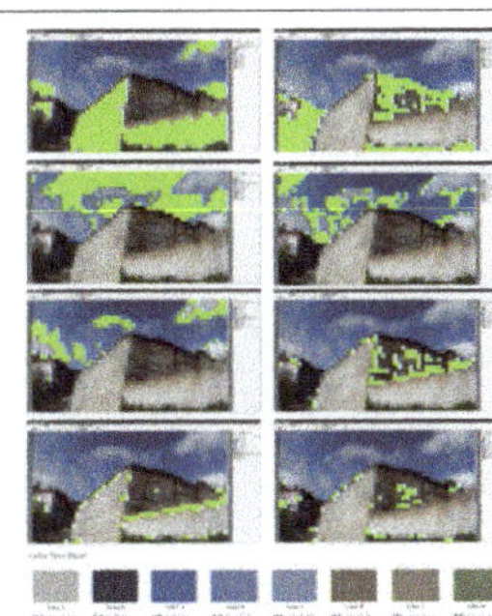

Table 11. *Cont.*

Type	No.	Samples	Type	No.	Samples
Street	S7	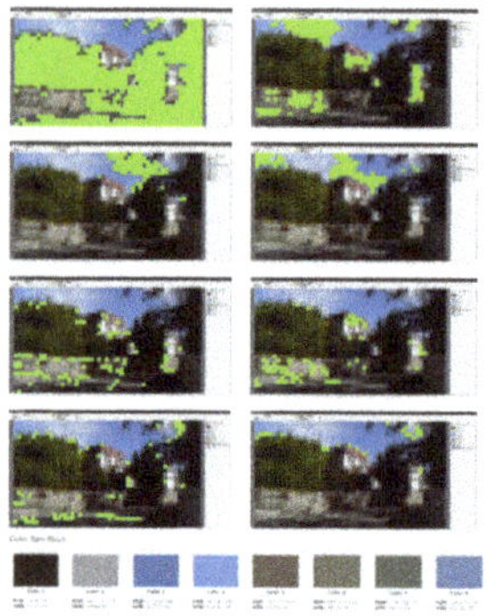	Materials	S14	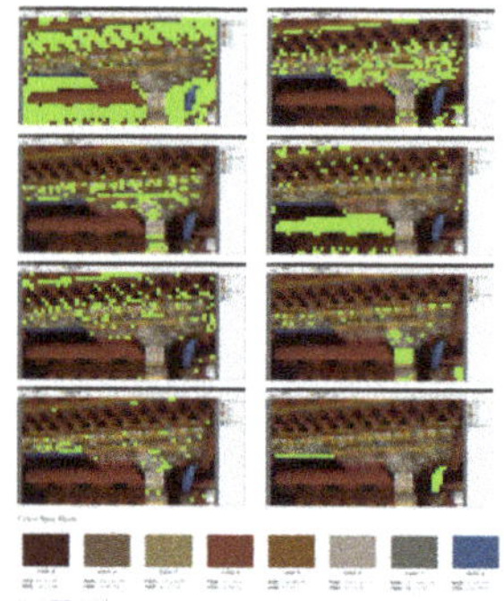

5.2. Analysis of Main and Auxiliary Colors and Embellishments

According to the evaluation value obtained by the SD method, the top five samples with high aesthetic degrees (S5, S3, S14, S6, and S9) were classified as group A, and the last five samples with low aesthetic degrees (S10, S2, S8, S1, and S13) were classified as group B. Color quantitative analysis was performed on the two groups of samples using ColorImpact based on the color HSB information from Table 11. All sample color modes were set as 32 colors to ensure the unity of the quantitative analysis and color balance.

A comparison of Tables 12 and 13 shows that group A's main and auxiliary colors are prominent. Group A is mainly composed of white, reddish brown, yellow, black, and natural colors such as mountain green and sky blue as the main, and auxiliary colors with yellow, red, green, black, and blue in the same color tones as embellishments that represent the theme of the color landscape. Therefore, the whole picture is rich in color without affecting the expression of the overall tone. In contrast, the color distribution in Group B is more balanced between the main and auxiliary colors. The main color in Group B does not stand out as a dominant single hue, resulting in a more subtle and uniform color composition. Additionally, the embellishment colors used in Group B are more monotonous and less varied when compared to the diverse palette employed in Group A.

Table 12. Color quantitative analysis of the samples in group A.

No.	Samples	Main and Auxiliary Colors	Embellishments
S5			
S3			
S14			No

Table 12. *Cont.*

No.	Samples	Main and Auxiliary Colors	Embellishments
S_6			
S_9			No

Table 13. Color quantitative analysis of samples in group B.

No.	Samples	Main and Auxiliary Colors	Embellishments
S_{10}			No
S_2			No
S_8			
S_1			No
S_{13}			

5.3. Color Layout

According to the color layout analysis of the samples in groups A and B, the influence of the color layout on the aesthetic evaluation was obtained (Tables 14 and 15). The color layout of group A has the characteristics of rich colors, strong contrast, and coordinated pictures, reflecting the characteristics of Xiangcheng's color–area ratio. The color layout of group B is monotonous, and the contrast is not apparent. Although the color tone in group B is uniform, the color richness is weak and cannot reflect the characteristics of Xiangcheng's color–area ratio. Therefore, color richness and coordination in the picture are essential for the color layout, which can affect the aesthetic degree.

Table 14. Group A color layout.

No.	S_5	S_3	S_{14}	S_6	S_9
Samples					
Color layout	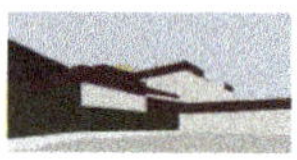				
Single analysis	48% Gray, 10% white, and 22% green make up the main area of the picture, occupying a balanced proportion, and the picture is coordinated. The 18% reddish brown and 2% yellow of the building reflect the characteristics of ethnic temples.	34% Blue and 18% white occupy the main area of the picture, and the facade of the building is decorated in many colors and rich in colors, reflecting the ethnic color.	The colors are rich, reflecting the ethnic characteristics of rural areas.	The prayer flags' colour is the most direct embodiment of the ethic color, and the picture is coordinated.	The colors of the fields, paths, and mountains, and buildings are in strong contrast.
Overall analysis	The pictures in the color layout of group A have rich colors, strong contrast, and coordinated pictures, which can reflect the color characteristics of Xiangcheng's landscape.				

Table 15. Group B color layout.

No.	S_{10}	S_2	S_8	S_1	S_{13}
Samples					
Color layout			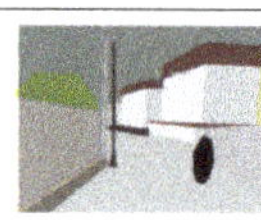	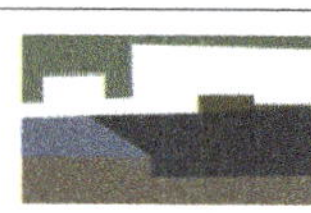	
Single analysis	The picture is coordinated, but the color is monotonous, without the unique color of Xiangcheng, and cannot reflect the ethnic characteristics.	The green in the foreground occludes the white of the building, causing the space to be fragmented and the color monotonous.	White takes up a large proportion, and the color is monotonous.	The environmental color ratio is too large, and the main color is not prominent.	Blue and white are in contrast, the contrast is strong, but the color is monotonous and cannot reflect ethnic characteristics.
Overall analysis	The color layout of group B is monotonous, and the contrast is not apparent. Although the color tone is uniform, it does not reflect Xiangcheng's characteristics.				

6. Discussion

6.1. Colorscape's Quantitative Model Should Be Coordinated and Unified with the Environment

The quantitative expression of Xiangcheng's landscape color is a research process based on a comprehensive interpretation of the objective laws of the color characteristics of static viewing environments. The use of analysis software to objectively and rationally analyze the HSB measurement thresholds of the color effects of spatial elements. It is different from the subjective judgment of color that relies on human eye function and perceptual cognition. The color average quantitative data obtained in the study are typical representative data extracted after classifying and filtering the data. From the qualitative and quantitative research process and methods of the color effects of Ming city walls [4], it can be seen that the selection of sample sheets and quadrats in this study can fully represent the color composition characteristics of Xiangcheng and the presentation of color visual effects under ideal outdoor viewing conditions. Xiangcheng's color data, obtained through quantitative data analysis of hue, saturation, and brightness (HSB), can be used as the basis for color planning and in the design of rural and urban landscapes.

Furthermore, the results of the study indicated that colors should be coordinated and unified with the environment. Local materials and plants should be fully utilized as much as possible to coordinate the landscape and the original environment of the area. The interrelationship between color–area ratios also determines the effect of the color–area ratio. Using and processing the law of unity and change between colors correctly can create a rich color change effect in a significant positive relationship.

6.2. The Quantitative Influences of Landscape Color Evaluation Factors

The quantitative influences of various landscape color evaluation factors on the landscape color in Tibetan areas are as follows: color richness (X3) > color brightness (X5) > attraction (X4) > aesthetic degree (X6) > sense of rhythm (X2) > spatial openness (X1). Among these factors, color richness and color brightness, which rank as the top two, are more intuitive for color expression and stimulate vision more easily. Therefore, the more attention paid to the color richness and color brightness by people, the more popular the landscape, indicating that the richness and brightness of colors are vital in color–area ratio design. The factors of color brightness, attraction, and aesthetic degree, which are partial to the psychological perception of landscape color descriptions, have received less attention than color richness. However, these factors are also important for design expressions in landscape color moods. The sense of rhythm ranks fifth among these six factors. Color spatial openness has received the lowest attention, indicating no absolute relationship between the color–area ratio design and spatial openness. Therefore, the intuitive visual expression of color, psychological emotion, and artistic conception is indispensable in color–area ratio planning and design.

6.3. The Different Color Landscapes with Specific Color Layouts

The component characteristics of the color landscape are rich in color without affecting the expression of the overall tone in Xiangcheng. At the same time, the color landscape design in Xiangcheng is mainly composed of white, reddish brown, yellow, black, and natural colors, such as mountain green and sky blue, as the main and auxiliary colors with yellow, red, green, black, and blue in the same color tones as embellishments. Most of the embellishments are colors with cultural contexts in Xiangcheng. The color landscape in the color layout should have rich colors, strong contrast, and a coordinated color ratio that can reflect the color characteristics of Xiangcheng's landscape. The results from Section 5.3, Tables 14 and 15, show different color landscapes with specific quantitative color layouts.

(1) For religious architecture design, 48% Gray, 10% white, and 22% green occupy a balanced proportion, and the color landscape is coordinated. At the same time, the 18% reddish brown and 2% yellow of the building reflect the characteristics of ethnic temples. From the perspective of the relationship between cultural heritage and color, these buildings serve as centers of cultural and religious activities. Their colors retain rich

traditional arts and craftsmanship contexts, demonstrating the Tibetan people's spiritual pursuits and cultural values. Analyzing architectural color can provide insight for designers to enhance the beauty of a building and its relationship to its surroundings. Attention is paid to of conserving and restoring buildings to maintain their historical and cultural value. Nonetheless, the application of traditional colors in modern architecture can be further studied;

(2) For residential architecture design, 34% blue and 18% white are needed, and the facade of the building is decorated in many colors, reflecting the ethnic culture. The layout and proportion of the colors of the surrounding environment, such as the Baizangfang and the sky, align with the aesthetic values of nature. It can also reflect the structure and cultural identity of Tibetan society, such as the social status of the family (such as the color and area of Baizangfang, the number of building floors, the form of painting, etc.) and the climatic conditions of the region environment (such as the blue sky, clean and pollution-free surroundings, etc.);

(3) For materials design and applications, the colors are rich, reflecting the ethnic characteristics of rural areas. The richness of colors of the materials not only reflects the characteristics of the natural environment but also embodies the Tibetan culture's emphasis on the harmonious symbiosis of nature. Therefore, the relationship between culture and materials is very important. The color selection and processing (such as painting and carving) techniques of traditional materials reflect Tibetan environmental protection concepts and commitment to sustainable development. The natural colors of wood and stone are often used to construct residences and temples. Analyzing the colors of these materials can help designers use different materials to reveal their unique color properties under the influence of natural light, making them harmonious with their surroundings;

(4) For street design, the color of the prayer flags has the most direct embodiment of ethnic colors, and the picture is coordinated. In addition, street elements also include pavement materials, street trees, street buildings and other components. The color combination of these elements can affect people's emotions and behavioral patterns. For example, bright and colorful streets may attract more tourists and shoppers. Combined with the application of color psychology, street color can enhance the spiritual outlook of the community and happiness of residents, and enhance the cultural confidence and identity of the region. However, a comparative analysis showed that, in one of the streetscape samples appearing in Group B, white takes up a large proportion of the sample; the color is monotonous, and the results show a relatively negative result. The streetscape in this area may be too monochromatic due to the monotony of landscape elements. Future color planning can be optimized concerning the proportion and type of architectural colors;

(5) For farmland design, the colors of the fields, paths, mountains, and buildings are in strong contrast. This reflects the characteristics of strong local color contrast but overall coordination between farmland and the surrounding natural and cultural environments. Additionally, by analyzing the color of farmlands, crop maturity, planting patterns, and their integration with the natural landscape can be observed. From the perspective of color and environmental sustainability, color management on farmlands emphasises ecological sustainability, such as using multiple crop rotations to increase biodiversity. Future research can collect farmland samples in different seasons for analysis. Seasonal changes in farmland color not only improve the beauty of farmlands and promote ecological balance.

(6) On the contrary, from an aerial view, the white color of traditional Tibetan roofs and walls stands out against the green, natural background. White has special significance in Xiangcheng Tibetan culture. There is a special local festival, "White Filling Ceremony". It is an ancient custom in which Tibetans use a local white clay diluted with water and then pour a layer of white clay on the outer walls and courtyard walls of Tibetan houses. However, the green in the sample's foreground blocks the building's white, resulting in fragmented space and monotonous colors. Although the color richness is weak and cannot reflect the characteristics of Xiangcheng's color–area ratio, it can reflect whether the whole color landscape is uniform. Thus, the color layout of the bird's-eye-view sample provides a

unique perspective. It can help analyze the color transition between different areas and be used to study the spatial layout and color application of Tibetan areas to reflect their social structure and cultural values.

6.4. Research Limitations

Studying Tibetan color landscapes is not merely an investigation of colors themselves, but a deep exploration of Tibetan culture, religion, social structure, and interactions with the natural environment. This research provides a comprehensive perspective to understand and appreciate the rich and colorful cultural heritage of Tibetan area. However, this research has certain limitations, as follows: (1) The complex terrain of Tibetan area and the inaccessibility of many areas may limit field investigations and data collection in certain regions [60,61]; (2) Due to language and cultural differences, non-Tibetan researchers may face challenges in fully comprehending the deep meanings of colors in Tibetan culture; (3) Current color analysis technologies and methodologies might not adequately capture and interpret the complex cultural and environmental factors influencing color landscapes; and (4) The selection of a limited sample of investigation, 14 images, and only with 6 factors to do factor analysis and one common factor could be a limitation of this study. When estimating factor loadings, a problem we may face is specifying too few factors (under-decomposition) or too many (over-decomposition), although the latter results in less error [62]. However, specifying too many factors can lead to the creation of constructs that have little theoretical value [62]. One of the fundamental questions for multivariate observations is the true actual number of principal components or factors in the underlying data-generating model. Determining this number of factors is a complicated and long standing problem [63]. Furthermore, the difference in whether conditions were detected by pictures could represent a bias in the study.

7. Conclusions

With the updating of digital technology, color physical properties and visual and psychological perception are described using quantitative and qualitative methods in color landscape in forests, urban and rural areas, etc. [4]. However, the lack of a common and good cognition standard for colorscapes in ethnic minority areas has led to a separation of planning from the local public and cultural environments and to a lack of identity. Quantitatively selecting and using traditional ethnic minority color elements in landscape design in Tibetan areas is a research gap in current landscape research. Therefore, the evaluation and analysis of the color–area ratio, the color quantification process, and the construction of quantification standards are all problems faced by color–area ratio quantitative research in Tibetan areas. This study combined the SD method and the color quantitative analysis method to systematically analyze color–area ratio quantitative research in Tibetan areas. Based on the SD method evaluation, the factor analysis for dimensionality reduction was carried out to test whether the correlation and overlap of the SD evaluation factors were reasonable. The common factors of color–area ratio design were extracted based on qualified inspection, making the quantitative study of the color–area ratio in minority areas objective and reasonable, enhancing the operability of the design. In the survey process, it is also necessary to strengthen collaboration with local researchers and communities, leveraging their deep understanding of local culture to overcome barriers to cultural comprehension.

8. Further Research Directions

(1) Develop advanced color analysis tools and methods to more accurately capture and analyze the subtle variations in Tibetan color landscapes, encourage interdisciplinary team collaborations, integrate perspectives from anthropology, cultural studies, psychology, and more, for a comprehensive understanding of Tibetan color landscapes;

(2) Conduct long-term studies to explore the changes in Tibetan color landscapes over time and the socio-cultural and environmental factors these changes reflect. For example, the samples about distinguished color landscapes may be comparatively studied

in different seasons; or studied in different periods during the day and night to compare colorscapes under natural light and artificial light;

(3) Comparing the color landscapes of Xiangcheng County with other Tibetan regions can reveal cultural and environmental differences among regions. Comparing Tibetan color landscape research with similar studies in other regions or cultures can be used to explore the commonalities and differences in color usage across different cultures. Using the same methodology to study other urban/rural areas outside Tibetan areas could be a future research direction and make the results generalizable for other urban/rural areas.

Author Contributions: Conceptualization, L.Z. and R.L.; methodology, L.Z. and R.Y.M.L.; software, R.L. and L.Z.; validation, L.Z. and R.Y.M.L.; formal analysis, L.Z. and R.Y.M.L.; investigation, L.Z. and R.L.; resources, L.Z., R.L. and R.Y.M.L.; data curation, L.Z.; writing—original draft preparation, L.Z. and R.L.; writing—review and editing, L.Z. and R.Y.M.L.; visualization, L.Z. and R.L.; supervision, R.Y.M.L.; project administration, L.Z. and R.Y.M.L.; funding acquisition, L.Z. All authors have read and agreed to the published version of the manuscript.

Funding: This research was funded by (1) Panzhihua City's Municipal Guiding Science and Technology Program Project in 2023: Research on evaluation of green building environment and energy-saving design in resource-based industrial cities [Grant No. 2023ZD-S-46]. (2) Panzhihua University Scientific Research Project (Economic Environmental Impact Assessment of Rural Ecotourism [Grant No. 035001411]; (3) Panzhihua University Science and Technology Park Development Co., Ltd. Seed Fund Innovation and Entrepreneurship Project [Grant No. CJY 2020-2].

Institutional Review Board Statement: The study was approved by the Human Research Ethics Committee of School of Civil and Architectural Engineering, Panzhihua University (Approval number: HRECA002) and date of approval is 20 December 2022.

Informed Consent Statement: Informed consent was obtained from all subjects involved in the study.

Data Availability Statement: The data used to support the findings of this study is available from the corresponding author upon request.

Acknowledgments: We would like to thank the anonymous reviewers for their helpful remarks. We thank the editors for their useful feedback that improved this paper. We deeply appreciate their contributions.

Conflicts of Interest: The authors declare that there are no conflicts of interest regarding the publication of this paper.

References

1. Lu, H.; Hu, H.; Tan, Y. Sustainable Development of Color Design of Urban Landscapes. *J. Shandong Agric. Univ.* **2005**, *36*, 402–406.
2. Shen, S.G.; Yao, Y.; Li, C.L. Quantitative Study on Landscape Colors of Plant Communities in Urban Parks Based on Natural Color System and M-S Theory in Nanjing, China. *Color Res. Appl.* **2021**, *47*, 152–163. [CrossRef]
3. Sun-Wook, M. A Plan and Guideline for the Urban Landscape Color of Dobong-Gu, Seoul. *J. Recreat. Landsc.* **2012**, *6*, 113–126.
4. Cheng, Y.N.; Tan, M. The Quantitative Research of Landscape Color: A Study of Ming Dynasty City Wall in Nanjing. *Color Res. Appl.* **2018**, *43*, 436–448. [CrossRef]
5. Saito, M. Comparative Studies on Color Preference in Japan and Other Asian Regions, with Special Emphasis on the Preference for White. *Color Res. Appl.* **1996**, *21*, 35–49. [CrossRef]
6. Lengen, C. The Effects of Colours, Shapes and Boundaries of Landscapes on Perception, Emotion and Mentalising Processes Promoting Health and Well-Being. *Health Place* **2015**, *35*, 166–177. [CrossRef] [PubMed]
7. Lee, M.H. A Study on Urban Landscape Color Design to Strengthen Regional Identity—Focusing on the External Color Design of the Jeonbuk Jeonju-Wanju Innovation City Apartments. *J. Ind. Des. Stud.* **2014**, *8*, 91–98.
8. Ji, D.; Xiao, J.; Piao, Y.; Deng, Q. Research of the Pubic Opinion Survey Reerch of Color Landscape Garden in Taian City Park. *J. Shandong Agric. Univ.* **2013**, *44*, 199–204.
9. Feng, W.W.; Huang, Z.S.; Zhang, Y.B.; Liu, Y.F.; Pang, M. Landscape Scenic Beauty of Traditional Dong Minority Villages in Southeast of Guizhou Province. *Shengtaixue Zazhi* **2019**, *38*, 3820–3830. [CrossRef]
10. Asarzadeh, K.; Ghazanfari, P.; Pirbazari, A.G. Recoveringfigure-Groundperception in Tehran's Color Plan. *Color Res. Appl.* **2020**, *45*, 1179–1189. [CrossRef]
11. Zhang, C.F. The Importance of Visual Identity Graphic Design in Cities. In Proceedings of the 2nd International Conference on Social Science and Technology Education (ICSSTE), Guangzhou, China, 14–15 May 2016; pp. 708–714.

12. Zhou, Y.; Fu, S.P. The Research of "Five Colored" in Chinese Traditional Culture and the Built Environment. In Proceedings of the International Conference on Manufacturing Construction and Energy Engineering (MCEE), Hong Kong, China, 17–18 August 2016; pp. 511–514.
13. Brox, T. Landscapes of Little Lhasa: Materialities of the Vernacular, Political and Commercial in Urban China. *Geoforum* **2019**, *107*, 24–33. [CrossRef]
14. Guo, F.; Li, F.X.; Nagamachi, M.; Hu, M.C.; Li, M.M. Research on Color Optimization of Tricolor Product Considering Color Harmony and Users' Emotion. *Color Res. Appl.* **2020**, *45*, 156–171. [CrossRef]
15. Ding, M.; Dong, W. Product Color Emotional Design Considering Color Layout. *Color Res. Appl.* **2019**, *44*, 285–295. [CrossRef]
16. Ma, C.X. Study on the Application of Color in Landscape Design. In Proceedings of the 7th International Conference on Social Science, Education and Humanities Research (SSEHR), Xian, China, 15–16 December 2018; pp. 106–110.
17. Liu, Z.J.Y.; Liu, Y. Reasonable Allocation Strategy of Garden Landscape Space Color Based on Decomposition and Combination Method. *Fresenius Environ. Bull.* **2021**, *30*, 6137–6143.
18. Rhee, J.-S. The Study on Landscape Colors in Gunsan City. *J. Korean Hous. Assoc.* **2011**, *22*, 29–36. [CrossRef]
19. Dong, Z.L. An Analysis of Colors Used in Gardening and Landscape Design. In Proceedings of the 2nd Global Conference on Civil, Structural and Environmental Engineering (GCCSEE 2013), Shenzhen, China, 28–29 September 2013; pp. 3031–3034.
20. Zhu, X.Y.; Zhang, H.; Lan, S.; Huang, Q. Research on Traditional Village Color Landscape Optimization Based on Quantitative Analysis and Public Perception: Taking Xunpu Village in Southern Fujian as an Example. *J. Cent. China Norm. Univ. Nat. Sci. Ed.* **2020**, *54*, 50–59.
21. Wang, Y.Q.; Qu, H.H.; Bai, T.; Chen, Q.B.; Li, X.; Luo, Z.H.; Lv, B.Y.; Jiang, M.Y. Effects of Variations in Color and Organ of Color Expression in Urban Ornamental Bamboo Landscapes on the Physiological and Psychological Responses of College Students. *Int. J. Environ. Res. Public Health* **2021**, *18*, 1151. [CrossRef] [PubMed]
22. Montero-Parejo, M.J.; Moruno, L.G.; Rodriguez, A.M.R.; Blanco, J.H.; Velarde, J.G. Analysis of Facade Color and Cost to Improve Visual Integration of Buildings in the Rural Environment. *Sustainability* **2020**, *12*, 840. [CrossRef]
23. Fan, R.; Fan, J.X.; Song, J.Y.; Li, K.Y.; Ji, W.L. Naturalness in the City: Demographic Groups' Differences in Preference for Deciduous Landscape. *Sustainability* **2021**, *13*, 7615. [CrossRef]
24. Tan, C.; Yang, S.Y. Automatic Extraction of Color Features from Landscape Images Based on Image Processing. *Trait. Du Signal* **2021**, *38*, 747–755. [CrossRef]
25. Wang, H.X.; Wang, H.J.; Hu, X.M. Artistic Expression of Urban Community Landscape Color. In Proceedings of the 2nd International Conference on Education Technology and Information System (ICETIS), Jinan, China, 28 March 2024.
26. Wan, Y.H.; Wu, F.; Zhu, P.J. Color Design of Architectures in Yuelu-Mountain University Group. In Proceedings of the 4th International Conference on Technology of Architecture and Structure (ICTAS 2011), Xi'an University of Architecture and Technology, Xi'an, China, 22–24 September 2011.
27. Grigoryan, A.M.; Agaian, S.S. Evidence of Golden and Aesthetic Proportions in Colors of Paintings of the Prominent Artists. *IEEE Multimed.* **2020**, *27*, 8–16. [CrossRef]
28. Gou, A.P.; Wang, X.Y.; Wang, J.B. The Development of Color of Historic Buildings on the North Bund of Shanghai. *Color Res. Appl.* **2021**, *46*, 402–429. [CrossRef]
29. Jonauskaite, D.; Tremea, I.; Burki, L.; Diouf, C.N.; Mohr, C. To See or Not to See: Importance of Color Perception to Color Therapy. *Color Res. Appl.* **2020**, *45*, 450–464. [CrossRef]
30. Zhang, X.X.; Yang, M.G.; Su, J.N.; Yang, W.J.; Qiu, K. Research on Product Color Design Decision Driven by Brand Image. *Color Res. Appl.* **2020**, *45*, 1202–1216. [CrossRef]
31. (Consultants/Designers), IACC (International Association of Color. "Who We Are." IACC (International Association of Color Consultants/Designers). Available online: https://www.iaccna.com/about (accessed on 8 May 2023).
32. Zhang, X.J.; Chen, J.; Li, Q.Y.; Liu, J.C.; Tao, J.P. Color Quantification and Evaluation of Landscape Aesthetic Quality for Autumn Landscape Forest Based on Visual Characteristics in Subalpine Region of Western Sichuan, China. *Yingyong Shengtai Xuebao* **2020**, *31*, 45–54. [CrossRef] [PubMed]
33. Beza, B.B. The Aesthetic Value of a Mountain Landscape: A Study of the Mt. Everest Trek. *Landsc. Urban Plan.* **2010**, *97*, 306–317. [CrossRef]
34. Osgood, C.E.; Luria, Z. A Blind Analysis of a Case of Multiple Personality Using the Semantic Differential. *J. Abnorm. Psychol.* **1954**, *49*, 579–591. [CrossRef]
35. Huang, S.; van den Bosch, C.; Fu, W.C.; Qi, J.D.; Chen, Z.R.; Zhu, Z.P.; Dong, J.W. Does Adding Local Tree Elements into Dwellings Enhance Individuals' Homesickness? Scenario-Visualisation for Developing Sustainable Rural Landscapes. *Sustainability* **2018**, *10*, 3943. [CrossRef]
36. Office, Government. "Xiangcheng Overview". The Department of Government Office in Xiangcheng. Available online: http://www.xcx.gov.cn/xcgk/article/136856 (accessed on 9 May 2023).
37. Liu, Y.M.; Pan, X.X.; Liu, Q.; Li, G.C. Establishing a Reliable Assessment of the Green View Index Based on Image Classification Techniques, Estimation, and a Hypothesis Testing Route. *Land* **2023**, *12*, 1030. [CrossRef]
38. Johnson, M. Navigating the Cultural Landscape through Publishing Brands: A Theoretical, Gendered Perspective. *Publ. Res. Q.* **2023**, *39*, 162–177. [CrossRef]
39. Liu, T. Application of Traditional Cultural Elements in Landscape Design. *Appl. Math. Nonlinear Sci.* **2023**, *1*, 1–17. [CrossRef]

40. Wu, M.; Sun, Y.; Jiang, S. Adaptive Color Transfer from Images to Terrain Visualizations. *IEEE Trans. Vis. Comput. Graph.* 2023; 1–11, *Online ahead of print*. [CrossRef]
41. Bijker, R.A.; Sijtsma, F.J. A Portfolio of Natural Places: Using a Participatory Gis Tool to Compare the Appreciation and Use of Green Spaces inside and Outside Urban Areas by Urban Residents. *Landsc. Urban Plan.* **2017**, *158*, 155–165. [CrossRef]
42. Tuaycharoen, N.; Tregenza, P.R. View and Discomfort Glare from Windows. *Light. Res. Technol.* **2007**, *39*, 185–200. [CrossRef]
43. Wang, L.L.; Huang, Y.P. Fast Vehicle Detection Based on Colored Point Cloud with Bird's Eye View Representation. *Sci. Rep.* **2023**, *13*, 7447. [CrossRef] [PubMed]
44. Li, S.J.; Geng, K.K.; Yin, G.D.; Wang, Z.W.; Qian, M. MVMM: Multiview Multimodal 3-D Object Detection for Autonomous Driving. *IEEE Trans. Ind. Inform.* **2024**, *20*, 845–853. [CrossRef]
45. Döllner, J.; Buchholz, H.; Nienhaus, M.; Kirsch, F. Illustrative Visualization of 3D City Models. In Proceedings of the Visualization And Data Analysis, San Jose, CA, USA, 17–18 January 2005; pp. 42–51.
46. Wolff, M.; Collins, R.T.; Liu, Y.X. Regularity-Driven Building Facade Matching between Aerial and Street Views. In Proceedings of the 2016 IEEE Conference on Computer Vision and Pattern Recognition (CVPR), Las Vegas, NV, USA, 27–30 June 2016; IEEE: Piscataway, NJ, USA, 2016; pp. 1591–1600.
47. Zhuang, Y.; Guo, C.Y. City Architectural Color Recognition Based on Deep Learning and Pattern Recognition. *Appl. Sci.* **2023**, *13*, 1575. [CrossRef]
48. Ünver, R.; Öztürk, L.D. An Example of Facade Colour Design of Mass Housing. *Color Res. Appl.* **2002**, *27*, 291–299. [CrossRef]
49. Li, M.; Xu, J.G.; Zhang, X. Spatial-Sensitivity Analysis for Urban Color Planning: Study of Luoyang City, China. *J. Urban Plan. Dev.* **2017**, *143*, 1–9. [CrossRef]
50. Zhong, T.; Ye, C.; Wang, Z.; Tang, G.A.; Zhang, W.; Ye, Y. City-Scale Mapping of Urban Facade Color Using Street-View Imagery. *Remote Sens.* **2021**, *13*, 1591. [CrossRef]
51. Özcan, E.K.; Çelik, K. Environmental Color Analysis and Facade Color Design in a Street Rehabilitation: Adana, Kayalıbağ. *Color Res. Appl.* **2024**, 1–16. [CrossRef]
52. Hu, K.T.; Xu, Z.Q.; Wang, X.F.; Wang, Y.Y.; Li, H.R.; Zhang, Y.B. Research on Street Color Environment Perception Based on CEP-KASS Framework. *Buildings* **2023**, *13*, 2649. [CrossRef]
53. Qin, L.Z. A Study on "Overall Flexible Control" of Rural Urbanization-the Case of Juyuan Planning. Master's Thesis, Tsinghua University, Beijing, China, 2013.
54. Gao, C.L.; Iqbal, J. An Empirical Study of Thailand Cities' Color Landscapes. *Heliyon* **2023**, *9*, e17558. [CrossRef] [PubMed]
55. Hong, C.; Yang, Y.J.; Ge, S.W.; Chai, G.K.; Zhao, P.Z.; Shui, Q.X.; Gu, Z.L. Is the Design Guidance of Color and Material for Urban Buildings a Good Choice in Terms of Thermal Performance? *Sust. Cities Soc.* **2022**, *83*, 103927. [CrossRef]
56. Hairul, N.N.N.; Yazid, M.R.M.; Ismail, R.; Rose, R.A.C.; Tahir, Z.; Noordin, N.A.S.; Sitinjak, C. Factor Analysis of End-of-Life Vehicle Policy Evaluation. *J. Kejuruter.* **2023**, *35*, 767–778. [CrossRef] [PubMed]
57. Kanno, T.; Fukuyama, M.; Oku, T.; Sasaki, H.; Nagamachi, M. A Study of Images and Amenity of Grassland Landscape, Using SD Method. *Grassl. Sci.* **1998**, *44*, 127–137.
58. Zhao, Y.; Liu, J.H.; Zheng, Y.L. Preservation and Renewal: A Study on Visual Evaluation of Urban Historical and Cultural Street Landscape in Quanzhou. *Sustainability* **2022**, *14*, 8775. [CrossRef]
59. Camgoz, N.; Yener, C.; Guvenc, D. Effects of Hue, Saturation, and Brightness on Preference. *Color Res. Appl.* **2002**, *27*, 199–207. [CrossRef]
60. Zeng, L.; Li, R.Y.M.; Huang, X. Sustainable Mountain-Based Health and Wellness Tourist Destinations: The Interrelationships between Tourists' Satisfaction, Behavioral Intentions, and Competitiveness. *Sustainability* **2021**, *13*, 13314. [CrossRef]
61. Zeng, L.; Li, R.Y.M. Tourist Satisfaction, Willingness to Revisit and Recommend, and Mountain Kangyang Tourism Spots Sustainability: A Structural Equation Modelling Approach. *Sustainability* **2021**, *13*, 10620. [CrossRef]
62. Treiblmaier, H.; Filzmoser, P. Exploratory Factor Analysis Revisited: How Robust Methods Support the Detection of Hidden Multivariate Data Structures in Is Research. *Inf. Manag.* **2010**, *47*, 197–207. [CrossRef]
63. Iacobucci, D.; Ruvio, A.; Román, S.; Moon, S.; Herr, P.M. How Many Factors in Factor Analysis? New Insights About Parallel Analysis with Confidence Intervals. *J. Bus. Res.* **2022**, *139*, 1026–1043. [CrossRef]

applied sciences

MDPI

Article

Multi-Scale Cross-Attention Fusion Network Based on Image Super-Resolution

Yimin Ma [1,2,†], Yi Xu [1,*,†], Yunqing Liu [1,2], Fei Yan [1,2], Qiong Zhang [1,2], Qi Li [1,2] and Quanyang Liu [1,2]

[1] The College of Electronic and Information Engineering, Changchun University of Science and Technology, Changchun 130022, China; mayimincust@163.com (Y.M.); liuyunqing@cust.edu.cn (Y.L.); yanf@cust.edu.cn (F.Y.); zhangqiong@cust.edu.cn (Q.Z.); liqicust@163.com (Q.L.); 2018100409@mails.cust.edu.cn (Q.L.)

[2] Jilin Provincial Science and Technology Innovation Center of Intelligent Perception and Information Processing, Changchun 130000, China

* Correspondence: xuyicust@163.com; Tel.: +86-177-6771-1633

† These authors contributed equally to this work.

Abstract: In recent years, deep convolutional neural networks with multi-scale features have been widely used in image super-resolution reconstruction (ISR), and the quality of the generated images has been significantly improved compared with traditional methods. However, in current image super-resolution network algorithms, these methods need to be further explored in terms of the effective fusion of multi-scale features and cross-domain application of attention mechanisms. To address these issues, we propose a novel multi-scale cross-attention fusion network (MCFN), which optimizes the feature extraction and fusion process in structural design and modular innovation. In order to make better use of the attention mechanism, we propose a Pyramid Multi-scale Module (PMM) to extract multi-scale information by cascading. This PMM is introduced in MCFN and is mainly constructed by multiple multi-scale cross-attention modules (MTMs). To fuse the feature information of PMMs efficiently in both channel and spatial dimensions, we propose the cross-attention fusion module (CFM). In addition, an improved integrated attention enhancement module (IAEM) is inserted at the network's end to enhance the correlation of high-frequency feature information between layers. Experimental results show that the algorithm significantly improves the reconstructed images' edge information and texture details, and the benchmark dataset's performance evaluation shows comparable performance to current state-of-the-art techniques.

Keywords: image super-resolution; pyramid multi-scale features; inter-attention mechanism

1. Introduction

Image super-resolution (SR) is a fundamental task in computer vision, the primary goal of which is to reconstruct a low-resolution image (LR) into a high-resolution photo (HR). Image super-resolution (ISR) reconstruction is an ill-posed problem because multiple HR images may degrade into the same LR image, and details may be lost in the degradation process. Image super-resolution has been widely studied and applied to medical images, remote sensing images, video surveillance, and other fields needing high-frequency information. In recent years, as deep learning technology has made significant progress in computer vision, this technology has been applied to more tasks. Compared with the image super-resolution methods based on interpolation [1], reconstruction [2], and learning [3,4], the use of deep learning methods can reconstruct high-frequency information more effectively.

SRCNN [5] first applied a Convolutional Neural Network (CNN) to the field of image super-resolution and solved the problem through the mapping function from LR input to HR output. Since then, deep CNN-based methods have been widely used in ISR. Following SRCNN, methods such as FSRCNN [6], ESPCN [7], VDSR [8], EDSR [9], LapSRN [10], and DRRN [11] provide a wider sensory field by deepening the network structure and introducing a residual learning mechanism to alleviate the gradient vanishing problem that increases with network deepening.

Recently, CNN-based methods, such as MSRN [12], MSFRNE [13], and MSAR [14], have demonstrated the ability to further enhance network performance by making full use of multi-scale extracted feature information to increase image texture details. However, despite advances in these methods, more work still needs to be done on the effective fusion of multi-scale features and deep utilization of attention mechanisms. In particular, how to fully use different multi-scale information and enhance the ability of feature information expression while maintaining network efficiency. Therefore, to solve these problems, this paper proposes a multi-scale cross-attention fusion network (MCFN) for the image super-resolution task. The main contributions of this paper are as follows:

(1) A multi-scale cross-attention fusion network (MCFN) is proposed to achieve total extraction and compelling fusion of feature information at different scales and promote high-quality image reconstruction.
(2) A multi-scale Trans-attention module (MTM) is proposed to efficiently extract and fuse multi-scale feature information. MTM utilizes a pyramid multi-scale module (PMM) to extract feature information of various scales, which is then input into a Cross Attention Fusion module (CFM) in a cross-module manner. This approach incorporates a cross-connect strategy that combines channel and spatial attention mechanisms to fuse the multi-scale feature information effectively and capture the correlation dependence between them.
(3) An improved integrated Attention Enhancement module (IAEM) is proposed to extract more feature information from the middle layer through a dense connection strategy. The module learns the correlation between the middle layers and integrates the feature information of each module effectively.
(4) The objective metrics and subjective vision of public datasets show that our method is competitive compared with existing methods. At the same time, we prove the proposed method's effectiveness through many ablation and experimental studies.

This paper is organized as follows: Section 2 will introduce the relevant studies. Section 3 will elaborate on our proposed method and structure. Section 4 will show the experimental results of the method on a public benchmark dataset. The last section will summarize the main conclusions of the paper.

2. Related Works

2.1. Deep CNN-Based Image Super-Resolution

Methods based on deep learning have recently been widely used in image super-resolution [15] and have achieved significant advantages over traditional methods. Dong et al. proposed SRCNN [5], the first article to apply a convolutional neural network to the field of image super-resolution. They used a three-layer convolutional neural network to establish an end-to-end mapping SR method between LR images and their corresponding HR images. Kim et al. proposed the VDSR [8] algorithm, which used a deep convolutional neural network and added residual learning to improve the SRCNN network. At the same time, the DRCN [16] algorithm was proposed, which is the first method to introduce recursive learning to realize parameter sharing in SR. Although the initial application of the CNN method can improve the performance of traditional methods, it will increase the computational cost and produce artifacts. Therefore, Dong et al. proposed the FSRCNN [6] approach to improve computational efficiency by introducing deconvolution in up-sampling. The ESPCN [7] algorithm was suggested by Shi et al., which presents a sub-pixel convolutional layer to upsample the final LR features as HR output to improve the computational performance to achieve a complete end-to-end mapping. Due to the effectiveness of the sub-pixel convolutional layer, the EDSR [9] algorithm also directly uses it for upsampling and removes the BN layer at the same time to increase the amount of network calculation, reduce the model parameters, and improve image performance. Lai et al. proposed the LapSRN [10] algorithm to reduce the amount of network calculation by using a cascade structure to gradually enlarge image reconstruction. Tai et al. proposed the MemNet [17] algorithm, which uses dense blocks for deep networks. Jiang et al. proposed the HDRN [18] algorithm, which uses hierarchical thick blocks to reconstruct the image to reduce the amount of calculation brought by the dense residual method. These methods show that deep, residual, and dense connections can improve the network's performance. There are other ways to improve network performance.

2.2. Multi-Scale Feature Extraction Based on Image Super-Resolution

Multi-scale feature extraction is widely used in object detection [19] and semantic segmentation tasks [20]. Multi-scale feature extraction can fully use information features at different depths to improve accuracy. The classical scheme for multi-scale feature extraction is the Inception [21] module proposed by Szegedy et al., which uses multiple convolution kernels of different sizes at the same level to extract features, obtain various receptive fields, and improve image quality. Recently, multi-scale feature extraction has also been introduced into image super-resolution. Li et al. proposed an MSRN algorithm [12] that uses multi-scale feature extraction to extract image features of different scales adaptively. He et al. proposed the MRFN [22] algorithm, which uses a multi-receptive field module to remove parts of various receptive fields and proposed a new training loss to reduce reconstruction error. Feng et al. proposed the MSRFN [13] algorithm, which uses a multi-scale extraction module and adds multiple paths for fusion to improve image reconstruction quality. Although these methods are optimized at the network and training levels to enhance the performance of image reconstruction, there is still room for improvement in the extraction and fusion of feature information at different scales.

2.3. Attention Mechanism Based on Image Super-Resolution

Attention usually means that the human visual system adaptively focuses on salient areas in visual information. Therefore, the attention mechanism can help the network focus on essential details. A non-local neural network for image classification tasks [23] was first proposed by Wang et al. After that, Hu et al. designed a Squeeze and Excitation Network (SENet) [24] to improve image classification performance by introducing a channel attention mechanism. Attention-based networks have also been increasingly applied in image super-resolution (ISR) tasks. Inspired by the SENet network [25], Zhang et al. referred to the channel attention mechanism in SR [26] to improve image quality. The SAN [27] algorithm recently used a second-order channel attention mechanism to refine features adaptively. In the AIDN [28] algorithm, information recognition ability is enhanced using a refined attention mechanism to improve network performance. In the MSAR [14] algorithm, the multi-scale attention residual module of feature refinement is used to refine the edge of parts at each scale to improve performance. Therefore, using a multi-scale attention mechanism for feature correlation learning can achieve a more comprehensive and in-depth improvement in performance. We propose a multi-scale cross-attention fusion network (MCFN) to extract and effectively fuse image feature information fully.

3. Methods

The ISR aims to reconstruct a high-resolution image $I_{HR} \in R^{C\times rH\times rW}$ on top of a low-resolution image $I_{LR} \in R^{C\times H\times W}$. The height and width of the image are denoted as W and H, C is the number of channels in the color space, and r is the scale factor. LR images are usually obtained by down-sampling the HR image.

Firstly, this section shows the overall framework of the multi-scale cross-attention fusion network (MCFN). We will then detail each core component, including the pyramid multi-scale module (PMM) in the multi-scale trans-attention module (MTM), the cross-attention fusion module (CFM), and the optimized, integrated attention enhancement module (IAEM). In addition, we will provide an in-depth analysis and justification of the overall architecture strategy of the network.

3.1. Network Framework

We proposed a multi-scale cross-attention fusion network architecture, as shown in Figure 1, which consists of a shallow feature extraction module (SFM), a deep feature extraction module (DFM), and a feature reconstruction module (FRM).

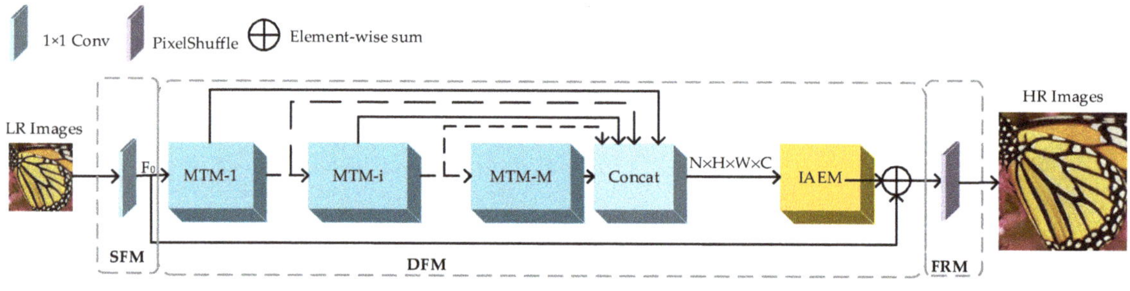

Figure 1. Framework of the multi-scale cross-attention fusion network.

First, the SFM extracts shallow feature information $F_0 \in R^{C \times H \times W}$, including edges and corners, through a single 3×3 convolution function $f_{sf}(\cdot)$, given an input LR image $I_{LR} \in R^{C \times H \times W}$.

$$F_0 = f_{SFM}(I_{LR}), \quad (1)$$

At the same time, F_0 is also the input to the Deep Feature Extraction Module (DFM). Inside the DFM, the F_0 is used as the input of the M multi-scale trans-attention modules and an optimized, Integrated Attention Enhancement Module (IEAM) in order to extract and fuse image feature information. The function of this process is called f_{DFM}. In addition, global skip and dense connections are introduced to make the central part of the network focus on high-frequency information, which can be formally expressed as follows:

$$\begin{aligned} F_R &= f_{DFM}(F_0) = F_0 + f_{IAEM}(Concat[F_1, F_2, \ldots, F_i, \ldots, F_M]), \\ F_i &= f^i_{MTM}(F_{i-1}), \end{aligned} \quad (2)$$

f^i_{MTM} denotes the mapping of the i-th multi-scale trans-attentive module, and $[\cdot]$ denotes concatenation. F_i denotes the output of the i-th MTM, and its input is a concatenation of the outputs of the previous $i-1$ MTM modules. *Concat* denotes the connectivity operator, and f_{IAEM} denotes the mapping in which the module learns feature information from the outputs of the M MTMs, enhancing the feature information for high-frequency information. The IAEM module is designed to enhance the feature layers that are highly informative in their contribution and suppress the feature layers that contain redundant information. Finally, the feature reconstruction module generates a high-resolution image $I_{SR} \in R^{C \times rH \times rW}$ according to the feature information F_R, which is upsampled to the required size by sub-pixel convolution:

$$I_{SR} = f_{PixelShuffle}(F_R), \quad (3)$$

where $f_{PixelShuffle}$ denotes sub-pixel convolution, which aggregates low-resolution feature information to reconstruct the image.

Currently, loss functions such as L_1, L_2, perceptual loss, and adversarial loss are commonly used to train SR models. In this paper, we choose loss L_1 to reduce computational complexity. In a given training set, $\{I^i_{LR}, I^i_{SR}\}^N_{i=1}$, N images, and corresponding images, L_1 loss is defined as:

$$L(\Theta) = \frac{1}{N}\sum_{i=1}^{n}(f_{MCFN}(I^i_{LR}) - I^i_{HR})_1 = \frac{1}{n}\sum_{i=1}^{n}(I^i_{SR} - I^i_{HR})_1, \quad (4)$$

where f_{MCFN} and Θ denote the proposed functional mapping and its learning parameters, respectively. The configuration of each module will be shown in detail next.

3.2. Multi-Scale Trans-Attention Module

The multi-scale trans-attention module (MTM) is the core of this method, where the extraction and fusion of multi-scale deep feature information are mainly carried out. Figure 2 shows the pyramid multi-scale module (PMM) and the cross-attention fusion module (CFM).

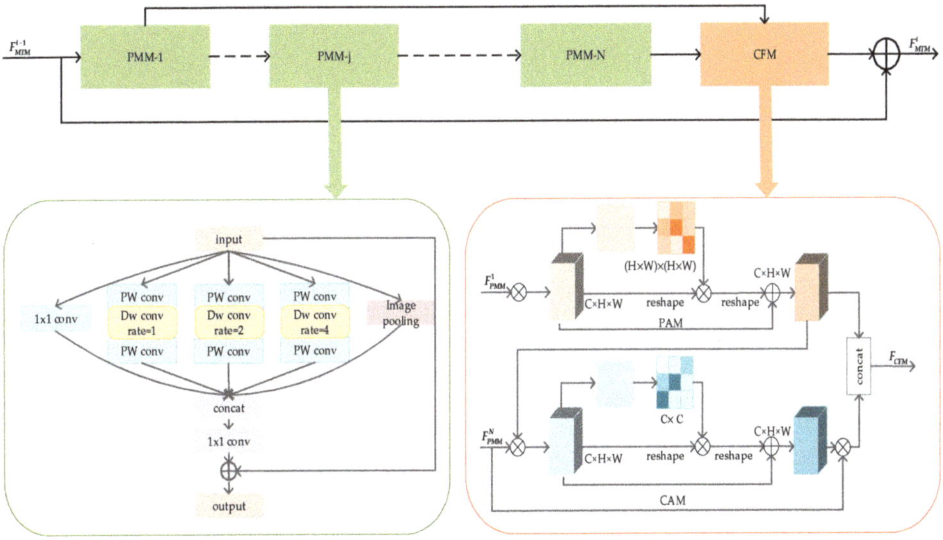

Figure 2. Architecture of the multi-scale trans-attentive module. The core consists of the PMM as a multi-scale pyramid module, which extracts feature information at different scales by incorporating depth-separable convolution to improve efficiency. In addition, CFM is the cross-attention fusion module, which fully fuses feature information by cross-learning the correlation of shallow and deep PMM output feature information.

We constructed a pyramid multi-scale module (PMM) to fully extract feature information and a cross-attention fusion module (CFM) for feature information fusion. We adopt the global residual to minimize loss in the feature information extraction process. The pyramid multi-scale module (PMM) we designed extracts features, such as detail texture and contour area, to extract feature information comprehensively. Then, the heads and tails of multiple modules are fed into the cross-attention fusion module as cross-module outputs for related learning. The specific process is as follows:

$$F^{j}_{MTM} = F^{j-1}_{MTM} + f_{CFM}(F^{1}_{PMM}, F^{N}_{PMM}), \quad (5)$$

where F^{1}_{PMM} and F^{N}_{PMM} denote the outputs of the 1st and Nth pyramid multi-scale modules, and f_{IFM} denotes the mapping of the cross-attention fusion module.

3.2.1. Pyramid Multi-Scale Module

The multi-scale CNN can provide more informative features and help generate high-quality super-resolution images. In order to extract the informative part of all scales more comprehensively, we designed a pyramid multi-scale module for feature lifting, as shown in Figure 2.

In feature extraction, the shallower convolutional layers contain more global information, so extracting more than one detailed texture information feature is crucial. Inspired by DEEP Lab V3 [29] and Mobile Net V2 [30], the ASPP module is improved to extract detailed texture feature information. ASPP uses multiple cavity convolutions with different expansion rates to extract sensory fields of different sizes and then uses standard convolutions to achieve multi-scale feature information fusion. In order to improve the efficiency and performance of ASPP as well as reduce its computational overhead, this paper improves ASPP. It proposes the pyramid multi-scale module to extract the feature information at different scales more effectively. A comparison is shown in Figure 3.

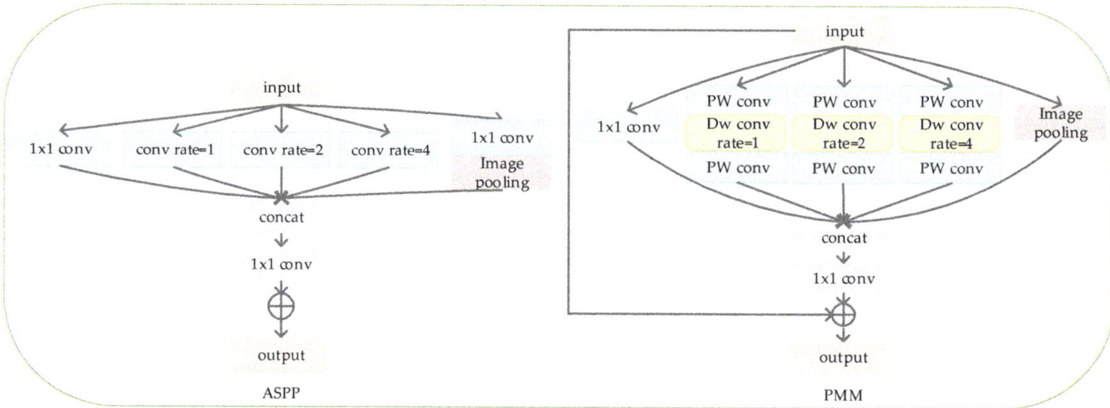

Figure 3. Comparative structural diagram of PMM and ASPP.

We replaced the dilated convolution module with depthwise separable and point convolutions to improve computational efficiency. Experiments [30] show that the number of channels has an essential impact on the overall performance. The comparison shows that the performance of the dilated dimension is better than that of the compressed dimension. This paper uses point convolution to expand and restore the dimension and control the number of channels. Point convolution can effectively promote the information exchange between different channels, and depthwise separable convolution can also focus on extracting multi-scale feature information on each channel independently. The leaky Relu function, which has smaller parameters and better feature extraction ability than Relu6, is selected in this paper. The representation process is as follows:

$$F_{pwconv}^{PMM} = f_{lrelu}(f_{1\times1conv}^{\exp and}(F_{MTM}^{j-1})), \tag{6}$$

$$F_{dwconv}^{PMM} = f_{lrelu}(f_{dwconv,rate=n}(F_{pwconv}^{PMM})), \tag{7}$$

$$F_{pwconv,rate=n}^{PMM} = f_{lrelu}(f_{1\times1conv}^{regain}(F_{dwconv}^{PMM})), \tag{8}$$

where F_{MTM}^{i-1} denotes the output of the *j*-1st MTM, $f_{1\times1conv}^{\exp and}$ denotes the convolution function of the expanded dimension, F_{pwconv}^{PMM} denotes the output after the expanded dimension, $f_{dwconv,rate=n}$ denotes the Depthwise Convolution function with expansion rate n, F_{dwconv} denotes the output after the expanded rate, $f_{1\times1conv}^{regain}$ denotes the convolution function of the recovered dimension, f_{lrelu} denotes the Leaky Relu function, and $F_{pwconv,rate=n}$ denotes the output after the recovered dimension. Thus, the process concludes with the introduction of global residual connectivity in this paper in order to increase the stability of the module. Formally, the process is described as follows:

$$
\begin{aligned}
F_{PMM}^{j} &= F_{PMM}^{j-1} + f_{PMM}^{j}\left(F_{PMM}^{j-1}\right), \\
f_{PMM}^{j}\left(F_{PMM}^{j-1}\right) &= Concat(F_{conv} + F_{global} + F_{pwconv,rate=1}^{PMM} + F_{pwconv,rate=2}^{PMM} + F_{pwconv,rate=4}^{PMM})
\end{aligned}
\tag{9}
$$

where f_{PMM}^{j} denotes the mapping of the PMM, F_{conv} denotes the feature mapping obtained after convolutional layer processing, and F_{global} denotes the feature information after pooling. Compared with the previous improvement, the module's parameters and computational overhead are reduced, and more detailed texture information features can be extracted.

3.2.2. Cross-Attention Fusion Module

The CNN convolution module is usually used to extract features and perform simple feature fusion. In order to comprehensively fuse information features, this paper proposes a cross-attention fusion module (CFM) to learn the correlation of feature information and fuse them. As shown in Figure 2, the PAM and CAM [31] modules are imported.

In the feature extraction process, the deeper layers can extract more advanced feature information, such as shape feature information, and reduce the deformation during image reconstruction. However, there will be a loss of feature information. Considering such a problem, we designed the cross-module input method, which focuses on shallow and deep feature information to complement the feature information. We designed a cross-attention fusion module (CFM), containing a channel attention module (CAM) [31] and a position attention module (PAM) [31]. Shallow feature information contains more comprehensive and rich spatial location information. After extracting feature information through the location attention module, spatial location features are weighted and selectively aggregated for each location. Deeply extracted feature information often contains rich semantic context, so the information is cross-processed after the output of the location attention module is combined with the deeply extracted feature information. Then, through the channel attention module, the correlation feature information between all channel mappings is learned to achieve the purpose of selectively emphasizing the interdependence. This information is then multiplied with the input features to refine the feature boundaries and finally cross-fertilized with spatial location feature information and semantic feature information. Formally, the process is described as:

$$F_{CFM} = Concat(f_{CAM}(F_{PMM}^{N} \otimes f_{PAM}(F_{PMM}^{1})) \otimes F_{PMM}^{N}, f_{PAM}(F_{PMM}^{1})), \tag{10}$$

where f_{CAM} and f_{PAM} denote spatial attention and position attention function mapping, F_{CFM} denotes cross-attention fusion function mapping, and $\otimes$ denotes element-wise multiplication. The module we designed adopts the strategy of cross-module learning and cross-learning to fuse the correlation of spatial location and semantic context of feature information, making the learning process more comprehensive and detailed.

3.3. *Integrating the Attention Enhancement Module*

Currently, most SR networks usually use standard convolutional connections and ultimately perform deep feature extraction. Adding an extra module enhances the feature learning capability and thus improves the network's overall performance. Therefore, we designed the Integrated Attention Enhancement Module (IAEM) according to this assumption. We continue with the attention mechanism, inspired by DANet [31], and optimize it. We treat the mapping of each deep feature extraction module as a specific response; different module responses correlate. The interdependence between module mappings is used to enhance the interdependent feature information mapping and the feature representation ability of modules, as shown in Figure 4.

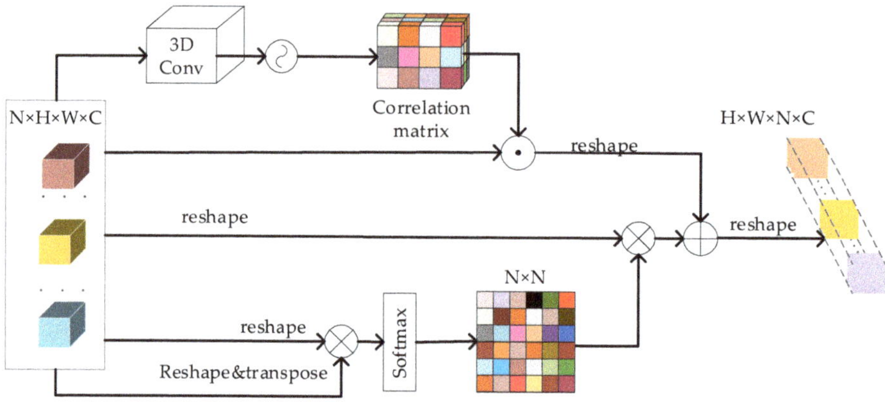

Figure 4. Integration of the Attention Enhancement Module architecture.

Different from the above CAM module, the input is the deep feature group $F_{IFG} \in R^{N \times H \times W \times C}$ output from N multi-scale cross-attention modules, and the dimension is $N \times H \times W \times C$. Through the change of dimension, the weight of feature information is re-learned to strengthen the attention of high-frequency information. Firstly, in this paper, the feature group is convolved by 3D convolution to strengthen the representation of local context features. Then, the sigmoid function is used to extract the feature information of the deep feature group and generate the corresponding attention map.

According to the dimensions of the feature groups, we chose a 3D convolution with kernel size three and step size 1 to generate the attention maps of the three feature groups. Then, in this paper, we multiply it element-by-element with the original input depth-extracted feature layer and multiply it by the scale parameter C to generate the attention map B. Formally, the process is described as:

$$F_{IAEM}^{CHW} = \mu(\sigma(f_{3dconv}(F_{IFG})) \cdot F_{IFG}), \tag{11}$$

where f_{3dconv} represents the 3D convolution function, σ represents the softmax function, $\cdot$ represents element-wise multiplication, and μ learns weights starting from initialization 0.

Secondly, this paper reshapes these deep extracted feature groups IFGs into a two-dimensional matrix of $N \times HWC$. After that, the reshaped feature group is matrix multiplied with its transpose, and then, softmax is applied to obtain the attention map $S \in R^{N \times N}$ that strengthens the correlation between modules. Formally, the process is described as follows:

$$s_{ji} = \frac{\exp(IFGs_i, IFGs_j)}{\sum_{i=1}^{N} \exp(IFGs_i, IFGs_j)}, i, j = 1, 2, \ldots, N, \tag{12}$$

where s_{ji} represents the influence between the i-th module and the j-th module, the attention map of the depth extraction feature layer is obtained by multiplying the reshaped depth extraction feature set with the original feature set matrix and then multiplying the result with the scale parameter λ. Finally, the two attention maps are summed element-wise to obtain the output $F_{IAEM} \in H \times W \times NC$. Formally, the process is described as follows:

$$F_{IAEM_j} = \lambda \sum_{i=1}^{N} (s_{ji} IFGs_i) + F_{CHW_j}^{IAEM}, \tag{13}$$

where λ learns the weights from the initialization of 0, and the final feature of each module represents a weighted sum of all the parts of the module that are related to the original quality and models the long-range semantic dependencies of the entire feature graph. Thus, integrating the attention enhancement modules by learning the interdependencies between the modules is a way to enhance and optimize the overall network's performance effectively.

4. Results

4.1. Datasets and Metrics

In this paper, DIV2K [32] is used as the training set of the model, and the DIV2K dataset contains 800 training images, 100 validation images, and 100 test images. Five standard test sets: Set5 [33], Set14 [34], B100 [35], Urban100 [36], and Manga109 [37] are used. According to the current work, all training and testing are performed based on the luminance channel of the YCbCr color space, and only the Y-channel is processed. This paper uses bicubic down-sampling (BI) to obtain the low-resolution image (LR). The commonly used evaluation metrics PSNR and SSIM are selected for quantitative comparison with other SR methods. Visualization results are also provided for a more intuitive comparison with other methods.

4.2. Implementation Details

In this paper, the LR image is randomly cropped into blocks of size 48×48 as training input, and the corresponding patch size of the HR image is $48r \times 48r$, where r is the scale factor. The minibatch is set to 16, and data enhancement such as horizontal flipping and random rotation of 90° are performed on the training set. This paper sets the number of MTMs M = 5 and the number of PMMs N = 7 for hyper-parameter settings. The model in this paper is trained using the ADAM optimizer [3–6] with $\beta 1 = 0.9$, $\beta 2 = 0.999$, and $\varepsilon = 10^{-8}$, L1 loss function, the number of channels (number of filters) C = 64, and sets the learning rate to 10^{-4} every 200 backpropagation iterations to reduce the learning rate to 0.5 per 100 iterations. Backpropagation iterations were reduced by half. In increasing the image resolution to 3× and 4× for model training, we adopt the trained 2× image upsampling model as a pre-trained model to further train the ×3 and ×4 models. This approach captures the underlying upsampling mechanism and features by learning with a small (×2) upsampling time. When this pre-trained model is trained on the task of upsampling to higher magnifications (×3 and ×4), it can learn the complex details required for the task more efficiently, accelerating training time and improving model performance at higher resolutions. This paper uses the PyTorch framework and NVIDIA GeForce RTX 3090 GPU for training and testing.

4.3. Comparison with State-of-the-Art Methods

In this section, we compare the performance of the MCFN network in detail with several state-of-the-art network models. The comparison covers the following network models: double cubic interpolation, A+ [38], SRCNN [5], VDSR [8], EDSR-baseline [9], Lap-SRN [10], CARN [39], IDN [40], MSRN [12], MSFRN [13], MIPN [41], MSCIF [42], and MSAR [14]. Through quantitative analysis and subjective visual evaluation methods, we aim to objectively assess the performance metrics of each model in order to comprehensively demonstrate the performance of the MCFN network in various aspects. This study performed detailed comparisons on different scaling factors, i.e., c2, ×3, ×4. The specific comparison results are shown in Table 1.

Table 1. Comparison of PSNR and SSIM values on standard datasets. In this table, the bolded numbers indicate the optimal values in each dataset, while the slanted numbers represent the suboptimal values.

Method	Scale	Set5		Set14		B100		Urban100		Manga109	
		PSNR	SSIM	PSNR	SSIM	PSNR	SSIM	PSNR	SSIM	PSNR	SSIM
BICUBIC	×2	33.66	0.9299	30.24	0.8688	29.56	0.8431	26.88	0.8403	30.80	0.9339
A+	×2	36.60	0.9542	32.42	0.9059	31.24	0.8870	29.25	0.8955	35.37	0.9663
SRCNN [5]	×2	36.66	0.9542	32.45	0.9067	31.36	0.8879	29.50	0.8946	35.60	0.9663
VDSR [8]	×2	37.53	0.9590	33.05	0.9130	31.90	0.8960	30.77	0.9140	37.22	0.9750
Lap-SRN [10]	×2	37.52	0.9591	33.08	0.9130	31.08	0.8950	30.41	0.9101	37.27	0.9740
EDSR-baseline [9]	×2	37.99	0.9604	33.57	0.9175	32.16	0.8994	31.98	0.9272	38.54	0.9769
CARN [39]	×2	37.76	0.9590	33.52	0.9166	32.09	0.8978	31.92	0.9256	38.36	0.9765
IDN [40]	×2	37.83	0.9600	33.30	0.9148	32.08	0.8985	31.27	0.9196	38.01	0.9749
MSRN [12]	×2	38.08	0.9605	33.74	0.9170	32.23	0.9002	32.22	*0.9326*	38.82	0.9772
MSCIF [42]	×2	37.89	0.9605	33.41	0.9153	32.15	0.8892	*31.47*	0.9220	--------	---------
MSFRN [13]	×2	38.02	0.9606	33.68	0.9184	32.19	0.8998	32.17	0.9287	38.59	0.9770
MIPN [41]	×2	38.12	*0.9610*	33.73	0.9180	32.25	0.9006	32.42	0.9310	*38.88*	*0.9773*
MSAR [14]	×2	**38.22**	**0.9616**	*33.79*	*0.9189*	*32.27*	**0.9108**	32.46	0.9322	--------	---------
MCFN	×2	*38.17*	*0.9610*	**33.95**	**0.9211**	**32.29**	*0.9011*	**32.80**	**0.9345**	**38.93**	**0.9775**
BICUBIC	×3	30.39	0.8682	27.55	0.7742	27.21	0.7385	24.46	0.7349	26.95	0.8556
A+	×3	32.63	0.9085	29.25	0.8194	28.31	0.7828	26.05	0.8019	29.93	0.9089
SRCNN [5]	×3	32.75	0.9090	29.30	0.8215	28.41	0.7863	26.24	0.7989	30.48	0.9117
VDSR [8]	×3	33.67	0.9210	29.78	0.8320	28.83	0.7990	27.14	0.8290	32.01	0.9340
Lap-SRN [10]	×3	33.82	0.9227	29.87	0.8320	28.82	0.7980	27.07	0.8280	32.21	0.9350
EDSR-baseline [9]	×3	34.37	0.9270	30.28	0.8417	29.09	0.8052	28.15	0.8527	33.45	0.9439
CARN [39]	×3	34.29	0.9255	30.29	0.8407	29.06	0.8034	28.06	0.8493	33.50	0.9440
IDN [40]	×3	34.11	0.9253	29.99	0.8354	28.95	0.8013	27.42	0.8359	32.71	0.9381
MSRN [12]	×3	34.38	0.9262	30.34	0.8395	29.08	0.8041	28.08	0.8554	33.44	0.9427
MSCIF [42]	×3	34.24	0.9266	30.09	0.8371	29.01	0.8024	27.69	0.8411	-------	-------
MSFRN [13]	×3	34.40	0.9272	30.34	0.8423	29.10	0.8052	28.19	0.8530	33.59	0.9447
MIPN [41]	×3	34.53	0.9280	*30.43*	0.8440	29.15	*0.8060*	28.38	0.8570	33.86	0.9460
MSAR [14]	×3	*34.59*	*0.9285*	**30.53**	*0.8446*	**29.35**	0.8044	*28.44*	*0.8586*	**33.98**	**0.9470**
MCFN	×3	**34.63**	**0.9289**	**30.53**	**0.8458**	*29.29*	**0.8087**	**28.73**	**0.8635**	**33.98**	*0.9469*
BICUBIC	×4	28.43	0.8020	26.10	0.6940	25.96	0.6600	23.150	0.6590	21.460	0.6138
A+	×4	30.33	0.8560	27.44	0.7450	26.83	0.7000	24.340	0.7210	22.390	0.6454
SRCNN [5]	×4	30.48	0.8630	27.49	0.7500	26.90	0.7100	24.520	0.7260	27.580	0.8555
VDSR [8]	×4	31.35	0.8840	28.01	0.7670	27.29	0.7250	25.18/	0.7520	28.830	0.8870
Lap-SRN [10]	×4	31.54	0.8850	28.19	0.7720	27.32	0.7280	25.210	0.7560	29.090	0.8900
EDSR-baseline [9]	×4	32.09	0.8938	28.58	0.7813	27.50	0.7357	26.040	0.7849	30.350	0.9067
CARN [39]	×4	32.13	0.8937	28.60	0.7806	27.58	0.7349	26.070	0.7837	30.470	0.9084
IDN [40]	×4	31.82	0.8900	28.25	0.7730	27.41	0.7300	25.410	0.7630	29.410	0.8942
MSRN [12]	×4	32.26	0.8960	28.63	0.7836	27.61	0.7380	26.220	0.7911	30.570	0.9103
MSCIF [42]	×4	31.91	0.8923	28.35	0.7751	27.46	0.7308	25.640	0.7692	-------	-------
MSFRN [13]	×4	32.16	0.8947	28.62	0.7823	27.57	0.7362	26.090	0.7868	30.470	0.9082
MIPN [41]	×4	32.31	0.8970	28.65	0.7830	27.61	0.7370	26.230	0.7900	*30.670*	*0.9107*
MSAR [14]	×4	*32.29*	**0.8989**	*28.67*	*0.7841*	**27.95**	**0.7410**	*26.250*	*0.7907*	30.660	0.9100
MCFN	×4	**32.43**	*0.8976*	**28.78**	**0.7858**	*27.71*	*0.7405*	**26.637**	**0.8012**	**31.008**	**0.9133**

It can be observed in these results that the MCFN network shows a significant advantage in most of the performance metrics compared to the recently proposed methods. In particular, compared to the more extensive network MSRN proposed by ECCV, the MCFN network shows higher PSNR and SSIM values by 0.21dB and 0.0041, respectively, on the Set14 test set with a scaling factor of 2. On Set5, with a scaling factor of 3, compared to the MIPN, the MCFN also improves its PSNR and SSIM values by 0.1 dB and 0.0009. As the scaling factor increases, the low-resolution image loses more high-frequency information, limiting the high-quality reconstruction of super-resolution images. In the Urban100 dataset, which is rich in detailed information, MCFN outperforms the following highest method, MSAR, by 0.387 dB and 0.0105 in PSNR and SSIM metrics, respectively, when the scaling factor is four. In summary, our network exhibits recognizable performance, which initially proves the validity of the network that we designed.

In order to present a more comprehensive picture of the performance of our model, we selected several representative detail parts from different super-resolution images. We reconstructed the images with ×2, ×3, and ×4 for these detail parts to show and compare these key details more obviously. As shown in Figures 5–8, the selected details were marked with rectangular boxes and enlarged three times to show and contrast these key details more obviously.

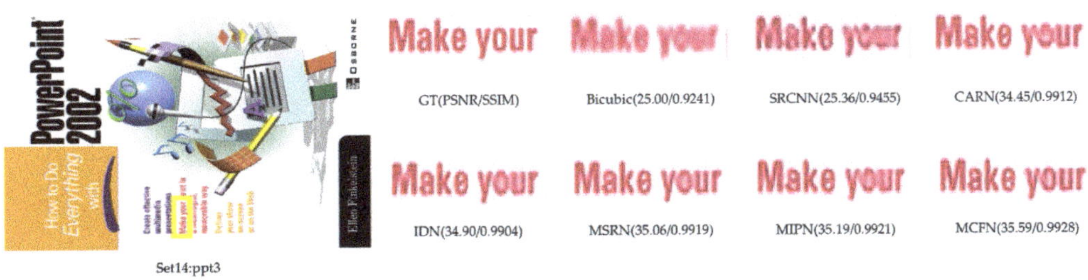

Figure 5. Visual comparison of our method with other methods (×2).

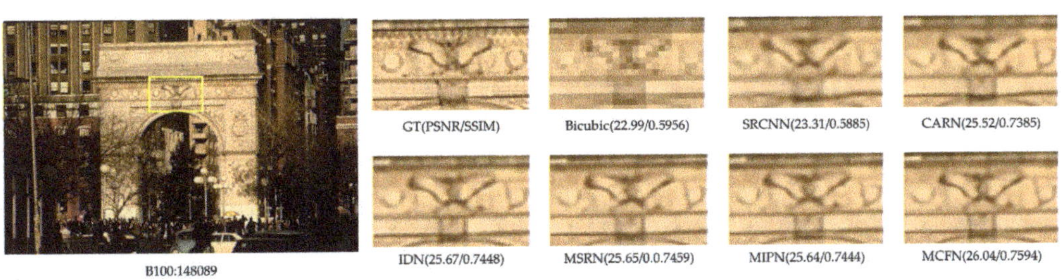

Figure 6. Visual comparison of our method with other methods (×3).

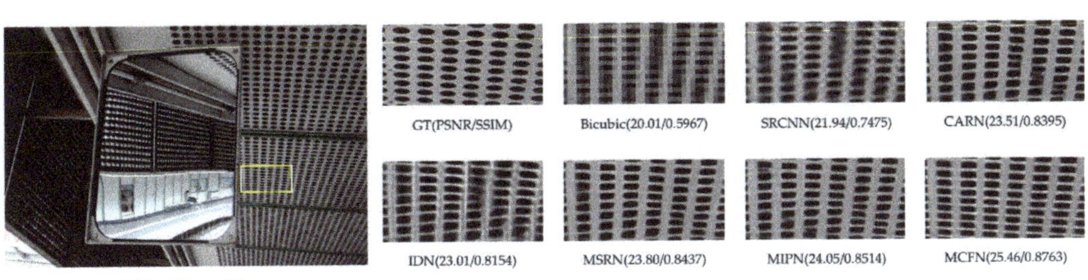

Figure 7. Visual comparison of our method with other methods (×4).

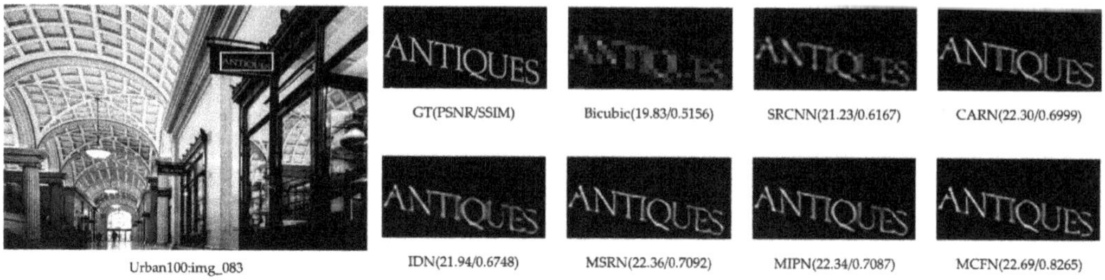

Figure 8. Visual comparison of the proposed method with other methods in terms of letters (×4).

In Figure 5, a significant difference in the clarity of the letters reconstructed by the different algorithms can be observed when the magnification factor is two times. For example, the letters reconstructed by SRCNN and CARN could be more precise and quieter. Although IDN, MSRN, and MIPN methods have improved the clarity, some details of the letter shape still need to be recovered. In contrast, the letters reconstructed by MCFN are more transparent and less noisy.

In Figure 6, a building at sunset at 3× magnification shows that MCFN performs better in preserving the edge texture and reducing the artifacts. Figure 7 shows a car roof image at 4× magnification. MCFN demonstrates less distortion and effectively reduces ringing effects, with richer information on the edge contours.

In addition, in Figure 8, the selected sign text in the scene is displayed under a magnification factor of 4, and our method improves the edge clarity while also improving the brightness to obtain a better visual effect. In general, our network performs well in objective indicators and shows significant advantages in subjective visual effects.

4.4. Ablation Study

4.4.1. Study of Ablation of Network Structures

In this part of the study, we demonstrate the effectiveness of each module in the proposed MCFN and their contribution to the network performance. We design a series of ablation experiments, as shown in Table 2. We evaluate their contribution to network performance by adding or replacing critical modules in the network. Firstly, we construct a base network consisting of a series of PMMs, called the PMMs network. The base network adopts a multi-scale mechanism of depth-separable convolution and pointwise convolution, improving computational efficiency while ensuring adequate feature information extraction at different scales. Then, IAEM was added to our study to evaluate the network performance of PMMs, denoted as MTMs_PMMs + IAEM. Subsequently, CFMs were added to the PMMs to assess the effect of the addition on the network's performance, denoted as MTMs (PMMs + CFM). It is worth noting that we did not perform ablation experiments on the combination of PMMs and CFM alone. Instead, we chose to perform ablation experiments on MTMs (a combination of PMMs and CFMs) together with IAEM, aiming to assess the impact of CFM on performance in the presence of IAEM. Therefore, we used the strategy of replacing CFMs with PAMs and CAMs, denoted as MTMs _PAM + IAEM and MTMs_CAM + IAEM, and similarly, in order to assess the performance of IAEMs, we replaced IAEMs with CAMs in the MCFN structure, denoted as MTMs + CAM. Although this design scheme for ablation experiments may be different from traditional ablation methods, it provides us with an effective way to assess the interactions of the individual modules. In addition, this design approach aligns more with our experimental resource realities, allowing us to perform the most effective performance evaluation under limited conditions. We select most of the modeling methods, PSNR, and SSIM values on Set5, Set14, and B100 test sets for 200 cycles of comparison to ensure the necessity and validity of the experiments. In order to show the experimental results more intuitively, we plotted the experimental data of the last 50 cycles as a line graph-Figure 9.

Table 2. Ablation study of MCFN properties.

Method	Scale	Set5		Set14		B100	
		PSNR	SSIM	PSNR	SSIM	PSNR	SSIM
PMMs	×4	31.797	0.889	28.362	0.776	27.424	0.731
MTMs_PMMs + IAEM		31.828	0.889	28.413	0.776	27.444	0.731
MTMs_PAM + IAEM		31.861	0.890	28.391	0.776	27.459	0.732
MTMs_CAM + IAEM		31.943	0.891	28.447	0.777	27.487	0.732
MTMs (PMMs + CFM)		31.995	0.891	28.517	0.780	27.529	0.734
MTMs + CAM		31.997	0.890	28.372	0.776	27.430	0.731
MCFN (MTMs + IAEM)		32.047	0.893	28.520	0.780	27.543	0.735

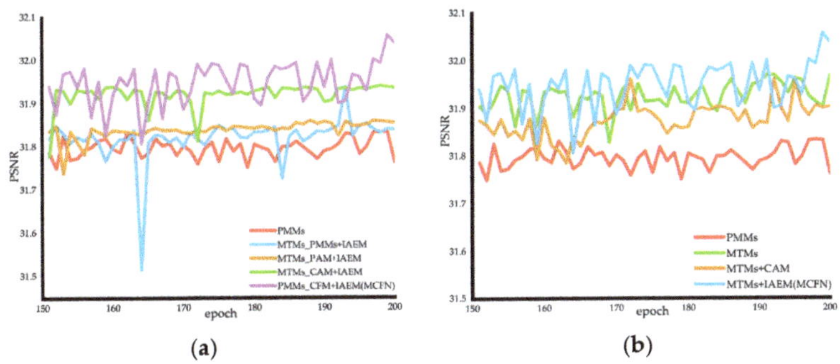

Figure 9. Line plots of the training process: (**a**) plot comparing the results of the fusion module network and (**b**) plot comparing the results of integrating the augmentation module and CAM.

Table 2 and Figure 9a demonstrate a clear trend: adding the fusion and enhancement networks to the base network significantly improves the network's performance metrics, proving the effectiveness of the individual modules and indicating that better results can be obtained. The performance improvement is pronounced in the MTMs_CAM + IAEM network. This network effectively focuses on critical feature information by learning the relevance between different channels, which demonstrates the importance of correlation learning after deep extraction of high-frequency information. In particular, in the MCFN network, we design an innovative cross-attention fusion module. This network not only effectively learns the spatial locations of shallow feature information through the cross-module learning approach but also combines this spatial location feature information with deep feature information through the cross-connection strategy to deeply learn the relevance of the information in the channel. This hierarchical approach improves the comprehensiveness of information utilization. In CFM, by integrating spatial and channel features, we achieve a more comprehensive fusion of information, enabling the network to achieve the best results in several performance metrics.

When analyzing the performance of IAEM, we used CAM as a control group to learn the difference in performance between the two. As shown in Table 2 and Figure 9b, our network performs better in PSNR and SSIM than the control group in the above test set experimental results. The results of the above analyses demonstrate the effectiveness of our module in performing relevant learning. In contrast to accessing channel attention only at the tail, our integrated attention-enhanced network employs a dimensionality transformation technique to fuse feature information at different stages. This strategy enhances the learning of feature information weights and effectively helps the network's performance during the fusion reconstruction process.

4.4.2. Study of Multi-Scale Trans-Module Synthesis

In this part of this study, we analyze the influence of MTM and the number of PMMs in MTM on the network performance and conduct a series of ablation experiments. As shown in Table 3, we set the number of MTMS M to 4, 5, and 6 and evaluate its impact on the number of parameters and network performance in the test set Set 5. The results show that with the increase in M, the PSNR value of the network improves, and the network performance improves, but the growth rate becomes gradually smaller. In addition, we analyze the number N of PMMs, setting them to 6, 7, and 8, respectively, and record the comparative experimental results, as shown in Table 4. The experimental results show that when N increases from 6 to 7, the PSNR value increases by 0.034. However, when N grows to 8, the increase in PSNR value is only 0.01. Therefore, to effectively balance the reconstruction quality and the number of parameters, we set the number of MTM and PMM to 5 and 7.

Table 3. Analysis of the number of MTMs.

Number	Scale	Parameters	Set5	
			PSNR	SSIM
M = 4	×2	1.43	37.108	0.960
M = 5	×2	1.70	38.166	0.961
M = 6	×2	1.98	38.233	0.962

Table 4. Analysis of the number of PMMs in MTM.

Number	Scale	Parameters	Set5	
			PSNR	SSIM
N = 6	×2	1.62	38.132	0.960
N = 7	×2	1.70	38.166	0.961
N = 8	×2	1.79	38.167	0.961

4.4.3. Study of Parameters and FLOPs

As shown in Figure 10, this study compares the number of parameters, the number of floating-point operations (FLOPs), and the average peak Signal-to-Noise Ratio (PSNR) (Avg. PSNR) between MCFN and other advanced methods when 4× magnification (output image resolution is 1280 × 720) is performed on the Set 5 dataset. In order to provide a more intuitive comparison perspective, the relevant data are summarized in Table 5. Compared with other methods, MCFN achieves superior performance with low computational overhead. Although not optimal regarding the number of parameters, MCFN has half the number of parameters compared to MSRN. In summary, MCFN performs well in model efficiency and objective evaluation indicators.

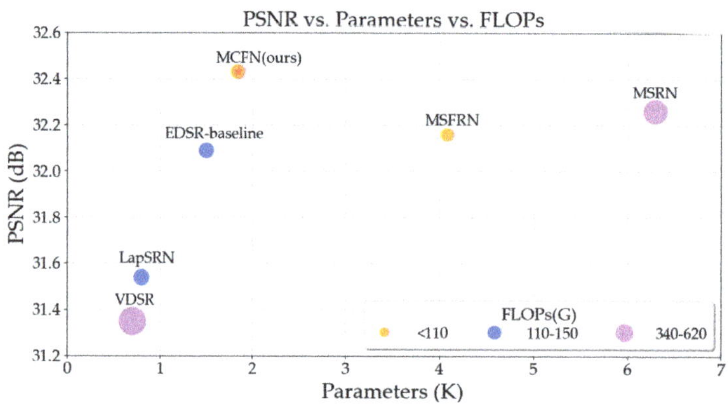

Figure 10. Visualization of PSNR, parameters, and FLOPs. PSNR values were evaluated in Set 5 with scaling factor × 4.

Table 5. Comparison of performance, parameters, and FLOPs with some state-of-the-art ISR methods under a scaling factor of 4 in the Set 5 dataset. Comparison results of the number of parameters, FLOPS, and average PSNR values of the SR method on the Set 5 test set. FLOPs are calculated based on 320 × 180 input features.

	VDSR	Lap-SRN	EDSR-Baseline	MSFRN	MSRN	MCFN
Para (M)	0.665	0.812	1.5	4.1	6.3	1.85
FLOPs (G)	612.6	149.9	114.2	94.99	349.8	110.12
PSNR	31.35	31.54	32.09	32.16	32.26	32.426

5. Conclusions

This paper proposes a multi-scale cross-attention fusion network (MCFN) to improve the image quality of image super-resolution tasks. The network combines the advantages of the multi-scale and attention mechanisms, aiming to extract and fuse the feature information of the image more thoroughly. The multi-scale trans-attention module (MTM) we designed includes the pyramid multi-scale module (PMM) and the cross-attention fusion module (CFM). In the pyramid multi-scale module (PMM), to extract feature information of each scale while maintaining the operation efficiency, depth separable convolution and point convolution are introduced using a residual strategy. In the cross-attention fusion module (CFM), the image feature information extracted by cross-fusion is designed to reconstruct the high-frequency information of the image. At the same time, to effectively fuse the cascaded multiple pyramid multi-scale modules (PMMs), a cross-module learning method is designed to learn the multi-scale information extracted by different deep features. In addition, an improved integrated attention enhancement module (IAEM) is inserted in the tail, which fuses the deep parts of different stages through dense connection, enhances the learning feature weight by changing the dimension, and introduces 3D convolution to learn context features to realize the effective fusion of image feature information to improve the quality of image reconstruction more accurately. Finally, experimental results show that MCFN has a certain competitiveness in key performance indicators compared with existing leading methods on public benchmark datasets. In particular, when quadrupled upsampling was performed on the Set 5 dataset, MCFN reached a PNSR of 32.43 dB, 0.14 dB higher than MSAR. In addition, through visual contrast, MCFN has rich texture details and a high level of high-frequency information in the reconstructed images, further proving the method's effectiveness. Although MCFN has shown some competitive performance in the experiment, we also recognize its limitations. Future work plans include training with more realistic datasets to enhance the generalization and practicality of the model. In addition, it includes the introduction of subjective evaluation and other methods to evaluate image quality more comprehensively.

Author Contributions: Conceptualization, Y.M. and Y.X.; methodology, Y.M. and Y.X.; data curation, Y.M.; writing—original draft preparation, Y.M. and Y.L.; writing—review and editing, Y.X., F.Y. and Q.Z.; supervision, Q.L. (Qi Li) and Q.L. (Quanyang Liu); project administration, Y.X.; funding acquisition, Y.L. All authors have read and agreed to the published version of the manuscript.

Funding: This research was funded by the Science and Technology Department Project of Jilin Province, China (20210203039SF).

Institutional Review Board Statement: Not applicable.

Informed Consent Statement: Not applicable.

Data Availability Statement: Publicly available datasets were analyzed in this study. The set Div2K is available online at: https://data.vision.ee.ethz.ch/cvl/DIV2K/, (accessed on 5 January 2023). The Set 5 set is available online at http://people.rennes.inria.fr/Aline.Roumy/results/SR_BMVC12.html, (accessed on 5 January 2023). The Set 14 set is available online at https://doi.org/10.1007/978-3-642-27413-8_47, (accessed on 5 January 2023). The set BSD10 is available online at https://www2.eecs.berkeley.edu/Research/Projects/CS/vision/bsds/, (accessed on 5 January

2023). The Urban100 set is available online at https://drive.google.com/drive/folders/1B3DJGQKB6eNdwuQIhdskA64qUuVKLZ9u, (accessed on 5 January 2023). The set Mange109 is available online at http://www.manga109.org/en/, (accessed on 5 January 2023).

Conflicts of Interest: The authors declare no conflicts of interest.

References

1. Lu, W.; Tan, Y.P. Color filter array demosaicking: New method and performance measures. *IEEE Trans. Image Process.* **2003**, *12*, 1194–1210. [CrossRef] [PubMed]
2. Irani, M.; Peleg, S. Improving resolution by image registration. CVGIP: Graph. *Model. Image Process.* **1991**, *53*, 231–239. [CrossRef]
3. Dong, B.Z.; Yu, M.C.; Zhao, P. Image super-resolution reconstruction method based on wavelet domain. *Liquid Cryst. Displays* **2021**, *36*, 10. [CrossRef]
4. Chen, Z.; Hu, H.; Yao, J.; Yan, Q.; Lin, Z. Single frame image super-resolution reconstruction based on improved generative adversarial network. *Liquid Cryst. Displays* **2021**, *36*, 8. [CrossRef]
5. Dong, C.; Loy, C.C.; He, K.; Tang, X. Image super-resolution using deep convolutional networks. *IEEE Trans. Pattern Anal. Mach. Intell.* **2015**, *38*, 295–307. [CrossRef] [PubMed]
6. Dong, C.; Loy, C.C.; Tang, X. Accelerating the Super-Resolution Convolutional Neural Network. In *Computer Vision–ECCV 2016: 14th European Conference, Amsterdam, The Netherlands, 11–14 October 2016, Proceedings, Part II*; Springer: Cham, Switzerland, 2016; Volume 14, pp. 391–407. [CrossRef]
7. Shi, W.; Caballero, J.; Huszár, F.; Totz, J.; Aitken, A.P.; Bishop, R.; Rueckert, D.; Wang, Z. Real-time single image and video super-resolution using an efficient sub-pixel convolutional neural network. In Proceedings of the 2016 IEEE Conference on Computer Vision and Pattern Recognition (CVPR), Las Vegas, NV, USA, 27–30 June 2016; pp. 1874–1883. [CrossRef]
8. Kim, J.; Lee, J.K.; Lee, K.M. Accurate Image Super-Resolution Using Very Deep Convolutional Networks. In Proceedings of the 2016 IEEE Conference on Computer Vision and Pattern Recognition (CVPR), Las Vegas, NV, USA, 27–30 June 2016; pp. 1646–1654. [CrossRef]
9. Lim, B.; Son, S.; Kim, H.; Nah, S.; Lee, K.M. Enhanced Deep Residual Networks for Single Image Super-Resolution. In Proceedings of the 2017 IEEE Conference on Computer Vision and Pattern Recognition Workshops (CVPRW), Honolulu, HI, USA, 21–26 July 2017; pp. 136–144. [CrossRef]
10. Lai, W.S.; Huang, J.B.; Ahuja, N.; Yang, M.H. Deep Laplacian Pyramid Networks for Fast and Accurate Super-Resolution. In Proceedings of the 2017 IEEE Conference on Computer Vision and Pattern Recognition Workshops (CVPRW), Honolulu, HI, USA, 21–26 July 2017; pp. 624–632. [CrossRef]
11. Tai, Y.; Yang, J.; Liu, X. Image Super-Resolution via Deep Recursive Residual Network. In Proceedings of the 2017 IEEE Conference on Computer Vision and Pattern Recognition Workshops (CVPRW), Honolulu, HI, USA, 21–26 July 2017; pp. 3147–3155. [CrossRef]
12. Li, J.; Fang, F.; Mei, K.; Zhang, G. Multi-Scale Residual Network for Image Super-Resolution. In Proceedings of the European Conference on Computer Vision (ECCV), Munich, Germany, 8–14 September 2018; pp. 517–532. [CrossRef]
13. Feng, X.; Li, X.; Li, J. Multi-Scale Fractal Residual Network for Image Super-Resolution. *Appl. Intell.* **2021**, *51*, 1845–1856. [CrossRef]
14. Mehta, N.; Murala, S. MSAR-Net: Multi-Scale Attention Based Light-Weight Image Super-Resolution. *Pattern Recognit. Lett.* **2021**, *151*, 215–221. [CrossRef]
15. Hou, J.; Si, Y.; Yu, X. A Novel and Effective Image Super-Resolution Reconstruction Technique via Fast Global and Local Residual Learning Model. *Appl. Sci.* **2020**, *10*, 1856. [CrossRef]
16. Kim, J.; Lee, J.K.; Lee, K.M. Deeply-Recursive Convolutional Network for Image Super-Resolution. In Proceedings of the 2016 IEEE Conference on Computer Vision and Pattern Recognition (CVPR), Las Vegas, NV, USA, 27–30 June 2016; pp. 1637–1645. [CrossRef]
17. Tai, Y.; Yang, J.; Liu, X.; Xu, C. MemNet: A Persistent Memory Network for Image Restoration. In Proceedings of the 2017 IEEE International Conference on Computer Vision (ICCV), Venice, Italy, 22–29 October 2017; pp. 4539–4547. [CrossRef]
18. Jiang, K.; Wang, Z.; Yi, P.; Jiang, J. Hierarchical Dense Recursive Network for Image Super-Resolution. *Pattern Recognit.* **2020**, *107*, 107475. [CrossRef]
19. Cheng, R.; He, X.; Zheng, Z.; Wang, Z. Multi-Scale Safety Helmet Detection Based on SAS-YOLOv3-Tiny. *Appl. Sci.* **2021**, *11*, 3652. [CrossRef]
20. Wu, Y.; Liu, Z.; Chen, Y.; Zheng, X.; Zhang, Q.; Yang, M.; Tang, G. FCNet: Stereo 3D Object Detection with Feature Correlation Networks. *Entropy* **2022**, *24*, 1121. [CrossRef] [PubMed]
21. Szegedy, C.; Vanhoucke, V.; Ioffe, S.; Shlens, J.; Wojna, Z. Rethinking the Inception Architecture for Computer Vision. In Proceedings of the 2016 IEEE Conference on Computer Vision and Pattern Recognition (CVPR), Las Vegas, NV, USA, 27–30 June 2016; pp. 2818–2826. [CrossRef]
22. He, Z.; Cao, Y.; Du, L.; Xu, B.; Yang, J.; Cao, Y.; Zhuang, Y. MRFN: Multi-Receptive-Field Network for Fast and Accurate Single Image Super-Resolution. *IEEE Trans. Multimed.* **2019**, *22*, 1042–1054. [CrossRef]

23. Wang, F.; Jiang, M.; Qian, C.; Yang, S.; Li, C.; Zhang, H.; Tang, X. Residual Attention Network for Image Classification. In Proceedings of the 2017 IEEE Conference on Computer Vision and Pattern Recognition Workshops (CVPRW), Honolulu, HI, USA, 21–26 July 2017; pp. 3156–3164. [CrossRef]
24. Hu, J.; Shen, L.; Sun, G. Squeeze-and-Excitation Networks. In Proceedings of the 2018 IEEE/CVF Conference on Computer Vision and Pattern Recognition, Salt Lake City, UT, USA, 18–23 June 2018; pp. 7132–7141. [CrossRef]
25. Zhang, Y.; Li, K.; Li, K.; Wang, L.; Zhong, B.; Fu, Y. Image Super-Resolution Using Very Deep Residual Channel Attention Networks. In Proceedings of the European Conference on Computer Vision (ECCV), Munich, Germany, 8–14 September 2018; pp. 286–301. [CrossRef]
26. Guo, T.; Dai, T.; Liu, L.; Zhu, Z.; Xia, S.-T. S2A:Scale Attention-Aware Networks for Video Super-Resolution. *Entropy* **2021**, *23*, 1398. [CrossRef] [PubMed]
27. Dai, T.; Cai, J.; Zhang, Y.; Xia, S.T.; Zhang, L. Second-Order Attention Network for Single Image Super-Resolution. In Proceedings of the 2019 IEEE/CVF Conference on Computer Vision and Pattern Recognition (CVPR), Long Beach, CA, USA, 15–20 June 2019; pp. 11065–11074. [CrossRef]
28. Zang, H.; Zhao, Y.; Niu, C.; Zhang, H.; Zhan, S. Attention Network with Information Distillation for Super-Resolution. *Entropy* **2022**, *24*, 1226. [CrossRef] [PubMed]
29. Chen, L.C.; Papandreou, G.; Schroff, F.; Adam, H. Rethinking Atrous Convolution for Semantic Image Segmentation. *arXiv* **2017**, arXiv:1706.05587. [CrossRef]
30. Sandler, M.; Howard, A.; Zhu, M.; Zhmoginov, A.; Chen, L.C. MobileNetV2: Inverted Residuals and Linear Bottlenecks. In Proceedings of the 2018 IEEE/CVF Conference on Computer Vision and Pattern Recognition, Salt Lake City, UT, USA, 18–23 June 2018; pp. 4510–4520. [CrossRef]
31. Fu, J.; Liu, J.; Tian, H.; Li, Y.; Bao, Y.; Fang, Z.; Lu, H. Dual Attention Network for Scene Segmentation. In Proceedings of the 2019 IEEE/CVF Conference on Computer Vision and Pattern Recognition (CVPR), Long Beach, CA, USA, 15–20 June 2019; pp. 3146–3154. [CrossRef]
32. Agustsson, E.; Timofte, R. NTIRE 2017 Challenge on Single Image Super-Resolution: Dataset and Study. In Proceedings of the 2017 IEEE Conference on Computer Vision and Pattern Recognition Workshops (CVPRW), Honolulu, HI, USA, 21–26 July 2017; pp. 126–135. [CrossRef]
33. Bevilacqua, M.; Roumy, A.; Guillemot, C.; Alberi-Morel, M.L. Low-Complexity Single-Image Super-Resolution Based on Nonnegative Neighbor Embedding. In Proceedings of the British Machine Vision Conference, BMVC 2012, Surrey, UK, 3–7 September 2012. [CrossRef]
34. Zeyde, R.; Elad, M.; Protter, M. On Single Image Scale-Up Using Sparse Representations. In *Curves and Surfaces: 7th International Conference, Avignon, France, 24–30 June 2010, Revised Selected Papers*; Springer: Berlin/Heidelberg, Germany, 2012; Volume 7, pp. 711–730. [CrossRef]
35. Martin, D.; Fowlkes, C.; Tal, D.; Malik, J. A Database of Human Segmented Natural Images and Its Application to Evaluating Segmentation Algorithms and Measuring Ecological Statistics. In Proceedings of the Eighth IEEE International Conference on Computer Vision, ICCV 2001, Vancouver, BC, Canada, 7–14 July 2001; Volume 2, pp. 416–423. [CrossRef]
36. Huang, J.B.; Singh, A.; Ahuja, N. Single Image Super-Resolution from Transformed Self-Exemplars. In Proceedings of the 2015 IEEE Conference on Computer Vision and Pattern Recognition (CVPR), Boston, MA, USA, 7–12 June 2015; pp. 5197–5206. [CrossRef]
37. Matsui, Y.; Ito, K.; Aramaki, Y.; Fujimoto, A.; Ogawa, T.; Yamasaki, T.; Aizawa, K. Sketch-Based Manga Retrieval Using Manga109 Dataset. *Multimed. Tools Appl.* **2017**, *76*, 21811–21838. [CrossRef]
38. Timofte, R.; De Smet, V.; Van Gool, L. A+: Adjusted Anchored Neighborhood Regression for Fast Super-Resolution. In *Computer Vision—ACCV 2014. Lecture Notes in Computer Science*; Cremers, D., Reid, I., Saito, H., Yang, M.H., Eds.; Springer: Cham, Switzerland, 2015; Volume 9006. [CrossRef]
39. Ahn, N.; Kang, B.; Sohn, K.A. Fast, Accurate, and Lightweight Super-Resolution with Cascading Residual Network. In Proceedings of the European Conference on Computer Vision (ECCV), Munich, Germany, 8–14 September 2018; pp. 252–268. [CrossRef]
40. Hui, Z.; Wang, X.; Gao, X. Fast and Accurate Single Image Super-Resolution via Information Distillation Network. In Proceedings of the 2018 IEEE/CVF Conference on Computer Vision and Pattern Recognition, Salt Lake City, UT, USA, 18–23 June 2018; pp. 723–731. [CrossRef]
41. Lu, T.; Wang, Y.; Wang, J.; Liu, W.; Zhang, Y. Single Image Super-Resolution via Multi-Scale Information Polymerization Network. *IEEE Signal Process. Lett.* **2021**, *28*, 1305–1309. [CrossRef]
42. Hu, Y.; Gao, X.; Li, J.; Huang, Y.; Wang, H. Single Image Super-Resolution with Multi-Scale Information Cross-Fusion Network. *Signal Process.* **2021**, *179*, 107831. [CrossRef]

entropy

MDPI

Article

Ref-MEF: Reference-Guided Flexible Gated Image Reconstruction Network for Multi-Exposure Image Fusion

Yuhui Huang, Shangbo Zhou *, Yufen Xu, Yijia Chen and Kai Cao

College of Computer Science, Chongqing University, Chongqing 400044, China
* Correspondence: shbzhou@cqu.edu.cn

Abstract: Multi-exposure image fusion (MEF) is a computational approach that amalgamates multiple images, each captured at varying exposure levels, into a singular, high-quality image that faithfully encapsulates the visual information from all the contributing images. Deep learning-based MEF methodologies often confront obstacles due to the inherent inflexibilities of neural network structures, presenting difficulties in dynamically handling an unpredictable amount of exposure inputs. In response to this challenge, we introduce Ref-MEF, a method for color image multi-exposure fusion guided by a reference image designed to deal with an uncertain amount of inputs. We establish a reference-guided exposure correction (REC) module based on channel attention and spatial attention, which can correct input features and enhance pre-extraction features. The exposure-guided feature fusion (EGFF) module combines original image information and uses Gaussian filter weights for feature fusion while keeping the feature dimensions constant. The image reconstruction is completed through a gated context aggregation network (GCAN) and global residual learning GRL. Our refined loss function incorporates gradient fidelity, producing high dynamic range images that are rich in detail and demonstrate superior visual quality. In evaluation metrics focused on image features, our method exhibits significant superiority and leads in holistic assessments as well. It is worth emphasizing that as the number of input images increases, our algorithm exhibits notable computational efficiency.

Keywords: multi-exposure fusion; image processing; computational photography; convolutional neural networks

1. Introduction

Leveraging high dynamic range (HDR) imaging technology allows for a more intricate and expanded color palette in different media forms, including videos and images. However, the dynamic range captured by traditional image sensors like CCD or CMOS deviates significantly from the actual scene due to their ability to capture only low dynamic range images. Direct acquisition of HDR images imposes the need for more advanced and costly equipment. As a cost-effective alternative, multi-exposure image fusion (MEF) offers substantial advantages. It creates a comprehensive exposure map of a scene by merging low dynamic range (LDR) images obtained under various exposure settings, thereby producing an HDR image and enhancing visual perception. Moreover, the fused image retrieves and accentuates details otherwise lost due to underexposure or overexposure.

The extensive study of MEF is attributable to its effectiveness in generating high-quality images. Traditional MEF techniques [1–3] necessitate the manual creation of feature extraction methods and fusion rules. However, this process is not only laborious and intricate but also demonstrates limited robustness under varying input conditions. Recently, Convolutional Neural Networks (CNNs) have made significant progress in low-level tasks [4–6], such as image reconstruction and fusion, due to their robust representational capabilities. DeepFuse [7], a pioneering application of CNNs in the MEF domain, leverages the Multi-Exposure Structural Similarity Index (MEF-SSIM) [8] as a loss function, thereby overcoming the constraints of manual feature design.

Existing MEF algorithms predominantly employ feature concatenation [9,10], which restricts the input exposure sequence length to the number of input neurons, limiting fusion to merely two or three images. This insufficiency in exposure sequence numbers hinders the achievement of comprehensive exposure coverage, highlighting the necessity for MEF algorithms adept at handling sequences of infinite length. To circumvent this issue, most methods adopt a model nesting approach, which inadvertently leads to a linear escalation in model fusion time, undermining real-time performance. Although DeepFuse's [7] feature addition method overcomes this numerical limit, it may result in significant value range discrepancies when dealing with image sequences of varying lengths. The mean or average method for feature fusion proposed by IFCNN [11] indeed mitigates this issue, but it can inadvertently lead to significant feature degradation.

MEF-Net [12] proposes a single-input network that eliminates the connection between images in the same exposure sequence. It calculates weights for each image and uses a weighted fusion method. However, this approach assumes that the image sequences are independent of each other, ignoring the redundancy and complementarity of images captured under the same exposure conditions. Consequently, this assumption results in a loss of detail and color information.

This paper introduces an MEF method capable of accommodating an uncertain quantity of inputs, facilitating the recovery of static scenes while preserving color information. The contributions of this paper are outlined as follows:

- We introduce a reference-guided exposure correction (REC) module, rooted in the reference image, which incorporates both channel and spatial attention. This module significantly alleviates color discrepancies and artifacts in the fused image.
- Within the reconstruction network, we deploy an exposure-guided feature fusion (EGFF) module designed to standardize features of varying lengths to a common dimension. Simultaneously, we enhance the gated context aggregation network (GCAN) to efficiently gather deeper contextual information, preserve spatial resolution, and effectively suppress grid artifacts.
- An optimized loss function is proposed to uphold lighting and texture information, ensuring the comprehensive retention of color information from the exposure sequence images.

Ultimately, we introduce Ref-MEF, a novel and flexible MEF algorithm, specifically designed for multi-exposure image fusion with unpredictable input quantities and resolutions. We carry out end-to-end training on static multi-exposure image sequences processed by registration algorithms [13–15] using the loss function we develop. Several experiments indicate that, compared to most MEF algorithms, our method displays a significant advantage, both in subjective visual effects and objective evaluation metrics. Additionally, our method holds a clear computational time advantage when dealing with an increased number of exposure sequences.

2. Related Work

In this section, we begin with an explanation of different existing MEF methodologies, followed by an incisive review of relevant research endeavors closely related to our own work.

2.1. Existing MEF Methods

MEF algorithms are categorized into dynamic and static types based on the inherent characteristics of the shooting scene. Designing dynamic MEFs requires addressing object motion and camera shake to minimize ghosting effects. Predominantly, these algorithms involve motion detection, image registration, and image reconstruction. Image registration is crucial in counteracting camera shake. Starting with image alignment and registration enables the conversion of dynamic MEFs into static ones. This paper focuses primarily on static MEFs.

Static MEF algorithms are categorized into traditional and deep learning-based approaches. The traditional methods are subdivided into spatial domain-based and transformation domain-based methods. Within the spatial domain, the strategies include: (1) Pixel-level techniques adhere to a paradigm of fusion weighting, at the heart of which lies the development of efficacious weighting functions. For example, Liu et al. [16] proposed an MEF approach that employed dense Scale-Invariant Feature Transform (SIFT) descriptors and guided filtering. This method constructed a weight map informed by spatial consistency, exposure quality, and local contrast, leveraging guided filters to refine weights and mitigate noise. The dense SIFT descriptors gauged activity levels, rendering the method apt for dynamic scenes. (2) Patch-based techniques segment images into patches to compose the fused imagery. A notable method by Ma et al. [2] segmented patches into distinct components of signal strength, signal structure, and mean intensity. Through assessing patch intensity and exposure, these components were integrated to form the fused patches, which were subsequently amalgamated into the final fused image. SPD-MEF [17], developed by Ma's team, employed signal structure decomposition of patches to compute consistency maps for ghosting elimination. APS-MEF [18] improves dynamic contrast by integrating image patch structure decomposition, image cartoon texture decomposition, and the structural similarity index. (3) Optimization-based techniques, exemplified by MEF-Opt [8], aimed to optimize the MEF-SSIMc [8] index within the image domain. Although there is no universally accepted benchmark for appraising MEF algorithms, this method's forte is its adaptability to metrics that more accurately assess fusion outcomes. Notwithstanding, it necessitated extensive computational time due to its iterative global optimization in the image domain.

Regarding transformation domain-based methods, they typically encompass domain transformation, fusion within the transformed domain, and the subsequent inverse transformation. Effective fusion strategies are enacted within the transformed domain, with prevalent techniques involving multi-scale transformations, such as principal component analysis, wavelets, pyramids, and dense invariant feature transformations. Karakaya et al. [1] introduced PAS-MEF, grounded in principal component analysis, adaptive exposure, and saliency maps, harnessing pyramid decomposition for fusion. This preserved the richest information from each exposure image and boasted a rapid processing speed.

Recent advancements in the application of Convolutional Neural Networks (CNNs) in the MEF field underscored their remarkable image representation capabilities. These capabilities eliminated the need for complex manual fusion strategy design found in traditional methods, thus exhibiting high robustness. Deep learning methods predominantly fell into two categories: unsupervised and supervised. DeepFuse [7], the pioneer in incorporating deep learning technology in the MEF field, used an unsupervised measure, MEF-SSIM [19], as the loss function. This breakthrough approach transformed RGB images into YCbCr color space, focusing fusion design solely on the Y channel, whereas the network structure remained simple; the concept of unsupervised metric fusion and the design on the Y channel sparked various subsequent studies. FusionDN [20] and U2Fusion [21] consolidated multiple image tasks into one densely connected network, employing elastic weight merging. This approach enabled a single network model to tackle multiple image fusion tasks, inclusive of multi-modal, multi-exposure, and multi-focus. U2Fusion, building on FusionDN, refined the information preservation distribution strategy and loss function. FusionDN's losses comprised structural similarity Index (SSIM), perceptual loss, and gradient loss. Conversely, U2Fusion replaced the gradient loss with mean squared error (MSE) loss, effectively reducing the brightness bias in fusion outcomes. ACE-MEF [22] preserves the texture and environmental light details in the source image by constructing the clarity preservation network (CPN) network. The illumination adjustment network (IAN) network corrects locally severe exposure, and a specific MEF loss is built to guide CPN in adaptively retaining light and detail information in clear areas.

Supervised methods require a significant amount of ground truth for training; however, a large-scale ground truth dataset in the MEF field is currently non-existent. Consequently, it becomes necessary to either manually generate or simulate "ground truth". Wang et al. [23] generated "ground truth" by manipulating the pixel intensities of the ILSVRC 2012 validation image set [24]. Nevertheless, the authenticity of the ground truth generated by this method could be disputable as it may not accurately reflect the actual shooting effect of real-world scenes. An alternate approach involves the use of outcomes from prior algorithms to simulate "ground truth". For instance, the SCIE dataset [25] not only offered 500 sets of multi-exposure image sequences from static scenes but also presented fusion results from 13 representative algorithms. IFCNN [11] employed a dual-branch architecture with shared weights, merged features extracted from convolution based on element mean, and proceeded to train the model utilizing perceptual loss and the fundamental loss between the source image sequence and the simulated "ground truth". CFMSAN [26] employs a multi-scale attention-guided network to extract features across various scales, generating attention weight maps of multiple sizes. These weight maps guide the fusion result generation. The model undergoes training on the SCIE [25] dataset through a supervised manner.

Apart from CNNS, an alternative category of methodologies based on Generative Adversarial Networks (GANs) is employed to tackle the MEF issue. Taking inspiration from the FusionGAN [27] model, which effectively fuses infrared and visible images, GAN-Fuse [28] enhances adversarial learning by increasing the number of discriminators. This augmentation facilitates the assimilation of valuable information from pairs of images with extreme exposure. MEF-GAN [9] and Chen [29] et al. establish a GAN wherein the generator produces fused images, and the discriminator determines the distinguishability of the fusion results from the forged "real labels". To achieve feature fusion based on attention and long-term dependencies, MEF-GAN [9] incorporates a self-attention mechanism within the generator. However, the imposed constraints on MEF-GAN (requiring image dimensions to be multiples of 8,somewhat curtail its versatility, rendering it unsuitable for arbitrary resolutions. It is noteworthy that Chen [29] et al. integrate a Homography network into their model to compensate for camera motion. This incorporation renders their method applicable to dynamic MEF fusion scenes afflicted by camera jitter.

TransMEF [30] presently introduced a self-supervised, multi-task learning framework premised on the Transform architecture. This framework underwent training on extensive natural datasets, circumventing the need for ground truth. However, the MS-COCO dataset [31], primarily utilized for object detection and segmentation, fell short of meeting rigorous requirements due to its inherent image dynamic range and texture detail information. The brightness and texture data gathered from the MS-COCO dataset failed to adhere to the high-quality standards set forth for MEF image reconstruction. Moreover, the method TransMEF employed for the reconstruction of brightness channels was incapable of restoring the color information in the scene with precision.

2.2. Most Relevant Work

Our research work is intimately related to MEF-Net [12]. The MEF-Net also has the ability to solve network flexibility issues and can receive inputs of varying lengths. This network achieved this by constructing a single-input network, setting the number of input images equal to the batch size, disconnecting the correlation between image sequences, independently calculating the weights of each input, and performing image weighting operations. MEF-Net only used the brightness channel of the image for training, and only took MEF-SSIM [19] as the loss function, so it cannot retain the chroma information in the captured scene.

In contrast, our network fully utilizes the relationship between source image sequences and builds a weight map that has been smoothed by Gaussian after acquiring exposure information between source sequences, forming regional characteristics. By weighting and merging the corrected features, we send a fixed number of feature channels into the reconstruction network for training. Ref-MEF combines MEF-SSIMc [8] and gradient fidelity items to construct the loss function, not only preserving the chroma information in the scene as much as possible but also retaining the high-frequency components and texture integrity of the fusion results.

It is worth noting that both approaches adopt the context aggregation network (CAN) [32]. The CAN in MEF-Net was used to generate a weight map. Our enhancements to the CAN include the introduction of separable convolutions before dilated convolutions, thereby substantially strengthening the interdependence of the input units in the dilated convolutions and significantly diminishing grid artifacts. Furthermore, we have integrated a gating structure, combined multi-scale information, and employed global residual learning (GRL) for image reconstruction learning.

3. Methodology

We present Ref-MEF, a highly flexible and superior multi-exposure image fusion method. As illustrated in Figure 1, our approach can accommodate multi-exposure image sequences of varying lengths by first converting them into feature maps through the encoder section. We then refine these features using the reference-guided exposure correction (REC) module. In the reconstruction network section, we utilize the exposure-guided feature fusion (EGFF) module to ensure adaptability to different exposure levels. Additionally, we employ the reference-guided exposure correction (GCAN) and global residual (GRL) connections to facilitate efficient network reconstruction and information enhancement, ultimately improving the quality of image fusion. Finally, the reconstructed feature maps are decoded back into the original image space, producing a high-quality fused image.

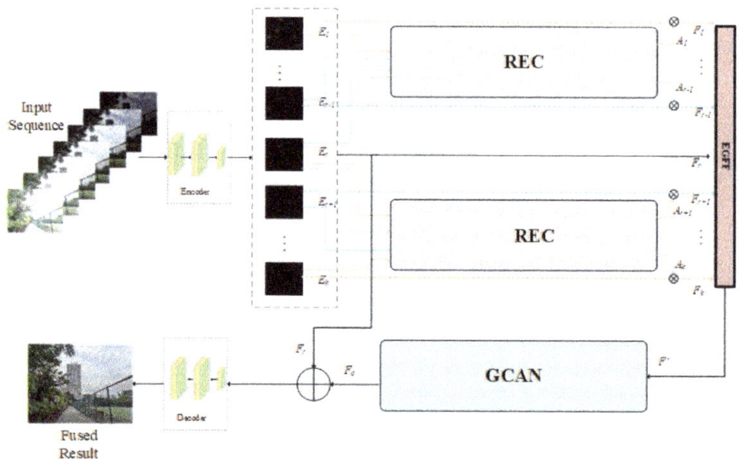

Figure 1. The overall network architecture of Ref-MEF, as proposed, follows a basic autoencoder framework. It consists of an encoder section with three convolutional layers. The reference-guided exposure correction (REC) module is responsible for feature correction, exposure-guided feature fusion (EGFF) handles feature fusion, and gated context aggregation network (GCAN) along with global residual connections are responsible for feature reconstruction. The decoder section is tasked with restoring the image to the RGB image space.

3.1. *Reference-Guided Exposure Correction*

As depicted in Figure 1, initial processing is performed on the input sequence images of multiple exposures. This procedure is facilitated by a universal encoder, which consists of three convolution layers and is tasked to map the images from the LDR domain to a distinct feature space for extraction and pre-processing of image features. For uniform feature space distribution and semantic information across LDR images, we have utilized a parameter-sharing approach to facilitate comparisons. This technique uses the identical encoder for all LDR images, providing superior operational efficiency and substantial reduction in network parameters compared to multiple autonomous encoders. Despite the shared-weight encoder's ability to efficiently extract generic image features, it falls short in characterizing the relationships among images with varying exposure levels and their associated features. Therefore, to improve image feature representation precision and foster a more profound study of exposure sequence interrelations, we introduce the reference-guided exposure correction (REC) module.

To determine the reference image essential for the REC module, we utilized the Peak-to-Average Ratio (PAR) for histogram quantization. The PAR signifies the ratio between the peak and valley of the histogram, serving as an indicator of the histogram's uniformity, specifically the uniform distribution of image brightness. An image with a diminished PAR generally suggests the absence of conspicuous overexposed or underexposed regions, as overexposure and underexposure result in abnormally elevated or diminished peaks and valleys in the histogram. Opting for such an image as a reference mitigates the introduction of unwarranted distortions during the fusion process. Furthermore, a lower PAR is frequently linked to superior preservation of image details, contributing to the overall retention of scene intricacies. We assume that the brightness has been sorted from low to high, and the reference image's index is defined as:

$$r = \arg\min PAR_i, \text{for} \quad i = 1, 2, \ldots, K, \tag{1}$$

where $\arg\min(\cdot)$ is a search operator used to locate the index of the image with the smallest PAR value within the exposure sequence, where K represents the current length of the exposure sequence. Here, r divides the image sequence into two parts: the underexposed images L_{u} and the overexposed images L_{o}, with the corresponding encoders extracting the features as E_{u} and E_{o}, respectively.

As depicted in Figure 2, the REC module combines spatial attention and channel attention to adjust the impact of non-reference features on image reconstruction by utilizing spatial information, exposure intensity information, and channel color information of the reference image.

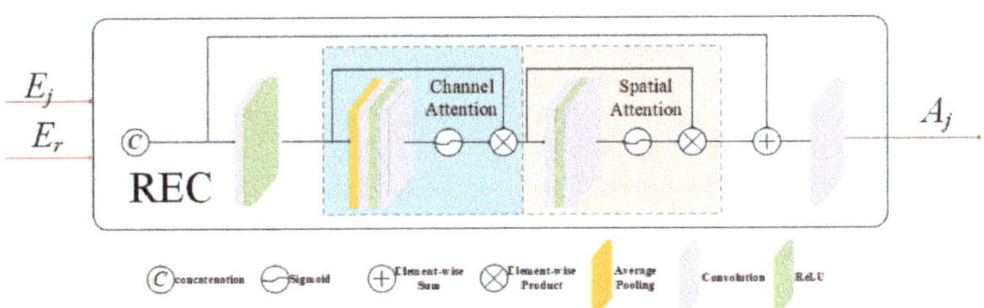

Figure 2. Reference-guided exposure correction module (REC).

Consider the underexposed feature E_{j}, an element of E_{u}. The $REC_u(\cdot)$ refines E_{j}'s contribution to image reconstruction by utilizing spatial, exposure, and color information from the reference image. The module automatically adjusts the weight A_{j} of the LDR image, specifically for those images with relatively lower exposure levels. This weight encapsulates not only the image's own exposure information but also integrates related content from the reference image. This integration allows the enhancement of non-reference images through the reference image's information, thus uncovering the relationships among images with differing exposure degrees.

In a similar way, we can also obtain the feature F_o adjusted by $REC_o(\cdot)$ in the overexposed area. To ensure that the network can cope with the image reconstruction problem of the exposure sequence of indefinite length, we adopt a parameter-sharing strategy for its implementation module.

$$\begin{aligned} F_j = E_j \bigotimes A_j &= E_j \bigotimes REC_i(concat(E_j, E_r)) \\ &= e(L_j) \bigotimes REC_i([e(L_j); e(L_r)]). \end{aligned} \tag{2}$$

$REC_i(\cdot)$, comprising $REC_u(\cdot)$ and $REC_o(\cdot)$, employs "concat" for channel dimension concatenation, with $e(\cdot)$ denoting the encoder and $\otimes$ indicating element-wise multiplication.

3.2. Reconstruction Network

3.2.1. Exposure-Guided Feature Fusion

To integrate the variably quantified correction features derived from the REC module into the reconstruction network for further processing, it is crucial to amalgamate and stabilize the features to a designated number of channels. Existing feature-merging methods, employing average-featured or maximum value selection [11], lead to suboptimal network flexibility and feature degeneration. Thus, we propose an exposure-guided feature fusion (EGFF) strategy.

This innovative method is built upon the principle that during the merging process, the weights corresponding to well-exposed regions should be accentuated, whereas those associated with poorly exposed regions should be significantly reduced. After establishing this objective, we use average brightness as a metric, setting the ideal brightness level away from 0 (indicating underexposure) and 1 (indicating overexposure), specifically at 0.5.

Following a Gaussian curvature measurement, pixel-level weights are derived. Nonetheless, given that F_j is a regionally distinctive feature with asymmetric spatial information, a direct weighting process is not feasible. Instead, we necessitate a subsequent transformation process to endow the weights with region-centric properties. Concurrently, the unity of features should maintain receptive fields similar to or the same as F_j. Using Gaussian curvature as a measuring scale, w_{gaussian_j} are obtained as outlined in Equation (3).

$$w_{\text{gaussian}_j} = \exp\left(-\frac{\|\overline{L}_j - 0.5\|_F^2}{2\sigma^2}\right), \quad \sigma = 0.2, \quad 1 \le j \le K, \tag{3}$$

wherein $\overline{L}_j$ denotes the mean brightness of the image, computed as the numeric mean of the three color channels of the image. The term $\|\cdot\|_F$ signifies the computation of the Frobenius norm, whereas K designates the length of the present exposure sequence.

We implement a Gaussian filtering procedure on the weight map, utilizing a Gaussian filtering kernel with standard deviation σ^* and Gaussian convolution kernel G_{σ^*}. This procedure enhances the weight's regional attributes, redresses its uneven distribution and smoothness, and enhances its resistance to noise interference. The entire process can be demonstrated as a convolution operation, with the Gaussian kernel acting as a filter to enhance the quality of the weight data.

$$w_i = G_{\sigma^*} * w_{\text{gaussian}_j}, \quad 1 \le j \le K. \tag{4}$$

Finally, we employ a normalization process to the weights, accompanied by a pixel-level weighting methodology, to accrue a feature map F' post the feature fusion:

$$F' = \sum_{j=1}^{K} \widetilde{\omega}_j \cdot F_j, \quad \widetilde{\omega}_j = \frac{\omega_j}{\sum_{k=1}^{K} \omega_k}. \tag{5}$$

Incorporating this mapping relationship enables the creation of networks capable of accommodating input sequences of unlimited length while maintaining fixed-dimensional features in the results. On the one hand, the network exhibits minimal structural and parametric expansion as the input image sequence length K increases. On the other hand, it associates input images with their respective image features, effectively preserving the original image information alongside the significance of feature maps. Simultaneously, this module's operation is straightforward and effectively manages computational complexity. In comparison to fusion techniques utilizing maximum or minimum values, this training approach offers superior stability and mitigates gradient truncation concerns. Unlike the use of the mean value for fusion, it takes into account the allocation of exposure information weights in input images, thereby averting bias issues stemming from inconsistent exposure information. Employing normalization for weight calculation, rather than simple summation [7], ensures the stability of weight values, preventing abrupt value range expansion as K increases. Hence, adopting a weighted approach represents the optimal method for feature fusion. We denote this fusion strategy as 'Exposure-Guided Feature Fusion' (EGFF).

3.2.2. Gated Context Aggregation Network

The primary objective of the context aggregation network (CAN) [32] is to aggregate context information at a deeper level without compromising spatial resolution in order to capture context information at various scales. In their research, they examined multiple convolutional network architectures and determined that the context aggregation network based on dilated convolutions has significant advantages in terms of approximate accuracy, speed, and convergence. Building upon their work, we have adopted a similar CAN architecture and made enhancements by incorporating a gate fusion structure to extract features at different levels, which we refer to as GCAN, as shown in Figure 3.

The fundamental component of CAN is dilated convolutions; although dilated convolutions are widely acknowledged as effective, they can generate a phenomenon known as gridding artifacts [33]. To mitigate this issue, Wang et al. [34] proposed either introducing interactions between input units before dilated convolutions or appending a convolutional layer with a kernel size of 2r-1 after dilated convolutions. In this study, we have chosen to employ a similar approach by incorporating depthwise separable convolutions as a pre-convolution layer prior to dilated convolutions.

Depthwise separable convolutions typically consist of two stages: depthwise convolutions and pointwise convolutions (also referred to as 1×1 convolutions), which independently address spatial and cross-channel correlations in the input. In the depthwise convolution stage, each input channel undergoes convolution with a distinct set of filters to effectively capture spatial correlations within each channel. Subsequently, in the pointwise convolution stage, the output of the depthwise convolution is convolved with 1×1 filters, taking into account cross-channel correlations. These shared filters enable each output feature to be a function of all input channels, thereby enhancing the dependency of the output on the input units.

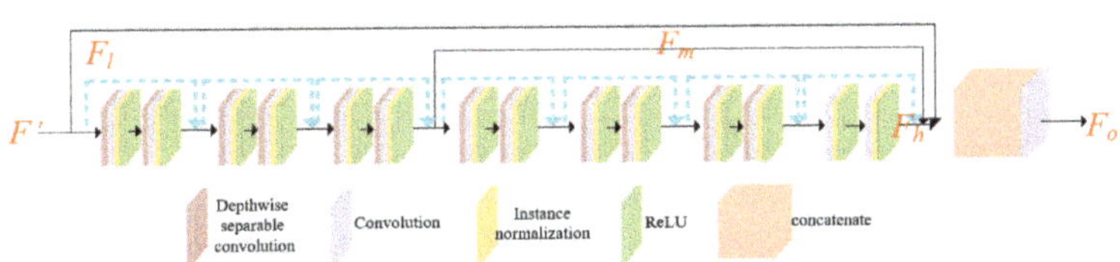

Figure 3. The architecture of gated context aggregation network (GCAN).

In computer vision, the integration of features from diverse layers can foster both low-level and high-level tasks. With this in mind, we have developed a structure, $\mathcal{G}$, for gated fusion. Initially, this structure extracts feature mappings from an array of levels F, subsequently feeding them into a fusion block. The fusion block's role is to compute weights for three distinct levels, each corresponding to a unique feature level. This design aims to achieve gated fusion weights that can efficiently aggregate information across various levels.

$$\begin{aligned} (\mathcal{W}_l, \mathcal{W}_m, \mathcal{W}_h) &= \mathcal{G}(F_l, F_m, F_h), \\ F_o &= \mathcal{W}_l * F_l + \mathcal{W}_m * F_m + \mathcal{W}_h * F_h, \end{aligned} \tag{6}$$

In our proposed GCAN module, F_l, F_m, and F_h denote the feature information at the low, middle, and high layers, correspondingly. Concurrently, $\mathcal{W}_l$, $\mathcal{W}_m$, and $\mathcal{W}_h$ serve as the output weights of the gated structure. F_o signifies not just the weight post-information aggregation, but also embodies the outcome of the whole GCAN module.

Simultaneously, the reconstruction network was enhanced by incorporating a global residual structure, thereby transforming the feature fusion process into a residual learning process, which facilitates network training. The inclusion of skip connections not only enables more comprehensive utilization of image information but also ensures that the fused image closely resembles the reference image, thereby preserving the color and brightness relationships within the image. More specifically, this design effectively reuses shallow features from the reference image, injecting spatial information containing these shallow features into middle-level features with a larger receptive field. This facilitates further integration and modulation of spatial and neighborhood information. This reuse of features can also be interpreted as learning the residual between the fused image features and the reference image features. Finally, a decoder structure symmetrical to the encoder is employed to maintain the original resolution and convert the feature maps back into the original image space, resulting in the successful fusion of multi-exposure images.

3.3. Loss Function

The Multiple Exposure Image Fusion Structural Similarity (MEF-SSIM) [19] evaluates the quality of image fusion by measuring the local similarity between the input image sequence and the fused image. This evaluation metric not only inherits the excellent mathematical properties of Structural Similarity Index (SSIM) but also aligns with people's subjective perception of image quality. It also satisfies the requirement of unsupervised learning without the need for labels, making it widely applicable. However, this operator is only applicable to brightness information, which weakens the color information of the image to some extent. Based on this, Ma [8] proposed MEF-SSIMc to extend it to the color space. MEF-SSIMc is an evaluation index for multiple exposure image fusion that contains rich texture, color, and spatial structural information. The representation of MEF-SSIMc is:

$$Q(\{L_k\}, F) = \frac{1}{M} \sum_{j=1}^{M} \frac{(2\mu_{\hat{L}}\mu_F + C_1)(2\sigma_{\hat{L}F} + C_2)}{(\mu_{\hat{L}}^2 + \mu_F^2 + C_1)(\sigma_{\hat{L}}^2 + \sigma_F^2 + C_2)}. \tag{7}$$

Among these variables, M denotes the number of patches, and $\hat{\mu}_L$ and F represent the expected mean intensity of image sequence patches and the fusion result, respectively. For brevity, please refer to reference X for the specific calculation formula of the mean intensity. $\mu_{\hat{L}}\mu_F$ signifies the covariance between $\hat{\mu}_L$ and F, whereas C_1 and C_2 are small constants introduced to prevent instability when the denominator approaches 0. Formula X is employed to compute the comprehensive quality measurement of the MEF-SSIMc indicator.

However, experiments have revealed that the use of MEF-SSIMc alone to formulate the loss function is considerably effective in preserving the main structural and color components of the image. Nonetheless, it also introduces blurring to the fused image, leading to a substantial loss of mid-to-high frequency details. Consequently, it becomes necessary to incorporate certain constraint terms into the loss function to ensure the preservation of mid-to-high frequency details in the image. To this end, we strive to introduce a gradient fidelity term into the loss function. The definition of the gradient fidelity term E_∇ is provided below:

$$E_\nabla = | \sum_{k=1}^{K} \widetilde{\omega_k} \nabla L_k - \nabla F |_2, \tag{8}$$

where ∇ is the gradient operator, $\widetilde{\omega_k}$ is the normalized weight. The specific calculation formula can be referred to in Equation (6). F represents the fused image. Our ultimate optimization goal is to simultaneously maximize MEF-SSIMc and minimize the gradient fidelity term. Maximizing MEF-SSIMc is used to optimize the general quality of the fused image, including spatial information, color information, exposure information, and mid-to-low frequency components. Minimizing E_∇ is used to optimize the details of the mid-to-high frequency components. Therefore, we can construct the following loss function:

$$\mathcal{L} = \alpha \cdot E_\nabla - E_{MEF-SSIM_c} + 1. \tag{9}$$

In this paper, the balance parameter α is set to 0.9.

Throughout the experiments conducted on the window size of MEF-SSIMc, a significant improvement in the overall fusion effect was observed as the window size was increased from 8 to 19. However, surpassing a window size of 35 did not result in the anticipated performance improvement, but rather led to an increase in computational time. As a result, for this paper, the window size for MEF-SSIMc has been set to 34.

Consequently, the construction of the loss function involves only the input image sequence and the output of the algorithm, without any ground truth. Therefore, our network is trained in an unsupervised manner.

4. Experimental Results and Comparisons

In this section, we conducted experiments to validate the fusion performance of the proposed Ref-MEF. First, we provided a detailed description of the experimental setup. Second, we compared Ref-MEF with recent classical MEF methods through subjective evaluation and objective assessment. Finally, we performed a series of ablation experiments to assess the effectiveness of the core components.

4.1. Training

We collected a comprehensive dataset for Ref-MEF. Initially, we gathered over 842 exposure sequences from six different sources [7,8,19,25,35,36]. Additionally, we used handheld devices and tripods to capture 30 sets of multi-exposure image sequences. We first eliminated sequences containing obvious object movement and retained only those successfully aligned using existing image registration algorithms [13–15]. After strict screening, a total of 794 static sequences were preserved. These sequences included rich HDR content, covering indoor and outdoor environments, static objects, and daytime and nighttime scenes. Their spatial resolution ranged from 0.2 to 20 million pixels, with exposure counts varying between three and nine times. Among them, 700 sequences were designated for Ref-MEF training, whereas the remaining 94 sequences were reserved for testing purposes.

During the training process, we adjusted the dimensions of the exposure sequences to three different resolutions: 128 s, 512 s, and 1024 s, representing low, medium, and high resolutions, respectively. Specifically, 128 s denotes resizing the shorter side to 128 while preserving the aspect ratio. We trained the entire network using the Adam optimizer for 100 epochs, with a learning rate of 10^{-4}. The remaining parameters in the Adam optimizer were kept at their default values. The batch size was set to match the number of exposures in the current sequence. To strike a balance between runtime and performance, we configured the seven dilation rates of GCAN as follows: (2, 2, 2, 4, 4, 4, 1). Additionally, we set the channel count for all intermediate convolutional layers to 64.

4.2. Main Result

Our study involved a comparative analysis of Ref-MEF with twelve state-of-the-art MEF techniques. These encompass traditional spatial and transformation domain-based algorithms such as SPD-MEF [17], MEF-Opt [8], FMMEF [37], and GD [3]. Additionally, we scrutinized several advanced deep learning methodologies, including DeepFuse [7], MEFCNN [38], IFCNN [11], FusionDN [20], U2Fusion [21], MEF-GAN [9], MEF-Net [12], and Trans-MEF [30].

In deep learning methods, aside from MEF-Net [12] which can flexibly handle multiple inputs, the number of multiple exposure images processed by other networks is fixed. To ensure the consistency of the comparison, we adopted a nested model strategy, that is; first selecting two images to merge to obtain an intermediate result, then merging this result with other LDR images, and repeating this process until the final result is obtained, thus ensuring that the number of inputs for all networks is the same.

Partial results of our algorithm's execution are depicted in Figure 4.

Figure 4. Results from partial execution of the Ref-MEF method.

4.2.1. Qualitative Comparison

The scene depicted in Figure 5 captures the exterior of a 7-Eleven convenience store during the night, encompassing both nocturnal and illuminative conditions. Under conditions of extreme exposure, the integration of information within the underexposed and overexposed regions becomes exceedingly challenging, presenting a formidable task for the algorithm. In contrast to both DeepFuse and our proposed method, alternative approaches generally prove inadequate in effectively mitigating highlights within the vicinity of street lamps. Within SPD-MEF, MEF-Opt, and MEF-Net, substantial errors manifest in the region illuminated by street lamps. Despite these challenges, our algorithm adeptly magnifies the light bulb in the area illuminated by street lamps. Regarding the section depicting the convenience store, SPD-MEF, MEF-Opt, MEF-Net, and TransMEF tend to manifest color deviations or insufficient brightness, resulting in a substantial loss of details. IFCNN exhibits an overall diminished brightness, and the fusion outcomes of DeepFuse and FusionDN demonstrate reduced clarity. Upon meticulous examination of the results, our algorithm excels in preserving the nuanced texture details of ground tiles and the internal information of the convenience store. Consequently, in the context of the current intricate scene examination, our algorithm emerges as particularly proficient in both information preservation and the suppression of highlights.

Figure 6's environment, atop a shopping mall, presents a wide exposure range challenge for fusion algorithms. MEF-Opt, FMMEF, MEF-CNN, MEF-Net, and Trans-MEF suffer from pronounced ghosting artifacts, particularly near windows with direct sunlight, impacting the overall visual quality. Additionally, SPD-MEF produces an overly bright and sharp image, whereas GD and DeepFuse yield overall dark results. IFCNN shows significant color deviation, with a predominant greenish tint. In contrast, FusionDN, U2Fusion, and Ref-MEF offer superior subjective visual effects. Notably, Ref-MEF adeptly handles multiple exposure challenges, such as ghosting, over-sharpening, and color deviation, providing balanced visuals in the challenging top-floor indoor setting, positioning it among the best in this context.

Figure 5. The qualitative performance comparison on the "SevenElevenNight" image sequence.

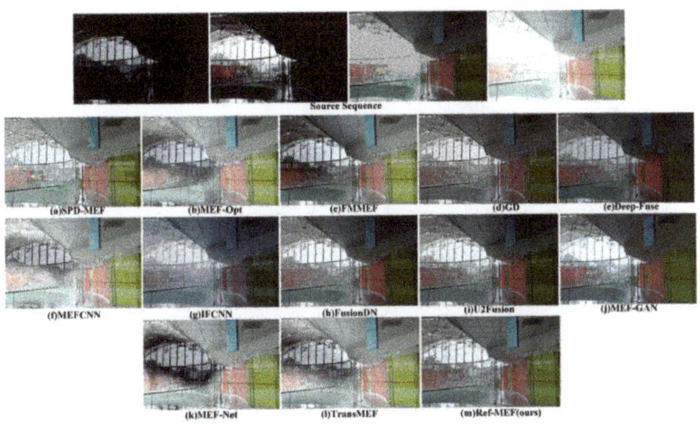

Figure 6. The qualitative performance comparison on the "Preschool" image sequence.

In Figure 7's coastal scene, comprising coastline, sunset, clouds, and waves, several fusion algorithms face hurdles. U2Fusion, MEF-GAN, and TransMEF exhibit notable errors; MEF-GAN shows clear color deviation, and both MEF-GAN and TransMEF significantly lose detail, obscuring the coastline. FMMEF, DeepFuse, IFCNN, and FusionDN produce overall dark images with limited dynamic range. MEF-Net and MEF-CNN struggle with texture detail degradation, especially in distant clouds and waves. For SPD-MEF, MEF-Opt, GD, and Re-MEF, the lack of Ground Truth hampers further subjective evaluation, though they show a high dynamic range.

Figure 8 depicts the "ColorChecker" scenario, wherein the original scene comprises two color palettes separated by a barrier for light control. One side of the barrier is exposed to extremely dim light, whereas the other side receives direct illumination. The distribution of lighting information in the scene is highly variable, presenting a formidable challenge for the MEF algorithms in recovering authentic scene details. Figure 8 showcases the outcomes of various algorithms, revealing substantial lens flare errors in SPD-MEF. IFCNN, FusionDN, U2Fusion, and MFE-GAN demonstrate perceptible shortcomings in restoring and preserving color palette details within shaded regions. The fusion results of GD, Deep-Fuse, IFCNN, FusionDN, U2Fusion, MEF-GAN, and Trans-MEF all manifest pronounced shifts in white balance, significantly diverging from the genuine color information of the scene. MEF-Opt, FMMEF, and MEFNet produce results more closely aligned with the authentic color tones of the scene. Regrettably, MEF-Opt yields somewhat blurry images. Given the current scenario, we posit that the outcomes from FMMEF, MEFNet, and our approach most faithfully represent the true scene.

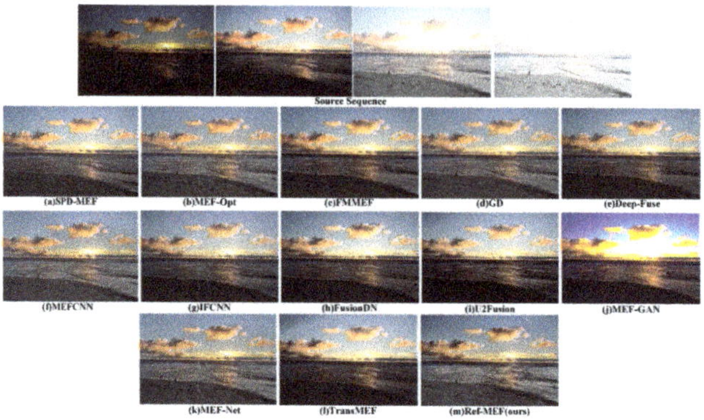

Figure 7. The qualitative performance comparison on the "Sky" image sequence.

Figure 8. The qualitative performance comparison on the "ColorChecker" image sequence.

Figure 9 portrays the nocturnal scene outside Waffle House, featuring a stationary red car that serves as a focal point in the current context. The comparison of fusion results is focused on these key elements. In the fusion outcomes, FMMEF manifests conspicuous errors. The majority of algorithms encounter challenges in rendering visible details, particularly in the bicycle's front window and the driver's cabin, with U2Fusion and MEF-GAN verging on operational failure. Although IFCNN adeptly retains finer details, the overall image significantly diverges from human perceptions of a nocturnal setting, exhibiting excessive brightness and suffering from overexposure in the Waffle House window area. In this specific scenario, we contend that our algorithm, when juxtaposed with alternative methods, meticulously preserves details and aligns most closely with the human perception of a nighttime scene.

Figure 10 illustrates the garden scene. In the current context, the overall outputs of IFCNN, U2Fusion, MEF-GAN, and TransMEF appear dim, revealing noticeable shortcomings in detail preservation. Notably, MEF-GAN introduces artificial clouds in the sky to enhance natural color transitions; however, a distinct boundary between the white clouds and the blue sky should be maintained. MEF-Net exhibits pronounced ghosting effects, particularly evident in color deviations surrounding the leaves on the right side of the image. In this scenario, the subjective representations of alternative algorithms are generally satisfactory, primarily reflecting subjective selection differences rather than significant errors. Our algorithm, in this particular scenario, effectively retains both detailed and color information.

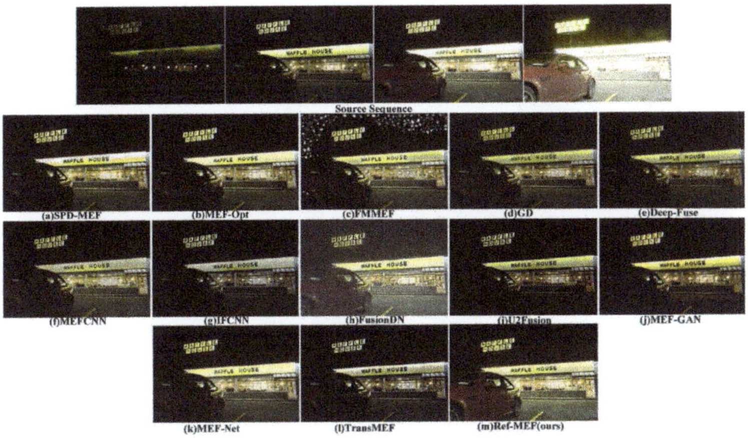

Figure 9. The qualitative performance comparison on the "WaffleHouse" image sequence.

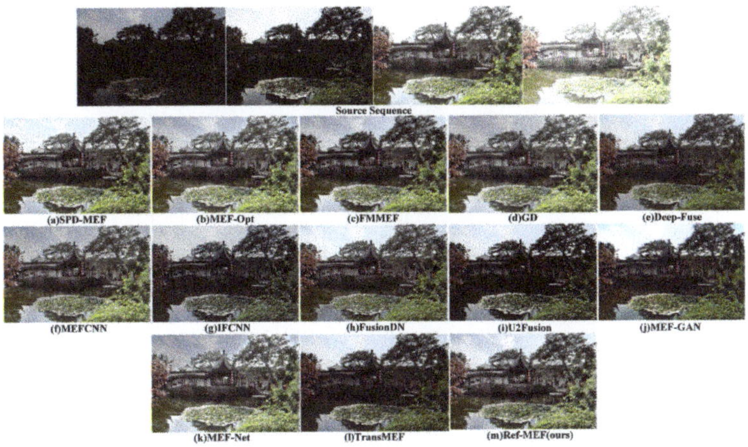

Figure 10. The qualitative performance comparison on the "ChineseGarden" image sequence.

In summary, our algorithm exhibits exceptional robustness in managing intricate scenes, particularly in the context of sequence fusion. The majority of learning-based algorithms typically embrace a design that limits the input to a pair of images, achieved through nested models for sequence image fusion. However, this approach falls short of fully capitalizing on exposure information across the entire sequence. It is noteworthy that, in certain relatively uncomplicated scenarios, even when errors are infrequent, there may be variations in subjective assessment results among individuals. Nevertheless, our algorithm delves into the correlations within the entire exposure sequence, meticulously addressing aspects such as color accuracy, image details, and overall effectiveness, with the aim of attaining satisfactory outcomes in diverse situations.

4.2.2. Quantitative Comparison

Numerous methods primarily utilize MEF-SSIM [19] as an evaluation metric in MEF research. This metric primarily assesses the structural similarity between the fused image and the inputted image sequence, correlating with intuitive human cognition. However, this method predominantly considers brightness details, partially disregarding color information. To rectify this limitation, Ma [8] expanded MEF-SSIM into a color space, generating MEF-SSIMc. This updated evaluation metric simultaneously considers the image's color, texture, and spatial structure details, offering a more thorough assessment of the effect of multiple exposure image fusion.

Table 1 shows the numerical comparison results of MEF-SSIM and MEF-SSIMc. Among all the compared methods, MEF-Opt [8] performed the best, which is not surprising, because its algorithm is designed to optimize these two indicators in the global image space. Compared with other methods, Ref-MEF is close to the best in MEF-SSIMc and ranks third in MEF-SSIM, which fully proves the effectiveness of our Ref-MEF network training.

Table 1. Comparison of MEF-SSIM and MEF-SSIMc index values for various multi-exposure image fusion methods.

Metrics	SPD-MEF [17]	MFE-Opt [8]	FMMEF [37]	GD [3]	DeepFuse citedeepfuse	MEFCNN [38]	IFCNN [11]
MEF-SSIM	0.9382	0.9762 [1]	0.9324	0.9645 [2]	0.8968	0.9364	0.9432
MEF-SSIMc	0.9271	0.9775 [1]	0.9403	0.9527 [3]	0.862	0.9126	0.9237
Metrics	FusionDN [20]	U2Fusion [21]	MEF-GAN [9]	MEFNet [12]	TransMEF [30]	Ref-MEF	
MEF-SSIM	0.924	0.9304	0.7722	0.9139	0.8972	0.9496 [3]	
MEF-SSIMc	0.9123	0.9203	0.7802	0.9026	0.9032	0.9582 [2]	

x [y] signifies that the method's value is 'x' under the present indicator, and its ranking stands at 'y'.

Furthermore, given that the MEF task remains within the scope of image fusion, several prevalent image quality assessment metrics are appropriate for evaluating its outcomes. Specifically, image fusion results should maximize detail retention and minimize artifact presence for enhanced visual appeal. Consequently, to evaluate the MEF method comprehensively, we have incorporated an expanded set of standard image quality assessment metrics. As illustrated in Table 2, we utilized 13 standard metrics to perform a thorough analysis of MEF fusion results, focusing on three domains: information theory-based, image feature-based, and human perception-inspired.

Table 2. Evaluation metrics used in this paper.

Category	Name	Meaning	+/−
Information theory-based	EN [39]	Entropy	+
	CE [40]	Cross entropy	−
	TE [41]	Tsallis entropy	+
	PSNR [42]	Peak signal-to-noise ratio	+
	NMI [43]	Normal mutual information	+
Image feature-based	AG [44]	Average gradient	+
	EI [45]	Edge intensity	+
	SD [46]	Standard deviation	+
	SF [47]	Spatial frequency	+
	$Q^{AB/F}$ [48]	Gradient-based fusion performance	+
Human perception-inspired	Q^{CB} [49]	Chen–Blum metric	+
	Q^{CV} [50]	Chen–Varshney metric	−
	VIF [51]	Visual information fidelity	+

"+" indicates better performance with larger values, and "−" indicates better performance with smaller values.

Table 3 demonstrates the calculated results derived from our chosen evaluation metrics. With respect to the image feature-based metrics, the Ref-MEF method exhibits substantial superiority. Simultaneously, in measurements grounded on information theory and human visual perception, it ascends to the benchmark level of contemporary algorithms. We apply an average to the rankings corresponding to each method across varied metrics, subsequently organizing them in accordance with their scores. These findings serve to confirm that our methodology secures a leading position, thereby authenticating its preeminent stature in the realm of objective evaluation metrics.

Table 3. Average results obtained using various evaluation metrics by different MEF methods on the test dataset.

Methods	EN	CE	TE	PNSR	NMI	AG	EI	SD	SF	$Q^{AB/F}$	Q^{CB}	Q^{CV}	VIF
SPD-MEF ^{6}	7.1811	3.234	17,394	58.5365	0.6984	5.8798	54.6891	56.7475	20.7963	0.6376	0.4546	354.9691	0.774
MFE-OPT ^{5}	7.2264	3.2354	**152,840**	**58.5998**	0.5926	5.7986	58.7073	51.5027	19.5281	0.6898	0.4627	729.1273	0.6959
FMMEF ^{4}	**7.4264**	2.9075	53,255	57.6855	0.4809	5.69	53.4626	53.508	18.9879	0.7006	0.4558	621.063	0.9041
GD ^{10}	7.2257	3.7746	30,000	56.6983	0.5465	5.4076	53.4681	55.8072	17.8313	0.6749	0.4305	336.0762	0.8511
DeepFuse ^{12}	6.8395	3.1395	93,099	57.9744	0.7403	3.4418	35.2964	47.8109	10.6415	0.3866	0.391	361.694	0.5178
MEFCNN ^{11}	7.3061	**2.6457**	101,951	54.2667	0.5974	4.9264	51.0512	55.7865	17.1608	0.6667	0.4297	750.0043	0.7355
IFCNN ^{7}	7.153	3.3971	47,282	55.3554	0.7796	6.1824	62.1918	51.5826	21.0011	0.5919	0.41	**238.3928**	0.7146
FusionDN ^{2}	7.4243	2.9392	9673	54.9748	0.7383	6.9693	**69.3412**	**67.7641**	21.6542	0.536	0.4355	322.5755	**0.9505**
U2Fusion ^{9}	6.6785	3.018	20,326	56.0697	0.7639	5.4728	59.3588	65.1615	18.5468	0.5354	0.4159	242.4821	0.8281
MEF-GAN ^{13}	6.9109	2.773	21,360	54.857	0.5699	4.5945	48.5215	63.734	13.9918	0.2829	0.3822	618.3198	0.5859
MEFNet ^{3}	7.3035	3.059	83,157	57.7134	0.6077	5.8818	62.828	58.5405	19.7768	0.6767	**0.4863**	622.814	0.8342
TransMEF ^{8}	7.2123	3.0568	18,812	56.9614	**0.8031**	5.5395	54.5106	62.901	18.3247	0.5705	0.4197	281.2867	0.8175
Ref-MEF ^{1}	7.4247 ^{2}	2.93 ^{4}	97,332 ^{3}	58.5548 ^{2}	0.7606 ^{4}	**6.9852** ^{1}	67.9798 ^{2}	67.103 ^{2}	**21.7384** ^{1}	**0.7013** ^{1}	0.4474 ^{5}	292.275 ^{4}	0.8681 ^{3}

x ^{y} represents that x is ranked as the yth in the column. Here, x can refer to either a method or a specific evaluation metric. The data highlighted in bold indicates that the current method outperforms all contrastive methods within the current evaluation Metrics.

4.2.3. Running Time Comparison

In order to compare the computational costs of the MEF algorithm, we demonstrate the running time with varying numbers of exposure shots, as depicted in Figure 11. These times are the average fusion times under a scenario with a fixed spatial resolution of 512 s (resizing the shorter side to 512 while preserving the aspect ratio). Among these algorithms, MEF-Opt [8] has the longest running time, which is not surprising as it employs iterative methods to perform global image optimization to satisfy the MEF-SSIM [19] criterion. Compared to other learning-based methods, Ref-MEF does not require more model layers due to its unique network structure when the number of exposure shots increases, and therefore the running time does not change much. However, other deep learning methods show a linear growth trend when the number of exposure shots increases. Although the algorithm of MEF-Net [12] is slightly faster than ours, our algorithm significantly outperforms MEF-Net in both objective and subjective assessments of the fusion results.

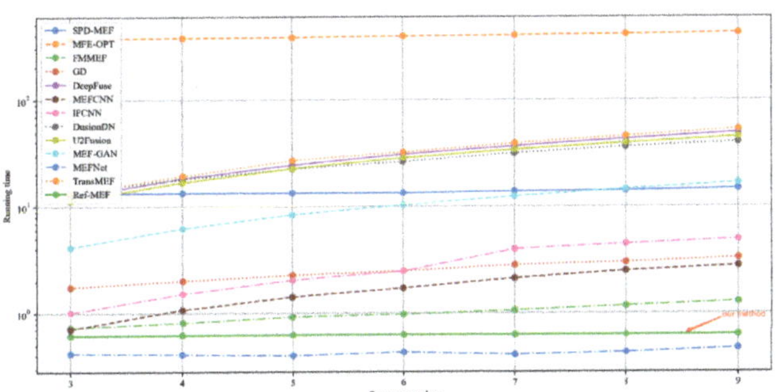

Figure 11. The change in the runtime of the MEF algorithms corresponds to an increase in the number of exposure lenses.

4.3. Ablation Experiments

To evaluate the significance of each component in Ref-MEF, we conducted an ablation analysis to explore the impact of different components on network performance. Special attention was directed towards the REC module, EGFF module, separable convolution, and gate fusion block in the GCAN, as well as the gradient fidelity term in the loss function. The influence of each component was systematically assessed by individually removing them. Upon removal of the REC module, we substitute the original structure with conventional convolution. For the exclusion of the EGFF module, a strategy akin to the weighted averaging of IFCNN [11] was employed to compute features. The GCAN was substituted with the CAN baseline network without separable convolution and gate fusion structures. In the discourse on the loss function, the gradient fidelity term was omitted, and only MEF-SSIMc was utilized for unsupervised training. Detailed configurations and experimental metric values can be found in Table 4.

Beyond the gradient fidelity term in the loss function, the removal of these components during the ablation process resulted in varying degrees of suppression on the performance of MEF-SSIM [19] and MEF-SSIMc [8]. It is crucial to note that the exclusion of the gradient fidelity term led to an improvement in the metrics of MEF-SSIM [19] and MEFSSIMc [8]. Nevertheless, we recommend retaining the gradient fidelity term due to its pivotal role in preserving texture and high-frequency information in images.

Table 4. Specific ablation settings and training configurations were implemented for each component, which demonstrate the optimal performance achieved by the combination of our designed modules.

component	configuration1	configuration2	configuration3	configuration4	configuration5	configuration6
REC		✓	✓	✓	✓	✓
EGFF	✓		✓	✓	✓	✓
Spe Conv	✓	✓		✓	✓	✓
Gated Fusion	✓	✓	✓		✓	✓
Loss with E_∇	✓	✓	✓	✓		✓
MEF-SSIM	0.8633	0.8479	0.8555	0.8958	**0.9588**	0.9496
MEF-SSIMc	0.8711	0.8578	0.8632	0.9039	**0.9673**	0.9582

In Figure 12, We showcase fusion outcomes related to scenes involving books, achieved by adjusting various balance factors, represented as α. Upon closer inspection of the image text details, it is observed that in the absence of the fidelity term for gradients ($\alpha = 0$), even though MEF-SSIMc based on the image structure reaches its maximum, the image details remain incomplete, resulting in inadequate clarity. Experimental findings reveal that as α increases to 0.7, there is a notable enhancement in image clarity, as evidenced by metrics such as average gradient (AG) and edge intensity (EI), describing image features. A further increment of α to 0.9 leads to a stabilization of image clarity. However, metrics related to image features, such as AG and EI, exhibit limited improvement at this stage. To achieve a balance between image features and the preservation of the main image structure, the balance factor α is set to 0.9. This decision is made with performance considerations in mind, aiming to retain texture and details while maximizing the maintenance of the image's primary structure.

It is noteworthy that, following the incorporation of the REC module, a substantial improvement in objective evaluation metrics has been achieved, evidenced by an almost 10% increase in MEF-SSIM and MEF-SSIMc on the test set. Furthermore, after the introduction of the REC module, notable enhancements in color deviation and scene tone consistency have been observed in the fusion results, as depicted in Figure 13. The REC module, utilizing an attention mechanism, thoroughly explores the color and exposure information within the exposure sequence, playing a pivotal role in providing essential corrective enhancements to features of other LDR images.

Utilizing separated convolution in CAN significantly strengthens the dependency of the dilated convolution input unit, aiding in the suppression of grid artifacts [34]. We contrast this approach with the classical CAN network [32] and present two examples. As depicted in Figure 14, in parts (a) near the leaves and railing, and (b) near the clock tower and leaves, grid artifacts and color deviations are evident at the edges of objects or texture regions. Nevertheless, employing separated convolution effectively resolves these issues while preserving the original fidelity of the image, thus demonstrating the efficacy of our design.

$\alpha = 1.0$	$\alpha = 0.9$	$\alpha = 0.8$	$\alpha = 0.7$	$\alpha = 0.0$
MEF-SSMIc = 0.9413	MEF-SSMIc = 0.9582	MEF-SSMIc = 0.9617	MEF-SSMIc = 0.9641	MEF-SSMIc = 0.9673
AG = 7.04 EI = 69.02	AG = 6.99 EI = 67.98	AG = 6.56 EI = 66.25	AG = 5.28 EI = 65.67	AG = 4.23 EI = 47.57
(a)	(b)	(c)	(d)	(e)

Figure 12. The fusion results obtained with different settings of the gradient fidelity term's balance factor α in the "ICCV02" scenario. (**a**) When the balance factor is 1.0, (**b**) when the balance factor is 0.9, (**c**) when the balance factor is 0.8, (**d**) when the balance factor is 0.7, (**e**) when the gradient fidelity term is not used, the balance factor is 0.

(a) source sequence

(b) (c)

Figure 13. Subjective experimental results of the ablation of the REC module. In the first row, item (**a**) depicts the provided multi-exposure image sequence. The second row, item (**b**), presents outcomes in the absence of the REC module, whereas item (**c**) illustrates enhancements upon the module's integration.

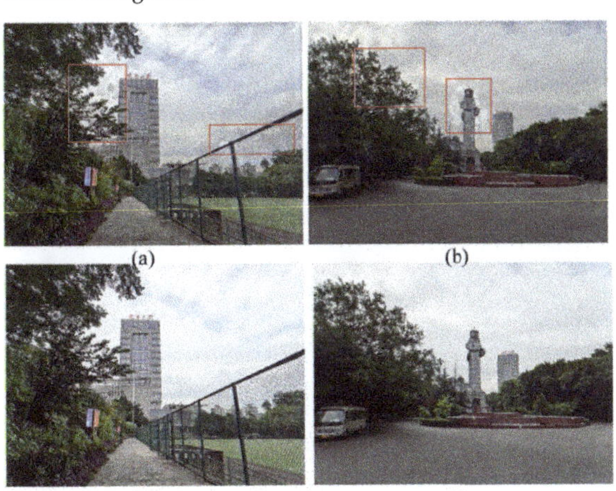

(a) (b)

(c) (d)

Figure 14. Subjective experimental results of the ablation of the separated convolution. The regions identified by the red boxes display notable grid artifacts. The first row (**a**,**b**) displays the results absent the use of separated convolution, whereas the effects of applying separated convolution are exhibited in the second row (**c**,**d**).

5. Conclusions

We propose a flexible multi-exposure image fusion method for static scenes, named Ref-MEF, which can accept an uncertain number of multi-exposure image inputs. To correct the color difference and inconsistency in hue in the fusion results, we have constructed a module called reference-guided exposure correction (REC). Using the exposure-guided feature fusion (EGFF) module, we have realized adaptive weighting to construct a fixed feature dimension. In addition, we use the reference-guided exposure correction (GCAN) to aggregate multi-scale contexts, reducing grid artifacts. In the loss function, we introduce a gradient fidelity term to ensure the completeness of detail information and high-frequency information in the fusion results. Our method shows excellent performance both qualitatively and quantitatively and is more flexible in handling an increasing number of multi-exposure inputs.

Author Contributions: Conceptualization, Y.H.; methodology, Y.H. and S.Z.; software, Y.H.; validation, Y.H. and Y.X.; formal analysis, Y.H. and S.Z.; investigation, Y.H. and Y.X.; resources, S.Z.; data curation, Y.C. and K.C.; writing—original draft preparation, Y.H.; writing—review and editing, S.Z.; visualization, Y.H. and Y.X.; supervision, S.Z.; project administration, S.Z.; funding acquisition, S.Z. All authors have read and agreed to the published version of the manuscript.

Funding: This research was funded by a General Program of National Natural Science Foundation of China under grant 62272070.

Institutional Review Board Statement: Not applicable.

Data Availability Statement: Data are contained within the article.

Acknowledgments: The authors thank the GPU computing resources provided by Zhou.

Conflicts of Interest: The authors declare no conflicts of interest.

References

1. Karakaya, D.; Ulucan, O.; Turkan, M. Pas-Mef: Multi-Exposure Image Fusion Based On Principal Component Analysis, Adaptive Well-Exposedness Furthermore, Saliency Map. In Proceedings of the ICASSP 2022 IEEE International Conference on Acoustics, Speech and Signal Processing (ICASSP), Singapore, 23–27 May 2022; pp. 2345–2349. [CrossRef]
2. Ma, K.; Wang, Z. Multi-exposure image fusion: A patch-wise approach. In Proceedings of the 2015 IEEE International Conference on Image Processing (ICIP), Quebec City, QC, Canada, 27–30 September 2015; pp. 1717–1721. [CrossRef]
3. Paul, S.; Sevcenco, I.S.; Agathoklis, P. Multi-Exposure and Multi-Focus Image Fusion in Gradient Domain. *J. Circuits Syst. Comput.* **2016**, *25*, 1650123. [CrossRef]
4. Ma, X.; Wang, Z.; Hu, S.; Kan, S. Multi-Focus Image Fusion Based on Multi-Scale Generative Adversarial Network. *Entropy* **2022**, *24*, 582. [CrossRef]
5. Wang, L.; Hu, Z.; Kong, Q.; Qi, Q.; Liao, Q. Infrared and Visible Image Fusion via Attention-Based Adaptive Feature Fusion. *Entropy* **2023**, *25*, 407. [CrossRef]
6. Jiang, Y.; Liu, Y.; Zhan, W.; Zhu, D. Improved Thermal Infrared Image Super-Resolution Reconstruction Method Base on Multimodal Sensor Fusion. *Entropy* **2023**, *25*, 914. [CrossRef]
7. Prabhakar, K.R.; Srikar, V.S.; Babu, R.V. DeepFuse: A Deep Unsupervised Approach for Exposure Fusion with Extreme Exposure Image Pairs. In Proceedings of the 2017 IEEE International Conference on Computer Vision (ICCV), Venice, Italy, 22–29 October 2017; pp. 4724–4732. [CrossRef]
8. Ma, K.; Duanmu, Z.; Yeganeh, H.; Wang, Z. Multi-Exposure Image Fusion by Optimizing A Structural Similarity Index. *IEEE Trans. Comput. Imaging* **2018**, *4*, 60–72. [CrossRef]
9. Xu, H.; Ma, J.; Zhang, X.P. MEF-GAN: Multi-Exposure Image Fusion via Generative Adversarial Networks. *IEEE Trans. Image Process.* **2020**, *29*, 7203–7216. [CrossRef]
10. Qi, Y.; Zhou, S.; Zhang, Z.; Luo, S.; Lin, X.; Wang, L.; Qiang, B. Deep unsupervised learning based on color un-referenced loss functions for multi-exposure image fusion. *Inf. Fusion* **2021**, *66*, 18–39. [CrossRef]

11. Zhang, Y.; Liu, Y.; Sun, P.; Yan, H.; Zhao, X.; Zhang, L. IFCNN: A general image fusion framework based on convolutional neural network. *Inf. Fusion* **2020**, *54*, 99–118. [CrossRef]
12. Ma, K.; Duanmu, Z.; Zhu, H.; Fang, Y.; Wang, Z. Deep Guided Learning for Fast Multi-Exposure Image Fusion. *IEEE Trans. Image Process.* **2020**, *29*, 2808–2819. [CrossRef] [PubMed]
13. Tang, Z.; Zhang, Z.; Chen, W.; Yang, W. An SIFT-Based Fast Image Alignment Algorithm for High-Resolution Image. *IEEE Access* **2023**, *11*, 42012–42041. [CrossRef]
14. Liu, C.; Yuen, J.; Torralba, A. SIFT Flow: Dense Correspondence across Scenes and Its Applications. *IEEE Trans. Pattern Anal. Mach. Intell.* **2011**, *33*, 978–994. [CrossRef]
15. Zhu, A.Z.; Yuan, L.; Chaney, K.; Daniilidis, K. Unsupervised Event-Based Learning of Optical Flow, Depth, and Egomotion. In Proceedings of the 2019 IEEE/CVF Conference on Computer Vision and Pattern Recognition (CVPR), Long Beach, CA, USA, 15–20 June 2019; pp. 989–997. [CrossRef]
16. Hayat, N.; Imran, M. Ghost-free multi exposure image fusion technique using dense SIFT descriptor and guided filter. *J. Vis. Commun. Image Represent.* **2019**, *62*, 295–308. [CrossRef]
17. Ma, K.; Li, H.; Yong, H.; Wang, Z.; Meng, D.; Zhang, L. Robust Multi-Exposure Image Fusion: A Structural Patch Decomposition Approach. *IEEE Trans. Image Process.* **2017**, *26*, 2519–2532. [CrossRef] [PubMed]
18. Li, Y.; Sun, Y.; Zheng, M.; Huang, X.; Qi, G.; Hu, H.; Zhu, Z. A Novel Multi-Exposure Image Fusion Method Based on Adaptive Patch Structure. *Entropy* **2018**, *20*, 935. [CrossRef] [PubMed]
19. Ma, K.; Zeng, K.; Wang, Z. Perceptual Quality Assessment for Multi-Exposure Image Fusion. *IEEE Trans. Image Process.* **2015**, *24*, 3345–3356. [CrossRef] [PubMed]
20. Xu, H.; Ma, J.; Le Z.; Jiang, J.; Guo, X. FusionDN: A Unified Densely Connected Network for Image Fusion. In Proceedings of the AAAI Conference on Artificial Intelligence, New York, NY, USA, 7–12 February 2020. [CrossRef]
21. Xu, H.; Ma, J.; Jiang, J.; Guo, X.; Ling, H. U2Fusion: A Unified Unsupervised Image Fusion Network. *IEEE Trans. Pattern Anal. Mach. Intell.* **2022**, *44*, 502–518. [CrossRef] [PubMed]
22. Wu, K.; Chen, J.; Yu, Y.; Ma, J. ACE-MEF: Adaptive Clarity Evaluation-Guided Network With Illumination Correction for Multi-Exposure Image Fusion. *IEEE Trans. Multimed.* **2023**, *25*, 8103–8118. [CrossRef]
23. Wang, J.; Wang, W.; Xu, G.; Liu, H. End-to-End Exposure Fusion Using Convolutional Neural Network. *IEICE Trans. Inf. Syst.* **2018**, *101*, 560–563. [CrossRef]
24. Russakovsky, O.; Deng, J.; Su, H.; Krause, J.; Satheesh, S.; Ma, S.; Huang, Z.; Karpathy, A.; Khosla, A.; Bernstein, M.; et al. ImageNet Large Scale Visual Recognition Challenge. *Int. J. Comput. Vis.* **2015**, *115*, .211–252. [CrossRef]
25. Cai, J.; Gu, S.; Zhang, L. Learning a Deep Single Image Contrast Enhancer from Multi-Exposure Images. *IEEE Trans. Image Process.* **2018**, *27*, 2049–2062. [CrossRef]
26. Zhao, H.; Zheng, J.; Shang, X.; Zhong, W.; Liu, J. Coarse-to-fine multi-scale attention-guided network for multi-exposure image fusion. *Vis. Comput.* **2023**, *39*, 1–14. [CrossRef]
27. Ma, J.; Yu, W.; Liang, P.; Li, C.; Jiang, J. FusionGAN: A generative adversarial network for infrared and visible image fusion. *Inf. Fusion* **2019**, *48*, 11–26. [CrossRef]
28. Yang, Z.; Chen, Y.; Le, Z.; Ma, Y. GANFuse: A novel multi-exposure image fusion method based on generative adversarial networks. *Neural Comput. Appl.* **2021**, *33*, 6133–6145. [CrossRef]
29. Chen, S.Y.; Chuang, Y.Y. Deep Exposure Fusion with Deghosting via Homography Estimation and Attention Learning. In Proceedings of the ICASSP 2020 IEEE International Conference on Acoustics, Speech and Signal Processing (ICASSP), Barcelona, Spain, 4–8 May 2020; pp. 1464–1468. [CrossRef]
30. Qu, L.; Liu, S.; Wang, M.; Song, Z. TransMEF: A Transformer-Based Multi-Exposure Image Fusion Framework using Self-Supervised Multi-Task Learning. In Proceedings of the AAAI Conference on Artificial Intelligence, Vancouver, BC, Canada, 22 February–1 March 2021. [CrossRef]
31. Microsoft COCO: Common Objects in Context. Available online: https://link.springer.com/chapter/10.1007/978-3-319-10602-1_48 (accessed on 8 August 2023).
32. Yu, F.; Koltun, V. Multi-Scale Context Aggregation by Dilated Convolutions. *arXiv* **2016**, arXiv:1511.07122. Available online: http://arxiv.org/abs/1511.07122 (accessed on 8 August 2023).
33. Hamaguchi, R.; Fujita, A.; Nemoto, K.; Imaizumi, T.; Hikosaka, S. Effective Use of Dilated Convolutions for Segmenting Small Object Instances in Remote Sensing Imagery. In Proceedings of the 2018 IEEE Winter Conference on Applications of Computer Vision (WACV), Lake Tahoe, NV, USA, 12–15 March 2018. [CrossRef]
34. Wang, Z.; Ji, S. Smoothed Dilated Convolutions for Improved Dense Prediction. In Proceedings of the Proceedings of the 24th ACM SIGKDD International Conference on Knowledge Discovery & Data Mining, New York, NY, USA, 19–23 August 2018; pp. 2486–2495. [CrossRef]
35. Zeng, K.; Ma, K.; Hassen, R.; Wang, Z. Perceptual evaluation of multi-exposure image fusion algorithms. In Proceedings of the 2014 Sixth International Workshop on Quality of Multimedia Experience (QoMEX), Singapore, 18–20 September 2014; pp. 7–12. [CrossRef]
36. Merianos, I.; Mitianoudis, N. Multiple-Exposure Image Fusion for HDR Image Synthesis Using Learned Analysis Transformations. *J. Imaging* **2019**, *5*, 32. [CrossRef] [PubMed]

37. Li, H.; Ma, K.; Yong, H.; Zhang, L. Fast Multi-Scale Structural Patch Decomposition for Multi-Exposure Image Fusion. *IEEE Trans. Image Process.* **2020**, *29*, 5805–5816. [CrossRef] [PubMed]
38. Li, H.; Zhang, L. Multi-Exposure Fusion with CNN Features. In Proceedings of the 2018 25th IEEE International Conference on Image Processing (ICIP), Athens, Greece, 7–10 October 2018; pp. 1723–1727. [CrossRef]
39. Van Aardt, J. Assessment of image fusion procedures using entropy, image quality, and multispectral classification. *J. Appl. Remote Sens.* **2008**, *2*, 023522. [CrossRef]
40. Bulanon, D.; Burks, T.; Alchanatis, V. Image fusion of visible and thermal images for fruit detection. *Biosyst. Eng.* **2009**, *103*, 12–22. [CrossRef]
41. Cvejic, N.; Canagarajah, C.N.; Bull, D.R. Image fusion metric based on mutual information and Tsallis entropy. *Electron. Lett.* **2006**, *42*, 626–627. [CrossRef]
42. Jagalingam, P.; Hegde, A.V. A Review of Quality Metrics for Fused Image. *Aquat. Procedia* **2015**, *4*, 133–142. [CrossRef]
43. Qu, G.; Zhang, D.; Yan, P. Information measure for performance of image fusion. *Electron. Lett.* **2002**, *38*, 313. [CrossRef]
44. Cui, G.; Feng, H.; Xu, Z.; Li, Q.; Chen, Y. Detail preserved fusion of visible and infrared images using regional saliency extraction and multi-scale image decomposition. *Opt. Commun.* **2015**, *341*, 199–209. [CrossRef]
45. Balakrishnan, R.; Priya, R. Hybrid Multimodality Medical Image Fusion Technique for Feature Enhancement in Medical Diagnosis. *Int. J. Eng. Sci. Invent.* **2018**, *2*, 52–60.
46. Rao, Y.J. In-fibre Bragg grating sensors. *Meas. Sci. Technol.* **1997**, *8*, 355–375. [CrossRef]
47. Eskicioglu, A.; Fisher, P. Image quality measures and their performance. *IEEE Trans. Commun.* **1995**, *43*, 2959–2965. [CrossRef]
48. Xydeas, C.; Petrović, V. Objective image fusion performance measure. *Electron. Lett.* **2000**, *36*, 308. :20000267. [CrossRef]
49. Chen, Y.; Blum, R.S. A new automated quality assessment algorithm for image fusion. *Image Vis. Comput.* **2009**, *27*, 1421–1432. [CrossRef]
50. Chen, H.; Varshney, P.K. A human perception inspired quality metric for image fusion based on regional information. *Inf. Fusion* **2007**, *8*, 193–207. [CrossRef]
51. Han, Y.; Cai, Y.; Cao, Y.; Xu, X. A new image fusion performance metric based on visual information fidelity. *Inf. Fusion* **2013**, *14*, 127–135. [CrossRef]

entropy

MDPI

Article

Nighttime Image Stitching Method Based on Image Decomposition Enhancement

Mengying Yan [1], Danyang Qin [1,2,*], Gengxin Zhang [1], Huapeng Tang [1] and Lin Ma [3]

1 Department of Electronic Engineering, Heilongjiang University, Harbin 150080, China; 2211723@s.hlju.edu.cn (M.Y.); 2211779@s.hlju.edu.cn (G.Z.); 2211781@s.hlju.edu.cn (H.T.)
2 National Mobile Communications Research Laboratory, Southeast University, Nanjing 210096, China
3 Department of Electronics and Information Engineering, Harbin Institute of Technology, Harbin 150080, China; malin@hit.edu.cn
* Correspondence: qindanyang@hlju.edu.cn

Abstract: Image stitching technology realizes alignment and fusion of a series of images with common pixel areas taken from different viewpoints of the same scene to produce a wide field of view panoramic image with natural structure. The night environment is one of the important scenes of human life, and the night image stitching technology has more urgent practical significance in the fields of security monitoring and intelligent driving at night. Due to the influence of artificial light sources at night, the brightness of the image is unevenly distributed and there are a large number of dark light areas, but often these dark light areas have rich structural information. The structural features hidden in the darkness are difficult to extract, resulting in ghosting and misalignment when stitching, which makes it difficult to meet the practical application requirements. Therefore, a nighttime image stitching method based on image decomposition enhancement is proposed to address the problem of insufficient line feature extraction in the stitching process of nighttime images. The proposed algorithm performs luminance enhancement on the structural layer, smoothes the nighttime image noise using a denoising algorithm on the texture layer, and finally complements the texture of the fused image by an edge enhancement algorithm. The experimental results show that the proposed algorithm improves the image quality in terms of information entropy, contrast, and noise suppression compared with other algorithms. Moreover, the proposed algorithm extracts the most line features from the processed nighttime images, which is more helpful for the stitching of nighttime images.

Keywords: night image stitching; image enhancement; feature extraction; edge enhancement

1. Introduction

Images can help humans understand the world most intuitively. It is an important channel for human and nature to conduct information interaction with nature and the basis of the research of computer vision. With the development of computer vision technology, a limited perspective can no longer meet people's needs, and a broader perspective and richer information demand under the field of views are becoming increasingly urgent. When people obtain high-resolution and wide-viewed images, because wide-angle lenses still have perspective limitations, fish-eyed lenses are serious, panoramic cameras are expensive and complicated, and there are great limitations for obtaining broad-vision images in hardware. Therefore, digital image stitching technology shows unique advantages. Image stitching is the technology of two or more images taken in a certain environment through image processing into a wider panoramic image technology. This technology can also take into account the high field of view and high distortion, thereby meeting people's needs for scene observation, and is used in the fields of autonomous driving, virtual tourism, and video surveillance [1].

The main steps of the image stitching technique include image pre-processing, feature extraction, feature matching, and image fusion. Previous splicing algorithms focused on improving the extraction and alignment of feature points, however, in recent years, more and more researchers have begun to introduce linear features to assist in the alignment. Real-life scenes are full of rich linear structures, and it is obviously very positive to protect the linear structures in image stitching. Especially in some low-texture images where it is difficult to extract enough effective matching points, the line features can compensate well to obtain more matching information. Moreover, the human eye has a good perception of linear structures, and matching linear structures in image stitching, building alignment relationships between images, and thus protecting linear structures is also of great benefit for enhancing the natural look and feel of the stitching results.

Night is one of the important scenes of human life, and the night image stitching technology can be applied to security monitoring, night intelligent driving, and other fields. However, most of the current mature image stitching techniques use images with good lighting conditions, while image stitching techniques in low-light scenes such as at night are not yet perfect. The night scene light source is complex, containing both weak natural light (such as moonlight, starlight, etc.) and light generated by artificial light sources (such as streetlights, headlights, etc.). Within the scene of artificial light source, the influence produced by natural illumination becomes weaker. The average brightness of the night images containing artificial light sources is improved compared with the night images under natural illumination fields. However, since artificial light sources can only affect local scenes, it causes the problems of uneven luminance distribution, low visibility of darker luminance areas, and serious loss of details in the captured night images. Moreover, the brightness of the area near the light source is high, and the detail information is also masked, making the degradation of the night image serious. When feature extraction is performed on nighttime images, it is found that the line features of the images are mainly concentrated in the bright areas of the images. When the image is matched, the stitching fails due to the lack of feature information of the image when the bright area is in the non-stitching overlap area. In order to improve the image quality and stitching success rate, we use the enhancement technique to pre-process the nighttime images. The effect of line feature extraction before and after the nighttime image enhancement is shown in Figure 1.

Figure 1. Line feature extraction effect before and after night image enhancement.

2. Related Work

In this paper, we use enhancement algorithms to pre-process the images to be stitched at night for the purpose of complementing the image line features while improving the night image quality. The low-light image enhancement algorithm mainly enhances the overall contrast and brightness of the image by improving the brightness of dark areas and suppressing the gray value of overly bright areas. Low-illumination image enhancement, a classical problem in the field of digital image processing, has been evolving for a long time. Common enhancement methods for low-illumination color images include Retinex theory-based methods, histogram equalization-based methods, and image fusion-based enhancement methods.

Multi-scale Retinex (MSR) [2] and multi-scale Retinex with color restoration (MSRCR) [3] are representative Retinex algorithms. However, these algorithms are prone to color distortion, halation, and over-enhancement. Adaptive multi-scale Retinex (AMSR) [4] is a weighting strategy based on the SSR (single scale retinex) algorithm. Tang et al. [5] used the Retinex model in the Y channel to enhance the luminance, but the image edges were blurred due to denoising and smoothing, resulting in a decrease in the contrast of the image. Based on Retinex theory, Guo et al. [6] proposed a detail enhancement method based on guided filtering to optimize the reflectance map and generate enhanced ocean images. Wang et al. [7] proposed a color image correction method based on nonlinear function transform to improve the image brightness, but the method parameters need to be set manually and the image processing effect depends on the selection of parameters.

Histogram equalization can effectively improve the brightness and contrast of the image, and the principle is simple and easy to implement. The dual histogram [8] equalization method is an algorithm to adjust the brightness of the input image. Lu et al. [9] proposed an image enhancement method based on adaptive detail equalization, which enhances the image brightness and contrast by adaptive dual-interval histogram equalization. Veluchamy and Subramani [10] used a new adaptive gamma correction method to enhance the image contrast while employing a weighted histogram distribution to maintain the natural color and detail of the image. Liu et al. [11] proposed an adaptive contrast enhancement method based on a histogram correction framework to improve the local detail features of the image by spatially segmenting the original image. Gautam and Tiwari [12] combined the limiting dual histogram equalization with adaptive gamma correction to effectively enhance low-contrast color images.

Fusion-based image enhancement techniques can recover image details very well. Li et al. [13] used the wavelet image fusion technique to highlight the details of the image so that the enhanced image has higher clarity and visual effect. Ren et al. [14] proposed an effective low-light image enhancement method to maintain naturalness and obtain a natural image of the picture. Fu et al. [15] proposed a fusion-based low-light image enhancement method to improve image brightness and contrast by selecting appropriate inputs and weights from the estimated illumination. Lee et al. [16] adaptively segmented the input image into a dark background region and bright background region. Subsequently, contrast stretching is performed only in the dark region, which can effectively enhance the contrast of backlit images without oversaturation problems but requires precise segmentation of the dark regions of the image. Lu and Zhang [17] proposed a highly adaptive two-branch fusion strategy to enhance weakly illuminated images with targeted enhancement for slightly distorted and severely distorted images and further proposed an adaptive fusion mechanism.

In recent years, intelligent algorithms have developed rapidly and have also been applied to image enhancement. Qian et al. [18] proposed an adaptive image enhancement algorithm based on visual saliency. This algorithm introduced a cuckoo search algorithm and a bilateral gamma adjustment function in the HIS color space to improve the overall brightness of the image. Kanmani and Narasimhan [19] established a population intelligence-based color image contrast enhancement algorithm that uses an adaptive gamma correction factor selected by a particle swarm algorithm (PSO) to improve the image entropy and enhance the image details. Li et al. [20] proposed an adaptive chaotic particle swarm optimization algorithm (ACPSO) combined with gamma correction to iteratively find the best image for global brightness adjustment. The problem of low brightness and low contrast of low-illumination color images is effectively improved.

These algorithms are commonly validated using images from publicly available datasets and are not validated on actual collected low-light images. Since the light in the nighttime environment tends to be very scattered, it results in multiple dark and bright regions in different locations of the image. In contrast, the dark and bright regions of low-illumination images tend to be more concentrated, and ordinary low-illumination image enhancement algorithms cannot handle nighttime images well. In addition, the dark areas of nighttime images usually contain a lot of noise. When enhancing a nighttime image, the amplified noise while restoring the image details seriously affects the image quality. Moreover, these dark areas often have rich linear structures, and when stitching the nighttime images, the point features and line features of the images are hidden and difficult to extract, which affects the subsequent stitching. Therefore, we propose a nighttime image enhancement method based on image decomposition in which the image is decomposed by the rolling guidance filter to obtain the structural layer and texture layer, followed by a brightness enhancement function to improve the brightness of the V component of the structural layer and saturation stretching of the S component to obtain the image of the structural layer after brightness enhancement. After that, the texture layer containing noise is smoothed and denoised, and the enhanced structural layer and the smoothed texture layer are fused. To highlight the edge information of the image, the contrast of the fused image is enhanced to highlight the edge detail information of the image. The proposed algorithm obtains higher quality nighttime images with richer details and sharper edges. When line features are extracted from the enhanced images, line features are extracted from the dark light areas of the images, which proves that the present algorithm also achieves greater improvement in line feature extraction and improves the stitching accuracy. The framework of the proposed algorithm is shown in Figure 2.

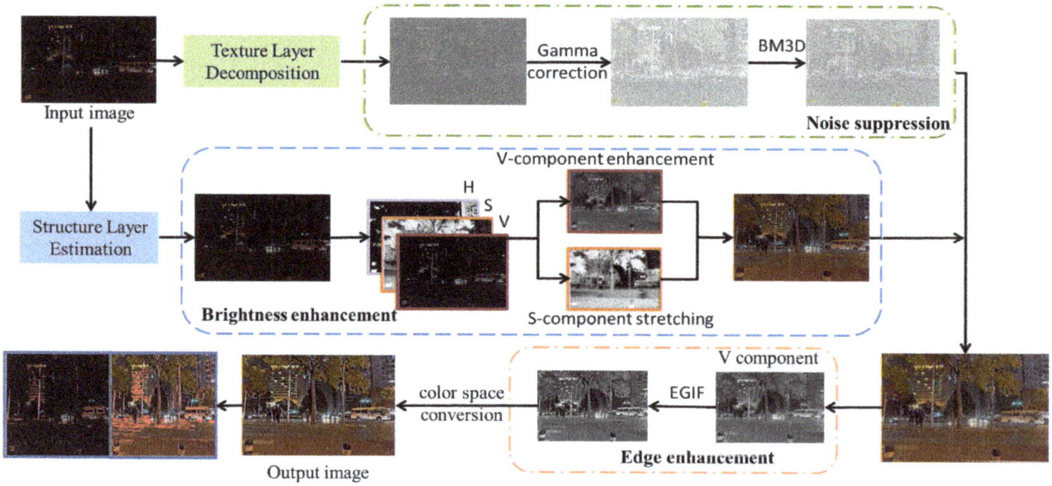

Figure 2. Overall framework of proposed enhancement method.

The remaining contents of this paper are arranged as follows. Section 3 presents the proposed enhancement algorithm. Section 4 contains the experimental results and discussion. Finally, Section 5 gives the conclusion.

3. The Proposed Night Image Enhancement Method

3.1. Image Decomposition Model

Most low-illumination image enhancement algorithms inevitably enlarge the image noise while enhancing the brightness, which will affect the quality of the image. The image decomposition framework can effectively solve this problem. We use the image decomposition method to decompose the night image into the structure layer and texture layer. The structural layer component is the smooth renderings of the input image. We increase the brightness of the structure layer to avoid noise amplification due to enhancement of brightness.

Input image I consists of a large-scale structure layer I_S and fine-scale texture layer I_T. The expression is shown below.

$$I = I_S + I_T \tag{1}$$

In order to obtain the structure layer, we choose the rolling guidance filter to smooth the night image. The rolling guidance filter is a new edge-retaining filter proposed by Zhang [21]. The difference from other edges to retain the filter is that the rolling guidance filter can be iterated into the implementation process, which can achieve rapid convergence. The implementation of this filter is simple and fast, and the scale separation is achieved in the space-overlapping characteristics. The rolling guidance filter includes two processes: small structure removal and edge recovery. The schematic diagram is shown in Figure 3.

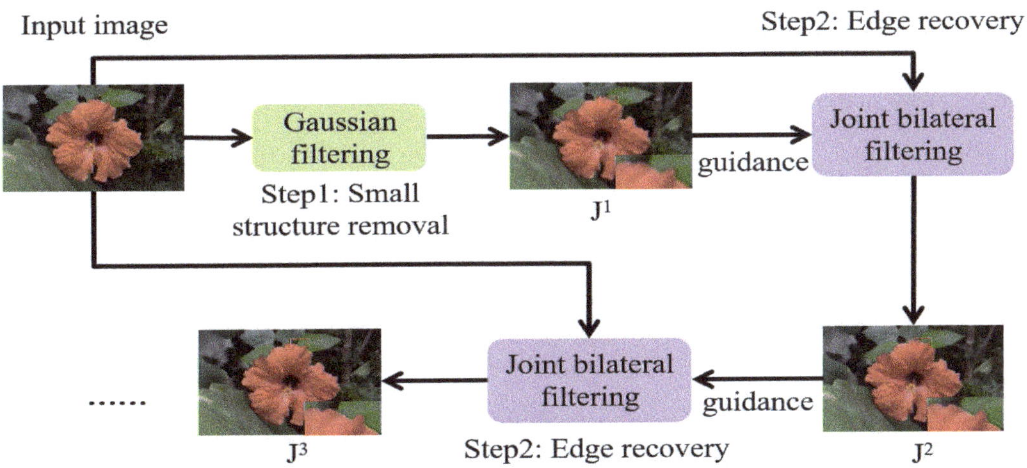

Figure 3. Principle diagram of the rolling guidance filter.

Small structure removal is achieved through Gaussian filtering. A small structure is usually detailed information, including information such as texture, noise, and small goals. The filter expression is as follows.

$$G(p) = \frac{1}{K_p} \sum_{q \in N(p)} \exp\left(-\frac{\|p-q\|^2}{2\sigma_s^2}\right) I(q) \tag{2}$$

where

$$K(p) = \sum_{q \in N(p)} \exp\left(-\frac{\|p-q\|^2}{2\sigma_s^2}\right) \tag{3}$$

where I represents the input image, G represents the output image, p and q are pixels in the input image I, and $N(p)$ is a neighboring pixel set centered on pixel p. $\| p - q \|$ indicates the distance between the two pixels. σ_s is the standard deviation in the neighborhood, which is a scale threshold. When the structure in the image is greater than σ_s, it will be retained, otherwise it will be eliminated.

The edge recovery uses iterative form to achieve continuously updating the output image J. We denote J^{t+1} as the result of the t-th iteration. The initial value J^1 is obtained by the Gaussian filtering shown in Equation (2). The output image J^{t+1} of the t-th iteration is obtained by the input image I and the previous iteration output image J^t through combining bilateral filtering methods, as shown in the following formula.

$$J^{t+1}(p) = \frac{1}{K_p} \sum_{q \in N(p)} \exp\left(-\frac{\|p-q\|^2}{2\sigma_s^2} - \frac{\|J^t(p) - J^t(q)\|^2}{2\sigma_r^2} \right) I(q) \tag{4}$$

where

$$K_p = \sum_{q \in N(p)} \exp\left(-\frac{\|p-q\|^2}{2\sigma_s^2} - \frac{\|J^t(p) - J^t(q)\|^2}{2\sigma_r^2} \right) \tag{5}$$

Equation (4) can be understood as a guidance image with the structure of J^t and can smoothly enter the filter form of image I. The process of constantly updating the guidance image is called rolling guidance filtering.

The nighttime image is processed by a rolling guide filter to obtain a structural layer image, as shown in Equation (6). RGF represents rolling guidance filter, t is the number of iterations. The texture layer is obtained by the difference between the original image and the structure layer, as shown in Equation (7).

$$I_S = RGF(I, \sigma_s, \sigma_r, t) \tag{6}$$

$$I_T = I - I_S \tag{7}$$

The effect of image decomposition is shown in Figure 4. In order to make the texture layer easy to observe, a gamma transform is used to improve the brightness of the texture layer. The texture layer is offset by 0.5 and then displayed.

Figure 4. Top row: original image; middle row: structure layer; bottom row: texture layer.

3.2. Brightness Enhancement of Structural Layer

The enhancement processing of RGB color space easily causes the color distortion of the image, so we choose the HSV color space closer to the human visual expectations to enhance the image. We convert the RGB space of the image to HSV space and obtain three components, namely H (hue), S (saturation), and V (luminance), respectively, as $I_h(x,y)$, $I_s(x,y)$, and $I_v(x,y)$.

In the Retinex-based image enhancement algorithm, Gaussian filtering and bilateral filtering are usually used as a surround function to estimate the light component [22]. Gaussian filtering can be used to extract light components, but as the filter window increases, the calculation complexity will increase significantly. When the bilateral filtering is treated with color images, the gradient reversal is generated near the edge of the object in the image, causing the halo to appear [23]. This article uses a linear guidance filter with smooth and bordering functions to estimate the light component and uses brightness component $I_v(x,y)$ as input images and guide images. Considering that the slow change of light in most areas leads to sudden changes in local area luminance, the luminance components are processed by two guidance filters and fused together by averaging and weighting as the final light component estimate. The expression is shown below.

$$F_1(x,y) = GF_{r1,\lambda 1}[I_v(x,y), I_v(x,y)] \tag{8}$$

$$F_2(x,y) = GF_{r2,\lambda 2}[I_v(x,y), F_1(x,y)] \tag{9}$$

$$I_{v\_gif} = 0.5 * F_1(x,y) + 0.5 * F_2(x,y) \tag{10}$$

where $GF_{(r,\lambda)}$ represents the guided filter function with the window radius as r and the regularization parameter as λ. I_{v_gif} denotes the filtered illumination component.

Weber–Fechner's law shows that the human vision system is a non-linear processing process. The enhanced function is formulated according to Weber–Fechner's law, and the image obtained is more in line with human vision [7]. Due to the height complexity of the number of calculations, the following functions are used to fit the lighting component.

$$I'_v = \frac{I_v(255 + \bar{I}_s \times \bar{I}_v)}{\max\left(I_v, I_{v\_gif}\right) + (\bar{I}_s \times \bar{I}_v)} \tag{11}$$

where $\bar{I}_s = \frac{1}{N}\sum_{i=1}^{N} I_s$, $\bar{I}_v = \frac{1}{N}\sum_{i=1}^{N} I_v$, and N is the number of pixels of image I_v.

After the image brightness is improved, the saturation of the image will be reduced to a certain extent. In order to prevent the impact of brightness on saturation, we quote the adaptive non-linear stretching function proposed by the literature [24] to stretch the saturation of the image. After using this function to process S components, the saturation of the image is higher and the color information of the image is richer.

$$I'_s = (0.5 + 0.5 * \frac{\max(R,G,B) + \min(R,G,B) + 1}{2 * \text{mean}(R,G,B) + 1}) * I_s \tag{12}$$

where I_s and I'_s are the saturation of the image before and after stretching. $max(R,G,B)$ indicates maximum value of pixels in R, G, and B color channels. $min(R,G,B)$ refers to minimum value of pixels in the three channels. $mean(R,G,B)$ refers to the average value of pixels in the three color channels.

The brightness improvement of the V channel, the saturation stretch of the S component, and the H component remain unchanged. Finally, the enhanced structural layer $I_{S\_E}(x,y)$ is obtained by converting it to RGB color space. The effect is shown in Figure 5. The enhanced structural layer has greatly improved in terms of brightness and color saturation.

Figure 5. First row: structural layer of the original image; Second row: structural layer after brightness enhancement.

3.3. Noise Suppression of Texture Layer

The night image minus the structure layer is used to obtain the original texture layer. The original texture layer is a positive and negative piece of data that is distributed around the zero value, which is rich in detail information and a lot of noise. After obtaining the texture layer, the gamma correction function is used to increase the brightness of the texture layer. Then, the BM3D denoising algorithm [25] is used to smooth the texture layer. The expression is as follows.

$$I_{T\_F} = BM3D((I_T)^{\frac{1}{g}}) \tag{13}$$

where I_T is the texture of the night image. g is a gamma correction parameter, which is generally taken as 2.2. I_{T_F} is the smooth image layer of the image. After using the BM3D algorithm to deal with the texture layer, the large amount of noise in the image is removed.

3.4. Edge Enhancement

The enhanced structural layer I_{S_E} plus the smooth texture layer I_{T_F} results in a fusion image $R(x,y)$.

$$R(x,y) = I_{S\_E}(x,y) + I_{T\_F}(x,y) \tag{14}$$

In addition, the noise of night images is often distributed in the dark area, but the BM3D performs the same operation on all areas of the image, resulting in excessive smoothness in some areas, and the edge of the image is unclear, which affects line feature extraction. Therefore, it is necessary to enhance the edge of enhanced images. In order to avoid the loss of details of the foreground objects from smoothing, the edge enhancement of the fusion image is enhanced to supplement the detail texture information of the image to make the edge of the image clearer. This article uses effective guide filtering (EGIF) [26] with strong edge maintenance capabilities to smooth the fusion image and then estimate the texture layer of the image. After that, the texture layer is enhanced by the amplifier factor to highlight the edge of the image. The principle of EGIF processing is as follows.

The output image q is represented as a linear model related to the guidance image I. The formula is as follows:

$$q_i = a_k I_i + b_k, \quad \forall i \in \omega_k \tag{15}$$

where q_i is the gray value of the linear transformation at the i pixel in the window ω_k of the image I, k is the central pixel of the window ω_k, and a_k and b_k are the linear coefficients of the guided image within a local window ω_k with a radius of r centered on pixel k. The value function settings are as follows:

$$E(a_k, b_k) = \sum_{i \in \omega_k} \left((a_k I_i + b_k - p_i)^2 + \lambda \Gamma a_k^2 \right) \tag{16}$$

where

$$\Gamma = \bar{\sigma}^2 = \frac{1}{N} \sum_{k=1}^{N} \sigma_k^2 \tag{17}$$

where λ is a parameter used to prevent the regularization parameter of a_k becoming too large, which is used to regulate the filter effect of the filter. p is the input image, and N is the number of pixels in the guidance image I. Local linear coefficients a_k and b_k can be solved through the minimum dwellings:

$$a_k = \frac{\frac{1}{N_{\omega_k}} \sum_{i \in \omega_k} I_i p_i - \mu_k \bar{p}_k}{\sigma_k^2 + \lambda \Gamma} \tag{18}$$

$$b_k = \bar{p}_k - a_k \mu_k \tag{19}$$

When GIF is used to enhance image contrast, I and q are equal, so the following equations are established,

$$\frac{1}{N_{\omega_k}} \sum_{i \in \omega_k} I_i p_i - \mu_k \bar{p}_k = \sigma_k^2 \tag{20}$$

$$\bar{p}_k = \mu_k \tag{21}$$

where the pixel average and standard deviation of the guidance image in the window ω_k with radius r and central pixel k are μ_k and σ_k, $\bar{p}_k$ is the mean of the filtering image in the window ω_k, and N_{ω_k} is the total number of pixels in the window ω_k.

Bring Equations (20) and (21) into Equations (18) and (19).

$$a_k = \frac{\sigma_k^2}{\sigma_k^2 + \lambda \Gamma} \tag{22}$$

$$b_k = (1 - a_k)\mu_k \tag{23}$$

After calculating $E(a_k, b_k)$ in all windows ω_k of the image, the final output of the filter is calculated as follows:

$$\begin{aligned} q_i &= \frac{1}{N_{\omega_k}} \sum_{i \in \omega_k} (a_k I_i + b_k) \\ &= \bar{a}_i I_i + \bar{b}_i \end{aligned} \tag{24}$$

The calculation formula of the texture layer defined by the image decomposition model is as follows:

$$l = I - q \tag{25}$$

where q is a structure layer processed by Equation (24). The texture layer is multiplied with β.

$$l' = \beta \cdot l = \beta \cdot (I - q) \tag{26}$$

l' is the enhanced texture layer. Output image f is the sum of q and l'.

$$f = q + l' \tag{27}$$

Substitute Equation (24) into Equation (26).

$$l' = \beta \cdot (I - \bar{a}I - \bar{b}) = \beta \cdot (1 - \bar{a}) \cdot I - \beta \cdot \bar{b} \tag{28}$$

The gradient of the enhanced texture layer is calculated as follows:

$$\bigtriangledown l' = \beta \cdot (1 - \bar{a}) \cdot \bigtriangledown I \tag{29}$$

Calculate the gradient of the structure layer on the basis of Equation (15), as follows,

$$\bigtriangledown q = \bar{a} \cdot \bigtriangledown I \tag{30}$$

The gradient of the texture layer should not be larger than the gradient of the structure layer. Otherwise, the noise in the texture layer will be amplified. Therefore, the following is not equal to the establishment:

$$\bigtriangledown l' \leq \bigtriangledown q \tag{31}$$

Bring Equations (29) and (30) to Equation (31).

$$\beta \cdot (1 - \bar{a}) \cdot \bigtriangledown I \leq \bar{a} \cdot \bigtriangledown I \tag{32}$$

Therefore,

$$\beta \leq \frac{\bar{a}}{1 - \bar{a}} \tag{33}$$

When the value of β is very small, the details will be suppressed. On the other hand, noise will be amplified for larger β values. Therefore, considering the balance between noise suppression and enhancement of details, the value of β is set as follows:

$$\beta = \frac{\bar{a}}{1 - \bar{a}} \tag{34}$$

According to Equation (34), when $\bar{a}$ is close to 1, the value of β will be very large, and it is easy to excessively enhance the edge of the image. Therefore, the introduction coefficient γ in Equation (34) is as follows:

$$\beta = (\frac{\bar{a}}{1 - \bar{a}})^{\gamma} \tag{35}$$

where $0 \leq \gamma \leq 1$. In order to prevent the image from excessive enhancement, this article converts the input image to the HSV channel and only enhances the edges for the V channel, while the H component and S component remain unchanged. The formula used is as follows:

$$output_v = R_v(x,y) + \beta \cdot (R_v(x,y) - q_v(x,y)) \tag{36}$$

where $R_v(x,y)$ is the V component of $R(x,y)$. $q_v(x,y)$ is obtained by EGIF processing $R_v(x,y)$. $output_v$ is the V component of the output image. Finally, the color space of the image is transferred to RGB to obtain the night image enhanced. The edges of the image obtained by the proposed method are clear. By controlling the parameters of image enhancement, excessive enhancement of the image is avoided.

4. Experiment

In order to verify the superiority of the proposed algorithm in processing nighttime images, Ammen [27], Dong [28], SRIE [29], NPE [22], MF [15], Jiep [30], Ying [31], LIME [32], AIEM [7], and RBMP [33] have been chosen as the comparison algorithms. Nighttime images in the dataset of literature [34], which have a lot of dark light regions and contain artificial light sources, are selected to evaluate the proposed algorithm. Experimental results are shown for eight groups of images with different degrees of richness of texture structure in dark light regions to verify the effectiveness of the proposed algorithm in detail supplementation, edge protection, and noise suppression. All experiments in this research were run on MATLAB R2018a on a PC with 1.6 GHz CPU and 8 GB RAM. The proposed image decomposition-based enhancement algorithm is implemented as follows Algorithm 1:

Algorithm 1 Image decomposition-based enhancement algorithm.

Step 1: Enter a low-illumination image I.
Step 2: Obtain the structure layer I_S using Formula (6).
Step 3: Obtain the texture layer I_T using Formula (7).
Step 4: Enhance the brightness of the structural layer using Formula (11).
Step 5: Stretch the structural layer saturation using Formula (12).
Step 6: Denoise the texture layer using Formula (13).
Step 7: Obtain the fused image $R(x,y)$ using Formula (14).
Step 8: Enhance edge to fused image using Formula (36).
Step 9: Output enhanced image $output$.

In this section, we adopt an evaluation method combined with subjective evaluation and objective evaluation and use the performance of image decomposition night image enhancement methods proposed by night image verification, including noise suppression and edge details. Subjective evaluation can evaluate the quality of the results from the direction of human perception, and objective evaluation can calculate the image quality score from the statistical characteristics of various natural images.

4.1. Experimental Parameter Settings

The results of the comparison algorithms are generated by the code downloaded from the author's website, and the parameters are set as in the paper. The proposed algorithm uses a rolling guide filter to decompose the image. The decomposition effect is related to σ_s, σ_r, and the number of iterations t. The effect of different parameter settings is shown in Figure 6. $\|\cdot\|_F$ represents Frobenius norm, and the closer the value of the Frobenius norm of the two images, the more similar the two pictures are. The convergence curve shows that generally an optimal solution can be obtained within four iterations even with different parameter settings. Thus, for all experiments, we let $t = 4$. It is seen from Figure 6 that the larger the σ_s and σ_r, the smoother the images. When the σ_s and σ_r are too large, the image is blurred and the edges are lost, as shown in the lights of Figure 6a,d. If s is too small, it will cause noise residue, as shown in the window in Figure 6c. Therefore, this article sets $\sigma_s = 1.5$, $\sigma_r = 0.05$.

The proposed algorithm uses the effective guidance filter (EGIF) to enhance the edges, and the enhancement strength is related to γ. The value range of γ is usually [0, 1], and different γ will obtain different edge enhancement results. As shown in Figure 7, in general, the larger γ is, the greater the contrast and information entropy of the image, indicating sharper edges and richer details. However, too much γ will cause the over-enhancement phenomenon of the image, resulting in an unnatural image. Taking this into account, the value of γ is set to 0.9 in this paper.

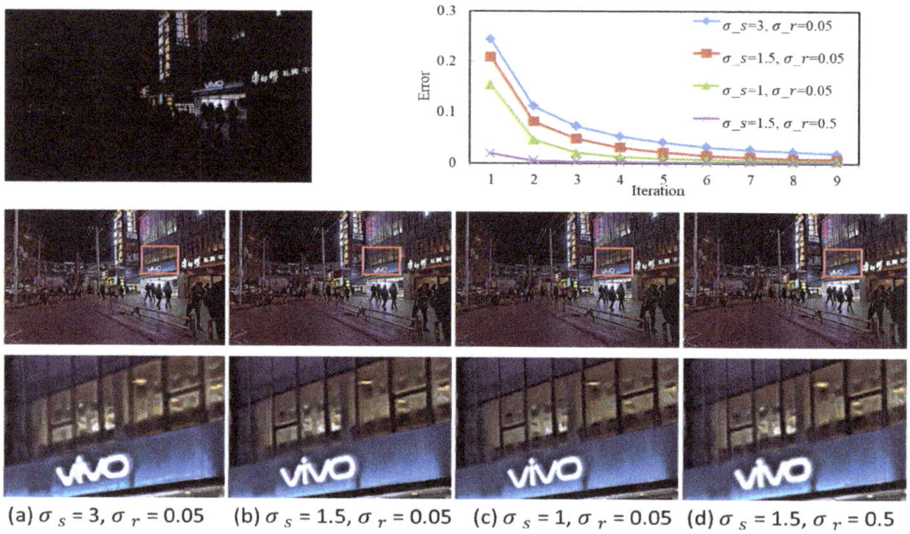

Figure 6. Enhancement effect for different σ_s and σ_r. First row: convergence curves of $||I_s^{t+1} - I_s^t||_F / ||I_s^t||_F$ for the original image and different parameters. Second row: the resultant image after enhancement. Third row: local enlargement image.

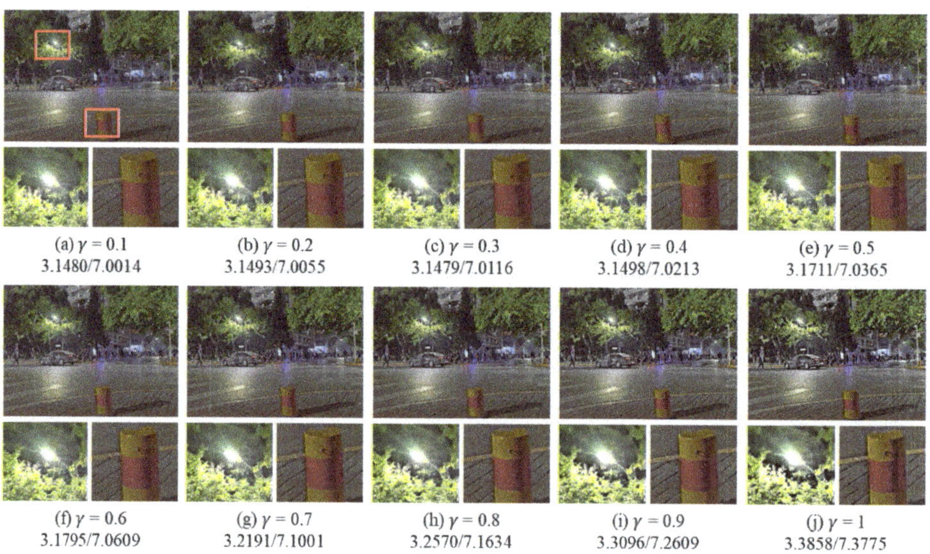

Figure 7. Enhancement results for different γ. A/B: A represents the CEIQ value, B represents the image discrete information entropy.

4.2. Subjective Comparison Experiments of Noise Suppression and Edge Detail Retention

The subjective evaluation method is still the main evaluation method to evaluate the performance of image enhancement methods, especially for the lack of reference images such as night image enhancement methods. The subjective perception of vision is more reflective of the overall image quality improvement, including image contrast, noise suppression, and detail retention, as well as the naturalness of the enhanced resultant image.

Figure 8 shows the enhancement results of the nighttime images by different algorithms, and the details are marked with red boxes and enlarged on the enhanced images. From the analysis of Figure 8, it can be seen that the SRIE and Jiep algorithms fail to improve the overall brightness of the image in terms of dark light enhancement. In terms of noise suppression, combined with the enlarged "wall" in Figure 8, it can be observed that the enhancement results of Ammen, Dong, NPE, MF, and AIEM algorithms all contain a large amount of noise, which seriously affects the image quality. The Jiep algorithm adds denoising processing and achieves noise suppression by smoothing the reflective layer of the image, but the brightness of the enhanced image obtained by the Jiep algorithm is darker. In terms of color correction, the RBMP algorithm has more severe color distortion, such as the overall color distortion of the enlarged vase and wall in Figure 8k. In terms of detail protection, LIME algorithm loses the detail information of the image due to the over-smoothing of the image caused by denoising, such as the blurred texture of the wall shown in Figure 8i. The proposed algorithm improves the brightness of the image while ensuring the effect of image noise suppression, the noise of the wall is smoothed, and the edge texture information of the wall is preserved with clear image edge contours.

As observed in Figure 9, the Dong algorithm boosts the brightness of the image in terms of luminance enhancement but produces an over-enhancement phenomenon in the high-brightness areas of the image, such as the light sign shown in Figure 9c, where some details are lost due to excessive brightness. The SRIE and Jiep algorithms do not improve the brightness of the image enough, and the average brightness of the image is low. The proposed algorithm makes the image brighter while avoiding overexposure of the bright areas, which significantly improves the visibility of the image. In terms of noise suppression, the LIME algorithm has a good denoising effect, but the image details are blurred due to over-smoothing. For example, the details of the car in Figure 9i are missing more seriously, the ground texture is lost, and the edges are blurred. The proposed algorithm enhances the edge details of the image compared with the LIME algorithm, and the edges are more prominent, which improves the clarity of the image and has a better image denoising effect.

As shown in Figure 10, the Ammen, NPE, MF, and AIEM algorithms improve the image brightness but, at the same time, significant noise appears, such as the presence of obvious noise points around the vehicle in Figure 10, indicating that these algorithms lack effective noise suppression. The RBMP algorithm processes images with high brightness, resulting in loss of details and the overall white color of the image due to the lack of color correction of the image. The Ying algorithm does not correct the color of the image and also shows some color distortion. The texture details of the image processed by the LIME algorithm are obviously lost. As shown in the enlarged floor image in Figure 10i, the texture of the floor tiles is blurred, leading to difficulties in extracting line features. In terms of texture details, the proposed algorithm is able to improve the image brightness and contrast while being able to maintain the image detail information due to the inclusion of edge enhancement. As shown in Figure 10l, the edges of the electric car are more clearly defined, which proves that the proposed algorithm makes the image richer in detail information and the visual effect of the image is greatly improved.

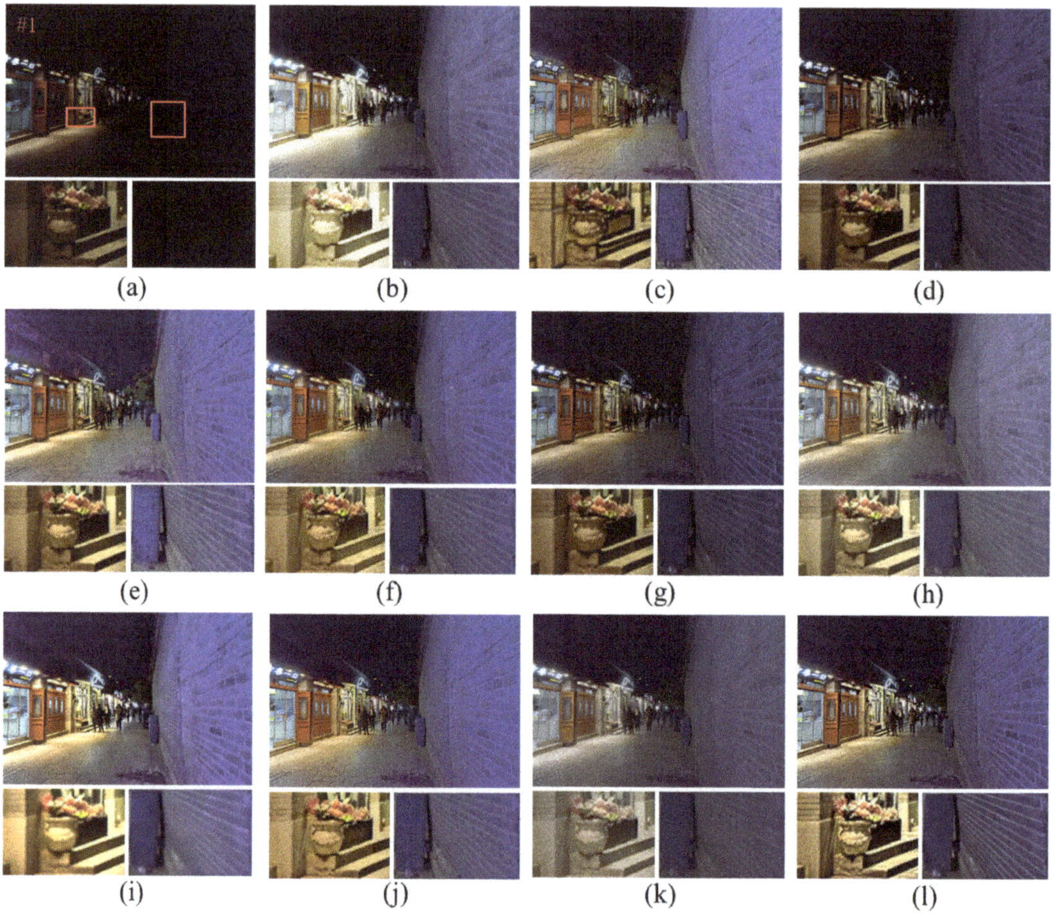

Figure 8. Comparison of different enhancement methods for nighttime images. (a) Original image. (b) Ammen. (c) Dong. (d) SRIE. (e) NPE. (f) MF. (g) Jiep. (h) Ying. (i) LIME. (j) AIEM. (k) RBMP. (l) Ours.

From the observation of Figure 11, it can be seen that the RBMP algorithm shows a fading phenomenon, and many objects have white color and more serious fading phenomenon. The proposed method can better maintain the light distribution and color information of the image. As shown in the enlarged image of the light sign in Figure 11, the image brightness is moderate and there is no over-enhancement. The saturation of the image is in accordance with the visual effect of human eyes, and the image is more natural. As can be observed from the partial zoomed image of the bicycle, the image processed by the proposed algorithm retains more edge texture information and the texture of the seat is clearly visible, so the proposed algorithm has a better edge preservation effect than other comparative algorithms.

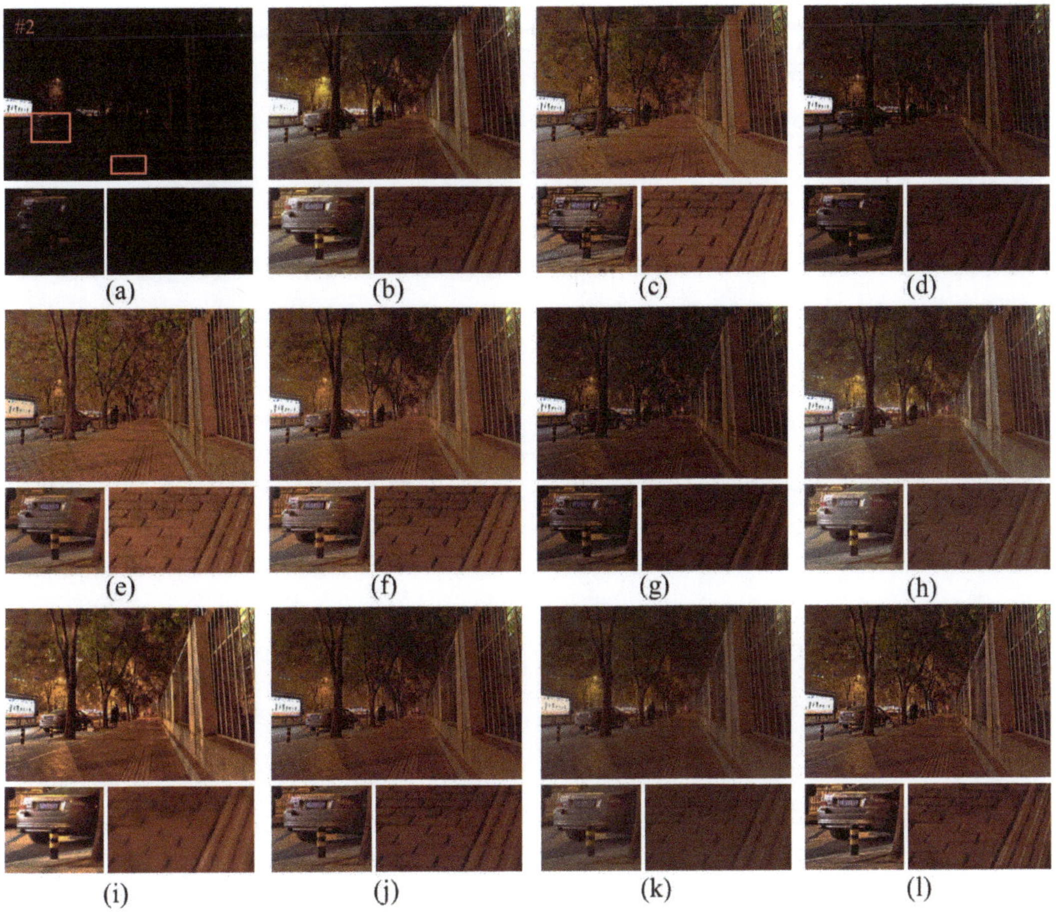

Figure 9. Comparison of different enhancement methods for nighttime images. (a) Original image. (b) Ammen. (c) Dong. (d) SRIE. (e) NPE. (f) MF. (g) Jiep. (h) Ying. (i) LIME. (j) AIEM. (k) RBMP. (l) Ours.

In Figure 12, more nighttime image enhancement results are shown in this paper to demonstrate the effectiveness of the proposed nighttime image enhancement method. Comparing the input image and the enhanced image, it can be seen that the brightness of the enhanced image is improved, the detail information in the dark areas that is difficult to distinguish but contains rich structure becomes clear, the overall visual effect of the image is improved, and the image noise is suppressed while the texture edge information is protected.

Figure 10. Comparison of different enhancement methods for nighttime images. (**a**) Original image. (**b**) Ammen. (**c**) Dong. (**d**) SRIE. (**e**) NPE. (**f**) MF. (**g**) Jiep. (**h**) Ying. (**i**) LIME. (**j**) AIEM. (**k**) RBMP. (**l**) Ours.

4.3. Objective Comparison Experiments of Noise Suppression and Edge Detail Preservation

In order to objectively reflect the enhancement effect of each algorithm in processing low-light images, ARISMC [35], AG (average gradient), CEIQ [36], DE (discrete information entropy) [37], and PSNR (peak signal-to-noise ratio) are used in this paper to measure the quality of the enhanced nighttime images. DE is used to represent the information content of an 8-bit image. The resolution of the histogram is usually 256. Discrete entropy is a statistical measure of stochasticity, the maximum value of the information entropy of an image is eight, and the closer it is to eight implies that the image contains more details. The formula is shown as follows.

$$\mathrm{DE} = -\sum_{i=0}^{255} p(i) \times \log_2(p(i)) \tag{37}$$

where $p(i)$ represents the probability of gray value i. Figure 13 lists the comparison of objective evaluation metrics of different algorithms for processing nighttime images.

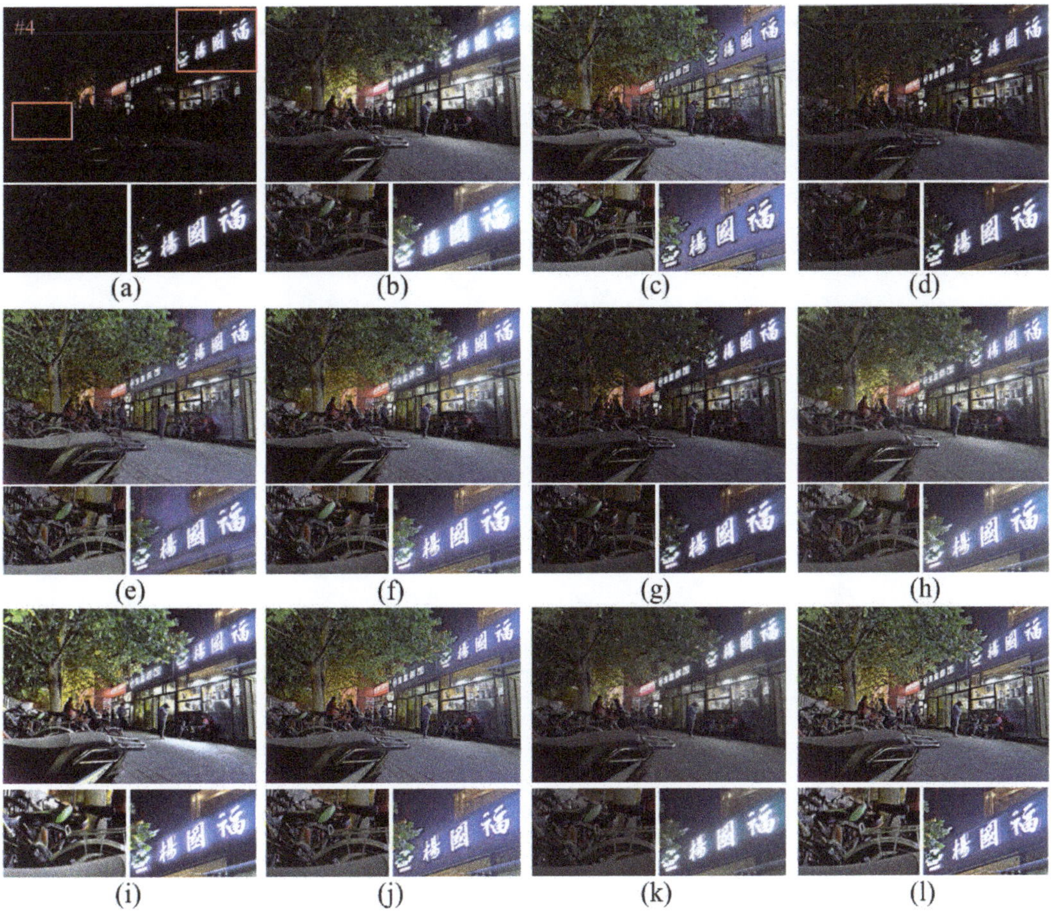

Figure 11. Comparison of different enhancement methods for nighttime image. (**a**) Original image. (**b**) Ammen. (**c**) Dong. (**d**) SRIE. (**e**) NPE. (**f**) MF. (**g**) Jiep. (**h**) Ying. (**i**) LIME. (**j**) AIEM. (**k**) RBMP. (**l**) Ours.

From Figure 13, it can be seen that the proposed algorithm outperforms the other algorithms in ARISMC. The average gradient value of the proposed algorithm only lags behind Dong, NPE, and MF algorithms, indicating that the proposed algorithm can effectively improve the sharpness of images. The CEIQ index only lags behind LIME, indicating that the proposed algorithm achieves good results in the improvement of nighttime image contrast, which reflects the effectiveness of the proposed algorithm. Discrete entropy is a statistical measure of randomness, and higher entropy value usually indicates more details. The proposed algorithm only lags behind the LIME algorithm in DE index, which indicates that the nighttime images processed by the proposed algorithm are enriched in detail content.

Figure 12. More night image enhancement results.

The proposed algorithm does not perform well on the PSNR index, which is a reference measure of image noise and distortion. However, due to the lack of good quality reference images for nighttime images, the original nighttime image is used as the reference image in this paper. However, due to the low brightness and high implied noise of the original night image, the use of the PSNR metric cannot evaluate the denoising effect of the algorithm well. Therefore, we use the SNR (signal-to-noise ratio) metric to continue to verify the image denoising effect. In a large homogeneous area, the ratio of the mean value of image elements to the standard deviation can be considered as the signal-to-noise ratio of the image. The more homogeneous the image is, the closer the estimated value is to the true value [38]. The SNR expression is as follows.

$$\mathrm{SNR} = \frac{mean(I)}{\sqrt{\frac{1}{m*n} * \sum_{i=1}^{m}\sum_{j=1}^{n}(I(i,j) - mean(I))^2}} \tag{38}$$

where $m * n$ represents the size of the image, $I(i,j)$ represents the pixel value of the i-th row and j-th column, and $mean(I)$ represents the mean value of the image.

We intercept part of the uniform region in Figure 8 for testing, and the test results are shown in Table 1. The proposed algorithm has a low SNR value, and the Ying and RBMP algorithms have a high SNR value. We show the effect graph of these three algorithms as shown in Figure 14, and we can see that the denoising effect of the Ying and RBMP algorithms is not good. The noise of the processed image by the proposed algorithm disappears, but the SNR index is the lowest instead. We explain it as follows. In the proposed algorithm, the method used to enhance the image contrast consists of two parts: gamma correction before denoising the texture layer and edge enhancement at the end. To verify the effect of contrast on the SNR index, we process the images with and without gamma correction and edge enhancement, respectively, and then calculate the SNR values. The results are shown in Table 2. The SNR value after removing these two steps reaches 16.5549, which is the largest value in the comparison algorithm. Gamma correction and edge enhancement work on contrast enhancement but will amplify noise if noise removal is not effective. However, in terms of the effect of the image shown in Figure 14c, the proposed algorithm has a good effect on noise removal and does not amplify the noise, and the image has a high contrast and clear edge texture. In contrast, the images processed by the Ying and RBMP algorithms have noise visible to the naked eye and low contrast. Therefore, we suppose that the reason for the low SNR value of the images processed by the proposed algorithm is the increase in contrast, not the high noise. It further verifies the effectiveness of the algorithm in this paper in improving the contrast and suppressing the noise.

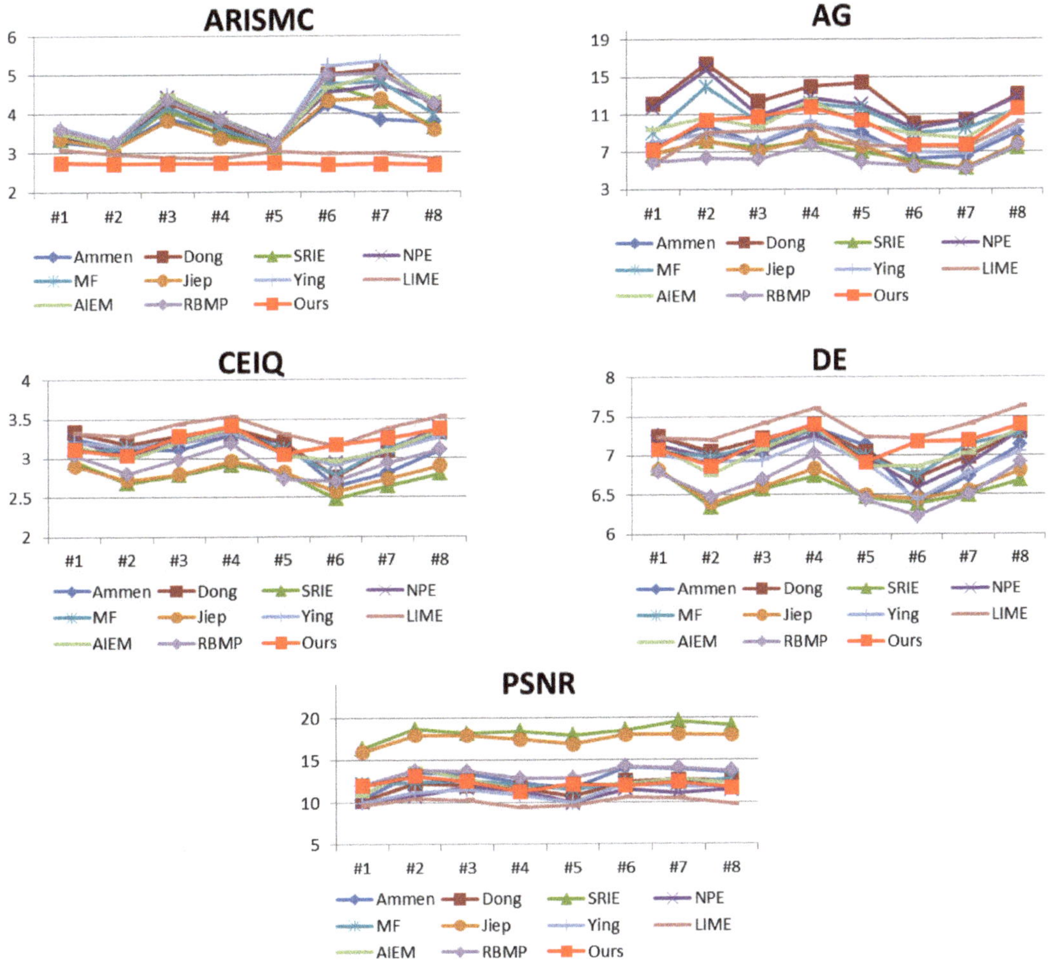

Figure 13. Comparison of objective evaluation metrics for 8 enhanced nighttime images.

(a) (b) (c)

Figure 14. The results of the three algorithms after processing. (**a**) Ying. (**b**) RBMP. (**c**) Ours.

Table 1. SNR evaluation results of locally enhanced images of #1.

Methods	Ammen	Dong	SRIE	NPE	MF	Jiep	Ying	LIME	AIEM	RBMP	Ours
SNR	9.1678	7.7301	7.7478	7.5599	8.5608	7.6108	13.4639	11.8873	9.6383	15.8182	5.0489

Table 2. SNR evaluation results of the local image enhanced by the proposed algorithm for image #1.

Methods	Ours (without Gamma Correction)	Ours (without Gamma Correction and Edge Enhancement)
SNR	11.3355	16.5549

Overall, the results of the comparison experiments show that the proposed algorithm improves the image contrast and brightness while enhancing the detailed texture and suppressing the noise in dark areas. The proposed algorithm processes images with clear details, effectively improves the quality of low-illumination images, and better preserves the edges of objects.

4.4. Comparison with Illumination Images

In order to illustrate more intuitively the effectiveness of the proposed algorithm in detail recovery and brightness enhancement of the image, the low-light image is enhanced and compared with the corresponding illuminated image. The experiment is performed using three sets of images: 'vehicle', 'umbrella', and 'table'. The experimental results are shown in Figure 15. The objective evaluation results are shown in Table 3. As seen in Figure 15, the proposed algorithm is able to recover the scene in the dark light image with appropriate brightness and no overexposure or under-enhancement, which is similar to the illuminated image. From Table 3, it can be seen that the image processed by the proposed algorithm has more obvious improvement in DE and CEIQ values, which is close to the illuminated image.

Table 3. The assessment results on the 'vehicle', 'umbrella' and 'table' images.

Image Name	Image Index	AG	DE	CEIQ
vehicle	(a)	9.5308	7.5610	3.5549
	(b)	2.3725	5.7367	2.1842
	(c)	8.9704	7.4100	3.3822
umbrella	(a)	10.7415	7.6450	3.5293
	(b)	1.7601	5.5031	2.1237
	(c)	4.0315	6.9612	3.0986
table	(a)	7.2880	7.2186	3.2175
	(b)	2.0186	5.3812	2.2509
	(c)	3.8058	6.6435	2.9434

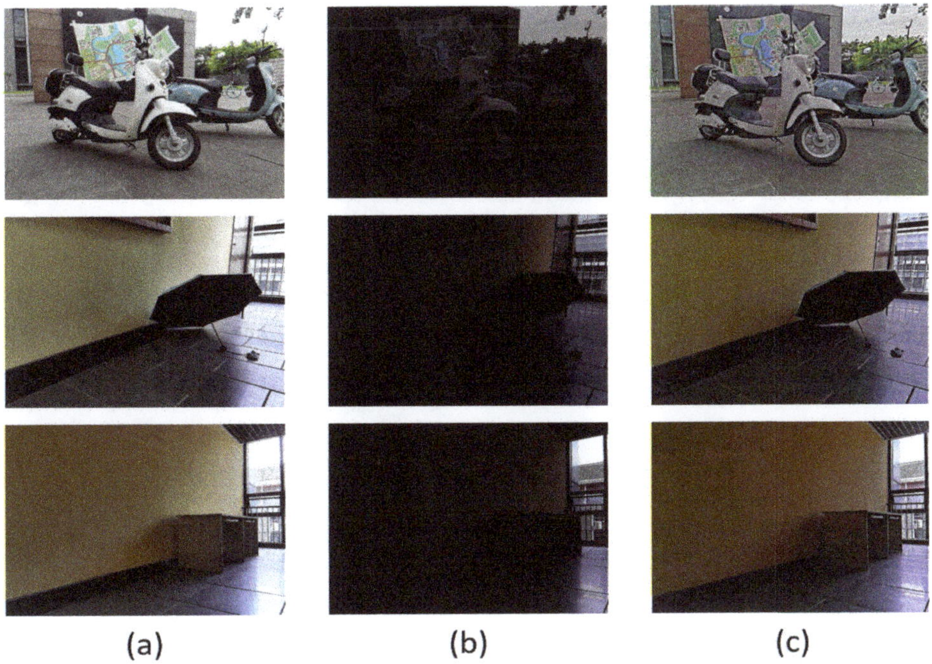

Figure 15. Comparison between enhanced images and illuminated images. (**a**) Illuminated image. (**b**) Low-light image. (**c**) Image enhanced by proposed algorithm for low-light image.

4.5. Comparison of Line Feature Extraction

The night image is processed by the enhancement algorithm, which supplements the detailed features of the dark light area of the image and contributes greatly to the line feature extraction of the image. The effect of line feature extraction of the night image is shown in Figure 16. The comparison data of the number of line features with other enhancement algorithms are shown in Figure 17.

As shown in Figure 16, the processing of the nighttime image by the proposed algorithm enhances the brightness of the dark light region of the image and suppresses the image noise. Due to the image texture enhancement algorithm, the texture edge details of the nighttime image are clearer, the detail information hidden in the dark light region of the image is also restored, and the number of extracted line features is substantially increased. The richness of line features in the dark light region of the image is beneficial to nighttime image stitching.

Figure 17 shows the comparative effect of the proposed algorithm and the comparison algorithm in terms of online feature extraction capability. The results show that the proposed algorithm is significantly better than other comparison algorithms in terms of enriching image structure and line feature extraction, which proves the effectiveness of the proposed algorithm in image feature extraction and helps to improve the success rate of nighttime image stitching.

Figure 16. Comparison of line feature extraction for nighttime images. First row: original image; second row: proposed algorithm; third row: original image; fourth row: proposed algorithm.

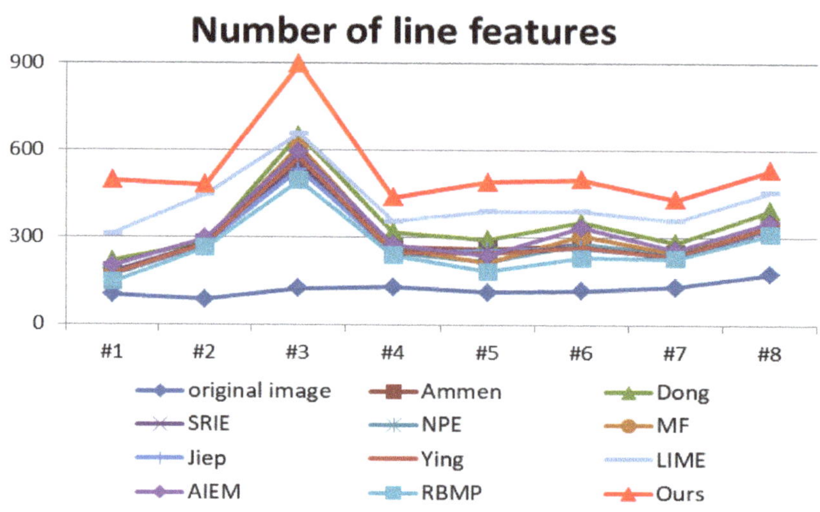

Figure 17. Comparison of the number of line features extracted by nighttime image enhancement algorithms.

4.6. Comparison of Nighttime Images for Stitching

In this paper, the nighttime images from the dataset [34] are clipped and segmented into two images with overlapping regions for stitching experiments. We extract feature points by using the SIFT algorithm, eliminate the mis-matched pairs applying the RANSAC algorithm, extract line features using the LSD algorithm, and generate the stitched images by the linear fusion method. The four sets of images to be stitched are shown in Figure 18. The comparison effect of matching point and line features for the four groups of images to be stitched before and after enhancement is shown in Figure 19.

As can be seen from Figure 19, the number of extracted and aligned line features and point features of the image is increased after processing by the proposed enhancement algorithm. As shown on the pavement of Figure 19b, the details of the dark light areas of the image processed by the proposed enhancement algorithm are visible, and the number of line features and point features extracted and aligned is increased. As shown in Figure 19d, mis-matched pairs are caused due to the presence of faint bright spots in the nighttime images, which directly led to stitching failure. As seen in Figure 19d, the pre-processing of the nighttime image by the proposed enhancement algorithm increases the number of feature point pairs in the image and no mismatched pairs appear.

In order to make the details of the night stitched image visible and easy to compare, we enhance the brightness of the stitched night image by the histogram equalization method, and the effect is shown in the enlarged figure in Figure 20. The effect of night image stitching and the effect of night image stitching after the enhancement process are shown in Figure 20. The objective quality of the stitched images is evaluated using AG (average gradient), DE (discrete information entropy), and CEIQ. The results are shown in Table 4, and the image names in the table are consistent with the image names in Figure 20.

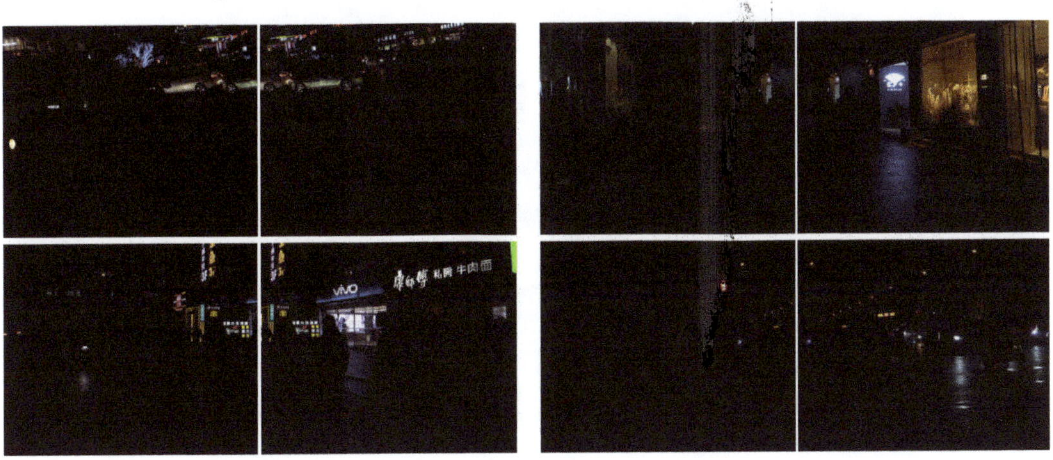

Figure 18. Experimental images of night stitching.

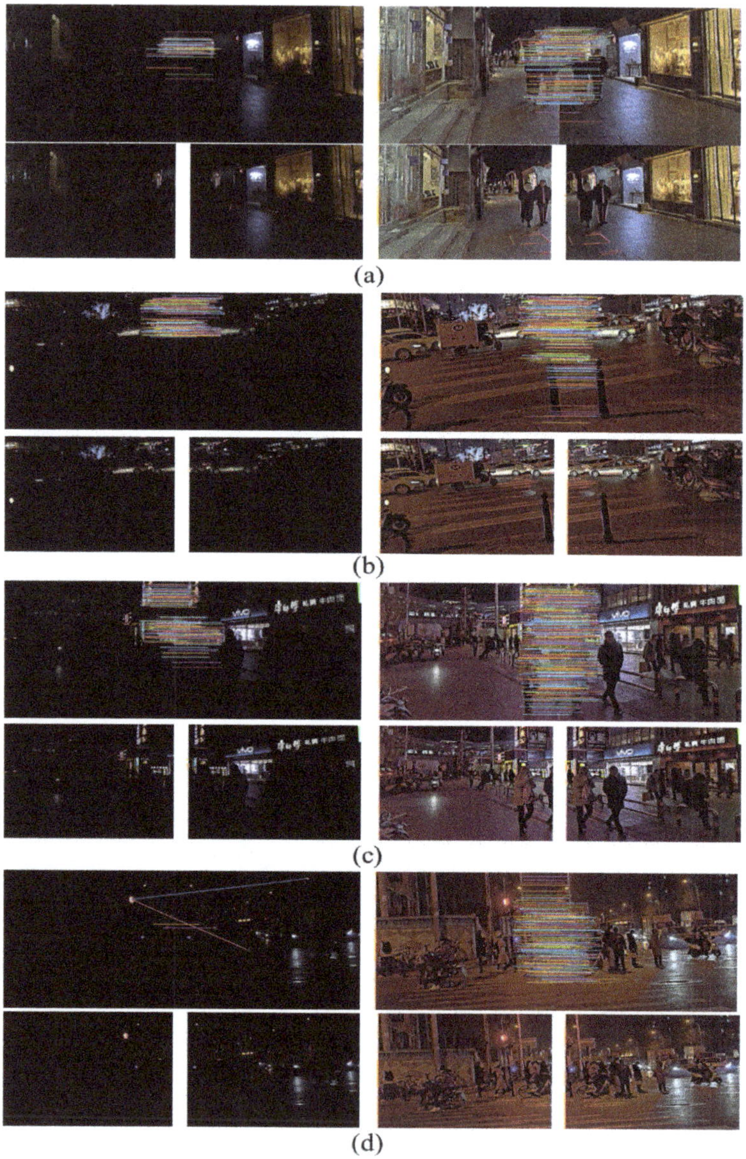

Figure 19. Comparison of the matching effect of point and line features before and after image enhancement in four groups. The first column: comparison of point feature matching; the second column: comparison of line feature matching.

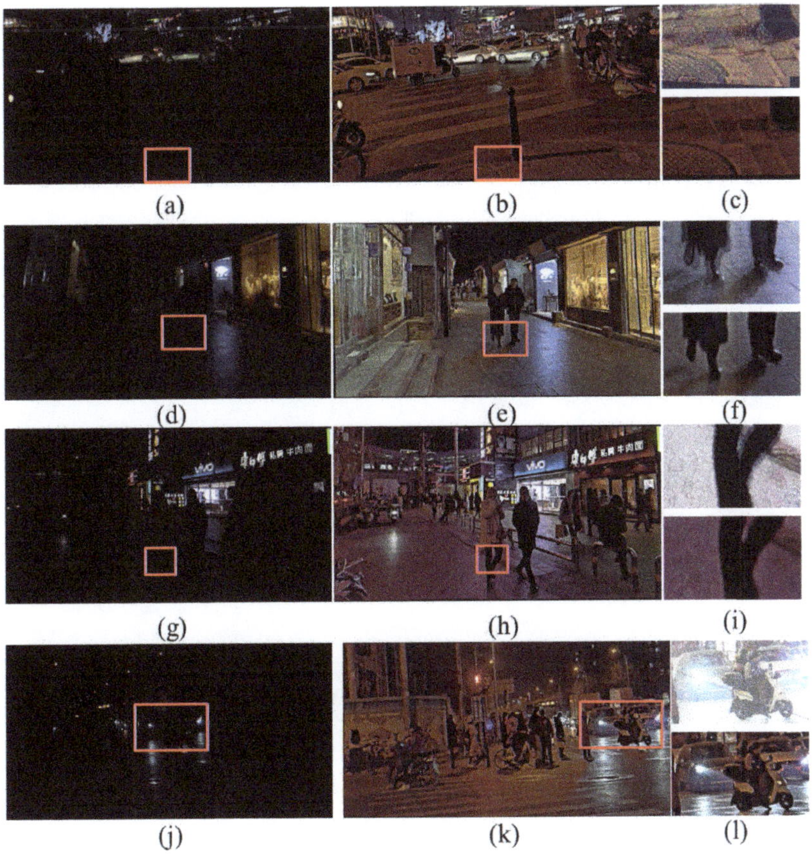

Figure 20. First column: stitching of nighttime images; second column: stitching of nighttime images after enhancement; third column: local enlargement.

Table 4. Objective evaluation of stitched images.

Metric \ Images	(a)	(b)	(d)	(e)	(g)	(h)	(j)	(k)
AG	2.5148	8.9469	2.3347	7.9535	2.9061	8.4843	1.1548	7.1729
DE	5.6975	7.3219	4.2336	6.4785	4.5531	7.0246	3.3175	6.8408
CEIQ	2.1882	3.3638	1.8909	2.6831	1.9174	3.1295	1.8664	3.0218

From Figure 20c,f,i, it can be seen that when stitching the nighttime images directly, the stitched images obtained are misaligned and overlapped due to the lack of feature information. Figure 20j shows that this group of nighttime images failed to be stitched together, which is highly likely to cause image stitching failure due to the small number of feature points and the presence of mis-matched pairs. Table 4 shows that the stitched images (b,e,h,k) after the enhancement process are significantly improved in terms of image sharpness and contrast. These four sets of stitched images show that the line features and point features are complemented by the enhanced nighttime stitched images, which results in a more accurate transformation matrix, and the ghosting misalignment disappears. Meanwhile, The quality of the stitched images is improved. This experiment proves that the proposed enhancement algorithm is suitable for nighttime image stitching.

5. Conclusions

Aiming at the problem of insufficient line feature extraction during the splicing process of night images, a nighttime image stitching method based on image decomposition enhancement is proposed. The proposed method decomposes the image using the rolling guidance filter to obtain a higher quality structural layer. The structural layer brightness is enhanced using an improved enhancement function, and the texture layer is denoised using the BM3D algorithm. After the enhanced structure layer and the smoothed texture layer are fused, the fused night image is then contrast enhanced by the edge enhancement function, and finally a higher quality and more detailed night enhanced image is obtained.

In this paper, the proposed algorithm is validated using nighttime images and compared with ten other enhancement algorithms. From the experimental results, we can see that the nighttime images processed by the proposed enhancement algorithm are processed to obtain images with rich details, clear textures, and natural colors. By comparing the enhanced images with other algorithms for line feature extraction, the proposed algorithm has a more obvious advantage in the number of line features extracted. In addition, through the image stitching experiments, it is proved that the proposed algorithm improves the efficiency of nighttime image stitching and reduces the phenomenon of misalignment and ghosting. In summary, the proposed nighttime image stitching method based on image decomposition enhancement can improve the quality of nighttime images, supplement texture information, and increase the number of line features in dark light areas of images, resulting in efficient and accurate stitching, which provides value for nighttime security surveillance applications.

Author Contributions: Software, writing—original draft preparation, writing—review and editing, M.Y.; formal analysis, D.Q.; project administration, D.Q.; investigation, G.Z.; validation, H.T.; supervision, D.Q. and L.M. All authors have read and agreed to the published version of the manuscript.

Funding: This research was funded by the Open Research Fund of National Mobile Communications Research Laboratory, Southeast University (No. 2023D07), Outstanding Youth Program of Natural Science Foundation of Heilongjiang Province (YQ2020F012) and National Natural Science Foundation of China (61971162, 61771186), Fundamental Scientific Research Funds of Heilongjiang Province (2022-KYYWF-1050).

Informed Consent Statement: Informed consent was obtained from all subjects involved in the study, for studies not involving humans.

Data Availability Statement: The data presented in this study are available on request from the corresponding author. The data are not publicly available due to privacy.

Conflicts of Interest: The authors declare no conflict of interest.

References

1. Cao, M.; Zheng, L.; Jia, W.; Liu, X. Constructing big panorama from video sequence based on deep local feature. *Image Vis. Comput.* **2020**, *101*, 103972. [CrossRef]
2. Rahman, Z.; Jobson, D.J.; Woodell, G.A. Multiscale retinex for color image enhancement. In Proceedings of the 3rd IEEE International Conference on Image Processing, Lausanne, Switzerland, 19 September 1996.
3. Jobson, D.J.; Rahman, Z.U.; Woodell, G.A. A multiscale retinex for bridging the gap between color images and the human observation of scenes. *IEEE Trans. Image Process.* **1997**, *6*, 965–976. [CrossRef] [PubMed]
4. Lee, C.H.; Shih, J.L.; Lien, C.C.; Han, C.C. Adaptive multiscale retinex for image contrast enhancement. In Proceedings of the 2013 International Conference on Signal-Image Technology & Internet-Based Systems, Kyoto, Japan, 2–5 December 2013; pp. 43–50.
5. Tang, H.; Zhu, H.; Tao, H.; Xie, C. An improved algorithm for low-light image enhancement based on RetinexNet. *Appl. Sci.* **2022**, *12*, 7268. [CrossRef]
6. Guo, Y.; Lu, Y.; Liu, R.W.; Yang, M.; Chui, K.T. Low-light image enhancement with regularized illumination optimization and deep noise suppression. *IEEE Access* **2020**, *8*, 145297–145315. [CrossRef]
7. Wang, W.; Chen, Z.; Yuan, X.; Wu, X. Adaptive image enhancement method for correcting low-illumination images. *Inf. Sci.* **2019**, *496*, 25–41. [CrossRef]
8. Chen, S.D.; Ramli, A.R. Minimum mean brightness error bi-histogram equalization in contrast enhancement. *IEEE Trans. Consum. Electron.* **2004**, *49*, 1310–1319. [CrossRef]

9. Lu, H.; Liu, Z.; Pan, X. An Adaptive Detail Equalization for Infrared Image Enhancement Based on Multi-Scale Convolution. *IEEE Access* **2020**, *8*, 156763–156773. [CrossRef]
10. Veluchamy, M.; Subramani, B. Image Contrast and Color Enhancement using Adaptive Gamma Correction and Histogram Equalization. *Optik* **2019**, *183*, 329–337. [CrossRef]
11. Liu, C.; Sui, X.; Liu, Y.; Kuang, X.; Chen, Q. Adaptive contrast enhancement based on histogram modification framework. *J. Mod. Opt.* **2019**, *66*, 1–12. [CrossRef]
12. Gautam, C.; Tiwari, N. Efficient color image contrast enhancement using Range Limited Bi-Histogram Equalization with Adaptive Gamma Correction. In Proceedings of the 2015 International Conference on Industrial Instrumentation and Control (ICIC), Pune, India, 28–30 May 2015.
13. Li, Z.; Jia, Z.; Yang, J.; Kasabov, N. Low illumination video image enhancement. *IEEE Photonics J.* **2020**, *12*, 1–13. [CrossRef]
14. Ren, Y.; Ying, Z.; Li, T.H.; Li, G. LECARM: Low-Light Image Enhancement Using the Camera Response Model. *IEEE Trans. Circuits Syst. Video Technol.* **2019**, *29*, 968–981. [CrossRef]
15. Fu, X.; Zeng, D.; Huang, Y.; Liao, Y.; Ding, X.; Paisley, J. A fusion-based enhancing method for weakly illuminated images. *Signal Process.* **2016**, *129*, 82–96. [CrossRef]
16. Lee, S.; Kim, N.; Paik, J. Adaptively partitioned block-based contrast enhancement and its application to low light-level video surveillance. *SpringerPlus* **2015**, *4*, 431. [CrossRef]
17. Lu, K.; Zhang, L. TBEFN: A two-branch exposure-fusion network for low-light image enhancement. *IEEE Trans. Multimed.* **2020**, *23*, 4093–4105. [CrossRef]
18. Qian, S.; Shi, Y.; Wu, H.; Liu, J.; Zhang, W. An adaptive enhancement algorithm based on visual saliency for low illumination images. *Appl. Intell.* **2022**, *52*, 1770–1792. [CrossRef]
19. Kanmani, M.; Narasimhan, V. Swarm intelligent based contrast enhancement algorithm with improved visual perception for color images. *Multimed. Tools Appl.* **2018**, *77*, 12701–12724. [CrossRef]
20. Li, C.; Liu, J.; Wu, Q.; Bi, L. An adaptive enhancement method for low illumination color images. *Appl. Intell.* **2021**, *51*, 202–222. [CrossRef]
21. Zhang, Q.; Shen, X.; Xu, L.; Jia, J. Rolling guidance filter. In Proceedings of the Computer Vision–ECCV 2014: 13th European Conference, Zurich, Switzerland, 6–12 September 2014; Springer: Berlin/Heidelberg, Germany, 2014; pp. 815–830.
22. Wang, S.; Zheng, J.; Hu, H.M.; Li, B. Naturalness preserved enhancement algorithm for non-uniform illumination images. *IEEE Trans. Image Process.* **2013**, *22*, 3538–3548. [CrossRef]
23. Zhang, Y.; Huang, W.; Bi, W.; Gao, G. Colorful image enhancement algorithm based on guided filter and Retinex. In Proceedings of the 2016 IEEE International Conference on Signal and Image Processing (ICSIP), Beijing, China, 13–15 August 2016; pp. 33–36.
24. Wang, D.; Han, P.; Fan, J.; Liu, Y.; Xu, Z.; Wang, J. A Multispectral Image Enhancement Algorithm Based on Illumination Reflection Imaging Model and Morphological Operations. *Acta Phys. Sin.* **2016**, *65*, 160701.
25. Dabov, K.; Foi, A.; Katkovnik, V.; Egiazarian, K. Image denoising by sparse 3-D transform-domain collaborative filtering. *IEEE Trans. Image Process.* **2007**, *16*, 2080–2095. [CrossRef]
26. Lu, Z.; Long, B.; Li, K.; Lu, F. Effective guided image filtering for contrast enhancement. *IEEE Signal Process. Lett.* **2018**, *25*, 1585–1589. [CrossRef]
27. Al-Ameen, Z. Nighttime image enhancement using a new illumination boost algorithm. *IET Image Process.* **2019**, *13*, 1314–1320. [CrossRef]
28. Dong, X.; Pang, Y.; Wen, J. Fast efficient algorithm for enhancement of low lighting video. In *ACM SIGGRAPH 2010 Posters*; Association for Computing Machinery: New York, NY, USA, 2010; p. 1.
29. Fu, X.; Zeng, D.; Huang, Y.; Zhang, X.P.; Ding, X. A weighted variational model for simultaneous reflectance and illumination estimation. In Proceedings of the IEEE Conference on Computer Vision and Pattern Recognition, Las Vegas, NV, USA, 27–30 June 2016; pp. 2782–2790.
30. Cai, B.; Xu, X.; Guo, K.; Jia, K.; Hu, B.; Tao, D. A joint intrinsic-extrinsic prior model for retinex. In Proceedings of the IEEE International Conference on Computer Vision, Venice, Italy, 22–29 October 2017; pp. 4000–4009.
31. Ying, Z.; Li, G.; Ren, Y.; Wang, R.; Wang, W. A new low-light image enhancement algorithm using camera response model. In Proceedings of the IEEE international Conference on Computer Vision Workshops, Venice, Italy, 22–29 October 2017; pp. 3015–3022.
32. Guo, X. LIME: A method for low-light image enhancement. In Proceedings of the 24th ACM international Conference on Multimedia, Amsterdam, The Netherlands, 15–19 October 2016; pp. 87–91.
33. Al-Hashim, M.A.; Al-Ameen, Z. Retinex-Based Multiphase Algorithm for Low-Light Image Enhancement. *Trait. Signal* **2020**, *37*, 733–743. [CrossRef]
34. Liang, J.; Wang, J.; Quan, Y.; Chen, T.; Liu, J.; Ling, H.; Xu, Y. Recurrent exposure generation for low-light face detection. *IEEE Trans. Multimed.* **2021**, *24*, 1609–1621. [CrossRef]
35. Gu, K.; Zhai, G.; Lin, W.; Yang, X.; Zhang, W. No-reference image sharpness assessment in autoregressive parameter space. *IEEE Trans. Image Process.* **2015**, *24*, 3218–3231. [PubMed]
36. Yan, J.; Li, J.; Fu, X. No-reference quality assessment of contrast-distorted images using contrast enhancement. *arXiv* **2019**, arXiv:1904.08879.

37. Ye, Z.; Mohamadian, H.; Ye, Y. Discrete entropy and relative entropy study on nonlinear clustering of underwater and arial images. In Proceedings of the 2007 IEEE International Conference on Control Applications, Singapore, 1–3 October 2007; pp. 313–318.
38. Zhang, L.; Huang, W.; Zhang, Y.; Xu, Y.; Zhou, C. Evaluation of Signal to Noise Ratio of HJ-1 Satellite CCD Image. *Geospat. Inf.* **2013**, *11*, 73–75.

Journal of
Imaging

MDPI

Article

Order Space-Based Morphology for Color Image Processing

Shanqian Sun, Yunjia Huang, Kohei Inoue * and Kenji Hara

Department of Media Design, Faculty of Design, Kyushu University, 4-9-1, Shiobaru, Minami-ku, Fukuoka 815-8540, Japan; sunshanqian@outlook.com (S.S.); yuichi0507@163.com (Y.H.); hara@design.kyushu-u.ac.jp (K.H.)
* Correspondence: k-inoue@design.kyushu-u.ac.jp

Abstract: Mathematical morphology is a fundamental tool based on order statistics for image processing, such as noise reduction, image enhancement and feature extraction, and is well-established for binary and grayscale images, whose pixels can be sorted by their pixel values, i.e., each pixel has a single number. On the other hand, each pixel in a color image has three numbers corresponding to three color channels, e.g., red (R), green (G) and blue (B) channels in an RGB color image. Therefore, it is difficult to sort color pixels uniquely. In this paper, we propose a method for unifying the orders of pixels sorted in each color channel separately, where we consider that a pixel exists in a three-dimensional space called order space, and derive a single order by a monotonically non-decreasing function defined on the order space. We also fuzzify the proposed order space-based morphological operations, and demonstrate the effectiveness of the proposed method by comparing with a state-of-the-art method based on hypergraph theory. The proposed method treats three orders of pixels sorted in respective color channels equally. Therefore, the proposed method is consistent with the conventional morphological operations for binary and grayscale images.

Keywords: mathematical morphology; color image processing; order space; noise removal; exponentially weighted averaging; log-sum-exp; softmax; fuzzy

1. Introduction

Mathematical morphology is a theory that originated in the 1960s for treating the shape of objects in images based on set theory and lattice theory. Mathematical morphology has a wide range of applications in digital image processing. At the present time, there are a large number of theoretical and practical studies on mathematical morphology, where the development of basic techniques for binary and grayscale images is almost complete. For a comprehensive introduction to morphological image analysis, one may refer to the book by Soille [1].

Unlike the case of binary or grayscale images, mathematical morphology for color images and higher-dimensional images is still under study because of the difficulty and uncertainty of ordering vector data, such as color vectors or pixels, in color images. That is, there is no canonical ordering of pixels in color images, and an arbitrary choice of order function that assigns an order to any pixel will provide good results for some problems or images and bad results for others.

Recently, a number of morphological techniques for color images have been presented to overcome the above difficulty. Sartor and Weeks [2] proposed a method based on the $(C-Y)$ color space, which has the luminance coordinate (Y) and the chromatic coordinates $(R-Y,\ B-Y)$, where a generalized distance between a color and reference color is used for ordering color vectors. For computing the generalized distance, one requires a 3×3 covariance matrix. They also provided a brief introduction to lattice theory. Angulo also proposed a method to use a reference color for computing color distance, where the distance-based and lexicographical approaches are generalized in RGB, LSH and Lab color spaces [3]. d'Ornellas and Costa proposed an ordering relation for colors that is based on the natural ordering of spectra [4]. As a result, they derived a color-model-independent approach for color mathematical morphology. However, in compensation for the independency, their method requires reconstructing the fundamental spectrum from a conventional 3D color vector. Benavent et al. proposed a method based on the color histogram of a quantized color image [5], where the pixels are sorted on the basis of the frequency recorded in the histogram. In their method, the results may be affected by the number of quantized colors. Comer and Delp defined erosion and dilation for color morphology using marginal ordering, which uses only one component of a vector for ordering pixels, and reduced ordering, which uses a dimensionality reduction function for ordering three-dimensional pixel data [6]. Zhao also proposed a method for color morphology based on marginal ordering, where no new color artifacts are produced [7]. Van de Gronde and Roerdink pointed out that the false color problem lies in violating certain invariances, and demonstrated the effectiveness of hue-invariant and rotation-invariant methods [8]. Gimenez and Evans [9] analyzed the convex color sieve (CCS) by Gibson et al. [10] and the vector area morphology sieve (VAMS) by Evans [11] algorithmically and experimentally. Evans also described a chapter devoted to color area morphology scale spaces [12]. Burgeth et al. extended morphological maximum and minimum operations to tensor-valued settings by employing Loewner ordering for symmetric matrices [13]. Naegel and Passat extended the gray-level definition of component trees to multi-value images, and compared some strategies for color image processing based on component trees in the color image filtering and color document binarization fields [14]. Tushabe and Wilkinson proposed a color filtering method using max-tree representation, where a color image is converted into a grayscale image that is then subjected to the conventional filtering techniques, and demonstrated three restitution mechanisms that reconstruct the filtered image back into color: nearest color, nearest neighbor and mean of parent approaches [15]. Lezoray et al. proposed a method for the graph-based ordering of color vectors, and demonstrated the proposed mathematical morphology operations in RGB, IHSL [16], $L^*a^*b^*$ and CIECAM02 [17] color models [18]. Wang et al. proposed color morphological operators on a hypergraph to avoid the loss of details caused by fixed structuring elements [19]. The hypergraph-based method has two parameters for controlling spatial and color similarities between pixels.

In this paper, we propose a method for morphologically operating color images on the basis of an order space, which is a three-dimensional space with the axes of orders of pixels in three color channels. Specifically, we take the RGB (red, green and blue) color channels of RGB color images as a typical example, and sort the pixels in each channel separately. As a result, we obtain a triplet of orders for each pixel, which is then represented as a point in the order space. After that, we compute a single order from the obtained triplet of orders by a function from 3D to 1D, and then apply morphological operations based on the single order of pixels. In our experiments, we compere the proposed method with Wang's hypergraph-based method [19], and demonstrate the performance of the proposed method in a noise-removal task. Moreover, we present the fuzzy version of the proposed order space-based method, which improves the performance further.

Since a color image is a stack of three grayscale images corresponding to three color channels, it would be consistent with the conventional morphological operation for binary and grayscale images to take into account the triplet of orders of pixels in the color version of the morphological operations. Therefore, the proposed order space-based method can be a plausible candidate for the extension of a grayscale morphology to a color one.

The rest of this paper is organized as follows: Section 2 briefly summarizes binary and grayscale morphological operations. Section 3 proposes the order space-based morphological operations for color images. Section 4 proposes an exponentially weighted averaging method for fuzzifying the order space-based method. Section 5 shows the experimental results obtained from a standard image dataset. Section 6 discusses the results obtained in Section 5. Finally, Section 7 concludes this paper.

2. Morphology for Binary and Grayscale Image Processing

In this section, we briefly summarize the basics of mathematical morphology for binary and grayscale images in preparation for the subsequent sections. In the following definitions of morphological operations, since binary images can be regarded as a special case of grayscale images, we focus on grayscale morphology [20].

Let $G = [g_{ij}]$ be a grayscale image, where $g_{ij} \in \{0, 1, \ldots, L-1\}$ for $i = 1, 2, \ldots, m$ and $j = 1, 2, \ldots, n$ denotes the pixel value at the ith row and jth column in G with m rows and n columns, where $L - 1$ denotes the maximum pixel value, e.g., $L = 256 = 2^8$ for an 8-bit grayscale image. The grayscale pixel values $g_{ij} = 0$ and $g_{ij} = L - 1$ denote black and white pixels, respectively. To perform a morphological operation on G, we need a structuring element S, which is a set of relative coordinates, e.g., a 3×3 'Cross' (or 'Rhombus') structuring element $S = \{(-1,0),\ (0,-1),\ (0,0),\ (0,1),\ (1,0)\}$ and a 'Square' one $S = \{(-1,-1),\ (-1,0),\ (-1,1),\ (0,-1),\ (0,0),\ (0,1),\ (1,-1),\ (1,0), (1,1)\}$, which are illustrated in Figure 1. We assume that all structuring elements used in this paper are point-symmetric, which is a reasonable assumption for isotropic image processing tasks and simplifies the definitions of morphological operations as follows. (In a formal description, dilation is defined as the Minkowski set addition by a given structuring element. On the other hand, erosion is defined as the Minkowski set subtraction by the reflection of the structuring element. With the symmetric structuring elements, we can skip the reflection step.)

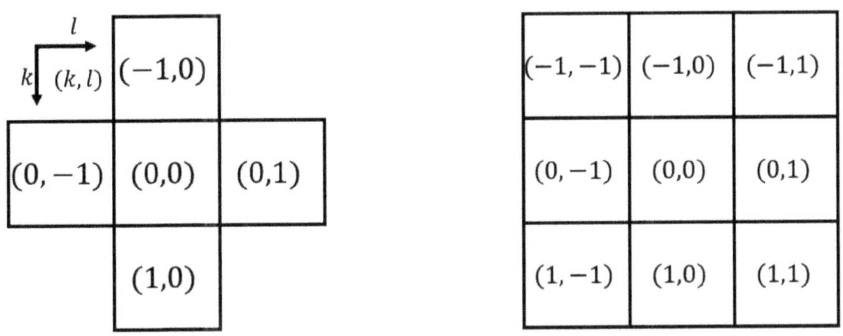

(**a**) Cross (**b**) Square

Figure 1. The 3×3 structuring elements: (**a**) The 3×3 'Cross' structuring element is defined by a set of relative coordinates as $S = \{(-1,0),\ (0,-1),\ (0,0),\ (0,1),\ (1,0)\}$. (**b**) The 3×3 'Square' structuring element is defined by a set of relative coordinates as $S = \{(-1,-1),\ (-1,0),\ (-1,1),\ (0,-1),\ (0,0),\ (0,1),\ (1,-1),\ (1,0), (1,1)\}$.

The dilation of G by a symmetric structuring element S is defined as

$$D(G,S) = [d_{ij}], \quad d_{ij} = \max_{(k,l)\in S}\left\{g_{i+k,\, j+l}\right\}, \tag{1}$$

and the erosion of G by the same S is defined as

$$E(G,S) = [e_{ij}], \quad e_{ij} = \min_{(k,l)\in S}\left\{g_{i+k,\, j+l}\right\}, \tag{2}$$

where we note that if $i + k \notin \{1, 2, \ldots, m\}$ or $j + l \notin \{1, 2, \ldots, n\}$, then the corresponding value $g_{i+k,j+l}$ is excluded from the candidates for output pixel.

The above dilation and erosion operations change the mean brightness of a given image. To compensate for such bias caused by dilation and erosion operations, they are often combined with each other as follows: the opening of G by S is defined as

$$O(G,S) = D(E(G,S),S), \tag{3}$$

and the closing of G by S is defined as

$$C(G,S) = E(D(G,S),S), \tag{4}$$

i.e., the opening operation is composed of an erosion followed by a dilation, and the closing operation is composed of a dilation followed by an erosion. The opening and closing operations are also combined with each other as follows: the open–closing of G by S is defined as

$$OC(G,S) = C(O(G,S),S), \tag{5}$$

and the close–opening of G by S is defined as

$$CO(G,S) = O(C(G,S),S), \tag{6}$$

i.e., the open–closing operation is composed of an opening followed by a closing, and the close–opening operation is composed of a closing followed by an opening (the definitions of the open–closing and close–opening operations are convertible into each other as mentioned by Schevenels and Sigmund [21]).

Here, we note that if $L = 2$, then these definitions are reduced to those for binary images.

3. Order Space-Based Morphology for Color Image Processing

The above morphological operations for binary and grayscale images include the maximum and minimum selection, which is based on the assumption that the pixels in an image can be sorted in ascending or descending order of their pixel values. For a binary or grayscale image, it is easy to sort the pixels by their values. However, for a color image, it is not easy because each color pixel has three values, e.g., red, green and blue components, the orders of which may conflict with each other. Therefore, sorting each color component separately frequently causes undesirable colors.

In this section, we propose a method for morphologically processing color images in an appropriate manner, which can alleviate the drawback of the naive separable method.

Let $F = [f_{ij}]$ be an RGB color image, where $f_{ij} = [f_{ij}^{\mathrm{R}}, f_{ij}^{\mathrm{G}}, f_{ij}^{\mathrm{B}}]$ for $i = 1,2,\ldots,m$ and $j = 1,2,\ldots,n$ denotes the RGB color vector at the position (i,j) in F, where $f_{ij}^{\mathrm{R}}, f_{ij}^{\mathrm{G}}$ and f_{ij}^{B} denote the red (R), green (G) and blue (B) components of the pixel f_{ij}, respectively. Then, we can sort the color components covered by a structuring element in ascending order of their values, e.g., $f^{\mathrm{R}}_{i+k(a_1^{\mathrm{R}}),\, j+l(a_1^{\mathrm{R}})} \leq f^{\mathrm{R}}_{i+k(a_2^{\mathrm{R}}),\, j+l(a_2^{\mathrm{R}})} \leq \cdots \leq f^{\mathrm{R}}_{i+k(a_5^{\mathrm{R}}),\, j+l(a_5^{\mathrm{R}})}$ for the R component with a structuring element S with five pixels, as shown in Figure 1a, where $a_1^{\mathrm{R}}, a_2^{\mathrm{R}}, \ldots, a_5^{\mathrm{R}}$ denote the sorted indices of pixels covered by S, and $k(a_1^{\mathrm{R}})$ and $l(a_1^{\mathrm{R}})$ denote the vertical and horizontal relative coordinates of the pixel corresponding to a_1^{R}, respectively.

Let $\xi = a_\eta^{\mathrm{R}}$ (for $\eta = 1,2,\ldots,5$) be a function where a pixel index ξ is related to an order η given by the above sorting procedure. Then, we consider the inverse function of $\xi = a_\eta^{\mathrm{R}}$ as $\eta = o_\xi^{\mathrm{R}} = (a^{\mathrm{R}})_\xi^{-1}$, where an order η is related to a pixel index ξ. That is, each pixel ξ has the corresponding order η. According to the order, we can arrange the five pixels on an axis as shown in Figure 2a, where each black point denotes a pixel ξ, which is placed at the position designated by the order η.

Similarly, we can sort the set of pixels in the ascending order of the G components to have the sorted indices $a_1^{\mathrm{G}}, a_2^{\mathrm{G}}, \ldots, a_5^{\mathrm{G}}$ satisfying $f^{\mathrm{G}}_{i+k(a_1^{\mathrm{G}}),\, j+l(a_1^{\mathrm{G}})} \leq f^{\mathrm{G}}_{i+k(a_2^{\mathrm{G}}),\, j+l(a_2^{\mathrm{G}})} \leq \cdots \leq$

$f^{G}_{i+k(a^{G}_{5}),\, j+l(a^{G}_{5})}$. We also consider the inverse function of $\xi = a^{G}_{\eta}$ as $\eta = o^{G}_{\xi} = (a^{G})^{-1}_{\xi}$. Then, we can plot the five pixels on a two-dimensional coordinate system with the axes o^{R} and o^{G} as shown in Figure 2b, where we note that no two pixels are aligned with one another vertically and horizontally.

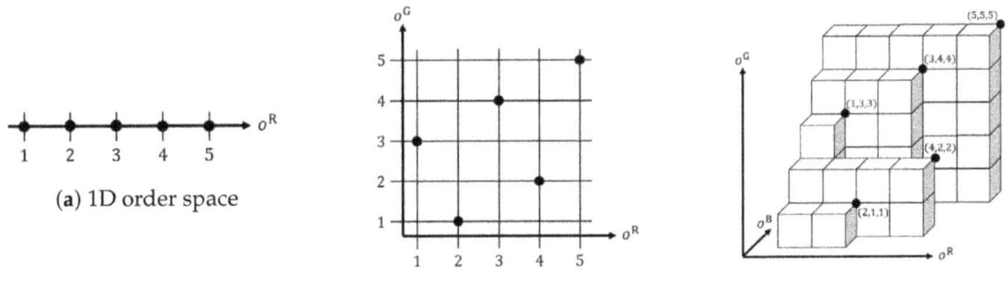

(a) 1D order space

(b) 2D order space

(c) 3D order space

Figure 2. Illustrations of 1D, 2D and 3D order spaces for RGB color images: (**a**) Five pixels are arranged in a line (or a one-dimensional order space) according to the ascending order of their R components. For binary and grayscale images, we can consider the similar 1D order space. (**b**) If we take into account R and G components simultaneously, then we have a two-dimensional order space onto which five pixels are located according to their orders. (**c**) If we take into account R, G and B components simultaneously, then we have a three-dimensional order space onto which five pixels are located according to their orders.

By sorting the B components, we also have the sorted indices $a^{B}_{1}, a^{B}_{2}, \ldots, a^{B}_{5}$ satisfying $f^{B}_{i+k(a^{B}_{1}),\, j+l(a^{B}_{1})} \leq f^{B}_{i+k(a^{B}_{2}),\, j+l(a^{B}_{2})} \leq \cdots \leq f^{B}_{i+k(a^{B}_{5}),\, j+l(a^{B}_{5})}$, which are summarized as a function $\xi = a^{B}_{\eta}$ for $\eta = 1, 2, \ldots, 5$, the inverse function of which is given by $\eta = o^{B}_{\xi} = (a^{B})^{-1}_{\xi}$. Then, we can plot each pixel on a three-dimensional coordinate system with the axes o^{R}, o^{G} and o^{B} as shown in Figure 2c. We call the space determined by the above coordinate system *order space*. As a result, an RGB color pixel identified by an index ξ is mapped to a point on the order space as $(o^{R}_{\xi}, o^{G}_{\xi}, o^{B}_{\xi})$. This is a natural consequence of the generalization of the basics of morphological operations for binary and grayscale images, since there are no advantages and disadvantages among the three color channels. Therefore, it is reasonable to construct morphological operations for color images on the basis of the 3D order space.

Algorithm 1 summarizes the procedure for mapping from an RGB color space to the order space. In Algorithm 1, line 3, the function 'argsort' sorts the arguments $f^{X}_{1}, f^{X}_{2}, \ldots, f^{X}_{|S|}$ in ascending order as $f^{X}_{a^{X}_{1}} \leq f^{X}_{a^{X}_{2}} \leq \cdots \leq f^{X}_{a^{X}_{|S|}}$, and returns their indices $a^{X}_{1}, a^{X}_{2}, \ldots, a^{X}_{|S|}$, where $|S|$ denotes the number of elements of S. Each value of the coordinates in the order space is given at line 5.

Algorithm 1 Mapping from RGB color space to order space

Require: a set of pixels $\{f_{i+k,j+l} = [f^{R}_{i+k,j+l}, f^{G}_{i+k,j+l}, f^{B}_{i+k,j+l}] \mid (k,l) \in S\}$

Ensure: a set of coordinates in order space $\{(o^{R}_{\xi}, o^{G}_{\xi}, o^{B}_{\xi}) \mid \xi \in \{1, 2, \ldots, |S|\}\}$

1: Assign serial numbers $\xi \in \{1, 2, \ldots, |S|\}$ to all pixels in the required set to have a set of re-indexed pixels $\{f_{\xi} = [f^{R}_{\xi}, f^{G}_{\xi}, f^{B}_{\xi}] \mid \xi \in \{1, 2, \ldots, |S|\}\}$.
2: **for** $X \in \{R, G, B\}$ **do**
3: $\quad [a^{X}_{1}, a^{X}_{2}, \ldots, a^{X}_{|S|}] = \mathrm{argsort}(f^{X}_{1}, f^{X}_{2}, \ldots, f^{X}_{|S|})$
4: $\quad$ **for** $\xi \in \{1, 2, \ldots, |S|\}$ **do**
5: $\quad\quad o^{X}_{a^{X}_{\xi}} = \xi$
6: $\quad$ **end for**
7: **end for**
8: Return $\{(o^{R}_{\xi}, o^{G}_{\xi}, o^{B}_{\xi}) \mid \xi \in \{1, 2, \ldots, |S|\}\}$

In the 3D order space, an RGB color pixel with an index ξ is represented by a triplet $(o_\xi^R, o_\xi^G, o_\xi^B)$. To define dilation and erosion for an RGB color image, we need to reduce the triplet $(o_\xi^R, o_\xi^G, o_\xi^B)$ to a singlet o_ξ. If we have $o_\xi^R \le o_{\xi'}^R$, $o_\xi^G \le o_{\xi'}^G$ and $o_\xi^B \le o_{\xi'}^B$ for two pixels ξ and ξ', then we can assign an order satisfying $o_\xi \le o_{\xi'}$. For example, the following equations for obtaining a singlet o_ξ from the triplet $(o_\xi^R, o_\xi^G, o_\xi^B)$ satisfy this condition:

$$o_\xi^S = o_\xi^R + o_\xi^G + o_\xi^B, \tag{7}$$
$$o_\xi^P = o_\xi^R o_\xi^G o_\xi^B, \tag{8}$$
$$o_\xi^M = \mathrm{med}\left\{o_\xi^R, o_\xi^G, o_\xi^B\right\}, \tag{9}$$

where 'med' means to select the median value from a given set of elements. We chose these equations here for their simplicity and easy implementation. Other choices may include weighted average, mode and nonlinear transformations of the order triplet. For example, let us consider three pixels in 3D order space: $a = (1,2,3)$, $b = (3,1,2)$ and $c = (2,3,1)$. Then, the above three Equations (7)–(9) give the same orders $o^S = 1+2+3 = 6$, $o^P = 1 \times 2 \times 3 = 6$ and $o^M = \mathrm{med}\{1,2,3\} = 2$ for a, b and c. To assign different orders to different points in 3D order space, we need more sophisticated equations than the above.

Figure 3 shows the contour lines of o_ξ^S, o_ξ^P and o_ξ^M in their order spaces, where the top, middle and bottom rows correspond to o_ξ^S, o_ξ^P and o_ξ^M, respectively. In each row, the five figures from left to right show cross sections for $o^B = 1, 2, \ldots, 5$. In each figure, the horizontal and vertical axes denote o^R and o^G. For example, in Figure 3a, feasible orders are denoted by color points, and contour lines for fixed values of $o^S = 6, 7, \ldots, 10$ are denoted by color lines with the corresponding colors. For fixed o^S and o^B, we have a straight line $o^G = (o^S - o^B) - o^R$ with slope -1. On the other hand, in the middle row of Figure 3, for fixed o^P and o^B, we have a hyperbola $o^G = (o^P/o^B)/o^R$. In the bottom row of Figure 3, we have no analytical expressions for the contour lines. However, we can draw them as shown in this figure. It is interesting that there are contour 'areas' as shown in Figure 3l–n with light blue, light orange and light green colors.

Once a function from $(o_\xi^R, o_\xi^G, o_\xi^B)$ to o_ξ is given like in (7)–(9), we can define the dilation and erosion of F by S as follows:

$$D(F,S) = [d_{ij}], \quad d_{ij} = f_{\xi^{\max}}, \quad \xi^{\max} = \arg \max_{\xi \in \{1,2,\ldots,|S|\}} o_\xi, \tag{10}$$

$$E(F,S) = [e_{ij}], \quad e_{ij} = f_{\xi^{\min}}, \quad \xi^{\min} = \arg \min_{\xi \in \{1,2,\ldots,|S|\}} o_\xi. \tag{11}$$

Next, we combine the above dilation and erosion operations for defining opening and closing operations as follows:

$$O(F,S) = D(E(F,S),S), \tag{12}$$
$$C(F,S) = E(D(F,S),S). \tag{13}$$

Here, we define an image $Z = [z_\xi]$ whose pixel value z_ξ denotes the order o_ξ of the corresponding pixel of F. Then, the above morphological operations correspond to the grayscale morphological operations applied to Z. Therefore, idempotence, increasingness and (anti-)extensiveness hold for the application of morphological opening and closing operations to Z as well as the conventional opening and closing operations.

Combining the above opening and closing operations, we can define open–closing and close–opening operations as follows:

$$OC(F,S) = C(O(F,S),S), \tag{14}$$
$$CO(F,S) = O(C(F,S),S), \tag{15}$$

which are consistent with the definitions of the corresponding operations for binary and grayscale images summarized in the previous section.

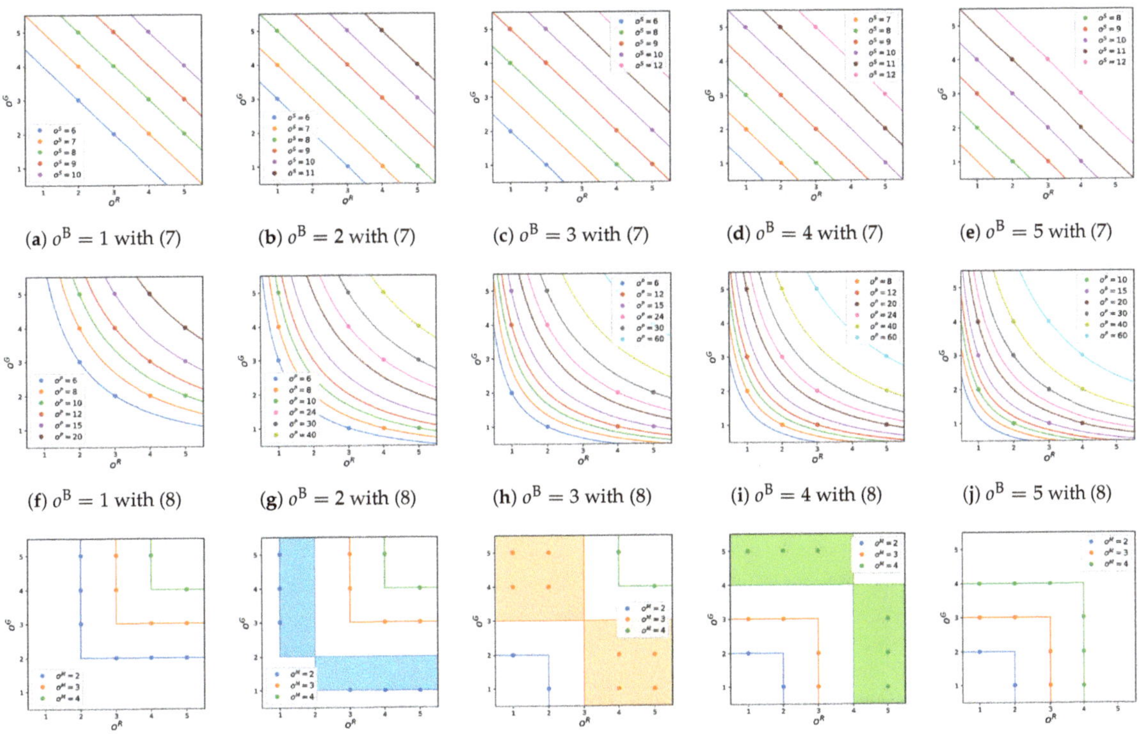

(a) $o^{\mathrm{B}} = 1$ with (7) (b) $o^{\mathrm{B}} = 2$ with (7) (c) $o^{\mathrm{B}} = 3$ with (7) (d) $o^{\mathrm{B}} = 4$ with (7) (e) $o^{\mathrm{B}} = 5$ with (7)

(f) $o^{\mathrm{B}} = 1$ with (8) (g) $o^{\mathrm{B}} = 2$ with (8) (h) $o^{\mathrm{B}} = 3$ with (8) (i) $o^{\mathrm{B}} = 4$ with (8) (j) $o^{\mathrm{B}} = 5$ with (8)

(k) $o^{\mathrm{B}} = 1$ with (9) (l) $o^{\mathrm{B}} = 2$ with (9) (m) $o^{\mathrm{B}} = 3$ with (9) (n) $o^{\mathrm{B}} = 4$ with (9) (o) $o^{\mathrm{B}} = 5$ with (9)

Figure 3. Contour lines in three order spaces corresponding to (7)–(9): (**a–e**) o^S_{ξ} given by (7) with fixed $o^{\mathrm{B}} = 1, 2, \ldots, 5$, respectively. (**f–j**) o^P_{ξ} given by (8) with fixed $o^{\mathrm{B}} = 1, 2, \ldots, 5$, respectively. (**k–o**) o^M_{ξ} given by (9) with fixed $o^{\mathrm{B}} = 1, 2, \ldots, 5$, respectively. In (**l–n**), the contour lines for $o^M = 2$, 3 and 4 are spread over the plane $o^{\mathrm{B}} = 2$, 3 and 4 as illustrated by light blue, light orange and light green areas, respectively.

We applied the proposed order space-based morphological operations to a color image in Figure 4, and obtained the images in Figure 5, where the top, middle and bottom rows were obtained with o^S, o^P and o^M in (7)–(9), and the six columns from left to right show the results of dilation, erosion, opening, closing, open–closing and close–opening operations, respectively. We observe that the three kinds of ordering, o^S, o^P and o^M, give similar output images to each other.

Figure 4. Original color image selected from SIDBA [22].

(**a**) Dilat. with (7) (**b**) Eros. with (7) (**c**) Open. with (7) (**d**) Clos. with (7) (**e**) O.-c. with (7) (**f**) C.-o. with (7)

(**g**) Dilat. with (8) (**h**) Eros. with (8) (**i**) Open. with (8) (**j**) Clos. with (8) (**k**) O.-c. with (8) (**l**) C.-o. with (8)

(**m**) Dilat. with (9) (**n**) Eros. with (9) (**o**) Open. with (9) (**p**) Clos. with (9) (**q**) O.-c. with (9) (**r**) C.-o. with (9)

Figure 5. Order space-based morphological operations for a color image in Figure 4: The **top**, **middle** and **bottom** rows show the results with (7)–(9), respectively. The six columns from left to right show the results of dilation (Dilat.), erosion (Eros.), opening (Open.), closing (Clos.), open–closing (O.-c.) and close–opening (C.-o.) operations, respectively.

4. Fuzzy Morphological Operations by Exponentially Weighted Averaging

In this section, we extend the above order space-based morphological operations, which are crisp operations, to fuzzy ones by introducing an exponentially weighted averaging method.

Assume that an order o_ξ for $\xi \in \{1,2,\ldots,|S|\}$ is obtained from a set of triplets $\{(o_\xi^{\mathrm{R}}, o_\xi^{\mathrm{G}}, o_\xi^{\mathrm{B}})\}$. Then, we define a fuzzy dilation by introducing an exponentially weighted averaging to (10) as follows:

$$D^{\mathrm{FUZ}}(F,S,\alpha) = \left[d_{ij}^{\mathrm{FUZ}}\right], \quad d_{ij}^{\mathrm{FUZ}} = \frac{\sum_{\xi=1}^{|S|} \exp(\alpha o_\xi) f_\xi}{\sum_{\xi=1}^{|S|} \exp(\alpha o_\xi)}, \tag{16}$$

where exp denotes the exponential function defined by $\exp(x) = e^x$, where e is a constant called Euler's number and α is a positive constant for controlling the fuzziness. Here, we note that the second equation in (16) includes the softmax function [23], which is the gradient of the log-sum-exp function [24]. Therefore, the equation can be rewritten as

$$d_{ij}^{\mathrm{FUZ}} = \arg\min_{d} \sum_{\xi=1}^{|S|} \frac{\partial}{\partial o_\xi}\left(\log \sum_{\nu=1}^{|S|} \exp(\alpha o_\nu)\right) \|f_\xi - d\|^2, \tag{17}$$

which explicitly describes the relationship between the exponentially weighted averaging and the log-sum-exp function, where $\partial/\partial o_\xi$ denotes a partial derivative with respect to o_ξ and $\|\cdot\|$ denotes the Euclidean norm. This expression accepts vectors f_ξ and d of any dimension. Therefore, we can fuzzify morphological operations for not only color images but also binary and grayscale images by the proposed method.

Similarly, we can define a fuzzy erosion as follows:

$$E^{\mathrm{FUZ}}(F,S,\alpha)=\left[e_{ij}^{\mathrm{FUZ}}\right],\quad e_{ij}^{\mathrm{FUZ}}=\frac{\sum_{\xi=1}^{|S|}\exp(-\alpha o_\xi)f_\xi}{\sum_{\xi=1}^{|S|}\exp(-\alpha o_\xi)}. \tag{18}$$

Combining these operations, we have fuzzy opening and closing operations as follows:

$$O^{\mathrm{FUZ}}(F,S,\alpha)=D^{\mathrm{FUZ}}\left(E^{\mathrm{FUZ}}(F,S,\alpha),S,\alpha\right), \tag{19}$$

$$C^{\mathrm{FUZ}}(F,S,\alpha)=E^{\mathrm{FUZ}}\left(D^{\mathrm{FUZ}}(F,S,\alpha),S,\alpha\right). \tag{20}$$

From these, we further define fuzzy open–closing and close–opening operations as follows:

$$OC^{\mathrm{FUZ}}(F,S,\alpha)=C^{\mathrm{FUZ}}\left(O^{\mathrm{FUZ}}(F,S,\alpha),S,\alpha\right), \tag{21}$$

$$CO^{\mathrm{FUZ}}(F,S,\alpha)=O^{\mathrm{FUZ}}\left(C^{\mathrm{FUZ}}(F,S,\alpha),S,\alpha\right). \tag{22}$$

The value of α is empirically determined in the following section.

5. Experimental Results

In this section, we show the experimental results of noise removal from color images by the proposed order space-based morphological operations, which are compared with the state-of-the-art method of Wang et al. [19]. Figure 6 shows a noisy input image including 10% impulse noise.

Figure 6. Noisy input image including 10% impulse noise, where 6553 out of 256 × 256 = 65,536 pixels are corrupted with impulse noise.

Figure 7 shows the output images by Wang's hypergraph-based method [19] and the proposed method with 'Cross' and 'Square' structuring elements in Figure 1a and Figure 1b, respectively, where the order o^S in (7) is used. Wang's method has two parameters, μ and β, which are set as $\mu = 250$ and $\beta = 1$ by adjusting for this noise removal task through preliminary experiments. The top row in this figure shows the results of Wang's method with a structural hypergraph denoted by 'HG' as an alternative to structuring elements for the dilation, erosion, opening, closing, open–closing and close–opening operations, the output images of which are arranged from left to right in columns, where we observe that the dilation Figure 7a and erosion Figure 7b tend to enlarge impulse noise, but the following operations Figure 7c–f can suppress the noise effectively. The middle and bottom rows in Figure 7 show the results of the proposed method with 'Cross' and 'Square' structuring elements shown in Figure 1a and Figure 1b, respectively. The 3 × 3 'Square' structuring element corresponds to the structuring hypergraph with $\beta = 1$ in Wang's method in terms of size.

(a) Dilat./'HG' (b) Eros./'HG' (c) Open./'HG' (d) Clos./'HG' (e) O.-c./'HG' (f) C.-o./'HG'

(g) Dilat./'Cross' (h) Eros./'Cross' (i) Open./'Cross' (j) Clos./'Cross' (k) O.-c./'Cross' (l) C.-o./'Cross'

(m) Dilat./'Square' (n) Eros./'Square' (o) Open./'Square' (p) Clos./'Square' (q) O.-c./'Square' (r) C.-o./'Square'

Figure 7. Noise removal results using Wang's method (**top** row) and the proposed order space-based morphological operations (**middle** and **bottom** rows) with o^S in (7) for a noisy image in Figure 6, where their subcaptions denote the 'operation/structuring element' used for computing respective images: The top row shows the results of Wang's method, where 'HG' indicates that the structuring elements are given by hypergraphs. The middle and bottom rows show the results of the proposed method with 'Cross' and 'Square' structuring elements shown in Figure 1. The six columns from left to right show the results of dilation (Dilat.), erosion (Eros.), opening (Open.), closing (Clos.), open–closing (O.-c.) and close–opening (C.-o.) operations, respectively.

Table 1 shows the values of the peak signal-to-noise ratio (PSNR) [25] between the output images in Figure 7 and the original noise-free image in Figure 4, where Wang's method with the 'HG' structuring element achieves the highest PSNR 21.59 dB by the close–opening operation. On the other hand, the proposed method with 'Cross' and 'Square' structuring elements achieves 25.14 and 25.83 dB by open–closing and close–opening, respectively.

Table 1. PSNR for output images in Figure 7 with 'HG', 'Cross' and 'Square' structuring elements (SEs). In each row, the highest value is boldfaced.

SE	Dilation	Erosion	Opening	Closing	Open-Closing	Close-Opening
'HG' [19]	15.31	16.22	20.11	20.52	20.88	**21.59**
'Cross'	18.82	18.80	22.96	23.11	**25.14**	25.13
'Square'	17.79	17.73	23.67	23.97	25.74	**25.83**

Figure 8 shows the noise removal results on the SIDBA image dataset [22], where the top row lists all 12 original color images, which are corrupted by impulse noise as shown in the second row, where the noise density increases from the left to right columns. We adopted open–closing and close–opening operations for removing the noise on the basis of the observation in Table 1, where those operations achieved higher PSNR values than the other morphological operations. In this figure, we compared the proposed method based on the ordering o^S, o^P and o^M in (7)–(9), computed with the 3×3 'Square' structuring element in Figure 1b with Wang's method using the parameters $\mu = 250$ and $\beta = 1$.

Figure 8. Noise removal results for 12 color images in the SIDBA dataset [22]: The original images in the top row receive impulse noise with densities varying from 10% (the leftmost two columns) to 60% (the rightmost two columns), as shown in the second row. The third and subsequent rows show the corresponding output images from the open–closing and close–opening operations in Wang's method and the proposed method with o^S, o^P and o^M in (7)–(9), respectively.

The performance of noise removal is evaluated by the mean PSNR among the 12 different images as summarized in Figure 9, where Figure 9a,b show the results of open–closing and close–opening, respectively. In each graph, the vertical and horizontal axes denote the mean PSNR among the 12 images and the density of impulse noise varying from 10% to 60%, respectively, and the line colors, blue, orange, green and red correspond to Wang's method and the proposed methods with o^S, o^P and o^M, respectively. In both graphs, Wang's method (blue line) obtains higher values of mean PSNR than the proposed methods with o^P and o^M (green and red lines), and the proposed method with o^S (orange line) outperforms Wang's method.

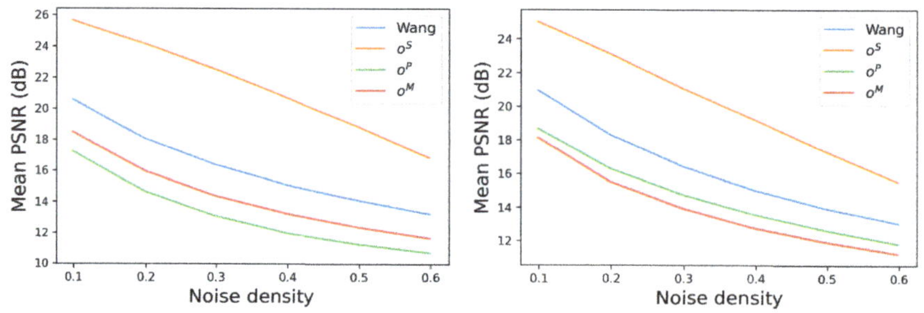

(**a**) Open–closing (**b**) Close–opening

Figure 9. Mean PSNR vs. noise density on SIDBA dataset [22]: (**a**) Open–closing operations of Wang's and the proposed methods are compared with each other, where the proposed method with o^S (orange line) outperforms Wang's method (blue line). (**b**) Similarly, close–opening operations are compared, where the proposed method with o^S (orange line) also outperforms Wang's method (blue line).

We also compared the performance of grayscale and color morphological operations as illustrated in Figure 10, where a color original image (top left box) is corrupted by Gaussian or impulse noise to produce a noisy image (top right box). Both images are converted to grayscale images through the outside clockwise and counterclockwise routes. Then, the standard method for grayscale images is applied to those grayscale images (bottom leftmost and rightmost boxes). On the other hand, color original and noisy images pass through inner routes, where Wang's and our methods for color images are applied to them. Then, the resultant images are converted to grayscale images (bottom middle two boxes). Finally, we compute PSNR or the structural similarity index measure (SSIM) [26] for the resultant grayscale images processed by the same method. Figure 11 shows the results of Gaussian noise removal with the SIDBA dataset [22], where the vertical axes denote Figure 11a PSNR and Figure 11b SSIM, and the horizontal axes denote the compared methods. In this figure, the grayscale operation achieved the highest PSNR and SSIM values, and the proposed method outperformed Wang's method.

On the other hand, Figure 12 shows the results of impulse noise removal, where the settings of axes are the same as Figure 11. In Figure 12a, the proposed method achieved the highest PSNR value, while in Figure 12b, the grayscale operation achieved the highest SSIM value. The reason why the grayscale operation achieves higher values than color ones is speculated to be that the conversion from color to gray has a noise-reduction effect. This speculation is investigated in Table 2, where color noisy images are compared with grayscale noisy images by PSNR and SSIM for Gaussian and impulse noises. The values of the image quality measure for R, G and B components are improved by grayscale conversion for all combinations of noises and measures. This result shows that the grayscale conversion has a noise-reduction effect.

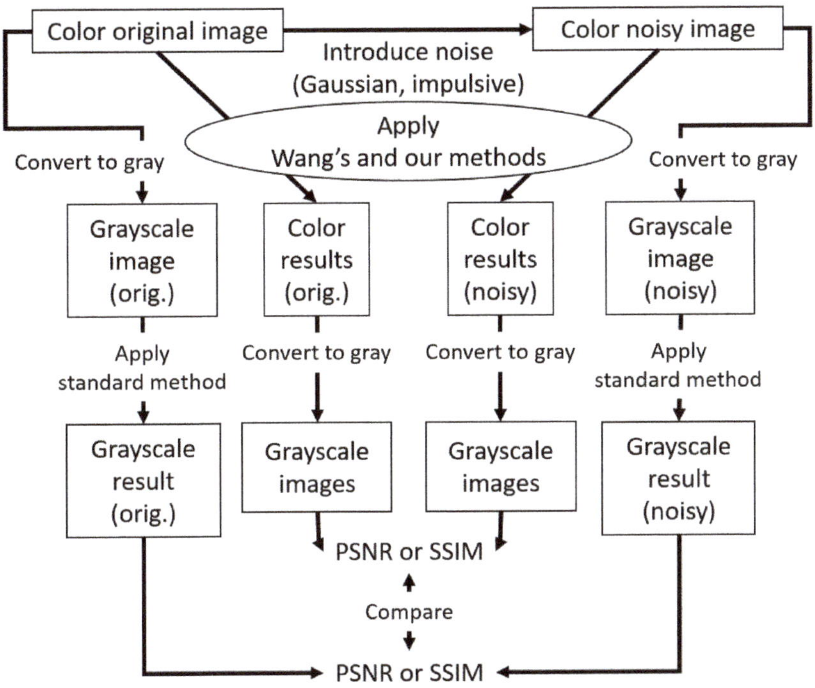

Figure 10. Comparison of grayscale and color morphological operations with Gaussian and impulse noises. In this flow chart, grayscale conversions are followed by grayscale morphological operations (outer routes), and color morphological operations are followed by grayscale conversions (inner routes). Finally, the corresponding grayscale images are compared by computing PSNR or SSIM.

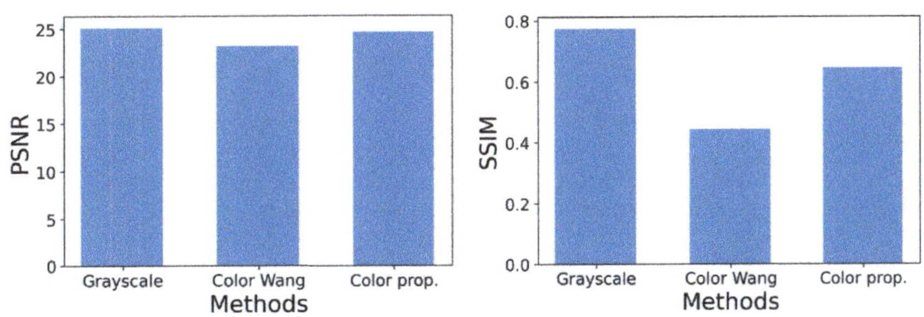

(**a**) PSNR vs. methods (**b**) SSIM vs. methods

Figure 11. Results of Gaussian noise removal, where Gaussian noise with mean 0 and standard deviation 30 are added to the original images in Figure 8: (**a**) PSNR values are compared for grayscale, Wang's and our open–closing operations. (**b**) SSIM values are compared for grayscale, Wang's and our open–closing operations.

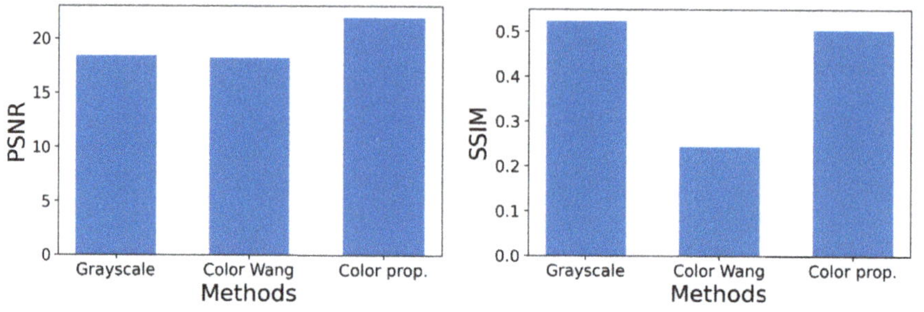

(**a**) PSNR vs. methods (**b**) SSIM vs. methods

Figure 12. Results of impulse noise removal, where 50% impulse noise is added to the original images in Figure 8: (**a**) PSNR values are compared for grayscale, Wang's and our open–closing operations. (**b**) SSIM values are compared for grayscale, Wang's and our open–closing operations.

Table 2. Comparison of the quality of noisy images used in Figure 10 between color and gray. In each row, the highest value is boldfaced.

Noise	Quality Measure	R	G	B	Gray
Gaussian	PSNR	18.90	19.06	19.03	**22.71**
Gaussian	SSIM	0.306	0.350	0.315	**0.417**
Impulse	PSNR	12.16	11.94	12.01	**16.63**
Impulse	SSIM	0.118	0.144	0.122	**0.183**

In terms of the color morphological operations in this experiment, the proposed method achieved better PSNR and SSIM values than Wang's method.

For impulse noise removal, it is well known that simple marginal processing based on marginal ordering works well, although it can generate false colors. Thus, we compared the proposed method with the marginal open–closing and Max-tree-based area open–closing proposed by Tushabe and Wilkinson [15], where we adopted an area threshold of $T = 150$ and a nearest color (NC) approach for image restoration as recommended in their paper. Figure 13 shows the results of noise removal, where 12 color images in the SIDBA dataset [22] were corrupted by 50% impulse noise, and we applied the three open–closing operations to those noisy images. The performance of noise removal was evaluated with PSNR and SSIM, which are shown in Figure 13a and Figure 13b, respectively. In Figure 13a, the proposed method achieved the highest PSNR value among the three methods. On the other hand, in Figure 13b, the simple marginal method achieved the highest SSIM value, which matches the above knowledge that the marginal method removes impulse noise well.

Figure 14 shows the output images computed by the three methods, where the image in Figure 14a given by the simple marginal open–closing operation appears to be the best among three output images. However, the image in Figure 14a includes new colors that do not exist in the input image. This violates a desirable property that color morphological operations should have, i.e., no new colors should be introduced [27].

Next, we show the experimental results for the fuzzy morphological operations described in Section 4. Here, we would like to determine the value of α in the fuzzy operations with the open–closing operation, which outperforms the close–opening operation as shown in Figure 9; that is, the orange line in Figure 9a exceeds that in Figure 9b. Figure 15 shows the PSNR values for different values of α varying from 0.1 to 1.0, where we applied the fuzzy open–closing in (21) to the noisy image in Figure 6. We observe that $\alpha = 0.5$ achieves the highest PSNR value, and use $\alpha = 0.5$ below.

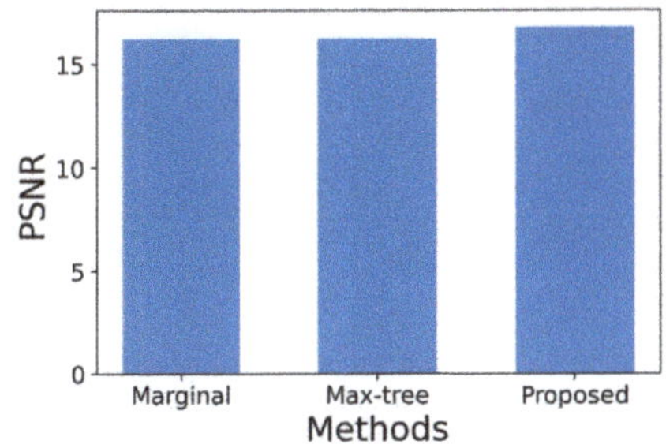

(**a**) PSNR vs. methods

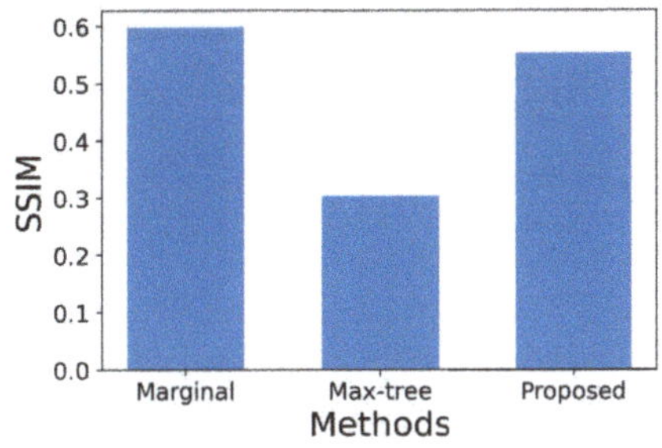

(**b**) SSIM vs. methods

Figure 13. Comparison of marginal open–closing, Max-tree-based area open–closing and the proposed order space-based open–closing for impulse noise removal: (**a**) PSNR values are compared for marginal, Max-tree-based area and the proposed open–closing operations. (**b**) SSIM values are compared for marginal, Max-tree-based area and the proposed open–closing operations.

(**a**) Marginal

(**b**) Max-tree

(**c**) Proposed

Figure 14. Output images obtained by (**a**) marginal open–closing, (**b**) Max-tree-based area open–closing and (**c**) the proposed order space-based open–closing.

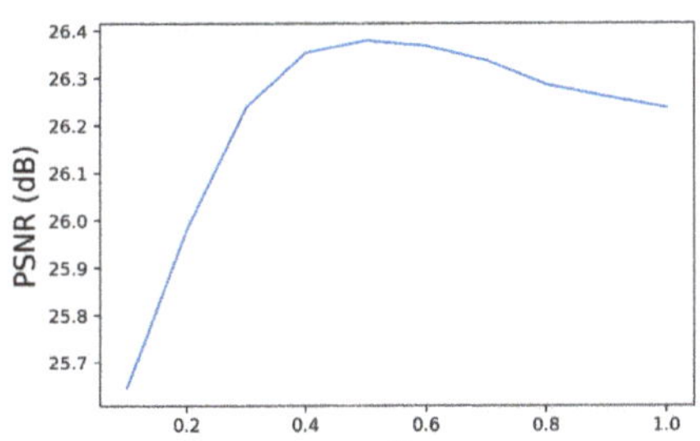

Figure 15. PSNR vs α for controlling the fuzziness of the proposed fuzzy morphological operations. This figure shows that $\alpha = 0.5$ gives the highest PSNR value in the proposed fuzzy open–closing operation applied to the noisy image in Figure 6.

Figure 16 shows the results of the proposed fuzzy morphological operations defined in (16)–(22). A visual comparison between Figures 16 and 7 demonstrates the effectiveness of the proposed fuzzification, and Figure 17 shows the effectiveness quantitatively by comparing the mean PSNR values computed with the SIDBA dataset [22] between crisp and fuzzy operations, where the vertical and horizontal axes denote the mean PSNR and noise density as well as the settings from Figure 9, and Figure 17a,b which show the results of open–closing and close–opening operations, respectively. For both operations, the fuzzy ones denoted by purple lines outperform the crisp ones denoted by orange lines.

(a) Dilat. (b) Eros. (c) Open. (d) Clos. (e) O.-c. (f) C.-o.

Figure 16. Noise removal results by fuzzy morphological operations with $\alpha = 0.5$ applied to the noisy image in Figure 6. The order of the output images (**a**–**f**) by six morphological operations, dilation (Dilat.), erosion (Eros.), opening (Open.), closing (Clos.), open–closing (O.-c.) and close–opening (C.-o.), is the same as that of Figure 7.

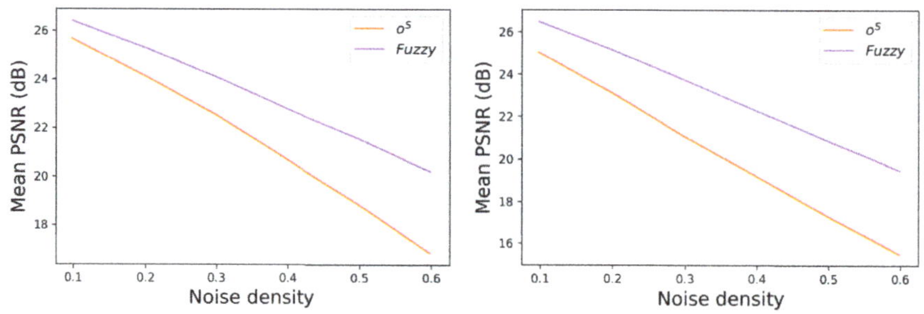

(**a**) Open–closing (**b**) Close–opening

Figure 17. Comparison of mean PSNR between crisp and fuzzy morphological operations: (**a**) Crisp (orange line) and fuzzy (purple line) open–closing operations are compared, where the former is the same as the orange line in Figure 9a. (**b**) Similarly, crisp (orange line) and fuzzy (purple line) close–opening operations are compared, where the former is the same as the orange line in Figure 9b.

6. Discussion

In the above experimental results, we demonstrated the effectiveness of the proposed order space-based morphological operations, which are compared with Wang's method based on hypergraph theory [19]. Generally, color images have three color channels, e.g., red, green and blue channels for RGB color images, and we can sort the pixel values in each channel separately. Therefore, it would be appropriate to consider three orders derived from the three channels in morphological operations for color images. The proposed method is a method by which the obtained three orders, which form a 3D order space, can be unified into a single order of pixels in a suitable manner for a given application. In this paper, we presented three ways of unifying three orders corresponding to three color channels into a single order, i.e., o^S, o^P and o^M defined in (7), (8) and (9), respectively. In the application of morphological operations to noise removal demonstrated in Section 5, Wang's method [19] achieved better performance than the proposed method with o^P and o^M, but the remaining option o^S outperformed Wang's method, which shows the potential of the proposed order space-based method. The ways of unifying three orders are not restricted to the three methods presented in this paper. Investigating better ways to unify plural orders into one will be a promising future research direction.

We also extended the proposed order space-based morphological operations to their fuzzy version, where we proposed a method for fuzzifying morphological operations by exponentially weighted averaging. Conventional morphological operations for binary and grayscale images include maximum and minimum selection. The max function for selecting the maximum value from a set of scalar values can be approximated by the log-sum-exp function [24], which has a relationship with fuzzy techniques [28]. However, it is difficult to use the log-sum-exp function directly for fuzzifying morphological operations for color images because of the dimensional discrepancy between scalar and vector data. On the other hand, the proposed exponentially weighted averaging method can be used for both scalar and vector data. Therefore, we can also fuzzify conventional morphological operations for binary and grayscale images by the proposed method. In the above experiments, we demonstrated the effectiveness of the fuzzification of the order space-based morphological operations in the noise-removal application. The applicability of the proposed fuzzification method to any dimensional data will expand its application areas into the area of multidimensional data processing.

7. Conclusions

In this paper, we proposed a method for applying morphological operations to color images. The proposed method is based on a three-dimensional (3D) order space, which has three coordinate axes corresponding to the orders of pixels in three color channels, e.g., R (red), G (green) and B (blue) color channels for RGB color images. That is, a color pixel is represented by a point on the 3D space specified by the set of orders of pixels sorted in R, G and B color channels, separately. Then, the triplet was shrunk to a single order by an appropriate function, e.g., sum, product and median functions were investigated in this paper. We conducted experiments on noise removal with a standard image dataset, and demonstrated that the sum function achieved the best performance among the three functions and a state-of-the-art method based on hypergraph theory by Wang et al. [19]. We can consider other options for the shrinkage functions and the structuring elements in morphological operations that may further improve the performance.

We also proposed an exponentially weighted averaging method for fuzzifying the order space-based morphological operations. As a result, the noise removal performance was further improved by the fuzzification for both open–closing and close–opening operations, both of which achieved better performance than dilation, erosion, opening and closing operations in a conventional crisp situation.

Our future work will include the extension of the proposed method for color image processing to multidimensional data processing, which will also be fuzzified by the proposed exponentially weighted averaging method to improve the performance.

Author Contributions: Conceptualization, K.I.; methodology, S.S., Y.H. and K.I.; software, S.S., Y.H. and K.I.; validation, K.I. and K.H.; formal analysis, K.I.; investigation, S.S., Y.H. and K.I.; resources, K.I. and K.H.; data curation, K.I.; writing—original draft preparation, S.S., Y.H. and K.I.; writing—review and editing, S.S., Y.H. and K.I.; visualization, S.S., Y.H. and K.I.; supervision, K.H.; project administration, K.I.; funding acquisition, K.I. All authors have read and agreed to the published version of the manuscript.

Funding: This work was supported by JSPS KAKENHI, Grant Number JP21K11964.

Institutional Review Board Statement: Not applicable.

Informed Consent Statement: Not applicable.

Data Availability Statement: Not applicable.

Conflicts of Interest: The authors declare no conflict of interest.

Abbreviations

The following abbreviations are used in this manuscript:

RGB	Red, green and blue
PSNR	Peak signal-to-noise ratio
SSIM	Structural similarity index measure
SIDBA	Standard Image DataBAse
SE	Structuring element

References

1. Soille, P. *Morphological Image Analysis*; Springer: Berlin/Heidelberg, Germany, 1999. [CrossRef]
2. Sartor, L.J.; Weeks, A.R. Morphological operations on color images. *J. Electron. Imaging* **2001**, *10*, 548–559. [CrossRef]
3. Angulo, J. Morphological colour operators in totally ordered lattices based on distances: Application to image filtering, enhancement and analysis. *Comput. Vis. Image Underst.* **2007**, *107*, 56–73. [CrossRef]
4. d'Ornellas, M.C.; da Costa, J.A.T.B. Color Mathematical Morphology Based on Partial Ordering of Spectra. In Proceedings of the XX Brazilian Symposium on Computer Graphics and Image Processing (SIBGRAPI 2007), Minas Gerais, Brazil, 7–10 October 2007; pp. 37–44. [CrossRef]
5. Benavent, X.; Dura, E.; Vegara, F.; Domingo, J. Mathematical Morphology for Color Images: An Image-Dependent Approach. *Math. Probl. Eng.* **2012**, *2012*, 678326. [CrossRef]
6. Comer, M. L.; Delp, E.J., III. Empirical study of morphological operators in color image enhancement. *Image Process. Algorithms Tech. III* **1992**, *1657*, 314–325. [CrossRef]
7. Zhao, C. A new vectorial ordering for color morphology based on marginal ordering. In Proceedings of the 5th International Conference on Computer Science & Education, Hefei, China, 24–27 August 2010; pp. 1769–1772. [CrossRef]
8. van de Gronde, J.J.; Roerdink, J.B.T.M. Group-Invariant Frames for Colour Morphology. In *International Symposium on Mathematical Morphology and Its Applications to Signal and Image Processing*; Lecture Notes in Computer Science; Hendriks, C.L.L., Borgefors, G., Strand, R., Eds.; Springer: Berlin/Heidelberg, Germany, 2013; Volume 7883. [CrossRef]
9. Gimenez, D.; Evans, A.N. An evaluation of area morphology scale-spaces for colour images. *Comput. Vis. Image Underst.* **2008**, *110*, 1, 32–42. [CrossRef]
10. Gibson, S.; Harvey, R.W.; Finlayson, G.D. Convex Colour Sieves. In *Scale Space Methods in Computer Vision*; Lecture Notes in Computer Science; Griffin, L.D., Lillholm, M., Eds.; Springer: Berlin/Heidelberg, Germany, 2003; Volume 2695, pp. 550–563. [CrossRef]
11. Evans, A.N. Vector area morphology for motion field smoothing and interpretation. *IEEE Proc.-Vis. Image Signal Process.* **2003**, *150*, 219–226. [CrossRef]
12. Evans, A.N. Chapter 2—Color Area Morphology Scale-Spaces. In*Advances in Imaging and Electron Physics*; Elsevier: 1Amsterdam, The Netherlands, 2010; Volume 160, pp. 35–74. [CrossRef]
13. Burgeth, B.; Papenberg, N.; Bruhn, A.; Welk, M.; Feddern, C.; Weickert, J. Morphology for Higher-Dimensional Tensor Data Via Loewner Ordering. In *Mathematical Morphology: 40 Years On, Proceedings of the 7th International Symposium on Mathematical Morphology, Paris, France, 18–20 April 2005*; Ronse, C., Najman, L., Decencière, E., Eds.; Springer: Dordrecht, The Netherlands, 2005. [CrossRef]
14. Naegel, B.; Passat, N. Component-Trees and Multi-value Images: A Comparative Study. In *Mathematical Morphology and Its Application to Signal and Image Processing*; Lecture Notes in Computer Science; Wilkinson, M.H.F., Roerdink, J.B.T.M., Eds.; Springer: Berlin/Heidelberg, Germany, 2009; Volume 5720. [CrossRef]
15. Tushabe, F.; Wilkinson, M.H.F. Color processing using max-trees: A comparison on image compression. In Proceedings of the 2012 International Conference on Systems and Informatics (ICSAI2012), Yantai, China, 19–20 May 2012; pp. 1374–1380. [CrossRef]
16. Angulo, J. Unified morphological color processing framework in a lum/sat/hue representation. In *Mathematical Morphology: 40 Years On, Proceedings of the 7th International Symposium on Mathematical Morphology, Paris, France, 18–20 April 2005*; Springer: Dordrecht, The Netherlands, 2005; pp. 387–396.
17. Moroney, N.; Fairchild, M.; Hunt, R.; Li, C.; Luo, M.; Newman, T. The CIECAM02 color appearance model. In Proceedings of the IS&T/SID 10th Color Imaging Conference, Scottsdale, AZ, USA, 12–15 November 2002.
18. Lezoray, O.; Elmoataz, A.; Meurie, C. Mathematical Morphology in Any Color Space. In Proceedings of the 14th International Conference of Image Analysis and Processing—Workshops (ICIAPW 2007), Modena, Italy, 10–13 September 2007; pp. 183–187. [CrossRef]
19. Wang, J.; Liang, G.; Wu, Y.; Li, Y.; Hu, J. New colour morphological operators on hypergraph. *IET Image Process.* **2018**, *12*, 690–695. [CrossRef]
20. Sternberg, S.R. Grayscale morphology. *Comput. Vis. Graph. Image Process.* **1986**, *35*, 333–355. [CrossRef]
21. Schevenels, M.; Sigmund, O. On the implementation and effectiveness of morphological close-open and open-close filters for topology optimization. *Struct. Multidisc. Optim.* **2016**, *54*, 15–21. [CrossRef]
22. Sakauchi, M.; Ohsawa, Y.; Sone, M.; Onoe, M. Management of the Standard Image Database for Image Processing Researches (SIDBA). *ITEJ Tech. Rep.* **1984**, *8*, 7–12. (In Japanese)
23. Goodfellow, I.; Bengio, Y.; Courville, A. *Deep Learning*; MIT Press: Cambridge, MA, USA, 2016; pp. 180–184. Available online: https://www.deeplearningbook.org/ (accessed on 5 July 2023).
24. Boyd, S.; Vandenberghe, L. *Convex Optimization*; Cambridge University Press: Cambridge, MA, USA, 2004.
25. Martini, M.G. On the relationship between SSIM and PSNR for DCT-based compressed images and video: SSIM as content-aware PSNR. *TechRxiv* **2022** . [CrossRef]
26. Wang, Z.; Bovik, A.C.; Sheikh, H.R.; Simoncelli, E.P. Image quality assessment: From error visibility to structural similarity. *IEEE Trans. Image Process.* **2004**, *13*, 600–612. [CrossRef]

27. Köppen, M.; Nowack, C.; Rösel, G. Pareto-Morphology for Color Image Processing: A Comparative Study of Multivariate Morphologies. *Pattern Recognit. Image Anal.* **2000**, *10*, 478–491.
28. Inoue, K.; Hara, K. An equivalence between log-sum-exp approximation and entropy regularization in K-means clustering. *Nonlinear Theory Its Appl. IEICE* **2020**, *11*, 454–465. [CrossRef]

entropy

MDPI

Article

Enhanced CycleGAN Network with Adaptive Dark Channel Prior for Unpaired Single-Image Dehazing

Yijun Xu [1], Hanzhi Zhang [2], Fuliang He [2,3,*], Jiachi Guo [1] and Zichen Wang [1]

[1] Westa College, Southwest University, Chongqing 400715, China
[2] College of Electronic and Information Engineering, Southwest University, Chongqing 400715, China
[3] Chongqing Key Laboratory of Nolinear Circuits and Intelligent Information Processing, Southwest University, Chongqing 400715, China
* Correspondence: lighter@swu.edu.cn

Abstract: Unpaired single-image dehazing has become a challenging research hotspot due to its wide application in modern transportation, remote sensing, and intelligent surveillance, among other applications. Recently, CycleGAN-based approaches have been popularly adopted in single-image dehazing as the foundations of unpaired unsupervised training. However, there are still deficiencies with these approaches, such as obvious artificial recovery traces and the distortion of image processing results. This paper proposes a novel enhanced CycleGAN network with an adaptive dark channel prior for unpaired single-image dehazing. First, a Wave-Vit semantic segmentation model is utilized to achieve the adaption of the dark channel prior (DCP) to accurately recover the transmittance and atmospheric light. Then, the scattering coefficient derived from both physical calculations and random sampling means is utilized to optimize the rehazing process. Bridged by the atmospheric scattering model, the dehazing/rehazing cycle branches are successfully combined to form an enhanced CycleGAN framework. Finally, experiments are conducted on reference/no-reference datasets. The proposed model achieved an SSIM of 94.9% and a PSNR of 26.95 on the SOTS-outdoor dataset and obtained an SSIM of 84.71% and a PSNR of 22.72 on the O-HAZE dataset. The proposed model significantly outperforms typical existing algorithms in both objective quantitative evaluation and subjective visual effect.

Keywords: dehaze; atmospheric scattering model; cycle generative adversarial network; dark channel prior

1. Introduction

With the rapid development of digital society, computer vision technology is increasingly being applied in the fields of autonomous driving, remote sensing imaging, and intelligent monitoring. However, the quality of the images acquired by photographic equipment in hazy weather is severely affected, with the target object being obscured and the image losing a lot of detailed information. Furthermore, degraded images are not conducive to subsequent high-level vision tasks. Therefore, a method for processing and clarifying hazy degraded images is highly desired.

At present, single-image dehazing has become a mainstream method for image clarification because it is cost-effective and requires no additional constraint information. Single-image dehazing methods can be classified into image enhancement, image restoration and learning-based approaches based on their mechanism.

Traditional image enhancement methods for dehazing include Retinex theory [1], histogram equalization [2], and wavelet transforms. These methods adjust the contrast and saturation of the image to achieve dehazing without considering the physical nature of haze formation. However, these global enhancements often cause the loss of some local information and perform poorly when facing hazy images in complex scenes. In recent years, many methods combining image fusion have been widely proposed. Zheng et al. [3] used gamma correction to obtain a sequence of multiple exposed images from a single hazy image, then integrated the best region of saturation using adaptive decomposition to produce a clear image. Similarly, Galdran [4] utilized a multiscale Laplacian transform to fuse artificially exposed images to achieve dehazing. Zhu et al. [5] implemented feature extraction of a single image based on the idea of image space domain transformation; these authors then used a multiscale fusion algorithm based on fast filtering and saturation curve analysis to fuse the transformed image. These image fusion-based methods have improved traditional image enhancement, but the complexity of the algorithms used in these methods is high, and there are certain limitations to the stability of the dehazing they can provide.

Image restoration [6–9] uses prior knowledge or assumptions to establish a physical model of image degradation to achieve clarity. He et al. [7] discovered the dark channel prior (DCP) and mapped it to the atmospheric scattering model [10], designing an effective haze removal method. Zhu et al. [8] revealed the connection between haze concentration, image brightness, and saturation and developed the color attenuation prior. Berman et al. [9] proposed that haze alters the original tight color clusters in RGB space and forms haze lines through atmospheric light coordinates. Wang et al. [11] estimated the transmittance based on a prior for which there exists a linear relationship between the minimum channel of a hazy image and a clear image; these authors also introduced a weakening strategy combined with a quad-tree method of subdividing additional channels to restore the atmospheric light. Physical-model-based methods have been widely adopted since they are simple and efficient. Unfortunately, this type of algorithm requires high accuracy in parameter estimation and fails in regions that do not satisfy the prior; thus, the defogging results are often accompanied by negative effects such as color distortion and halos.

Recently, learning-based methods have significantly pushed the state of the art of unpaired image dehazing. Cai et al. [12] devised DehazeNet by integrating four different traditional defogging algorithms with deep learning. Zhang et al. [13] set two sub-networks in the pyramid network to obtain the transmittance and the atmospheric light, respectively. Li et al. [14] proposed a light-weight CNN network that they combined with the atmospheric scattering model to achieve dehazing. Chen et al. [15] developed GCANet on the basis of generative adversarial networks and adopted smooth convolution instead of extended convolution to solve the problem of grid artifacts. Similarly, a series of networks [16–19] were designed to derive clear images directly from the input hazy images without considering the degradation mechanism. Compared to conventional image enhancement and prior-based haze removal models, learning-based methods have achieved great progress. However, most of these methods are trained based on paired data and rely on clear images for positive supervision. This training process of supervision leads to excessive sensitivity to samples and the poor generalization of real-world haze removal. To address this issue, various unsupervised learning methods have been proposed. Li et al. [20] presented an unsupervised, unpaired defogging algorithm based on layer disentanglement, breaking away from training on large-scale datasets. However, this algorithm often produces images with serious color distortion and poor stability during defogging. Zhao et al. [21] proposed a weakly supervised RefineDNet, which combines the dark channel prior with a learning-based method using unpaired data for adversarial learning to improve the quality of the defogged images. Li et al. [22] integrated multi-scale feature representation with an attention mechanism and designed an enhanced decoder to improve the extraction of haze information. Ding et al. [23] unified the haze removal and noise suppression tasks and introduced a region similarity fusion module to obtain the final results. The development of unsupervised defogging algorithms has significantly alleviated the overfitting problem associated with supervised methods, but the defogging results lack realism, and the network structures tend to be complex, requiring higher computational resources.

Known as a powerful tool for unpaired image processing, CycleGAN (cycle generative adversarial network) [24] is characterized by its structure, which enables images to be converted between two domains. Recently, many unpaired CycleGAN-based dehazing approaches have been widely proposed to solve the problem that paired samples are nearly unavailable in the real world. Engin et al. [25] designed a CycleDehaze system that combines a pyramid network for high-resolution images and introduces a cyclic perception loss to improve the dehazing quality. Zheng et al. [26] introduced an enhanced attention mechanism in the CycleGAN framework and applied it to the task of defogging remote sensing images. Most CycleGAN-based dehazing methods ignore the physical properties of the hazy environment; thus, the results lack realism and variability. In order to make progress on this issue, Yang et al. [27] combined CycleGAN with the atmospheric scattering model to recover the scene depth and haze density of images to improve dehazing quality and achieved better results on synthetic datasets; however, their network, with its high-complexity structure, is still limited regarding the accuracy of estimation for transmittance.

In this paper, we specifically propose a novel unpaired dehazing network termed ADCP-CycleGAN (adaptive DCP combined with CycleGAN). The network consists of two branches that implement the reconstruction of hazy and clear images, respectively. In the dehazing process, we use the scale-adaptive DCP to accurately recover the transmittance and atmospheric light and combine the variable scattering coefficient with depth to achieve a more realistic rehazing process.

The contributions of this paper can be summarized as follows:

- A novel unpaired single-image dehazing model is proposed to fuse the dark channel prior and the enhanced CycleGAN.
- An adaptive DCP is designed to rely on the Wave-ViT semantic segmentation model, and it can accurately recover the transmittance and atmospheric light.
- In the enhanced CycleGAN method, the scattering coefficient β is obtained from two different approaches in order to generate haze of various thicknesses and uneven distributions. β_1 is derived from the atmospheric scattering model, while β_2 is randomly sampled.

The article is organized as follows. Section 2 explains the preliminary knowledge of the atmospheric scattering model and the dark channel prior, as well as the basic structure of the cycle generative adversarial network. Section 3 elaborates the proposed image dehazing method based on CycleGAN with the adaptive dark channel. The experimental results, along with relevant discussions, are illustrated in Section 4. Conclusions and future work are summarized in Section 5.

2. Preliminaries

2.1. Atmospheric Scattering Model

To describe the mechanism of haze generation, McCartney et al. [10] proposed an atmospheric scattering model in 1977,

$$I(x) = J(x)t(x) + A(1 - t(x)), \tag{1}$$

where $I(x)$ and $J(x)$ indicate a hazy degraded image and a clear image, respectively. A is the value of the global atmospheric light, and the transmission map, $t(x)$, can be derived from the following relationship:

$$t(x) = \mathrm{e}^{-\beta d(x)} \tag{2}$$

where β is called the scattering coefficient, which can reflect the haze density. $d(x)$ is the depth of field.

Based on the atmospheric scattering model, a series of dehazing algorithms using prior knowledge [6–9] have been proposed. Among them, the most representative one is the dark channel prior [7] discovered by He et al.

2.2. Dark Channel Prior

The prior refers to certain pixels with lower intensities in at least one RGB channel as the dark channel, which can be represented as

$$J^{dark}(x) = \min_{y\in\Omega(x)}(\min_{c\in\{r,g,b\}} J^c(y)) \rightarrow 0, \tag{3}$$

where $J^c(y)$ denotes one of the RGB channels of a clear image, and $\Omega(x)$ is a patch centered on pixel x. The internal transmittance of $\Omega(x)$ can be approximated as a constant provided that the patch scale is sufficiently small. Substituting this into Equation (1), a mathematical derivation gives an estimate of the transmittance:

$$\tilde{t}(x) = 1 - \min_{y\in\Omega(x)}(\min_{c\in\{r,g,b\}} \frac{I^c(y)}{A^c}) \tag{4}$$

where $I^c(y)$ and A^c represent the original hazy image and the atmospheric ambient light in one of the RGB components, respectively. The subtraction term in Equation (4) is actually the dark channel intensity of $\frac{I^c(y)}{A^c}$. Combined with Equation (1), a clear result can be obtained as follows:

$$J(x) = \frac{I(x) - A}{max(t(x), t_0)} + A, \tag{5}$$

in which t_0 is a tiny constant set to prevent the value of the denominator from being zero.

The patch size of the crucial parameter $\Omega(x)$ has a decisive impact on the defogging result. As shown in Figure 1b–d, an oversized patch ($\Omega(x) = 30$) would invalidate the assumption that "the transmittance in the patch is constant", and the patch tends to cross the edge of the depth of field, leading to the halo effect. Conversely, as shown in Figure 1e–g, if the patch scale is too small ($\Omega(x) = 3$), the intensity of the dark pixels increases; thus, the transmittance obtained from Equation (4) is less than the real value, which may result in oversaturation, distortion, and an overall darkening of the image. Therefore, a single-scale $\Omega(x)$ will cause many unexpected negative effects and reduce the image quality.

Figure 1. Effect of different patch sizes on dark channel prior (DCP) defogging. (**a**) Hazy input. (**b–d**) represent the dark channel map, transmission map, and dehazing result, respectively, based on $\Omega(x) = 30$. (**e–g**) are the corresponding groups, while $\Omega(x) = 3$.

Based on this, a number of algorithms were subsequently proposed to optimize DCP performance. Chen et al. [28] proposed the concept of a "bright channel", as opposed to the dark channel, in order to solve the problem of the misalignment of brightness in dehazing results. Zhu et al. [29] and Jackson et al. [30] introduced the energy minimization theory and Raleigh scattering theory, respectively, to remove artifacts and halos. To some extent, these approaches that introduce external theories act as a correction and complement to the original DCP, while they also undermine the advantages of DCP, i.e., its efficiency and simplicity. From the perspective of parameter adaption, Song et al. [31] compared the defogging effect at different scales in detail and adaptively adjusted the scale range of the dark channel according to the color and edge characteristics of the hazy image. Hu et al. [32] and Guo et al. [33] focused on segmenting the sky region, which does not satisfy the prior, to improve the accuracy of transmittance recovery. Inspired by previous research, we attempt to further subdivide the feature regions of the images and apply more accurate segmentation techniques to improve the quality of parameter adaptation. In Section 3.2, we will elaborate on the detailed optimization method.

2.3. CycleGAN

Cycle generative adversarial network was first designed by Zhu et al. [24]. It has a network structure with two generators and dual discriminators by mirror-symmetrizing the traditional GAN. Based on this special network structure, CycleGAN can convert images in the original and target domains without the supervision of paired datasets, a property that makes it widely preferred for unpaired dehazing tasks [25,26,34,35].

As shown in Figure 2, the previous CycleGAN-based dehazing networks contain a rehazing cycle and a dehazing cycle. In essence, most of them simply treat "hazy" and "clear" as two style domains for image transformation, with poor network interpretability and severe traces of artificial recovery. Specifically, the rehazing operation ignores real hazy environments that occur with various thicknesses and uneven distributions in the natural world, resulting in a large gap between the generated hazy images and the actual photographed hazy dataset. This means that the rehazing cycle has little significance for the enhancement of dehazing processing and can even negatively affect the quality of outputs, resulting in issues such as obvious artificial recovery traces and distortion.

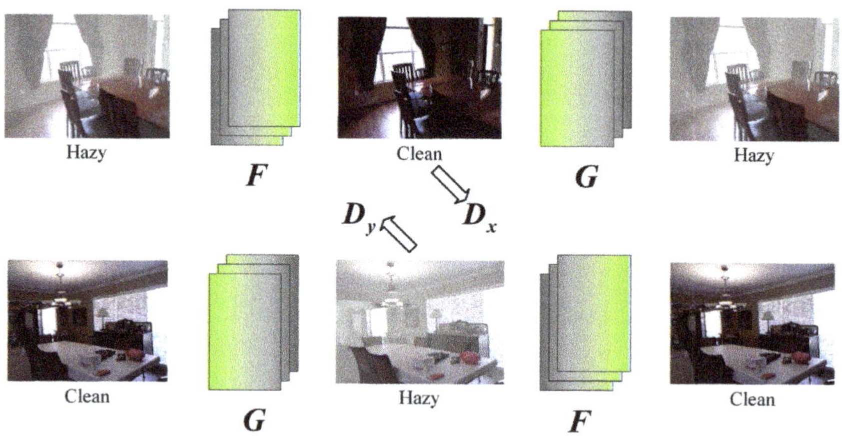

Figure 2. Structure of previous CycleGAN-based dehazing.

In order to improve the above issues, we introduce critical physical information to realize the enhancement of the dehazing and rehazing cycle. More details will be illustrated in Section 3.1.

3. Proposed Method

In this section, we elaborate on an unsupervised unpaired dehazing network termed ADCP-CycleGAN. We adopt adaptive DCP to accurately recover transmittance and atmospheric light for dehazing and achieve rehazing based on the depth and scattering coefficients. The two cycle branches of hazy/clarity reconstruction are connected by the atmospheric scattering model to form enhanced CyleGAN. The algorithm and network structure are detailed as follows.

3.1. Network Structure

The network consists of a hazy image reconstruction **H-H branch** and a clear image reconstruction **C-C branch**, as shown in Figure 3.

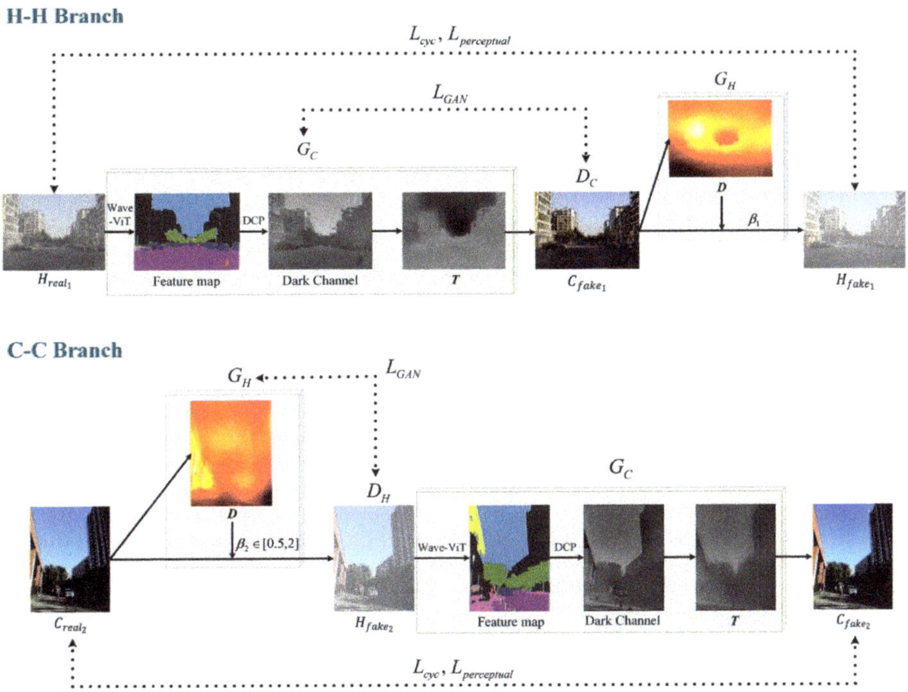

Figure 3. The structure of ADCP-CycleGAN.

H-H Branch. Given a hazy image H_{real_1}, we first perform Wave-ViT segmentation of the image to obtain the regional feature map. After the DCP operation, a dark channel map is obtained to deduce the transmittance T and atmospheric light A according to Equation (4). Then, the clear image C_{fake_1} can be acquired as follows:

$$C_{fake_1} = \frac{H_{real_1} - A}{T} + A \tag{6}$$

Based on the clear image, we can restore the depth D, at which time the scattering coefficient β_1 can be recovered to reflect the density of the haze distribution. With the depth and scattering coefficients, we ultimately obtain the reconstructed hazy H_{fake_1}. In this branch, the generator G_C is the dehazing processor, and D_C is the discriminator that identifies whether C_{fake_1} pertains to the clean domain.

C-C Branch. We initially derive the depth information from the input clear image C_{real_2}. The scattering coefficient β_2 is randomly sampled in the range of $[0.5, 2]$. The corresponding hazy image H_{fake_2} is subsequently acquired, and the same dehazing process as in the **H-H branch** is then adopted to acquire the final reconstructed clear image C_{fake_2}; that is,

$$C_{fake_2} = \frac{H_{fake_2} - A}{T} + A \tag{7}$$

In this branch, the generator G_H produces the haze, and the discriminator D_H is used for recognizing if H_{fake_2} belongs to the hazy domain.

3.2. Adaptive DCP

In Section 2.2, we discussed in detail the drawbacks of the global fixedness of Ω in DCP. In this section, we continue the idea of parameter adaption to make further improvements.

To achieve a more refined segmentation of the feature regions, we here adopt the Wave-ViT model proposed by Yao et al. [36]. This model unites the wavelet transform with the Transformer network. With reversible downsampling for the lossless recovery of object texture details, it shows good performance in semantic segmentation tasks. The image division effect is shown in Figure 4.

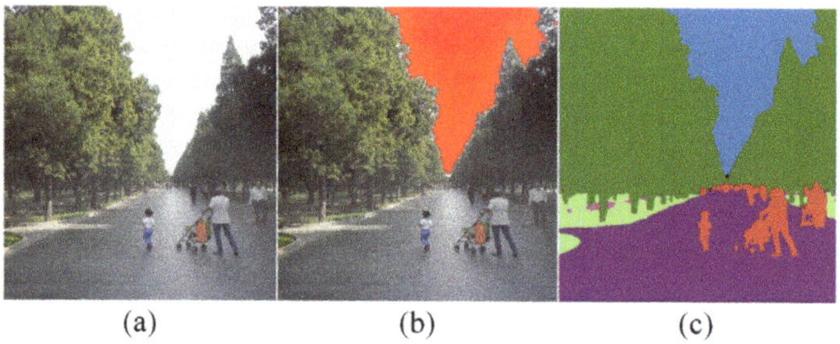

Figure 4. Hazy image region division. (**a**) Hazy image. (**b**) Sky region identification. (**c**) Foreground region segmentation.

We determine distinct patch sizes based on the essential properties of different areas in the image to achieve parameter self-adaption. The image can be divided into 3 regions: (a) The **Foreground** region, which consists of complex objects with rich colors and high saturation. An undersized patch may further aggravate the oversaturation phenomenon, whereas an oversized patch will violate the change of transmittance distribution in this region, causing an obviously distorted visual effect. Therefore, we set the patch scale of the foreground area in a normal interval that varies uniformly with the saturation. Specifically, the patch size of foreground area Ω_{fore} can be determined based on the saturation S and luminance L as follows:

$$L(x) = rI_r(x) + gI_g(x) + bI_b(x) \tag{8}$$

$$S(x) = 1 - \frac{\underset{c\in\{r,g,b\}}{min} I_c(x)}{L(x)} \tag{9}$$

$$\Omega_{fore} = max\{5, round(k \cdot \underset{c\in\{r,g,b\}}{min} I_c(x)\} \tag{10}$$

where the max and round operators are used to set the patch scale as a positive integer. Based on previous research [7,28,31–33] on the defogging quality at different scales, we further conducted a validation experiment on the RESIDE dataset [37]. The results demonstrate that [5, 15] is a scale range that enables dark channel defogging to achieve optimal results, and other patch scales below or above this range experience significant negative effects, such as halos, luminance distortion, and oversaturation. Therefore, we take the value of k as 15 to ensure that Ω in the foreground region is adaptive in this range. As we calculate the brightness and saturation of the image in the HSI color space, the saturation value is in the range of [0, 1]. In order to change the patch scale uniformly with the saturation, we construct a linear mapping relationship between [5, 15] and [0, 1] so that pixel blocks with different levels of saturation in the foreground area can correspond to the suitable patches. (b) The **Sky** region has high brightness and low saturation. We choose a larger patch scale in the $[25, 30]$ range in this area to intensify the defogging effect. At the same time, partitioning out the region helps us find the atmospheric light values using the method in [7]. Notably, though we set the patch scale in the sky region to be much larger than in the foreground area, the sky area usually does not contain too much detail, the color saturation is more homogeneous, and the composition of the scene is simpler. At this point, the negative effects of large patches can be reduced. (c) The **Edge mutation** region. We set a smaller patch value in the range of [0, 3] in the depth of field border area to prevent halo effect and to preserve richer detail information.

3.3. Acquisition of Scattering Coefficient

In order to simulate the generation of real haze environments, which occur with various thicknesses and uneven distributions in the natural world, we optimize the rehazing process based on the atmospheric scattering model by combining the depth and density.

In the **H-H branch**, the scattering coefficient β_1 can be recovered according to Equation (2), as shown below:

$$\beta_1 = -\frac{\ln T}{D} \tag{11}$$

Based on this, the reconstructed hazy H_{fake_1} can be described as:

$$H_{fake_1} = C_{fake_1} e^{-\beta_1 D} + A(1 - e^{-\beta_1 D}) \tag{12}$$

Different from the **H-H branch**, the scattering coefficient β_2 in the **C-C branch** is randomly sampled in the range of $[0.5, 2]$. By altering the scattering coefficients, the generator G_H can produce hazy environments with arbitrary density distributions, as shown in Figure 5. Correspondingly, the hazy image H_{fake_2} is subsequently acquired as follows:

$$H_{fake_2} = C_{real_2} e^{-\beta_2 D} + A(1 - e^{-\beta_2 D}) \tag{13}$$

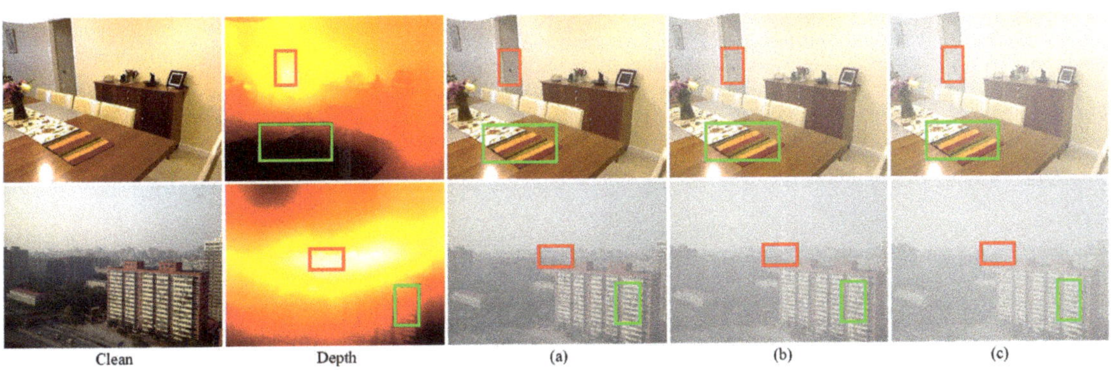

Figure 5. Different hazy images generated by G_H based on diverse depth-of-field and variable scattering coefficients. (**a**) $\beta = 0.5$. (**b**) $\beta = 1$. (**c**) $\beta = 2$.

It is noteworthy that, based on the atmospheric scattering model, the transmittance T and atmospheric light A derived from G_C can be applied in G_H to generate haze. Furthermore, these variable foggy images can also be used to augment the training of G_C. This mutually reinforcing haze removal/generation process constitutes the enhanced CycleGAN.

3.4. Calculation of Losses

GAN losses are incurred during the adversarial game between the generator and the discriminator. In our network, this occurs to ensure the quality of the dehazing and rehazing process. In the **H-H branch**, the losses of the generator G_C and the discriminator D_C can be expressed as follows:

$$L_{GAN}(G_C) = E[(D_C(C_{fake_1}) - 1)^2] \quad (14)$$

$$L_{GAN}(D_C) = E[(D_C(C_{real_1}) - 1)^2] + E[(D_C(C_{fake_1}))^2] \quad (15)$$

in which C_{fake_1} is a clear image constructed by the generator G_c, and C_{real_1} is sampled from the clear image set $Set\{C\}$. In the **C-C Branch**, correspondingly, H_{fake_2}, which is derived from the rehazing generator G_H, and H_{real_2}, which is sampled from the hazy image $Set\{H\}$, are adopted to calculate the loss, which can be described as

$$L_{GAN}(G_H) = E[(D_H(H_{fake_2}) - 1)^2] \quad (16)$$

$$L_{GAN}(D_H) = E[(D_H(H_{real_2}) - 1)^2] + E[(D_H(H_{fake_2}))^2]. \quad (17)$$

Cycle-consistency losses calculate the consistency between the original and the target domain at both ends of the loop branch. In the **H-H branch**, the input H_{real_1} and the reconstructed hazy image H_{fake_1} must display sufficient levels of consistency. Likewise, C_{real_2} should agree with C_{fake_2}. Thus, the cycle-consistency losses can be written as Equation (18), where $|| \ ||_1$ denotes the $L1$ norm.

$$L_{cyc} = E_{H_{real_1} \sim Set\{H\}} ||H_{real_1} - H_{fake_1}||_1 + E_{C_{real_2} \sim Set\{C\}} ||C_{real_2} - C_{fake_2}||_1 \quad (18)$$

Cycle-perceptual losses. Although the cycle-consistency losses can be used to remove part of the noise, we also add cycle-perceptual losses to extract richer details and advanced features based on the VGG16 network to further enhance the structural similarity and ensure more realistic visual effects. The perceptual loss can be seen as Equation (19), where φ is the feature extractor and $|| \ ||_2$ denotes the $L2$ norm.

$$L_{perceptual} = ||\varphi(H_{real_1}) - \varphi(H_{fake_1})||_2 + ||\varphi(C_{real_2}) - \varphi(C_{fake_2})||_2 \quad (19)$$

Thus, the total loss function of ADCP-CycleGAN can be derived as:

$$L_{total} = \lambda_1 L_{GAN} + \lambda_2 L_{cyc} + \lambda_3 L_{perceptual} \quad (20)$$

λ_1, λ_2, and λ_3 are the weight-balancing factors of the three loss functions.

4. Experiment

4.1. Experimental Configuration

Datasets. In the experiment, four diverse datasets were adopted. (a) The RESIDE datasets [37] contain large amounts of hazy images synthesized artificially. SOTS-indoor and SOTS-outdoor contain 500 hazy/clear images indoors and outdoors, respectively, while ITS and OTS include 13,990 and 72,135 indoor and outdoor hazy and clear images, respectively. (b) The O-HAZE [38] dataset from the 2018 NTIRE Single Image Defogging Challenge contains 45 pairs of outdoor fogged/clear images with 10 pairs for testing. The images within this dataset are of high resolution and originate from real shots. (c) The BeDDE [39] dataset contains 208 real-world paired fogged/clear images of high quality captured in 23 different Chinese cities. We conducted qualitative comparison experiments on this dataset to evaluate its generalization ability and assess the subjective visual quality of real-world defogging effects. (d) In addition to the validation on the reference dataset, to compare the visual effects, we additionally introduced 30 hazy images captured in real life, as well as Fattal's dataset [40], which contains 31 real hazy images as non-reference samples.

Competitors & Metrics. We compared the proposed method with several state-of-art algorithms, including the most representative prior-based defogging algorithm, DCP [7]; supervised methods, including DehazeNet [12], GCANet [15], and FFANet [19]; and unsupervised methods, including ZID [20], RefineDNet [21], D4 [27], and USID [22]. For persuasive and reliable comparisons, the parameter settings were still implemented according to the content in Refs. [7,12,15,19–22,27]. We chose SSIM, PSNR [41], and LPIPS [42] as objective evaluation metrics for the dehazing performance on the reference dataset. For the test on the non-reference dataset, we focused on the evaluation of the visual effect of the dehazed image; thus, the information entropy (IE) and average gradient (AG) were employed to reflect the overall information and the local detail performance of the image, respectively. Moreover, we introduce the $NIQE$ [43] (natural image quality evaluator) metric, which can be expressed as

$$D(v_1, v_2, \sum_1, \sum_2) = \sqrt{(v_1 - v_2)^T (\frac{\sum_1 + \sum_2}{2})^{-1} (v_1 - v_2)}, \tag{21}$$

where $v_1, v_2, \sum_1$, and $\sum_2$ represent the mean MVG value and variance matrices of the natural and distorted image, respectively. $NIQE$ evaluates the test image by extracting features from the natural landscape, and its smaller value means the image is more compatible with human eye perception.

Training Settings. In the training phase, we randomly select 6000 images each from ITS and OTS, 380 images each from SOTS-indoor and SOTS-outdoor, and the training set from O-HAZE as input samples. Notably, due to the small sample size and high image resolution in the O-HAZE dataset, we cropped the 35 images into 700 copies to achieve sample expansion. All training images were rescaled to 256 × 256. We set λ_1, λ_2, and λ_3 as discussed in Section 3.4 to 0.2, 1, and 0.0001, respectively, to balance the weights of the three loss functions. The learning rate of the Adam optimizer was set to 0.0001, with a batch size of 2; furthermore, $\beta_1 = 0.5$, and $\beta_2 = 0.999$. We trained our model with an Nvidia GeForce RTX 2080 Ti graphics card and conducted our experiments on PyTorch.

4.2. Results on Reference and No-Reference Datasets

Comparison of reference datasets. Table 1 summarizes the average value of SSIM, PSNR, and LPIPS for every dehazing method tested on the SOTS-indoor (120 remaining images that differed from the training set, SOTS-outdoor (120 remaining images that differed from the training set), and O-HAZE datasets (10 test images cropped into 500 copies). On the SOTS-indoor test set, the supervised algorithms FFANet and GCANet demonstrate their strong capabilities and significant advantages. This is due to the fact that the supervised algorithms can sufficiently learn the image features based on paired datasets, thus performing well in simpler indoor scenes. Our proposed method achieves the best results among unsupervised algorithms. In outdoor haze removal, our algorithm performs the best among all nine algorithms on both SOTS-Outdoor and O-HAZE datasets, demonstrating that the proposed method maintains better generalization and high-quality defogging effects even in complex outdoor scenes. Meanwhile, it is worth noting that the supervised methods lose their dominant positions. To some extent, the results reflect the overfitting issues of supervised algorithms and their poor generalization abilities in handling complex scene defogging tasks.

Furthermore, we display visual comparisons in Figure 6. As can be observed, DCP results in an overall low brightness with obvious color distortion in the sky area. This is due to the fact that the prior is not met in the sky region. While ZID can remove haze, it suffers from significant color distortion in the fogged image. In the case of indoor defogging, RefineDNet produces some unpredictable noises in certain localized areas, such as the color block in the upper left corner of (g) and (h). The indoor defogging results of D4 suffer from serious over-brightening in the deep field due to its inaccurate estimation of atmospheric light, which is determined by taking the brightest pixel point as atmospheric light. This estimation method may lead to over-brightening of the image, especially in indoor images with artificial noise, such as light sources and mirrors. On the other hand, FFANet, GCANet, and our supervised algorithm perform better in indoor defogging, with the former two being better at preserving the details of distant indoor objects. The outdoor defogging results, as shown in Figure 6c–f, reveal the overfitting problem of FFANet, as evidenced by the noticeable color halos on the gable roof in rows d and f. The proposed method exhibits better removal of residual haze in distant parts of the image, such as the distant buildings in row f. Overall, our algorithm shows good generalization ability for various types of defogging tasks, achieving thorough defogging and satisfactory subjective visual perception.

Table 1. Quantitative evaluation of nine algorithms on RESIDE and O-HAZE datasets. The best score is indicated in **Bolded**.

Type	Methods	SOTS-Indoor			SOTS-Outdoor			O-HAZE		
		PSNR↑	SSIM↑	LPIPS↓	PSNR↑	SSIM↑	LPIPS↓	PSNR↑	SSIM↑	LPIPS↓
Prior	DCP [7]	16.61	0.855	0.225	19.41	0.861	0.122	12.32	0.516	0.473
Supervised	DehazeNet [12]	19.82	0.821	0.186	24.75	0.927	0.065	16.47	0.624	0.229
	GCANet [15]	30.23	0.975	0.161	24.36	0.894	0.115	18.51	0.693	0.332
	FFANet [19]	**34.31**	**0.977**	**0.152**	21.23	0.835	0.173	18.36	0.829	0.170
Unsupervised	RefineDNet [21]	25.06	0.929	0.199	23.58	0.914	0.047	19.27	0.853	0.152
	ZID [20]	17.26	0.801	0.244	12.19	0.614	0.396	9.82	0.437	0.528
	D4 [27]	25.40	0.934	0.207	25.75	0.936	0.035	19.90	0.844	0.147
	USID [22]	20.09	0.873	0.218	24.97	0.930	0.044	20.12	0.862	0.140
	Ours	25.98	0.941	0.157	**26.95**	**0.949**	**0.031**	**22.72**	**0.871**	**0.136**

Figure 6. Comparative test of nine algorithms on RESIDE datasets. Rows (**a**),(**b**),(**g**),(**h**) show indoor defogging results, and rows (**c**–**f**) show outdoor defogging results. ADCP-CycleGAN dehazes well in different defogging scenarios.

Additionally, we compared the number of trainable parameters and the running time of our proposed ADCP-CycleGAN with other methods under the same experimental environment and summarized the results in Table 2. Of these methods, the prior-based DCP [7] does not require trainable parameters, and USID [22] outperforms the other algorithms in terms of the number of parameters and running time since it does not rely on calculating physical parameters in the atmospheric scattering model. The proposed method demonstrates acceptable network complexity and defogging efficiency, with fewer parameters and faster running speed compared to other state-of-the-art algorithms.

Table 2. Comparison of the number of trainable parameters and average running time of different dehazing methods.

Type	Methods	Number of Parameters	Runtime (s)
Prior	DCP [7]	-	0.2930
Supervised	DehazeNet [12]	0.008×10^6	1.6200
	GCANet [15]	0.660×10^6	0.9275
	FFANet [19]	4.964×10^6	1.3418
Unsupervised	RefineDNet [21]	63.378×10^6	0.7053
	ZID [20]	48.232×10^6	57.3681
	D4 [27]	11.707×10^6	0.0579
	USID [22]	4.022×10^6	0.0432
	Ours	4.275×10^6	0.0656

Comparison on no-reference real datasets. To verify the generalization ability of the network and the realism of the defogging results, we additionally introduced no-reference datasets. The quantitative evaluation results are reported in Table 3. Our method obtains the best scores in all three metrics, which means that the defogged images achieve acceptable results in terms of information content, detail representation, and visual effect.

Table 3. Quantitative evaluation of nine algorithms on no-reference datasets. The best score is indicated in **Bolded**.

Type	Methods	IE↑	AG↑	NIQE↓
Prior	DCP [7]	7.2658	7.4342	9.3858
Supervised	DehazeNet [12]	7.2945	7.0627	7.7306
	GCANet [15]	7.3098	6.4246	6.9544
	FFANet [19]	7.1056	7.1901	7.3398
Unsupervised	RefineDNet [21]	7.0903	7.9750	6.8427
	ZID [20]	7.2770	5.1849	12.4221
	D4 [27]	7.2251	7.4858	7.1425
	USID [22]	7.3560	8.0217	7.0951
	Ours	**7.5238**	**9.8605**	**6.5364**

In order to demonstrate the defogging effect more clearly, we framed some local details of the image and zoomed in for comparison, as shown in Figure 7. In rows a and c, we framed the text area and zoomed in. Our method successfully preserved more edge details and restored the text information well. For the nature landscape image in row b, our method has effectively removed the residual haze, resulting in a natural color perception of the defogged image. Though GCANet also produces results with less residual haze, there are noticeable distortions in the sky region in rows b and d. FFANet defogging in real-world scenes is not desirable, as there are noticeable haze residues in the results and a large number of artifacts in the sky area of row d. In addition, the hues of USID dehazing results in rows c and d lacking naturalness and realism, resulting in poor visual effects. To summarize, our algorithm consistently shows good defogging performance on real-world no-reference datasets, providing appealing subjective and visually realistic effects.

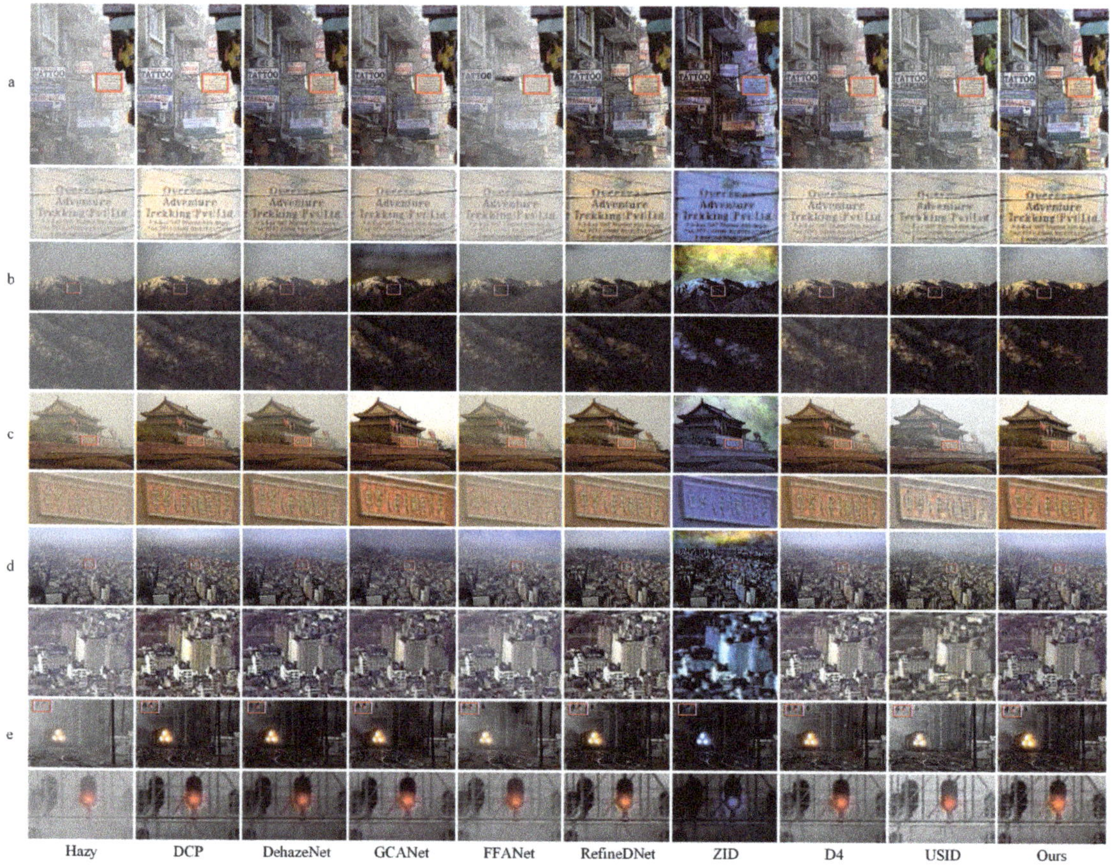

Figure 7. Comparative test of nine algorithms on no-reference datasets. The proposed method shows strong generalization ability and robustness in various real-world defogging tasks, with satisfactory overall picture quality and detailed information performance (**a**–**e**).

In addition, we conducted abundant extended experiments on the BeDDE dataset, and the visual comparison of the defogging results is shown in Figures 8 and 9. The satisfactory defogging effects further reveal the strong generalization ability and defogging stability of the proposed algorithm.

Figure 8. Comparative test of nine algorithms on BeDDE datasets.

Figure 9. Comparative test of nine algorithms on BeDDE datasets.

4.3. Ablation Study

To verify the effectiveness of the different components in ADCP-CycleGAN, we conducted an ablation study on the network. Three additional models were trained and compared with our proposed model on the SOTS dataset as follows: (a) Model A removes the Wave-ViT semantic segmentation and parameter adaptation module, and thus, the transmittance and the atmospheric light are recovered by the original DCP method; (b) the value of the scattering coefficient in Model B is set to a fixed constant; and (c) Model C deletes the cycle perceptual loss.

The dehazing results of the four models are reported in Figure 10. After removing the semantic segmentation module for the parameter adaptation of DCP, the defogging results of Model A show an obvious distortion. For the areas where the prior fails (such as the white floor tiles in row b), the distortion phenomenon appears, and the brightness of the picture in row c is also significantly darker. Model B lacks realism in the subjective visual effect of the defogging result since the scattering coefficient is set to a fixed value. Model C has a degraded performance regarding detail recovery after removing the cycle perceptual loss. The flowers in the far field in row c show an oversaturation of color, indicating that the deletion of cycle perceptual loss has an impact on defogging stability.

Figure 10. Ablation study on RESIDE datasets. The defogging results of Model A showed obvious oversaturation and color distortion. Model B showed significant haze residue. The defogging stability of Model C was reduced compared with ADCP-CycleGAN (**a–c**).

It is worth noting that in the quantitative analysis (as shown in Table 4), the degradation of Model B compared to ADCP-CycleGAN is different in indoor and outdoor dehazing tasks. This may due to the fact that the haze distribution in indoor scenes is more uniform compared to outdoors; thus, the scattering coefficient may have a more significant impact on the outdoor haze removal. This also confirms that the scattering coefficient is not negligible in the outdoor dehazing.

Table 4. Quantitative evaluation of ablation study. The best score is indicated in **Bolded**.

Methods	**SOTS-Indoor**			**SOTS-Outdoor**		
	PSNR↑	**SSIM↑**	**LPIPS↓**	**PSNR↑**	**SSIM↑**	**LPIPS↓**
Model A	21.60	0.872	0.209	22.78	0.904	0.046
Model B	24.22	0.921	0.166	24.19	0.916	0.043
Model C	23.09	0.919	0.173	24.48	0.925	0.037
ADCP-CycleGAN	**25.98**	**0.941**	**0.157**	**26.95**	**0.949**	**0.031**

5. Conclusions and Future Work

In this paper, we propose ADCP-CycleGAN, a novel enhanced CycleGAN network with adaptive DCP for unpaired single-image dehazing. In the network, we achieve the parameter adaption of DCP through a Wave-ViT semantic segmentation model to recover the transmittance and atmospheric light accurately. We optimize the rehazing process by deriving the scattering coefficient from both physical calculation and random sampling means to simulate the real haze distribution. The atmospheric scattering model is applied to realize the connection between the dehazing and rehazing branch in order to build the enhanced CycleGAN. The extended experiments on both reference/no-reference datasets with diverse evaluation metrics confirm the effectiveness of our method. Specifically, our approach can generate haze that is more consistent with real-world scenarios based on depth and density. This could be particularly meaningful for tasks that require clear vision but lack unpaired datasets, such as remote sensing images, autonomous driving, and intelligent monitoring. Furthermore, we hope that our innovative combination of physical prior models with CycleGAN for dehazing can contribute to future developments in unsupervised learning for low-level vision tasks. However, there are also some aspects of our algorithm that deserve improvement. The accuracy of the depth estimation of the proposed method is affected when there is noise such as strong light and obscuration in the image. Meanwhile, due to the incorporation of a physical model in the proposed method, its inherent limitations may result in the local over-enhancement in a few defogged results. In our future work, we will also investigate the post-processing of the defogged images to further improve the image quality.

Author Contributions: Methodology, Y.X.; Software, H.Z.; Supervision, Project administration, F.H.; Data curation, J.G.; Writing—review and editing, Z.W. All authors have read and agreed to the published version of the manuscript.

Funding: This work is supported by the National Training Program of Innovation and Entrepreneurship for Undergraduates (Grant No. 202310635096), Venture Innovation Support Program for Chongqing Overseas Returnees (Grant No. cx2019133) and the Chongqing Research Project of the Foal Eagle Program (Grant No. CY220231).

Data Availability Statement: Data sharing no applicable.

Conflicts of Interest: The authors declare no conflict of interest.

References

1. Jobson, D.; Rahman, Z.; Woodell, G. A multi-scale retinex for bridging the gap between color images and the human observation of scenes. *IEEE Trans. Image Process.* **1997**, *6*, 965–976. [CrossRef]
2. Zou, X.; Liu, Y.; Tan, Z. A fog-removing treatment based on combining high-frequency emphasis filtering and histogram equalization. *Key Eng. Mater.* **2011**, *474*, 2198–2202. [CrossRef]
3. Zheng, M.; Qi, G.; Zhu, Z.; Li, Y.; Wei, H.; Liu, Y. Image dehazing by an artificial image fusion method based on adaptive structure decomposition. *IEEE Sens. J.* **2020**, *20*, 8062–8072. [CrossRef]
4. Galdran, A. Image dehazing by artificial multiple-exposure image fusion. *Signal Process.* **2018**, *149*, 135–147. [CrossRef]
5. Zhu, Z.; Wei, H.; Hu, G.; Li, Y.; Qi, G.; Mazur, N. A novel fast single image dehazing algorithm based on artificial multiexposure image fusion. *IEEE Trans. Instrum. Meas.* **2020**, *70*, 1–23. [CrossRef]
6. Fattal, R. Single Image Dehazing. *ACM Trans. Graph.* **2008**, *27*, 1–9. [CrossRef]
7. He, K.; Sun, J.; Tang, X. Single image haze removal using dark channel prior. *IEEE Trans. Pattern Anal. Mach. Intell.* **2010**, *33*, 2341–2353.
8. Zhu, Q.; Mai, J.; Shao, L. A fast single image haze removal algorithm using color attenuation prior. *IEEE Trans. Image Process.* **2015**, *24*, 3522–3533.
9. Berman, D. Non-local image dehazing. In Proceedings of the IEEE Conference on Computer Vision and Pattern Recognition, Las Vegas, NV, USA, 27–30 June 2016; pp. 1674–1682.
10. Mccartney, E.J. Optics of the atmosphere: Scattering by molecules and particles. *Phys. Bull.* **1977**, *28*, 521. [CrossRef]
11. Wang, W.; Yuan, X.; Wu, X.; Liu, Y. Fast image dehazing method based on linear transformation. *IEEE Trans. Multimed.* **2017**, *19*, 1142–1155. [CrossRef]
12. Cai, L.B.; Xu, X.M.; Jia, K.; Qing, C.M.; Tao, D.C. Dehazenet: An end-to-end system for single image haze removal. *IEEE Trans. Image Process.* **2016**, *25*, 5187–5198. [CrossRef] [PubMed]
13. Zhang, H.; Patel, V.M. Densely connected pyramid dehazing network. In Proceedings of the IEEE Conference on Computer Vision and Pattern Recognition, Salt Lake City, UT, USA, 18–23 June 2018; pp. 3194–3203.
14. Li, B.; Peng, X.; Wang, Z.; Xu, J.; Feng, D. Aod-net: All-in-one dehazing network. In Proceedings of the IEEE International Conference on Computer Vision, Venice, Italy, 22–29 October 2017; pp. 4770–4778.
15. Chen, D.; He, M.; FAN, A. Gated context aggregation network for image dehazing and deraining. In Proceedings of the 2019 IEEE Winter Conference on Applications of Computer Vision (WACV), Waikoloa, HI, USA, 7–11 January 2019; pp. 1375–1383.
16. Li, R.; Pan, J.; Li, Z.; Tang, J. Single image dehazing via conditional generative adversarial network. In Proceedings of the IEEE Conference on Computer Vision and Pattern Recognition, Salt Lake City, UT, USA, 18–23 June 2018; pp. 8202–8211.
17. Qu, Y.; Chen, Y.; Huang, J.; Xie, Y. Enhanced pix2pix dehazing network. In Proceedings of the IEEE/CVF Conference on Computer Vision and Pattern Recognition, Long Beach, CA, USA, 15–20 June 2019; pp. 8160–8168.

18. Liu, X.; Ma, Y.; Shi, Z.; Chen, J. Griddehazenet: Attention-based multi-scale network for image dehazing. In Proceedings of the IEEE International Conference on Computer Vision, Seoul, Republic of Korea, 27 October–2 November 2019; pp. 7314–7323.
19. Qin, X.; Wang, Z.; Bai, Y.; Xie, X.; Jia, H. FFA-Net: Feature fusion attention network for single image dehazing. In Proceedings of the AAAI Conference on Artificial Intelligence, New York, NY, USA, 7–12 February 2020; Volume 34, pp. 11908–11915.
20. Li, B.; Gou, Y.; Liu, J.Z.; Zhu, H.; Zhou, J.T.; Peng, X. Zero-shot image dehazing. *IEEE Trans. Image Process.* **2020**, *29*, 8457–8466. [CrossRef] [PubMed]
21. Zhao, S.; Zhang, L.; Shen, Y.; Zhou, Y. RefineDNet: A weakly supervised refinement framework for single image dehazing. *IEEE Trans. Image Process.* **2021**, *30*, 3391–3404. [CrossRef]
22. Li, J.; Li, Y.; Zhuo, L.; Kuang, L.; Yu, T. USID-Net: Unsupervised single image dehazing network via disentangled representations. *IEEE Trans. Multimed.* **2022**. [CrossRef]
23. Ding, B.; Zhang, R.; Xu, L.; Liu, G.; Yang, S.; Liu, Y.; Zhang, Q. U^2D^2 Net: Unsupervised Unified Image Dehazing and Denoising Network for Single Hazy Image Enhancement. *IEEE Trans. Multimed.* **2023**. [CrossRef]
24. Zhu, J.; Park, T.; Isola, P. Unpaired image-to-image translation using cycle-consistent adversarial networks. In Proceedings of the IEEE International Conference on Computer Vision, Venice, Italy, 22–29 October 2017; pp. 2223–2232.
25. Engin, D.; Genc, A.; Ekenel, H.K. Cycledehaze: Enhanced cyclegan for single image dehazing. In Proceedings of the IEEE Conference on Computer Vision and Pattern Recognition Workshops, Salt Lake City, UT, USA, 18–23 June 2018; pp. 825–833.
26. Zheng, Y. Dehaze-AGGAN: Unpaired Remote Sensing Image Dehazing Using Enhanced Attention-Guide Generative Adversarial Networks. *IEEE Trans. Geosci. Remote. Sens.* **2022**, *60*, 1–13. [CrossRef]
27. Yang, Y.; Wang, C.; Liu, R.; Zhang, L.; Guo, X.; Tao, D. Self-augmented Unpaired Image Dehazing via Density and Depth Decomposition. In Proceedings of the IEEE Conference on Computer Vision and Pattern Recognition, New Orleans, LA, USA, 18–24 June 2022; pp. 2037–2046.
28. Chen, Y.; Lu, C.T. Single Image Dehazing Based on Superpixel Segmentation Combined with Dark-Bright Channels. *Laser Optoelectron. Prog.* **2020**, *57*, 161023. [CrossRef]
29. Zhu, M.; He, B.; Wu, Q. Single image dehazing based on dark channel prior and energy minimization. *IEEE Signal Process. Lett.* **2017**, *25*, 174–178. [CrossRef]
30. Jackson, J.; Kun, S.; Agyekum, K.O. A fast single-image dehazing algorithm based on dark channel prior and rayleigh scattering. *IEEE Access* **2020**, *8*, 73330–73339. [CrossRef]
31. Song, Y.; Luo, H.; Hui, B.; Chang, Z. Haze removal using scale adaptive dark channel prior. *Infrared Laser Eng.* **2016**, *45*, 928002. [CrossRef]
32. Hu, Q.; Zhang, Y.; Zhu, Y.; Jiang, Y.; Song, M. Single image dehazing algorithm based on sky segmentation and optimal transmission maps. *Vis. Comput.* **2023**, *39*, 997–1013. [CrossRef]
33. Guo, F.; Qiu, J.; Tang, J. Single Image Dehazing Using Adaptive Sky Segmentation. *IEEJ Trans. Electr. Electron. Eng.* **2021**, *16*, 1209–1220. [CrossRef]
34. Liu, W.; Hou, X.; Duan, J.; Qiu, G. End-to-end single image fog removal using enhanced cycle consistent adversarial networks. *IEEE Trans. Image Process.* **2020**, *29*, 7819–7833. [CrossRef]
35. Zhao, J.; Zhang, J.; Li, Z.; Hwang, J.N.; Gao, Y.; Fang, Z.; Jiang, X.; Huang, B. Dd-cyclegan: Unpaired image dehazing via double-discriminator cycle-consistent generative adversarial network. *Eng. Appl. Artif. Intell.* **2019**, *82*, 263–271. [CrossRef]
36. Yao, T.; Pan, Y.; Li, Y.; Ngo, C.W.; Mei, T. Wave-vit: Unifying wavelet and transformers for visual representation learning. In Proceedings of the Computer Vision-ECCV 2022: 17th European Conference, Tel Aviv, Israel, 23–27 October 2022; pp. 328–345.
37. Li, B.; Ren, W.; Fu, D.; Tao, D.; Feng, D.; Zeng, W.; Wang, Z. Benchmarking singleimage dehazing and beyond. *IEEE Trans. Image Process.* **2018**, *28*, 492–505. [CrossRef]
38. Ancuti, C.O.; Ancuti, C.; Timofte, R.; Vleeschouwer, C.D. O-HAZE: A Dehazing Benchmark with Real Hazy and Haze-Free Outdoor Images. In Proceedings of the IEEE Conference on Computer Vision and Pattern Recognition Workshops, Salt Lake City, UT, USA, 18-22 June 2018; pp. 754–762.
39. Zhao, S.; Zhang, L.; Huang, S.; Shen, Y.; Zhao, S.; Yang, Y. Evaluation of defogging: A real-world benchmark dataset, a new criterion and baselines. In Proceedings of the 2019 IEEE International Conference on Multimedia and Expo (ICME), Shanghai, China, 8–12 July 2019; pp. 1840–1845.
40. Fattal, R. Dehazing using color-lines. *ACM Trans. Graph.* **2014**, *34*, 1–14. [CrossRef]
41. Wang, Z.; Bovik, A.C.; Sheikh, H.R.; Simoncelli, E.P. Image quality assessment: From error visibility to structural similarity. *IEEE Trans. Image Process.* **2004**, *13*, 600–612. [CrossRef]
42. Zhang, R.; Isola, P.; Efros, A.A.; Shechtman, E.; Wang, O. The unreasonable effectiveness of deep features as a perceptual metric. In Proceedings of the IEEE Conference on Computer Vision and Pattern Recognition, Salt Lake City, UT, USA, 18–23 June 2018; pp. 586–595.
43. Mittal, A.; Soundararajan, R.; Bovik, A.C. Making a "completely blind" image quality analyzer. *IEEE Signal Process. Lett.* **2012**, *20*, 209–212. [CrossRef]

Journal of *Imaging*

MDPI

Article

Manipulating Pixels in Computer Graphics by Converting Raster Elements to Vector Shapes as a Function of Hue

Tajana Koren Ivančević *, Nikolina Stanić Loknar, Maja Rudolf and Diana Bratić

Faculty of Graphic Arts, University of Zagreb, 10000 Zagreb, Croatia
* Correspondence: tajana.koren.ivancevic@grf.unizg.hr

Abstract: This paper proposes a method for changing pixel shape by converting a CMYK raster image (pixel) to an HSB vector image, replacing the square cells of the CMYK pixels with different vector shapes. The replacement of a pixel by the selected vector shape is done depending on the detected color values for each pixel. The CMYK values are first converted to the corresponding RGB values and then to the HSB system, and the vector shape is selected based on the obtained hue values. The vector shape is drawn in the defined space, according to the row and column matrix of the pixels of the original CMYK image. Twenty-one vector shapes are introduced to replace the pixels depending on the hue. The pixels of each hue are replaced by a different shape. The application of this conversion has its greatest value in the creation of security graphics for printed documents and the individualization of digital artwork by creating structured patterns based on the hue.

Keywords: pixel shape; hue; color systems; computer graphics; security graphics

1. Introduction

There has been a desire to modify and refine digital pictures since the beginning of computer graphics and even today. This work was inspired in part by a series of articles published in the 1990s, which dealt with the artistic rasterization (screening) of images [1,2]. In these papers, artistic screening was described as a new image reproduction technique in which freely designed screening elements were used to create halftones. These were black and white images. In artistic screening, the shape of the screen dots can be customized according to the designer's will. Various screen shapes created in Adobe Illustrator were used. They are used in the creation of graphic designs of high artistic quality and in the field of security graphics [3]. In addition, the development of computer graphics allows for the research and creation of mathematical tools for computer-generated ornamental patterns to create images [4]. To improve image quality without increasing the resolution of the square pixels, variable shaped pixels are used [5,6]. The Mathematica program can be used to test the output shapes of future screen elements. By translating mathematical functions into the Postscript programming language, a database of screen elements of various shapes was developed and created [7,8]. Experiments with variable shapes of screen elements, so-called mutants, have also been performed [9]. Multicolor dithering is applied to generate color images whose screen dots consist of artistic shapes (letters, symbols, ornaments, etc.) [10]. An algorithm is also presented for extracting a resolution-independent vector representation from pixel art images, which can be used to arbitrarily enlarge the results without image degradation [11].

Images can be manipulated by applying various filters that enhance certain properties of the image. In particular, the application of the Gaussian filter is frequently cited in the literature as a basis for further research [12–15]. The Gaussian filter is an important component of many algorithms in image processing. The bilateral filter was originally introduced for the task of image denoising as an edge-preserving filter [16–19]. There are works in which joint bilateral filtering improves the quality of photographs by combining an image taken with daylight and one taken with flash [20,21]. Trilateral filters for high contrast images and meshes built from two modified forms of Tomasi and Manduchi's bilateral filter for edge-preserving smoothing and visual detail removal for n-dimensional signals in computer graphics, image processing, and computer vision applications have also been presented [22].

One of the most important and commonly used manipulations of images is pseudo-coloring, which has applications in various fields. There are several techniques for coloring satellite images SAR. Deep learning has become the main method of SAR colorization, with the most advanced pix2pix method [23]. One of the methods is based on transferring black and white images to the RGB system through the CIE Lab system [24]. Various techniques are also used to enhance the colors in the images. For example, there is a method to improve saturation in the context of hue-preserving color image enhancement in an RGB color space. The proposed method handles colors in an RGB color space that has the shape of a cube, and improves the contrast of a given image by histogram manipulation [25]. There are also methods to improve contrast by reversible data hiding [26].

In the field of security graphics, various methods are used to protect the originality of the image. There are various techniques to secure digital images such as encryption, steganography, and watermarking [27–29]. Using fractal geometry, Hilbert curve-based image protection software has been developed in Postscript programming language [30].

However, to our knowledge, there are no scientific studies in which the appearance (shape) of the pixels themselves has been changed. Our research provides a suggestion on a method to change the shape and appearance of pixels by inserting the various vector shapes into an empty pixel cell. For this purpose, different vector shapes have been designed to represent pixels in different ways for each hue in the HSB color space. The aim of this research is to show that it is possible to change the appearance of each pixel and thereby affect the appearance of the entire image on the basis of the hue value. In the results of the research, we were able to present a multi-color graphic in which a different shape is automatically displayed for each hue instead of the original pixels.

2. Materials and Methods

According to CIE, colors are represented geometrically in space, usually in 3 dimensions. Color spaces are divided into device-dependent and device-independent spaces, according to the 1996 IFRA Special Report. Device specific color spaces represent colors relative to device properties. The most commonly used device-dependent color spaces are RGB, CMY, CMYK, and YCC color spaces. Device-independent color spaces are based on consistency with a standard observer's perception, as well as perceptual uniformity. The most common ones are: HSB, CIE XYZ, CIE xyY, CIE Lab, CIELAB, and CIE Luv. In this document, the color systems CMYK, RGB, and HSB are used [31].

CMYK is a subtractive color system whose primary colors are cyan, magenta, and yellow, with black added. In this system, also known as "printer inks", colors are viewed from the perspective of the reflection of white light on a surface. The color obtained is the result of subtraction from the white color. Theoretically, if all the colors in this system are mixed together, the result is the color black. The values of the CMYK colors range from 0 to 100% [32].

The additive or RGB color model consists of three primary colors: red, green, and blue. The RGB model is used by RGB monitors and LCD screens. When all three components are added together, white is (theoretically) obtained. The color values in the RGB system range from 0 to 255 [33].

The HSB color model is a model of secondary and complementary colors. In it, the combination of primary colors from the two previously mentioned systems leads to all other colors or tones. The color wheel is used to represent hues and their 'positions'. The hue is given in degrees, and the values for the primary colors of the additive color model can be easily determined by dividing 360 degrees into thirds (R = 0 or 360, G = 120, B = 240). By combining the primary colors of the additive color model, the primary colors of the subtractive color model are also determined (R + G = Y = 60, G + B = C = 180, B + R = M = 300 degrees). In this way, all other color tones can be defined. Moreover, each primary color of the additive system is complementary to one color of the subtractive system (R~C, G~M, B~Y). Saturation is a property which defines full hues or shades of gray, while brightness controls the lightness or darkening of the color [34–37].

In this research, the Postscript programming language is used for image analysis and pattern creation [38–41]. Instead of classical halftone elements, individual shapes are created whose position is defined by the location of the pixel cell in the coordinate space of the image. The shapes are first sketched and then programmed. A square cell is created in which new vector shapes are programmed. The shapes are programmed to use data about the dimensions of a particular square shape, which is the pixel size, so they can easily be sized in relation to the dimensions of the original pixel. To apply new vector shapes, graphics with division into CMYK system channels are used. Each image channel is defined by a hexadecimal matrix, and the color component of each pixel is described by two values from 00 to FF. Converted to the decimal system, it is possible to represent 256 hues for each CMYK channel. The hue of each pixel is determined by representing all four components of the CMYK channels. The original hexadecimal code of the image is translated into the decimal system and normalized (where 0 represents the absence of color and 1 represents the maximum tone intensity). Figure 1 shows the research plan of image transformation from the original image in jpeg format to the image with applied vector shapes based on the hue value.

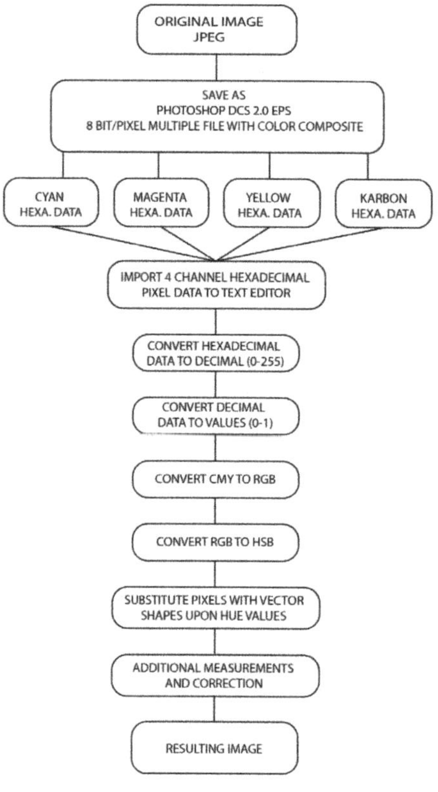

Figure 1. Translation of the original image in jpeg to resulting image with shapes defined by color hue.

The algorithm reads the CMYK values of each pixel and converts them to values between 0 and 1. The rows and columns of the matrix are defined programmatically, based on the image width and height. To correctly represent the pixels from all four CMYK channels, a pixel width offset is defined on the x-axis for the columns and a pixel height offset is defined on the y-axis for the rows. It is important to emphasize that in Postscript, it is possible within one program (one printable page) to use all three-color systems—CMYK, RGB, and HSB—simultaneously. This possibility will prove to be very necessary when continuing the experimental part of the work.

Algorithm for creating a matrix of cells based on the image pixel position:

- Define the width (w) and height (h) of the cell at the position of the original pixel;
- Define the total number of columns (S) and rows (R) of the matrix;
- Construct a matrix in which the cell positions x and y are defined as $x = w \times s$; $y = h \times r$, where 's' and 'r' are the values of the current column and row.

When a cell is created with its own dimensions and position, an arbitrary shape is created that defines a new raster element with the dimensions of the cell itself. This raster element contains information about the coloring that was previously associated with the pixel. The plan for conducting the experiment is shown in Figure 2.

Figure 2. Shows 12 pixels of different hues and their replacement with a new fish shape.

For the first phase of the research, an 8-bit raster image is used, consisting of 3 rows and 4 columns. In the first example, four solids of the CMYK system were used in the top row, while different hues were mixed in the other two rows. The color data are expressed in hexadecimal values, and their image is displayed with these values, i.e., an image of 12 pixels with different hues. The same image was used to manipulate the pixels that now represent the vector shape of the "fish". The vector shape is placed in the previously defined square shape with pixel width and height. The data of each color channel are converted from hexadecimal values to values between 0 and 1, adapted to the Postscript programming language. The newly obtained data for each pixel are then plotted in the shape of a fish.

In the next phase of the research, a different shape is used for each of the CMYK channels. The experiment consists of four solid squares of C, M, Y, and K. The image is saved with the separation of the channels. A new alternative pixel shape is defined for each channel (Figure 3a,b).

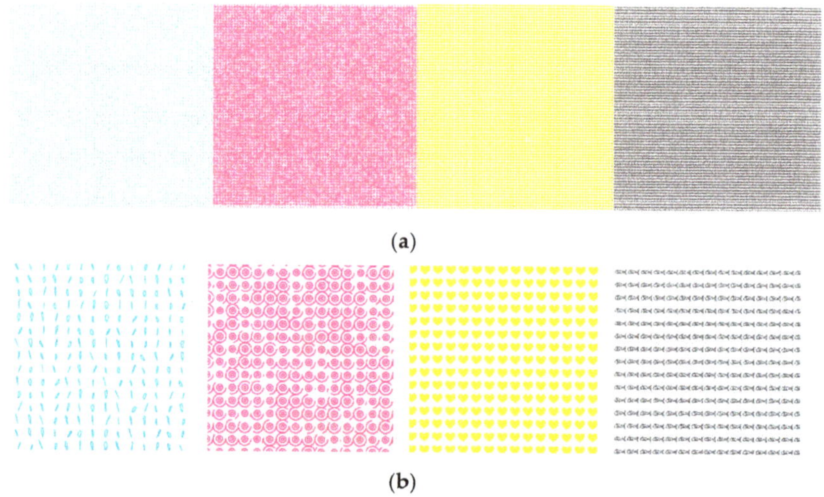

Figure 3. (**a**) Shows four colors where the original pixels are replaced by four new shapes, and (**b**) shows enlarged details of the pixel layout.

The pixels in the cyan channel are replaced by a Bezier curve to which a pseudorandom number has been added as the x value in the first control point and the x and y values in the second control point. In this way, the curves are drawn differently for each pixel, randomly but predefined by the seed of the pseudorandom numbers.

In the magenta channel, the pixels are replaced by three circles, with the initial angle at the largest of the three circles also determined by pseudorandom numbers.

The pixels in the yellow channel are replaced by heart shapes.

In the last K channel, the pixels are replaced by a fish shape. The conditions are set to split the image so that a different replacement shape for the pixels is chosen for each channel.

In the continuation, the investigation has been extended to the three basic colors of the RGB system (Figure 4). Seven new shapes were used: random curves (lines), the letter 'a', a star, a wave, a diamond, and rotating squares.

Seven new shapes were used: random curves (lines), the letter 'a', a star, a wave, a diamond, and rotating squares (Figure 4).

In the next phase of research, we wanted to extend the sampling of new replacement shapes for the classic pixels to more hues, not just the basic ones from the CMYK and RGB systems, for which it is easy to set the conditions. We encountered an obstacle in that it was not possible for us to achieve an appropriate response by combining these two-color systems and setting conditions for selecting another element for a particular hue. Setting the condition would result in at least one hue popping out and displaying the wrong vector element or no vector element at all. Therefore, the conversion was made from the CMYK system to the RGB system to the HSB system. Figure 5 shows the result of displaying different hues after conversion.

Figure 4. Four basic colors of the CMYK system and three basic colors of the RGB system in which the new shapes replace the original pixel shape.

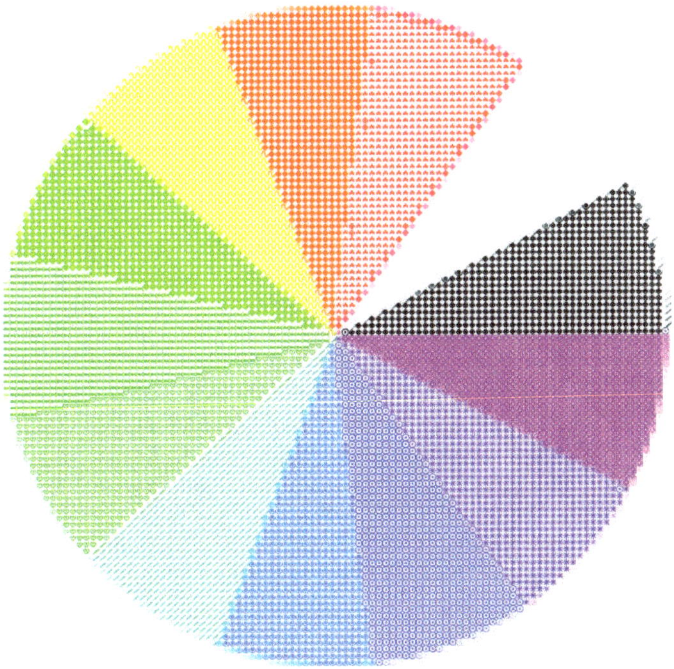

Figure 5. Shows the pixels replaced by vector shapes for 11 hues by the HSB system and 1 for black.

The first step is to read the cyan, magenta, yellow, and black values from the hexadecimal data contained in the image.

To perform the conversion from CMYK to RGB, the CMYK values read from the image are converted to CMY (K = 0) using the "gray component replacement" (GCR) method with the minimization of the black component.

The formulas in Equation (1) show the conversion from CMYK to CMY (K = 0):

$$\begin{aligned} C1 &= C + K \\ M1 &= M + K \\ Y1 &= Y + K \\ K1 &= K - K = 0 \end{aligned} \tag{1}$$

In the next step, the values of the newly obtained C, M, and Y are converted to the RGB system using the complementarity method shown in Equation (2):

$$\begin{aligned} R &= 1 - C1 \\ G &= 1 - M1 \\ B &= 1 - Y1 \end{aligned} \tag{2}$$

The last step is the conversion from RGB to HSB. First, the largest and smallest values of the RGB components must be determined (e.g., for R = 25, G = 70, B= 15, the smallest value would be the B component and the largest would be the G component). The highest value 'max' is appended to the brightness component of the HSB.

Hue and saturation are defined by the difference between the maximal and minimal RGB value. If the difference is zero, then the saturation is also zero, otherwise it is calculated as follows in the formula:

$$S = (\max - \min)/\max \tag{3}$$

For hue, the following conditions apply: If the difference $\Delta_{max-min}$ between the max and min is zero, then the hue is zero. If this is not the case, then the highest value of the three RGB components is searched for (max) and calculated according to the following expressions in Equation (4):

$$\begin{aligned} &\text{For R} = \max, H = (G - B/\Delta_{\text{max-min}}) \times 60/360 \\ &\text{For G} = \max, H = 2 + (B - R/\Delta_{\text{max-min}}) \times 60/360 \\ &\text{For B} = \max, H = 4 + (R - G/\Delta_{\text{max-min}}) \times 60/360 \end{aligned} \tag{4}$$

if H turns out to be a negative number in a calculation, 1 is added to it.

This experiment led to the final phase, where a problem was also encountered. The HSB color wheel was used, which is divided into 20 hues. The pixels of each hue were to be replaced by a vector shape. However, while some hues responded correctly to the program's requirements, others did not. The result is shown in Figures 6b and 7 (enlarged detail of Figure 6b). Figure 6a presents the original image that was used totest our method. The Postscript code of this example can be found in the supplementary material under the name Code S1.

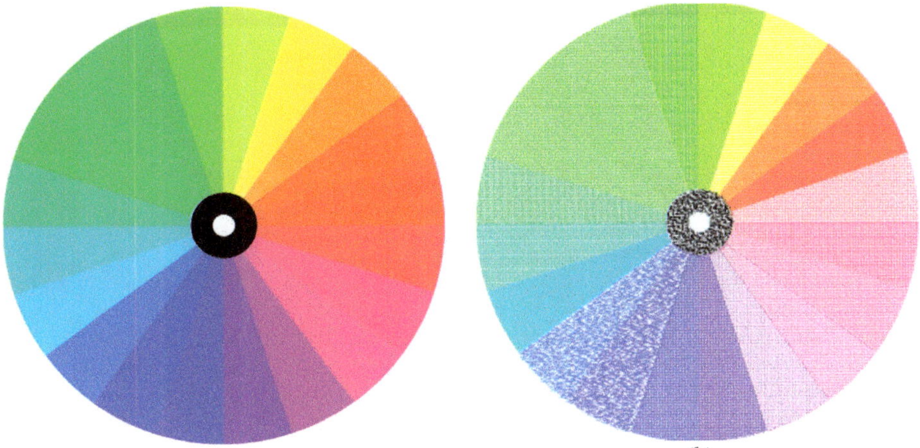

(a) (b)

Figure 6. (a) Showing the color wheel divided into 20 hues and (b) the result obtained by replacing the pixels with vector shapes.

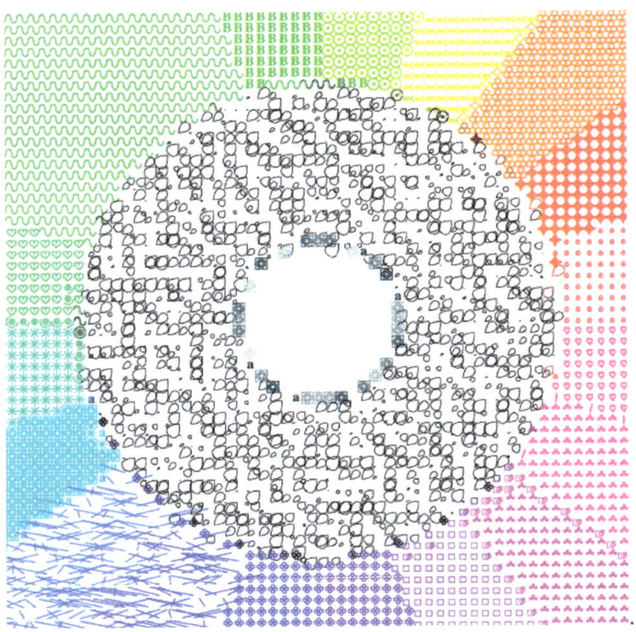

Figure 7. Shows enlarged details of Figure 6b. Some hues responded correctly to the program's requirements, others did not. Some shapes appear in more than one hue interval (green waves, blue lines).

3. Results

Since the shapes were not distributed according to the hues and conditions set, additional measurements and corrections were made. It was found that the color settings affect the way of conversion from the CMYK system to the HSB system, and also the distribution of the shapes within a certain interval. The colors are grouped around some tones, i.e., they are too similar to each other, and this is exactly the reason why the program uses the same shape for several neighboring tones, despite the precisely set conditions (Figure 7). The measurements gave different results. The hues group around certain hue angles. This is particularly pronounced for green, green-blue, blue, and blue-violet hues, hue (72, 90), hue (90, 108, 126, 144), hue (234, 252), hue (252, 270), and the general absence of cyan (hue 180). Although the hues constantly increase by a constant angle of 18 degrees, in reality, the C, M, and Y values do not exactly follow this change. For example, at angles 90, 108, 126, and 144, the equivalent of the C, M, and Y values are almost the same (53, 0, 100; 65, 0, 100; 68, 0, 100; 66, 0, 91). After extensive analysis and measurements, we concluded that the hue spacing must be increased for certain hues and decreased for others to achieve an appropriate distribution of hues across all twenty parts and black. To produce the desired hue separations, five different color settings were used to analyze the hue behavior of C, M, and Y. The hue of each of the five color settings was then used to produce the desired hue separations. These color settings provide different separation methods and are designed to use different inks under different printing conditions and on different papers. Euroscale Coated V2, for example, uses specifications designed to produce high-quality separations with Euroscale inks at 300% total ink coverage, positive plate, and bright white coated paper. Fogra was developed by the German Graphic Technology Research Organization, Japan was developed by the Japan Magazine Publisher Association, and the U.S. was developed to produce quality separations using U.S. inks. Using these color settings and the differences in the C, M, and Y values in correlation to hue, as shown in Table 1, will result in the correct color setting and the correct distribution of shapes as a function of hue. The first column of Table 1 contains the data used for the example in Figure 7. The other columns contain measurement data as a function of various color settings. Chart 1 shows the poor distribution of C, M, and Y in certain parts of the spectrum. Table 1 shows the C, M, and Y values correlated with the hue angle. Viewed from left to right, the mathematically calculated values are shown first, followed by the measured values using five different color settings.

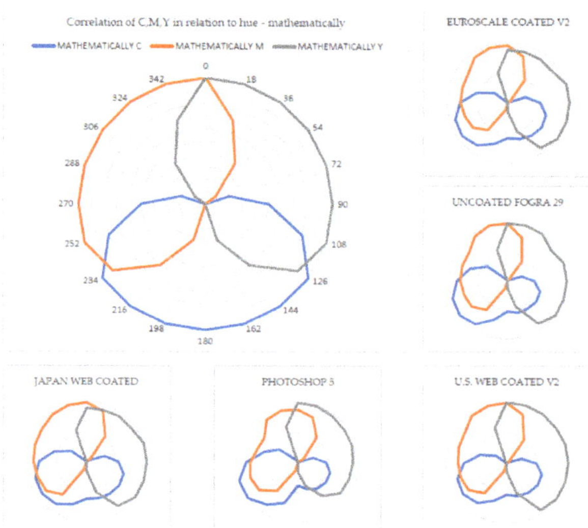

Chart 1. Shows the values from Table 1 for the first four columns, i.e., the correlation of C, M, Y as a function of hue, the mathematically determined values (**large image**), and the values obtained by measurement for different color settings (**5 small images**).

Table 1. Shows the differences in the correlations of C, M, Y on hue (H) with respect to the mathematically determined angle relative to the measured values for five different color settings.

Mathematecally				Euroscale Coated V2				Uncoated Fogra 29			
H	C	M	Y	H	C	M	Y	H	C	M	Y
0	0	100	100	0	0	94	87	0	0	98	99
18	0	70	100	18	0	80	88	18	0	78	100
36	0	40	100	36	0	46	89	36	0	41	100
54	0	10	100	54	2	4	89	54	3	1	91
72	20	0	100	72	30	0	100	72	25	0	100
90	50	0	100	90	53	0	100	90	45	0	100
108	80	0	100	108	65	0	100	108	58	0	100
126	100	0	90	126	68	0	100	126	60	0	100
144	100	0	60	144	66	0	91	144	58	0	90
162	100	0	30	162	62	0	49	162	57	0	46
180	100	0	0	180	58	0	14	180	52	0	12
198	100	30	0	198	71	12	0	198	69	13	0
216	100	60	0	216	86	55	0	216	92	61	0
234	100	90	0	234	92	70	0	234	100	75	0
252	80	100	0	252	90	73	0	252	98	77	0
270	50	100	0	270	78	77	0	270	86	80	0
288	20	100	0	288	53	78	0	288	67	81	0
306	0	100	10	306	27	80	0	306	42	81	0
324	0	100	40	324	0	92	0	324	3	94	0
342	0	100	70	342	0	95	52	342	0	100	56
Japan Web Coated				**Photoshop 5**				**Web Coated V2 U.S.**			
H	C	M	Y	H	C	M	Y	H	C	M	Y
0	0	98	89	0	0	87	99	0	0	99	100
18	0	88	90	18	0	78	98	18	0	84	100
36	0	52	93	36	0	51	95	36	0	47	100
54	2	7	93	54	1	11	93	54	2	4	99
72	31	0	100	72	26	0	93	72	25	0	100
90	53	0	100	90	46	0	90	90	48	0	100
108	65	0	100	108	55	0	88	108	60	0	100
126	67	0	100	126	56	0	86	126	62	0	100
144	65	0	90	144	53	0	68	144	60	0	95
162	63	0	53	162	46	0	41	162	57	0	51
180	61	0	15	180	38	0	16	180	52	0	13
198	74	14	0	198	70	15	0	198	65	15	0
216	86	67	0	216	86	58	0	216	81	61	0
234	90	82	0	234	100	78	0	234	87	76	0
252	88	84	0	252	100	81	0	252	84	78	0
270	78	87	0	270	84	77	0	270	69	79	0
288	56	89	0	288	58	70	0	288	45	82	0
306	30	91	0	306	37	68	0	306	21	84	0
324	0	96	0	324	6	87	0	324	0	96	0
342	0	98	55	342	0	90	62	342	0	99	61

Chart 1 shows the values from Table 1 for the first four columns, i.e., the correlation of C, M, and Y as a function of hue. The mathematically determined values (large image) show the equal distribution of the values. The values obtained by the measurement for different color settings (five small images) show how the measured values deviate from the mathematical model. The greatest changes are visible in the cyan (C) and magenta (M) values, while the yellow (Y) values remain close to the mathematical model.

By correcting the interval, the correct distribution of shapes was achieved by the hue spectrum, which was divided into 20 parts, and the added black component, which was the goal of this research.

The final result is shown in Figure 8. All 21 shapes were used, each in its own segment or interval. It can also be seen that individual elements appear in other segments, as already shown for the most challenging blues and greens.

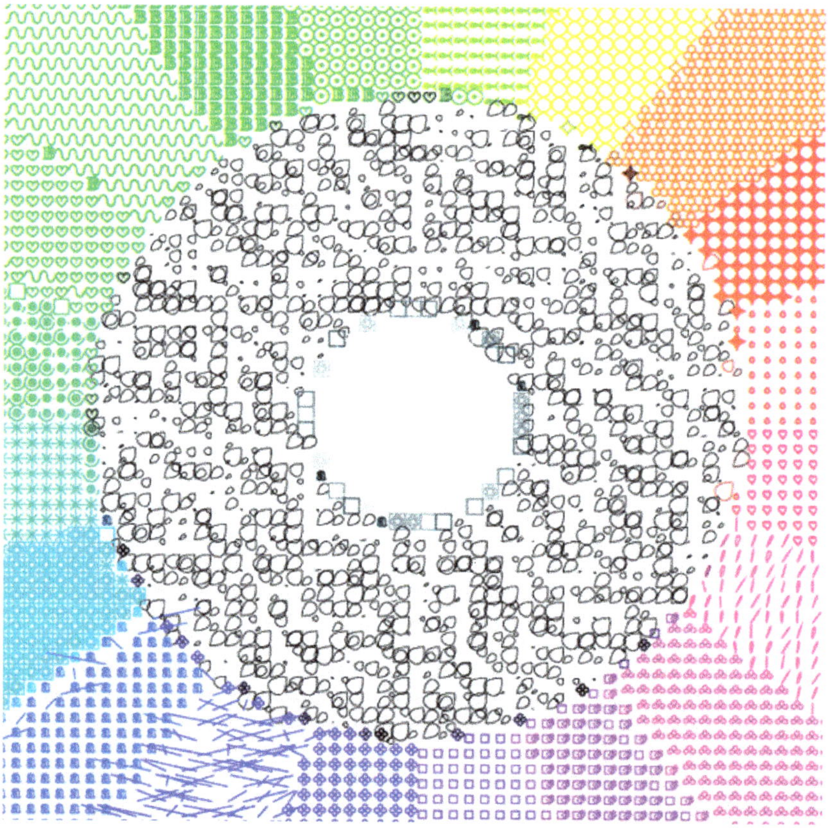

Figure 8. Showing a color wheel with 21 different shapes (20 + black) replacing the original pixels with corrected intervals of hue values.

Figure 7 shows variations in individual hue intervals where the program did not use different shapes for different intervals, but used the same shape to represent several adjacent intervals. After correcting the tones, the result shown in Figure 8 was obtained so that all 20 tones and the black color are displayed. The Postscript code of Figure 8 can be found in the supplementary material under the name Code S2. Chart 2 shows the deviations of the values of each hue interval from the values obtained by calculation. The differences in degrees between the initial and final angles within which a shape or hue value is displayed for both cases are shown. The correct distribution of the difference values of 18 degrees is shown in blue, and the visibly fluctuating difference is shown in red.

Chart 3 not only shows the difference between the calculated intervals and those after correction, but also the possibility to visualize parts of the spectrum. The difference with the color wheel example (Figure 8) is that the distribution of colors and shapes in the example starts at 90° (3 of the clock) and moves counterclockwise, while in Graph 3, it starts at 0° (12 of the clock) and moves clockwise.

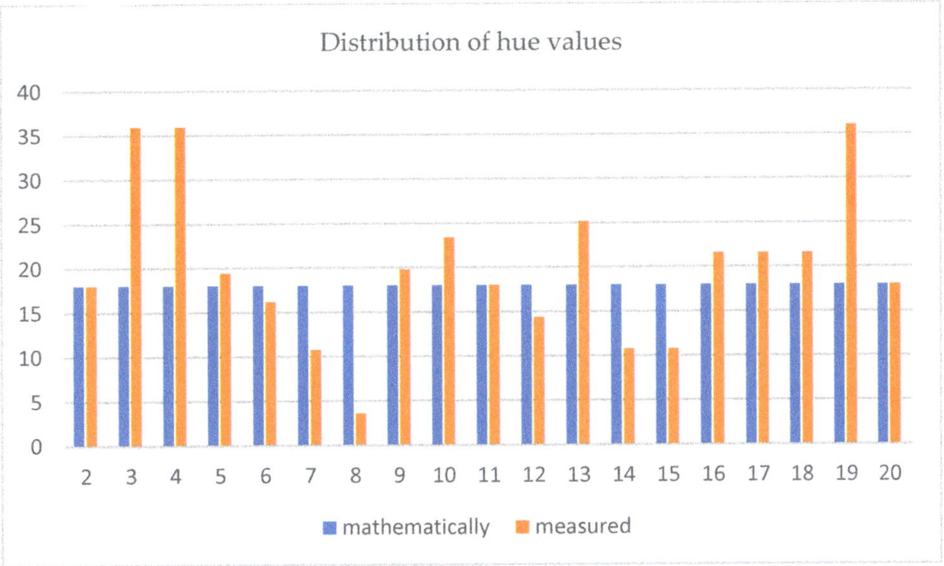

Chart 2. The comparison of the distribution of hue values obtained mathematically by dividing the circle into 20 equal parts (delta) and hue intervals for correctly displayed shape distributions. Table 2 shows the values obtained mathematically at the beginning, with intervals of 18 degrees and the values for the correct representation of the shape by the individual segments.

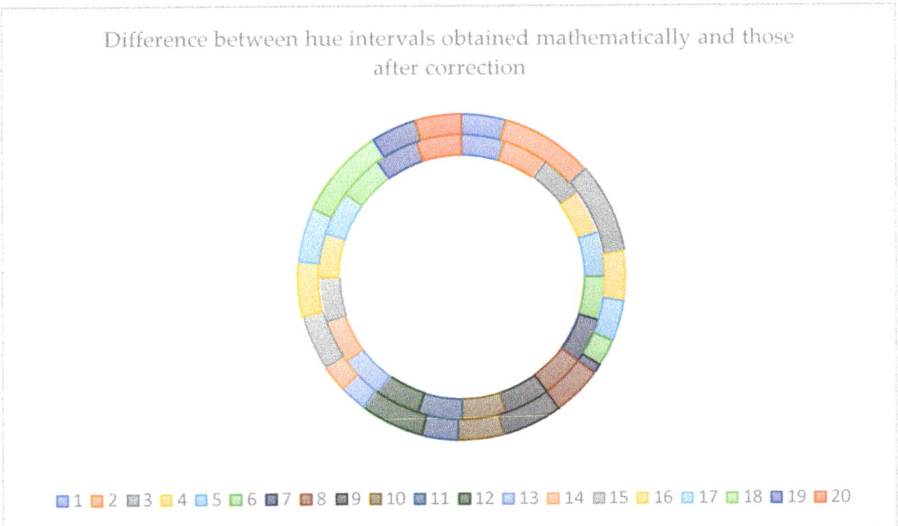

Chart 3. The difference between the mathematically determined hue intervals (inner circle data—intervals of 18 degrees) and those after correction showing the result of our method (outer circle data—different hue intervals). Chart 4 shows the difference between the initial and final values of the hue interval determined by the program and those measured in the case of a regular shape distribution on the color wheel. Since the differences between the initial and final values of the hue interval in the program solution are always 18, straight lines (blue and orange) are obtained, while oscillations (gray and yellow) can be seen in the corrected values.

Table 2. The values from Chart 1 obtained mathematically, with intervals of 18 degrees and the values for the correct representation of shapes by each segment of hue.

	H Mathematically (Degrees)	H Mathematically (Values 0–1)	Interval (Degrees)	H Displaying Correctly (Degrees)	H Displaying Correctly (Values 0–1)	Interval (Degrees)
1	0–18	0–0.05	18	0–18	0–0.05	18
2	18–36	0.05–0.1	18	18–36	0.05–0.01	36
3	36–54	0.1–0.15	18	34.2–70.2	0.095–0.195	36
4	54–72	0.15–0.2	18	70.56–90	0.196–0.25	19.44
5	72–90	0.2–0.25	18	90–106.2	0.25–0.295	16.2
6	90–108	0.25–0.3	18	104.4–115.2	0.29–0.32	10.8
7	108–126	0.3–0.35	18	115.2–118.8	0.32–0.33	3.6
8	126–144	0.35–0.4	18	117–136.8	0.325–0.38	19.8
9	144–162	0.4–0.45	18	138.6–162	0.385–0.45	23.4
10	162–180	0.45–0.5	18	162–180	0.45–0.5	18
11	180–198	0.5–0.55	18	180–194.4	0.5–0.54	14.4
12	198–216	0.55–0.6	18	198–223.2	0.55–0.62	25.2
13	216–234	0.6–0.65	18	223.2–234	0.62–0.65	10.8
14	234–252	0.65–0.7	18	234–244.8	0.65–0.68	10.8
15	252–270	0.7–0.75	18	244.8–266.4	0.68–0.74	21.6
16	270–288	0.75–0.8	18	266.4–288	0.74–0.8	21.6
17	288–306	0.8–0.85	18	284.4–306	0.79–0.85	21.6
18	306–324	0.85–0.9	18	298.8–334.8	0.83–0.93	36
19	324–342	0.9–0.95	18	324–342	0.9–0.95	18
20	342–360	0.95–1	18	342–360	0.95–1	18

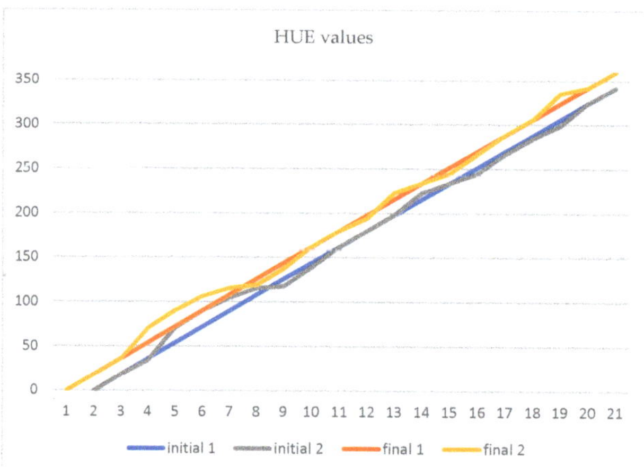

Chart 4. Shows the difference between the initial and final values of the hue interval determined mathematically by the program, and those measured in the case of a regular shape distribution on the color wheel.

Once the proper distribution of shapes is determined according to a particular hue, the search is extended to color images. The image of a colorful bouquet of flowers is used in the next example, as shown in Figure 9a. Figure 9b shows the result according to the distribution of shapes depending on the determined values of the hue for each pixel. Figure 10 shows the enlarged details of Figure 9.

(a) (b)

Figure 9. (**a**) Original image of colorful bouquet of flowers (Source: https://i.pinimg.com/originals/92/a5/3f/92a53f294d9309d526e2469765028a75.jpg, visited on 29 April 2023) and (**b**) the resulting image after the pixels were replaced by different shapes based on the detected hue values.

Figure 10. The enlarged details of Figure 9.

The next example used in our research is the image of Easter eggs (Figure 11). Figure 11a shows the original image, while Figure 11b shows the result after applying our method. Figure 12 shows the enlarged detail of the Figure 11 b).

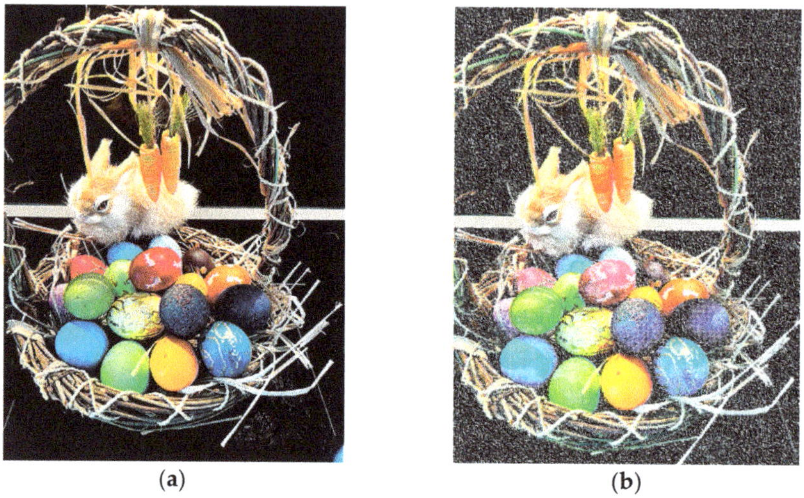

Figure 11. The image of Easter eggs. (**a**) Shows the original image and (**b**) shows the result after applying our method.

Figure 12. Shows the enlarged details of Figure 11.

In addition to real nature images, we also tested our method on pop art images of Marilyn Monroe. Figure 13 shows the artwork obtained by changing the shapes for the detected hue. In this way, numerous completely different results can be obtained. In this example, there is no right or wrong shape distribution. It is a matter of taste as to which looks better than the other.

Figure 13. Proposed method implemented on pop art image of Marilyn Monroe (Source: https://www.pxfuel.com/en/desktop-wallpaper-eejre, visited on 2 May 2023), creating numerous different solutions based on the change of shapes for the same hue.

The next example shows the difference in selecting shapes by detected hue on images created with different color settings (Figure 14). Figure 14a shows the distributions of the shapes depending on the detected hue using our method, while Figure 14b shows the deviations in shape distribution using color setting Uncoated Fogra 29. Additional figures can be found in the supplementary material under Figures S1–S4. The figures show the deviations of the shape distribution depending on the detected hue for different color settings as follows: Figure S1: Euroscale Coated V2; Figure S2: Japan web coated; Figure S3: Photoshop 5; and Figure S4: U.S. web coated V2. This example also shows that even using the original graphics for protective printing can lead to an incorrect result. Using an incorrect color setting can result in different shapes being displayed that represent pixels for a detected hue.

(a)

(b)

Figure 14. (**a**) Right distribution of the shapes obtained with our method. (**b**) The distribution of the shapes obtained using Uncoated Fogra 29 color setting—deviations are visible in the letters S, C, I, Y, P, A, S, S.

The last example was created to show the possibility of counterfeit protection. The example shows the original graphic and what happens to it after printing and rescanning. The graphic would be very difficult to reconstruct using vector graphics software because some shapes are created using random numbers, i.e., they are built and distributed randomly. The shadow of the first red letter S, which passes over the letter P, has lost the structure of the shape. The letters 'P' and 'A' show too much light detail from the shadow. The yellow letter 'S' has practically lost its shadow. The colors are completely different, especially visible in the letters 'C', 'U', 'P', and 'A'. This experiment was performed with the Canon ImagePress C165. The use of different shapes, algorithms known only to the authors, and the correct distribution of shapes according to the detected hue make our proposed method a good way to protect graphics from forgery. Figure 15a shows the original security graphic and Figure 15b shows the result after printing and rescanning the graphic.

(a) (b)

Figure 15. (**a**) Shows the original security graphic and (**b**) shows the result after printing and rescanning the graphic.

Figure 16a,b show the enlarged details of security graphics from those displayed in Figure 15.

(a) (b)

Figure 16. Enlarged details of Figure 15; (**a**) original security graphics and (**b**) enlarged details of rescanned graphics.

4. Discussion and Conclusions

This work shows that by converting from CMYK to RGB and then to the HSB system, it is possible to manipulate pixels more easily and influence their replacement by different vector shapes depending on the hue. We managed to represent 20 different vector shapes by replacing 20 hue intervals and one additional interval for black. When converting from the CMYK system to the HSB system, deviations and anomalies were encountered. These anomalies are particularly pronounced for greens and blues, as shown in the paper. These hues are an area where research could be expanded. Several other conclusions follow from this research. It is possible to manage different hues and replace the pixels representing their values with different vector shapes. There are numerous graphic elements that can be used as a replacement for square pixels. Thus, it is possible to fill the image with different elements that change the shape of the pixels. This conclusion could be used for protection against counterfeiting, including in art and in the economic sense.

Pixel manipulation creates great value in creating security graphics for printed documents. Pixel size can also be controlled so that vector shapes can be reduced so that they are not visible to the human eye, but only with the aid of a magnifying device. When scanning and reprinting, the structures of the various vector shapes that replace the pixels would be completely lost. The appearance of the pixels displayed in this way is simply impossible to reproduce without the knowledge of all the algorithms used in the work. In addition to the individualized shapes to replace standard pixel shapes, algorithms to convert to and from different color systems also contribute, and there are few programs that allow the use of three-color systems in one document. Furthermore, even if the algorithm is known, additional measurements, analysis, and corrections are required at certain intervals to achieve the desired result.

There are several software solutions for manipulating an image or its parts. At the time of writing, we have not yet found one that can process so many hues simultaneously and in different ways. The original image can be rendered quite differently, either on an artistic basis or on a strictly programmable basis. Moreover, a multicolor graphic can be represented in innumerable ways by changing the parameters or the vector shape that represents a particular hue.

Supplementary Materials: The following supporting information can be downloaded at: https://www.mdpi.com/article/10.3390/jimaging9060106/s1, Figure S1: The deviations of the shape distribution depending on detected hue for Euroscale coated V2 color setting; Figure S2: The deviations of the shape distribution depending on detected hue for Japan web coated color setting; Figure S3: The deviations of the shape distribution depending on detected hue for Photoshop 5 color setting; Figure S4: The deviations of the shape distribution depending on detected hue for U.S. web coated V2 color setting; Code S1: Postscript code for Figure 6; Code S2: Postscript code for Figure 8.

Author Contributions: Conceptualization, T.K.I.; methodology, T.K.I., M.R. and N.S.L.; software, T.K.I., M.R. and N.S.L.; validation, M.R. and T.K.I.; formal analysis, T.K.I. and D.B.; resources, N.S.L. and D.B.; data curation, M.R. and T.K.I.; writing—original draft preparation, T.K.I.; writing—review and editing, N.S.L. and D.B.; visualization, T.K.I. and D.B.; supervision, T.K.I. All authors have read and agreed to the published version of the manuscript.

Funding: This research received no external funding.

Institutional Review Board Statement: Not applicable.

Informed Consent Statement: Not applicable.

Data Availability Statement: Not applicable.

Conflicts of Interest: The authors declare no conflict of interest.

References

1. Ostromoukhov, V.; Hersch, R.D. Artistic Screening. In Proceedings of the SIGGRAPH'95: 22nd Annual Conference on Computer Graphics and Interactive Techniques, Los Angeles, CA, USA, 6–11 August 1995; pp. 219–228.
2. Rudaz, N.; Hersch, R.D.; Ostromoukhov, V. An interface for the interactive design of artistic screens. In *Electronic Publishing, Artistic Imaging and Digital Typography*; Lecture Notes in Computer Science; Springer: Berlin/Heidelberg, Germany, 1998; Volume 1375, pp. 1–10.
3. Ostromoukhov, V.; Rudaz, N.; Amidror, I.; Emmel, P.; Hersch, R.D. Anti-Counterfeiting Feature of Artistic Screening. In *Holographic and Diffractive Techniques*; SPIE: Bellingham, WA, USA, 1996; Volume 2951, pp. 126–133.
4. Ostromoukhov, V. Mathematical Tools for Computer-Generated Ornamental Patterns. In *Electronic Publishing, Artistic Imaging and Digital Typography*; Lecture Notes in Computer Science; Springer: Berlin/Heidelberg, Germany, 1998; Volume 1375, pp. 193–223.
5. Sugathan, S.; Scaria, R.; James, A.P. Adaptive Digital Scan Variable Pixels. In Proceedings of the 2015 International Conference on Advances in Computing, Communications and Informatics (ICACCI), Kochi, India, 10–13 August 2015.
6. Sugathan, S.; James, A.P. Irregular pixel imaging. In Proceedings of the 2014 International Conference on Advances in Computing, Communications and Informatics (ICACCI), Delhi, India, 24–27 September 2014; pp. 2459–2463.
7. Pap, K.; Žiljak, I.; Žiljak Vujić, J. *Design of Digital Screening*; FS Ltd.: Zagreb, Croatia, 2008.
8. Koren, T.; Žiljak, V.; Rudolf, M.; Stanić Loknar, N.; Bernašek, A. Mathematical Models of the Sinusoidal Screen Family. *Acta Graph. J. Print. Sci. Graph. Commun.* **2017**, *22*, 11–20.

9. Pap, K.; Žiljak Vujić, J.; Ziljak, I.; Agić, D. Screen Element Shape 'R73' Mutation. In *DAAAM International Scientific Book*; DAAAM International: Vienna, Austria, 2009; pp. 763–770.
10. Ostromoukhov, V.; Hersch, R.D. Multi-Color and Artistic Dithering. In Proceedings of the SIGGRAPH 99: 26th Annual Conference on Computer Graphics and Interactive Techniques, Los Angeles, CA, USA, 8–13 August 1999; pp. 425–432.
11. Kopf, J.; Lischinski, D. Depixelizing pixel art. *ACM Trans. Graph.* **2011**, *30*, 1–8. [CrossRef]
12. Kabbai, L.; Sghaier, A.; Douik, A.; Machhout, M. FPGA implementation of filtered image using 2D Gaussian filter. *Int. J. Adv. Comput. Sci. Appl.* **2016**, *7*, 514–520. [CrossRef]
13. Teutsch, M.; Trantelle, P.; Beyerer, J. Adaptive real-time image smoothing using local binary patterns and Gaussian filters. In Proceedings of the 2013 IEEE International Conference on Image Processing, Melbourne, VIC, Australia, 15–18 September 2013; pp. 1120–1124.
14. Yang, C.; Liu, C.; Shen, C. Guided Gaussian range kernel filtering based on similarity-aware window. *J. Electron. Imaging* **2022**, *31*, 043022. [CrossRef]
15. Wei, Z.; Yan, Q.; Lu, X.; Zheng, Y.; Sun, S.; Lin, J. Compression Reconstruction Network with Coordinated Self-Attention and Adaptive Gaussian Filtering Module. *Mathematics* **2023**, *11*, 847. [CrossRef]
16. Aurich, V.; Weule, J. Non-Linear Gaussian Filters Performing Edge Preserving Diffusion. In *Mustererkennung 1995*; Sagerer, G., Posch, S., Kummert, F., Eds.; Informatik Aktuell; Springer: Berlin/Heidelberg, Germany, 1995.
17. Smith, S.M.; Brady, J.M. SUSAN—A New Approach to Low Level Image Processing. *Int. J. Comput. Vis.* **1997**, *23*, 45–78. [CrossRef]
18. Tomasi, C.; Manduchi, R. Bilateral filtering for gray and color images. In Proceedings of the Sixth International Conference on Computer Vision (IEEE Cat. No.98CH36271), Bombay, India, 7 January 1998; pp. 839–846.
19. Cheng, S.W.; Lin, Y.T.; Peng, Y.T. A Fast Two-Stage Bilateral Filter Using Constant Time *O*(1) Histogram Generation. *Sensors* **2022**, *22*, 926. [CrossRef] [PubMed]
20. Petschnigg, G.; Agrawala, M.; Hoppe, H.; Szeliski, R.; Cohen, M.; Toyama, K. *Digital Photography with Flash and No-Flash Image Pairs*; Association for Computing Machinery: New York, NY, USA, 2004; Volume 23, pp. 664–672.
21. Eisemann, E.; Durand, F. *Flash Photography Enhancement via Intrinsic Relighting*; Association for Computing Machinery: New York, NY, USA, 2004; Volume 23, pp. 673–678.
22. Choudhury, P.; Tumblin, J. *The Trilateral Filter for High Contrast Images and Meshes*; Association for Computing Machinery: New York, NY, USA, 2005; p. 5–es.
23. Ji, G.; Wang, Z.; Zhou, L.; Xia, Y.; Zhong, S.; Gong, S. SAR Image Colorization Using Multidomain Cycle-Consistency Generative Adversarial Network. *IEEE Geosci. Remote Sens. Lett.* **2021**, *18*, 296–300. [CrossRef]
24. Koukiou, G. Perceptually Optimal Color Representation of Fully Polarimetric SAR Imagery. *J. Imaging* **2022**, *8*, 67. [CrossRef] [PubMed]
25. Inoue, K.; Jiang, M.; Hara, K. Hue-Preserving Saturation Improvement in RGB Color Cube. *J. Imaging* **2021**, *7*, 150. [CrossRef] [PubMed]
26. Guo, G.; Han, T.; Wu, B.; Fu, J.; Xia, Z. A hue preservation lossless contrast enhancement method with RDH for color images. *Digit. Signal Process.* **2023**, *136*, 103965. [CrossRef]
27. Moussa, M.I.; Abd El-Latif, E.I.; Majid, N. Enhancing the Security of Digital Image Encryption using Diagonalize Multidimensional Nonlinear Chaotic System. *Int. J. Adv. Comput. Sci. Appl. (IJACSA)* **2022**, *13*, 524–533. [CrossRef]
28. Razzaq, M.A.; Shaikh, R.A.; Baig, M.A.; Memon, A.A. Digital Image Security: Fusion of Encryption, Steganography and Watermarking. *Int. J. Adv. Comput. Sci. Appl. (IJACSA)* **2017**, *8*, 224–228.
29. Zhang, S.; Liu, L. A novel image encryption algorithm based on SPWLCM and DNA coding. *Math. Comput. Simul.* **2021**, *190*, 723–744. [CrossRef]
30. Dronyuk, I.; Kalinchuk, V.; Greguš, M. Protection of images based on fractal geometry. *Procedia Comput. Sci.* **2019**, *160*, 515–520. [CrossRef]
31. Hussein, Q.M.; Abdullah, A.S.; Mohammed, N.Q. The efficiency of Color Models layers at Color Images as Cover in text hiding. *Tikrit J. Pure Sci.* **2016**, *21*, 130–139. [CrossRef]
32. Shevell, S.K. *The Science of Color*, 2nd ed.; Elsevier: Oxford, UK, 2003; pp. 192–197.
33. Saravanan, G.; Yamuna, G.; Nandhini, S. Real time implementation of RGB to HSV/HSI/HSL and its reverse color space models. In Proceedings of the 2016 International Conference on Communication and Signal Processing (ICCSP), Melmaruvathur, India, 6–8 April 2016; pp. 462–466.
34. Huang, Z.K.; Liu, D.H. Segmentation of Color Image Using EM algorithm in HSV Color Space. In Proceedings of the 2007 International Conference on Information Acquisition, Seogwipo, Republic of Korea, 8–11 July 2007; pp. 316–319.
35. Converting RGB to HSV. Available online: https://mattlockyer.github.io/iat455/documents/rgb-hsv.pdf (accessed on 1 October 2022).
36. Ford, A.; Roberts, A. Colour Space Conversions. 1998, pp. 11–17. Available online: https://poynton.ca/PDFs/coloureq.pdf (accessed on 22 December 2022).
37. Gomes, J.; Velho, L.; Costa Sousa, M. *Computer Graphics: Theory and Practice*, 1st ed.; Peters, A.K., Ed.; CRC Press: New York, NY, USA, 2012; pp. 108–136. [CrossRef]
38. Žiljak, V.; Pap, K. *Postscript Programiranje*; FS Ltd.: Zagreb, Croatia, 1999.

39. Reid, G.C. *Thinking in PostScript®*; Addison-Wesley Publishing Company: Boston, MA, USA, 1990.
40. Michael, L. *Scott Programming Language Pragmatics*, 2nd ed.; Morgan Kaufmann Publishers: San Francisco, CA, USA, 2006; pp. 679–767.
41. *Adobe Systems Incorporated PostScript® LANGUAGE REFERENCE*, 3rd ed.; Addison-Wesley Publishing Company: Boston, MA, USA, 1999; Retrieved 18 June 2004; Available online: https://www.adobe.com/jp/print/postscript/pdfs/PLRM.pdf (accessed on 2 December 2022).

Journal of
Imaging

MDPI

Article

Comparing Different Algorithms for the Pseudo-Coloring of Myocardial Perfusion Single-Photon Emission Computed Tomography Images

Abdurrahim Rahimian [1], Mahnaz Etehadtavakol [1], Masoud Moslehi [1] and Eddie Y. K. Ng [2,*]

1 Department of Medical Physics, School of Medicine, Isfahan University of Medical Sciences, Isfahan 81745-33871, Iran
2 School of Mechanical and Aerospace Engineering, College of Engineering, Nanyang Technological University, 50 Nanyang Avenue, Singapore 639798, Singapore
* Correspondence: mykng@ntu.edu.sg

Abstract: Single-photon emission computed tomography (SPECT) images can significantly help physicians in diagnosing patients with coronary artery or suspected coronary artery diseases. However, these images are grayscale with qualities that are not readily visible. The objective of this study was to evaluate the effectiveness of different pseudo-coloring algorithms of myocardial perfusion SPECT images. Data were collected using a Siemens Symbia T2 dual-head SPECT/computed tomography (CT) scanner. After pseudo-coloring, the images were assessed both qualitatively and quantitatively. The qualities of different pseudo-color images were examined by three experts, while the images were evaluated quantitatively by obtaining indices such as mean squared error (MSE), peak signal-to-noise ratio (PSNR), normalized color difference (NCD), and structure similarity index metric (SSIM). The qualitative evaluation demonstrated that the warm color map (WCM), followed by the jet color map, outperformed the remaining algorithms in terms of revealing the non-visible qualities of the images. Furthermore, the quantitative evaluation results demonstrated that the WCM had the highest PSNR and SSIM but the lowest MSE. Overall, the WCM could outperform the other color maps both qualitatively and quantitatively. The novelty of this study includes comparing different pseudo-coloring methods to improve the quality of myocardial perfusion SPECT images and utilizing our collected datasets.

Keywords: pseudo-coloring; quality assessment; quantitative indicators; SPECT image

1. Introduction

Some applications of single-photon emission computed tomography (SPECT) include tumor growth estimation, genetic therapies, brain function diagnosis, and cardiovascular and coronary artery disease [1,2]. Radionuclide myocardial perfusion imaging (MPI) is a common non-invasive procedure in nuclear medicine. The SPECT-MPI method can provide valuable information about coronary perfusion and myocardial function in patients with or suspected of having coronary artery diseases [3]. In nuclear imaging, a gamma camera receives gamma rays emitted by radiopharmaceuticals. The signal then passes through internal components, including scintillation crystals, photomultiplier tubes, positioning circuits, and pulse-height analyzers. Eventually, image reconstruction algorithms are used to determine the distribution of radionuclide species. As a result of the attenuation and scattering of gamma rays, SPECT images are generally noisy [4]. Furthermore, these images are grayscale, and grayscale images have relatively low contrast between adjacent gray levels, as well as relatively few just noticeable differences (60–90 JNDs) [5]. Consequently, some of these images' qualities are not readily visible. Pseudo-coloring images can help reveal those elements and help physicians to observe the details more clearly. Pseudo-color image processing is a method in which colors are assigned to a grayscale image based on a particular approach. The pseudo-coloring algorithm should be designed in such a way as to facilitate the accurate identification of individual data elements. In other words, the target can be distinguished from the non-target objects. In addition, the number of colors should be optimal for visual judgment [6]. Various fields benefit from pseudo-color images, including medicine and industry [7,8], since they can enhance the ability of the human visual system to perceive color.

In a study, Levin et al. (2004) [9], suggested a coloring method based on the assumption that neighboring pixels in space-time with similar intensities should have similar colors. They used a quadratic cost function and obtained an optimization problem. In their method, in order to produce a fully colorized image, a user is required to manually margin the image with a few color scratches. Moreover, Ironi et al. (2005) [10] presented a method for a grayscale image to be colorized by transferring color from a segmented example image and using a robust supervised classification scheme. Their method requires less manual effort than previous user-assisted methods.

In a study conducted by Varga and Szirányi (2016) [11], a fully automatic method was presented to colorize a grayscale image. Based on a Convolutional Neural Network, they presented a feed-forward, two-stage architecture to predict the U and V color channels. They utilized the SUN database and other images. They realized that the Quaternion Structural Similarity (QSSIM) index was a good base for quantitative evaluation. Sharma (2017) [12] developed a false-coloring method for medical-image processing and declared that the images were clear for diagnosing ligaments, tissues, and bones at a glance. Likewise, Selvapriya and Raghu (2019) [13] demonstrated that the quality and presentation of the images were improved by a pseudo-coloring process. In this study, magnetic resonance images were pseudo-colored with different algorithms such as jet color (JCM), cool color, hot color, and copper color maps. They concluded that the JCM had better performance compared to the other color maps. Whitehead et al. (2021) [14] also examined the magnetic resonance images of 26 children with sensorineural hearing loss with an average age of 7.6 ± 3 years and 13 healthy children with an average age of 7.3 ± 4 years using pseudo-color post-processing. Pseudo-color image enhancement techniques were found to improve the detection of cochlear pathology and could have therapeutic implications.

However, a few studies have evaluated the pseudo-coloring of myocardial perfusion SPECT images. Therefore, the current study aimed to evaluate the effectiveness of different pseudo-coloring algorithms.

Subsequently, the materials and methods are explained in Section 2. Section 3 presents the results and discussion, and Section 4 presents the conclusion.

2. Materials and Methods

First, the myocardial perfusion SPECT gray images were collected in Chamran Hospital, Iran. Second, a Wiener filter with a kernel size of 5×5 was used to reduce the noise of the images. Third, the images were colored using pseudo-colorization algorithms, including warm color map (WCM), hot color map (HCM), sine color map (SCM), Zahedi-proposed color map (ZCM), and jet color map (JCM). Then, the quality of the pseudo-color images was evaluated qualitatively by three experts, and quantitatively by obtaining the mean squared error (MSE), peak signal-to-noise ratio (PSNR), normalized color difference (NCD), and structure similarity index metric (SSIM) indices. Moreover, statistical analysis was performed using a one-way analysis of variance (ANOVA) test. Finally, the obtained indices were compared, and the best pseudo-coloring algorithms were selected and introduced for our dataset. Figure 1 shows the steps of this study.

2.1. Image Preparation and Data Collection

Our dataset was collected according to the European Association of Nuclear Medicine procedural guidelines for radionuclide MPI with SPECT and SPECT/CT [15]. Figure 2 illustrates the process of patient inclusion and exclusion. As shown, 32 patients were considered, including 17 women and 15 men. Due to pregnancy, two women were excluded from our dataset. As a result, the myocardial perfusion SPECT images from 30 patients (15 men and 17 women) in the age range of 47–75 years were included in this study. It should be mentioned that the number of images per patient was 32. These images were provided in Shahid Chamran Hospital of Isfahan, Iran, using the Siemens Symbia T2 dual-head SPECT/CT scanner with a low-energy, high-resolution collimator. A standard energy window (20%) centered at 140 keV was adjusted, and a 64 × 64 matrix size was selected as well. Sixteen views were taken for any head, and the radius of the rotation of the gamma camera head was set at 27.5 cm. The intended time for each view was 20 s. The acquisition SPECT images were reconstructed using the filtered back projection.

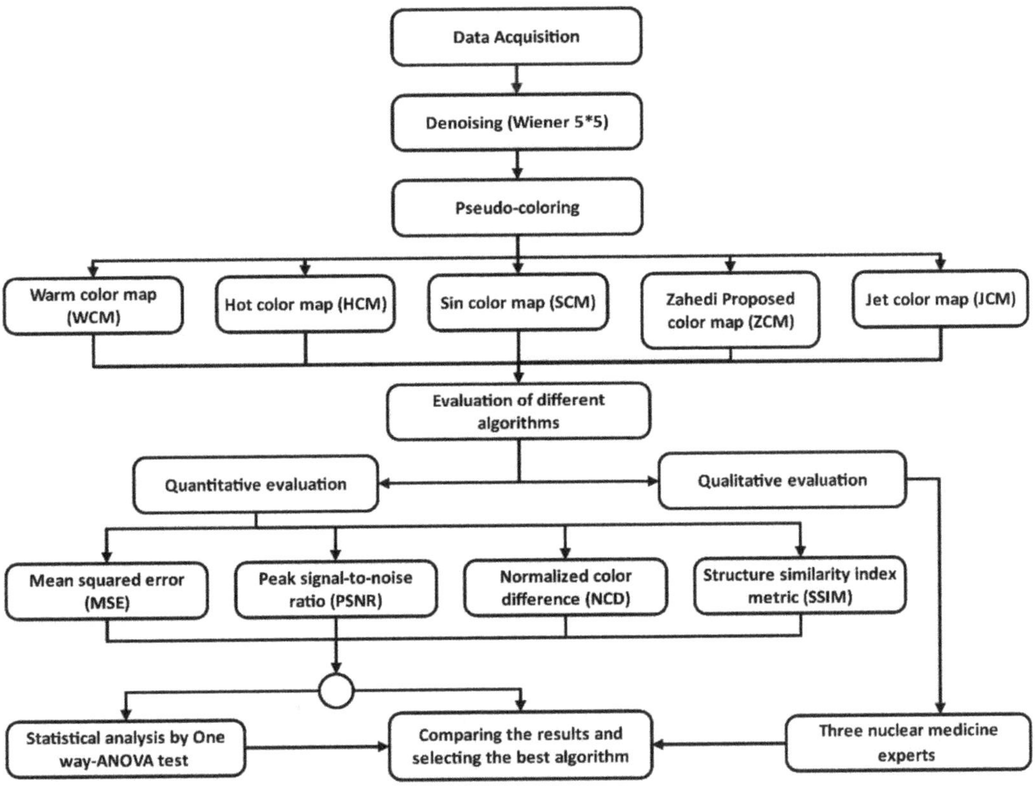

Figure 1. Steps of the study.

There were two phases in the imaging procedure, including rest and stress tests. In the rest test, based on the patient's weight, 15–20 mCi $^{99m}Tc - MIBI$ (99m Tc-methoxy isobutyl isonitrile) was intravenously injected into the patient, and imaging was repeated after 45 min. The administration of drugs such as dipyridamole or Exercise (treadmill) was used to increase the patient's heart rate, followed by the injection of 20–25 mCi $^{99m}Tc - MIBI$. Then, another image was taken approximately 15–45 min later. A flowchart of the patient inclusion and exclusion is depicted in Figure 2.

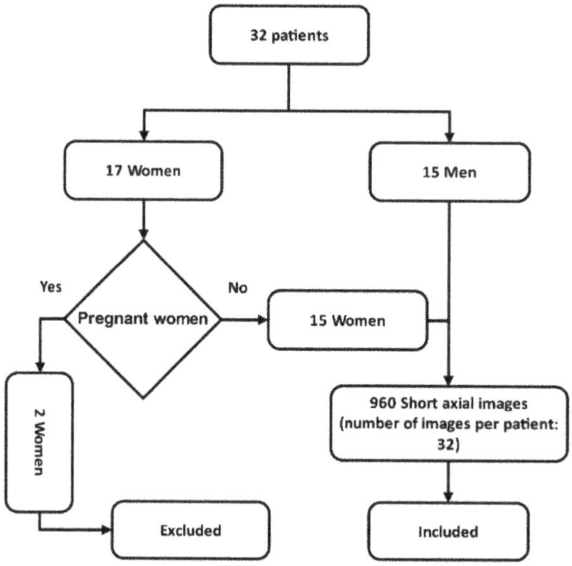

Figure 2. Flowchart of patient inclusion and exclusion.

2.2. *Preprocessing (Denoising)*

SPECT images are commonly noisy because gamma rays are attenuated and scattered before hitting the detector. These images are identified using low contrast and high noise levels. Therefore, images must be denoised before the pseudo-coloring process. In one study, Masoomi et al. [16], found that the Wiener filter was effective for denoising myocardial perfusion SPECT images. Therefore, this filter with kernel size 5 × 5 was applied in this study, which is defined as follows:

$$\mu = \frac{1}{xy} \sum_{x,y \in \eta} a(x, y) \tag{1}$$

$$\sigma^2 = \frac{1}{xy} \sum_{x,y \in \eta} a(x,y)^2 - \mu^2 \tag{2}$$

$$F_W(x,y) = \mu + \frac{\sigma^2 + \nu^2}{\sigma^2} \cdot (a(x,y) - \mu) \tag{3}$$

where μ and σ^2 represent the mean value of the pixel and the variance of the Gaussian noise in the image, respectively. Moreover, $x \times y$ and ν^2 denote the size of the neighborhood area in kernel size η and the value of the noise variance in the kernel size, respectively. The average of all local variances estimated for each kernel can be used if the noise variance is not given as input [17]. The second variance adjustment was applied in the present study.

2.3. *Pseudo-Coloring*

An RGB color image is represented as an M × N × 3 array of color pixels, where each color pixel corresponds to the three values of red (R), green (G), and blue (B) components of the image at a specific spatial location. Figure 3 shows the basic principle of the pseudo-coloring process by assigning a color to each gray pixel. Each gray pixel I (x, y) is converted into three R (x, y), G (x, y), and B (x, y) values through a specific function P [I (x, y)]. Next, R (x, y), G (x, y), and B (x, y) pixels are stacked, creating a color image RGB. Differently colored images can be obtained by changing the functions P [I (x, y)].

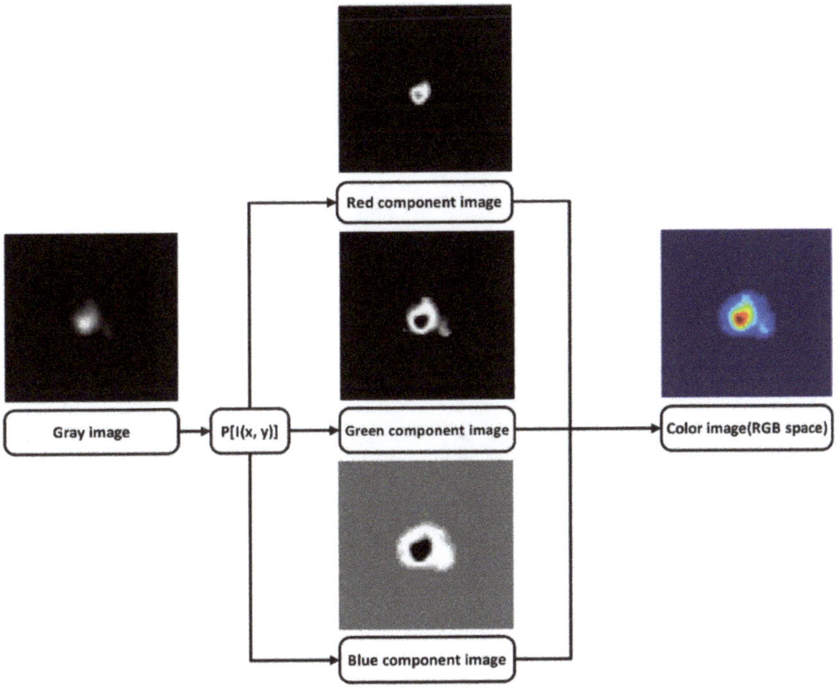

Figure 3. The basic principle of the pseudo-coloring process.

In this study, five different pseudo-coloring algorithms, including WCM, HCM, SCM, ZCM, and JCM, were employed. Their equations are presented below in full. It is noteworthy that in all these equations, the parameter "t" represents the intensity value of the gray image I (x, y) after denoising.

2.3.1. Warm Color Map (WCM)

In this color map, the distance between adjacent colors is understandably equal, while the color scale varies from dark blue, magenta, and orange to light yellow.

$$\begin{pmatrix} R(t) \\ G(t) \\ B(t) \end{pmatrix} = \left(\frac{1}{2\sqrt{3}}\right) \cdot \begin{pmatrix} 1+\sqrt{3} & 1-\sqrt{3} & 2 \\ 1-\sqrt{3} & 1+\sqrt{3} & 2 \\ -2 & -2 & 2 \end{pmatrix} \cdot \begin{pmatrix} r(t)\sin(\omega t+\varphi) \\ r(t)\cos(\omega t+\varphi) \\ z(t) \end{pmatrix} \quad (4)$$

$$z(t) = \sqrt{3}\,t \quad (5)$$

$$r(t) = \begin{cases} \sqrt{\frac{3}{2}}\,t & 0 \le t < \frac{1}{2} \\ \sqrt{\frac{3}{2}}\,(1-t) & others \end{cases} \quad (6)$$

2.3.2. Hot Color Map (HCM)

The most important advantage of HCM is that it clearly shows the areas with high t; therefore, the viewer is attracted to these areas. In this scale, the color slowly changes from black through red, orange, and yellow to white, all of which are classified into one color group.

$$R(t) = \begin{cases} 2.7027\,t & t < 0.37 \\ 1 & t \ge 0.37 \end{cases} \quad (7)$$

$$G(t) = \begin{cases} 0 & t < 0.37 \\ 2.7027\, t - 1 & 0.37 \leq t \leq 0.74 \\ 1 & t > 0.74 \end{cases} \quad (8)$$

$$B(t) = \begin{cases} 0 & t < 0.74 \\ 3.8461\, t - 2.8461 & t > 0.74 \end{cases} \quad (9)$$

2.3.3. Sine Color Map (SCM)

This color map depicts targets with orange and red colors and non-targets as the background with a blue color.

$$\begin{aligned} R(t) &= -0.5\cos(\pi t) + 0.5 \\ G(t) &= \sin(\pi t) \\ B(t) &= 0.5\cos(\pi t) + 0.5 \end{aligned} \quad (10)$$

2.3.4. Zahedi-Proposed Color Map (ZCM)

This color map changes from blue, shades of turquoise, green, yellow, orange, and red to white.

$$R(t) = \begin{cases} 0 & 0 \leq t \leq \frac{11}{20} \\ 4t - \frac{11}{5} & \frac{11}{20} < t < \frac{4}{5} \\ 1 & \frac{4}{5} \leq t \leq 1 \end{cases} \quad (11)$$

$$G(t) = \begin{cases} 5t & 0 \leq t \leq \frac{1}{5} \\ -\frac{20}{9}t + \frac{13}{9} & \frac{1}{5} < t < \frac{7}{20} \\ \frac{20}{27}t + \frac{11}{27} & \frac{7}{20} \leq t \leq \frac{4}{5} \\ -\frac{15}{2}t + 7 & \frac{4}{5} < t < \frac{14}{15} \\ 60t - 56 & \frac{14}{15} \leq t < \frac{19}{20} \\ 1 & \frac{19}{20} \leq t \leq 1 \end{cases} \quad (12)$$

$$B(t) = \begin{cases} 1 & 0 \leq t \leq \frac{1}{5} \\ -4t + \frac{9}{5} & \frac{1}{5} < t < \frac{2}{5} \\ \frac{1}{5} & \frac{2}{5} \leq t \leq \frac{14}{15} \\ 60t - 56 & \frac{14}{15} < t < \frac{19}{20} \\ 1 & \frac{19}{20} \leq t \leq 1 \end{cases} \quad (13)$$

2.3.5. Jet Color Map (JCM)

This color scale bar starts from blue and ends with turquoise, yellow, orange, and then red. The JCM can be considered when it is necessary to use different colors for an image.

$$f(x) = \begin{cases} 0 & x < 0 \\ x & 0 \leq x \leq 1 \\ 1 & x > 1 \end{cases} \quad (14)$$

$$R(t) = f(1.5 - |2\,t - 1|) \qquad -1 \leq t \leq 1 \quad (15)$$

$$G(t) = f(1.5 - |2\,t|) \qquad -1 \leq t \leq 1 \quad (16)$$

$$B(t) = f(1.5 - |2\,t + 1|) \qquad -1 \leq t \leq 1 \quad (17)$$

It is worth noting that the parameter "t" is between -1 and 1 in the above equations. To employ these equations, the intensity of gray images must be converted from [0 to 255] to [-1 to 1] accordingly. The following formula demonstrates the process in detail.

$$I_{new} = (I - Min)\frac{newMax - newMin}{Max - Min} + newMin \rightarrow I_{new} = (I - 0)\frac{1 - (-1)}{255 - 0} - 1 = \frac{2I}{255} - 1 \quad (18)$$

where I, Max, and Min are the intensity, maximum intensity, and minimum intensity of the original image. In addition, I_{new}, $newMax$, and $newMin$ are the intensity, maximum intensity, and minimum intensity of the new image, respectively.

2.4. Quantitative Indicator Calculations

Digital images are subject to a wide variety of distortions during acquisition, processing, compression, storage, transmission, and reproduction, any of which may result in a degradation of visual quality. There are many visual quality criteria to measure the quality of these images. However, the four indicators used in this study are explained in the following section.

2.4.1. Mean Squared Error (MSE)

MSE measures the difference between two images in a color space. As a consequence, it is useless to calculate MSE between grayscale and color images. For this reason, each gray image was converted to an RGB image with equal values of R, G, and B. Then, the MSE was computed for the RGB and pseudo-colored images. In general, an image with a high MSE exhibits more visible distortions than an image with a low MSE. The MSE is defined as follows:

$$MSE = \frac{\sum_{i=1}^{M} \sum_{j=1}^{N} (G_{ij} - X_{ij})^2}{3\,MN} \quad (19)$$

G and X represent the filtered and unfiltered images, respectively. Additionally, M and N indicate the size of the image matrix.

2.4.2. Peak Signal-to-Noise Ratio (PSNR)

To determine the display quality, PSNR is calculated as the ratio of the maximum possible value of the signal to the power of noise distortion. The PSNR is usually expressed using a logarithmic decibel scale due to the wide dynamic range of many signals. The PSNR equation is as follows [18]:

$$PSNR = 10 \log_{10}\left(\frac{{I_{max}}^2}{MSE(G, X)}\right) \quad (20)$$

2.4.3. Normalized Color Difference (NCD)

Several researchers have employed NCD as an objective measure [19]. In a particular color space (typically a laboratory color space), NCD is a measure of the distance between colors. The lower the NCD, the better the image quality. The NCD index is determined using the following formula:

$$NCD = \frac{\sum_{i=1}^{M} \sum_{j=1}^{N} \sqrt{\sum_{q \in [L,a,b]} [G_q(i,j) - Cl_q(i,j)]^2}}{\sum_{i=1}^{M} \sum_{j=1}^{N} \sqrt{\sum_{q \in [L,a,b]} Cl_q(i,j)^2}} \quad (21)$$

where G_q and Cl_q are gray and color images with q channel (in laboratory space), respectively.

2.4.4. Structure Similarity Index Metric (SSIM)

SSIM index is another objective measure that is proposed in this study. It is based on how the human visual system works [20] and has been presented for analyzing the structure of an image after the coloring process. For the color image, SSIM can be separately calculated for each color channel, and then their average is computed accordingly. Different windows can be used in an image to calculate the SSIM index. The measure between two windows x and y of common size N × N is:

$$SSIM = \frac{(2\mu_x\mu_y + c_1)(2\sigma_{xy} + c_2)}{({\mu_x}^2 + {\mu_y}^2 + c_1)({\sigma_x}^2 + {\sigma_y}^2 + c_2)} \quad (22)$$

where μ_x and μ_y are the average x and y, respectively. Further, ${\sigma_x}^2$ and ${\sigma_y}^2$ represent the variance of x and y, respectively, and σ_{xy} is the covariance of x and y.

2.5. Statistical Analysis

PSNR, SNR, and CNR were analyzed using IBM SPSS software, version 26. It is worth noting that the one way-ANOVA test was applied in this study with a significance level of <0.05.

2.6. Qualitative Assessment

A qualitative assessment was performed with trained human users. In this study, the quality of each pseudo-color image was visually evaluated by three nuclear medicine experts with many years of experience. It is noteworthy that all three experts evaluated the images under the same conditions.

3. Results

A myocardial perfusion SPECT image of a 61-year-old male was implemented by WCM, HCM, SCM, ZCM, and JCM pseudo-coloring algorithms, and the visual results are depicted in Figure 4.

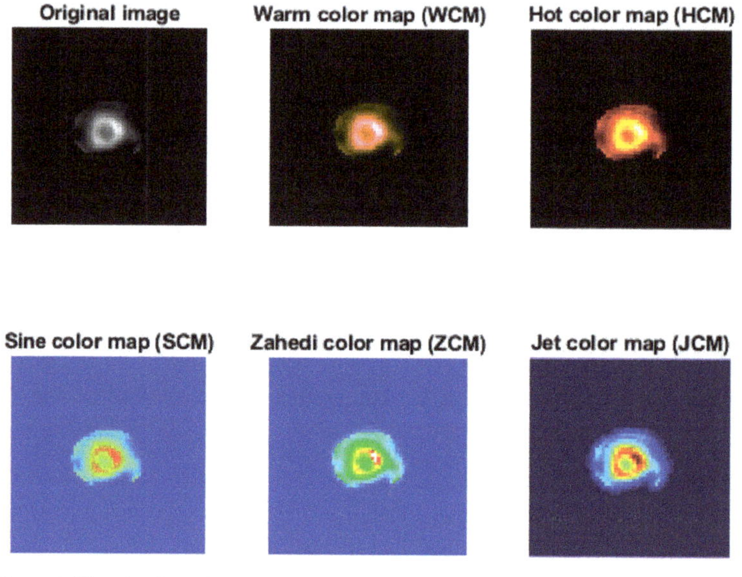

Figure 4. The visual results of WCM, HCM, SCM, ZCM, and JCM pseudo-coloring algorithms for a 61-year-old male. *Note*: WCM: Warm color map; HCM: Hot color map; SCM: Sine color map; ZCM: Zahedi-proposed color map; JCM: Jet color map.

In addition, for this case, MSE, PSNR, NCD, and SSIM indices were obtained for different pseudo-coloring algorithms and are shown in Table 1.

In addition, the graphs of the mean of MSE, PSNR, NCD, and SSIM for all cases are illustrated in Figure 5 as well as the related box plots in Figure 6. These indices were obtained using different pseudo-coloring algorithms such as WCM, HCM, SCM, ZCM, and JCM. Additionally, the related results are provided in Table 2.

Table 1. Obtained MSE, PSNR, NCD, and SSIM indices by applying different pseudo-coloring algorithms for the myocardial perfusion SPECT image of a 61-year-old male. The up arrow (↑) indicates that the larger the average value, the better the model performance. The down arrow (↓) has the opposite meaning.

Pseudo-Coloring/Index	MSE (↓)	PSNR (dB) (↑)	NCD (↓)	SSIM (↑)
Warm color map (WCM)	**0.0027**	**26.3055**	0.1584	**0.9577**
Hot color map (HCM)	0.0075	21.9380	0.3284	0.9147
Sine color map (SCM)	0.3234	4.9026	**0.0732**	0.6139
Zahedi-proposed color map (ZCM)	0.3256	4.8732	0.2232	0.5906
Jet color map (JCM)	0.0938	10.2779	0.1914	0.6115

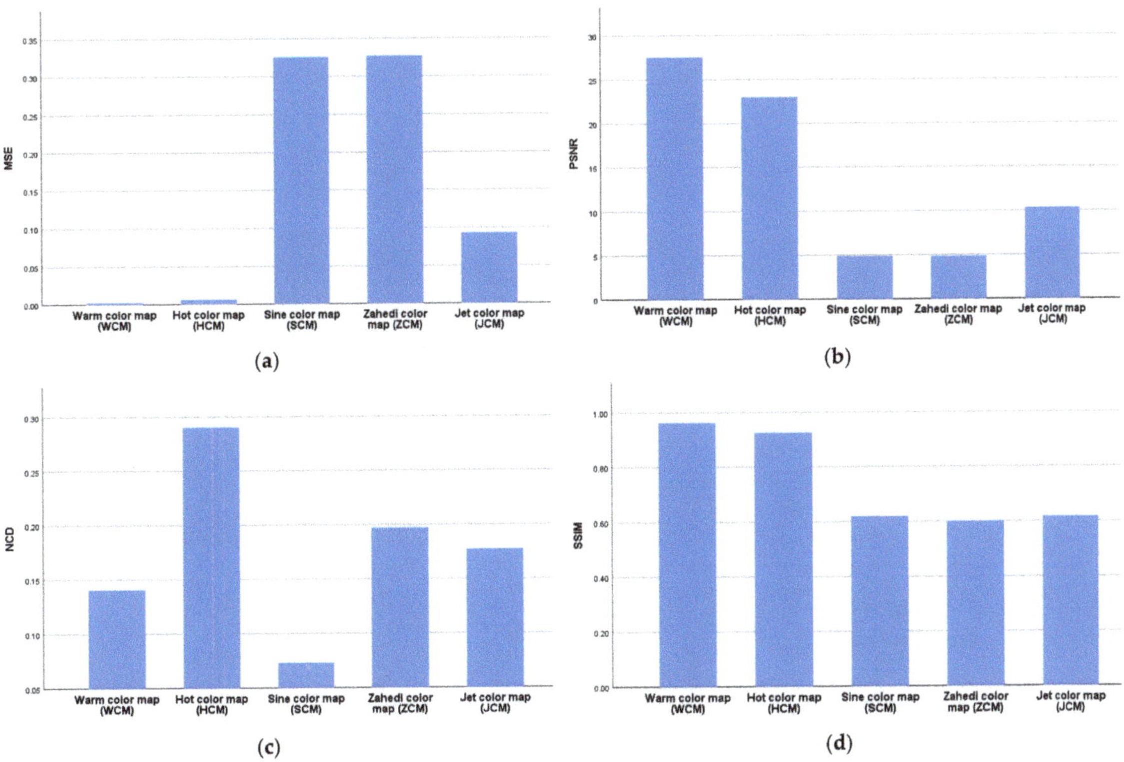

Figure 5. The graphs of the mean of (**a**) MSE, (**b**) PSNR, (**c**) NCD, and (**d**) SSIM. *Note.* MSE: Mean squared error; PSNR: Peak signal-to-noise ratio; NCD: Normalized color difference; SSIM: Structure similarity index metric.

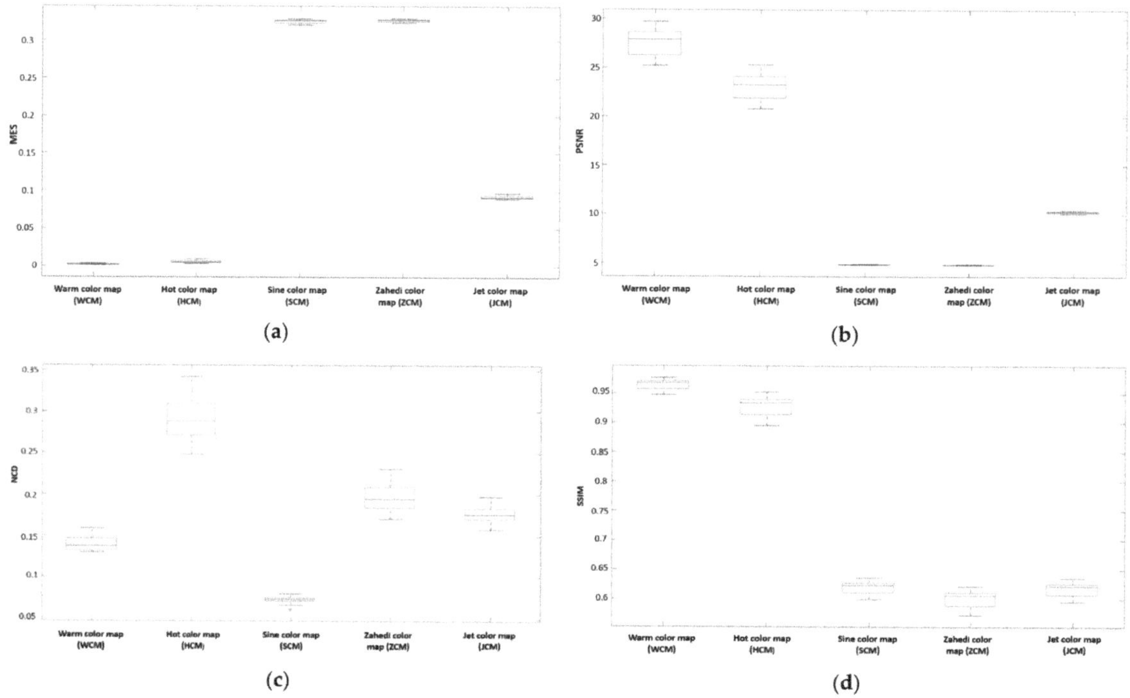

Figure 6. The box plots of (**a**) MSE, (**b**) PSNR, (**c**) NCD, and (**d**) SSIM. *Note.* MSE: Mean squared error; PSNR: Peak signal-to-noise ratio; NCD: Normalized color difference; SSIM: Structure similarity index metric.

Table 2. Average (± standard deviation (SD)) indices of mean squared error (MSE), peak signal-to-noise (PSNR), normalized color difference (NCD), and structure similarity index metric (SSIM) for different applied pseudo-coloring algorithms in this study. The up arrow (↑) indicates that the larger the average value, the better the model performance. The down arrow (↓) has the opposite meaning.

Pseudo-Coloring/Index	MSE ± SD (↓)	PSNR (dB) ± SD (↑)	NCD ± SD (↓)	SSIM ± SD (↑)
Warm color map (WCM)	**0.0021 ± 0.0006**	**27.5484 ± 1.3041**	0.1406 ± 0.0089	**0.9643 ± 0.0086**
Hot color map (HCM)	0.0060 ± 0.0017	22.9967 ± 1.2585	0.2903 ± 0.0232	0.9268 ± 0.0170
Sine color map (SCM)	0.3254 ± 0.0023	4.8754 ± 0.0313	**0.0730 ± 0.0039**	0.6196 ± 0.0102
Zahedi-proposed color map (ZCM)	0.3269 ± 0.0015	4.8551 ± 0.0208	0.1971 ± 0.0154	0.6001 ± 0.0142
Jet color map (JCM)	0.0931 ± 0.0022	10.3115 ± 0.1015	0.1774 ± 0.0092	0.6175 ± 0.0116

4. Discussion

To the best of our knowledge, this is the first study for pseudo-coloring of myocardial perfusion SPECT images. Results were obtained via two approaches: (1) by qualitative assessment and (2) by quantitative assessment. In the first approach, all three experts concluded that the WCM followed by the JCM algorithms revealed the non-visible qualities of the images better than the other algorithms. In the second approach, the WCM algorithm had the highest PSNR and SSIM values. However, it had the lowest MSE values. Moreover, the SCM algorithm obtained the lowest NCD values.

As shown in Figure 5a, WCM and HCM outperformed the remaining algorithms by each achieving the lowest mean of MSE. Figure 5b also shows that WCM achieved the largest mean of PSNR compared to the other algorithms. However, based on the results shown in Figure 5c, SCM and WCM could outperform the remaining algorithms by both obtaining the lowest mean of NCD. As illustrated in Figure 5d, the largest mean of SSIM was achieved by WCM.

Based on Table 1, the WCM algorithm had the highest PSNR and SSIM values of 27.5484 ± 1.3041 (dB) and 0.9643 ± 0.0086, respectively, while it had the lowest MSE value of 0.0021 ± 0.0006. Moreover, the SCM algorithm obtained the lowest NCD value of 0.0730 ± 0.0039.

For different pseudo-coloring algorithms used in this study, the difference between MSE, PSNR, NCD, and SSIM indices was statistically significant ($p < 0.05$). However, in terms of the PSNR index, the difference between SCM and ZCM algorithms was not significantly substantial ($p = 0.932$); similarly, the difference between SCM and JCM algorithms in the SSIM index was not meaningful ($p = 0.518$). As we can see from Figure 6c, the boxplot of NCD, the only outlier data with a value of 0.061 were related to SCM.

According to Table 2, the SCM, ZCM, and JCM algorithms had high MSE values but low PSNR and SSIM values, implying that they underperformed in this regard. However, the WCM and HCM algorithms outperformed the rest by both achieving lower MSE, higher PSNR values, and SSIM values close to 1. As a result, the comparison of the results of MSE, PSNR, and SSIM indices for different algorithms used in this study revealed that the WCM algorithm was chosen quantitatively. Additionally, the WCM algorithm was also qualitatively selected by the three experts. NCD indicates the distance between colors in a specific color space; it was the best output achieved by the SCM algorithm compared to the other color-map algorithms. However, the WCM algorithm had the second best NCD after the SCM algorithm.

As mentioned earlier, the WCM algorithm performs better in both quantitative and qualitative evaluations in comparison to the other investigated algorithms. It should be noted that the second performance in quantitative and qualitative evaluations was related to HCM and JCM, respectively. The experts chose the JCM algorithm because, in their opinion, it has better contrast and visually distinguishes normal points from abnormal points more effectively compared to the other algorithms.

5. Conclusions

Myocardial perfusion SPECT images are usually available as grayscale images. Increasing visual clarity is beneficial to physicians for making an accurate diagnosis. Pseudo-coloring myocardial perfusion SPECT can be helpful in this regard. This study was conducted qualitatively and quantitatively to evaluate the effectiveness of pseudo-coloring algorithms such as WCM, HCM, SCM, ZCM, and JCM to increase the quality and visual clarity of myocardial perfusion SPECT. The qualitative evaluations performed by the three experts revealed that WCM and JCM algorithms both outperformed the remaining methods. Eventually, MSE, PSNR, and SSIM indices also demonstrated that the WCM algorithm could quantitatively outperform the other methods.

Author Contributions: Study concept and design A.R., M.E.; acquisition of data M.M.; analysis and interpretation of data A.R., M.E.; drafting of the manuscript A.R., M.E.; critical revision of the manuscript for important intellectual content M.E., E.Y.K.N.; administrative, technical, or material support M.E., E.Y.K.N.; and study supervision M.E. All authors have made a significant contribution to this study and have approved the final manuscript. All authors have read and agreed to the published version of the manuscript.

Funding: This research received no specific grant from any funding agency in the public, commercial, or not-for-profit sectors. This article is the result of the thesis entitled "Review and comparison of pseudo-coloring techniques of single-photon emission computed tomography (SPECT) images of myocardial perfusion images" with the code 3400838, which was approved at Isfahan University of Medical Sciences, Iran.

Institutional Review Board Statement: The study was performed following the Helsinki Declaration on ethical principles for medical research involving human subjects and was approved by the Institutional Committee for Ethics in Biomedical Research of the Isfahan University of Medical Sciences (approval ID: IR.MUI.MED.REC.1400.790). Written informed consent was obtained from all individual participants to be included in the study and to publish the accompanying images.

Informed Consent Statement: Informed consent was obtained from all subjects involved in the study.

Data Availability Statement: Data will be provided if required.

Acknowledgments: This article is the result of the thesis entitled "Review and comparison of pseudo-coloring techniques of single-photon emission computed tomography (SPECT) images of myocardial perfusion images" with the code 3400838, which was approved at Isfahan University of Medical Sciences, Iran. The efforts of the research assistant of Isfahan University of Medical Sciences are hereby appreciated and thanked. Furthermore, the cooperation of nuclear medicine department personnel of Shahid Chamran Hospital in Isfahan is appreciated and acknowledged.

Conflicts of Interest: The authors have no conflicts of interest related to this publication.

References

1. Popa, T.; Ibanez, L.; Elliot Levy, M.D.; White, A.; Bruno, J.; Cleary, K. Tumor volume measurement and volume measurement comparison plug-ins for VolView using ITK. *SPIE* **2006**, *6141*, 395–402.
2. Dutour, A.; Monteil, J.; Paraf, F.; Charissoux, J.L.; Kaletta, C.; Sauer, B.; Naujoks, K.; Rigaud, M. Endostatin cDNA/Cationic liposome complexes as a promising therapy to prevent lung metastases in osteosarcoma: Study in a human-like rat orthotopic tumor. *Mol. Ther.* **2005**, *11*, 311–319. [CrossRef] [PubMed]
3. Slomka, P.J.; Miller, R.J.H.; Hu, L.H.; Germano, G.; Berman, D.S. Solid-state detector SPECT myocardial perfusion imaging. *J. Nucl. Med.* **2019**, *60*, 1194–1204. [CrossRef] [PubMed]
4. Tsui, B.M.W. The AAPM/RSNA Physics Tutorial for Residents: Physics of SPECT. *Radiographics* **1996**, *16*, 173–183. [CrossRef] [PubMed]
5. Zhang, X.; Bai, T.; Li, H. Pseudo-color coding method of infrared images based on human vision system. In Proceedings of the SPIE—The International Society for Optical Engineering, San Jose, CA, USA, 24–25 January 2007.
6. Zahedi, Z.; Soltani, M.; Sadri, S.; Moosavi, A. Breast thermography and pseudo-coloring presentation for improving gray infrared images. In Proceedings of the 2012 Photonics Global Conference (PGC), Singapore, 13–16 December 2012; pp. 1–5.
7. Zare, M.; Lari, K.B.; Jampour, M.; Shamsinejad, P. Multi-GANs and its application for Pseudo-Coloring. In Proceedings of the 4th International Conference on Pattern Recognition and Image Analysis, Teheran, Iran, 6–7 March 2019; pp. 1–6.
8. Zhang, J.; Lu, S.; Chen, J. Application of Pseudo-color Image Feature-Level Fusion in Nondestructive Testing of Wire Ropes. *J. Fail. Anal. Prev.* **2020**, *20*, 1541–1553. [CrossRef]
9. Levin, A.; Lischinski, D.; Weiss, Y. Colorization using optimization. In *ACM SIGGRAPH 2004 Papers*; Association for Computing Machinery: New York, NY, USA, 2004; pp. 689–694.
10. Ironi, R.; Cohen-Or, D.; Lischinski, D. Colorization by Example. *Render Tech.* **2005**, *29*, 201–210.
11. Varga, D.; Szirányi, T. Fully automatic image colorization based on Convolutional Neural Network. In Proceedings of the 2016 23rd International Conference on Pattern Recognition (ICPR), Cancun, Mexico, 4–8 December 2016; pp. 3691–3696.
12. Sharma, A. Enhanced False Coloring in Medical Image Processing. *Int. J. Adv. Res. Ideas Innov. Technol.* **2017**, *3*, 75–78.
13. Selvapriya, B.; Raghu, B. Pseudocoloring of medical images: A research. *Int. J. Eng. Adv. Technol.* **2019**, *8*, 3712–3716.
14. Whitehead, M.T.; Guillot, L.M.; Reilly, B.K. Cochlear signal alterations using pseudo-color perceptual enhancement for patients with sensorineural hearing loss. *Pediatr. Radiol.* **2021**, *51*, 1448–1456. [CrossRef]
15. Verberne, H.J.; Acampa, W.; Anagnostopoulos, C.; Ballinger, J.; Bengel, F.; De Bondt, P.; Buechel, R.R.; Cuocolo, A.; van Eck-Smit, B.L.; Flotats, A.; et al. EANM Procedural Guidelines for Radionuclide Myocardial Perfusion Imaging with SPECT and SPECT/CT: 2015 revision. *Eur. J. Nucl. Med. Mol. Imaging* **2015**, *42*, 1929–1940. [CrossRef] [PubMed]
16. Masoomi, M.A.; Al-Shammeri, I.; Kalafallah, K.; Elrahman, H.M.; Ragab, O.; Ahmed, E.; Al-Shammeri, J.; Arafat, S. Wiener filter improves diagnostic accuracy of CAD SPECT images-comparison to angiography and CT angiography. *Medicine* **2019**, *98*, e14207. [CrossRef] [PubMed]
17. Cannistraci, C.V.; Montevecchi, F.M.; Alessio, M. Median-modified Wiener filter provides efficient denoising, preserving spot edge and morphology in 2-DE image processing. *Proteomics* **2009**, *9*, 4908–4919. [CrossRef] [PubMed]

18. Hore, A.; Ziou, D. Image quality metrics: PSNR vs. SSIM. In Proceedings of the 2010 20th International Conference on Pattern Recognition, Istanbul, Turkey, 23–26 August 2010.
19. Popowicz, A.; Smolka, B. Fast image colourisation using the isolines concept. *Multimed Tools Appl.* **2017**, *76*, 15987–16009. [CrossRef]
20. Wang, Z.; Bovik, A.; Simoncelli, E.P. Structural Approaches to Image Quality Assessment. 2005. Available online: https://www.ece.uwaterloo.ca/~{}z70wang/publications/HIVP_chapter83.pdf (accessed on 1 April 2021).

MDPI AG
Grosspeteranlage 5
4052 Basel
Switzerland
Tel.: +41 61 683 77 34

MDPI Books Editorial Office
E-mail: books@mdpi.com
www.mdpi.com/books

www.ingramcontent.com/pod-product-compliance
Lightning Source LLC
Chambersburg PA
CBHW061811210926
51850CB00006B/676
* 9 7 8 3 7 2 5 8 7 9 5 5 7 *